SOLUTIONS MANUAL

Merrill
Geometry
Applications and Connections

GLENCOE
McGraw-Hill

New York, New York
Columbus, Ohio
Mission Hills, California
Peoria, Illinois

The copy in this text was word processed using ChiWriter Software from Horstmann
Software, P.O. Box 5039 San Jose, California 95192

Send all inquires to:
Glencoe/McGraw-Hill
936 Eastwind Drive
Westerville, OH 43081

ISBN 0-02-824448-6

2 3 4 5 6 7 8 9 10 BANT 03 02 01 00 99 98 97 96 95

Contents

Chapter 1 The Language of Geometry 1

Chapter 2 Reasoning and Introduction to Proof 19

Chapter 3 Parallels 36

Chapter 4 Congruent Triangles 49

Chapter 5 Applying Congruent Triangles 68

Chapter 6 Quadrilaterals 91

Chapter 7 Similarity 111

Chapter 8 Right Triangles and Trigonometry 130

Chapter 9 Circles 156

Chapter 10 Polygons and Area 178

Chapter 11 Surface Area and Volume 199

Chapter 12 More Coordinate Geometry 219

Chapter 13 Loci and Transformations 245

Chapter 1　The Language of Geometry

Connections from Algebra: The Coordinate Plane

PAGE 10　CHECKING FOR UNDERSTANDING

1. (3, 5) x-coordinate is 3, y-coordinate is 5.
   (5, 3) x-coordinate is 5, y-coordinate is 3.

2. to differentiate between "vertical" rows and "horizontal" rows of seats

3. Check to see if the point (-2, 3) satisfies both equations.

4. Draw a line connecting each of the two cities, and see if the other city is on that line.

5. III　　6. IV　　7. y-axis　　8. Q; (2, -2)

9. R; (-3, 4)　　10. right angle

11. Find the length of each leg. Then use the Pythagorean Theorem to find the length of the hypotenuse. Then add the sides together.

PAGES 11-12　EXERCISES

12. (-4, -1)　　13. (3, -1)　　14. (3, 4)

15. (-2, 4)

16-21.

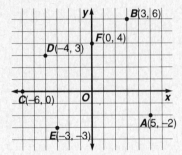

22. (0, 14)　　23. (0, -11)　　24. (5, 0)

25. (15, 0)　　26. (5, 14)　　27. (15, -11)

28. yes; (2) $\overset{?}{=}$ (0) + 2　　29. no; (-1) $\overset{?}{=}$ (1) + 2
   　　　2 = 2　　　　　　　　　　　　-1 ≠ 3

30. no; (-2) $\overset{?}{=}$ (-3) + 2　　31. yes; (-1) $\overset{?}{=}$ (-3) + 2
   　　　-2 ≠ -1　　　　　　　　　　　　-1 = -1

32. a. -1　　b. 6　　c. 22 units

33.

x	$3x + 5$	y	(x, y)
0	3(0) + 5	5	(0, 5)
2	3(2) + 5	11	(2, 11)
-2	3(-2) + 5	-1	(-2, -1)

a.

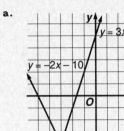

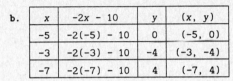

b.

x	$-2x - 10$	y	(x, y)
-5	-2(-5) - 10	0	(-5, 0)
-3	-2(-3) - 10	-4	(-3, -4)
-7	-2(-7) - 10	4	(-7, 4)

c. (-3, -4)

34. a. II or IV; If $xy < 0$, either $x < 0$ and $y > 0$ or $x > 0$ and $y < 0$. If $x < 0$ and $y > 0$, the point is in Quadrant II. If $x > 0$ and $y < 0$, the point is in Quadrant IV.

   b. I or III; If $xy > 0$, either $x > 0$ and $y > 0$ or $x < 0$ and $y < 0$. If $x > 0$ and $y > 0$, the point is in Quadrant I. If $x < 0$ and $y < 0$, the point is in Quadrant III.

   c. x-axis or y-axis; If $xy = 0$, either $x = 0$ or $y = 0$. If $y = 0$, the point is on the x-axis. If $x = 0$, the point is on the y-axis.

35. a. Magic Kingdom　　b. $(E, 3)$
   c. $(D, 5), (D, 6)$　　d. Epcot Center Drive
   e. $(C, 1), (D, 1), (D, 2), (E, 3), (E, 4),$
   　 $(F, 4), (F, 5), (F, 6)$

36. Answers will vary. A typical answer is to have a way of describing the location of an object in a plane numerically.

Points, Lines, and Planes

PAGES 15-16　CHECKING FOR UNDERSTANDING

1. points　　　　　　　　2. point, line, plane

3.

1

4. true   5. false

6. 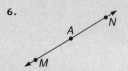   7.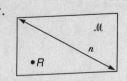

8. 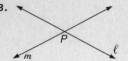   9.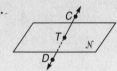

10. false   11. true   12. false   13. true
14. true   15. *E*   16. yes; yes   17. no; yes
18. *C*, *G*, *H*   19. line *TU*   20. yes   21. *R*, *U*
22. yes; infinitely many   23. no; infinitely many

PAGES 16-18   EXERCISES
24. line   25. plane   26. line   27. line
28. point   29. plane

30. 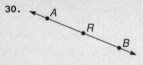   31.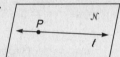

32. 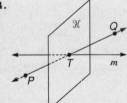   33.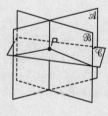

34. 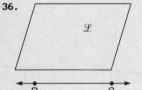   35.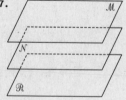

36. 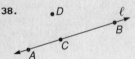   37.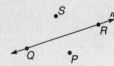

38.   • *D*   ℓ   39.   • *S*   *n*

40. planes *PAB*, *PBC*, *PCD*, *PAD*, *ABCD*   41. no
42. $\overleftrightarrow{AB}$, $\overleftrightarrow{CB}$, $\overleftrightarrow{PB}$ 43. planes *PDC* and *PDA*
44. Answers will vary. Sample answer: line *PD*,
    plane *PBC*.
45. parts of the figure that are hidden from view
46. See students' work.
47. The figure is not possible unless *P*, *Q*, and *R*
    are collinear. If points *P*, *Q*, and *R* determine
    a unique plane, it is not possible for *P*, *Q*, and
    R to be in a plane that does not contain *S* and a
    different plane that does contain *S*.

48.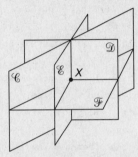

49. 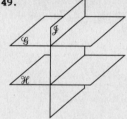   50.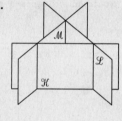

51. no   52. yes   53. no   54. yes
55. If Mr. Johnstone builds the chair with four
    legs, the fourth may not lie in the same plane
    defined by the other three. This would mean
    that the chair would be wobbly. Since three
    points determine a plane, he should use three
    legs.
56. 5 · 8 · 1200 or 48,000 colored dots
57-59.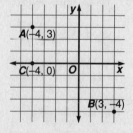

60. (0, 3)   61. (-1, -2)   62. 5   63. -2
64. point, line, plane; examples may vary; **sample**
    answers: point - corner of a box; line - guitar
    string; plane - parking lot
65. $\sqrt{961} = \sqrt{31^2} = 31$ 66. $\sqrt{3025} = \sqrt{55^2} = 55$
67. $\sqrt{775} \approx 27.84$ 68. $\sqrt{6436} \approx 80.22$

1-3 Problem-Solving Strategy: List the Possibilities

PAGE 21 CHECKING FOR UNDERSTANDING

1. to be sure that you list all of the possibilities and that you do not omit any important items

2. organized list, table, tree diagram

3. The sum of the lengths of its sides is 18 yards.

4. 24 arrangements:

President -
- V-P, Sec., Treas.
- V-P, Treas., Sec.
- Sec., V-P, Treas.
- Sec., Treas., V-P
- Treas., Sec., V-P
- Treas., V-P, Sec.

Vice President -
- Pres., Sec., Treas.
- Pres., Treas., Sec.
- Treas., Pres., Sec.
- Treas., Sec., Pres.
- Sec., Treas., Pres.
- Sec., Pres., Treas.

Secretary -
- Pres., V-P, Treas.
- Pres., Treas., V-P
- V-P, Treas., Pres.
- V-P, Pres., Treas.
- Treas., Pres., V-P
- Treas., V-P, Pres.

Treasurer -
- Pres., V-P, Sec.
- Pres., Sec., V-P
- V-P, Sec., Pres.
- V-P, Pres., Sec.
- Sec., Pres., V-P
- Sec., V-P, Pres.

5. 10 combinations:

quarters	dimes	nickels
2	0	0
0	5	0
0	0	10
1	2	1
1	1	3
1	0	5
0	4	2
0	3	4
0	2	6
0	1	8

6. $\overline{AB}$, $\overline{AC}$, $\overline{AD}$, $\overline{AE}$, $\overline{BC}$, $\overline{BD}$, $\overline{BE}$, $\overline{CD}$, $\overline{CE}$, $\overline{DE}$

7. 9:

People	Coats								
Sarah	V	V	V	J	J	J	K	K	K
Victor	S	K	J	S	K	K	S	J	J
Janel	K	S	K	K	S	V	V	S	V
Kirby	J	J	S	V	V	S	J	V	S

PAGE 22 EXERCISES

8. Renee, Sandra, Tim: Tim is not in the middle because he tells the truth and the person in the middle claims to be Renee. Tim cannot be in front because the student walking in front says Tim is in the middle, and Tim tells the truth. Tim is in back. The student in the back (Tim, who tells the truth) says that Sandra is in the middle. That leaves Renee in front.

9. 22 pieces; Each nth cut makes n new pieces.

Cut	New pieces	Total pieces
1	1	2
2	2	4
3	3	7
4	4	11
5	5	16
6	6	22

10.

11. Sample answer: $3 + 3 + 3 + 3 - (3 + 3) = 11$

12.

least often ← □ → most often

13. The old car used $\frac{12000}{22}$ or about 545.45 gallons per year.

The new car will use $\frac{12000}{37}$ or about 324.32 gallons per year. That is a savings of 221.13 gallons. At \$1.20 per gallon, Ted and Mary will save \$1.20(221.13) or about \$265 a year.

14. 12 outfits:

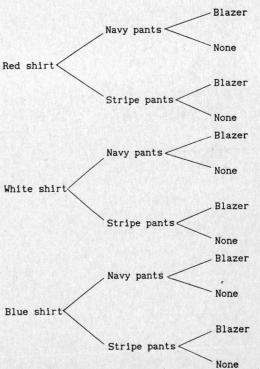

3

Cooperative Learning Project

PAGE 22

The student in the front is wearing a red hat.

The possible arrangements of hats, listed from front to back are

YYR; YRY; RYY; RRY; RYR; YRR; and RRR.

If the student in the back saw two yellow hats, he would know that he had to be wearing a red hat. So, he saw either one red and one yellow or two red hats. The arrangement of hats had to be either YRY, RYY, RRY, RYR, YRR, or RRR.

The student in the center knew that the student in the back saw either red and yellow or two red, so if she saw a yellow hat on the student in the front, she would have known that the arrangement of hats was either YRY or YRR and that she was wearing a red hat. Since she didn't know what color hat she was wearing, she must have seen a red hat on the student in the front.

1-4 Finding the Measures of Segments

PAGES 26-27   CHECKING FOR UNDERSTANDING

1. No; you can use 18 for x_2 as long as you use 8 for y_2, 5 for x_1, and 7 for y_1.

2. Since one lip was on the 6 and the other lip was on the 9, Sally knew that the length of Snoopy's mouth had to be 9 - 6, or 3 inches.

3. Answers will vary. Sample answers:

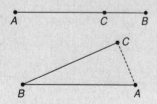

4. $GH < XY < AB < MN < KL$
5. $AB = |-4 - 0| = |-4| = 4$
6. $CD = |3 - 6| = |-3| = 3$
7. $BD = |0 - 6| = |-6| = 6$
8. $CB = |3 - 0| = |3| = 3$
9. $DA = |6 - (-4)| = |6 + 4| = 10$
10. $AC = |-4 - 3| = |-7| = 7$

11. $PQ = \sqrt{(-1 - (-1))^2 + (-6 - 4)^2} = \sqrt{100} = 10$

12. $SR = \sqrt{(14 - 5)^2 + (-4 + (-4))^2}$
$= \sqrt{9^2 + 0}$
$= \sqrt{81}$
$= 9$

13. $RP = \sqrt{(-1 - 5)^2 + (4 - (-4))^2}$
$= \sqrt{-6^2 + 8^2}$
$= \sqrt{100}$
$= 10$

14. $PS = \sqrt{14 - (-1)^2 + (-4 - 4)^2}$
$= \sqrt{15^2 + (-8)^2}$
$= \sqrt{225 + 64}$
$= 17$

15. $QR = \sqrt{5 - (-1)^2 + (-4 - (-6))^2}$
$= \sqrt{(5 + 1)^2 + (-4 + 6)^2}$
$= \sqrt{6^2 + 2^2} = \sqrt{36 + 4} = \sqrt{40}$
≈ 6.32

16. $QS = \sqrt{14 - (-1)^2 + (-4 - (-6))^2}$
$= \sqrt{(14 + 1)^2 + (-4 + 6)^2}$
$= \sqrt{15^2 + 2^2} = \sqrt{225 + 4} = \sqrt{229}$
≈ 15.13

17. $x + 2x + 1 = 22$
$3x = 21$
$x = 7$
$BC = 2x + 1 = 15$

18.

PAGES 27-29   EXERCISES

19. $CD = |0 - (-1)| = |1| = 1$
20. $BF = |9 - (-4)| = |13| = 13$
21. $CF = |9 - (-1)| = |10| = 10$
22. $EB = |-4 - 3| = |-7| = 7$
23. $BA = |-8 - (-4)| = |-4| = 4$
24. $FE = |3 - 9| = |-6| = 6$
25. $FA = |9 - (-8)| = |17| = 17$
26. $AC = |-1 - (-8)| = |7| = 7$
27. $HJ + JK = HK$
17 + 6 = 23
28. $HJ + JK = HK$
4.8 + 7 = 11.8
29. $HJ + JK = HK$
23.7 + JK = 35.2
$JK = 35.2 - 23.7$
$JK = 11.5$

4

30. $HJ + JK = HK$

$HJ + 2\frac{1}{2} = 6\frac{2}{5}$

$HJ = 6\frac{2}{5} - 2\frac{1}{2}$

$HJ = 3\frac{9}{10}$

31. $AB = \sqrt{(5-2)^2 + (-1-3)^2}$

$= \sqrt{3^2 + (-4)^2} = \sqrt{9+16}$

$= \sqrt{25}$

$= 5$

32. $CF = \sqrt{(3-(-3))^2 + (5-(-3))^2}$

$= \sqrt{6^2 + 8^2}$

$= \sqrt{36+64} = \sqrt{100}$

$= 10$

33. $DG = \sqrt{(10-(-2))^2 + (-1-4)^2}$

$= \sqrt{12^2 + (-5)^2}$

$= \sqrt{144+25} = \sqrt{169}$

$= 13$

34. $HE = \sqrt{(9-(-6))^2 + (-2-6)^2}$

$= \sqrt{15^2 + (-8)^2}$

$= \sqrt{225+64} = \sqrt{289}$

$= 17$

35. $JF = \sqrt{(0-3)^2 + (1-5)^2}$

$= \sqrt{3^2 + (-4)^2}$

$= \sqrt{9+16} = \sqrt{25}$

$= 5$

36. $AD = \sqrt{(-2-2)^2 + (4-3)^2}$

$= \sqrt{(-4)^2 + 1^2}$

$= \sqrt{16+1} = \sqrt{17}$

≈ 4.12

37. $GE = \sqrt{(9-10)^2 + (-2-(-1))^2}$

$= \sqrt{(-1)^2 + (-1)^2}$

$= \sqrt{1+1} = \sqrt{2}$

≈ 1.41

38. $JB = \sqrt{(0-5)^2 + (1-(-1))^2}$

$= \sqrt{(-5)^2 + (2)^2}$

$= \sqrt{25+9} = \sqrt{29}$

≈ 5.39

39. $CH = \sqrt{(-6-(-3))^2 + 6-(-3)^2}$

$= \sqrt{-3^2 + 9^2}$

$= \sqrt{9+81} = \sqrt{90}$

≈ 9.49

40. $HG = \sqrt{(10-(-6))^2 + (-1-6)^2}$

$= \sqrt{16^2 + (-7)^2}$

$= \sqrt{256+49} = \sqrt{305}$

≈ 17.46

41. $AB + BC = AC$

$3 + 4x + 1 = 8$

$4x = 4$

$x = 1$

$BC = 4x + 1$

$= 4(1) + 1$

$= 5$

$BC = 5$

42. $AB + BC = AC$

$x + 2 + 2x - 6 = 20$

$3x = 24$

$x = 8$

$BC = 2x - 6$

$= 2(8) - 6$

$= 10$

$BC = 10$

43. $AB + BC = AC$

$24 + 3x = 7x - 4$

$-4x = -28$

$x = 7$

$BC = 3x = 21$

44. $AB + BC = AC$

$3 + 2x + 5 = 11x + 2$

$-9x = -6$

$x = \frac{2}{3}$

$BC = 2x + 5 = 2\left(\frac{2}{3}\right) + 5 = \frac{19}{3}$

45.

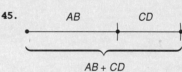

46.

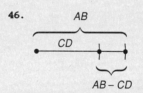

47.

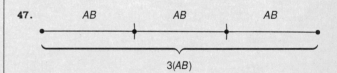

48.

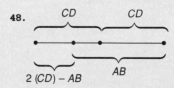

5

49. 29.31 units: $P = XY + YZ + ZX$
$$= 5 + 11.31 + 13$$
$$= 29.31 \text{ units}$$

$$XY = \sqrt{(5 - 2)^2 + (3 - (-1))^2}$$
$$= \sqrt{3^2 + 4^2} = \sqrt{25}$$
$$= 5$$

$$YZ = \sqrt{(-3 - 5)^2 + (11 - 3)^2}$$
$$= \sqrt{-8^2 + 8^2} = \sqrt{64 + 64}$$
$$\approx 11.31$$

$$ZX = \sqrt{(2 - (-3))^2 + (-1 - 11)^2}$$
$$= \sqrt{5^2 + (-12)^2} = \sqrt{169}$$
$$= 13$$

50. $a = 7$ or $a = 1$
$$AB = \sqrt{(a - 4)^2 + (3 - 7)^2}$$
$$5 = \sqrt{a^2 - 8a + 16 + (-4)^2}$$
$$= \sqrt{a^2 - 8a + 32}$$
$$25 = a^2 - 8a + 32$$
$$0 = a^2 - 8a - 7$$
$$0 = (a - 7)(a + 1)$$
$$|7| = a \qquad |-1| = a$$
$$7 = a \qquad 1 = a$$

51.

Z   V   X   Y   W

52. $TR = 10$, $RS = 5$, $TS = 15$. Since $TR - RS = TS$, R is between T and S, and R, S, and T are collinear.
$$TR = \sqrt{(1 - (-7))^2 + (1 - (-5))^2}$$
$$= \sqrt{8^2 + 6^2}$$
$$= \sqrt{64 + 36} = \sqrt{100}$$
$$= 10$$
$$RS = \sqrt{(5 - 1)^2 + (4 - 1)^2}$$
$$= \sqrt{4^2 + 3^2} = \sqrt{25}$$
$$= 5$$
$$TS = \sqrt{5 - (-7)^2 + (4 - (-5))^2}$$
$$= \sqrt{12^2 + 9^2}$$
$$= \sqrt{225}$$
$$= 15$$

53. A is between B and C.

54. about 132 miles
$$D = \sqrt{(387 - 158)^2 + (213 - 562)^2}$$
$$= \sqrt{229^2 + (-349)^2}$$
$$= \sqrt{52,441 + 121,801}$$
$$= 417.42 \text{ units}$$
$$D = 417.42 \text{ units} \times .316 \text{ miles} = \text{about } 132 \text{ miles}$$

55. a. distance formula   **b.** 10   **c.** ≈ 3.07
    d. ≈ 16.55

56. $(-1, 3)$ **57.** E **58.** A **59.** D, A, E, O

60.

61. 18 area codes: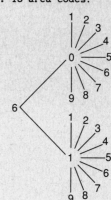

62. See students' work.

$\boxed{\textbf{1-5}}$ **Segment Relationships**

1. No; point B does not have to lie on $\overline{AC}$.

2. Answers will vary.   **3.** 1; infinitely many
Sample answer:

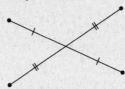

4. First fold the paper so that the fold contains both point X and point Y. The fold the paper so that point X falls on point Y. The point of intersection of the two folds is the midpoint of $\overline{XY}$.

5. $\dfrac{0 + 6}{2} = 3$ **6.** $\dfrac{-4 + 0}{2} = -2$ **7.** $\dfrac{6 + (-4)}{2} = 1$

8. $\dfrac{0 + 3}{2} = 1\frac{1}{2}$ **9.** $\dfrac{3 + 6}{2} = 4\frac{1}{2}$ **10.** $\dfrac{3 + (-4)}{2} = -\frac{1}{2}$

11. $(-1, -1)$ **12.** $\left(2, \dfrac{1}{2}\right)$

$\dfrac{-1 + (-1)}{2}, \dfrac{4 + (-6)}{2}$ $\dfrac{5 + (-1)}{2}, \dfrac{-3 + 4}{2}$

$\dfrac{-2}{2}, \dfrac{-2}{2}$ $\dfrac{4}{2}, \dfrac{1}{2}$

$-1, -1$ $2, \dfrac{1}{2}$

13. $\left(2, -4\dfrac{1}{2}\right)$ **14.** $\left(5\dfrac{1}{2}, 3\right)$

$\dfrac{-1 + 5}{2}, \dfrac{-6 + (-3)}{2}$ $\dfrac{-1 + 12}{2}, \dfrac{4 + 2}{2}$

$\dfrac{4}{2}, \dfrac{-9}{2}$ $\dfrac{11}{2}, \dfrac{6}{2}$

$2, -4\dfrac{1}{2}$ $5\dfrac{1}{2}, 3$

15. $\left(5\frac{1}{2}, -2\right)$

$\dfrac{12 + (-1)}{2}, \dfrac{2 + (-6)}{2}$

$\dfrac{11}{2}, \dfrac{-4}{2}$

$5\frac{1}{2}, -2$

16. $\left(8\frac{1}{2}, -\frac{1}{2}\right)$

$\dfrac{12 + 5}{2}, \dfrac{-3 + 2}{2}$

$\dfrac{17}{2}, -\dfrac{1}{2}$

$8\frac{1}{2}, -\frac{1}{2}$

17. $5x - 3 = 3x + 5$ $DF = DE + EF$

$2x = 8 \qquad = (5x - 3) + (3x + 5)$

$x = 4 \qquad = (5 \cdot 4 - 3) + (3 \cdot 4 + 5)$

$\qquad\qquad\qquad\qquad\;\; = 17 + 17$

$\qquad\qquad\qquad\qquad\;\; = 34$

18.

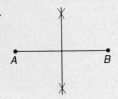

$A \qquad\qquad\qquad B$

PAGES 33-35   EXERCISES

19. true   **20.** false   **21.** true   **22.** true

23. false   **24.** true   **25.** true   **26.** false

27. false   **28.** true

29. $B\ (5, 5)$

$\dfrac{-1 + x_2}{2} = 2 \qquad\qquad \dfrac{5 + y_2}{2} = 5$

$-1 + x_2 = 4 \qquad\qquad 5 + y_2 = 10$

$x_2 = 5 \qquad\qquady_2 = 5$

30. $A\ (-9, 4)$

$\dfrac{3 + x_2}{2} = -3 \qquad\qquad \dfrac{-2 + y_2}{2} = 1$

$3 + x_2 = -6 \qquad\qquad -2 + y_2 = 2$

$x_2 = -9 \qquad\qquady_2 = 4$

31. $A\ (2, 8)$

$\dfrac{x_1 - 6}{2} = -2 \qquad\qquad \dfrac{y_2 - 4}{2} = 2$

$x_1 - 6 = -4 \qquad\qquad y_2 - 4 = 4$

$x_1 = 2 \qquad\qquady_2 = 8$

32. $B\ (2, -10)$

$\dfrac{-1 + x_2}{2} = .5 \qquad\qquad \dfrac{-3 + y_2}{2} = -6.5$

$-1 + x_2 = 1 \qquad\qquad -3 + y_2 = -13$

$x_2 = 2 \qquad\qquady_2 = -10$

33. $AX = XB \qquad\qquad AB = AX + XB$

$2x + 11 = 4x - 5 \qquad\quad = (2x + 11) + (4x - 5)$

$-2x = -16 \qquad\qquad = 2(8) + 11 + 4(8) - 5$

$x = 8 \qquad\qquad\quad = 54$

34. $\dfrac{AB}{2} = AX \qquad\qquad XB = AB - AX$

$\dfrac{x + 3}{2} = 3x - 1 \qquad\qquad = (x + 3) - (3x - 1)$

$x + 3 = 6x - 2 \qquad\qquad = (1 + 3) - (3 \cdot 1 - 1)$

$-5x = -5 \qquad\qquad = 4 - 2$

$x = 1 \qquad\qquad = 2$

35. $XY = YB$

$2x + 3 = 23 - 2x$

$4x = 20$

$x = 5$

$AX = XY + YB$

$ = 2x + 3 + 23 - 2x$

$ = (2 \cdot 5 + 3) + (23 - 2 \cdot 5)$

$ = 13 + 13$

$ = 26 \qquad\qquad AB = YB + XY + AX$

$\qquad\qquad\qquad\qquad\quad = 13 + 13 + 26$

$\qquad\qquad\qquad\qquad\quad = 52$

36. $AX = XB \qquad\qquad XY = \dfrac{XB}{2}$

$27 - x = 13 - 3x \qquad\qquad = \dfrac{13 - 3x}{2}$

$2x = -14 \qquad\qquad\qquad = \dfrac{13 - 3(-7)}{2}$

$x = -7 \qquad\qquad\qquad = \dfrac{13 + 21}{2} = \dfrac{34}{2}$

$\qquad\qquad\qquad\qquad\qquad\qquad = 17$

37. 8; 18

$\dfrac{AB}{2} = AX \qquad XB = 2(XY) \qquad \dfrac{5x - 4}{2} = 2(x + 1)$

$\dfrac{5x - 4}{2} = AX \qquad XB = AX \qquad 5x - 4 = 4(x + 1)$

$\qquad\qquad\qquad AX = 2(XY) \qquad 5x - 4 = 4x + 4$

$\qquad\qquad\qquad = 2(x + 1) \qquadx = 8$

$\qquad\qquad\qquad\qquad\qquad\qquad AX = 2(8 + 1)$

$\qquad\qquad\qquad\qquad\qquad\qquad = 18$

38. $\overline{XY} \cong \overline{YZ}$

$8x - 5 = 4x + 7$

$4x = 12$

$x = 3$

39. No; if $\overline{XY}$ and $\overline{YZ}$ are congruent, then $XY = YZ = $ 19 and $XY + YZ = 38 \neq 34$. Thus X, Y, and Z are not collinear.

40-42. See students' work.

43. $P\ (4, -1),\ Q\ (6, -5)$

$\overline{AP} \cong \overline{PQ} \cong \overline{QB}$

$2 + 3x = 8$

$3x = 6$

$x = 2$

$3 + 3y = -9$

$3y = -12$

$y = -4$

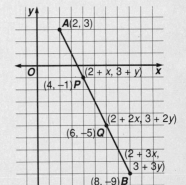

7

44. N (5, 9)

$KN = \frac{1}{4}KL$

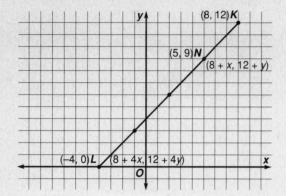

$8 + 4x = -4$ $12 + 4y = 0$

      $4x = -12$ $4y = -12$

        $x = -3$ $y = -3$

45. $RS + ST = RT$

$x^2 + 8 + 3x + 6 = 24$

$x^2 + 3x - 10 = 0$

$(x + 5)(x - 2) = 0$

$x = -5$ $x = 2$ yes

$x = 2$, yes

46. a., c. See students' work.

   b. The three lines intersect at one point.

47. $2(MN) = BC$ and $\overline{BC} \parallel \overline{MN}$.

48. a. Lay the 4-foot board and the 2-foot board
end-to-end on the piece of lumber with the
4-foot board at one end of the piece of
lumber. Now, pick up the 4-foot board and
place it at the other end of the 2-foot
board. Now cut the piece of lumber at the
end of the 4-foot board.

   b. He is using Segment Addition and Congruent
Segments.

49. (-1, 5) or (-1, -1)

$\sqrt{(-1 - (-1))^2 + (2 - y)^2} = 3$ x-coordinate is

$\sqrt{(-1 + 1)^2 + (2 - y)^2} = 3$ -1 because line

            $(2 - y)^2 = 9$ is vertical.

       $4 - 4y + y^2 = 9$

        $y^2 - 4y - 5 = 0$

     $(y - 5)(y + 1) = 0$

       $y = 5$ or $y = -1$

50. a. P, Q, R, S

   b. yes, since any three points are coplanar

51. 12 ways:

---

52. 25

$AB = \sqrt{(6 - (-1))^2 + (-20 - (4))^2}$

      $= \sqrt{(6 + 1)^2 + (-24)^2}$

      $= \sqrt{49 + 576} = \sqrt{625}$

      $= 25$

53. F is between D and E.

54. The coordinates of the midpoint of a line
segment in the coordinate plane are the average
of the x-coordinates and y-coordinates of the
endpoints of the line segment.

Mid-Chapter Review

PAGE 35

1. (1, 3)   **2.** (-1, 1)   **3.** (4, -2)   **4.** true

5. -2   **6.** U, V, W, or X **7.** $\overrightarrow{RS}$, $\overrightarrow{TS}$, $\overrightarrow{VS}$

8. $\overleftrightarrow{XY}$ **9.** true

10. 3 unicycles, 4 bicycles, 23 tricycles

    Let x = number of unicycles

    $x + 1$ = number of bicycles

       y = number of tricycles

   $2[(x) + (x + 1) + y] = 60$

    $2(x + x + 1 + y) = 60$

    $2x + 2x + 2 + 2y = 60$

         $4x + 2y = 58$

          $2x + y = 29$

             $y = 29 - 2x$

$x + 2(x + 1) + 3y = 80$

  $x + 2x + 2 + 3y = 80$

       $3x + 3y = 78$

         $x + y = 26$

       $x + y = 26$

$x + (29 - 2x) = 26$

          $-x = -3$

           $x = 3$ unicycles

       $x + 1 = 4$ bicycles

           $y = 23$ tricycles

11. If S is between R and T:

       $RS + ST = RT$

   $3x - 6 + 2x + 9 = 13$

        $5x + 3 = 13$

          $5x = 10$

           $x = 2$

If $x = 2$, $RS = 3(2) - 6$ or 0.

Therefore, S is not between R and T.

If R is between S and T:

       $RS + RT = ST$

   $3x - 6 + 13 = 2x + 9$

       $3x + 7 = 2x + 9$

          $x = 2$

If $x = 2$, $RS = 3(2) - 6$ or 0.

Therefore, R is not between S and T.

If T is between R and S:

$$RT + ST = RS$$
$$13 + 2x + 9 = 3x - 6$$
$$2x + 22 = 3x - 6$$
$$28 = x$$

If $x = 28$, $ST = 2(28) + 9$ or 65 and $RS = 3(28) - 6$ or 78. Therefore, T is between R and S.

12. 5, 13
$$4x - 9 + (7 - x) = 2x + 3$$
$$x = 5$$
$$AC = 2x + 3 = 13$$

13. 10; (3, 4) $\dfrac{7 - 1}{2} = 3$ $\dfrac{7 + 1}{2} = 4$

$$MN = \sqrt{(7 - (-1))^2 + (7 - 1)^2}$$
$$= \sqrt{8^2 + 6^2} = \sqrt{100}$$
$$= 10$$

14. $DE = EF$
$$4x - 9 = 7 + 2x$$
$$x = 8$$

1–6 Rays and Angles

1. $130°$ 2. the common endpoint

3. A straight angle is formed by two collinear, not noncollinear, rays.

4.

5.

6.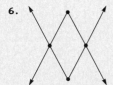

7.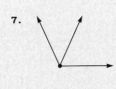

8. negative number   9. $\overrightarrow{QR}$, $\overrightarrow{QT}$ 10. S

11. false   12. $\overrightarrow{RX}$, $\overrightarrow{RY}$ 13. Y, R, S, or T

14. $\angle PRY$, $\angle XRY$, $\angle TRY$ 15. N, S, or T 16. $m\angle 3$

17. 10   18. 25   19. 105   20. $40 - 10 = 30$

21. $120 - 40 = 80$ 22. $75 - 25 = 50$
23. $105 - 10 = 95$ 24. $155 - 10 = 145$
25. J 26. $\angle HUK$ 27. V 28. $\angle HJK$, $\angle HJU$, $\angle UJK$
29. No   30. No. $\angle J$ could refer to $\angle 1$, $\angle 2$, or $\angle HJK$.

31. 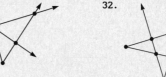   32.

33.

34. $m\angle SXT + m\angle RXS = m\angle RXT$
$$3x - 4 + 2x + 5 = 111$$
$$5x = 111 - 1$$
$$x = 22$$
$$m\angle RXS = 49$$

35. $m\angle PXQ + m\angle QXT = 180$
$$2x + 5x - 23 = 180$$
$$7x = 203$$
$$x = 29$$
$$m\angle QXT = 122$$

36. $m\angle QXR + m\angle RXS = m\angle QXS$
$$x + 10 + 91 = 4x - 1$$
$$-3x = -102$$
$$x = 34$$
$$m\angle QXS = 135$$

37. $m\angle QXP + m\angle QXR = m\angle RXP$
$$2x - 3 + 3x + 5 = x + 50$$
$$4x = 48$$
$$x = 12$$
$$m\angle RXP = 62$$
$$m\angle RXT = 180 - m\angle RXP$$
$$= 180 - 62$$
$$= 118$$

38. $m\angle TXS + m\angle SXR + m\angle RXP = 180$
$$x + 4 + 3x + 4 + 2x + 4 = 180$$
$$6x = 168$$
$$x = 28$$
$$m\angle TXS = 32$$
$$m\angle PXS = 180 - m\angle TXS$$
$$= 180 - 32$$
$$= 148$$

39.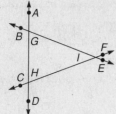

12 angles:

∠AGB, ∠BGH, ∠HGI,

∠IGA, ∠CHB, ∠GHI,

∠IHD, ∠DHC, ∠FIE,

∠GIH, ∠FIG, ∠EIH

40.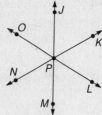

12 angles

∠JPK, ∠KPL, ∠LPM,

∠MPN, ∠NPO, ∠OPJ,

∠JPL, ∠KPM, ∠LPN,

∠MPO, ∠NPJ, ∠OPK

41.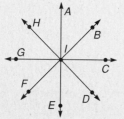

24 angles:

∠AIB, ∠BIC, ∠CID,

∠DIE, ∠EIF, ∠FIG,

∠GIH, ∠HIA, ∠AIC,

∠BID, ∠CIE, ∠DIF,

∠EIG, ∠FIH, ∠GIA,

∠HIB, ∠AID, ∠BIE,

∠CIF, ∠DIG, ∠EIH,

∠FIA, ∠GIB, ∠HIC

42.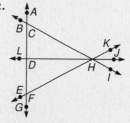

24 angles:

∠ACB, ∠BCD, ∠DCH,

∠HCA, ∠LDC, ∠LDF,

∠FDH, ∠HDC, ∠EFD,

∠HFD, ∠HFG, ∠EFG,

∠IHJ, ∠JHK, ∠IHK,

∠KHF, ∠KHD, ∠FHD,

∠FHC, ∠DHC, ∠CHI,

∠JHC, ∠JHF, ∠IHD

43. 1; 2 if $PQ \geq 2$. 1 if $PQ < 2$.

44. a. 4 rays = 6 angles;

5 rays = 10 angles;

6 rays = 15 angles;

b. 21 angles; 45 angles

c. $\dfrac{n(n-1)}{2}$

45. a. As the loft of the club increases, the ball will travel higher in the air and for a shorter distance, as long as the ball is struck with the same amount of force.

b.

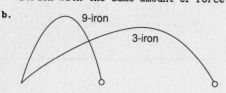

9-iron

3-iron

46. Answers may vary.   **47.** (2, −1)

48.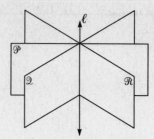

49. greater than 0

50.
$$AB + BC = AC$$
$$(5x - 3) + (3x - 1) = 12$$
$$8x = 16$$
$$x = 2$$
$$3x - 1 = BC = 5$$

51. $\dfrac{-5+3}{2}, \dfrac{-2+6}{2}$

$\dfrac{-2}{2}, \dfrac{4}{2}$

(−1, 2)

52.
$$WX = XZ$$
$$2x - 3 = 5x - 24$$
$$-3x = -21$$
$$x = 7$$

53. See students' work.

Developing Reasoning Skills

PAGE 42

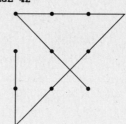

1–7 Classifying Angles

PAGES 46–47   CHECKING FOR UNDERSTANDING

1. exactly one; protractor postulate

2. Right angles all have a measure of 90°. Thus, right angles all have the same measure and are therefore congruent.

3. Acute angles do not always have the same measure. For example, a 30° angle and a 70° angle are both acute. Since they do not have the same measures, they cannot be congruent.

4.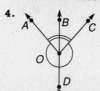

5.

45°

6.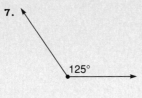

60°

7. 125°

8.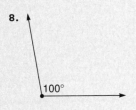

100°

9.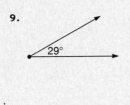

29°

10.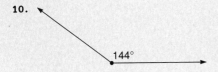

144°

11. acute   **12.** right   **13.** straight

14. obtuse   **15.** right   **16.** acute

17. $0 < 3x + 12 < 90$ or $-4 < x < 26$

18. obtuse: $8n - 17 = 7n - 3$

$$n = 20$$

$$m\angle N = 7n - 3 = 137$$

PAGES 47-48   EXERCISES

19. acute   **20.** right   **21.** obtuse

22. acute   **23.** straight   **24.** obtuse

25. acute   **26.** obtuse

27. $\angle MHA$ and $\angle HMT$, $\angle MAH$ and $\angle TAH$, $\angle ATM$ and $\angle HTM$

28. $\overrightarrow{TM}$ bisects $\angle HTA$; $\overrightarrow{AH}$ bisects $\angle MAT$.

29. $m\angle AHM = m\angle TMH$

$$3x + 5 = 7x - 27$$

$$x = 8$$

$$m\angle AHM = 3x + 5 = 29$$

30. $m\angle MAH = m\angle TAH$

$$2x + 5 = 7x - 10$$

$$x = 3$$

$$m\angle MAH = 2x + 5 = 11$$

$$m\angle TAH = 7x - 10 = 11$$

$$m\angle MAT = m\angle MAH + m\angle TAH$$

$$= 11 + 11$$

$$= 22$$

31. $m\angle HTA - m\angle HTM = m\angle MTA$

$$\frac{m\angle HTA}{2} = m\angle HTA - m\angle HTM$$

$$\frac{130 - x}{2} = 130 - x - (3x + 2)$$

$$130 - x = 2(130 - x - 3x - 2)$$

$$130 - x = 260 - 2x - 6x - 4$$

$$7x = 126$$

$$x = 18$$

$$m\angle HTA = 130 - x = 112$$

$$m\angle HTM = 3x + 2 = 56$$

$$m\angle MTA = m\angle HTA - m\angle HTM = 112 - 56$$

$$= 56$$

32. $m\angle MAR = m\angle MAL$

$$2x + 13 = 4x - 3$$

$$x = 8$$

$$m\angle RAL = m\angle MAR + m\angle MAL$$

$$= (2x + 13) + (4x - 3)$$

$$= 58$$

33. $m\angle MAR = \dfrac{m\angle RAL}{2}$

$$x - 31 = \frac{x + 32}{2}$$

$$2(x - 31) = x + 32$$

$$x = 94$$

$$m\angle LAM = m\angle MAR = x - 31$$

$$= 94 - 31$$

$$= 63$$

34. $m\angle RAS = m\angle SAM$

$$25 - 2x = 3x + 5$$

$$-5x = -20$$

$$x = 4$$

$$m\angle LAR = 2(m\angle RAS + m\angle SAM)$$

$$= 2(25 - 2(4) + 3(4) + 5)$$

$$= 2(17 + 17)$$

$$= 68$$

35. $m\angle RAM = m\angle LAM$

$$31 - x = 17 - 3x$$

$$2x = -14$$

$$x = -7$$

$$m\angle SAR = \frac{m\angle RAM}{2} = \frac{31 - (-7)}{2}$$

$$= 19$$

36. $m\angle RAL = 4(m\angle MAS)$

$$5x - 7 = 4(x + 3)$$

$$5x - 7 = 4x + 12$$

$$x = 19$$

$$m\angle MAR = 2(m\angle MAS) = 2(x + 3)$$

$$= 2(19 + 3)$$

$$= 44$$

37. Let $x = m\angle TQR$

$$x + 4x = 90$$

$$x = 18 = m\angle TQR$$

38. $90 < 5x + 25 < 180$ or $13 < x < 31$

39. yes; $m\angle KOJ = m\angle KOL$

$$8x - 17 = 3x + 28$$

$$x = 9$$

40. See students' work.

11

41. $x = 6$, $y = 8$

$$23x - 6y = 7x + 6y \qquad 23x - 6y = 90$$
$$23x - 7x - 6y - 6y = 0 \qquad 23\left(\frac{3}{4}y\right) - 6y = 90$$
$$16x - 12y = 0 \qquad \frac{69}{4}y - 6y = 90$$
$$4x - 3y = 0 \qquad 69y - 24y = 360$$
$$4x = 3y \qquad 45y = 360$$
$$x = \frac{3}{4}y \qquad y = 8$$

$$x = \frac{3}{4}y$$
$$x = \frac{3}{4}(8)$$
$$x = 6$$

42. $n = 7$; no

$$(n^2 - 12) + (4n + 11) = 76$$
$$n^2 + 4n - 77 = 0$$
$$(n + 11)(n - 7) = 0$$
$$\text{choose } n = 7$$
$$4n + 11 = 39$$
$$n^2 - 12 = 37$$

43. 24 times (twice each hour)

44. **a.** The three rays intersect at one point.
b. See students' work.

45. $m\angle IMP = 40$, $m\angle IMN = 50$: Since $m\angle IMR = 80$,
$m\angle IMP = \frac{80}{2} = 40$. Since $m\angle PMN = 90$,
$m\angle IMN = 90 - 40 = 50$.

46. point

47. $x = 3$: $\qquad SP + PM = SM$
$$(3x + 11) + (2x + 1) = 27$$
$$5x = 15$$
$$x = 3$$

48. $PT = 12$
$$PQ + PT = TQ$$
$$PQ = PT$$
$$2PQ = TQ$$
$$PQ = x + 7$$
$$2(x + 7) = 5x - 1$$
$$x = 5$$
$$PT = x + 7 = 12$$

49. false; since R is not in the interior of $\angle TPM$

50. $m\angle QPM = 58$
$$m\angle SPR + m\angle RPM = 180$$
$$(3d - 11) + (7d + 1) = 180$$
$$10d = 190$$
$$d = 19$$
$$m\angle QPM = m\angle RPM - m\angle RPQ$$
$$= (7d + 1) - (3d + 19)$$
$$= (7(19) + 1) - (3(19) + 19)$$
$$= 134 - 76$$
$$= 58$$

51. See students' work.

Technology: Using LOGO

PAGE 49   EXERCISES

1. vertical segment 80 units long
2. The turtle disappears when you type HT and reappears when you type ST.
3. Draw FD 50, RT 90, FD 25, RT 90, FD 50, BK 25, LT 90, FD 50, RT 90, FD 25, RT 90, FD 75
4. Draw FD 100, RT 90, FD 100, RT 90, FD 100, RT 90, FD 100, RT 90, FD 50, RT 90, FD 100, RT 90, FD 50, RT 90, FD 50, RT 90, FD 100
5. Draw FD 100, RT 90, FD 100, RT 90, FD 100, RT 90, FD 100, BK 25, RT 90, FD 25, LT 90, FD 25, RT 90, FD 25, RT 90, FD 50, RT 90, FD 50, LT 90, FD 25, LT 90, FD 75, LT90, FD75

1-8   Pairs of Angles

PAGES 52-53   CHECKING FOR UNDERSTANDING

1. Two sides of the pair of angles form a line.
2. False; any two angles whose measures have a sum of 180 are supplementary.
3. vertex; side; interior points
4. The sum of the measures of complementary angles is 90, while the sum of the measures of supplementary angles is 180.
5. $90 - 38 = 52$; $180 - 38 = 142$
6. $90 - 63 = 27$; $180 - 63 = 117$
7. no complement; $180 - 110 = 70$
8. $(90 - x)$, $(180 - x)$
9. $\angle NML$ and $\angle PMK$ **10.** $\angle JMK$ and $\angle KML$
11. $\angle JMP$ and $\angle JML$
12. Sample answers: $\angle NMP$ and $\angle PMK$, $\angle NMJ$ and $\angle JMK$, $\angle NML$ and $\angle KML$
13. Sample answers: $\angle NMP$ and $\angle PMJ$, $\angle PMJ$ and $\angle JMK$, $\angle JMK$ and $\angle KML$
14. $\angle JMK$ and $\angle NMP$
15. $\qquad m\angle A + m\angle B = 90$
$$(7x + 4) + (4x + 9) = 90$$
$$11x = 77$$
$$x = 7$$
$$m\angle A = 7x + 4 = 53$$
$$m\angle B = 4x + 9 = 37$$
16. $\qquad m\angle P + m\angle Q = 180$
$$(6x + 4) + 10x = 180$$
$$16x = 176$$
$$x = 11$$
$$m\angle P = 6x + 4 = 70$$
$$m\angle Q = 10x = 110$$

17. $3x - 5 = 94$

$3x = 99$

$x = 33$

18. $(4x + 1) + 53 = 90$

$4x = 36$

$x = 9$

19. $5x + 11 + 69 = 180$

$5x = 100$

$x = 20$

20. adjacent   21. adjacent, complementary

22. vertical   23. adjacent, supplementary, linear pair   24. adjacent, complementary

25. supplementary

26. $3x + 22 = 6x - 8$

$-3x = -30$

$x = 10$

$m\angle ABC = 3x + 22 = 52$

27. $(6x + 13) + (7x - 2) = 180$

$13x = 169$

$x = 13$

$m\angle ABC = 7x - 2 = 89$

28. $(4x + 23) + (2x + 1) = 90$

$6x = 66$

$x = 11$

$m\angle ABC = 3x = 33$

29. Let x = measure of smaller angle

$x + 44$ = measure of larger angle

$x + x + 44 = 180$

$2x = 136$

$x = 68$

$x + 44 = 112$

30. Let x = measure of larger angle

$x - 12$ = measure of smaller angle

$x + (x - 12) = 90$

$x = 51$

$x - 12 = 39$

31. Let x = measure of angle

$180 - x$ = measure of supplement

$x = \frac{1}{3}(180 - x)$

$3x = 180 - x$

$x = 45$

32. Let x = measure of angle

$90 - x$ = measure of complement

$x = \frac{1}{4}(90 - x)$

$4x = 90 - x$

$x = 18$

33. Let x = measure of angle

$90 - x$ = measure of complement

$2(90 - x) + 6 = x$

$180 - 2x + 6 = x$

$-3x = -186$

$x = 62$

$90 - x = 28$

34. Let x = measure of angle

$180 - x$ = measure of supplement

$4(180 - x) - 5 = x$

$720 - 4x - 5 = x$

$-5x = -715$

$x = 143$

$180 - x = 37$

35. Let x = measure of angle

$90 - x$ = complement

$180 - x$ = supplement

$180 - x = 6(90 - x)$

$180 - x = 540 - 6x$

$5x = 360$

$x = 72$

$90 - x = 18$

$180 - x = 108$

36. Let x = measure of angle

$90 - x$ = complement

$180 - x$ = supplement

$180 - x = 3(90 - x) - 60$

$180 - x = 270 - 3x - 60$

$2x = 30$

$x = 15$

$90 - x = 75$

$180 - x = 165$

37. $m\angle X + m\angle Y = 180$

$(x^2 - 9x) + (11x + 12) = 180$

$x^2 + 2x - 168 = 0$

$(x + 14)(x - 12) = 0$

$x = -14 \qquad x = 12$

choose $x = 12$

$m\angle X = x^2 - 9x = 36$

$m\angle Y = 11x + 12 = 144$

38. 36, 17, 75, 15, 55, 35

$m\angle A + m\angle B = 90$

$(2x + 3) + (y - 2) = 90$

$2x + y = 89$

$y = 89 - 2x$

$m\angle C + m\angle D = 90$

$(2x - y) + (x - 1) = 90$

$3x - y = 91$

$y = 3x - 91$

$89 - 2x = 3x - 91 \qquad\qquad x = 36$

$-5x = -91 - 89 \qquad m\angle A = 2x + 3 = 75$

$5x = 180 \qquad\qquad m\angle D = x - 1 = 35$

$x = 36$

$y = 3x - 91$

$y = 3(36) - 91 \qquad m\angle C = 2x - y = 55$

$y = 17$

$y - 2 = 15 = m\angle B$

39. Always true. Let x be the measure of the acute angle. Then $90 - x$ is the measure of its complement and $180 - x$ is the measure of its supplement. $(180 - x) - 2(90 - x) =$ $180 - x - 180 + 2x = x$. Thus the difference of the measure of the supplement and twice the measure of the complement is the measure of the angle.

40. Yes. $\angle 1 \cong \angle 2$ and $\angle 3 \cong \angle 4$, since they are vertical angles. So if $m\angle 2 + m\angle 3 = 90$, then by substitution $m\angle 1 + m\angle 4 = 90$ and $\angle 1$ and $\angle 4$ are complementary.

41. $180 - 10 = 170$

42. If $\angle N = 10$ then the coordinate of $N = 4$.
$NS = |8 - 4|$ or 4

43. $\dfrac{-6 + 8}{2} = 1$

44.
$$m\angle 1 + m\angle 2 = m\angle ADC$$
$$(3x + 2) + (4x - 1) = 148$$
$$7x = 147$$
$$x = 21$$

45. yes; $m\angle 1 = m\angle 2$
$$m\angle 1 + m\angle 2 = m\angle ADC$$
$$2x + 28 = 5x - 14$$
$$-3x = -42$$
$$x = 14$$
$$m\angle 1 = 2x = 28$$
$$m\angle 2 = 28$$
$$m\angle ADC = 5x - 14 = 56$$

46.
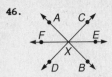

6 pairs: $\angle AXC$ and $\angle BXD$; $\angle EXB$ and $\angle FXA$; $\angle CXB$ and $\angle DXA$; $\angle CXE$ and $\angle DXF$; $\angle AXE$ and $\angle BXF$; $\angle EXD$ and $\angle FXC$

47. Adjacent angles are in the same plane and have a common vertex and a common side but no common interior points. Vertical angles are the two nonadjacent angles formed by two intersecting lines. Linear pairs of angles are adjacent and have noncommon sides that are opposite rays. Supplementary angles have measures that have a sum of 180. Complementary angles have measures that have a sum of 90. See students' drawings.

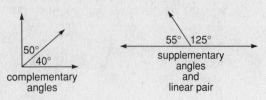

Both are also adjacent angles.

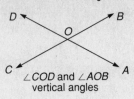
$\angle COD$ and $\angle AOB$
vertical angles

<table>
<tr><td>1-9</td><td>Right Angles and Perpendicular Lines</td></tr>
</table>

PAGES 59-60   CHECKING FOR UNDERSTANDING

1. in words, $\perp$; in a diagram, $\neg$ 2. congruent
3. $m \perp \ell$ 4. yes; no; yes   5. $\overline{CQ}$
6. $\angle AQB$ and $\angle CQD$
7. yes; $\angle BQD$ and $\angle CQE$ are right angles, so $m\angle BQD = 90$ and $m\angle CQE = 90$. Therefore $m\angle BQD = m\angle CQE$. $m\angle BQD = m\angle BQC + m\angle CQD$ and $m\angle CQE = m\angle CQD + m\angle DQE$ by the angle addition postulate. By substitution, $m\angle BQC + m\angle CQD = m\angle CQD + m\angle DQE$; $m\angle BQC = m\angle DQE$.
8.
$$m\angle AQB + m\angle BQC = m\angle AQC$$
$$(4x - 15) + (2x + 9) = 90$$
$$6x = 96$$
$$x = 16$$
$$m\angle CQD = m\angle AQB$$
$$= 4x - 15$$
$$= 49$$

9. yes   10. no   11. no   12. yes
13. no   14. no   15. yes   16. 9

PAGES 60-61   EXERCISES
17. no   18. yes   19. no   20. no
21. yes   22. no   23. yes
24. 19; yes
$$7x - 43 = 147 - 3x$$
$$10x = 190$$
$$x = 19$$
$$7x - 43 = 90$$
25. 25; no
$$(5x - 20) + (x + 50) = 180$$
$$6x = 150$$
$$x = 25$$
$$5x - 20 = 105$$
26. 10; no
$$4x + 9 = 5x - 1$$
$$-x = -10$$
$$x = 10$$
$$4x + 9 = 49$$

27. no   28. no   29. yes   30. no

31. no   32. no   33. yes   34. yes

35. a square:

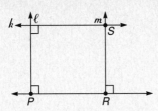

36.
$$3x - 24 = 2x + 10$$
$$x = 34$$
$$m\angle CEF = 3x - 24 = 78$$
$$m\angle FEA = 90 - m\angle CEF = 90 - 78$$
$$= 12$$

37.
$$m\angle RQC + m\angle AQR + m\angle DQA = 180$$
$$y + x + (2x - 4) = 180$$
$$3x = 180$$
$$x = 60$$
$$m\angle RQC + m\angle AQR = 90$$
$$y + x = 90$$
$$y + 60 = 90$$
$$y = 30$$

38.
$$m\angle BPC = 128$$
$$m\angle ACP + m\angle BCP = 90$$
$$(3x + 2y) + (3x + 4y) = 90$$
$$6x + 6y = 90$$
$$x + y = 15$$
$$y = 15 - x$$
$$m\angle APC + m\angle BPC = 180$$
$$(7x + 3) + 16y = 180$$
$$7x = 177 - 16y$$
$$x = \frac{177 - 16y}{7}$$

$$x = \frac{177 - 16y}{7} \qquad\qquad y = 15 - x$$
$$x = \frac{177 - 16(15 - x)}{7} \qquad = 15 - 7$$
$$7x = 177 - 240 + 16x \qquad y = 8$$
$$-9x = -63$$
$$x = 7$$
$$m\angle BPC = 16y$$
$$= 16(8)$$
$$= 128$$

39. $x = 15$, $y = 10$
$$m\angle MTB = 2x + 6y = 90$$
$$2x = 90 - 6y$$
$$x = 45 - 3y$$
$$m\angle ATN = 4x + 3y = 90$$
$$4(45 - 3y) + 3y = 90$$
$$180 - 12y + 3y = 90$$
$$-9y = -90$$
$$y = 10$$
$$x = 45 - 3y$$
$$= 45 - 3(10)$$
$$= 15$$

40. Suppose there were two lines in the plane perpendicular to the given line through the given point on the line as shown in the figure below. Since $\angle AXP$ and $\angle PXB$ are a linear pair, $m\angle AXP + m\angle PXB = 180$. Also $m\angle PXB = m\angle PXQ + m\angle QXB$ by angle addition postulate. Thus, $m\angle AXP + m\angle PXQ + m\angle QXB = 180$. But $m\angle AXP = 90$ and $m\angle QXB = 90$. This means $m\angle PXQ + 180 = 180$, or $m\angle PXQ = 0$ which is not possible. Therefore, there can be only one line perpendicular to the given line through the given point on the line.

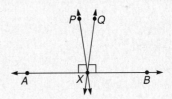

41. $90 - 45 = 45$

42.
$$AB + BC = AC$$
$$(2x - 3) + (3x + 13) = 30$$
$$5x = 20$$
$$x = 4$$

43. $\overline{CF}$, $\overline{AD}$, $\overline{AF}$, $\overline{FD}$, F 44. $\angle ACE$, $\angle FCE$, $\angle CEB$

45. If $\overline{CF}$ bisects $\angle ACE$,
$$m\angle BCF = m\angle FCD$$
$$5x + 11 = 3x + 23$$
$$2x = 12$$
$$x = 6$$

46. $m\angle DFE = m\angle AFB$ $m\angle CFD + m\angle DFE = 90$
      $= d + 10$ $(6d - 11) + (d + 10) = 90$
                                        $7d = 91$
                                        $d = 13$

   $m\angle DFE = d + 10$
             $= 13 + 10$
             $= 23$

47. See students' work.

Chapter 1 Summary and Review

PAGES 62-64   SKILLS AND CONCEPTS

1-4.

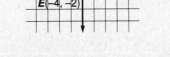

5. Quadrant IV   6. yes   7. point E

8. $\overleftrightarrow{ED}$, $\overleftrightarrow{AD}$, $\overleftrightarrow{CD}$

9. $AG = |15 - (-20)|$
   $= |35|$
   $= 35$

10. $EB = |10 - (-10)|$
    $= |20|$
    $= 20$

11. C and H

12. $\dfrac{-20 + 15}{2} = \dfrac{-5}{2}$

13. $\left(\dfrac{-2 + 8}{2}, \dfrac{7 + 1}{2}\right)$
    $\left(\dfrac{6}{2}, \dfrac{8}{2}\right)$
    $(3, 4)$

14. $2(x + 6) = 5x - 3$
    $2x + 12 = 5x - 3$
    $-3x = -15$
    $x = 5$
    $QR = PQ = x + 6 = 5 + 6 = 11$

15. $\overline{JK} \cong \overline{GH}$
    $|3 - x| = 17$

    $3 - x = 17$ $3 - x = -17$
    $-x = 14$ $-x = -20$
    $x = -14$ $x = 20$

16. $\overline{AB} \cong \overline{BC}$
    $8x - 7 = 4x + 9$
    $4x = 16$
    $x = 4$

17. yes

    A ———|——— B ———|——— C

18. $m\angle 1 + m\angle QXS = 180$
    $37 + m\angle QXS = 180$
    $m\angle QXS = 143$

19. $m\angle 2 + m\angle 3 = m\angle QXS$
    $(3x - 20) + (3x - 19) = 147$
    $6x = 186$
    $x = 31$

20. $m\angle 3 + m\angle 4 = m\angle RXT$
    $(77 - x) + (2x + 7) = 3x$
    $x + 84 = 3x$
    $-2x = -84$
    $x = 42$
    $m\angle 3 = 77 - x = 77 - 42 = 35$
    $m\angle 4 = 2x + 7 = 2(42) + 7 = 91$

21. yes; $\angle QXS$

22. $m\angle 1 = m\angle 2$
    $6x - 7 = 9x - 31$
    $-3x = -24$
    $x = 8$
    $m\angle 1 = 6x - 7 = 6(8) - 7 = 41$
    $m\angle 2 = 9x - 31 = 9(8) - 31 = 41$
    $m\angle PXR = m\angle 1 + m\angle 2$
    $= 41 + 41$
    $= 82$

23. acute $m\angle A = m\angle B$
    $3n + 55 = 8n$
    $55 = 5n$
    $11 = n$
    $m\angle B = 8n = 8(11) = 88$

24. $\angle 5$, $\angle 4$

25. Sample answer: $\angle FNA$ and $\angle 5$

26. $\angle CNF$ and $\angle 2$

27. Let x = measure of the angle
    $90 - x$ = complement
    $x = 3(90 - x) - 10$
    $x = 270 - 3x - 10$
    $4x = 260$
    $x = 65$
    $90 - x = 25$

28. $m\angle 4 + m\angle 5 = 90$
    $(2x - 1) + (3x - 4) = 90$
    $5x = 95$
    $x = 19$
    $m\angle 1 = m\angle 5 = 3x - 4 = 3(19) - 4 = 53$

29. no

30. $20x - 11 = 13x + 24$
    $7x = 35$
    $x = 5$
    $m\angle J = 20x - 11 = 20(5) - 11 = 89$
    $m\angle K = 13x + 24 + 13(5) + 24 = 89$
    no

PAGE 64   APPLICATIONS AND CONNECTIONS

31. No; there are only 32 different patterns.

32.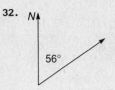

Chapter 1 Test

PAGE 65

1.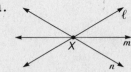

2.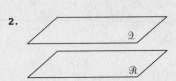

3.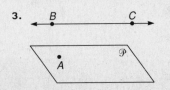

16

4.

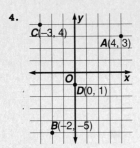

$C(-3, 4)$ $A(4, 3)$ $D(0, 1)$ $B(-2, -5)$

5. $(-2, 3)$

6. 5 units

$P(4, -1); Q(1, 3)$

$PQ = \sqrt{(1 - 4)^2 + (3 - (-1))^2}$

$= \sqrt{-3^2 + 4^2}$

$= \sqrt{25}$

$= 5$

7. $(-2, -1)$

$Q(1, 3); R(-5, -5)$

$\dfrac{1 - 5}{2}, \dfrac{3 - 5}{2}$

$\dfrac{-4}{2}, \dfrac{-2}{2}$

$-2, -1$

8. 3

9. $AC = |-2 - (-8)| = |6| = 6$

10. $\dfrac{-2 + 8}{2} = \dfrac{6}{2} = 3$

11. $\overline{AD}$

12.

$DG = 14$

$|4 - G| = 14$

$4 - G = 14$ or $4 - G = -14$

$-G = 10$ $\qquad$ $G = 18$

$G = -10$

G is negative because it is to the left of C on the number line and C is -2. $G = -10$

13. A, C, E **14.** $\overrightarrow{VA}$ and $\overrightarrow{VC}$ **15.** $\angle 7$

16. Sample answers: $\angle 3$ and $\angle 4$, $\angle 4$ and $\angle VCE$, $\angle VCE$ and $\angle VCA$, $\angle VCA$ and $\angle 3$

17. Sample answers: $\angle 6$ and $\angle 5$, $\angle 5$ and $\angle 2$, $\angle 2$ and $\angle 1$

18. yes **19.** false **20.** true

21.

$AC = CE$ $\qquad\qquad$ $AE = AC + CE$

$4x + 1 = 16 - x$ $\qquad$ $= 12.6 + 12.6$

$5x = 15$ $\qquad\qquad$ $= 25.2$

$x = 3$

$AC = 4x + 1 = 4(3) + 1 = 13$

$CE = 16 - x = 16 - 3 = 13$

$AE = AC + CE = 13 + 13 = 26$

22. yes **23.** $\angle 5$ and $\angle 6$ or $\angle 5$ and $\angle 1$

24.

$m\angle FVB = m\angle 5 + m\angle 6$

$9x - 11 = (3x + 14) + (x + 30)$

$5x = 55$

$x = 11$

$m\angle FVB = 9x - 11 = 9(11) - 11 = 88$

25. 10:

Darts in ring 3	3	2	2	0	1	0	0	0	1	1
Darts in ring 4	0	0	1	3	2	2	0	1	0	1
Darts in circle 9	0	1	0	0	0	1	3	2	2	1
Total	9	15	10	12	11	17	27	22	21	16

BONUS $\qquad \dfrac{-8 + 16}{2}, \dfrac{11 + 1}{2}$

$\dfrac{8}{2}, \dfrac{12}{2}$

$(4, 6)$ center

possible points: $(9, 18)$, $(-1, -6)$, $(-8, 1)$, $(16, 11)$

Algebra Review

PAGES 66-67

1. $17 + (-9) = 17 - 9 = 8$

2. $-7 + (-13) = -7 - 13 = -20$

3. $2.4 - 3.7 = -1.3$

4. $-3.72 - (-8.651) = -3.72 + 8.651 = 4.931$

5. $\dfrac{5}{4} + \left(-\dfrac{7}{8}\right) = \dfrac{10}{8} - \dfrac{7}{8} = \dfrac{3}{8}$

6. $-\dfrac{6}{5} - \dfrac{11}{12} = -\dfrac{72}{60} - \dfrac{55}{60} = -\dfrac{127}{60}$

7. $18 - (3 \cdot 4) + 5 = 11$

8. $18 - ((3 \cdot 4) + 5) = 1$

9. $18 - 3(4 + 5) = 18 - 27 = -9$

10. $(18 - 3)4 + 5 = 15(4) + 5 = 65$

11. $(18 - 3) \cdot (4 + 5) = 15 \cdot 9 = 135$

12. $6x + 7y + 8x - 2y = 14x + 5y$

13. $9r - 9s + 4s = 9r - 5s$

14. $3mn - 6m^2 - 4mn + 6n^2 = -mn - 6m^2 + 6n^2$

15. $\dfrac{3a^2}{4} + \dfrac{2ab}{3} + \dfrac{3ab}{3} - \dfrac{4a^2}{4} = \dfrac{5ab}{3} - \dfrac{a^2}{4}$

16. $-\dfrac{10}{7}\left(-\dfrac{5}{9}\right) = \dfrac{50}{63}$

17. $-\dfrac{10}{7} + \left(-\dfrac{5}{9}\right) = -\dfrac{10}{7} \cdot \left(-\dfrac{9}{5}\right) = \dfrac{18}{7}$

18. $\dfrac{33a - 66}{-11} = -3a + 6$

19. $-3\left(-\dfrac{7}{4}a + \dfrac{1}{6}\right) + \dfrac{5}{2}\left(3 - \dfrac{9}{2}\right) = \dfrac{21a}{4} - \dfrac{3}{6} + \dfrac{15}{2} - \dfrac{5a}{4} =$

$\dfrac{16a}{4} + \dfrac{45}{6} - \dfrac{3}{6} = \dfrac{16a}{4} + \dfrac{42}{6} = 4a + 7$

20. $|4 - (-2)| = |4 + 2| = 6$

21. $|-5| - |2 \cdot 1| = 5 - 2 = 3$

22. $-|3 + (-12)| = -|3 - 12| = -|-9| = -9$

23. $12 - a^2 = b$ **24.** $C = (2 + 3m)^3$ **25.** $xy^2 = t$

26. $x - 16 = 37$ $\qquad$ **27.** $z + 15 = -9$

$x = 53$ $\qquad\qquad$ $z = -24$

28. $r - (-4) = 21$ $\qquad$ **29.** $m + (-5) = 17$

$r = 17$ $\qquad\qquad\qquad$ $m = 22$

30. $-19 = -8 + d$
$-11 = d$

31. $9 = 18 + d$
$-9 = d$

32. $-7r = -56$
$r = 8$

33. $23y = 103.5$
$y = 4.5$

34. $-534 = 89a$
$-6 = a$

35. $\frac{x}{5} = 7$
$x = 35$

36. $-\frac{3}{4}n = 12$
$n = -16$

37. $\frac{-5}{3}z = \frac{-3}{2}$
$z = \frac{9}{10}$

38. $C = 3(113)$; $C = 339$

39. Let x = distance
$$\frac{x}{.75} = 13.65$$
$x = 10.2375$

40. Let x = Mark's score
$x - 4$ = Jessica's score
$x - 4 = 68$
$x = 72$

41. .75 liters $\quad \frac{89 \text{ cents}}{.75 \text{ liters}} \approx \$1.19$ per liter

1.25 liters $\quad \frac{\$1.31}{1.25 \text{ liters}} \approx \$1.05$ per liter

1.25 liters is better buy.

Chapter 2 Reasoning and Introduction to Proof

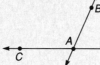 **2-1** **Inductive Reasoning and Conjecturing**

1. A conjecture is an educated guess based on observations of a particular situation.

2. You can prove a conjecture false by giving a counterexample.

3. He looked at several specific situations, none of which established the truth of his conjecture. He could have tested something that was not a form of water.

4. Answers will vary. Sample answer: Earth is the center of the universe.

5. False; A, B, and C could be as shown. They are not collinear.

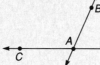

6. True; if $m\angle C = 25$, then
$m\angle A = 90 - 25 = 65$ and $m\angle B = 90 - 25$ or 65.
Since $m\angle A = m\angle B$, $\angle A \cong \angle B$.

Answers to Exercises 7-10 will vary. Sample answers are given. Given conjectures are not necessarily true.

7. $\angle A \cong \angle B$

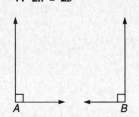

8. A, B, C, and D are collinear.

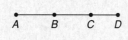

9. $\overline{PQ} \cong \overline{RQ}$

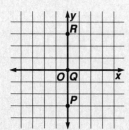

10. $\triangle ABC$ is a right triangle.

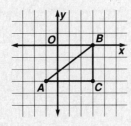

11. True; any three noncollinear points can be the vertices of a triangle.

12. False; collinear points cannot be the vertices of a triangle.

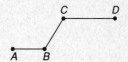

13. False. Counterexample:

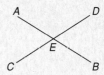

Answers for Exercises 14-18, 21-22 will vary. Sample answers are given.

14. A, B, and E are collinear and C, D, and E are collinear.

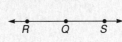

15. Points R, Q and S are collinear.

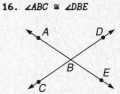

16. $\angle ABC \cong \angle DBE$

17. Points Q, P, and R are collinear.

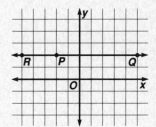

18. Points A, B, C, and D form a parallelogram.

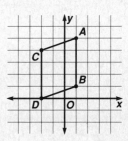

19. $1111^2 = 1,234,321$

20. $4^3 = 10^2 - 6^2$

21. $\overline{DE}$ is parallel to $\overline{BC}$.

22. $RSTU$ has four congruent sides.

23. False. Counterexample:

24. True; a positive or a negative squared will result in a positive, and zero squared equals zero. Therefore, any real number squared is a nonnegative number.

25. True; the diagonals of a rectangle are congruent.

26. True; the slopes of opposite sides are equal and the sloples of adjacent sides are opposite reciprocals. All sides are 5 units long.

Answers for Exercises 27 and 28 may vary. Sample answers are given.

27. *ABCDE* is a pentagon.

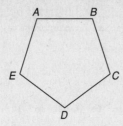

28. Segments *AB*, *BC*, *CD*, *DE*, and *EA* form a quadrilateral.

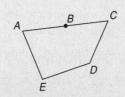

29. No three points are collinear.

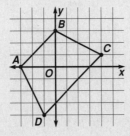

Answers for Exercises 30 and 32 will vary. Sample answers are given.

30. Quadrilaterals whose opposite sides are parallel have opposite angles that are congruent. Quadrilaterals whose sides are perpendicular have four right angles.

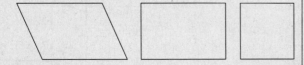

31. False, n = 41.

32. a. See students' work.
    b. A person's height is approximately three times the distance around his or her head.

33. a. Answers will vary.
    b. Yes, fungus is killing the plants.
    c. Introduce the fungus to some healthy plants and see if they grow taller and thinner.

34. Yes, they have a common side $\overline{CD}$.

35.

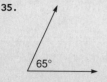

36.

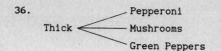

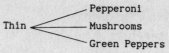

6 different pizzas can be made.

37. Plane

38. See students' work.

Technology: Conjectures

PAGE 75   EXERCISES

1. See students' work.

2. The diagonals of each rectangle and of each square are congruent.

<table>
<tr><td>2-2</td><td>**If-Then Statements, Converses, and Postulates**</td></tr>
</table>

PAGES 78-79   CHECKING FOR UNDERSTANDING

1. Answers will vary. A sample answer is given. A conditional statement is a statement that can be written in if-then form. A sample conditional is "If it rains tomorrow, then I will not go sailing."

2. If you waste not, then you will want not.

3. See students' work.

4. You form the converse of a statement by interchanging the hypothesis and conclusion of a conditional statement. If there is a rainbow, then it is raining.

5. Answers will vary. Sample answer: The existence of an atom is assumed in science.

6. Hypothesis: you work for 8 hours
   Conclusion: you work for one third of a day

7. Hypothesis: two lines are perpendicular
   Conclusion: they intersect

8. Hypothesis: you are sixteen years old
   Conclusion: you may get a driver's license

9. Hypothesis: $x = 4$
   Conclusion: $x^2 = 16$

10. If there are clouds, then it is raining. The converse is false since it may be cloudy and not be raining.

11. If an angle is acute, then it measures $37°$; false. Counterexample: An angle that measures $58°$ is acute, but its measure is not $37°$.

20

12. If three points lie in a straight line, then they are collinear; true.

13. If a person is President, then he or she must be a native-born United States citizen at least thirty-five years old; true.

14. If two angles are congruent, then they have the same measure.

15. If two planes intersect, then the intersection is a line.

16. If something goes up, then it must come down.

17. If an aluminum can is recycled, then it is remelted and back in the store within six weeks.

18. False   19. False

20. True   21. False

PAGES 79-81   EXERCISES

22. Hypothesis: it is Memorial Day
    Conclusion: it is a holiday

23. Hypothesis: a candy bar is a Milky Way®
    Conclusion: it contains caramel

24. Hypothesis: a container holds 32 ounces
    Conclusion: it holds a quart

25. True   26. True

27. False   28. False

29. True

30. If two angles are right angles, then they are congruent.

31. If a vehicle is a car, then it has four wheels.

32. If a figure is a square, then it has four sides.

33. If an angle is acute, then it is less than $90°$

34. If a figure is a triangle, then it has exactly three angles.

35. If two lines are parallel, then they do not intersect.

36. If a month has 31 days, then it is January; false. March, May, July, August, October, and December all have 31 days.

37. If it is about 6.2 miles, then the distance of the race is 10 kilometers; true.

38. If an animal is a dog, then it is a Springer Spaniel; false. German Shepherds are dogs and they are not Springer Spaniels.

39. Through any two points there is exactly one line.

40. A line contains at least two points.

41. If two points lie in a plane, then the entire line containing those two points lies in that plane.

42. A plane contains at least three points not on the same line.

43. If two planes intersect, then their intersection is a line.

44. one   45. one
46. three   47. six
48. ten   49. fifteen
50. twenty-one   51. one
52. infinitely many   53. ten

54. Answers will vary. Sample answers are given.

    a. If two line segments are congruent, then they have the same measure.

    b. If two lines are parallel, then they intersect at one point.

    c. If B is the midpoint of $\overline{AC}$, then $AB = BC$.

    d. If $\angle A$ and $\angle C$ are acute, then $m\angle A + m\angle C$ is less than 90.

55.
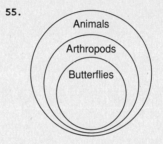

56. a. If you try Georgia, then you want a fabulous vacation.

    b. They are fabulous.

    c. No

57. a. 92
    b. 1023

58. In line 60, change > to <.

59. False; A, B, and P are not necessarily collinear.

60. $x + (x + 36) = 180$
    $2x + 36 = 180$
    $2x = 144$
    $x = 72$
    $x + 36 = 108$

61. $m\angle LON = x$
    $m\angle MOL = 5x$
    $x + 5x = 90$
    $6x = 90$
    $x = 15$

62. $\left(\dfrac{x_1 + x_2}{2}, \dfrac{y_1 + y_2}{2}\right) = (-3, 5)$

    $\dfrac{x_1 + x_2}{2} = -3 \qquad \dfrac{y_1 + y_2}{2} = 5$

    $\dfrac{-7 + x_2}{2} = -3 \qquad \dfrac{6 + y_2}{2} = 5$

    $-7 + x_2 = -6 \qquad 6 + y_2 = 10$

    $x_2 = 1 \qquad\qquad y_2 = 4$

    Coordinates of B are (1, 4).

63.
$$\overline{AB} + \overline{BC} = \overline{AC}$$
$$(6x - 1) + (2x + 4) = 9x - 3$$
$$8x + 3 = 9x - 3$$
$$6 = x$$
$$\overline{AC} = 9x - 3 = 9 \cdot 6 - 3 = 51$$

64.

65. No; $y = -2x + 5$
$$-2 \stackrel{?}{=} -2(7) + 5$$
$$-2 \stackrel{?}{=} -14 + 5$$
$$-2 \neq -9$$

66. See students' work.

2-3 Deductive Reasoning

PAGES 84-85   CHECKING FOR UNDERSTANDING

1. Sample answer: If Joan goes to the movies, she will spend half her allowance. Joan goes to the movies.
   Conclusion: Joan spends half her allowance.

2. a true conditional and given information that satisfies the hypothesis

3. a. I should choose Tint and Trim Hair Salon.
   b. Sample answer: Dogs have four legs. Kitty has four legs. Therefore, Kitty is a dog.

4. If two angles are a linear pair, then their measures total 180.

5. Yes; detachment
6. Yes; detachment
7. No
8. Yes; syllogism
9. No
10. No conclusion
11. $\overline{CD} \cong \overline{CD}$; detachment
12. If two angles form a linear pair, then they are adjacent; syllogism.
13. Planes M and N intersect in a line; detachment.
14. No conclusion
15. Bobby Rahal is a professional race car driver; detachment.

PAGES 85-87   EXERCISES

16. Yes; detachment
17. Yes; syllogism
18. No
19. Yes; detachment
20. Yes; syllogism
21. No
22. No conclusion
23. A, B, C are collinear; detachment.
24. No conclusion
25. p and q have a common point; detachment.
26. No conclusion
27. If an ordered pair for a point has 0 as its x-coordinate, then it is not contained in any of the four quadrants; syllogism.

28. No conclusion
29. No conclusion
30. Parallel lines have no points in common; syllogism.
31. No conclusion
32. No conclusion
33. Basalt was formed by volcanos; syllogism.

Answers for Exercises 34-37 will vary. Sample answers are given.

34. a. (2) I'm looking for a fun car to drive.
    (3) I need a Tigercub.
34. b. (2) Anyone who needs a Tigercub must have a good driving record.
    (3) If you are looking for a fun car to drive, then you must have a good driving record.

35. a. (2) Angles X and Y are adjacent and supplementary.
    (3) Angles X and Y are right angles.
35. b. (2) Right angles measure 90°.
    (3) Angles that are adjacent and supplementary measure 90°.

36. a. (2) (2, 3) satisfies the equation of a line.
    (3) (2, 3) lies on the line.
36. b. (2) If a point lies on a line, then it lies in the same plane as the line.
    (3) If the coordinates of a point satisfy the equation of a line, then the point lies in the same plane as the line.

37. a. (2) Dr. Garcia is a physician.
    (3) Dr. Garcia graduated from medical school.
37. b. (2) All medical school graduates have studied chemistry.
    (3) All physicians have studied chemistry.

38. You assumed the conditional was true.
39. If a mineral sample is quartz, then it can scratch glass; syllogism.
40. No valid conclusion
41. See students' work.
42. If a geometry test score is 89, then it is above average.
43. Acute
44. Let (4, 8) be (x_1, y_1) and (-3, 0) be (x_2, y_2).

$$\text{midpoint} = \left(\frac{x_1 + x_2}{2}, \frac{y_1 + y_2}{2} \right)$$

$$= \left(\frac{4 + (-3)}{2}, \frac{8 + 0}{2} \right)$$

$$\text{midpoint of } \overline{GH} = \left(\frac{1}{2}, 4 \right)$$

45. Let $(5, -3)$ be (x_1, y_1) and $(0, -5)$ be (x_2, y_2).

$$d = \sqrt{(x_2 - x_1)^2 + (y_2 - y_1)^2}$$
$$= \sqrt{(0 - 5)^2 + (-5 - (-3))^2}$$
$$= \sqrt{25 + 4}$$
$$= \sqrt{29}$$

The length of $\overline{XY}$ is $\sqrt{29}$ units.

46.

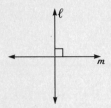

47. See students' work.

2-4   Properties from Algebra and Proof

PAGES 90-91   CHECKING FOR UNDERSTANDING

Answers for Exercises 2-3 will vary. Sample answers are given.

2. The reflexive property states that any single quantity is equal to itself; the symmetric property shows that if one quantity is equal to a second, then the second is equal to the first; the transitive property describes the relationship between three quantities.

3. A proof is a step-by-step reasoning from a hypothesis to a conclusion, where each step is justified by postulates, properties, or definitions.

4. hypothesis; conclusion

5. subtraction

6. distributive

7. division

8. addition

9. substitution

10. a. Given
    b. Subtraction property of equality
    c. Division property of equality

11. a. Given
    b. Reflexive property of equality
    c. Addition property of equality
    d. Angle addition postulate
    e. Substitution property of equality

PAGES 91-94   EXERCISES

12. subtraction

13. substitution

14. multiplication

15. transitive

16. substitution

17. reflexive

18. symmetric

19. subtraction

20. addition

21. addition

22. a. Given
    b. Multiplication property of equality
    c. Division property of equality

23. a. Given
    b. Symmetric property of equality
    c. Multiplication property of equality
    d. Distributive property
    e. Subtraction property of equality
    f. Multiplication property of equality

24. a. Given
    b. Multiplication property of equality
    c. Distributive property
    d. Subtraction property of equality
    e. Addition property of equality
    f. Division property of equality

25. a. Given
    b. Angle addition postulate
    c. Substitution property of equality
    d. Substitution property of equality
    e. Subtraction property of equality

26. Given: $4 - x = 10$
    Prove: $x = -6$

STATEMENTS	REASONS
a. $4 - x = 10$	a. Given
b. $-x = 6$	b. Subtraction property of equality
c. $x = -6$	c. Multiplication property of equality

27. Proof will vary. Sample proof given.
    Given: $m\angle M = m\angle P$
    $m\angle N = m\angle P$
    Prove: $m\angle M = m\angle N$

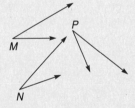

STATEMENTS	REASONS
a. $m\angle M = m\angle P$ $m\angle N = m\angle P$	a. Given
b. $m\angle M = m\angle N$	b. Substitution property of equality

28. Given: $x - 1 = \dfrac{x - 10}{-2}$

Prove: $x = 4$

STATEMENTS	REASONS
a. $x - 1 = \dfrac{x - 10}{-2}$	a. Given
b. $-2(x - 1) = x - 10$	b. Multiplication property of equality
c. $-2x + 2 = x - 10$	c. Distributive property of equality
d. $12 = 3x$	d. Addition property of equality
e. $4 = x$	e. Division property of equality
f. $x = 4$	f. Symmetric property of equality

29. Given: $m\angle ABC = 90$

$m\angle EDC = 90$

$m\angle 1 = m\angle 3$

Prove: $m\angle 2 = m\angle 4$

STATEMENTS	REASONS
a. $m\angle ABC = 90$ $m\angle EDC = 90$ $m\angle 1 = m\angle 3$	a. Given
b. $m\angle ABC = m\angle EDC$	b. Substitution property of equality
c. $m\angle ABC = m\angle 1 + m\angle 2$ $m\angle EDC = m\angle 3 + m\angle 4$	c. Angle addition postulate
d. $m\angle 1 + m\angle 2 = m\angle 3 + m\angle 4$	d. Substitution property of equality
e. $m\angle 1 + m\angle 2 = m\angle 1 + m\angle 4$	e. Substitution property of equality
f. $m\angle 2 = m\angle 4$	f. Subtraction property of equality

30. Answers will vary. Sample answer given. The method of scoring would have to be changed so that better play would be rewarded with higher, not lower, scores.

31. Given: $A = p + prt$

Prove: $p = \dfrac{A}{1 + rt}$

STATEMENTS	REASONS
a. $A = p + prt$	a. Given
b. $A = p(1 + rt)$	b. Distributive property of equality
c. $\dfrac{A}{1 + rt} = p$	c. Division property of equality
d. $p = \dfrac{A}{1 + rt}$	d. Symmetric property of equality

32. Given: $s = \frac{1}{2}at^2 + v_0 t$

Prove: $a = \dfrac{2s - 2v_0 t}{t^2}$

STATEMENTS	REASONS
a. $s = \frac{1}{2}at^2 + v_0 t$	a. Given
b. $s - v_0 t = \frac{1}{2}at^2$	b. Subtraction property of equality
c. $2(s - v_0 t) = at^2$	c. Multiplication property of equality
d. $2s - 2v_0 t = at^2$	d. Distributive property
e. $\dfrac{2s - 2v_0 t}{t^2} = a$	e. Division property of equality
f. $a = \dfrac{2s - 2v_0 t}{t^2}$	f. Symmetric property

33. See students' work.

34. $7 = 7$; detachment

35. $\dfrac{1}{9} = 0.\overline{1}$; $\dfrac{2}{9} = 0.\overline{2}$

$\dfrac{3}{9} = 0.\overline{3}$, $\dfrac{4}{9} = 0.\overline{4}$; $\dfrac{5}{9} = 0.\overline{5}$

36. Let $(9, 3)$ be (x_1, y_1) and $(-3, 8)$ be (x_2, y_2)

$$\text{midpoint} = \left(\frac{x_1 + x_2}{2}, \frac{y_1 + y_2}{2} \right)$$

$$= \left(\frac{9 + (-3)}{2}, \frac{3 + 8}{2} \right)$$

$$= \left(3, \frac{11}{2} \right)$$

37.

38. See students' work.

Mid-Chapter Review

PAGE 94

1. true, since a midpoint divides a segment into two congruent segments
2. true, since $x^3 = x \cdot x \cdot x$ and the reals are closed under multiplication
3. false

4. true, since all right angles have a measure of 90, and congruent angles are by definition angles with the same measure
5. If two lines are perpendicular, then they form four right angles.
6. If a substance is ordinary table sugar, then its chemical formula is $C_{12}H_{22}O_{11}$.
7. If it is a non-leap year, then the month of February has 28 days.

24

8. No conclusion

9. The diagonals of *ABCD* are congruent; detachment.

10. If two angles are right angles, then they have the same measure; syllogism.

11. Given: $x = 7$
Prove: $4x^2 = 196$

STATEMENTS	REASONS
a. $x = 7$	a. Given
b. $x \cdot x = 7 \cdot x$	b. Multiplication property of equality
c. $x^2 = 7 \cdot 7$	c. Substitution property of equality
d. $4x^2 = 196$	d. Multiplication property of equality

12. Given: $AC = AB$
$AC = 4x + 1$
$AB = 6x - 13$

Prove: $x = 7$

STATEMENTS	REASONS
a. $AC = AB$ $AC = 4x + 1$ $AB = 6x - 13$	a. Given
b. $4x + 1 = AB$	b. Substitution property of equality
c. $4x + 1 = 6x - 13$	c. Substitution property of equality
d. $1 = 2x - 13$	d. Subtraction property of equality
e. $14 = 2x$	e. Addition property of equality
f. $7 = x$	f. Division property of equality
g. $x = 7$	g. Symmetric property of equality

2-5 Problem-Solving Strategy: Process of Elimination

PAGE 96   CHECKING FOR UNDERSTANDING

1. Make a table and mark eliminations with an X.

2. No, you could not eliminate enough possibilities to make a conclusion.

3. 9th - Anthony, 10th - Erin,
11th - Brad, 12th - Lisa

4. 1 - mercury, 2 - gallium,
3 - lithium, 4 - calcium

5. x = people ahead of me
$x + 9$ = people behind me
$3x$ = total number of people in line
$$x + 1 + (x + 9) = 3x$$
$$2x + 10 = 3x$$
$$10 = x$$
$$19 = x + 9$$
19 people behind me

6. 5 corners:

 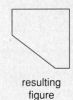

cut here   resulting figure

7. Umeko – Drama Club, delivery person
Jim – Spanish Club, tutor
Gwen – Marching band, lifeguard

8. 12 times: 1:11, 2:22, 3:33, 4:44, 5:55, and 11:11, both A.M. and P.M.

9. The jeans and T-shirts box contained T-shirts, the jeans box contained jeans and T-shirts, and the T-shirts box contained jeans.

10. 1773

Cooperative Learning Project

PAGE 97

		People					Days				
		Zach	Luisa	Marcus	Kelly	Mother	Monday	Tuesday	Wednesday	Thursday	Friday
A.M.	Swimming	√	x	x	x	x	x	√	x	x	x
	Chess	x	x	x	√	x	x	x	x	x	√
	Shoppng	x	x	x	x	√	x	x	√	x	x
	Biking	x	x	√	x	x	√	x	x	x	x
	Picnic	x	√	x	x	x	x	x	x	√	x
P.M.	Tennis	x	√	x	x	x	x	x	x	√	x
	Walking	x	x	√	x	x	√	x	x	x	x
	Radio	x	x	x	√	x	x	x	x	x	√
	Skateboarding	√	x	x	x	x	x	√	x	x	x
	Painting	x	x	x	x	√	x	x	√	x	x

Day	Person	Morning	Afternoon
Monday	Marcus	Biking	Walking
Tuesday	Zach	Swimming	Skateboarding
Wednesday	Mother	Shopping	Painting
Thursday	Luisa	Picnic	Tennis
Friday	Kelly	Chess	Radio

1. Answers will vary. A sample answer is given. A proof must include a statement of the theorem to be proved, a list of the given information, and a logical argument.

2. The measures of segments are real numbers.

3. a. Given
   b. Definition of congruent segments
   c. Transitive property of equality
   c. Definition of congruent segments

4. Given: $\overline{AB}$
   Prove: $\overline{AB} \cong \overline{AB}$

A————————B

STATEMENTS	REASONS
a. $\overline{AB}$ is a line segment.	a. Given
b. $AB = AB$	b. Reflexive property of equality
c. $\overline{AB} \cong \overline{AB}$	c. Definition of congruent segments

5. Congruence of segments is reflexive.
6. Subtraction property of equality
7. Congruence of segments is symmetric.
8. Division property of equality
9. Substitution property of equality
10. Congruence of segments is transitive.
11. Addition property of equality
12. Transitive property of equality or substitution property of equality

13. Given: $\angle A$ is a right angle.
    Prove: $m\angle A = 90$

14. Given: x is rational.
    Prove: x is a real number.

15. Given: $\angle 1$ and $\angle 2$ are vertical angles.
    Prove: $\angle 1 \cong \angle 2$

16. Given: Lines AB and XY are perpendicular.
    Prove: $\angle 1$, $\angle 2$, $\angle 3$, and $\angle 4$ are right angles.

17. Given: $\triangle QED$ is a triangle.
    Prove: $m\angle Q + m\angle E + m\angle D = 180$

18. Given: $QUAD$ is a rectangle.
    Prove: $\overline{QA} \cong \overline{UD}$

19. Given: $\overline{LE} \cong \overline{MR}$
    $\overline{EG} \cong \overline{RA}$
    Prove: $\overline{LG} \cong \overline{MA}$

L———E————————G

A————————R———M

STATEMENTS	REASONS
a. $\overline{LE} \cong \overline{MR}$ $\overline{EG} \cong \overline{RA}$	a. Given
b. $LE = MR$ $EG = RA$	b. Definition of congruent segments
c. $LE + EG = LG$ $MR + RA = MA$	c. Segment addition postulate
d. $LE + EG = MR + RA$	d. Addition property of equality
e. $LG = MA$	e. Substitution property of equality
f. $\overline{LG} \cong \overline{MA}$	f. Definition of congruent segments

20. Given: $DA = EL$
    Prove: $DE = AL$

D——E————A——L

STATEMENTS	REASONS
a. $DA = EL$	a. Given
b. $DA = DE + EA$ $EL = EA + AL$	b. Segment addition postulate
c. $DE + EA = EA + AL$	c. Substitution property of equality
d. $DE = AL$	d. Subtraction property of equality

21. Given: $\overline{AB} \cong \overline{CD}$
    M is the midpoint of $\overline{AB}$.
    N is the midpoint of $\overline{CD}$.
    Prove: $\overline{AM} \cong \overline{CN}$

A————M————B

C————N————D

STATEMENTS	REASONS
a. $\overline{AB} \cong \overline{CD}$ M is the midpoint of $\overline{AB}$. N is the midpoint of $\overline{CD}$.	a. Given
b. $AB = CD$	b. Definition of congruent segments
c. $AM = MB$ $CN = ND$	c. Definition of midpoint
d. $AM + MB = AB$ $CN + ND = CD$	d. Segment addition postulate

e. $AM + MB = CN + ND$ e. Substitution property of equality

f. $AM + AM = CN + CN$ f. Substitution property of equality

g. $2AM = 2CN$ g. Substitution property of equality

h. $AM = CN$ h. Division property of equality

i. $\overline{AM} \cong \overline{CN}$ i. Definition of congruent segments

---

22. Given: $RS = ST$
Prove: $RT = 2ST$

STATEMENTS	REASONS
a. $RS = ST$	a. Given
b. $RT = RS + ST$	b. Segment addition postulate
c. $RT = ST + ST$	c. Substitution property of equality
d. $RT = 2ST$	d. Substitution property of equality

23. Given: $MP = NP$
        $PO = PL$
Prove: $MO = NL$

STATEMENTS	REASONS
a. $MP = NP$ $PO = PL$	a. Given
b. $MP + PO = NP + PL$	b. Addition property of equality
c. $MP = MP + PO$ $NL = NP + PL$	c. Segment addition postulate
d. $MO = NL$	d. Substitution property of equality

24. Given: $AC = AD$
        $AB = AE$
Prove: $BC = ED$

STATEMENTS	REASONS
a. $AC = AD$ $AB = AE$	a. Given
b. $AC = AB + BC$ $AD = AE + ED$	b. Segment addition postulate
c. $AB + BC = AE + ED$	c. Substitution property of equality
d. $BC = ED$	d. Subtraction property of equality

25. Given: $\overline{SA} \cong \overline{ND}$
Prove: $\overline{SN} \cong \overline{AD}$

STATEMENTS	REASONS
a. $SA \cong ND$	a. Given
b. $SA = ND$	b. Definition of congruent segments
c. $SA + AN = AN + ND$	c. Addition property of equality
d. $SN = SA + AN$ $AD = AN + ND$	d. Segment addition postulate
e. $SN = AD$	e. Substitution property of equality
f. $SN \cong AD$	f. Definition of congruent segments

26. Given: $\overline{BC} \cong \overline{YX}$
        $\overline{AC} \cong \overline{ZX}$
Prove: $\overline{AB} \cong \overline{ZY}$

STATEMENTS	REASONS
a. $\overline{BC} \cong \overline{YX}$ $\overline{AC} \cong \overline{ZX}$	a. Given
b. $BC = YX$ $AC = ZX$	b. Definition of congruent segments
c. $AC = AB + BC$ $ZX = ZY + YX$	c. Segment addition postulate
d. $AB + BC = ZY + YX$	d. Substitution property of equality
e. $AB = ZY$	e. Subtraction property of equality
f. $\overline{AB} \cong \overline{ZY}$	f. Definition of congruent segments

27. Given: $\overline{QT} \cong \overline{RT}$
        $\overline{TS} \cong \overline{TP}$
Prove: $\overline{QS} \cong \overline{RP}$

STATEMENTS	REASONS
a. $\overline{QT} \cong \overline{RT}$ $\overline{TS} \cong \overline{TP}$	a. Given
b. $QT = RT$ $TS = TP$	b. Definition of congruent segments
c. $QT + TS = RT + TP$	c. Addition property of equality
d. $QS = QT + TS$ $RP = RT + TP$	d. Substitution property of equality
e. $QS = RP$	e. Substitution property of equality
f. $\overline{QS} \cong \overline{RP}$	f. Definition of congruent segments

28. Given: $\overline{AC} \cong \overline{CD} \cong \overline{DB}$

A   C   D   B

Prove: $AB = 3AC$

STATEMENTS	REASONS
a. $\overline{AC} \cong \overline{CD} \cong \overline{DB}$	a. Given
b. $AC = CD = DB$	b. Definition of congruent segments
c. $AB = AC + CB$	c. Segment addition postulate
d. $CB = CD + DB$	d. Segment addition postulate
e. $AB = AC + CD + DB$	e. Substitution property of equality
f. $AB = AC + AC + AC$	f. Substitution property of equality
g. $AB = 3AC$	g. Substitution property of equality

29. Given: $AB = CD$

M is the midpoint of $\overline{AB}$.

N is the midpoint of $\overline{CD}$.

A   M   B

C   N   D

Prove: $AM = MB = CN = ND$

STATEMENTS	REASONS
a. $AB = CD$ M is the midpoint of $\overline{AB}$. N is the midpoint of $\overline{CD}$.	a. Given
b. $AB = AM + MB$ $CD = CN + ND$	b. Segment addition postulate
c. $AM = MB$ $CN = ND$	c. Definition of midpoint
d. $AB = AM + AM$ $CD = CN + CN$	d. Substitution property of equality
e. $2AM = 2CN$	e. Substitution property of equality
f. $AM = CN$	f. Division property of equality
g. $AM = ND$	g. Transitive property of equality
h. $AM = MB = CN = ND$	h. Transitive property of equality

30. Answers will vary. Sample answers are given.
$\overline{EG} \cong \overline{JH}$ and $\overline{EF} \cong \overline{FG} \cong \overline{KL} \cong \overline{LM} \cong \overline{JI} \cong \overline{IH}$

31.

STATEMENTS	REASONS
a. The defendant drove through a red traffic light at the corner of Washington and Elm.	a. The defendant was seen.
b. The signal was not down.	b. The traffic computer shows no indication that the signal was down.
c. The defendant is subject to a $50 fine.	c. The law states that if a driver proceeds through a red traffic light that is in proper working order, the driver is subject to a $50 fine.

32. a. It is priced well below any comparable truck. It's fun to drive. It has room for four and plenty of cargo space.
   b. Answers will vary.
   c. Answers will vary. Sample answer: Fuel economy.

33.

	Jan	Feb	Aug	Sep
Amy	x	x	x	✓
Emma	x	x	✓	x
Timothy	x	✓	x	x
Pablo	✓	x	x	x

January – Pablo, February – Timothy, August – Emma, September – Amy

34. Division or multiplication property of equality

35. If a student maintains a C average, then he or she is eligible to play a varsity sport.

36. Answers will vary. Sample answer: a satellite

37. $x = m\angle NOR$; $4x = m\angle AND$

$$x + 4x = 90$$
$$5x = 90$$
$$x = 18$$

$m\angle NOR = 18$, $m\angle AND = 72$

38. a. $|-7 - (-2)| = |-5| = 5$ units
   b. $|-2 - 0| = |-2| = 2$ units
   c. $|-7 - 0| = |-7| = 7$ units
   d. $|1 - (-7)| = |8| = 8$ units

39. See students' work.

2-7 Two-Column Proofs with Angles

PAGES 107-108   CHECKING FOR UNDERSTANDING

1. Answers will vary. Sample answer: angles formed by the legs of a director's chair

2. Answers will vary. Sample answers are given.

   Theorem 2-2. Supplement Theorem

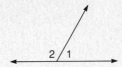

$m\angle 1 = 60$, $m\angle 2 = 120$

$\angle 1$ and $\angle 2$ form a linear pair. They are supplementary since $m\angle 1 + m\angle 2 = 180$.

Theorem 2-3. Congruence of angles is reflexive, symmetric, and transitive.

$m\angle 1 = 50$ $m\angle 2 = 50$ $m\angle 3 = 50$

a. $\angle 1 \cong \angle 1$ since $m\angle 1 = m\angle 1$
b. If $\angle 1 \cong \angle 2$, then $\angle 2 \cong \angle 1$
   since $m\angle 1 = 50$ and $m\angle 2 = 50$.
c. If $\angle 1 \cong \angle 2 \cong \angle 3$, then $\angle 1 \cong \angle 3$
   since $m\angle 1 = 50$, $m\angle 2 = 50$, $m\angle 3 = 50$.

Theorem 2-4. Angles supplementary to the same angle or to congruent angles, are congruent.

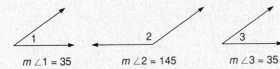

$m\angle 1 = 35$ $m\angle 2 = 145$ $m\angle 3 = 35$

$\angle 1$ and $\angle 2$ are supplements since
$m\angle 1 + m\angle 2 = 35 + 145 = 180$.
$\angle 2$ and $\angle 3$ are supplements since
$m\angle 2 + m\angle 3 = 145 + 35 = 180$.
$\angle 1 \cong \angle 3$ since $m\angle 1 = 35$ and
$m\angle 2 = 35$.

Theorem 2-5. Angles complementary to the same angle or to congruent angles are congruent.

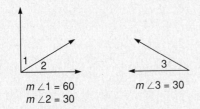

$m\angle 1 = 60$
$m\angle 2 = 30$ $m\angle 3 = 30$

$\angle 1$ and $\angle 2$ are complementary since
$m\angle 1 + m\angle 2 = 60 + 30 = 90$.
$\angle 1$ and $\angle 3$ are complementary since
$m\angle 1 + m\angle 3 = 60 + 30 = 90$.
$\angle 2 \cong \angle 3$ since $m\angle 2 = 30$ and $m\angle 3 = 30$.

Theorem 2-6. All right angles are congruent.

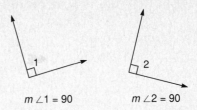

$m\angle 1 = 90$ $m\angle 2 = 90$

$\angle 1 \cong \angle 2$ since $m\angle 1 = 90$ and $m\angle 2 = 90$

Theorem 2-7. Vertical angles are congruent.

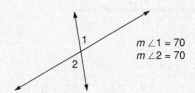

$m\angle 1 = 70$
$m\angle 2 = 70$

$\angle 1$ and $\angle 2$ are vertical angles
and $m\angle 1 = 70$ and $m\angle 2 = 70$.

Theorem 2-8. Perpendicular lines intersect to form four right angles.

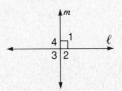

Lines ℓ and m are perpendicular,
$\angle 1$, $\angle 2$, $\angle 3$, and $\angle 4$ are all right angles since
$m\angle 1 = m\angle 2 = m\angle 3 = m\angle 4 = 90$.

3. sometimes   4. never
5. sometimes   6. never
7. sometimes   8. always
9. always   10. sometimes

11. $m\angle 1 = m\angle 2$
    $2x + 94 = 7x + 49$
         $45 = 5x$
          $9 = x$
    $m\angle 1 = 2x + 94 = 112$
    $m\angle 2 = 7x + 49 = 112$

12. $m\angle 1 + m\angle 2 = 180$
    $50 + 5x + 60x = 180$
       $50 + 65x = 180$
          $65x = 130$
            $x = 2$
    $m\angle 1 = 50 + 5x = 60$
    $m\angle 2 = 60x = 120$

13. $m\angle 1 + m\angle 2 = 180$
    $100 + 20x + 20x = 180$
        $100 + 40x = 180$
            $40x = 80$
              $x = 2$
    $m\angle 1 = 100 + 20x = 140$
    $m\angle 2 = 20x = 40$

14. $m\angle 1 = m\angle 2$

  $5x = x + 36$

  $4x = 36$

  $x = 9$

  $m\angle 1 = 5x = 45$

  $m\angle 2 = x + 36 = 45$

15. Given: $\angle 1$ and $\angle 2$ form a linear pair.

Prove: $\angle 1$ and $\angle 2$ are supplementary.

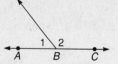

STATEMENTS	REASONS
1. $\angle 1$ and $\angle 2$ form a linear pair.	1. Given
2. $\overrightarrow{BA}$ and $\overrightarrow{BC}$ are opposite rays.	2. Definition of a linear pair
3. $m\angle ABC = 180$	3. Definition of straight angle
4. $m\angle ABC = m\angle 1 + m\angle 2$	4. Angle addition postulate
5. $180 = m\angle 1 + m\angle 2$	5. Substitution property of equality
6. $\angle 1$ and $\angle 2$ are supplementary.	6. Definition of supplementary

PAGES 108-109   EXERCISES

16. $\angle PLO$ or $\angle MLR$

17. $\angle MLN$ or $\angle PLQ$

18. $m\angle QLN - m\angle QLR - m\angle NLM = 180 - 30 - 40$ or 110

19. $m\angle OLP = m\angle MLR$ or 110

20. $\angle PLQ$ or $\angle MLN$

21. $m\angle NLO = m\angle QLR$ or 30

22. $m\angle RLP = m\angle RLQ + m\angle QLP = 30 + 40$ or 70

23. Given: $\angle ABC \cong \angle EFG$

  $\angle ABD \cong \angle EFH$

Prove: $\angle DBC \cong \angle HFG$

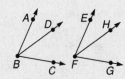

STATEMENTS	REASONS
a. $\angle ABC \cong \angle EFG$ $\angle ABC \cong \angle EFH$	a. Given
b. $m\angle ABC = m\angle EFG$ $m\angle ABD = m\angle EFH$	b. Definition of congruent angles
c. $m\angle ABC = m\angle ABD + m\angle DBC$ $m\angle EFG = m\angle EFH + m\angle HFG$	c. Angle addition postulate
d. $m\angle ABD + m\angle DBC =$ $m\angle EFH + m\angle HFG$	d. Substitution property of equality
e. $m\angle DBC = m\angle HFG$	e. Subtraction property of equality
f. $\angle DBC \cong \angle HFG$	f. Definition of congruent angles

24. Given: $\angle 1 \cong \angle 2$

  $\angle 3 \cong \angle 4$

Prove: $\angle ABC \cong \angle DCB$

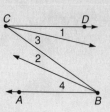

STATEMENTS	REASONS
a. $\angle 1 \cong \angle 2$ $\angle 3 \cong \angle 4$	a. Given
b. $m\angle 1 = m\angle 2$ $m\angle 3 = m\angle 4$	b. Definition of congruent angles
c. $m\angle ABC = m\angle 2 + m\angle 4$ $m\angle DCB = m\angle 1 + m\angle 3$	c. Angle addition postulate
d. $m\angle 1 + m\angle 3 =$ $m\angle 2 + m\angle 4$	d. Addition property of equality
e. $m\angle DCB = m\angle ABC$	e. Substitution property of equality
f. $m\angle ABC = m\angle DCB$	f. Symmetric property of equality
g. $\angle ABC \cong \angle DCB$	g. Definition of congruent angles

25. Given: $\angle A$ is an angle.

Prove: $\angle A \cong \angle A$

STATEMENTS	REASONS
a. $\angle A$ is an angle.	a. Given
b. $m\angle A = m\angle A$	b. Reflexive property of equality
c. $\angle A \cong \angle A$	c. Definition of congruent angles

26. Given: $\angle A \cong \angle B$

Prove: $\angle B \cong \angle A$

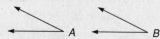

STATEMENTS	REASONS
a. $\angle A \cong \angle B$	a. Given
b. $m\angle A = m\angle B$	b. Definition of congruent angles
c. $m\angle B = m\angle A$	c. Symmetric property of equality
d. $\angle B \cong \angle A$	d. Definition of congruent angles

27. Given: $\angle X$ and $\angle Y$ are right angles.

Prove: $\angle X \cong \angle Y$

STATEMENTS	REASONS
a. $\angle X$ and $\angle Y$ are right angles.	a. Given
b. $m\angle X = 90$ $m\angle Y = 90$	b. Definition of right angle

c. $m\angle X = m\angle Y$	c. Substitution property of equality
d. $\angle X \cong \angle Y$	d. Definition of congruent angles

k. $m\angle 4 = 90$ $m\angle 2 = 90$	k. Subtraction property of equality
l. $\angle 4$ is a right angle. $\angle 2$ is a right angle.	l. Definition of right angle

28. Given: $\angle 1$ and $\angle 2$ are complementary.
$\angle 3$ and $\angle 2$ are complementary.
Prove: $\angle 1 \cong \angle 3$

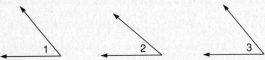

STATEMENTS	REASONS
a. $\angle 1$ and $\angle 2$ are complementary. $\angle 3$ and $\angle 2$ are complementary.	a. Given
b. $m\angle 1 + m\angle 2 = 90$ $m\angle 3 + m\angle 2 = 90$	b. Definition of complementary
c. $m\angle 1 + m\angle 2 =$ $m\angle 3 + m\angle 2$	c. Substitution property of equality
d. $m\angle 1 = m\angle 3$	d. Subtraction property of equality
e. $\angle 1 \cong \angle 3$	e. Definition of congruent angles

29. Given: $\ell \perp m$
Prove: $\angle 1$, $\angle 2$, $\angle 3$, and $\angle 4$ are right angles.

STATEMENTS	REASONS
a. $\ell \perp m$	a. Given
b. $\angle 1$ is a right angle.	b. Definition of perpendicular lines
c. $m\angle 1 = 90$	c. Definition of right angle
d. $\angle 1 \cong \angle 3$	d. Vertical angles are congruent.
e. $m\angle 3 = 90$	e. Definition of congruent angles
f. $\angle 3$ is a right angle.	f. Definition of right angle
g. $\angle 1$ and $\angle 4$ form a linear pair. $\angle 2$ and $\angle 1$ form a linear pair.	g. Definition of linear pair
h. $\angle 1$ and $\angle 4$ are supplementary. $\angle 1$ and $\angle 2$ are supplementary.	h. If two angles form a linear pair, they are supplementary.
i. $m\angle 1 + m\angle 4 = 180$ $m\angle 1 + m\angle 2 = 180$	i. Definition of supplementary
j. $90 + m\angle 4 = 180$ $90 + m\angle 2 = 180$	j. Substitution property of equality

30. Given: $\angle 1$ and $\angle 2$ form a linear pair.
$\angle 1$ is a right angle.
Prove: $\angle 2$ is a right angle.

STATEMENTS	REASONS
a. $\angle 1$ and $\angle 2$ form a linear pair. $\angle 1$ is a right angle.	a. Given
b. $\angle 1$ and $\angle 2$ are supplementary.	b. If two angles form a linear pair, they are supplementary.
c. $m\angle 1 + m\angle 2 = 180$	c. Definition of supplementary angle
d. $m\angle 1 = 90$	d. Definition of right angle
e. $90 + m\angle 2 = 180$	e. Substitution property of equality
f. $m\angle 2 = 90$	f. Subtraction property of equality
g. $\angle 2$ is a right angle.	g. Definition of right angle

31. Given: $\angle S \cong \angle T$
$\angle S$ and $\angle T$ are supplementary.
Prove: $\angle S$ and $\angle T$ are right angles.

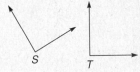

STATEMENTS	REASONS
a. $\angle S \cong \angle T$ $\angle S$ and $\angle T$ are supplementary.	a. Given
b. $m\angle S = m\angle T$	b. Definition of congruent angles
c. $m\angle S + m\angle T = 180$	c. Definition of supplementary angles
d. $2m\angle S = 180$	d. Substitution property of equality
e. $m\angle S = 90$	e. Division property of equality
f. $m\angle T = 90$	f. Substitution property of equality
g. $\angle S$ and $\angle T$ are right angles.	g. Definition of right angle

32. Given: ∠1 and ∠2
        are vertical angles.
        ∠1 is a right angle.
    Prove: ∠2 is a right angle.

STATEMENTS	REASONS
a. ∠1 and ∠2 are vertical angles. ∠1 is a right angle.	a. Given
b. ∠1 ≅ ∠2	b. Vertical angles are congruent.
c. m∠1 = m∠2	c. Definition of congruent angles
d. m∠1 = 90	d. Definition of right angle
e. 90 = m∠2	e. Substitution property of equality
f. ∠2 is a right angle.	f. Definition of a right angle

33. 90 pairs of angles. Look for a pattern.

Lines	1	2	3	4	5	6	7	8	9	10
Angles	0	2	6	12	20	30	42	56	72	90

+2 +4 +6 +8 +10 +12 +14 +16 +18

34. $180 - 57 = 123$

35. Reflexive property of equality

36.

STATEMENTS	REASONS
a. $F = \frac{9}{5}C + 32$	a. Given
b. $F - 32 = \frac{9}{5}C$	b. Subtraction property of equality
c. $\frac{5}{9}(F - 32) = C$	c. Multiplication property of equality

37. No conclusion

38. No complement, 21

39. See students' work.

Chapter 2 Summary and Review

PAGES 110-112   SKILLS AND CONCEPTS

1. True

2. False, not all supplementary angles are congruent.

3. If something is a cloud, then it has a silver lining.

4. If a polygon is a rectangle, then it has four right angles.

5. If a rock is obsidian, then it is a glassy rock produced by a volcano.

6. If two planes intersect, then their intersection is a line.

7. ∠A and ∠B have measures with a sum of 90; law of detachment.

8. No conclusion

9. The sun is in constant motion; syllogism

10. Given: $12x + 24 = 0$
    Prove: $x = -2$

STATEMENTS	REASONS
a. $12x + 24 = 0$	a. Given
b. $12x = -24$	b. Substraction property of equality
c. $x = -2$	c. Division property of equality

11. Given: MN = PN
          NL = NO
    Prove: ML = PO

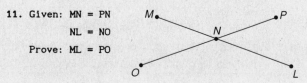

STATEMENTS	REASONS
a. MN = PN NL = NO	a. Given
b. MN + NL = PN + NO	b. Addition property of equality
c. ML = MN + NL PO = PN + NO	c. Segment addition postulate
d. ML = PO	d. Substitution property of equality

12. Given: m∠BAC + m∠BAD = 180
          m∠DAE + m∠CAE = 180
          m∠BAD = m∠CAE
    Prove: m∠DAE = m∠BAC

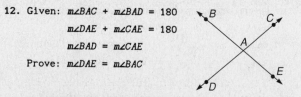

STATEMENTS	REASONS
a. m∠BAC + m∠BAD = 180 m∠DAE + m∠CAE = 180 m∠BAD = m∠CAE	a. Given
b. m∠BAC + m∠BAD = m∠DAE + m∠CAE	b. Substitution property of equality
c. m∠BAC + m∠CAE = m∠DAE + m∠CAE	c. Substitution property of equality
d. m∠BAC = m∠DAE	d. Subtraction property of equality
e. m∠DAE = m∠BAC	e. Symmetric property of equality

13. Given: $\overline{AM} \cong \overline{CN}$
    $\overline{MB} \cong \overline{ND}$
    Prove: $\overline{AB} \cong \overline{CD}$

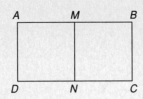

STATEMENTS	REASONS
a. $\overline{AM} \cong \overline{CN}$ $\overline{MB} \cong \overline{ND}$	a. Given
b. $AM = CN$ $MB = ND$	b. Definition of congruent segments
c. $AM + MB = CN + ND$	c. Addition property of equality
d. $AB = AM + MB$ $CD = CN + ND$	d. Segment addition postulate
e. $AB = CD$	e. Substitution property of equality
f. $\overline{AB} \cong \overline{CD}$	f. Definition of congruent segments

14. Given: $\angle 1$ and $\angle 3$ are supplementary. $\angle 3$ and $\angle 4$ form a linear pair.
    Prove: $\angle 1 \cong \angle 4$

STATEMENTS	REASONS
a. $\angle 1$ and $\angle 3$ are supplementary. $\angle 3$ and $\angle 4$ form a linear pair.	a. Given
b. $\angle 3$ and $\angle 4$ are supplementary.	b. If two lines form a linear pair, they are supplementary
c. $m\angle 1 + m\angle 3 = 180$ $m\angle 3 + m\angle 4 = 180$	c. Definition of supplementary
d. $m\angle 1 + m\angle 3$ $= m\angle 3 + m\angle 4$	d. Substitution property of equality
e. $m\angle 1 = m\angle 4$	e. Subtraction property of equality
f. $\angle 1 \cong \angle 4$	f. Definition of congruent angles

15. Given: $\angle 1$ and $\angle 2$ form a linear pair. $\angle 1 \cong \angle 2$
    Prove: $\angle 1$ and $\angle 2$ are right angles.

STATEMENTS	REASONS
a. $\angle 1$ and $\angle 2$ form a linear pair. $\angle 1 \cong \angle 2$	a. Given
b. $m\angle 1 = m\angle 2$	b. Definition of congruent angles
c. $\angle 1$ and $\angle 2$ are supplementary.	c. If two angles form a linear pair, they are supplementary.
d. $m\angle 1 + m\angle 2 = 180$	d. Definition of supplementary
e. $m\angle 1 + m\angle 1 = 180$	e. Substitution property of equality
f. $2m\angle 1 = 180$	f. Substitution property of equality
g. $m\angle 1 = 90$	g. Division property of equality
h. $m\angle 2 = 90$	h. Substitution property of equality
i. $\angle 1$ and $\angle 2$ are right angles.	i. Definition of right angle

PAGE 112   APPLICATIONS AND CONNECTIONS

16. If you are a hard-working person, then you deserve a night on the town at Gil's Grill. Hypothesis: You are a hard-working person. Conclusion: You deserve a night on the town at Gil's Grill. Converse: If you deserve a night on the town at Gil's Grill, then you are a hard-working person.

17. A sponge remains permanently attached to a surface for all of its adult life; syllogism.

18. Transitive property of equality

19.

STATEMENTS	REASONS
a. $t = 35d + 20$	a. Given
b. $t - 20 = 35d$	b. Subtraction property of equality
c. $\dfrac{t - 20}{35} = d$	c. Division property of equality

20.

	spaghetti	salad	macaroni
Alana	√	x	x
Becky	x	x	√
Carl	x	√	x

Alana - spaghetti, Becky - macaroni & cheese, Carl - salad

Chapter 2 Test

PAGE 113

1. False. Counterexample: $x = -1$
   -1 is real, but $-(-1) > 0$.
2. True. Congruent angles have the same measure, and the measure of the angles are real numbers; therefore, the symmetric property of equality holds true.

3. True. The angles form a straight angle which equals 180°.

4. False. It is possible that $x = -4$.

5. If there are any two points, then there is exactly one straight line through them. Hypothesis: there are any two points Conclusion: there is exactly one straight line through them. Converse: If there is exactly one line, then there are two points on it.

6. If something is a rolling stone, then it gathers no moss. Hypothesis: Something is a rolling stone. Conclusion: It gathers no moss. Converse: If something gathers no moss, then it is a rolling stone.

7. If you make a wise investment with Petty-Bates, then it pays off. Hypothesis: you make a wise investment with Petty-Bates. Conclusion: it pays off. Converse: If it pays off, then it is a wise investment with Petty-Bates.

8. If two planes are parallel, then they do not intersect. Hypothesis: two planes are parallel. Conclusion: they do not intersect. Converse: If two planes do not intersect, then they are parallel.

9. Wise investments with Petty-Bates build for the future; syllogism.

10. Lines ℓ and m intersect; detachment.

11. No conclusion

12. 7 is a real number; detachment.

13. Symmetric property of equality

14. Subtraction property of equality

15. Division property of equality

16. Substitution

17.

	Honda	Ford	Volkswagen
Anthony	x	✓	x
Eric	✓	x	x
Karen	x	x	✓

Anthony – Ford, Eric – Honda, Karen – Volkswagen

18. Given: $\overline{AC} \cong \overline{BD}$
Prove: $\overline{AB} \cong \overline{CD}$

STATEMENTS	REASONS
a. $\overline{AC} \cong \overline{BD}$	a. Given
b. $AC = BD$	b. Definition of congruent segments
c. $AC = AB + BC$ $BD = BC + DC$	c. Segment addition postulate
d. $AB + BC = BC + CD$	d. Substitution property of equality
e. $AB = CD$	e. Subtraction property of equality
f. $\overline{AB} \cong \overline{CD}$	f. Definition of congruent segments

19. Given: $m\angle 1 = m\angle 3 + m\angle 4$
Prove: $m\angle 3 + m\angle 4 + m\angle 2$
    $= 180$

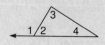

STATEMENTS	REASONS
a. $m\angle 1 = m\angle 3 + m\angle 4$	a. Given
b. $m\angle 1 + m\angle 2$ $= m\angle 3 + m\angle 4 + m\angle 2$	b. Addition property of of equality
c. $\angle 1$ and $\angle 2$ form a linear pair.	c. Definition of linear pair
d. $\angle 1$ and $\angle 2$ are supplementary.	d. If two angles form a linear pair, they are supplementary.
e. $m\angle 1 + m\angle 2 = 180$	e. Definition of supplementary
f. $m\angle 3 + m\angle 4 + m\angle 2$ $= 180$	f. Substitution property of equality

20. Given: $\angle 1$ and $\angle 2$ are supplementary. $\angle 1$ is a right angle.
Prove: $\angle 2$ is a right angle.

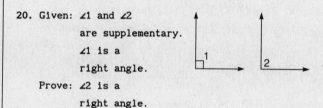

STATEMENTS	REASONS
a. $\angle 1$ and $\angle 2$ are supplementary. $\angle 1$ is a right angle.	a. Given
b. $m\angle 1 + m\angle 2 = 180$	b. Definition of supplementary
c. $m\angle 1 = 90$	c. Definition of right angle
d. $90 + m\angle 2 = 180$	d. Substitution property of equality
e. $m\angle 2 = 90$	e. Subtraction property of equality
f. $\angle 2$ is a right angle.	f. Definition of right angle

BONUS: If an animal is not a dog, then it is not a mammal.

College Entrance Exam Preview

PAGES 114-115

1. B; $0.06x = 24$
    $x = 400$

2. A; $c^2 = a^2 + b^2$
    $c^2 = 3^2 + 4^2$
    $c^2 = 25$
    $c = 5$ units

3. D; $x - y < 12 + 18$
    $x - y < 30$

4. A; $0.40(120) = x$

$$48 = x$$

$$3 \cdot 48 = 144$$

5. C; $AB = BC = x$

$$2x + 12 = 50$$

$$2x = 38$$

$$x = 19$$

$$BC = 19$$

6. D; $d = \sqrt{(x_2 - x_1)^2 + (y_2 - y_1)^2}$

$$d^2 = (x_2 - x_1)^2 + (y_2 - y_1)^2$$

$$(\sqrt{74})^2 = (4 - (-1))^2 + (2 - y_1)^2$$

$$74 = 25 + (2 - y_1)^2$$

$$49 = (2 - y_1)^2$$

$$7 = 2 - y_1 \text{ or } -7 = 2 - y_1$$

$$-5 = y_1 \qquad\qquad 9 = y_1$$

7. D; $x + 5 = \frac{1}{3}(3x - 5)$

$$x + 5 = x - \frac{5}{3}$$

$$x \ne x - \frac{20}{3}$$

No real number

8. B; $100\% - 25\% = 75\%$ (percent paid)

$$0.75n = 12.90$$

$$n = \$17.20$$

9. D; $\angle A$ and $\angle B$ are supplementary.

$\angle A$ and $\angle C$ are complementary.

Conclusions: $m\angle A < 90$, $m\angle C < 90$, $m\angle B > 90$

$$m\angle A < m\angle B$$

10. A; If two planes intersect, their intersection is a straight line.

11. C; $12^3 \cdot 12^8 = 12^{3 + 8} = 12^{11}$

12. B is the only possible answer. You cannot assume the cities lie in a straight line.

13. Cannot be determined from given information.

14. x = percentage salt in remaining solution

$$0.04(9) = 8x$$

$$0.045 = x$$

$$0.045 = 4.5\%$$

15. $(8, -3)$. Count down 2 units and left 4 units to locate the x- and y-axes, then determine the coordinates of Q.

16. $7200 - 80x = 5000 + 120x$

$$2200 = 200x$$

$$11 = x$$

17. x = large buckets y = jumbo buckets

$$x + y = 532$$

$$x = 532 - y$$

$$2.25x + 3.75y = 1489.50$$

$$2.25(532 - y) + 3.75y = 1489.50$$

$$1197 + 1.5y = 1489.50$$

$$1.5y = 292.5$$

$$y = 195 \text{ jumbo buckets}$$

18. $\dfrac{2 \text{ inches}}{3 \text{ feet}} = \dfrac{6\frac{1}{2} \text{ inches}}{x \text{ feet}}$

$$2x = 19.5$$

$$x = 9.75 \text{ ft or 9 ft 9 in.}$$

19. $180 - x - 90 = 90 - x$

20. x = correct

$20 - x$ = incorrect

$$5x - (20 - x) = 82$$

$$6x = 102$$

$$x = 17$$

Chapter 3   Parallels

3-1   Problem-Solving Strategy: Draw a Diagram

PAGES 119-120   CHECKING FOR UNDERSTANDING

1. help choose a strategy, organize your information, or provide the solution

2. 72 games; $(8 + 7 + 6 + 5 + 4 + 3 + 2 + 1) \times 2$

3. the given information

4. Let x = fraction of trip Gloria slept.

$$2\left(x + \frac{1}{2}x\right) = 1$$
$$2x + x = 1$$
$$x = \frac{1}{3}$$

5. 21

6. Given: $\overleftrightarrow{XY} \perp \overleftrightarrow{XZ}$
   Prove: $\angle YXW$ and $\angle WXZ$ are complementary.

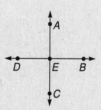

7. Given: $\angle AED$ and $\angle BEC$ are supplementary.
   Prove: $\angle AED$ is a right angle.
   $\angle BEC$ is a right angle.

PAGES 120-121   EXERCISES

8. 84 times

9. They are the same.
   Let x = smaller number;
   y = larger number.
   $x + y = 1$
   $x = 1 - y$

   $x^2 + y = (1 - y)^2 + y \qquad y^2 + x = y^2 + (1 - y)$
   $\qquad = 1 - 2y + y^2 + y \qquad\qquad = y^2 - y + 1$
   $\qquad = y^2 - y + 1$

10. Given: $\angle ABC$ is a right angle.
    $\angle CBD$ is a right angle.
    Prove: $\overrightarrow{BA}$ and $\overrightarrow{BD}$ are opposite rays.

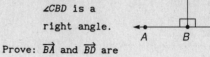

11. $33^2 = 1{,}089$
    $333^2 = 110{,}889$
    $3{,}333^2 = 11{,}108{,}889$
    $33{,}333^2 = 1{,}111{,}088{,}889$

12. $\dfrac{n(n - 1)}{2} = \dfrac{5(5 - 1)}{2} = 10$

13. 6;

10¢	5¢	1¢
2	1	0
1	3	0
1	2	5
1	1	10
1	0	15
2	0	5

14. infinitely many

15. See students' work.

16. length = 1.2(1760) = 2112 yd
    width = 3 feet or 1 yd
    height = 2 inches or $\dfrac{2}{36} = \dfrac{1}{18}$ yd
    volume = $2112(1)\left(\dfrac{1}{18}\right)$
    ≈ 117.3 yd^3

17. 11

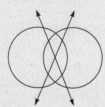

Cooperative Learning Project

PAGE 121

If there are 200 pages in the directory, the sum of the page numbers on each side of a sheet of paper is 201. For example, the pages 1 and 200 will appear on the same side of a sheet of paper. The numbers on the pages on the left are even and the numbers on the right are odd. So, if n is an even page number, then the odd-numbered page on that sheet will be 201 − n. On the other side of the sheet of paper the page numbers would be $n + 1$ and 201 − (n + 1). For example, if $n = 1$, one side of the sheet shows pages 1 and 200 and the other shows pages 2 and 199. Since four pages are printed on each sheet of paper, the number of pages in the

36

directory must be divisible by 4. If there are to be 150 pages in the directory, there will have to be blank pages at the end of the directory. If we consider the two blank pages to be pages 151 and 152, then the sum of the page numbers on each sheet would be 153. The pages on one side of a sheet would be n and $153 - n$. The other side would be $n + 1$ and $153 - (n + 1)$. If there were N pages in the directory and N is divisible by 4, then the sum of the page numbers is $N + 1$. If K is a natural number and $1 \leq K \leq \frac{N}{4}$, then number the pages as shown in the diagram. If there are N pages and N is not divisible by 4, then add blank pages at the end of the book until the number of pages is divisible by 4 and number the pages as shown below.

Back	$2k - 1$	$N - (2k - 2)$
Front	$2k$	$N - (2k - 1)$

3-2 Parallels and Transversals

1. Sample answer: arrows

2. See students' work.
3. Sample answer: Corresponding angles are the angles in the same position in relation to each line and the transversal.

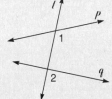

4. parallel, intersecting, skew
5. parallel
6. parallel and/or intersecting
7. parallel, intersecting, skew
8. intersecting and parallel
9. intersecting or parallel
10. False; a transversal and the lines it intersects are in the same plane.
11. false; could be skew
12. false, not in same plane
13. true   14. true   15. false
16. true   17. false   18. true
19. true   20. true   21. true

22. $\overleftrightarrow{RT}$; alternate interior angles
23. $\overleftrightarrow{RT}$; alternate interior angles
24. $\overleftrightarrow{TV}$; consecutive interior angles
25. $\overleftrightarrow{RV}$; consecutive interior angles
26. m; consecutive interior angles
27. m; corresponding angles
28. a; alternate interior angles
29. a; corresponding angles
30. a; alternate exterior angles
31. ℓ; consecutive interior angles
32. parallel
33. parallel and intersecting
34. parallel   35. intersecting
36. parallel   37. intersecting
38.   39.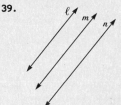

40. 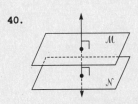   41.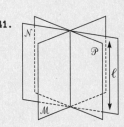

42. 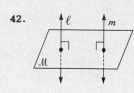   43.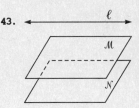

44. $\overline{RU}$, $\overline{ST}$, $\overline{CV}$, $\overline{BW}$, $\overline{AR}$, $\overline{RS}$, $\overline{CB}$, $\overline{BZ}$
45. $\overline{CV}$, $\overline{BW}$, $\overline{ZX}$, $\overline{AY}$, $\overline{RU}$
46. $\overline{UY}$, $\overline{CB}$, $\overline{RA}$ 47. plane BWX
48. No, because ℓ could be in plane N.

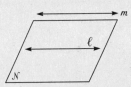

49. If a plane A is parallel to a plane B and plane B is parallel to a plane C, then plane A is parallel to plane C. The basement floor is parallel to the ground-level floor and the ground-level floor is parallel to the upstairs floor, so the basement floor is parallel to the upstairs floor.

50. They are congruent.
51. a. 2000 feet
    b. easy to keep track of which airplanes are eastbound and which are westbound; less worry about collisions
52. Given: $\overrightarrow{BA}$ and $\overrightarrow{BD}$ are opposite rays.
    Prove: ∠ABC and ∠CBD are supplementary

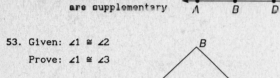

53. Given: ∠1 ≅ ∠2
    Prove: ∠1 ≅ ∠3

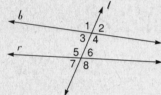

STATEMENTS	REASONS
1. ∠1 ≅ ∠2	1. Given
2. ∠2 ≅ ∠3	2. Vertical ∠s are ≅.
3. ∠1 ≅ ∠3	3. Congruence of angles is transitive.

54. Symmetric property of equality
55. If two lines lie in the same plane and do not intersect, then they are parallel.
56. $\left(\dfrac{10 - 6}{2}, \dfrac{-4 - 0}{2}\right)$

    $\left(\dfrac{4}{2}, \dfrac{-4}{2}\right)$

    $(2, -2)$

57. $RT + TS = RS$

    $RT + 7 = 20$

    $RT = 13$

58.

Interior Angles: ∠3, ∠4, ∠5, ∠6
Exterior Angles: ∠1, ∠2, ∠7, ∠8
Alternate Interior Angles: ∠3 and ∠6, ∠4 and ∠5
Alternate Exterior Angles: ∠1 and ∠8, ∠2 and ∠7
Corresponding Angles: ∠1 and ∠5, ∠2 and ∠6, ∠3 and ∠7, ∠4 and ∠8
Consecutive Interior Angles: ∠3 and ∠5, ∠4 and ∠6

3-3   Using Parallel Lines

PAGES 130-131   CHECKING FOR UNDERSTANDING
1. If two parallel lines are cut by a transversal, consecutive interior angles are supplementary.
2. Answers may vary. Sample answers: m∠1 = m∠3 because ∠1 and ∠3 are vertical angles.

$m\angle 3 + m\angle 5 = 180$, because if two parallel lines cut by a transversal, then consecutive interior angles are supplementary. Therefore, $70 + m\angle 5 = 180$ and $m\angle 5 = 110$. $m\angle 1 = m\angle 8$ because if two parallel lines are cut by a transversal, then alternate exterior angles are congruent. ∠5 and ∠8 are supplementary because ∠5 and ∠8 are a linear pair and if two angles form a linear pair they are supplementary. So $m\angle 5 + m\angle 8 = 180$ by definition of supplementary. Therefore, $m\angle 5 + 70 = 180$ and $m\angle 5 = 110$.

3. Lines are parallel.
4. If two parallel lines are cut by a transversal, corresponding angles are congruent.
5. If two parallel lines are cut by a transversal, alternate interior angles are congruent.
6. ∠1 ≅ ∠4
7. ∠5 and ∠2 are supplementary; ∠1 and ∠4 are supplementary; ∠3 ≅ ∠2; ∠3 and ∠5 are supplementary.
8. ∠2 and ∠6 are supplementary; ∠4 and ∠5 are supplementary; ∠1 ≅ ∠2; ∠3 ≅ ∠5; ∠3 and ∠4 are supplementary.
9. 82   10. 98   11. 82   12. 140
13. 40   14. 40   15. 140
16. $(9x + 12) + 5x = 180$ $6y + (13y - 10) = 180$
          $14x = 168$ $19y = 190$
          $x = 12$ $y = 10$
17. $(4x + 7) + (7x - 3) = 180$
          $11x = 176$
          $x = 16$

    $(7x - 3) + (6y + 5) = 180$
    $7(16) - 3 + 6y + 5 = 180$
    $112 - 3 + 6y + 5 = 180$
    $6y = 66$
    $y = 11$
18. $6x = 90$ $6x + 10y = 180$
    $x = 15$ $6(15) + 10y = 180$
                      $90 + 10y = 180$
                      $10y = 90$
                      $y = 9$

PAGES 131-134   EXERCISES
19. 90   20. 35   21. 125   22. 55   23. 35   24. 55
25. $x = 52$; $4y = 52$
          $y = 13$
26. $14x - 8 = 90$ $14x - 8 = 12y$
        $14x = 98$ $14(7) - 8 = 12y$
        $x = 7$ $98 - 8 = 12y$
                          $90 = 12y$
                          $7.5 = y$

27. $3y + 1 = 7x$

$y = \dfrac{7x - 1}{3}$

$12x + 6 = 5y + 10$

$12x + 6 = 5\left(\dfrac{7x - 1}{3}\right) + 10$

$12x + 6 = \dfrac{35x - 5}{3} + 10$

$36x + 18 = 35x - 5 + 30$

$x = 7$

$3y + 1 = 7x$

$3y = 7(7) - 1 = 48$

$y = 16$

28. 62   **29.** 77   **30.** 41   **31.** 62   **32.** 77   **33.** 103

34. $4y + 68 = 180$ $x = 4y$ $5z + 2 = x$

$4y = 112$ $x = 4(28)$ $5z + 2 = 112$

$y = 28$ $= 112$ $z = 22$

35. $z = 42$ $3x + 42 = 90$ $3x = y + 7$

$x = 16$ $3(16) = y + 7$

$41 = y$

36. $x = 90$ $(3y - 8) + (y + 12) = 180$

$4y = 176$

$y = 44$

$z + (y + 12) + x = 180$

$z + (44 + 12) + 90 = 180$

$z = 34$

37. $x = 127$ $(9y + 8) + 127 = 180$

$9y = 45$

$y = 5$

$(4z + 3) + (9y + 8) = 180$

$4z + 3 + 9(5) + 8 = 180$

$4z = 124$

$z = 31$

38. $x = 14; \; y = 11; \; z = 73$

$(11x - 1) + (2y + 5) = 180$

$z + (7x + 9) = 180$

$(7x + 9) + (7y - 4) = 180$

$(11x - 1) + (2y + 5) = (7x + 9) + (7y - 4)$

$4x - 5y = 1$

$x = \dfrac{1 + 5y}{4}$

$(11x - 1) + (2y + 5) = 180$

$\left(11\left(\dfrac{1 + 5y}{4}\right) - 1\right) + 2y + 5 = 180$

$\dfrac{11 + 55y}{4} - 1 + 2y + 5 = 180$

$11 + 55y - 4 + 8y + 20 = 720$

$63y = 693$

$y = 11$

$x = \dfrac{1 + 5y}{4}$

$= \dfrac{1 + 5(11)}{4}$

$= 14$

$z + (7x + 9) = 180$

$z + (7(14) + 9) = 180$

$z = 73$

---

39. 35   **40.** 35   **41.** 125

42. 35   **43.** 35   **44.** 110

45. **a.** Given

b. Perpendicular lines form 4 right angles.

c. $m\angle 1 = 90$

d. If two parallel lines are cut by a transversal, corresponding angles are congruent.

e. $m\angle 2 = 90$

f. Definition of right angle

g. m is perpendicular to p

46. Given: $\ell \parallel m$

Prove: $\angle 3 \cong \angle 6$,

$\angle 4 \cong \angle 5$

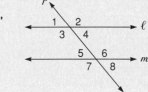

STATEMENTS	REASONS
1. $\ell \parallel m$	1. Given
2. $\angle 3 \cong \angle 2$ $\angle 4 \cong \angle 1$	2. Vertical $\angle$s are $\cong$.
3. $\angle 2 \cong \angle 6$ $\angle 1 \cong 5$	3. If 2 $\parallel$ lines are cut by a transversal, corr. $\angle$s are $\cong$.
4. $\angle 3 \cong \angle 6$ $\angle 4 \cong \angle 5$	4. Congruence of angles is transitive.

47. Given $\ell \parallel m$

Prove: $\angle 3$ and $\angle 5$ are supplementary.

$\angle 4$ and $\angle 6$ are supplementary.

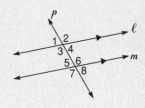

STATEMENTS	REASONS
1. $\ell \parallel m$	1. Given
2. $\angle 1 \cong \angle 5$ $\angle 2 \cong \angle 6$	2. If 2 $\parallel$ lines are cut by a transversal, corr. $\angle$s are $\cong$.
3. $\angle 1$ and $\angle 3$ form a linear pair. $\angle 2$ and $\angle 4$ form a linear pair.	3. Definition of linear pair
4. $\angle 1$ and $\angle 3$ are supplementary. $\angle 2$ and $\angle 4$ are supplementary.	4. If 2 $\angle$s form a linear pair, they are supplementary.
5. $m\angle 1 + m\angle 3 = 180$ $m\angle 2 + m\angle 4 = 180$	5. Definition of supplementary
6. $m\angle 5 + m\angle 3 = 180$ $m\angle 6 + m\angle 4 = 180$	6. Substitution property of equality
7. $\angle 3$ and $\angle 5$ are supplementary. $\angle 4$ and $\angle 6$ are supplementary.	7. Definition of supplementary

48. $x + 27 = 76$ $\qquad$ $y + 104 = 180$

$\qquad x = 49$ $\qquad\qquad\qquad y = 76$

49. Given: $\overline{MQ} \parallel \overline{NP}$

$\qquad\qquad \angle 1 \cong \angle 5$

Prove: $\angle 4 \cong \angle 3$

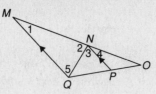

STATEMENTS	REASONS
1. $MQ \parallel NP$ $\angle 1 \cong \angle 5$	1. Given
2. $\angle 4 \cong \angle 1$	2. If 2 $\parallel$ lines are cut by a transversal, corr. $\angle$s are $\cong$.
3. $\angle 4 \cong \angle 5$	3. Congruence of angles is transitive.
4. $\angle 5 \cong \angle 3$	4. If 2 $\parallel$ lines are cut by a transversal, alt. int. $\angle$s are $\cong$.
5. $\angle 4 \cong \angle 3$	5. Congruence of angles is transitive.

50. $m\angle 3 = 73$

$m\angle 2 + m\angle 3 + m\angle 1 = 180$ and $\angle 3 \cong \angle 5 \cong \angle 1$

$\qquad 34 + m\angle 3 + m\angle 3 = 180$

$\qquad\qquad\qquad 2m\angle 3 = 146$

$\qquad\qquad\qquad\quad m\angle 3 = 73$

51. a. $\angle BDA$ $\qquad$ **b.** $\angle BCA$ $\qquad$ **c.** $\angle BAC$

52. The sides of the wallpaper are parallel, so if each new piece is parallel to the last one, they will all be vertical.

53. parallel

54. Given: $\overline{AB} \cong \overline{FE}$

$\qquad\qquad \overline{BC} \cong \overline{ED}$

Prove: $\overline{AC} \cong \overline{FD}$

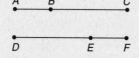

STATEMENTS	REASONS
1. $AB \cong FE$ $BC \cong ED$	1. Given
2. $AB = FE$, $BC = ED$	2. Definition of congruent segments
3. $AC = AB + BC$ $FD = FE + ED$	3. Segment addition postulate
4. $AB + BC = FE + ED$	4. Addition property of equality
5. $AC = FD$	5. Substitution property of equality
6. $AC \cong FD$	6. Definition of congruent segments

55. Lines p and m never meet; detachment.

56. $(9x + 14) + (12x + 19) = 180$

$\qquad\qquad\qquad\qquad 21x = 147$

$\qquad\qquad\qquad\qquad\quad x = 7$

57. 9 or −3 $\qquad\qquad$ **58.** quadrant III

59. 1. Corresponding angles are congruent.

  example: $\angle 1 \cong \angle 5$

2. Alternate interior angles are congruent.

  example: $\angle 4 \cong \angle 5$

3. Consecutive interior angles are supplementary.

  example: $\angle 3$ and $\angle 5$ are supplementary

4. Alternate exterior angles are congruent.

  example: $\angle 2 \cong \angle 7$

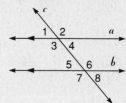

Mid-Chapter Review

PAGE 134

1. Given $a \parallel b$

$\qquad\qquad \angle 1 \cong \angle 2$

Prove: $a \perp t$

$\qquad\qquad b \perp t$

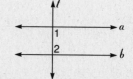

2. $\overline{EF}$ $\qquad$ **3.** $\overline{AC}$, $\overline{EF}$ $\qquad$ **4.** plane DEF

5. none $\qquad$ **6.** 65 $\qquad$ **7.** 65

8. 115 $\qquad$ **9.** 65 $\qquad$ **10.** 115

11. 115 $\qquad$ **12.** 65

3-4 **Proving Lines Parallel**

PAGES 137-138 $\qquad$ **CHECKING FOR UNDERSTANDING**

1. Sample answer: draw the sidelines, then draw all of the yardage lines perpendicular to those. The lines will be parallel to each other by Theorem 3-8.

2. Answers may vary. A sample answer is parking lot spaces.

3. $\angle AMH$ and $\angle MHT$ are consecutive interior angles that are supplementary.

4. If $\overline{AT} \parallel \overline{MH}$, then $\angle ATH$ and $\angle THM$ would be supplementary, but $m\angle ATH + m\angle THM = 119 + 52$ or 171. Therefore, $\overline{AT} \not\parallel \overline{MH}$.

5. Yes, because $\overline{AM} \parallel \overline{HT}$ and if 2 $\parallel$ lines are cut by a transversal alt. int. $\angle$s are $\cong$.

40

6. $180 - (4x - 7) = 43$
   $180 - 4x + 7 = 43$
   $-4x = -144$
   $x = 36$

7. $7x - 1 = 90$
   $7x = 91$
   $x = 13$

8. $(3x + 20) + (5x - 8) = 180$
   $8x = 168$
   $x = 21$

9. $(5x + 8) + (12x + 2) = 180$
   $17x = 170$
   $x = 10$

10. $8x + 5 = 10x - 7$
    $-2x = -12$
    $x = 6$

11. $180 - (3x - 2) = 122$
    $-3x + 2 = -58$
    $x = 20$

12. none

13. $\overline{AB} \parallel \overline{DC}$, Th. 3-5

14. $\ell \parallel m$, Th. 3-8

15. False; they must be in a plane.

16. true

17. False; the alternate interior angles would be congruent.

18. true

PAGES 138-141   EXERCISES

19. $\overleftrightarrow{GR} \parallel \overleftrightarrow{HL}$; corresponding angles are congruent (Postulate 3-2).

20. $\overleftrightarrow{GI} \parallel \overleftrightarrow{KM}$; alternate interior angles are congruent. (Theorem 3-5).

21. $\overleftrightarrow{FG} \parallel \overleftrightarrow{JR}$; alternate interior angles are congruent (Theorem 3-5).

22. $\overleftrightarrow{GJ} \parallel \overleftrightarrow{HL}$; consecutive interior angles are supplementary (Theorem 3-6).

23. none

24. $a \parallel b$; alternate interior angles are congruent (Theorem 3-5).

25. $c \parallel d$; corresponding angles are congruent (Postulate 3-2).

26. $a \parallel b$; alternate interior angles are congruent (Theorem 3-5).

27. none

28. $c \parallel d$; consecutive interior angles are supplementary (Theorem 3-6).

29. none

30. a. $\angle 2 \cong \angle 1$
    b. Vertical $\angle$s are $\cong$.
    c. $\angle 2 \cong \angle 3$
    d. If 2 lines in a plane are cut by a transversal and corr. $\angle$s are $\cong$ the lines are $\parallel$.

31. $(5x + 7) + (18x + 12) = 180$
    $23x = 161$
    $x = 7$
    $(5x + 7) + y = 180$
    $(5 \cdot 7 + 7) + y = 180$
    $y = 138$

32. $5x + 7 = 19y$
    $\dfrac{5x + 7}{19} = y$
    $4x - 8 = 11y - 1$
    $4x - 8 = 11\left(\dfrac{5x + 7}{19}\right) - 1$
    $4x - 8 = \dfrac{55x + 77}{19} - 1$
    $\dfrac{5(10) + 7}{19} = y$
    $3 = y$
    $76x - 152 = 55x + 77 - 19$
    $21x = 210$
    $x = 10$

33. $\angle 2$ and $\angle 3$; $\angle 6$ and $\angle 7$; $\angle 2$ and $\angle 8$; $\angle 6$ and $\angle 4$; $\angle 3$ and $\angle 5$; $\angle 7$ and $\angle 1$; $\angle 5$ and $\angle 8$; $\angle 1$ and $\angle 4$

34. No; if $x = 12$, then the angles are supplementary, and by Theorem 3-6, $\ell \parallel m$.

35. $\overleftrightarrow{AE} \parallel \overleftrightarrow{DF}$ since in a plane, if 2 lines are $\perp$ to the same line, they are $\parallel$. $\overline{EB} \parallel \overline{FH}$ since if 2 lines in a plane are cut by a transversal and alt. int. $\angle$s are $\cong$, then the lines are $\parallel$.

36. 60

37. a. given
    b. $\angle 1$ and $\angle 2$ form a linear pair.
    c. If 2 $\angle$s form a linear pair they are supp.
    d. $\angle 1 \cong \angle 3$
    e. If 2 lines in a plane are cut by a transversal and corr. $\angle$s are $\cong$, the lines are $\parallel$.

38. Given: $\ell \perp t$, $m \perp t$
    Prove: $\ell \parallel m$

STATEMENTS	REASONS
1. $\ell \perp t$, $m \perp t$	1. Given
2. $\angle 1$ is a right angle.	2. $\perp$ lines form four rt. $\angle$s.
3. $\angle 1 \cong \angle 2$	3. All rt. $\angle$s are $\cong$.
4. $\ell \parallel m$	4. If 2 lines are cut by a transversal and corr. $\angle$s are $\cong$, then the lines are $\parallel$.

39. Given: $\angle RQP \cong \angle PSR$
$\angle SRQ$ and $\angle PSR$ are
supplementary.
Prove: $\overline{QP} \parallel \overline{RS}$

STATEMENTS	REASONS
1. $\angle RQP \cong \angle PSR$, $\angle SRQ$ and $\angle PSR$ are supplementary.	1. Given
2. $m\angle RQP = m\angle PSR$	2. Definition of congruent angles
3. $m\angle SRQ + m\angle PSR = 180$	3. Definition of supplementary
4. $m\angle SRQ + m\angle RQP = 180$	4. Substitution prop. of equality
5. $\angle SRQ$ and RQP are supplementary.	5. Definition of supplementary
6. $\overline{QP} \parallel \overline{RS}$	6. If 2 lines are cut by a transversal and consec. int. $\angle$s are supp., then the lines are $\parallel$.

40. Given: $\overline{JK} \perp \overline{KM}$
$\angle 1 \cong \angle 2$
Prove: $\overline{LM} \perp \overline{KM}$

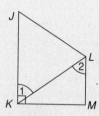

STATEMENTS	REASONS
1. $\overline{JK} \perp \overline{KM}$, $\angle 1 \cong \angle 2$	1. Given
2. $\overline{JK} \parallel \overline{LM}$	2. If 2 lines are cut by a transversal so that alt. int. $\angle$s are $\cong$, then the lines are $\parallel$.
3. $\overline{LM} \perp \overline{KM}$	3. In a plane, if a line is $\perp$ to one of 2 $\parallel$ lines, then it is $\perp$ to the other.

41. Given: $\angle ABD \cong \angle BEF$
$\overleftrightarrow{BC}$ bisects $\angle ABD$.
$\overleftrightarrow{EH}$ bisects $\angle BEF$.
Prove: $\overleftrightarrow{BC} \parallel \overleftrightarrow{EH}$

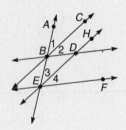

STATEMENTS	REASONS
1. $\angle ABD \cong \angle BEF$ $\overleftrightarrow{BC}$ bisects $\angle ABD$. $\overleftrightarrow{EH}$ bisects $\angle BEF$.	1. Given
2. $m\angle 1 + m\angle 2 = m\angle ABD$ $m\angle 3 + m\angle 4 = m\angle BEF$	2. Angle addition postulate

3. $m\angle 1 + m\angle 2$ $= m\angle 3 + m\angle 4$	3. Substitution property of equality
4. $m\angle 1 = m\angle 2$; $m\angle 3 = m\angle 4$	4. Defintion of angle bisector
5. $m\angle 1 + m\angle 1$ $= m\angle 3 + m\angle 3$	5. Substitution property of equality
6. $2m\angle 1 = 2m\angle 3$	6. Substitution property of equality
7. $m\angle 1 = m\angle 3$	7. Division property of equality
8. $\overleftrightarrow{BC} \parallel \overleftrightarrow{EH}$	8. If 2 lines in a plane are cut by a transversal and corresponding $\angle$s are $\cong$, the lines are $\parallel$.

42. If $\overline{AC} \perp \overline{AB}$ and $\overline{BC} \perp \overline{AB}$, then $\overline{AC} \parallel \overline{BC}$ by Theorem 3-8, but parallel lines don't meet.

43. Postulate 3-2   **44.** true

45. intersecting or skew

46.

STATEMENTS	REASONS
1. $A = 2\pi r^2 + 2\pi rh$	1. Given
2. $A - 2\pi r^2 = 2\pi rh$	2. Subtraction property of equality
3. $\dfrac{A - 2\pi r^2}{2\pi r} = h$	3. Division property of equality

47. If something is a cloud, then it is composed of millions of water droplets.

48. yes; $4x + 14 = 6x - 24$
$$-2x = -38$$
$$x = 19$$

$4x + 14 = 4(19) + 14$ $6x - 24 = 6(19) - 24$
$= 90$ $= 90$

49. 6   **50.** See students' work.

3-5   Slopes of Lines

1. 0-horizontal; 5 rises to the right.
2. The slope of a vertical line is undefined; yes.
3. horizontal
4. $\dfrac{5 - (-3)}{16 - 0} = \dfrac{8}{16} = \dfrac{1}{2}$; -2
5. Answers will vary.
   Sample answer:

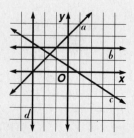

6. $\frac{1-1}{3-1} = 0$; horizontal

7. $\frac{-2-0}{3-(-1)} = \frac{-2}{4} = -\frac{1}{2}$; falling

8. $\frac{4-0}{0-5} = \frac{-4}{5}$; falling

9. $\frac{2-4}{1-3} = \frac{-2}{-2} = 1$; rising

10. $\frac{3-4}{-1-(-2)} = \frac{-1}{1} = -1$; falling

11. $\frac{-5-2}{8-8}$ = undefined; vertical

12. neither 13. perpendicular 14. parallel

15. $\frac{2-(-1)}{3-(-1)} = \frac{3}{4}$; $-\frac{4}{3}$ 16. $\frac{-1-2}{3-4} = \frac{-3}{-1} = 3$; $-\frac{1}{3}$

17. $\frac{2-5}{3-1} = \frac{-3}{2}$; $\frac{2}{3}$ 18. $\frac{1-5}{1-(-7)} = \frac{-4}{8} = -\frac{1}{2}$; 2

19. $\frac{8-(-3)}{1-(-2)} = \frac{11}{3}$; $-\frac{3}{11}$ 20. $\frac{6-(-2)}{1-(-2)} = \frac{8}{3}$; $-\frac{3}{8}$

PAGES 145-147   EXERCISES

21. $\frac{0-6}{-3-0} = \frac{-6}{-3} = 2$ 22. $\frac{6-6}{1-0} = 0$

23. $\frac{0-6}{-3-1} = \frac{-6}{-4} = \frac{3}{2}$ 24. $\frac{2-4}{-2-(-4)} = \frac{-2}{2} = -1$

25. undefined 26. 2 27. $-\frac{2}{3}$ 28. -1

29.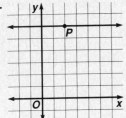

30.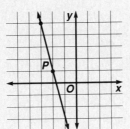

31.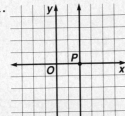

32.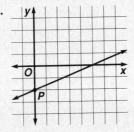

33.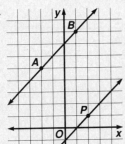

34.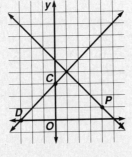

35. Slope of $\overleftrightarrow{AB}$ = $-\frac{1}{3}$; slope of $\overleftrightarrow{BC}$ = $-\frac{1}{3}$. Either $\overleftrightarrow{AB} \parallel \overleftrightarrow{BC}$ or $\overleftrightarrow{AB}$ and $\overleftrightarrow{BC}$ are the same line. Since B is a common point, $\overleftrightarrow{AB}$ is not parallel to $\overleftrightarrow{BC}$. Thus $\overleftrightarrow{AB}$ and $\overleftrightarrow{BC}$ are the same line and A, B, and C are collinear.

36. Slope of $\overleftrightarrow{MN}$ = 2; slope of $\overleftrightarrow{MO}$ = 2. Either $\overleftrightarrow{MN} \parallel \overleftrightarrow{MO}$ or $\overleftrightarrow{MN}$ and $\overleftrightarrow{MO}$ are the same line. Since M is a common point, $\overleftrightarrow{MN}$ is not parallel to $\overleftrightarrow{MO}$. Thus $\overleftrightarrow{MN}$ and $\overleftrightarrow{MO}$ are the same line and M, N, and O are collinear.

37. No. Slope of $\overleftrightarrow{AB}$ = 3; slope of $\overleftrightarrow{CD}$ = 3; slope of $\overleftrightarrow{DA}$ = 3. $\overleftrightarrow{AB}$ and $\overleftrightarrow{CD}$ are the same line and A, B, C, and D are collinear.

38. No. Slope of $\overleftrightarrow{AB}$ = 1; slope of $\overleftrightarrow{CD}$ = $-\frac{1}{3}$. $\overleftrightarrow{AB} \not\parallel \overleftrightarrow{CD}$ because they have different slopes.

39.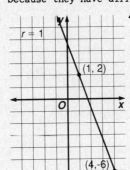

40.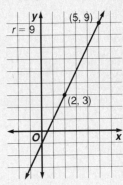

41.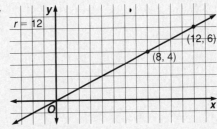

42.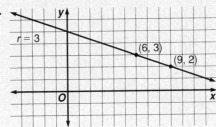

43. (7, 5), (5, -1), (-3, 3)

44. a. slope of $\overline{AB}$ = $\frac{3}{5}$; slope of $\overline{BC}$ = 3
    slope of $\overline{CD}$ = $\frac{3}{5}$; slope of $\overline{DA}$ = 3
    Since the opposite sides have the same slope, they are parallel.

    b. $AB = \sqrt{(-5-5)^2 + (-3-3)^2} = \sqrt{136}$
    $BC = \sqrt{(5-7)^2 + (3-9)^2} = \sqrt{40}$
    $CD = \sqrt{(7-(-3))^2 + (9-3)^2} = \sqrt{136}$
    $DA = \sqrt{(-3-(-5))^2 + (3-(-3))^2} = \sqrt{40}$
    Opposite sides have the same length, so they are congruent.

    c. parallelogram

43

45. The slope between $(9, 1)$ and $(5, 5)$ is $\frac{5 - 1}{5 - 9}$

$= \frac{4}{-4} = -1$.

The slope between $(5, 5)$ and $(0, 10)$ is $\frac{10 - 5}{0 - 5}$

$= \frac{5}{-5} = -1$.

The lines between $(9, 1)$ and $(5, 5)$ and $(5, 5)$ and $(10, 0)$ are either parallel or the same line. The lines share the point $(5, 5)$, so they must be the same line. Therefore, the line through $(9, 1)$ and $(5, 5)$ crosses the y-axis at $(10, 0)$.

46. $\overline{AB}$ – accelerating; starting out from a stop

$\overline{BC}$ – decelerating; slowing for traffic

$\overline{CD}$ – slowly accelerating; speeding up

$\overline{DE}$ – accelerating faster; speeding up more

$\overline{EF}$ – decelerating to a stop; stopping at a red light

$\overline{FG}$ – no movement; waiting for a light to change

$\overline{GH}$ – accelerating; starting after light turns green

47. a. 7,500 gain

b. The rate of change is the slope of the line that relates population and time.

c. 300,000

48. about 308 feet per mile

49. a.

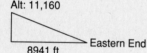

Alt: 11,160

8941 ft — Eastern End

b.

$$-0.00895 = \frac{y_2 - 11160}{8941 - 0}$$

$$-0.00895(8941) + 11160 = y_2$$

$$11,080 \text{ ft} = y_2$$

50. a. finds the slope

b. See students' work.

51. Given: $\angle 1 \cong \angle 2$

$\overline{PQ} \perp \overline{QR}$

Prove: $\overline{ST} \perp \overline{PQ}$

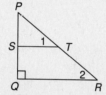

STATEMENTS	REASONS
1. $\angle 1 \cong \angle 2$ $\overline{PQ} \perp \overline{QR}$	1. Given
2. $\overline{ST} \parallel \overline{QR}$	2. If 2 lines in a plane are cut by a transversal and corr. $\angle$s are $\cong$, the lines are $\parallel$.
3. $\overline{ST} \perp \overline{PQ}$	3. In a plane, if a line is $\perp$ to one of 2 $\parallel$ lines, it is $\perp$ to the other.

52. Answers may vary. Sample answers: $\angle 1$ and $\angle 2$ are supplementary; $\angle 1 \cong \angle 3$; $\angle 2$ and $\angle 3$ are supplementary; $\angle 4$ and $\angle 5$ are supplementary; $\angle 4 \cong \angle 6$; $\angle 5$ and $\angle 6$ are supplementary.

53. Given: $5x - 7 = x + 1$

Prove: $x = 2$

STATEMENTS	REASONS
1. $5x - 7 = x + 1$	1. Given
2. $4x - 7 = 1$	2. Subtraction prop. of equality
3. $4x = 8$	3. Addition prop. of equality
4. $x = 2$	4. Division prop. of equality

54. $\left(\frac{1}{2}\right)^2 = \frac{1}{4}$ and $\frac{1}{2} < \frac{1}{4}$

55. $\frac{8 + (-4)}{2}, \frac{11 + 7}{2}$

$(2, 9)$

56.

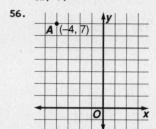

$A (-4, 7)$

57. same slopes; corresponding angles congruent; alternate interior angles congruent

---

3-6   Parallels and Distance

PAGES 151-152   CHECKING FOR UNDERSTANDING

1. Construct a line perpendicular to one line from a point on the line or from a point off the line.

2. Yes; they share a point and the distance between a line and a point on the line is zero.

3. distance

$$= \sqrt{(-2 - 1)^2 + (3 - 2)^2}$$

$$= \sqrt{10}$$

$$\approx 3.2 \text{ units}$$

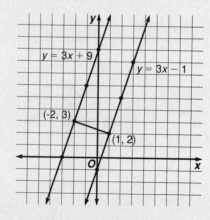

$y = 3x + 9$

$y = 3x - 1$

$(-2, 3)$

$(1, 2)$

4. Answers may vary. Sample answers:

point to point - the distance between two cities

point to line - the distance from your house to the street

line to line - finding the width of your classroom

5.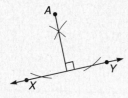

6.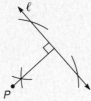

7.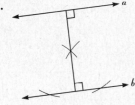

8. true   **9.** true

10. false; must be a ⊥ segment

11. true

12. no; not equidistant at all points

13. yes; equidistant at all points

PAGES 152–154   EXERCISES

14. 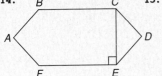   **15.**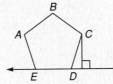

16.   **17.**

18.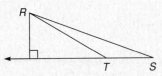

19. $d = 2\sqrt{10}$
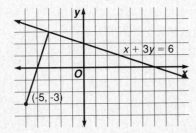

20. $d = \sqrt{5}$ **21.** $d = 0$

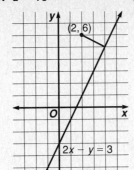   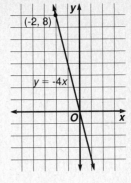

22. $d = 1$ **23.** $d = 5$

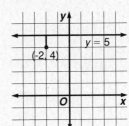   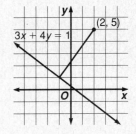

24. $d = 3$

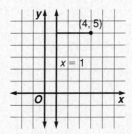

25. ∠CBA and ∠DBA are right angles. AB is the distance from A to $\overline{CD}$.

26. ∠MNO is a right angle. MN is the distance from M to $\overline{NO}$. NO is the distance from O to $\overline{MN}$.

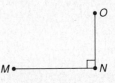

27. $\ell \parallel n$

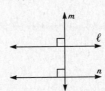

28. ∠Q and ∠D are supplementary, ∠U and ∠A are supplementary.

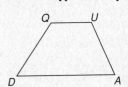

29. $\overline{PS}$ **30.** $\overline{RQ}$ **31.** $\overline{QR}$ **32.** $\overline{SR}$

33. Not necessarily; the lines may be skew.

34. Construct a line segment perpendicular to each plane and find its length.

35. yes

36. Yes. It is valid. See students' work.

Sample for Exercise 19. $x + 3y = 6$ $(-5, 3)$

$$d = \frac{|AX_1 + BY_1 + C|}{\sqrt{A^2 + B^2}}$$

$$= \frac{|1(-5) + 3(-3) - 6|}{\sqrt{1^2 + 3^2}}$$

$$= \left|\frac{-20}{\sqrt{10}}\right|$$

$$= 2\sqrt{10}$$

37. a. E. 69th. St; it is the perpendicular from the point to the line.

b. Answers may vary. Sample answers are heavy traffic and one-way streets.

38. Parallel lines are everywhere equidistant.

39. a. 2.1 kilometers

b. 2.7 kilometers

c. 4.1 kilometers

d. Riverboat; bird; bird is not restricted to traveling on the roads or in the rivers.

40. $\dfrac{0 - (-2)}{3 - 8} = \dfrac{2}{-5}$ or $-\dfrac{2}{5}$

41.

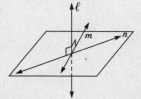

42. true

43. $2x = x + 43$; $x = 43$

44. yes; detachment

45. Hypothesis: two lines are parallel

Conclusion: they are everywhere equidistant

46.

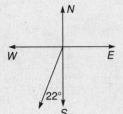

47. See students' work.

Technology: Finding the Distance between a Point and a Line

PAGE 155   EXERCISES

1. $\sqrt{2} \approx 1.4$ 2. $\sqrt{29} \approx 5.4$ 3. $\sqrt{10} \approx 3.2$

Chapter 3 Summary and Review

PAGES 156-158   SKILLS AND CONCEPTS

1. t, n 2. t, m 3. t, n, ℓ

4. plane WRA, plane VRA   5. t, m

6. ∠FAB, ∠ABE; ∠FAB, ∠HBC; ∠GAE, ∠AEB; ∠FAE, ∠DEB; ∠GAB, ∠EBC; ∠GAB, ∠ABH

7. ∠FAC, ∠ACD; ∠GAD, ∠ADC

8. ∠DCB, ∠FAB   9. ∠EBC, ∠ADH

10. $\overline{AD} \parallel \overline{EF}$; ∠1 ≅ ∠4 since vertical angles are congruent. So ∠4 and ∠2 are supplementary. So the lines are parallel since consecutive interior angles are supplementary.

11. $\overline{DE} \parallel \overline{CF}$; alternate interior angles are congruent.

12. $\overline{DA} \parallel \overline{EF}$, since corresponding angles are congruent.

13. $\dfrac{-2 - 4}{-1 - 0} = 6$

14. $\dfrac{-6 - 0}{0 - 2} = 3$

15. $\dfrac{4 - 2}{5 - 11} = -\dfrac{1}{3}$

16. $\dfrac{-7 + 5}{3 + 1} = -\dfrac{1}{2}$

17. $\dfrac{-2 - 7}{4 + 3} = -\dfrac{9}{7}, \dfrac{7}{9}$

18. $\dfrac{6 - 6}{3 - 0} = 0$, no slope

19. $\dfrac{-3 + 2}{1 - 7} = \dfrac{1}{6}$, -6

20. $\dfrac{4 + 2}{-1 - 9} = -\dfrac{3}{5}, \dfrac{5}{3}$

21. $\overline{PS}$

22. $\overline{RQ}$

23. $\overline{RQ}$ or $\overline{MP}$

24. $\overline{QP}$ or $\overline{RM}$

PAGE 158   APPLICATIONS AND CONNECTIONS

25. 36

26. a. –100 per year   b. 5000 deer

27. $\dfrac{455 \text{ mi} - 195 \text{ mi}}{\text{2:00 p.m.} - \text{10:00 a.m.}} = \dfrac{260 \text{ mi}}{4 \text{ hr}} = 65 \text{ mph}$

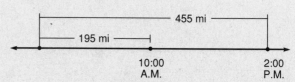

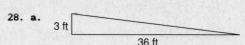

28. a.

3 ft
36 ft

b. $\dfrac{3}{36} = \dfrac{1}{12}$

Chapter 3 Test

PAGE 159

1. True; definition of alternate exterior angles

2. False; definition of consecutive interior angles

3. False; definition of vertical angles

4. True; if 2 || lines in a plane are cut by a transversal, consecutive interior angles are supplementary.

5. True; if 2 || lines in a plane are cut by a transversal, corr. ∠s are ≅.

6. True; vertical ∠s are ≅.

7. False

8. True; if 2 || lines in a plane are cut by a transversal consec. int. ∠s are supp.

9. a || ℓ; Postulate 3-2, corresponding angles

10. m || n; Theorem 3-5, alternate interior angles

11. a || ℓ; Theorem 3-6, consec. int. ∠s are supp.

12. $\frac{5 - 5}{-2 - 4} = 0$, undefined

13. $\frac{-3 - 8}{5 - 11} = \frac{11}{6}$, $-\frac{6}{11}$ 14. $\frac{-1 - 1}{7 + 3} = -\frac{1}{5}$, 5

15. $\overline{FD}$ 16. $\overline{FB}$ 17. $\overline{AC}$ 18. $\overline{DC}$

19. Given: ∠1 ≅ ∠2
    $\overline{ST}$ || $\overline{PR}$

Prove: ∠P ≅ ∠R

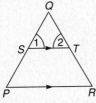

STATEMENTS	REASONS
1. ∠1 ≅ ∠2 $\overline{ST}$ || $\overline{PR}$	1. Given
2. ∠1 ≅ ∠P	2. If 2 || lines are cut by a transversal, corr. ∠s are ≅.
3. ∠P ≅ ∠R	3. Congruence of ∠s is transitive.

20. 5 min;

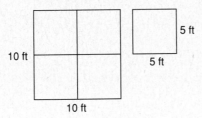

10 ft × 10 ft = 100 ft^2 room

5 ft × 5 ft = 25 ft^2 closet

$\frac{100 \text{ ft}^2}{25 \text{ ft}^2} = \frac{20 \text{ min}}{x}$

$100x = 500$

$x = 5$ min

BONUS

$180 - ∠1 = ∠2$

$180 - 40 = ∠2$

$140 = ∠2$

Algebra Review

1. $3x = 30$
   $x = 10$

2. $-4y = 30$
   $y = \frac{30}{-4}$
   $y = -\frac{15}{2}$

3. $.5n = -9$
   $n = -18$

4. $-12.4 = 3.1t$
   $-4 = t$

5. $\frac{x}{-3} = -23$
   $x = 69$

6. $8 - 5r = 18$
   $-5r = 10$
   $r = -2$

7. $15n = 6(45)$
   $15n = 270$
   $n = 18$

8. $35(11) = 55x$
   $385 = 55x$
   $7 = x$

9. $4t = 8(11)$
   $t = 22$

10. $5(4) = 6(a - 2)$
    $20 = 6a - 12$
    $32 = 6a$
    $\frac{32}{6} = \frac{6a}{6}$
    $\frac{16}{3} = a$

11. $3(y + 4) = 4(y - 1)$
    $3y + 12 = 4y - 4$
    $3y - 4y = -4 - 12$
    $-y = -16$
    $y = 16$

12. $7(z + 7) = 6(2 - 3)$
    $7z + 49 = 62 - 18$
    $7z - 62 = -18 - 49$
    $z = -67$

13. $\frac{60}{100} \times 80 = x$
    $48 = x$

14. $\frac{35}{100}x = 21$
    $35x = 2100$
    $x = 60$

15. $\frac{84}{96} = \frac{x}{100}$
    $100\left(\frac{84}{96}\right) = x$
    $87.5 = x$ 84 is 87.5% of 96.

16. $\frac{3}{1000}(62.7) = x$
    $1881 = x$

17.
    -5 -4 -3 -2 -1 0 1 2

18.
    -5 -4 -3 -2 -1 0 1 2

19. $n - 4 + 4 < 9 + 4$
    $n < 13$
    $\{n | n < 13\}$

20. $r + 8 - 8 \leq -3 - 8$
    $r \leq -11$
    $\{r | r \leq -11\}$

21. $a - 2.6 + 2.6 \geq -8.1 + 2.6$
    $a \geq -5.5$
    $\{a | a \geq -5.5\}$

22. $5z - 4z - 6 + 6 > 4z - 4z + 6$

                    $z > 6$

     $\{z \mid z > 6\}$

23. $3x - 2x \leq 2x - 2x + 7$

            $x \leq 7$

     $\{x \mid x \leq 7\}$

24. $y + \dfrac{7}{8} - \dfrac{7}{8} > \dfrac{13}{24} - \dfrac{7}{8}$

                $y > \dfrac{13}{24} - \dfrac{21}{24}$

                $y > -\dfrac{8}{24}$

                $y > -\dfrac{1}{3}$

     $\left\{y \mid y > -\dfrac{1}{3}\right\}$

25. y^8

26. $(3 \cdot -4)(m \cdot m^2)(n \cdot n^3) = -12m^3 n^4$

27. $(-4 \cdot -5)(a^2 \cdot a^3)(x \cdot x^4) = 20a^5 x^5$

28. $\left(\dfrac{42}{14}\right)\left(\dfrac{b^7}{b^4}\right) = 3b^3$ 29. $\left(\dfrac{y^3}{-y}\right)\left(\dfrac{x}{x}\right)\left(\dfrac{w}{w^2}\right) = \dfrac{-y^2}{w}$

30. $\left(\dfrac{-16}{-48}\right)\left(\dfrac{a^3}{a^4}\right)\left(\dfrac{b^2}{b}\right)\left(\dfrac{x^4}{x}\right)\left(\dfrac{y}{y^3}\right) = \dfrac{bx^3}{3ay^2}$

31. 5   32. 5   33. 3

34. $5ab$ 35. $2mr$ 36. $4n^2$ 37. xyz^3

38. Let x = First integer

    $x + 1$ = Next consecutive integer

    $2(x + 1) + x = 50$

      $2x + 2 + x = 50$

             $3x = 48$

              $x = 16$ First integer

        $x + 1 = 17$ Next integer

39. $(3.35)(50) = 45x$

        $167.5 = 45x$

    3.7 hours $= x$

40. $\dfrac{77}{100}(162{,}000{,}000) = 124{,}740{,}000$ people

41. $\dfrac{\$898.50 - \$420.75}{\$68.25} = 7$

Mei has made deposits for 7 weeks.

42. $74 \times 4 = 296$

    $80 \times 6 = 480$

  $296 + 2x = 480$

       $2x = 184$

        $x = 92$ or more

Namid needs at least a 92 on the final exam.

Chapter 4 Congruent Triangles

4-1 Classifying Triangles

PAGES 166-167 CHECKING FOR UNDERSTANDING

1. Answers may vary. A sample answer is a boy's bicycle frame. It is scalene and acute.

2. See students' work.
   Sample answer:

3. No; a scalene triangle has no two sides congruent and an isosceles triangle has at least two sides congruent.

4. See students' work. In this sample answer; $\overline{AC}$ is opposite the obtuse angle.

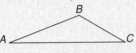

5. See students' work. A sample answer is the sides are all congruent.

Answers for 6-11 may vary sample answers are given.

6. some earrings
7. door brace
8. swing frame
9. gable
10. tortilla chips
11. campus walkways
12. $\triangle ADC$, $\triangle EDA$
13. $\triangle BCD$, $\triangle ABD$
14. $\triangle ABD$
15. $\triangle BCD$
16. $\overline{AD}$, $\overline{AC}$
17. $\overline{BD}$, $\overline{AD}$

18. Yes; the definition of isosceles says that the triangle has at least two sides congruent, so three sides could be congruent.

19. Since $\triangle JLK$ is isosceles, $JL = KJ$.

   $JL = KJ$ perimeter of $\triangle JLK = 3(JL)$
   $x + 3 = 2x - 5$ $= 3(x + 3)$
   $8 = x$ $= 3(8 + 3)$
                                 $= 33$ units

PAGES 167-169 EXERCISES

20. right scalene or right isosceles

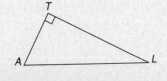

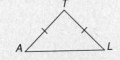

21. right isosceles

22. obtuse scalene or obtuse isosceles

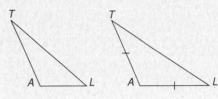

23. scalene

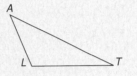

24. equilateral and equiangular

25. obtuse isosceles

26. $\overline{RO}$, $\overline{OM}$, $\overline{RM}$
27. $\angle R$, $\angle O$, $\angle M$
28. $\angle R$
29. $\angle O$, $\angle M$
30. $\overline{OM}$
31. $\overline{RO}$ and $\overline{RM}$
32. $\angle M$
33. true
34. true
35. true
36. false
37. false

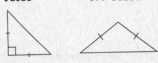

38. right scalene

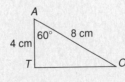

39. equiangular, equilateral

40. right, scalene

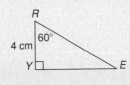

41. equiangular, equilateral

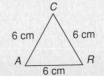

49

42. obtuse, isosceles

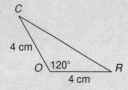

43. $\triangle OAT$ and $\triangle RYE$, and $\triangle WHT$ and $\triangle CAR$; $\triangle OAT$ and $\triangle RYE$

44. perimeter of $\triangle RLP = RL + RP + LP$

$62 = 4x - 5 + 2x + 11 + x$

$62 = 7x + 6$

$56 = 7x$

$8 = x$

$RL = 4x - 5$	$RP = x + 11$	$LP = x$
$= 4(8) - 5$	$= 2(8) + 11$	$= 8$
$= 27$	$= 27$	

The legs are 27 cm long.

45. obtuse, isosceles

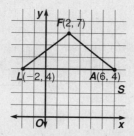

46. Given: $\overline{BC} \parallel \overline{DE}$

$\overline{AD} \perp \overline{DE}$

Prove: $\triangle ABC$ is a right triangle.

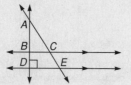

STATEMENTS	REASONS
1. $\overline{BC} \parallel \overline{DE}$ $\overline{AD} \perp \overline{DE}$	1. Given
2. $\overline{BC} \perp \overline{AD}$	2. In a plane, if a line is $\perp$ to one of 2 $\parallel$ lines, then it is $\perp$ to the other line.
3. $\angle ABC$ is a right angle.	3. $\perp$ lines form 4 rt. $\angle$s.
4. $\triangle ABC$ is a right triangle.	4. Definition of right triangle

47. Given: $m\angle NMO = 20$

Prove: $\triangle LMN$ is an obtuse triangle.

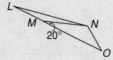

STATEMENTS	REASONS
1. $m\angle NMO = 20$	1. Given
2. $\angle LMN$ and $\angle NMO$ form a linear pair.	2. Definition of linear pair
3. $\angle LMN$ and $\angle NMO$ are supplementary.	3. If 2 $\angle$s form a linear pair, they are supp.

4. $m\angle LMN + m\angle NMO$ $= 180$	4. Definition of supplementary
5. $m\angle LMN + 20 = 180$	5. Substitution property of equality
6. $m\angle LMN = 160$	6. Subtraction property of equality
7. $\angle LMN$ is obtuse.	7. Definition of obtuse angle
8. $\triangle LMN$ is obtuse.	8. Definition of obtuse triangle

48. $ST = SR$

$6 = x + 4$

$2 = x$

perimeter of $\triangle STR = ST + TR + SR$

$= 6 + x + x + 4$

$= 6 + 2 + 2 + 4$

$= 14$ units

49. Write an inequality for the value of the perimeter.

$23 < 2x + 2 + 10 + x + 4 < 32$

$23 < 3x + 16 < 32$

$7 < 3x < 16$

$\dfrac{7}{3} < x < \dfrac{16}{3}$

Since $\triangle DEF$ is isosceles, one of the following is true.

$EF = ED$ or	$EF = FD$ or	$FD = ED$
$2x + 2 = 10$	$2x + 2 = x + 4$	$x + 4 = 10$
$2x = 8$	$x = 2$	$x = 6$
$x = 4$		

The only case that satisfies the inequality is $x = 4$, so $EF = ED$. The vertex angle is the angle between the congruent sides, so $\angle DEF$ is the vertex angle.

50. a line segment

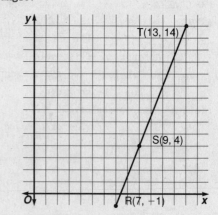

51. Isosceles triangles; the segments from the vertex A to B, C, D, and E will be congruent.

52. 4; $\triangle ABC$, $\triangle ADC$, $\triangle BCD$, $\triangle BAD$

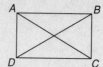

50

53. 2; ΔDEG, ΔEFG

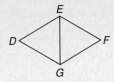

54. a. isosceles

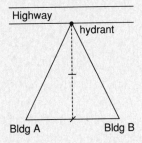

54. b. It is the same distance to each building.

55. a.

55. b. 36

56. Yes; the definition of parallel is that they are everywhere equidistant.

57. 0.1 or $\frac{1}{10}$

58. No; if they were parallel, $m\angle 1 = m\angle 5$.

59.

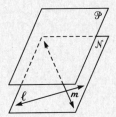

60. Substitution property of equality

61. $m\angle 1 = m\angle 2$ **62.** See students' work.
$$4x - 7 = 2x + 5$$
$$2x = 12$$
$$x = 6$$
$$m\angle 1 = 4x - 7$$
$$= 4(6) - 7$$
$$= 24 - 7$$
$$= 17$$

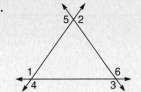

5. 42   **6.** 73   **7.** 73   **8.** 65
9. 65   **10.** 107   **11.** 51   **12.** 125

13.

exterior angle	remote interior angles
∠1	∠3 and ∠4
∠5	∠3 and ∠4
∠6	∠4 and ∠2
∠7	∠4 and ∠2
∠8	∠3 and ∠2
∠9	∠3 and ∠2

14. The sum of angle measures in a triangle is 180. The sum of the measures of two right angles is 180. If a triangle had two right angles, the measure of the third angle would be 0. That is impossible, so a right triangle can't have two right angles.

15. yes; sample answer:

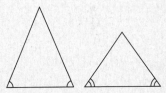

16. Answers may vary. Sample answers are that ∠ACE and ∠CAE are complementary and ∠EAB and ∠ABE are complementary.

17. Answers may vary. Sample answers are that $m\angle S + m\angle SUV = 90$ and $m\angle R + m\angle RUT = 90$.

PAGES 175-176   EXERCISES

18. $80 + 40 + x = 180$
$x = 60$

19. $20 + 70 + x = 180$
$x = 90$

20. $20 + 15 + x = 180$
$x = 145$

21. $x + x + 40 = 180$
$2x = 140$
$x = 70$

22. $x + 2x + 90 = 180$
$3x = 90$
$x = 30$

23. $3x + 16 + 45 + 68 = 180$
$3x = 51$
$x = 17$

24. $m\angle 1 + 70 = 180$
$m\angle 1 = 110$

25. $110 + 15 + m\angle 2 = 180$
$m\angle 2 = 55$

26. $m\angle 3 = 75$

27. $m\angle 4 + 75 + 50 = 180$
$m\angle 4 = 55$

28. $m\angle S = 50$

29. $35 + 90 + m\angle 6 = 180$
$m\angle 6 = 55$

30. $m\angle 7 = m\angle 6$
$m\angle 7 = 55$

31. $m\angle 8 = 90$

32. $m\angle 9 = 35$

33. $m\angle AEB + 150 = 180$
$m\angle AEB = 30$

4-2   **Angle Measures in Triangles**

PAGE 174 CHECKING FOR UNDERSTANDING

1. 180; all 180

2. complementary; $m\angle G + m\angle H + m\angle I = 180$ and $m\angle I = 90$

3. 60; 180 ÷ 3 = 60

34. $m\angle EBC + m\angle ECB + 150 = 180$
$2m\angle EBC = 30$
$m\angle EBC = 15$

35. $m\angle CED = m\angle AEB$
$m\angle CED = 30$

36. $m\angle BCE + m\angle ECD = 90$
$15 + m\angle ECD = 90$
$m\angle ECD = 75$

37. $m\angle ECB = 15$

38. $m\angle ABE = m\angle DCE$
$m\angle ABE = 75$

39. $m\angle BTD = 140$
$m\angle CTD = 40$
$m\angle ATB = 40$
$m\angle B = 20$
$m\angle A = 120$
$m\angle D = 120$

40. $m\angle MLN = 90$
$m\angle N + m\angle M = 90$
$m\angle M = 58$
$m\angle MPL = 90$
$m\angle NPL = 90$
$m\angle M + m\angle MLP = 90$
$m\angle N + m\angle NLP = 90$
$m\angle MLP = 32$
$m\angle NLP = 58$

41. Given: $\triangle RED$ is equiangular.
Prove: $m\angle R = m\angle E = m\angle D = 60$

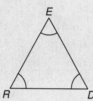

STATEMENTS	REASONS
1. $\triangle RED$ is equiangular.	1. Given
2. $\angle R \cong \angle E \cong \angle D$	2. Definition of equiangular
3. $m\angle R = m\angle E = m\angle D$	3. Definition of congruent angles
4. $m\angle R + m\angle E + m\angle D = 180.$	4. The sum of the $\angle$s in a $\triangle$ is 180°.
5. $m\angle R + m\angle R + m\angle R = 180$	5. Substitution property of equality
6. $3m\angle R = 180$	6. Substitution property of equality
7. $m\angle R = 60$	7. Division property of equality
8. $m\angle R = m\angle E = m\angle D = 60$	8. Substitution property of equality

42. Given: $\angle A \cong \angle D$
$\angle B \cong \angle E$
Prove: $\angle C \cong \angle F$

STATEMENTS	REASONS
1. $\angle A \cong \angle D$ and $\angle B \cong \angle E$	1. Given
2. $m\angle A = m\angle D$ and $m\angle B = m\angle E$	2. Definition of congruent angles

3. $m\angle A + m\angle B + m\angle C = 180$
$m\angle D + m\angle E + m\angle F = 180.$

3. The sum of the $\angle$s in a $\triangle$ is 180°.

4. $m\angle A + m\angle B + m\angle C$
$m\angle D + m\angle E + m\angle F$

4. Substitution property of equality

5. $m\angle C = m\angle F$

5. Subtraction property of equality

6. $\angle C \cong \angle F$

6. Definition of congruent angles

43. Given: $\triangle ABC$
Prove: $m\angle DCB = m\angle A + m\angle B$

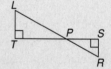

STATEMENTS	REASONS
1. $\angle ABC$	1. Given
2. $\angle DCB$ and $\angle ACB$ form a linear pair.	2. Definition of a linear pair
3. $\angle DCB$ and $\angle ACB$ are supplementary.	3. If 2 $\angle$s form a linear pair, they are supp.
4. $m\angle DCB + m\angle ACB = 180.$	4. Definition of supplementary
5. $m\angle ACB + m\angle A + m\angle B = 180$	5. The sum of the $\angle$s in a $\triangle$ is 180°.
6. $m\angle DCB + m\angle ACB = m\angle ACB + m\angle A + m\angle B$	6. Substitution property of equality
7. $m\angle DCB = m\angle A + m\angle B$	7. Subtraction property of equality

44. In $\triangle MNO$, $\angle M$ is a right angle. $m\angle M + m\angle N + m\angle O = 180$. $m\angle M = 90$, so $m\angle N + m\angle O = 90$. If $\angle N$ were a right angle, then $m\angle O = 0$. But that is impossible, so there cannot be two right angles in a triangle.

In $\triangle PQR$, $\angle P$ is obtuse. So $m\angle P > 90$. $m\angle P + m\angle Q + m\angle R = 180$. It must be that $m\angle Q + m\angle R < 90$. So $\angle Q$ and $\angle R$ must be acute.

45. Given: $\overline{LT} \perp \overline{TS}$ and $\overline{ST} \perp \overline{SR}$
Prove: $\angle TLR \cong \angle LRS$

STATEMENTS	REASONS
1. $\overline{LT} \perp \overline{TS}$ and $\overline{ST} \perp \overline{SR}$	1. Given
2. $\angle T$ and $\angle S$ are right angles.	2. $\perp$ lines form 4 rt. $\angle$s.
3. $\angle T \cong \angle S$	3. All right $\angle$s are $\cong$.
4. $\angle LPT \cong \angle RPS$	4. Vertical $\angle$s are $\cong$.
5. $\angle TLR \cong \angle LRS$	5. If 2 $\angle$s of a $\triangle$ are $\cong$ to 2 $\angle$s of another $\triangle$, the third $\angle$s are $\cong$ also.

46. Given: $\angle RUW \cong \angle VSR$

Prove: $\angle V \cong \angle W$

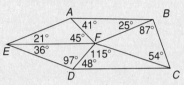

STATEMENTS	REASONS
1. $\angle RUW \cong \angle VSR$	1. Given
2. $\angle URW \cong \angle VRS$	2. Congruence of angles is reflexive.
3. $\angle V \cong \angle W$	3. If 2 ∠s of a Δ are ≅ to 2 ∠s of another Δ, the third ∠s are ≅ also.

47. $\angle 2 \cong \angle 3$

48. $m\angle A + m\angle ABC + m\angle ACB = 180$

$30 + m\angle ABC + m\angle ACB = 180$

$m\angle ABC + m\angle ACB = 150$

Since $\angle ABC$ and $\angle ACB$ are trisected, $m\angle CBT$

$= \frac{1}{3}m\angle ABC$, $m\angle CBM = \frac{2}{3}m\angle ABC$, $m\angle BCT = \frac{1}{3}m\angle ACB$, and

$m\angle BCM = \frac{2}{3}m\angle ACB$.

By the angle sum theorem

$m\angle M + m\angle CBM + m\angle BCM = 180$

$m\angle M + \frac{2}{3}m\angle ABC + \frac{2}{3}m\angle ACB = 180$

$m\angle M + \frac{2}{3}(m\angle ABC + m\angle ACB) = 180$

$m\angle M + \frac{2}{3}(150) = 180$

$m\angle M + 100 = 180$

$m\angle M = 80$

$m\angle T + m\angle CBT + m\angle BCT = 180$

$m\angle T + \frac{1}{3}m\angle ABC + \frac{1}{3}m\angle ACB = 180$

$m\angle T + \frac{1}{3}(m\angle ABC + m\angle ACB) = 180$

$m\angle T + \frac{1}{3}(150) = 180$

$m\angle T + 50 = 180$

$m\angle T = 130$

49. The sum of the measures of the angles in each triangle is 180. So since the quadrilateral contains two triangles, its angles will have a sum of 2(180) or 360.

50. Sum of angle measures > 180; no

51. Curved in; sum of angle measures < 180

52. $41 + 25 + m\angle AFB = 180$

$m\angle AFB = 114$

$21 + 45 + m\angle FAE = 180$

$m\angle FAE = 114$

$36 + 97 + m\angle EFD = 180$

$m\angle EFD = 47$

$115 + 48 + m\angle FCD = 180$

$m\angle FCD = 17$

$87 + 54 + m\angle BFC = 180$

$m\angle BFC = 39$

53. yes

54. $m \cdot 9 = -1$

$m = \frac{-1}{9}$

55. Congruence of angles is reflexive.

56. $x + 3x = 180$

$4x = 180$

$x = 45$

57. $5 = \sqrt{(5 - a)^2 + (6 - 10)^2}$

$25 = (5 - a)^2 + (-4)^2$

$25 = (5 - a)^2 + 16$

$9 = (5 - a)^2$

$3 = 5 - a$ or $-3 = 5 - a$

$a = 2$ $\qquad a = 8$

58. See students' work.

4-3   Congruent Triangles

PAGE 179   CHECKING FOR UNDERSTANDING

1.

2. See if the six pairs of corresponding parts are congruent.

3. The six pairs of corresponding parts are congruent. For example, if $\triangle ABC \cong \triangle RTS$, then $\angle A \cong \angle R$, $\angle B \cong \angle T$, $\angle C \cong \angle S$, $\overline{AB} \cong \overline{RT}$, $\overline{AC} \cong \overline{RS}$, and $\overline{BC} \cong \overline{TS}$.

4. $\triangle LEG$ **5.** $\triangle PSK$

6. $\triangle AND \cong \triangle BNC$

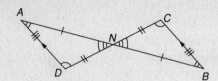

7. $\triangle WXY \cong \triangle WZY$

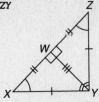

8. Answers may vary. A sample answer is a triangle with sides 4, 5, and 6, and a triangle with sides 6, 6, and 3.

PAGES 179-182   EXERCISES

9. $\triangle EFD$

10. $\angle R$

11. $\angle K$

12. $\overline{TA}$

13. $\overline{BR}$

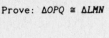

14. $\triangle OAB \cong \triangle AOD$ 15. $\triangle MIT \cong \triangle NIT$

16. $\triangle TAP \cong \triangle TOL$

17. The congruent parts are not corresponding.

18. The congruent parts are not corresponding.

19. $\triangle EAD$ 20. $\triangle YZX$

21. $\triangle ABR \cong \triangle ABS$, $\triangle ARO \cong \triangle ASO$, $\triangle BRO \cong \triangle BSO$, $\triangle ASR \cong \triangle BSR$

22. $TC = DG$
    $21 = 2x + 7$
    $14 = 2x$
    $7 = x$

23. $m\angle B + m\angle L + m\angle U = 180$
    $m\angle R + m\angle L + m\angle U = 180$
    $64 + 57 + 5x = 180$
    $5x = 55$
    $x = 11$

24. Given: $\triangle LMN \cong \triangle OPQ$
    Prove: $\triangle OPQ \cong \triangle LMN$

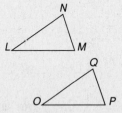

STATEMENTS	REASONS
a. $\triangle LMN \cong \triangle OPQ$	a. Given
b. $\angle L \cong \angle O$	b. CPCTC
$\angle M \cong \angle P$	
$\angle N \cong \angle Q$	
$\overline{LM} \cong \overline{OP}$	
$\overline{MN} \cong \overline{PQ}$	
$\overline{LN} \cong \overline{OQ}$	

c. $\angle O \cong \angle L$	c. Congruence of angles
$\angle P \cong \angle M$	is symmetric.
$\angle Q \cong \angle N$	
d. $\overline{OP} \cong \overline{LM}$	d. Congruence of segments
$\overline{PQ} \cong \overline{MN}$	is symmetric.
$\overline{OQ} \cong \overline{LN}$	
e. $\triangle OPQ \cong \triangle LMN$	e. Definition of congruent triangles

25. $\overline{BD} \cong \overline{AE}$ is true because the segments are corresponding parts of congruent triangles.

26. $\overline{AB} \cong \overline{DE}$ is true. $\overline{DB} \cong \overline{AE}$ because they are corresponding parts of congruent triangles. So $DB = AE$. By Segment Addition Postulate, $DB = DA + AB$ and $AE = AD + DE$, so $AB = DE$, by substitution and subtraction.

27. $\overline{BC} \cong \overline{AC}$ is not necessarily true. They are not corresponding parts of congruent triangles.

28. $\overline{AC} \cong \overline{DC}$ is true. $\triangle BCA \cong \triangle ECD$ and the segments are corresponding parts of these congruent triangles.

29. $\triangle CBA \cong \triangle CED$ is true because the angles are corresponding parts of congruent triangles.

30. $\angle BCA \cong \angle ACE$ is not necessarily true. $\angle BCA \ncong \angle ACE$ since $m\angle BCA < m\angle BCD$ and $m\angle BCD = m\angle ACE$.

Answers for 31-33 may vary. Sample answers are given.

31.

32.

33.

34. Given: $\overline{AB} \parallel \overline{RT}$
    $\overline{AR} \perp \overline{AB}$
    $\overline{BT} \perp \overline{RT}$
    $\overline{AB} \cong \overline{RT}$
    $\overline{AR} \cong \overline{TB}$

    Prove: $\triangle ABR \cong \triangle TRB$

54

STATEMENTS	REASONS
1. $\overline{AB} \parallel \overline{RT}$ $\overline{AR} \perp \overline{AB}$ $\overline{BT} \perp \overline{RT}$ $\overline{AB} \cong \overline{RT}$ $\overline{AR} \cong \overline{TB}$	1. Given
2. ∠A and ∠T are right angles.	2. ⊥ lines form right ∠s.
3. ∠A ≅ ∠T	3. All rt. ∠s are ≅.
4. ∠ABR ≅ ∠TRB	4. If 2 ∥ lines are cut by a transversal, alt. int. ∠s are ≅.
5. ∠ARB ≅ ∠TBR	5. If 2 ∠s in a △ are ≅ to 2 ∠s in another △, the third ∠s are also ≅.
6. $\overline{BR} \cong \overline{BR}$	6. Congruence of segments is reflexive.
7. △ABR ≅ △TRB	7. Definition of congruent triangles

35. Given: △XYZ
    Prove: △XYZ ≅ △XYZ

STATEMENTS	REASONS
1. ∠X ≅ ∠X, ∠Y ≅ ∠Y, ∠Z ≅ ∠Z	1. Congruence of ∠s is reflexive.
2. $\overline{XY} \cong \overline{XY}$, $\overline{YZ} \cong \overline{YZ}$, $\overline{XZ} \cong \overline{XZ}$	2. Congruence of segments is reflexive.
3. △XYZ ≅ △XYZ	3. Definition of congruent triangles

36. They are not necessarily congruent. The angles are all the same measure, but the sides may have different lengths. They are the same shape, but may not be the same size.

37. Given: △MNO ≅ △ONM
    Prove: △MNO is isosceles.

STATEMENTS	REASONS
1. △MNO ≅ △ONM	1. Given
2. $\overline{MN} \cong \overline{ON}$	2. CPCTC
3. △MNO is isosceles.	3. Definition of isosceles triangle

38. Given: △RST ≅ △TSR
    △RST ≅ △RTS
    Prove: △RST is equilateral and equiangular.

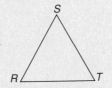

STATEMENTS	REASONS
1. △RST ≅ △TSR △RST ≅ △RTS	1. Given
2. $\overline{RS} \cong \overline{TS}$ $\overline{RS} \cong \overline{RT}$ ∠R ≅ ∠T ∠S ≅ ∠T	2. CPCTC
3. $\overline{TS} \cong \overline{RT}$	3. Congruence of segments is transitive.
4. ∠R ≅ ∠S	4. Congruence of angles is transitive.
5. △RST is equilateral and equiangular.	5. Definition of equilateral and equiangular

39. Answers may vary. Any pair of triangles with three congruent angles and two congruent sides, but not corresponding sides.

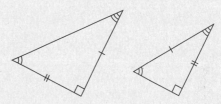

40. All the items described are the same size and shape.

41. Answers may vary. Sample answer:
    △CAE ≅ △EBG; △CAD ≅ △EAD ≅ △EBF ≅ △GBF

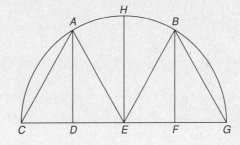

42. 54 + 79 or 133

43. $8x + 1 + 3x - 6 + 4x - 10 = 180$
    $15x - 15 = 180$
    $15x = 195$
    $x = 13$

    $8x - 1 = 8(13) + 1$
    $\quad = 104 + 1$
    $\quad = 105$

    $3x - 6 = 3(13) - 6$
    $\quad = 39 - 6$
    $\quad = 33$

    $4x - 10 = 4(13) - 10$
    $\quad = 52 - 10$
    $\quad = 42$

44. True; explanations may vary. Sample explanation: all right triangles are either scalene or isosceles.

55

45. $\dfrac{-3 - (-1)}{7 - 6} = \dfrac{-2}{1} = -2$　**46.**
$$m\angle L = m\angle S$$
$$3x + 7 = 43$$
$$3x = 36$$
$$x = 12$$

47. See students' work.

Technology: Congruent Triangles

PAGE 183　　EXERCISES

1. yes　　　　　　**2.** no

4-4　　**Tests for Congruent Triangles**

PAGES 187-188　　CHECKING FOR UNDERSTANDING

1. a. $\overline{AM} \cong \overline{PR}$　　　**b.** ASA
2. a. $\overline{TU} \cong \overline{QO}$　　　**b.** $\angle W \cong \angle S$
3. Not necessarily; for example, triangles with sides 4, 5, and 6 and 5, 6, and 10 are not congruent, but they have two parts congruent.
4. ASA　　　　　**5.** SSS
6. not congruent
7. Given: $\overline{AM} \parallel \overline{CR}$
　　　　B is the midpoint of $\overline{AR}$.
　　Prove: $\triangle ABM \cong \triangle RBC$

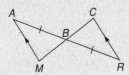

STATEMENTS	REASONS
a. B is the midpoint of $\overline{AR}$.	a. Given
b. $\overline{AB} \cong \overline{BR}$	b. Definition of midpoint
c. $\overline{AM} \parallel \overline{CR}$	c. Given
d. $\angle A \cong \angle R$	d. If 2 $\parallel$ lines are cut by a transversal, alt. int. $\angle$s are $\cong$.
e. $\angle ABM \cong \angle RBC$	e. Vertical $\angle$s are $\cong$.
f. $\triangle ABM \cong \triangle RBC$	f. ASA

8. ASA 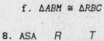　　**9.** SAS

10. SSS

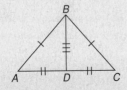

PAGES 189-191　　EXERCISES

11. True; since $\angle 3$ and $\angle 4$ are alt. int. angles and $\angle 3 \cong \angle 4$.
12. False; their non-common sides are not opposite rays.
13. Could be true
14. True; congruence of segments is reflexive.
15. Could be true　**16.** Could be true
17. Could be true　**18.** False; $\angle 2$ is not right.
19. SAS　　　　**20.** not possible
21. SSS
22. $\triangle MOL \cong \triangle MON$ by ASA　**23.** $\triangle EFH \cong \triangle GHF$ by SSS

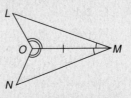　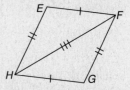

24. a. $\triangle ABD \cong \triangle CDB$ by SSS
　　b. $\angle A \cong \angle C$ by CPCTC

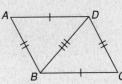

25. Given: $\angle A \cong \angle D$
　　　　$\overline{AO} \cong \overline{OD}$
　　Prove: $\triangle AOB \cong \triangle DOC$

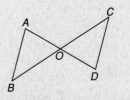

STATEMENTS	REASONS
1. $\angle A \cong \angle D$ $\overline{AO} \cong \overline{OD}$	1. Given
2. $\angle AOB \cong \angle DOC$	2. Vertical angles are congruent.
3. $\triangle AOB \cong \triangle DOC$	3. ASA

26. Given: $\overline{AD}$ bisects $\overline{BC}$.
　　　　$\overline{BC}$ bisects $\overline{AD}$.
　　Prove: $\triangle AOB \cong \triangle DOC$

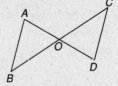

STATEMENTS	REASONS
1. $\overline{AD}$ bisects $\overline{BC}$. $\overline{BC}$ bisects $\overline{AD}$.	1. Given
2. $\overline{AO} \cong \overline{OD}$ $\overline{BO} \cong \overline{OC}$	2. Definition of bisector
3. $\angle AOB \cong \angle DOC$	3. Vertical angles are congruent.
4. $\triangle AOB \cong \triangle DOC$	4. SAS

27. Given: $\overline{MO} \cong \overline{PO}$

$\overline{NO}$ bisects $\overline{MP}$.

Prove: $\triangle MNO \cong \triangle PNO$

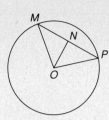

STATEMENTS	REASONS
1. $\overline{MO} \cong \overline{PO}$ $\overline{NO}$ bisects $\overline{MP}$.	1. Given
2. $\overline{MN} \cong \overline{NP}$	2. Definition of bisector
3. $\overline{NO} \cong \overline{NO}$	3. Congruence of segments is reflexive
4. $\triangle MNO \cong \triangle PNO$	4. SSS

28. Given: $\overline{NO}$ bisects $\angle POM$.

$\overline{NO} \perp \overline{MP}$

Prove: $\triangle MNO \cong \triangle PNO$

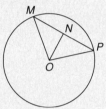

STATEMENTS	REASONS
1. $\overline{NO}$ bisects $\angle POM$. $\overline{NO} \perp \overline{MP}$	1. Given
2. $\angle MON \cong \angle PON$	2. Definition of angle bisector
3. $\angle MNO$ and $\angle PNO$ are right.	3. $\perp$ lines form 4 rt. $\angle$s.
4. $\angle MNO \cong \angle PNO$	4. All rt. $\angle$s are $\cong$.
5. $\overline{NO} \cong \overline{NO}$	5. Congruence of segments is reflexive.
6. $\triangle MNO \cong \triangle PNO$	6. ASA

29.

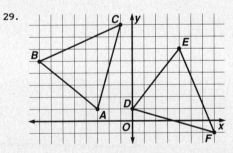

$AB = \sqrt{(-3 - (-8))^2 + (1 - 5)^2} = \sqrt{41}$

$BC = \sqrt{(-8 - (-1))^2 + (5 - 8)^2} = \sqrt{58}$

$AC = \sqrt{(-3 - (-1))^2 + (1 - 8)^2} = \sqrt{53}$

$DE = \sqrt{(0 - 4)^2 + (1 - 6)^2} = \sqrt{41}$

$EF = \sqrt{(4 - 7)^2 + (6 - (-1))^2} = \sqrt{58}$

$DF = \sqrt{(0 - 7)^2 + (1 - (-1))^2} = \sqrt{53}$

30. Given: $\angle 1 \cong \angle 6$

$\angle 3 \cong \angle 4$

Prove: $\overline{AD} \cong \overline{CB}$

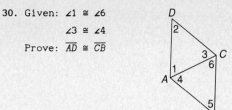

STATEMENTS	REASONS
1. $\angle 1 \cong \angle 6$ $\angle 3 \cong \angle 4$	1. Given
2. $\overline{AC} \cong \overline{AC}$	2. Congruence of segments is reflexive.
3. $\triangle ADC \cong \triangle CBA$	3. ASA
4. $\overline{AD} \cong \overline{CB}$	4. CPCTC

31. Given: $\angle 3 \cong \angle 4$

$\overline{DC} \cong \overline{BA}$

Prove: $\angle 1 \cong \angle 6$

STATEMENTS	REASONS
1. $\angle 3 \cong \angle 4$ $\overline{DC} \cong \overline{BA}$	1. Given
2. $\overline{AC} \cong \overline{AC}$	2. Congruence of segments is reflexive.
3. $\triangle ADC \cong \triangle CBA$	3. SAS
4. $\angle 1 \cong \angle 6$	4. CPCTC

32. $\overline{DB} \cong \overline{DC}$

$\overline{AD} \cong \overline{AD}$

$\angle DAB \cong \angle DAC$

No, the triangles are not congruent. SSA is not a test for congruent triangles.

33. a. $\triangle DCF$ **b.** $\triangle EFC$ **c.** $\triangle EDF$
d. $\triangle FCG$ **e.** $\triangle ECG$ **f.** $\triangle CGA$

34. $\angle B \cong \angle T$, $\angle I \cong \angle O$, $\angle G \cong \angle P$, $\overline{BT} \cong \overline{TO}$, $\overline{IG} \cong \overline{OP}$, $\overline{BG} \cong \overline{TP}$

35. $6x - 6 = x + 9$ $\qquad$ $6(3) - 6 = 18 - 6$
$\qquad$ $5x = 15$ $\qquad\qquad$ $= 12$ units
$\qquad\qquad$ $x = 3$

36. Hypothesis: - you want a great pizza; conclusion: - go to Katie's.

37. a straight angle   **38.** See students' work.

Mid-Chapter Review

PAGE 191

1. False, the hypotenuse must be longer than the legs.

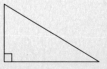

2. true   3. true   4. true

5. yes   6. no   7. yes

8. yes   9. ∠O   10. $\overline{TP}$

11. ∠T

12. Given: $\overline{QP} \cong \overline{ST}$

∠P and ∠T are right angles.

R is the midpoint of $\overline{PT}$.

Prove: $\overline{QR} \cong \overline{SR}$

STATEMENTS	REASONS
1. $\overline{QP} \cong \overline{ST}$ ∠P and ∠T are right angles. R is the midpoint of $\overline{PT}$.	1. Given
2. ∠P ≅ ∠T	2. All rt. ∠s are ≅.
3. $\overline{PR} \cong \overline{RT}$	3. Definition of midpoint
4. △QPR ≅ △STR	4. SAS
5. $\overline{QR} \cong \overline{SR}$	5. CPCTC

4-5   Another Test for Congruent Triangles

PAGES 194-195   CHECKING FOR UNDERSTANDING

1. SSS, ASA, SAS, AAS. Answers may vary. Sample answers: same - all have three parts of the triangle congruent; different - all have different combinations of parts.

2. a and d are congruent by ASA.

3. Answers may vary. Sample answers: show they are corresponding parts of congruent triangles or show they are vertical angles.

4. $\overline{AD}$ and $\overline{AO}$; $\overline{DO}$ and $\overline{AO}$; $\overline{DO}$ and $\overline{DA}$

5. ∠1 and ∠3; ∠1 and ∠2; ∠2 and ∠3

6. $\overline{AC} \cong \overline{DC}$ 7. $\overline{CE} \cong \overline{BA}$

8. ∠ABC ≅ ∠CEA   9. ∠ACB ≅ ∠CAE

10. ∠ACB ≅ ∠DCE, $\overline{BC} \cong \overline{EC}$; ∠ABC ≅ ∠DEC; $\overline{AC} \cong \overline{DC}$ ∠ACB ≅ ∠DCE, $\overline{AB} \cong \overline{DE}$; or ∠ABC ≅ ∠DEC; $\overline{BC} \cong \overline{EC}$

11. Given: $\overline{AB} \cong \overline{CD}$

$\overline{AB} \parallel \overline{CD}$

Prove: △AOB ≅ △DOC

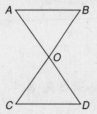

Proof: We are given that $\overline{AB} \cong \overline{CD}$ and $\overline{AB} \parallel \overline{CD}$. ∠A ≅ ∠D and ∠B ≅ ∠C since if parallel lines are cut by a transversal, alternate interior angles are congruent. Therefore, △ADB ≅ △DOC by ASA.

12. You cannot prove that △AOB ≅ △DOC given only that $\overline{AB} \parallel \overline{CD}$. This information would only give us two pairs of congruent angles: ∠A ≅ ∠D and ∠B ≅ ∠C since if parallel lines are cut by a transversal, alternate interior angles are congruent. To prove that △AOB ≅ △DOC, we would need to know that a pair of corresponding sides are congruent.

13. △ADO ≅ △CBO by AAS or ASA; △ADB ≅ △CBD by SAS

14. △BAO ≅ △DCO by ASA or AAS; △BAD ≅ △DCB by SAS △ABC ≅ △CDA by SAS

15. △AOD ≅ △COB by SAS; △AOB ≅ △COD by SAS

16. We are given that $\overline{PR}$ and $\overline{QS}$ bisect each other, so $\overline{PT} \cong \overline{TR}$ and $\overline{QT} \cong \overline{TS}$. ∠PTQ ≅ ∠STR because they are vertical angles. Therefore, △PQT ≅ △RST by SAS.

PAGES 195-197   EXERCISES

17. ∠E ≅ ∠S

18. ∠D ≅ ∠R

19. $\overline{DE} \cong \overline{RS}$ or $\overline{EF} \cong \overline{ST}$

20. $\overline{EF} \cong \overline{ST}$

21. △ABD ≅ △CDB by AAS

22. △AEC ≅ △DEB by AAS

23. One order of steps: 3, 1, 5, 9, 8, 2, 7, 6, 4.

Given: $\overline{AB} \perp \overline{BC}$, $\overline{AE} \perp \overline{DE}$, ∠1 ≅ ∠2, $\overline{AB} \cong \overline{AE}$

Prove: $\overline{AC} \cong \overline{AD}$

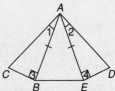

STATEMENTS	REASONS
1. ∠3 is a right angle.	1. ⊥ lines form rt ∠s.
2. ∠1 ≅ ∠2	2. Given
3. $\overline{AB} \perp \overline{BC}$	3. Given
4. $\overline{AC} \cong \overline{AD}$	4. CPCTC
5. $\overline{AE} \perp \overline{DE}$	5. Given
6. △ABC ≅ △AED	6. ASA
7. $\overline{AB} \cong \overline{AE}$	7. Given
8. ∠3 ≅ ∠4	8. All rt. ∠s are ≅.
9. ∠4 is a right angle.	9. ⊥ lines form four rt. ∠s.

24. not valid because there is only one pair of congruent parts: $\overline{BC} \cong \overline{DE}$.

25. not valid because the conditions of the theorems or postulates that prove the congruence of triangles are not met

26. We are given that ∠1 ≅ ∠2 and ∠L ≅ ∠M. $\overline{AE} ≅ \overline{EA}$ because congruence of segments is reflexive. Therefore, ΔEAM ≅ ΔAEL by AAS. So $\overline{EM} ≅ \overline{AL}$ by CPCTC.

27. $\overline{ST} ≅ \overline{QN}$, ∠S ≅ ∠Q, and $\overline{PS} ≅ \overline{PQ}$ is given. ΔTSP ≅ ΔNQP by SAS. $\overline{TP} ≅ \overline{NP}$ by CPCTC. So, ΔTPN is isosceles by definition of isosceles triangle.

28. Given $\overline{BC} ≅ \overline{AD}$
    $\overline{BD} ≅ \overline{AC}$

    Prove: ∠BAC ≅ ∠ABD

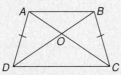

STATEMENTS	REASONS
1. $\overline{BC} ≅ \overline{AD}$, $\overline{BD} ≅ \overline{AC}$	1. Given
2. $\overline{AB} ≅ \overline{AB}$	2. Congruence of segments is reflexive.
3. ΔBAC ≅ ΔABD	3. SSS
4. ∠BAC ≅ ∠ABD	4. CPCTC

29. Given: $\overline{AB} ≅ \overline{AC}$
    D is the midpoint of $\overline{BC}$.

    Prove: ΔABD ≅ ΔACD

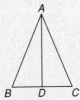

STATEMENTS	REASONS
1. $\overline{AB} ≅ \overline{AC}$ D is the midpoint of $\overline{BC}$.	1. Given
2. $\overline{BD} ≅ \overline{CD}$	2. Definition of midpoint
3. $\overline{AD} ≅ \overline{AD}$	3. Congruence of segments is reflexive.
4. ΔABD ≅ ΔACD	4. SSS

30. Given: ΔMNO is isosceles
    $\overline{QM}$ bisects ∠NMO.

    Prove: $\overline{QM} ⊥ \overline{NO}$

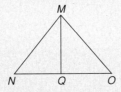

STATEMENTS	REASONS
1. ΔMNO is isosceles. $\overline{QM}$ bisects ∠NMO.	1. Given
2. $\overline{MN} ≅ \overline{MO}$	2. Definition of isosceles
3. ∠NMQ ≅ ∠OMQ	3. Definition of angle bisector
4. $\overline{MQ} ≅ MQ$	4. Congruence of segments is reflexive.
5. ΔNMQ ≅ ΔOMQ	5. SAS
6. ∠NQM ≅ ∠OQM	6. CPCTC
7. m∠NQM ≅ m∠OQM	7. Definition of congruent angles
8. ∠NQM and ∠OQM form	8. Definition of linear
a linear pair.	pair
9. m∠NQM + m∠OQM = 180	9. If 2 ∠s form a linear pair, they are supp.
10. 2m∠NQM = 180	10. Substitution property of equality
11. m∠NQM = 90	11. Division property of equality
12. m∠OQM = 90	12. Substitution property of equality
13. ∠NQM and ∠OQM are right.	13. Definition of right angle
14. $\overline{QM} ⊥ \overline{NO}$	14. Definition of perpendicular lines

31. AAA does not prove two triangles congruent. See students' justifications.

32. The distance from the shore to where the lines intersect is the distance from the shore to the ship. The triangle formed by the ship and P and Q is congruent to the triangle formed by the intersection point and P and Q. If S is the point of the ship, and I is the intersection point, then $\overline{PQ} ≅ \overline{PQ}$, ∠SPQ ≅ ∠IPQ, and ∠SQP ≅ ∠IQP. The triangles are congruent by ASA.

33.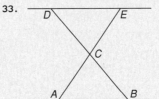

$\overline{DE}$ represents the ironing board and $\overline{AB}$ represents the floor. Since the legs bisect each other, $\overline{DC} ≅ \overline{BC}$ and $\overline{CE} ≅ \overline{CA}$. ∠DCE ≅ ∠BCA because vertical angles are congruent. Therefore, ΔDCE ≅ ΔBCA by SAS. Since corresponding parts of congruent triangles are congruent, ∠D ≅ ∠B. Since if two lines are cut by a transversal so that alt. int. ∠s are congruent, the lines are parallel, so $\overline{DE} \| \overline{AB}$.

34. Given: $\overline{PR} ≅ \overline{TR}$
    ∠1 ≅ ∠2
    ∠P and ∠T are right angles.

    Prove: $\overline{QR} ≅ \overline{SR}$

STATEMENTS	REASONS
1. $\overline{PR} ≅ \overline{TR}$ ∠1 ≅ ∠2 ∠P and ∠T are right angles.	1. Given
2. ∠P ≅ ∠T	2. All rt. ∠s are ≅.
3. ΔQPR ≅ ΔSTR	3. ASA
4. $\overline{QR} ≅ \overline{SR}$	4. CPCTC

35. ∠ACK

59

36. Alternate interior angles are congruent; corresponding angles are congruent; alternate exterior angles are congruent; consecutive interior angles are supplementary; two lines in a plane are parallel to a third line.

37. $d = \sqrt{(7 - (-3))^2 + (4 - 8)^2}$

$\quad = \sqrt{100 + 16}$

$\quad = 2\sqrt{29}$

$M = \left(\dfrac{7 + (-3)}{2}, \dfrac{4 + 8}{2}\right)$

$\quad = \left(\dfrac{4}{2}, \dfrac{12}{2}\right)$

$\quad = (2, 6)$

38. See students' work.

4-6 Problem-Solving Strategy: Identify Subgoals

PAGES 199-200 CHECKING FOR UNDERSTANDING

1. It breaks the problem into smaller steps.

2. Answers may vary. A typical answer is 2-column proof.

3. Any number divisible by 1, 2, 3, 4, 5, 6, and 7, will be divisible by their least common multiple, 420. 215 of the 90,000 five-digit whole numebrs are divisible by 420. So the fraction of the five-digit numbers divisible by 1, 2, 3, 4, 5, 6, and 7 is $\dfrac{215}{90,000}$ or $\dfrac{43}{18,000}$.

4. The possible digits are 008, 017, 026, 035, 044, 116, 125, 134, 224, or 233. There are 45 numbers with these combinations of digits.

5. The factors of 48 are 1, 2, 3, 4, 6, 8, 12, 16, and 48. The sum of their reciprocals is

$\dfrac{1}{1} + \dfrac{1}{2} + \dfrac{1}{3} + \dfrac{1}{4} + \dfrac{1}{6} + \dfrac{1}{8} + \dfrac{1}{12} + \dfrac{1}{16} + \dfrac{1}{48}$

$= \dfrac{48 + 24 + 16 + 12 + 8 + 6 + 4 + 3 + 2 + 1}{48}$

$= \dfrac{124}{48}$ or $2\dfrac{7}{12}$.

6. Use the strategy of guess and check. The number is 23.

7. $\triangle BCG \cong \triangle FCD$; $\overline{BG} \cong \overline{FD}$; $\triangle ABG \cong \triangle EFD$; $\angle A \cong \angle E$

PAGES 200-201 EXERCISES

8. The first two transactions yield a profit of $100 and the last two transactions yield a profit of $100; so the dealer made $200.

9. Use the strategy of guess and check. The number is 68^2 or 4624.

10. Cook one side of two hamburgers. After 5-minutes turn one hamburger over and cook one side of the raw hamburger. After 5 more minutes take off the fully cooked hamburger and cook the raw sides of the other two hamburgers. The total time is 15 minutes.

11. Subgoals: $\triangle ADB \cong \triangle ACB$, $\angle DAB \cong \angle CAB$

Given: $\overleftrightarrow{AB} \perp$ plane BCD

$\quad \overline{DB} \cong \overline{CB}$

Prove: $\angle DAB \cong \angle CAB$

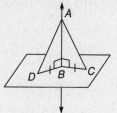

STATEMENTS	REASONS
1. $\overleftrightarrow{AB} \perp$ plane BCD	1. Given
2. $\overline{AB} \perp \overline{DB}$	2. Definition of
$\quad \overline{AB} \perp \overline{CB}$	$\quad$ perpendicular plane
3. $\angle ABC$ and $\angle ABD$ are right angles.	3. $\perp$ lines form four rt. $\angle$s.
4. $\angle ABD \cong \angle ABC$	4. All rt. $\angle$s are $\cong$.
5. $\overline{DB} \cong \overline{CB}$	5. Given
6. $\overline{AB} \cong \overline{AB}$	6. Congruence of segments is reflexive.
7. $\triangle ABD \cong \triangle ABC$	7. SAS
8. $\angle DAB \cong \angle CAB$	8. CPCTC

12. There are 16 product dates in the 1990s: 3/30/90; 5/18/90; 6/15/90; 9/10/90; 10/9/90; 7/13/91; 4/23/92; 3/31/93; 5/19/95; 4/24/96; 6/16/96; 8/12/96; 12/8/96; 7/14/98; 9/11/99; 11/9/99.

13. 3: 1 dog, 1 cat, and 1 hamster

14. Sample answer: $123 - 4 - 5 - 6 - 7 + 8 - 9 = 100$

15. You can roll the following combinations: 1 and 2, 2 and 1, 1 and 5, 5 and 1, 2 and 4, 4 and 2. 3 and 3, 3 and 6, 6 and 3, 4 and 5, 5 and 4, or 6 and 6. There are 12 combinations.

16. a.

	Justine	Vivian	Cynthia	Kim	Sarah
Art	X	X	✓	X	X
Naren	X	X	X	✓	X
Will	✓	X	X	X	X
Jared	X	X	X	X	✓
Anthony	X	✓	X	X	X

If all predictions were correct, the marriages would have been Art and Cynthia, Naren and Kim, Will and Justine, Jared and Sarah, and Anthony and Vivian.

16. b.

	Justine	Vivian	Cynthia	Kim	Sarah
Art	X	X	X	✓	X
Naren	X	X	X	X	✓
Will	X	✓	X	X	X
Jared	✓	X	X	X	X
Anthony	X	X	✓	X	X

If we know who is Anthony's sister, we can tell who is married to whom. If Anthony's sister is anyone but Justine we can not tell all of the marriages. So, Anthony's sister is Justine and the marriages are Art and Kim, Naren and Sarah, Will and Vivian, Jared and Justine, and Anthony and Cynthia.

Cooperative Learning Project

PAGE 201

10; number of rebounds = $a + b - 2$

4-7   Isosceles Triangles

PAGES 204-205   CHECKING FOR UNDERSTANDING

1. base angles congruent; two sides congruent; line of symmetry
2. isosceles
3. Yes; an equilateral is isosceles and an isosceles triangle has symmetry.

4.   base: $\overline{BC}$
         legs: $\overline{AB}$ and $\overline{AC}$
         vertex: $\angle A$
         base angles $\angle B$ and $\angle C$

5. $\angle 1 \cong \angle 2$
  $\overline{BD} \not\cong \overline{DC}$

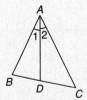

6. $\overline{AD} \perp \overline{BC}$
  $\overline{BD} \not\cong \overline{DC}$

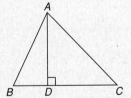

7. $\overline{BD} \cong \overline{DC}$
  $\overline{AD} \not\perp \overline{BC}$

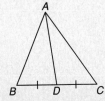

8. $\overline{BD} \cong \overline{DC}$
  $\angle 1 \not\cong \angle 2$

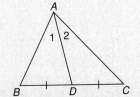

9. isosceles;
  $\triangle XWY \cong \triangle XWE$ by SAS so
  $\overline{XY} \cong \overline{XZ}$ by CPCTC

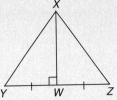

10. no; sample drawing

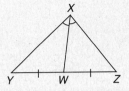

11. $\angle EAB$ and $\angle 4$ 12. $\angle 1$ and $\angle 2$
13. $\angle 5$ and $\angle 6$ or $\angle EFA$ and $\angle BGA$
14. $\angle 3$ and $\angle 7$
15. $x + x + 46 = 180$ 16. $x + x + 60 = 180$
             $2x = 134$ $2x = 120$
                $x = 67$ $x = 60$
17. $x = 21$

18.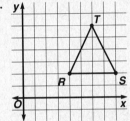

$RS = \sqrt{(4-8)^2 + (2-2)^2} = \sqrt{16} = 4$

$ST = \sqrt{(8-6)^2 + (2-6)^2} = \sqrt{20} = 2\sqrt{5}$

$RT = \sqrt{(4-6)^2 + (2-6)^2} = \sqrt{20} = 2\sqrt{5}$

19. Given: $\overline{AB} \cong \overline{BC}$
    Prove: $\angle 3 \cong \angle 5$

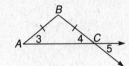

STATEMENTS	REASONS
1. $\overline{AB} \cong \overline{BC}$	1. Given
2. $\angle 3 \cong \angle 4$	2. Isosceles Triangle Theorem
3. $\angle 4 \cong \angle 5$	3. Vertical $\angle$s are $\cong$.
4. $\angle 3 \cong \angle 5$	4. Substitution property of equality

PAGES 205-207   EXERCISES

20. $x + x + 90 = 180$ 21. $4x - 6 = 18$
            $2x = 90$ $4x = 24$
              $x = 45$ $x = 6$
22. $2x + 11 + 2x + 11 + x - 2 = 180$
                   $5x + 20 = 180$
                       $5x = 160$
                          $x = 32$

23. $8x + 13 = 11x + 4$
    $9 = 3x$
    $3 = x$

24. $3x - 10 + 3x - 10 + 2x = 180$
    $8x - 20 = 180$
    $8x = 200$
    $x = 25$

25. $2x + 9 = 3x - 9$
    $18 = x$

26. $\overline{LB} \cong \overline{BF}$ – Theorem 4-7
    $\angle 3 \cong \angle 4$; If two $\angle$s are complements of $\cong$ $\angle$s, they are $\cong$.
    $\overline{LD} \cong \overline{DF}$; Theorem 4-7
    $\triangle LDF$ and $\triangle LBF$ are isosceles; definition of isosceles triangle

27. $\triangle TBR$ is isosceles; definition of isosceles triangle
    $\angle RQB \cong \angle BCR$; $\angle RQB$ and $\angle 1$ form a linear pair and so do $\angle BCR$ and $\angle 2$, so these pairs are supplementary. Since $\angle 1 \cong \angle 2$, $\angle RQB \cong \angle BCR$.
    $\triangle TQR \cong \triangle TCB$; AAS ($\angle 1 \cong \angle 2$, $\angle T \cong \angle T$, and $\overline{TB} \cong \overline{TR}$)
    $\angle TBR \cong \angle TRB$; Isosceles Triangle Theorem

28. Given: $\overline{AB} \cong \overline{BC}$
    Prove: $\angle 3 \cong \angle 4$

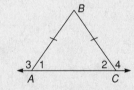

STATEMENTS	REASONS
1. $\overline{AB} \cong \overline{BC}$	1. Given
2. $\angle 1 \cong \angle 2$	2. If two sides of a $\triangle$ are $\cong$, then the $\angle$s opp. the sides are $\cong$.
3. $\angle 1$ and $\angle 3$ form a linear pair. $\angle 2$ and $\angle 4$ form a linear pair.	3. Definition of linear pair
4. $\angle 1$ and $\angle 3$ are supplementary. $\angle 2$ and $\angle 4$ are supplementary.	4. If 2 $\angle$s form a linear pair, they are supp.
5. $\angle 3 \cong \angle 4$	5. Angles that are supplementary to $\cong$ $\angle$s are $\cong$.

29. Given: $\overline{PS} \cong \overline{QR}$
    $\angle 3 \cong \angle 4$
    Prove: $\angle 1 \cong \angle 2$

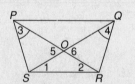

STATEMENTS	REASONS
1. $\overline{PS} \cong \overline{QR}$ $\angle 3 \cong \angle 4$	1. Given

2. $\angle 5 \cong \angle 6$ — 2. Vertical angles are congruent.
3. $\triangle POS \cong \triangle QOR$ — 3. AAS
4. $\overline{OS} \cong \overline{OR}$ — 4. CPCTC
5. $\angle 1 \cong \angle 2$ — 5. If two sides of a $\triangle$ are $\cong$, then the $\angle$s opp. the sides are $\cong$.

30. Given: $\overline{ZT} \cong \overline{ZR}$
    $\overline{TX} \cong \overline{RY}$
    Prove: $\angle 5 \cong \angle 7$

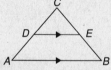

STATEMENTS	REASONS
1. $\overline{ZT} \cong \overline{ZR}$ $\overline{TX} \cong \overline{RY}$	1. Given
2. $\angle 2 \cong \angle 3$	2. Isosceles Triangle Theorem
3. $\angle 1$ and $\angle 2$ form a linear pair. $\angle 3$ and $\angle 4$ form a linear pair.	3. Definition of a linear pair
4. $\angle 1$ and $\angle 2$ are supplementary. $\angle 3$ and $\angle 4$ are supplementary.	4. If 2 $\angle$s form a linear pair, they are supp.
5. $\angle 1 \cong \angle 4$	5. If 2 $\angle$s are supplementary to $\cong$ $\angle$s, they are supp.
6. $\triangle XTZ \cong \triangle YRZ$	6. SAS
7. $\angle 5 \cong \angle 7$	7. CPCTC

31. Given: $\triangle ABC$ is isosceles.
    $\overline{DE} \parallel \overline{AB}$, $\overline{AB} \cong \overline{BC}$
    Prove: $\triangle DEC$ is isosceles.

STATEMENTS	REASONS
1. $\overline{DE} \parallel \overline{AB}$, $\overline{AB} \cong \overline{BC}$ $\triangle ABC$ is isosceles.	1. Given
2. $\angle A \cong \angle B$	2. If two sides of a $\triangle$ are $\cong$, then the angles opp. those sides are $\cong$.
3. $\angle A \cong \angle EDC$ $\angle B \cong \angle DEC$	3. If 2 $\parallel$ lines are cut by a transversal, then each pair of corresponding $\angle$s is $\cong$.
4. $\angle EDC \cong \angle DEC$	4. Substitution property of equality
5. $\overline{CD} \cong \overline{CE}$	5. If two $\angle$s of a $\triangle$ are $\cong$, the sides opp. those $\angle$s are $\cong$.
6. $\triangle DEC$ is isosceles.	6. Definition of isosceles triangle

32. Given: $\angle 5 \cong \angle 6$

$\overline{GJ} \perp \overline{FH}$

Prove: $\triangle FHJ$ is isosceles.

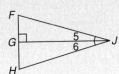

STATEMENTS	REASONS
1. $\angle 5 \cong \angle 6$ $\overline{GJ} \perp \overline{FH}$	1. Given
2. $\overline{GJ} \cong \overline{GJ}$	2. Congruence of segments is reflexive.
3. $\angle FGJ$ and $\angle HGJ$ are right.	3. $\perp$ lines form right $\angle$s.
4. $\angle FGJ \cong \angle HGJ$	4. Right $\angle$s are $\cong$.
5. $\triangle FGJ \cong \triangle HGJ$	5. ASA
6. $\overline{FJ} \cong \overline{HJ}$	6. CPCTC
7. $\triangle FHJ$ is isosceles.	7. Definition of isosceles triangle

33. Given: $\overline{AB} \cong \overline{AC}$

$\overline{BX}$ bisects $\angle ABC$.

$\overline{CX}$ bisects $\angle ACB$.

Prove: $\overline{BX} \cong \overline{CX}$

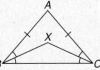

STATEMENTS	REASONS
1. $\overline{AB} \cong \overline{AC}$ $\overline{BX}$ bisects $\angle ABC$. $\overline{CX}$ bisects $\angle ACB$.	1. Given
2. $\angle ABX \cong \angle XBC$ $\angle ACX \cong \angle XCB$	2. Definition of angle bisector
3. $\angle ABC \cong \angle ACB$	3. If two sides of a $\triangle$ are $\cong$, then the $\angle$s opp. those sides are $\cong$.
4. $m\angle ABX = m\angle XBC$ $m\angle ACX = m\angle XCB$ $m\angle ABC = m\angle ACB$	4. Definition of congruent $\angle$s
5. $m\angle ABC = m\angle ABX +$ $m\angle XBC$ $m\angle ACB = m\angle ACX +$ $m\angle XCB$	5. Angle Addition Postulate
6. $m\angle ABC = 2m\angle XBC$ $m\angle ACB = 2m\angle XCB$	6. Substitution Property of equality
7. $2m\angle XBC = 2m\angle XCB$	7. Substitution Property of equality
8. $m\angle XBC = m\angle XCB$	8. Division Property of Equality
9. $\angle XBC \cong \angle XCB$	9. Definition of congruent $\angle$s.
10. $\overline{BX} \cong \overline{CX}$	10. If two $\angle$s of a $\triangle$ are $\cong$, then the sides opp. those $\angle$s are $\cong$.

34. $m\angle 3 = m\angle 1$ $m\angle 1 + m\angle 2 + m\angle 3 = 180$

$m\angle 3 = 30$ $30 + m\angle 2 + 30 = 180$

$m\angle 2 = 120$

$m\angle 2 + m\angle 4 = 180$ $m\angle 6 = m\angle 4$

$120 + m\angle 4 = 180$ $m\angle 6 = 60$

$m\angle 4 = 60$

$m\angle 4 + m\angle 5 + m\angle 6 = 180$ $m\angle 6 + m\angle 7 = 180$

$60 + m\angle 5 + 60 = 180$ $60 + m\angle 7 = 180$

$m\angle 5 = 60$ $m\angle 7 = 120$

$m\angle 3 + m\angle 5 + m\angle 8 = 180$

$30 + 60 + m\angle 8 = 180$

$m\angle 8 = 90$

35. Let $m\angle 1 = x$.

$m\angle 3 = m\angle 1$ $m\angle 2 + m\angle 1 + m\angle 3 = 180$

$m\angle 3 = x$ $m\angle 2 + x + x = 180$

$m\angle 2 = 180 - 2x$

$m\angle 4 + m\angle 2 = 180$ $m\angle 6 = m\angle 4$

$m\angle 4 + (180 - 2x) = 180$ $m\angle 6 = 2x$

$m\angle 4 = 2x$

$m\angle 5 + m\angle 4 + m\angle 6 = 180$

$m\angle 5 + 2x + 2x = 180$

$m\angle 5 = 180 - 4x$

$m\angle 7 + m\angle 6 = 180$ $m\angle 8 + m\angle 5 + m\angle 3 = 180$

$m\angle 7 + 2x = 180$ $60 + (180 - 4x) + x = 180$

$m\angle 7 = 180 - 2x$ $60 - 3x = 0$

$60 = 3x$

$20 = x$

$m\angle 1 = 20$ $m\angle 5 = 180 - 4(20)$

$m\angle 2 = 180 - 2(20)$ $= 100$

$= 140$ $m\angle 6 = 2(20)$

$m\angle 3 = 20$ $= 40$

$m\angle 4 = 2(20)$ $m\angle 7 = 180 - 2(20)$

$= 40$ $= 140$

36. $RS = \sqrt{(3 - (-2))^2 + (8 - 1)^2}$

$= \sqrt{5^2 + 7^2}$

$= \sqrt{25 + 49}$

$= \sqrt{74}$

$RT = \sqrt{(3 - 8)^2 + (8 - 1)^2}$

$= \sqrt{(-5)^2 + 7^2}$

$= \sqrt{25 + 49}$

$= \sqrt{74}$

$RS = RT$, so $\triangle RST$ is isosceles.

37. Given: △MNO is equilateral.

Prove: $m\angle M = m\angle N = m\angle O = 60$

STATEMENTS	REASONS
1. △MNO is equilateral.	1. Given
2. $\overline{MN} \cong \overline{MO} \cong \overline{NO}$	2. Definition of equilateral △
3. $m\angle M = m\angle N = m\angle O$	3. If two sides of a △ are ≅, then the ∠s opp. those sides are ≅.
4. $m\angle M + m\angle N + m\angle O = 180$	4. Angle Sum Theorem
5. $3m\angle M = 180$	5. Substitution Property of Equality
6. $m\angle M = 60$	6. Division Property of equality
7. $m\angle M = m\angle N = m\angle O = 60$	7. Substitution Property of equality

38. Given: △ABC is equilateral.

Prove: △ABC is equilangular.

STATEMENTS	REASONS
1. △ABC is equilateral.	1. Given
2. $\overline{AB} \cong \overline{AC} \cong \overline{BC}$	2. Definition of equilateral
3. $\angle A \cong \angle B \cong \angle C$	3. If two sides of a △ are ≅, then the ∠s opp. those sides are ≅.
4. △ABC is equilangular.	4. Definition of equilangular

Given: △ABC is equilangular.

Prove: △ABC is equilateral.

STATEMENTS	REASONS
1. △ABC is equilangular.	1. Given
2. $\angle A \cong \angle B \cong \angle C$	2. Definition of equilangular
3. $\overline{AB} \cong \overline{AC} \cong \overline{BC}$	3. If two ∠s of a △ are ≅, then the sides opp. those ∠s are ≅.
4. △ABC is equilateral.	4. Definition of equilateral

39. Given: △PQR; $\angle P \cong \angle R$

Prove: $\overline{PQ} \cong \overline{RQ}$

STATEMENTS	REASONS
1. Let $\overline{QT}$ bisect $\angle PQR$.	1. Auxiliary line; Protractor Postulate

2. $\angle P \cong \angle R$	2. Given
3. $\angle 1 \cong \angle 2$	3. Definition of angle bisector
4. $\overline{QT} \cong \overline{QT}$	4. Congruence of segments is reflexive.
5. △PQT ≅ △RQT.	5. AAS
6. $\overline{PQ} \cong \overline{RQ}$	6. CPCTC

40. Isosceles; the midpoints cut the sides of the triangle in half, so the halves will be congruent also. The small triangles, 1 and 2 can be proved congruent. This makes the small triangle isosceles by CPCTC.

41.
$$m\angle BAC = m\angle DAC$$
$$m\angle BAC + m\angle DAC = 90$$
$$2m\angle BAC = 90$$
$$m\angle BAC = 45$$

$$m\angle ABC = m\angle ACB$$
$$m\angle BAC + m\angle ABC + m\angle ACB = 180$$
$$45 + m\angle ABC + m\angle ACB = 180$$
$$m\angle ACB = 67.5$$

$$m\angle ACB = m\angle ACD$$
$$m\angle BCD = 2m\angle ACB$$
$$m\angle BCD = 135$$

42. point M. If the surface is level then it is horizontal. The plumb line will be vertical, so it is perpendicular to the surface. A perpendicular dropped from the vertex angle of an isosceles triangle will pass through the midpoint of the base.

43. a. 77 **b.** 30 **c.** 74 **d.** 51 **e.** 47.5 **f.** 39.5

44. △BLS ≅ △BES; ∠LBS ≅ ∠EBS; △LBU ≅ △EBU; ∠LUS ≅ ∠EUS

45. $\angle T \cong \angle C$, $\angle I \cong \angle A$, and $\overline{TN} \cong \overline{CN}$;

$\angle T \cong \angle C$, $\angle I \cong \angle A$, and $\overline{IN} \cong \overline{AN}$;

$\angle T \cong \angle C$, $\angle INT \cong \angle ANC$, and $\overline{TI} \cong \overline{CA}$;

$\angle T \cong \angle C$, $\angle INT \cong \angle ANC$, and $\overline{IN} \cong \overline{AN}$;

$\angle I \cong \angle A$, $\angle INT \cong \angle ANC$, and $\overline{TI} \cong \overline{CA}$;

$\angle I \cong \angle A$, $\angle INT \cong \angle ANC$, and $\overline{TN} \cong \overline{CN}$

46.
$$x + 14 + 3x + 1 + 6x - 5 = 180$$
$$10x + 10 = 180$$
$$10x = 170$$
$$x = 17$$

$$x + 14 = 17 + 14 \qquad\qquad 3x + 1 = 3(17) + 1$$
$$= 31 \qquad\qquad\qquad\qquad = 52$$

$$6x - 5 = 6(17) + 5$$
$$= 97$$

47. ∠1 ≅ ∠5, ∠1 and ∠2 are supplementary; ∠1 ≅ ∠4; ∠1 and ∠3 are supplementary; ∠1 and ∠6 are supplementary; ∠1 ≅ ∠8; ∠2 ≅ ∠3; ∠2 ≅ ∠7; ∠2 ≅ ∠6; ∠2 and ∠4 are supplementary; ∠2 and ∠6 are supplementary; ∠2 and ∠5 are supplementary; ∠3 and ∠4 are supplementary; ∠3 ≅ ∠6; ∠3 and ∠8 are supplementary; ∠3 ≅ ∠7; ∠4 and ∠6 are supplementary; ∠4 ≅ ∠8; ∠4 ≅ ∠5; ∠5 ≅ ∠8; ∠5 and ∠7 are supplementary; ∠5 and ∠6 are supplementary; ∠6 ≅ ∠7; ∠6 and ∠8 are supplementary; ∠7 and ∠8 are supplementary

48. Don will receive an A; detachment.

49. See students' work.

Chapter 4 Summary and Review

PAGES 208-210   SKILLS AND CONCEPTS

1. ΔABE, ΔDBE
2. ΔBCD
3. $\overline{BD}$
4. ΔBCD, ΔAFE, ΔBFD
5. ΔABF, ΔBFD, ΔDFE, ΔAFE, ΔBCD
6. ΔABF, ΔDFE
7. m∠OMN + m∠MON = 90
   m∠OMN + 37 = 90
   m∠OMN = 53
8. m∠MON = 90
9. m∠PON + m∠PNO = 90
   m∠PON + 37 = 90
   m∠PON = 53
10. m∠OMN + m∠MOP = 90
    53 + m∠MOP = 90
    m∠MOP = 37
11. $x = 120$
12. $w + 120 = 180$
    $w = 60$
13. $v = w$
    $v = 60$
14. $r + 65 + w = 180$
    $r + 65 + 60 = 180$
    $r = 55$
15. $s = r$
    $s = 55$
16. $t + s + v = 180$
    $t + 55 + 60 = 180$
    $t = 65$
17. $65 + y = 90$
    $y = 25$
18. $x + y + z = 180$
    $120 + 25 + z = 180$
    $z = 35$
19. ∠I
20. $\overline{JL}$
21. $\overline{HG}$
22. ∠IHG
23. $\overline{IG}$
24. ∠KLJ

25. Given: E is the midpoint of $\overline{AC}$.
    ∠1 ≅ ∠2
    Prove: ∠3 ≅ ∠4

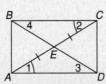

STATEMENTS	REASONS
1. E is the midpoint of $\overline{AC}$. ∠1 ≅ ∠2	1. Given
2. $\overline{AE} ≅ \overline{CE}$	2. Definition of midpoint
3. ∠BEC ≅ ∠DEA	3. Vertical angles are ≅.
4. ΔBEC ≅ ΔDEA	4. ASA
5. ∠3 ≅ ∠4	5. CPCTC

26. Given ΔWXZ is isosceles.
    Y is the midpoint of $\overline{XZ}$.
    Prove: $\overline{YW}$ bisects ∠XWZ.

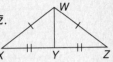

STATEMENTS	REASONS
1. ΔWXZ is isosceles. Y is the midpoint of $\overline{XZ}$.	1. Given
2. $\overline{WX} ≅ \overline{WZ}$	2. Definition of isosceles triangle
3. $\overline{WY} ≅ \overline{WY}$	3. Congruence of segments is reflexive.
4. $\overline{XY} ≅ \overline{YZ}$	4. Definition of midpoint
5. ΔWXY ≅ ΔWZY	5. SSS
6. ∠XWY ≅ ∠ZWY	6. CPCTC
7. WY bisects ∠XWZ.	7. Definition of angle bisector

27. Given: $\overline{KL} ≅ \overline{ML}$
    ∠J ≅ ∠N
    ∠1 ≅ ∠2
    Prove: $\overline{JK} ≅ \overline{NM}$

We are given that $\overline{KL} ≅ \overline{ML}$, ∠J ≅ ∠N, and ∠1 ≅ ∠2. Therefore, ΔJKL ≅ ΔNML by AAS. So, $\overline{JK} ≅ \overline{NM}$ by CPCTC.

28. Given: $\overline{JL} ≅ \overline{NL}$
    ∠1 ≅ ∠2
    $\overline{KL} ≅ \overline{ML}$
    Prove: ∠K ≅ ∠M

It is given that $\overline{JL} ≅ \overline{NL}$, ∠1 ≅ ∠2, and $\overline{KL} ≅ \overline{ML}$. So, ΔJKL ≅ ΔNML by SAS. Therefore, ∠K ≅ ∠M by CPCTC.

29. $8x - 21 = 6x + 3$
    $2x = 24$
    $x = 12$

30. $x + 42 + 42 = 180$
    $x = 96$

31. Given: $\angle A \cong \angle D$
$\overline{AB} \cong \overline{DC}$
E is the
midpoint of $\overline{AD}$.
Prove: $\angle 3 \cong \angle 4$

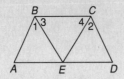

STATEMENTS	REASONS
1. $\angle A \cong \angle D$ $\overline{AB} \cong \overline{DC}$ E is the midpoint of $\overline{AD}$.	1. Given
2. $\overline{AE} \cong \overline{ED}$	2. Definition of midpoint
3. $\triangle ABE \cong \triangle DCE$	3. SAS
4. $\overline{BE} \cong \overline{CE}$	4. CPCTC
5. $\angle 3 \cong \angle 4$	5. If two sides of a $\triangle$ are $\cong$, then the $\angle$s opp. those sides are $\cong$.

PAGE 210 APPLICATIONS AND CONNECTIONS

32. $x + 54 = 90$
$x = 36$

33. $729 = 27^2 = 9^3$

34. Let A be the position of the ship when the lighthouse was first sighted.
Let B be the point where the angle to the lighthouse is twice the original angle.
Let L be the lighthouse, and P be a point on the the path of the ship.
Let x be the measure of the original angle.

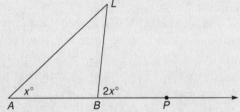

By the Exterior Angle Theorem, $m\angle A + m\angle L$ $= m\angle PBL$. So $x + m\angle L = 2x$, $m\angle L = x$. Therefore, $\overline{AB} \cong \overline{BL}$ by Theorem 4-7. Since $\overline{AB}$ represents the segment from the point where the lighthouse was first sighted to the second point and $\overline{BL}$ represents the segment from the second point to the lighthouse, the ship is as far from the lighthouse as it has traveled since the lighthouse was first sighted.

Chapter 4 Test

PAGE 211

1. $\triangle PSQ$, $\triangle PST$
2. $\triangle QRS$
3. $\overline{PS}$
4. $\triangle QRS$
5. 90
6. 90
7. $m\angle 3 + m\angle 8 + m\angle 9 = 180$
$30 + 90 + m\angle 9 = 180$
$m\angle 9 = 60$
8. $m\angle 6 = m\angle 9$
$m\angle 6 = 60$
9. $m\angle 2 + m\angle 6 + m\angle 7 = 180$
$m\angle 2 + 60 + 90 = 180$
$m\angle 2 = 30$
10. $m\angle 5 + m\angle 6 = 180$
$m\angle 5 + 60 = 180$
$m\angle 5 = 120$
11. $m\angle 9 + m\angle 10 = 180$
$60 + m\angle 10 = 180$
$m\angle 10 = 120$
12. $m\angle 4 + m\angle 10 + m\angle L = 180$
$20 + 120 + m\angle L = 180$
$m\angle L = 40$
13. $m\angle H = m\angle L$
$m\angle H = 40$
14. $m\angle 1 + m\angle 5 + m\angle H = 180$
$m\angle 1 + 120 + 40 = 180$
$m\angle 1 = 20$
15. $\overline{PB} \cong \overline{RW}$
16. $\overline{PB} \cong \overline{RW}$ or $\angle X \cong \angle H$
17. $\angle B \cong \angle R$ or $\angle X \cong \angle H$
18. $\angle X \cong \angle H$
19. A number with exactly three factors is the square of a prime. The greatest four-digit number that is the square of a prime is 97^2 or 9409.
20. Given: $\overline{AC} \perp \overline{BD}$
$\angle B \cong \angle D$
Prove: C is the midpoint of $\overline{BD}$.

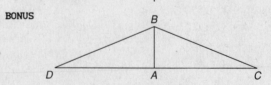

STATEMENTS	REASONS
1. $\overline{AC} \perp \overline{BD}$ $\angle B \cong \angle D$	1. Given
2. $\overline{CA} \cong \overline{CA}$	2. Congruence of segments is reflexive.
3. $\angle BCA$ and $\angle DCA$ are rt. $\angle$s.	3. $\perp$ lines form 4 rt $\angle$s.
4. $\angle 3 \cong \angle 4$	4. All right $\angle$s are $\cong$.
5. $\triangle BCA \cong \triangle DCA$	5. AAS
6. $\overline{BC} \cong \overline{DC}$	6. CPCTC
7. C is the midpoint of $\overline{BD}$.	7. Definition of midpoint

BONUS

Let A be the point where the soldier is standing. B is the soldier's eye-level. C is the opposite side of the stream, and D is the point on land that the soldier sighted.
The soldier's body is perpendicular to the ground, so $\angle CAB$ and $\angle DAB$ are right and are therefore

congruent. The soldier's height is constant, so $\overline{AB} \cong \overline{AB}$. SInce the soldier didn't raise or lower his head as he turned, $\angle ABC \cong \angle ABD$. Therefore, $\triangle ABC \cong \triangle ABD$ by ASA. So, $\overline{AD} \cong \overline{AC}$ and the distance the soldier paced off is the distance across the stream.

College Entrance Exam Preview

PAGES 212–213

1. *B*

2. *C* If x is odd, $2x$ is even.

    An even number is divisible by 2. Since 3 is not divisible by 2 and neither is x, then $3x$ is not divisible by 2. Therefore, the sum of an even and an odd is odd.

3. *B*
$$|6x - 8| = 10$$
$$6x - 8 = 10 \quad \text{or} \quad 6x - 8 = -10$$
$$6x = 18 \qquad\qquad 6x = -2$$
$$x = 3 \qquad\qquad\quad x = -\frac{1}{3}$$

4. *A*

5. *D* There are $65 - 13$ or 52 good apples.

    So $\frac{52}{65}$ or 80% are good.

6. *A* $m = \dfrac{8 - (-7)}{-4 - 3}$

    $ = -\dfrac{15}{7}$

7. *C* average $= \dfrac{a + 5 + 2a - 4 + 3a + 8}{3}$

    $ = \dfrac{6a + 9}{3}$

    $ = 2a + 3$

8. *B*

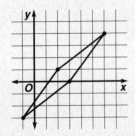

9. *D* $\dfrac{x^6 + x^6 + x^6}{x^3} = \dfrac{3x^6}{x^3} = 3x^3$

10. *B* Let a = adult tickets.

    $s + a = 250$

    $a = 250 - s$

    income $= 2s + 4a$

    $ = 2s + 4(250 - s)$

11. $m\angle 1 = m\angle 2$ since they are vertical angles.

    $m\angle 2 = m\angle 4$ since they are consecutive interior angles.

12. average $= \dfrac{9 \cdot 5 + 19 \cdot 6 + 52 \cdot 7 + 20 \cdot 8}{100}$

    $ = \dfrac{45 + 114 + 364 + 160}{100}$

    $ = \dfrac{683}{100}$

    $ = 6.83$ courses

13. Let x = cost per student

    $17x = 131.75$

    $x = 7.75$

    total cost $= 22x$

    $ = 22(7.75)$

    $ = \$170.50$

14. There are $\left(\dfrac{24}{100}\right)75$ or 18 red pens, so there are $75 - 18 - 17$ or 40 green pens. Therefore, the fraction of the pens that are green is $\dfrac{40}{75}$ or $\dfrac{8}{15}$.

15. At 45 words per minute, Mark can type 450 words in 10 minutes. That is 10 minutes or $\frac{1}{6}$ of an hour per page. So x pages would take $\frac{1}{6}x$ or $\frac{x}{6}$ hours.

Chapter 5   Applying Congruent Triangles

5-1   Special Segments in Triangles

PAGES 219-220   CHECKING FOR UNDERSTANDING

1. An angle bisector bisects an angle and a perpendicular bisector bisects a side.

2. Yes; isosceles

3. Theorem 5-2 is the converse of Theorem 5-1.

4. median   5. $\overline{AD}$ 6. isosceles

For Exercises 7-11, answers will vary. Sample answers are given.

7.
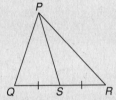

8.
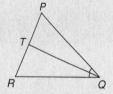

9.
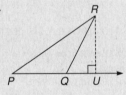

10.
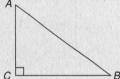

11.
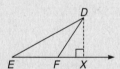

12. a. (0, 7)

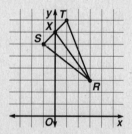

b. $d = \sqrt{(3-0)^2 + (3-7)^2}$

   $d = \sqrt{25} = 5$ units

c. $m = \dfrac{7-3}{0-3} = -\dfrac{4}{3}$

d. No. slope of $\overline{RX} = -\dfrac{4}{3}$

   slope of $\overline{ST} = \dfrac{8-6}{1+1} = 2$

   $-\dfrac{4}{3} \cdot 2 = -\dfrac{8}{3}$

   Product of slopes is not -1.

13. Given: $\overline{AB} \cong \overline{CB}$

    $\overline{BD}$ is a median of $\triangle ABC$.

    Prove: $\overline{BD}$ is an altitude of $\triangle ABC$.

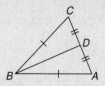

STATEMENTS	REASONS
a. $\overline{AB} \cong \overline{CB}$ $\overline{BD}$ is a median of $\triangle ABC$.	a. Given
b. D is the median of $\overline{CA}$.	b. Definition of median
c. $\overline{CD} \cong \overline{AD}$	c. Definition of midpoint
d. B is on the perpendicular bisector of $\overline{AC}$. D is on the perpendicular bisector of $\overline{AC}$.	d. A point equidistant from the endpoints of a segment lies on the ⊥ bisector of the segment.
e. $\overline{BD}$ is the perpendicular bisector of $\overline{AC}$.	e. Through any two points there is one line.
f. $\overline{BD} \perp \overline{AC}$	f. Definition of ⊥ bisector
g. $\overline{BD}$ is an altitude of $\triangle ABC$.	g. Definition of altitude

PAGES 220-222   EXERCISES

Answers for Exercises 14-18 will vary. Sample answers are given.

14.
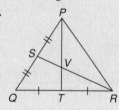

15.
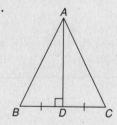

16.
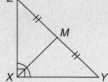

17.
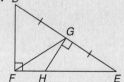

68

18. a. 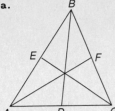 $\overline{BD}$, $\overline{AF}$, and $\overline{CE}$ are medians of $\triangle ABC$. They intersect in one point.

b. 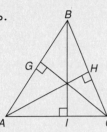 $\overline{CG}$, $\overline{BI}$, and $\overline{AH}$ are altitudes of $\triangle ABC$. They intersect in one point.

c. 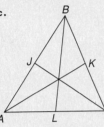 $\overline{AK}$, $\overline{BL}$, and $\overline{CJ}$ are angle bisectors of $\triangle ABC$. They intersect in one point.

d. 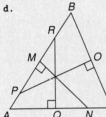 $\overline{MN}$, $\overline{OP}$, and $\overline{QR}$ are perpendicular bisectors of $\triangle ABC$. They interect in one point.

e. Only the triangle from part a balances.

f. The perpendicular bisectors and the altitudes would intersect at a point on or outside the triangle.

19. always   **20.** never

21. sometimes   **22.** sometimes

23. a. (7, 4)

b. Slope of $\overline{AB} = -\frac{1}{3}$

$-\frac{1}{3} \cdot$ (slope of perpendicular bisector) $= -1$

slope of perpendicular bisector $= 3$

c. slope of $\overline{BC} = \frac{2-12}{13+7} = -\frac{1}{2}$

slope of $\overline{AN} = \dfrac{\frac{38}{5}-6}{\frac{9}{5}-1} = 2$

Yes; the slope of $\overline{BC}$ times slope of $\overline{AN}$ equals -1.

24. $4x - 6 = 90$ **25.** $10x - 7 = 5x + 3$
$\quad\;\; 4x = 96$ $\qquad\quad\; 5x = 10$
$\quad\;\;\;\, x = 24$ $\qquad\quad\;\; x = 2$

26. $\frac{1}{2}(8x - 6) = 2x + 7$
$\qquad 4x - 3 = 2x + 7$
$\qquad\quad\; 2x = 10$
$\qquad\quad\;\, x = 5$
$\qquad 2x + 7 = 17$
$\qquad 8x - 6 = 34$

27. Given: $\overline{BD}$ is a median of $\triangle ABC$.
$\qquad\;\;$ $\overline{BD}$ is an altitude of $\triangle ABC$.
Prove: $\triangle ABC$ is isosceles.

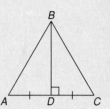

STATEMENTS	REASONS
a. $\overline{BD}$ is a median of $\triangle ABC$.	a. Given
b. D is the midpoint of $\overline{AC}$.	b. Definition of median
c. $\overline{AD} \cong \overline{CD}$	c. Definition of midpoint
d. $\overline{BD}$ is an altitude of $\triangle ABC$.	d. Given
e. $\overline{BD} \perp \overline{AC}$	e. Definition of altitude
f. $\angle ADB$, $\angle CDB$ are right $\angle$s.	f. $\perp$ lines form 4 rt. $\angle$s.
g. $\angle ADB \cong \angle CDB$	g. All rt. $\angle$s are $\cong$.
h. $\overline{BD} \cong \overline{BD}$	h. Congruence of segments is reflexive.
i. $\triangle ADB \cong \triangle CDB$	i. SAS
j. $\overline{AB} \cong \overline{CB}$	j. CPCTC
k. $\triangle ABC$ is isosceles.	k. Definition of isosceles triangle

28. Given: $\overline{UW}$ is perpendicular bisector of $\overline{XZ}$.
Prove: For any point V on $\overline{UW}$, $VX = VZ$.

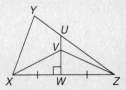

STATEMENTS	REASONS
a. $\overline{UW}$ is the $\perp$ bisector of $\overline{XZ}$.	a. Given
b. W is the midpoint of $\overline{XZ}$.	b. Definition of $\perp$ bisector
c. $\overline{XW} \cong \overline{WZ}$	c. Definition of midpoint
d. $\overline{UW} \perp \overline{XZ}$	d. Definition of $\perp$ bisector
e. $\angle XWV$, $\angle ZWV$ are right $\angle$s.	e. $\perp$ lines form 4 rt $\angle$s.
f. $\angle XWV \cong \angle ZWV$	f. All rt $\angle$s are $\cong$.

g. $\overline{VW} \cong \overline{VW}$	g. Congruence of segments is reflexive.
h. $\triangle XWV \cong \triangle ZWV$	h. SAS
i. $\overline{VX} \cong \overline{VZ}$	i. CPCTC
j. $VX = VZ$	j. Definition of congruence

29. Given: C is equidistant from A and B.
E is the midpoint of $\overline{AB}$.
Prove: C lies on the perpendicular bisector of $\overline{AB}$.

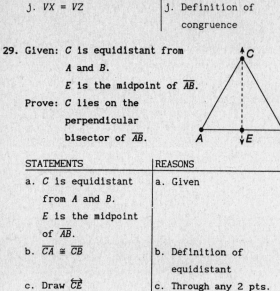

STATEMENTS	REASONS
a. C is equidistant from A and B. E is the midpoint of $\overline{AB}$.	a. Given
b. $\overline{CA} \cong \overline{CB}$	b. Definition of equidistant
c. Draw $\overleftrightarrow{CE}$	c. Through any 2 pts. there is 1 line.
d. $\overline{CE} \cong \overline{CE}$	d. Congruence of segments is reflexive.
e. $\overline{AE} \cong \overline{BE}$	e. Definition of midpoint
f. $\triangle CAE \cong \triangle CBE$	f. SSS
g. $\angle CEA \cong \angle CEB$	g. CPCTC
h. $\angle CEA$ and $\angle CEB$ form a linear pair.	h. Definition of linear pair
i. $\angle CEA$ and $\angle CEB$ are supplementary.	i. If 2 $\angle$s form a linear pair, they are supp.
j. $m\angle CEA + m\angle CEB = 180$	l. Definition of supplementary
k. $m\angle CEA + m\angle CEA = 180$	k. Substitution property of equality
l. $2m\angle CEA = 180$	l. Substitution property of equality
m. $m\angle CEA = 90$	m. Division property of equality
n. $m\angle CEB = 90$	n. Substitution property of equality
o. $\angle CEA$ and $\angle CEB$ are right angles.	o. Definition of right angle
p. $\overline{CE} \perp \overline{AB}$	p. Definition of perpendicular
q. $\overleftrightarrow{CE}$ is the perpendicular bisector of $\overline{AB}$.	q. Definition of perpendicular bisector
r. C is on the perpendicular bisector of $\overline{AB}$.	r. A line contains at least 2 pts.

30. Given: $\overline{BD}$ bisects $\angle ABC$.
Prove: $DE = DF$

STATEMENTS	REASONS
a. $\overline{BD}$ bisects $\angle ABC$.	a. Given
b. $\angle ABD \cong \angle CBD$	b. Definition of $\angle$ bisector
c. Let DE = distance from D to $\overline{AB}$; DF = distance from D to $\overline{BC}$.	c. Distance from point to to a line
d. $\overline{DE} \perp \overline{AB}$, $\overline{DF} \perp \overline{BC}$	d. Definition of distance from a point to a line
e. $\angle DEB$, $\angle DFB$ are right angles.	e. $\perp$ lines form 4 rt $\angle$s.
f. $\angle DEB \cong \angle DFB$	f. All rt $\angle$s are $\cong$.
g. $\overline{BD} \cong \overline{BD}$	g. Congruence of segments is reflexive.
h. $\triangle DEB \cong \triangle DFB$	h. AAS
i. $\overline{DE} \cong \overline{DF}$	i. CPCTC
j. $DE = DF$	j. Definition of congruence

31. Given: $\overline{AB} \cong \overline{AC}$
$\overline{AD}$ is an altitude of $\triangle ABC$.
Prove: $\overline{AD}$ is a median of $\triangle ABC$.

STATEMENTS	REASONS
a. $\overline{AD}$ is a altitude of $\triangle ABC$.	a. Given
b. $AD \perp BC$	b. Definition of altitude
c. $\angle ADB$ and $\angle ADC$ are right angles.	c. $\perp$ lines form 4 rt $\angle$s.
d. $\angle ADB \cong \angle ADC$	d. All rt $\angle$s are $\cong$.
e. $\overline{AB} \cong \overline{AC}$	e. Given
f. $\angle ABD \cong \angle ACD$	f. If 2 sides of a $\triangle$ are $\cong$, the $\angle$s opposite the sides are $\cong$.
g. $\triangle ADB \cong \triangle ADC$	g. AAS
h. $\overline{BD} \cong \overline{CD}$	h. CPCTC
i. $\overline{AD}$ is a median of $\triangle ABC$.	i. Definition of median

32. Given: $\triangle ABC \cong \triangle XYZ$
$\overline{AD}$ is a median
of $\triangle ABC$.
$\overline{XW}$ is a median
of $\triangle XYZ$.
Prove: $\overline{AD} \cong \overline{XW}$

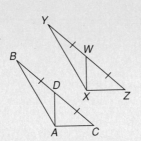

STATEMENTS	REASONS
a. $\triangle ABC \cong \triangle XYZ$; $\overline{AD}$ is a median of $\triangle ABC$; $\overline{XW}$ is a median of $\triangle XYZ$.	a. Given
b. $\overline{AB} \cong \overline{XY}$, $\angle B \cong \angle Y$, $\overline{BC} \cong \overline{YZ}$	b. CPCTC
c. $BC = YZ$	c. Definition of congruent
d. D is the midpoint of $\overline{BC}$. W is the midpoint of $\overline{YZ}$.	d. Definition of median
e. $\overline{BD} \cong \overline{DC}$, $\overline{YW} \cong \overline{WZ}$	e. Definition of midpoint
f. $BD = DC$, $YW = WZ$	f. Definition of congruent
g. $BC = BD + DC$, $YZ = YW + WZ$	g. Segment addition postulate
h. $BC = BD + BD$, $YZ = YW + YW$	h. Substitution
i. $2BD = 2YW$	i. Substitution
j. $BD = YW$	j. Division prop. of equality
k. $\overline{BD} \cong \overline{YW}$	k. Definition of $\cong$
l. $\triangle ABD \cong \triangle XYW$	l. SAS
m. $\overline{AD} \cong \overline{XW}$	m. CPCTC

33. Given: $\triangle ABC \cong \triangle XYZ$
$\overline{BD}$ is an angle
bisector of $\triangle ABC$.
$\overline{EH}$ is an angle
bisector of $\triangle DEF$.
Prove: $\overline{BG} \cong \overline{EH}$

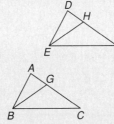

STATEMENTS	REASONS
a. $\triangle ABC \cong \triangle DEF$	a. Given
b. $\angle A \cong \angle D$, $\overline{AB} \cong \overline{DE}$ $\angle ABC \cong \angle DEF$	b. CPCTC
c. $\overline{BG}$ is an angle bisector of $\triangle ABC$. $\overline{EH}$ is an angle bisector of $\triangle DEF$.	c. Given
d. $\overline{BG}$ bisects $\angle ABC$. $\overline{EH}$ bisects $\angle DEF$.	d. Definition of $\angle$ bisector

STATEMENTS	REASONS
e. $m\angle ABG = \frac{1}{2}m\angle ABC$ $m\angle DEH = \frac{1}{2}m\angle DEF$	c. Definition of bisect
f. $m\angle ABC = m\angle DEF$	f. Definition of $\cong$ $\angle$s
g. $\frac{1}{2}m\angle ABC = \frac{1}{2}m\angle DEF$	g. Multiplication prop. of equality
h. $m\angle ABG = m\angle DEH$	h. Substitution prop. of equality
i. $\angle ABG \cong \angle DEH$	i. Definition of $\cong$ $\angle$s
j. $\triangle ABG \cong \triangle DEH$	j. ASA
k. $\overline{BG} \cong \overline{EH}$	k. CPCTC

34. Given: $\triangle LMN$ is isosceles.
$\overline{NO}$ and $\overline{LP}$ are
medians of $\triangle LMN$.
Prove: $\overline{NO} \cong \overline{LP}$

STATEMENTS	REASONS
a. $\triangle LMN$ is isosceles.	a. Given
b. $\overline{LM} \cong \overline{NM}$	b. Definition of isosceles $\triangle$
c. $LM = NM$	c. Definition of $\cong$
d. $\angle M \cong \angle M$	d. Congruence of $\angle$s is reflexive.
e. $\overline{NO}$ and $\overline{LP}$ are medians of $\triangle LMN$.	e. Given
f. O is the midpoint of $\overline{LM}$. P is the midpoint of $\overline{MN}$.	f. Definition of median
g. $\overline{LO} \cong \overline{OM}$, $\overline{NP} \cong \overline{PM}$	g. Definition of midpoint
h. $LO = OM$, $NP = PM$	h. Definition of $\cong$
i. $LM = LO + OM$ $NM = NP + PM$	i. Segment addition postulate
j. $LO + OM = NP + PM$	j. Substitution
k. $2OM = 2PM$	k. Substitution
l. $OM = PM$	l. Division prop. of equality
m. $\overline{OM} \cong \overline{PM}$	m. Definition of $\cong$
n. $\triangle LMP \cong \triangle NMO$	n. SAS
o. $\overline{NO} \cong \overline{LP}$	o. CPCTC

35. They are parallel.

36. It lies on the hypotenuse of the right triangle.

37.

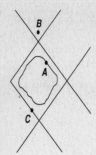

38. $3x - 8 = 13$
$3x = 21$
$x = 7$

39. $\angle BNC$ and $\angle BCN = x$
$2x + 34 = 180$
$2x = 146$
$x = 73$
$\angle ANB + 73 = 180$
$\angle ANB = 107$

40. $4y - 7 = 9 + 2y$
$2y = 16$
$y = 8$

41. slope of $\overleftrightarrow{PQ} = \dfrac{-2 - 0}{3 - 0} = -\dfrac{2}{3}$

slope of $\overleftrightarrow{RS} = \dfrac{-3 + 7}{-5 - 1} = \dfrac{4}{-6} = -\dfrac{2}{3}$

Yes; both lines have a slope of $-\dfrac{2}{3}$.

42. $\overline{AX}$ is an altitude of $\triangle ABC$; detachment.

43.

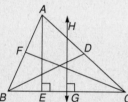

$\overline{AE}$ is an altitude of $\triangle ABC$. It is a segment perpendicular to $\overline{BC}$ and extends to vertex A. $\overline{BD}$ is a median of $\triangle ABC$. It extends from vertex B to the midpoint of $\overline{AC}$. $\overline{CF}$ is an angle bisector of $\triangle ABC$. It extends from vertex C to side $\overline{AB}$ such that $\angle ACF \cong \angle BCF$. $\overline{HG}$ is a perpendicular bisector of $\triangle ABC$. It extends through the midpoint of $\overline{BC}$ and is perpendicular to $\overleftrightarrow{BC}$.

| 5-2 | **Right Triangles** |

PAGES 226-227   CHECKING FOR UNDERSTANDING

1. Right triangles all have a right angle in common.

2. SAS

3. The side given may be either an included or a non-included leg.

4. HA or AAS

5. none

6. HL

7. HA or AAS

8. LA or AAS

9. none

10. $3x + 4 = 16$
$3x = 12$
$x = 4$

11. $11x - 3 = 9x + 9$
$2x = 12$
$x = 6$

---

12. $7x + 4 = 5(x + 2)$
$7x + 4 = 5x + 10$
$2x = 6$
$x = 3$

13. Given: $\angle Q$ and $\angle S$ are right angles.
$\angle 1 \cong \angle 2$
Prove: $\triangle PQR \cong \triangle RSP$

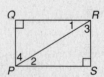

STATEMENTS	REASONS
a. $\angle Q$ and $\angle S$ are right angles. $\angle 1 \cong \angle 2$	a. Given
b. $\triangle QRP$ and $\triangle SPR$ are right triangles.	b. Definition of rt $\triangle$
c. $\overline{PR} \cong \overline{PR}$	c. Congruence of segments is reflexive.
d. $\triangle PQR \cong \triangle RSP$	d. HA

PAGES 227-229   EXERCISES

14. Yes; LA

15. No; there is no AA or AAA congruence theorem.

16. Yes; LL

17. Yes; HA

18. Yes; HL

19. $10x - 19 = 6x + 1$ $5y - 7 = 8$
$4x = 20$ $5y = 15$
$x = 5$ $y = 3$

20. $3x - 11 = 13$ $2y + 13 = 5y - 2$
$3x = 24$ $15 = 3y$
$x = 8$ $5 = y$

21. $8x - 3 = 7x + 4$ $y - 8 = 12$
$x = 7$ $y = 20$

22. $3x + 8 = 32$ $5y - 3 = 17$
$3x = 24$ $5y = 20$
$x = 8$ $y = 4$

23. Given: $\overline{QP} \cong \overline{SR}$
$\angle Q$ and $\angle S$ are right angles.
Prove: $\angle 1 \cong \angle 2$

STATEMENTS	REASONS
a. $QP \cong SR$ $\angle Q$ and $\angle S$ are right angles.	a. Given
b. $\triangle RQP$ and $\triangle PSR$ are right triangles.	b. Definition of rt $\triangle$
c. $\overline{PR} \cong \overline{PR}$	c. Congruence of segments is reflexive.
d. $\triangle RQP \cong \triangle PSR$	d. HL
e. $\angle 1 \cong \angle 2$	e. CPCTC

24. Given: ∠Q and ∠S are
right angles.
$\overline{QR} \parallel \overline{PS}$
Prove: $\overline{PQ} \cong \overline{RS}$

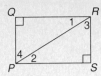

STATEMENTS	REASONS
a. ∠Q and ∠S are right angles. $\overline{QR} \parallel \overline{PS}$	a. Given
b. ΔRQP and ΔPSR are right triangles.	b. Definition of rt Δ
c. ∠1 ≅ ∠2	c. If 2 ‖ lines are cut by a transversal, alt. int. ∠s are ≅.
d. $\overline{PR} \cong \overline{PR}$	d. Congruence of segments is reflexive.
e. ΔPQR ≅ ΔRSP	e. HA
f. $\overline{PQ} \cong \overline{RS}$	f. CPCTC

25. Given: ΔABY and ΔCBY
are right
triangles.
$\overline{AB} \cong \overline{CB}$
$\overline{YX} \perp \overline{AC}$
Prove: $\overline{AX} \cong \overline{CX}$

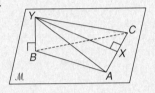

STATEMENTS	REASONS
a. ΔABY and ΔCBY are right triangles. $\overline{AB} \cong \overline{CB}$	a. Given
b. $\overline{YB} \cong \overline{YB}$	b. Congruence of segments is reflexive.
c. ΔYBA ≅ ΔYBC	c. LL
d. $\overline{YA} \cong \overline{YC}$	d. CPCTC
e. $\overline{YX} \perp \overline{AC}$	e. Given
f. ∠YXA and ∠YXC are right angles.	f. ⊥ lines form 4 rt ∠s.
g. ΔYXA and ΔYXC are right triangles.	g. Definition of rt Δ
h. $\overline{YX} \cong \overline{YX}$	h. Congruence of segments is reflexive.
i. ΔYXA ≅ ΔYXC	i. HL
j. $\overline{AX} \cong \overline{GX}$	j. CPCTC

26. Given: $\overline{YX}$ is an altitude
of ΔAYC.
∠AYX ≅ ∠CYX
$\overline{YB} \perp$ plane M
Prove: ∠AYB ≅ ∠CYB

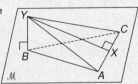

STATEMENTS	REASONS
a. $\overline{YX}$ is an altitude of ΔAYC. ∠AYX ≅ ∠CYX	a. Given
b. $\overline{YX}$ is an angle bisector of ΔAYC.	b. Definition of ∠ bisector

---

	c. If an ∠ bisector is also an altitude, then the Δ is isosceles.
c. ΔAYC is isosceles.	
d. $\overline{AY} \cong \overline{CY}$	d. Definition of isosceles Δ
e. $\overline{YB} \perp$ plane M	e. Given
f. $\overline{YB} \perp \overline{BA}$, $\overline{YB} \perp \overline{BC}$	f. Definition of line ⊥ to a plane
g. ∠YBA and ∠YBC are right angles.	g. ⊥ lines form 4 rt ∠s.
h. ΔYBA and ΔYBC are right triangles.	h. Definition of rt Δ
i. $\overline{YB} \cong \overline{YB}$	i. Congruence of segments is reflexive.
j. ΔYBA ≅ ΔYBC	j. HL
k. ∠AYB ≅ ∠CYB	k. CPCTC

27. Given: ΔABC and ΔDEF are
right triangles.
$\overline{AB} \cong \overline{DE}$
$\overline{AC} \cong \overline{DF}$
Prove: ΔABC ≅ ΔDEF

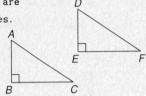

STATEMENTS	REASONS
a. ΔABC and ΔDEF are right triangles.	a. Given
b. ∠BAC and ∠DEF are right angles.	b. Definition of rt Δ
c. ∠ABC ≅ ∠DEF	c. Rt ∠s are ≅.
d. $\overline{AB} \cong \overline{DE}$, $\overline{BC} \cong \overline{EF}$	d. Given
e. ΔABC ≅ ΔDEF	e. SAS

28. Case 1:
Given: ΔABC and ΔDEF are
right triangles.
$\overline{AC} \cong \overline{DF}$
∠C ≅ ∠F
Prove: ΔABC ≅ ΔDEF

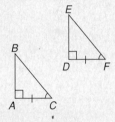

STATEMENTS	REASONS
a. ΔABC and ΔDEF are right triangles.	a. Given
b. ∠A and ∠D are right angles.	b. Definition of rt Δ
c. ∠A ≅ ∠D	c. Rt ∠s are ≅.
d. $\overline{AC} \cong \overline{DF}$, ∠C ≅ ∠F	d. Given
e. ΔABC ≅ ΔDEF	e. ASA

Case 2:

Given: △ABC and △DEF are
right triangles.
$\overline{AC} \cong \overline{DF}$
∠B ≅ ∠E

Prove: △ABC ≅ △DEF

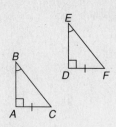

STATEMENTS	REASONS
a. △ABC and △DEF are right triangles.	a. Given
b. ∠A and ∠D are right angles.	b. Definition of rt △
c. ∠A ≅ ∠D	c. Rt ∠s are ≅.
d. $\overline{AC} \cong \overline{DF}$, ∠B ≅ ∠E	d. Given
e. △ABC ≅ △DEF	e. AAS

29. Given: △ABC ≅ △DEF
$\overline{AG}$ is the altitude to $\overline{BC}$.
$\overline{DH}$ is the altitude to $\overline{EF}$.

Prove: $\overline{AG} \cong \overline{DH}$

STATEMENTS	REASONS
a. △ABC ≅ △DEF	a. Given
b. $\overline{AC} \cong \overline{DF}$, ∠C ≅ ∠F	b. CPCTC
c. $\overline{AG}$ is the altitude to $\overline{BC}$. $\overline{DH}$ is the altitude to $\overline{EF}$.	c. Given
d. $\overline{AG} \perp \overline{BC}$, $\overline{DH} \perp \overline{EF}$	d. Definition of altitude
e. ∠AGC and ∠DHF are right angles.	e. ⊥ lines form 4 rt ∠s.
f. △AGC and △DHF are right triangles.	f. Definition of rt △
g. △AGC ≅ △DHE	g. LA
h. $\overline{AG} \cong \overline{DH}$	h. CPCTC

30. Given: △LMN is isosceles.
O is the midpoint of $\overline{LM}$.
P is the midpoint of $\overline{NM}$.
$\overline{OQ} \perp \overline{LN}$, $\overline{PR} \perp \overline{LN}$

Prove: $\overline{OQ} \cong \overline{PR}$

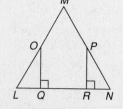

STATEMENTS	REASONS
a. △LMN is an isosceles triangle.	a. Given
b. $\overline{LM} \cong \overline{NM}$	b. Definition of isosceles △
c. LM = NM	c. Definition of congruence

d. ∠L ≅ ∠N	d. If two sides of a △ are ≅, then the ∠s opposite the sides are ≅.
e. O is the midpoint of $\overline{LM}$. P is the midpoint of $\overline{NM}$.	e. Given
f. $\overline{LO} \cong \overline{OM}$, $\overline{NP} \cong \overline{PM}$	f. Definition of midpoint
g. LO = OM, NP = PM	g. Definition of ≅
h. LM = LO + OM NM = NP + PM	h. Segment addition postulate
i. LO + OM = NP + PM	i. Substitution
j. 2LO = 2NP	j. Substitution
k. LO = NP	k. Division prop. of equality
l. $\overline{LO} \cong \overline{NP}$	l. Definition of ≅
m. $\overline{OQ} \perp \overline{LN}$, $\overline{PR} \perp \overline{LN}$	m. Given
n. ∠OQL and ∠PRN are right angles.	n. ⊥ lines form 4 rt. ∠s.
o. △OQL and △PRN are right triangles.	o. Definition of rt △
p. △OQL ≅ △PRN	p. HA
q. $\overline{OQ} \cong \overline{PR}$	q. CPCTC

31. Proof 1: It is given that $\overline{AC} \perp \overline{BE}$ and $\overline{CE} \perp \overline{AD}$, so ∠CBE and ∠CDA are right angles. By definition △CBE and △CDA are right triangles. ∠C ≅ ∠C by the reflexive property. $\overline{AC} \cong \overline{CE}$ is given, so △CBE ≅ △CDA by HA. Therefore, $\overline{BE} \cong \overline{AD}$ by CPCTC.

Proof 2: Given that $\overline{AC} \perp \overline{BE}$ and $\overline{CE} \perp \overline{AD}$, so ∠ABE and ∠EDA are right angles, which makes △ABE and △EDA right triangles. $\overline{AC} \cong \overline{CE}$ is given. Therefore ∠BAE ≅ ∠DEA, since if two sides of a triangle are congruent, then the angles opposite the sides are also congruent. $\overline{AE} \cong \overline{AE}$ by the reflexive property. Therefore, △ABE ≅ △EDA by HA. and $\overline{BE} \cong \overline{AD}$ by CPCTC.

32. Mr. Owens needs to give only two pieces of information, so he can chose any of the following sets of information.
legs: 108 in., 144 in.;
hypotenuse and an angle: 180 in., 37° or
180 in., 53°;
leg and an angle: 108 in., 53°; 108 in., 37°;
144 in., 53°; or 144 in., 37°
hypotenuse and a leg: 180 in., 144 in. or
180 in., 108 in.

33.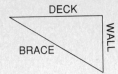

DECK

BRACE

WALL

The brace represents the hypotenuse of a right triangle as shown in the diagram, assuming the deck will be attached at a right angle to the wall. If each brace is attached at the same distance from the wall, this distance represents a leg of the triangle. HL says that the four triangles will be congruent and hence all will be attached at the same distance on the wall since that distance represents the other leg of the triangle.

34. $\angle 1 \cong \angle 6$

35. $\angle 1 \cong \angle 6$ and $\angle 4 \cong \angle 5$

36.
$$
\begin{aligned}
(3d + 11) + (5d - 2) &= 97 \\
8d + 9 &= 97 \\
8d &= 88 \\
d &= 11
\end{aligned}
$$

37. If a segment is a median of a triangle, then it bisects one side of the triangle.

38. See students' work.

5-3 Problem-Solving Strategy: Work Backward

PAGE 231 CHECKING FOR UNDERSTANDING

1. Guess a price and find the total after discounts and sales tax. Then make a revised guess if necessary and repeat.

2. Start with the original price of the computer, apply the discounts and tax, and you should end up with $1491.21.

3. Work backward from the statement to be proved to the given information.

4.
$$
\begin{aligned}
3(x + 6 \cdot 20 - 50 - 80) &= 270 \\
3(x - 10) &= 270 \\
3x &= 300 \\
x &= 100
\end{aligned}
$$

5.
$$
\begin{aligned}
\frac{(x - 52)12 + 20}{4} &= 32 \\
12x - 604 &= 128 \\
12x &= 732 \\
x &= 61
\end{aligned}
$$

6. x = number of baseball cards

$\frac{1}{2}x + 1$ = number given Leila

$$
\begin{aligned}
x - \left(\frac{1}{2}x + 1\right) = \frac{1}{2}x - 1 &= \text{number left} \\
\frac{1}{2}\left(\frac{1}{2}x - 1\right) + 1 = \frac{1}{4}x + \frac{1}{2} &= \text{number given Karl} \\
\left(\frac{1}{2}x - 1\right) - \left(\frac{1}{4}x + \frac{1}{2}\right) = \frac{1}{4}x - \frac{3}{2} &= \text{number left} \\
\frac{1}{2}\left(\frac{1}{4}x - \frac{3}{2}\right) + 1 = \frac{1}{8}x + \frac{1}{4} &= \text{number given Jarrod} \\
\left(\frac{1}{4}x - \frac{3}{2}\right) - \left(\frac{1}{8}x + \frac{1}{4}\right) = 74 &= \text{number given Charlene} \\
\frac{1}{8}x - \frac{7}{4} &= 74 \\
\frac{1}{8}x &= \frac{303}{4} \\
x &= 606
\end{aligned}
$$

Tom had 606 cards in his collection.

PAGES 231-232 EXERCISES

7. x = boxes of 15; $7 - x$ = boxes of 25
$$
\begin{aligned}
15x + 25(7 - x) &= 125 \\
175 - 10x &= 125 \\
50 &= 10x \\
5 &= x
\end{aligned}
$$

8. There are 14 combinations to equal 65¢:

quarters	dimes	nickels	quarters	dimes	nickels
2	1	1	0	5	3
1	4	0	0	4	5
1	3	2	0	3	7
1	2	4	2	0	3
1	1	6	0	2	9
1	0	8	0	1	11
0	6	1	0	0	13

9. $\frac{1}{2}x + 20$ = amount saved and concert ticket

$$
\begin{aligned}
x - \left(\frac{1}{2}x + 20\right) = \frac{1}{2}x - 20 &= \text{amount left} \\
\frac{1}{8}\left(\frac{1}{2}x - 20\right) = \frac{1}{16}x - \frac{5}{2} &= \text{cost of pizza} \\
\left(\frac{1}{2}x - 20\right) - \left(\frac{1}{16}x - \frac{5}{2}\right) = \frac{7}{16}x - \frac{35}{2} &= \text{amount left} \\
\frac{7}{16}x - \frac{35}{2} &= 42 \\
\frac{7}{16}x &= \frac{119}{2} \\
x &= \$136
\end{aligned}
$$

Enrico's paycheck was $136.

10. $10^2 - 6^2$; $15^2 - 10^2$

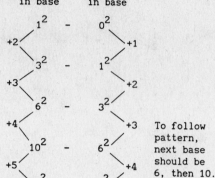

To follow pattern, next base should be 10, then 15.

To follow pattern, next base should be 6, then 10.

11. If $O = 2$, $N = 3$, $G = 9$: $23 + 23 + 23 + 23 = 92$

If $O = 0$, $N = 5$, $G = 2$: $5 + 5 + 5 + 5 = 20$

12. a.

FIRST DIE	SECOND DIE
1	1
2	2
3	3
4	4
5	5
6	4

She could roll a sum of 2, 3, 4, 5, 6, 7, 8, 9, 10, or 11. So there are ten possible sums.

b.

Sum	Number of ways to roll
2	1
3	2
4	4
5	6
6	6
7	7
8	5
9	2
10	2
11	1

7 is the most likely sum.

13. $\frac{4}{9}x^2 = (x - 5)^2$

$\frac{5}{9}x^2 - 10x + 25 = 0$

$x^2 - 18x + 45 = 0$

$(x - 3)(x - 15) = 0$

$x = 3$ or $x = 15$

$x \neq 3$ because $3 - 5 = -2$ and a square cannot have a negative length. Therefore, $x = 15$ and $x^2 = 225$ units.^{2}

14. Regular price is $270. $x - 50 =$ sale price

$0.85(x - 50) = 0.85x - 42.5 =$ employee discount price

$1.06(0.85x - 42.5) =$ employee price plus sales tax

$1.06(0.85x - 42.5) = 198.22$

$0.901x = 243.27$

$x = 270$

Cooperative Learning Project

PAGE 232

The least number of steps is the number of different letters. Answers will vary. Sample answers are given:

TOP $\rightarrow$ HOP $\rightarrow$ HOT $\rightarrow$ HAT

SEED $\rightarrow$ SLED $\rightarrow$ SLEW $\rightarrow$ SLOW $\rightarrow$ GLOW $\rightarrow$ GROW

WILD $\rightarrow$ WIND $\rightarrow$ WAND $\rightarrow$ WANE $\rightarrow$ SANE $\rightarrow$ SAME $\rightarrow$ TAME

5-4 Indirect Proof and Inequalities

PAGES 235-236 CHECKING FOR UNDERSTANDING

1. The alibi provides a contradiction to being guilty—therefore, not guilty.

2. The comparison property differentiates between *less than*, *equal to*, and *greater than*. The symmetric and reflexive properties apply only to equalities, while the transitive property applies to inequalities as well. Addition, subtraction, multiplication, and division properties exist for both equalities and inequalities, although there is a significant difference between the multiplication and division properties for equalities and inequalities.

3. a. Let $a = 2$, $b = 1$, $c = 5$, and $d = 4$. Then $a > b$ and $c > d$, but $a + b \not> c + d$ since $3 \not> 9$.

3. b. If $a > b$ and $c > d$, then $a + c > b + d$.

4. Points M, N, and P are not collinear.

5. Triangle ABC is not acute; it is right or obtuse.

6. The disk is not defective.

7. If two parallel lines are cut by a transversal, then alternate exterior angles are not congruent.

8. The angle bisector of the vertex angle of an isosceles triangle is not an altitude of the triangle.

9. $m\angle UNK > m\angle 1$

10. $m\angle 5 < m\angle 4$

11. $m\angle 1 < m\angle 7$

12. If $m\angle 1 < m\angle 3$ then $m\angle 5 > m\angle 1$.

13. Division property of inequality

14. Subtraction property of inequality

15. Transitive property of inequality

16. Comparison property

17. Given: $\overline{PQ} \cong \overline{PR}$

        $\angle 1 \not\cong \angle 2$

    Prove: $\overline{PZ}$ is not a

    median of $\triangle PQR$.

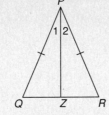

    Proof: Assume $\overline{PZ}$ is a median of $\triangle PQR$. We are
given that $\overline{PQ} \cong \overline{PR}$ and that $\angle 1 \not\cong \angle 2$.
Since $\overline{PZ}$ is a median of $\triangle PQR$, $\overline{QZ} \cong \overline{ZR}$
because Z is the midpoint of $\overline{QR}$ by the
definition of median. If two sides of a
triangle are congruent, then the angles
opposite these sides are congruent; so
$\angle Q \cong \angle R$. Therefore, $\triangle PZQ \cong \triangle PZR$ by SAS.
Then $\angle 1 \cong \angle 2$ by CPCTC. This is a
contradiction of a given fact. Therefore,
the assumption that $\overline{PZ}$ is a median of
$\triangle PQR$ must be false, which means $\overline{PZ}$ is not
a median of $\triangle PQR$.

PAGES 236-239   EXERCISES

18. a. $\overleftrightarrow{PQ}$ is not the only line through P
perpendicular to ℓ. Call this other line $\overleftrightarrow{PR}$,
where R is a point on ℓ different from Q.

    b. It is assumed.

    c. Perpendicular lines form four right angles.

    d. definitions of right angle

    e. The sum of the angles in a triangle is 180.

    f. substitution property of equality

    g. subtraction property of equality

    h. Angle measures must be greater than 0.

    i. $\overleftrightarrow{PQ}$ is the only line through P perpendicular
to ℓ.

19. $m\angle 6 > m\angle 4$

20. $m\angle 11 < m\angle 8$

21. $m\angle 9 < m\angle 1$

22. If $m\angle 10 = m\angle 13$, $m\angle 10 < m\angle 6$.

23. Given: $\triangle KNL$

        $\overline{NM} \cong \overline{OM}$

    Prove: $m\angle 1 > m\angle 2$

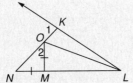

STATEMENTS	REASONS
a. $\overline{NM} \cong \overline{OM}$	a. Given
b. $\angle 2 \cong \angle N$	b. If two sides of a triangle are congruent, then the angles opposite the sides are also congruent.

c. $m\angle 1 > m\angle N$ c. The measure of an exterior
angle of a triangle is
greater than the measure of
either of its corr. interior
angles.

d. $m\angle 2 = m\angle N$ d. Definition of congruent
angles

e. $m\angle 1 > m\angle 2$ e. Substitution property of
equality

24. Given: $\triangle SQR$

        $\overline{SP} \cong \overline{QP}$

    Prove: $m\angle SQR > m\angle 2$

STATEMENTS	REASONS
a. $\overline{SP} \cong \overline{QP}$	a. Given
b. $\angle 1 \cong \angle 2$	b. If two sides of a triangle are congruent, then the angles opposite the sides are also congruent.
c. $m\angle SQR = m\angle 1 + m\angle 3$	c. Angle addition postulate
d. $m\angle SQR > m\angle 1$	d. Definition of inequality
e. $m\angle 1 = m\angle 2$	e. Definition of congruent angles
f. $m\angle SQR > m\angle 2$	f. Substitution property of equality

25. Given $\triangle ABC$

        $m\angle ABC = m\angle BCA$

    Prove: $x < y$

STATEMENTS	REASONS
a. $m\angle ABC = m\angle BCA$	a. Given
b. $m\angle ABC = x + c$	b. Angle addition postulate
c. $m\angle ABC > x$	c. Definition of inequality
d. $m\angle BCA > x$	d. Substitution prop. of equality
e. $m\angle ADB > m\angle BCA$	e. The measure of an ext. $\angle$ of a $\triangle$ is greater than the measure of either of its corr. remote int. $\angle$s.
f. $m\angle ADB > x$	f. Transitive prop. of inequality
g. $y > x$	g. Substitution prop. of equality

26. Given: ΔAEC
    ΔCFB

Prove: m∠4 < m∠1

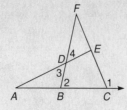

STATEMENTS	REASONS
a. m∠1 > m∠2 and m∠2 > m∠3	a. The measure of an ext. ∠ of a Δ is greater than the measure of either corr. remote int. ∠.
b. ∠3 ≅ ∠4	b. Vertical ∠s are ≅.
c. m∠3 = m∠4	c. Definition of ≅ ∠s
d. m∠2 > m∠4	d. Substitution property of equality
e. m∠1 > m∠4	e. Transitive prop. of inequality

27. Given: ∠2 ≇ ∠1

Prove: ℓ is not parallel to m.

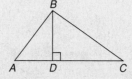

Proof: We are given that ∠2 ≇ ∠1. Assume that ℓ is parallel to m. Since ∠1 and ∠2 are corresponding angles, the corresponding angles postulate says that ∠1 ≅ ∠2. This is a contradiction of our given fact. Therefore, the assumption that ℓ is parallel to m must be false, and hence ℓ is not parallel to m.

28. Given: ΔABC is equilateral.
    ΔABX is equilateral.
    ΔACX is not equilateral.

Prove: ΔBCX is not equilateral.

Proof: Assume ΔBCX is equilateral. By definition CX ≅ BX. Since ΔABX is equilateral, BX ≅ AX, and CX ≅ AX by the transitive property. ΔABC equilateral means AC ≅ AB, and ΔABX equilateral means AB ≅ AX, so AC ≅ AX, by the transitive property. So AC ≅ AX ≅ CX and ΔACX is equilateral. But this contradicts our given information. Therefore, our assumption that ΔBCX is equilateral is false. Hence, ΔBCX is not equilateral.

29. Given: Intersecting lines ℓ and m.

Prove: ℓ and m intersect in no more than one point.

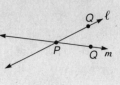

Proof: Assume lines ℓ and m intersect in more than one point. This means a point P is on both lines ℓ and m, and point Q is on both lines ℓ and m. Therefore points P and Q determine both lines ℓ and m. But this contradicts the postulate that states that through any two points there is exactly one line. So, the assumption must be false, and lines ℓ and m intersect at only one point.

30. Given: AB ≇ CB

Prove: ∠A ≇ ∠C

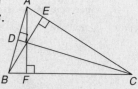

Proof: Assume the angles opposite the sides are congruent; therefore, ∠A ≅ ∠C. It is given that AB ≇ BC. Let BD be an altitude of ΔABC. By definition of altitude BD ⊥ AC and ∠ADB and ∠CDB are right angles since perpendicular lines form four right angles. All right angles are congruent, so ∠ADB ≅ ∠CDB. BD ≅ BD by the reflexive property. Therefore, ΔADB ≅ ΔCDB by AAS. AB ≅ CB by CPCTC. This is a contradiction, so ∠A ≇ ∠C.

31. Given: CD, BE and AF are altitudes of ΔABC.
    CD ≇ BE ≇ AF

Prove: ΔABC is scalene.

Proof: Assume ΔABC is not scalene. Then at least two sides must be congruent by the definition. Say AB ≅ AC. Now consider ΔABE and ΔACD. Since CD and BE are altitudes and altitudes are perpendicular to the opposite side by definition, and perpendicular lines form right angles, we have that ΔABE and ΔACD are right triangles. By the reflexive property of congruent angles, ∠BAC ≅ ∠BAC, and hence ΔABE ≅ ΔACD by HA. Then by CPCTC, BE ≅ CD. But this contradicts our given statement and hence our assumption must be false. AB ≇ BC and AC ≇ BC can be proved in a similar manner. Therefore, ΔABC is scalene.

32. Given: $\overleftrightarrow{AB}$ and $\overleftrightarrow{PQ}$ are skew.
Prove: $\overleftrightarrow{AP}$ and $\overleftrightarrow{BQ}$ are skew.

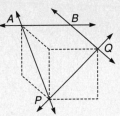

Proof: Assume $\overleftrightarrow{AP}$ and $\overleftrightarrow{BQ}$ are not skew lines. Then either $\overleftrightarrow{AP} \parallel \overleftrightarrow{BQ}$ or $\overleftrightarrow{AP}$ and $\overleftrightarrow{BQ}$ intersect. In either case, A, B, P, Q are coplanar. It given that $\overleftrightarrow{AB}$ and $\overleftrightarrow{PQ}$ are skew lines, so $\overleftrightarrow{AB}$ and $\overleftrightarrow{PQ}$ do not lie in the same plane, and A and B are not coplanar with P and Q. This is a contradiction, so $\overleftrightarrow{AP}$ and $\overleftrightarrow{BQ}$ must be skew.

33. Given: X is in the interior of $\triangle PQR$.

Prove: $m\angle X > m\angle Q$

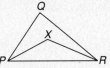

STATEMENTS	REASONS
a. $m\angle X + m\angle XPR + m\angle XRP$ $= 180$ $m\angle Q + m\angle QPR + m\angle QRP$ $= 180$	a. The sum of the measures of the $\angle$s of a $\triangle$ is 180.
b. $m\angle X + m\angle XPR + m\angle XRP =$ $m\angle Q + m\angle QPR + m\angle QRP$	b. Substitution prop. of equality
c. $m\angle QPR = m\angle QPX + m\angle XPR$ $m\angle QRP = m\angle QRX + m\angle XRP$	c. $\angle$ addition postulate
d. $m\angle X + m\angle XPR + m\angle XRP =$ $m\angle Q + (m\angle QPX + m\angle XPR)$ $+ (m\angle QRX + m\angle XRP)$	d. Substitution prop. of equality
e. $m\angle X =$ $m\angle Q + (m\angle QPX + m\angle QRX)$	e. Subtraction prop. of equality
f. $m\angle X > m\angle Q$	f. Definition of inequality

34. The prisoner should choose the door on the left. If the sign on the door on the right were true, then both signs would be true. But one sign is false, so the sign on the door on the right must be false.

35. Mr. Sopher, "killed" Mr. Block. Inspector Photos and Ms. Tebbe each have alibis and Mrs. Bloom couldn't shoot an arrow with the sling on.

36. S; $RS + ST = RT$

37. Distributive and division properties of equality

38. $x = 4$; The figure is a square because the two triangles are congruent by HA.

39. $2,187,000 \div 3^{n-1}$; $n = 7$ days

$2,187,000 \div 3^{6} = 3,000$

There were 3000 bacteria the first day.

40. See students' work.

Mid-Chapter Review

PAGE 239

1. $8a - 11 = 3a + 4$
$5a = 15$
$a = 3$

2. $11a - 9 = 90$
$11a = 99$
$a = 9$

3. Yes; $\triangle XYM \cong \triangle XZM$ by SAS or LL.

4. $\overline{XY} \cong \overline{XZ}$

5. <; Exterior angle inequality theorem

6. $8a - 11 < 12a - 19$
$8 < 4a$
$2 < a$ or $a > 2$

7. We are given that we have two lines that are noncoplanar and that do not intersect. Assume the lines are not skew. Then we have two possibilities for the lines.
Case 1: The lines intersect. This contradicts the given statement that the lines do not intersect.
Case 2: The lines are parallel. By the definition of parallel, this contradicts the given statement that the lines are noncoplanar. In each case we are led to a contradiction. Hence, our assumption must be false and therefore, the lines are skew.

8. Work backward and make a chart. Sally won the last hand, making the score Eric-8, Jon-8, Sally-8. To get the score for the second hand, divide Eric's and Jon's scores by 2 and add the results to Sally's score. This makes the second hand score Eric-4, Jon-4, Sally-16. Jon won the second hand, so to find the first hand score, divide Eric's and Sally's scores by 2 and add the results to Jon's score. This makes the score after the first hand Eric-2, Sally-8, Jon-14. Eric won the first hand, so divide Jon's and Sally's scores by 2 and add the results to Eric's score to get the beginning score of Eric-13, Jon-7, Sally-4.

	Eric	Jon	Sally
last hand	8	8	8
second hand	4	4	16
first hand	2	14	8
beginning points	13	7	4
	lost 5 points	gained 1 point	gained 4 points

Eric lost the most points.

1. Construct a 30° angle. Then mark off segments of 5 cm and 4 cm on each of the rays. Connect the endpoints of those segments.

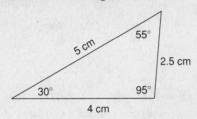

2. In an obtuse triangle, there is one obtuse angle and it must be the largest angle of the triangle. The longest side must be opposite this angle.

3. a. $\angle A \cong \angle L$ b. $PL > PA$ c. $m\angle L < m\angle A$

4. $\angle D$, $\angle E$, $\angle F$ 5. $\angle H$, $\angle G$, $\angle I$

6. $\angle L$, $\angle K$, $\angle M$ 7. $\overline{MN}$, $\overline{LN}$, $\overline{LM}$

8. $\overline{SV}$, $\overline{TV}$, $\overline{ST}$ 9. $\overline{PQ}$, $\overline{RQ}$, $\overline{RP}$

10. $\overline{PA}$ 11. $\overline{HT}$

12. $\overline{PA}$ is longer than $\overline{HT}$.   13. $\overline{PA}$

14. Given: $\triangle DEF$
    $\angle D$ is a right angle.
    Prove: $EF > ED$

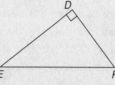

STATEMENTS	REASONS
a. $\angle D$ is a right angle.	a. Given
b. $m\angle D = 90$	b. Definition of a rt $\angle$
c. $\angle F$ is an acute angle.	c. There can be at most one rt or obtuse $\angle$ in a $\triangle$.
d. $m\angle F < 90$	d. Definition of acute $\angle$
e. $m\angle F < m\angle D$	e. Substitution prop. of equality
f. $ED < EF$	f. If one $\angle$ of a $\triangle$ is greater than another $\angle$ then the side opposite the greater $\angle$ is longer than the side opposite the lesser $\angle$.

15. $\angle CBA$; $\angle A$ 16. $\angle D$; $\angle CBD$

17.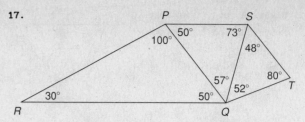

$\overline{PQ}$ is the shortest side of $\triangle PQR$, $\overline{SQ}$ is the shortest side of $\triangle PSQ$, so $SQ < PQ$, $\overline{QT}$ is the shortest side of $\triangle SQT$, so $QT < SQ$. Therefore, $\overline{QT}$ is the shortest side in the figure.

18. 3

19. $AD = \sqrt{(10 - 0)^2 + (3 - 0)^2} = \sqrt{109} \approx 10.44$

    $AE = \sqrt{(10 - 0)^2 + (0 - 0)^2} = \sqrt{100} = 10$

    $DE = \sqrt{(10 - 10)^2 + (3 - 0)^2} = \sqrt{9} = 3$

    $\angle EAD$, $\angle ADE$, $\angle E$

20. C is the midpoint of BD.

    $C = \left(\dfrac{-2 + 10}{2}, \dfrac{7 + 3}{2}\right)$ or $(4, 5)$

    $AB = \sqrt{(0 - (-2))^2 + (0 - 7)^2} = \sqrt{4 + 49} = \sqrt{53}$
    ≈ 7.3

    $AC = \sqrt{(0 - 4)^2 + (0 - 5)^2} = \sqrt{16 + 25} = \sqrt{41} \approx 6.4$

    $BC = \sqrt{(-2 - 4)^2 + (7 - 5)^2} = \sqrt{36 + 4} = \sqrt{40} \approx 6.3$

    $\angle CAB$, $\angle B$, $\angle BCA$

21. $AB = \sqrt{53} \approx 7.28$

    $BD = \sqrt{(-2 - 10)^2 + (7 - 3)^2} = \sqrt{160} \approx 12.65$

    $AD = \sqrt{(0 - 10)^2 + (0 - 3)^2} = \sqrt{100 + 9} = \sqrt{109}$
    ≈ 10.4

    $\angle ADB$, $\angle B$, $\angle BAD$

22. $AC = \sqrt{41} \approx 6.40$

    $CD = \sqrt{(4 - 10)^2 + (5 - 3)^2} = \sqrt{36 + 4} = \sqrt{40} \approx 6.3$

    $AD = \sqrt{109} \approx 10.4$

    $\angle CAD$, $\angle CDA$, $\angle ACD$

23. $(7x + 8) + (8x - 10) + (7x + 6) = 180$

    $22x + 4 = 180$

    $22x = 176$

    $x = 8$

    $m\angle P = 64$, $m\angle Q = 54$, $m\angle R = 62$
    $\overline{QR}$, $\overline{PQ}$, $\overline{PR}$

24. $(3x + 44) + (68 - 3x) + (x + 61) = 180$

    $x + 173 = 180$

    $x = 7$

    $m\angle P = 65$, $m\angle Q = 47$, $m\angle R = 68$
    $\overline{PQ}$, $\overline{QR}$, $\overline{PR}$

25. Given: $QR > QP$
    $\overline{PR} \cong \overline{PQ}$

Prove: $m\angle P > m\angle Q$

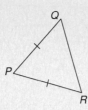

STATEMENTS	REASONS
a. $QR > QP$	a. Given
b. $m\angle P > m\angle R$	b. If one side of a Δ is longer than another side, then the $\angle$ opposite the longer side is greater than the $\angle$ opposite the shorter side.
c. $\overline{PR} \cong \overline{PQ}$	c. Given
d. $\angle Q \cong \angle R$	d. If 2 sides of a Δ are $\cong$, the $\angle$s opposite the sides are $\cong$.
e. $m\angle Q = m\angle R$	e. Definition of $\cong$ $\angle$s
f. $m\angle P > m\angle Q$	f. Substitution prop. of equality

26. Given: $\overline{AC} \cong \overline{AE}$
    $\overline{AE} \cong \overline{KE}$

Prove: $m\angle 1 > m\angle 2$

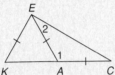

STATEMENTS	REASONS
a. $\overline{AE} \cong \overline{KE}$	a. Given
b. $\angle EKA \cong \angle EAK$	b. If 2 sides of a Δ are $\cong$, then the $\angle$s opposite those sides are $\cong$.
c. $m\angle EKA = m\angle EAK$	c. Definition of congruence
d. $m\angle 1 > m\angle EKA$	d. The measure of an ext. $\angle$ of a Δ is greater than the measure of either corr. remote int. $\angle$.
e. $m\angle 1 > m\angle EAK$	e. Substitution prop. of equality
f. $m\angle EAK > m\angle 2$	f. The measure of an ext. $\angle$ of a Δ is greater than the measure of either corr. remote int. $\angle$.
g. $m\angle 1 > m\angle 2$	g. Transitive prop. of inequality

27. Given: $TE > AE$
    $m\angle P > m\angle PAE$

Prove: $TE > PE$

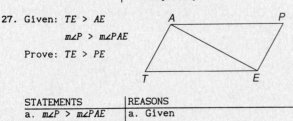

STATEMENTS	REASONS
a. $m\angle P > m\angle PAE$	a. Given

b. $AE > PE$

c. $TE > AE$

d. $TE > PE$

b. If one $\angle$ of a Δ is greater than another $\angle$, then the side opposite the greater $\angle$ is longer than the side opposite the lesser $\angle$.

c. Given

d. Transitive prop. of inequality

28. Given: $m\angle A > m\angle ABC$

Prove: $BC > AC$

Assume $BC \not> AC$. By the comparison property, $BC = AC$ or $BC < AC$.

Case 1: If $BC = AC$, then $\angle ABC \cong \angle A$ by the Isosceles Triangle Theorem (If two sides of a triangle are congruent, then the angles opposite those sides are congruent). But, $\angle ABC \cong \angle A$ contradicts the given statement that $m\angle A > m\angle ABC$. So, $BC \neq AC$.

Case 2: If $BC < AC$, then there must be a point D between A and C so that $\overline{DC} \cong \overline{BC}$. Draw the auxiliary segment $\overline{BD}$. Since $DC = BC$, by the Isosceles Triangle Theorem $\angle BDC \cong \angle DBC$. Now $\angle BDC$ is an exterior angle of ΔBAD, and by the Exterior Angle Inequality Theorem (the measure of an exterior angle of a triangle is greater than the measure of either corresponding remote interior angle) $m\angle BDC > m\angle A$. By the Angle Addition Postulate, $m\angle ABC = m\angle ABD + m\angle DBC$. Then by the definition of inequality, $m\angle ABC > m\angle DBC$. By substitution and the transitive property of inequality, $m\angle ABC > m\angle A$. But this contradicts the given statement that $m\angle A > m\angle ABC$.

In both cases, a contradiction was found, and hence our assumption must have been false. Therefore, $BC > AC$.

29. Given: $\overline{PQ} \perp$ plane $\mathcal{M}$

Prove: $\overline{PQ}$ is the shortest segment from P to plane $\mathcal{M}$.

Proof: By definition, $\overline{PQ}$ is perpendicular to plane $\mathcal{M}$ if it is perpendicular to every line in $\mathcal{M}$ that intersects it. But by Theorem 5-11, that perpendicular segment is the shortest segment from the point to each of these lines. Therefore, $\overline{PQ}$ is the shortest segment from P to $\mathcal{M}$.

30. $\overline{BN}$, $\overline{AM}$, $\overline{CO}$

31. C; distance from C to the line is the greatest.

32. $21 - 4x < 33$ and $21 - 4x > 0$

$$-4x < 12 \qquad 21 > 4x$$

$$x > -3 \quad \text{and} \quad \frac{21}{4} > x$$

$$-3 < x < \frac{21}{4}$$

33. $4x - 1 = 19$

$$4x = 20$$

$$x = 5$$

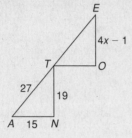

34. Answers will vary. A sample answer is given.

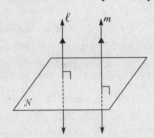

$\ell \parallel m$

$\ell \perp$ plane N

$m \perp$ plane N

35. $7d - 1 = 11d - 53$

$$52 = 4d$$

$$13 = d$$

$$m\angle B = 11d - 53$$

$$m\angle B = 11 \cdot 14 - 53$$

$$m\angle B = 90; \text{ right}$$

36. See students' work.

5-6 The Triangle Inequality

PAGES 248-249   CHECKING FOR UNDERSTANDING

1. Answers may vary. Sample answer: The length of the third side of a triangle is less than the combined lengths of the other two sides.

2. Answers may vary. Sample answers:

3, 4, 5   3, 4, 8

 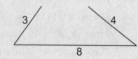

3. $2x > 8$

$$x > 4$$

The legs can be any length greater than 4 inches.

4. $13 - 5 < x < 13 + 5$

$8 < x < 18$ by the triangle inequality theorem. 13 will not necessarily be the longest side.

5. $1 + 2 = 3$
   $2 + 5 = 7$
   $5 + 1 = 6$
   No; $3 \not> 5$

6. $11 + 10 = 21$
   $10 + 17 = 27$
   $17 + 11 = 28$
   Yes

7. $2.4 + 6.8 = 9.2$
   $6.8 + 4.5 = 11.3$
   $4.5 + 2.4 = 6.9$
   Yes

8. $15 - 12 < x < 15 + 12$
   $3 < x < 27$

9. $13 - 4 < x < 13 + 4$
   $9 < x < 17$

10. $21 - 17 < x < 21 + 17$
    $4 < x < 38$

11. No, the points are collinear.

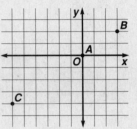

12. Given: $\angle B \cong \angle ACB$

Prove: $AD + AB > CD$

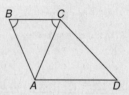

STATEMENTS	REASONS
a. $\angle B \cong \angle ACB$	a. Given
b. $\overline{AB} \cong \overline{AC}$	b. If 2 ∠s of a Δ are ≅ the sides opposite the ∠s are ≅.
c. $AB = AC$	c. Definition of ≅ Δs
d. $AD + AC > CD$	d. Δ inequality
e. $AD + AB > CD$	e. Substitution property of equality

PAGES 249-250   EXERCISES

13. yes

14. $1 + 2 = 3$; no

15. $4.7 + 4.1 = 8.8$; no

16. yes

17. $12 + 2.2 = 14.2$; no

18. yes

19. yes

20. yes

21. $7 + 215 = 222$; no

22. yes

23. $40 + 18 = 58$; no

24. yes

25. yes

26. $18 + 3 = 21$; no

27. $18 + 57 = 75$; no

28. $AB = \sqrt{(4 - 0)^2 + (-3 - 0)^2} = \sqrt{16 + 9} = 5$

$BC = \sqrt{(0 - (-4))^2 + (0 - 3)^2} = \sqrt{16 + 9} = 5$

$AC = \sqrt{(4 - (-4))^2 + (-3 - 3)^2} = \sqrt{64 + 36} = 10$

No; $AB + BC \not> AC$.

29. $DE = \sqrt{(-2 - 2)^2 + (1 - (-1))^2} = \sqrt{16 + 4} = \sqrt{20}$

$DF = \sqrt{(-2 - (-6))^2 + (1 - 3)^2} = \sqrt{16 + 4} = \sqrt{20}$

$EF = \sqrt{(2 - (-6))^2 + (-1 - 3)^2} = \sqrt{64 + 16} = \sqrt{80}$
$$= 2\sqrt{20}$$

No; $DE + DF \not> EF$.

30. $GH = \sqrt{(-2 - (-6))^2 + (4 - 5)^2} = \sqrt{16 + 1} = \sqrt{17}$
$$\approx 4.1$$

$GI = \sqrt{(-2 - (-3))^2 + (4 - (-3))^2} = \sqrt{1 + 49} = \sqrt{50}$
$$\approx 7.1$$

$HI = \sqrt{(-6 - (-3))^2 + (5 - (-3))^2} = \sqrt{9 + 64} = \sqrt{73}$
$$\approx 8.5$$

Yes; these satisfy the triangle inequality.

31. $JK = \sqrt{(3 - 8)^2 + (-3 - 2)^2} = \sqrt{25 + 25} = \sqrt{50}$
$$\approx 7.1$$

$JL = \sqrt{(3 - 5)^2 + (-3 - 5)^2} = \sqrt{4 + 64} = \sqrt{68} \approx 8.2$

$LK = \sqrt{(5 - 8)^2 + (5 - 2)^2} = \sqrt{9 + 9} = \sqrt{18} \approx 4.2$

Yes; these satisfy the triangle inequality.

32. a. 4(3, 4, 5; 3, 5, 6; 4, 5, 6; 3, 4, 6)

   b. 2(3, 4, 5; 4, 5, 6)

   c. $\frac{4}{10} = \frac{2}{5}$ or 0.4

33. $(3x + 2) + (8x - 10) > 5x + 8$
$$x > \frac{8}{3}$$

$(8x - 10) + (5x + 8) > 3x + 2$
$$x > \frac{2}{5}$$

$(5x + 8) + (3x + 2) > 8x - 10$
$$x \text{ is all real numbers}$$

Intersection of $x > \frac{8}{3}$, $x > \frac{2}{5}$ and all real

numbers is $x > \frac{8}{3}$.

34. $2x + (15 - x) > 4x - 6$
$$x < 7$$

$(15 - x) + (4x - 6) > 2x$
$$x > 9$$

$(4x - 6) + 2x > 15 - x$
$$x > 3$$

Intersection of $x < 7$, $x > 9$, and $x > 3$ is
$3 < x < 7$.

35. 1

36. Given: $MN = MQ$

   Prove: $OP + ON > PQ$

STATEMENTS	REASONS
a. $MN = MQ$	a. Given
b. $OP + ON > PN$	b. The sum of the lengths of any two sides of a $\triangle$ is greater than the length of third side.
c. $PN = PM + MN$	c. Segment addition postulate
d. $PN = PM + MQ$	d. Substitution prop. of equality
e. $OP + ON > PM + MQ$	e. Substitution prop. of equality
f. $PM + MQ > PQ$	f. $\triangle$ inequality
g. $OP + ON > PQ$	g. Transitive prop. of inequality

37. Given: $\overline{AD}$, $\overline{BE}$, $\overline{CF}$ are
   altitudes of $\triangle ABC$.

   Prove: $AB + BC + AC >$
   $AD + BE + CF$

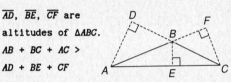

STATEMENTS	REASONS
a. $\overline{AD}$, $\overline{BE}$, and $\overline{CF}$ are altitudes of $\triangle ABC$.	a. Given
b. $\overline{AD} \perp \overleftrightarrow{DC}$; $\overline{BE} \perp \overleftrightarrow{AC}$; $\overline{CF} \perp \overleftrightarrow{AB}$	b. Definiton of altitude
c. $AB > AD$; $BC > BE$; $AC > CF$	c. The $\perp$ segment from a point to a line is the shortest segment from the point to the line.
d. $AB = AD + x$ $BC = BE + y$ $AC = CF + z$	d. Definition of inequality
e. $AB + BC + AC =$ $AD + BE + CF +$ $x + y + z$	e. Addition prop. of equality
f. $AB + BC + AC >$ $AD + BE + CF$	f. Definition of inequality

38. Given: $\triangle PQR$

   Prove: $PQ + PR > RQ$

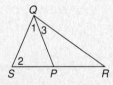

STATEMENTS	REASONS
a. Construct $\overline{PS}$ such that P is between S and R and $\overline{PQ} \cong \overline{PS}$.	a. Ruler postulate
b. $PQ = PS$	b. Definition of $\cong$ line segments
c. $PS + PR = RS$	c. Segment addition postulate
d. $\angle 1 \cong \angle 2$	d. If 2 sides of a $\triangle$ are $\cong$, then the $\angle$s opposite these sides are also $\cong$.

e. $m\angle 1 = m\angle 2$	e. Definition of $\cong$ $\angle$s
f. $m\angle SQR = m\angle 1 + m\angle 3$	f. $\angle$ addition postulate
g. $m\angle SQR = m\angle 2 + m\angle 3$	g. Substitution property of equality
h. $m\angle SQR > m\angle 2$	h. Definition of inequality
i. $RS > RQ$	i. If the measures of 2 $\angle$s of a Δ are unequal, then the measures of the sides opposite those $\angle$s are unequal in the same order.
j. $PS + PR > RQ$	j. Substitution prop. of equality
k. $PQ + PR > RQ$	k. Substitution prop. of equality

39. Theorem: The measure of the longest side of a quadrilateral is less than the sum of the measures of the other three sides.

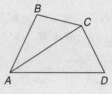

Given: $ABCD$ is a quadrilateral.
$\overline{AD}$ is the longest side.
Prove: $AD < AB + BC + CD$

STATEMENTS	REASONS
a. $ABCD$ is a quadrilateral.	a. Given
b. $AD < AC + CD$	b. Δ inequality theorem
c. $AC < AB + BC$	c. Δ inequality theorem
d. $AC + CD < AB + BC + CD$	d. Addition prop. of inequality
e. $AD < AB + BC + CD$	e. Transitive prop. of inequality

40. See students' work.

41. a. 1 in., 4 in., 4 in.; 4 in., 2 in., 3 in.; 3 in., 3 in., 3 in.

    b. Isosceles triangle with side 1 in., 4 in., 4 in.

42. One of three sets of flower beds can be made:
    3 ft, 3 ft, 5 ft and 4 ft, 5 ft, 7 ft;
    3 ft, 3 ft, 4 ft and 5 ft, 5 ft, 7 ft;
    3 ft, 5 ft, 7 ft and 3 ft, 4 ft, 5 ft.

43. $m\angle X + m\angle Y + m\angle Z = 180$
    $4n + 61 + 67 - 3n + n + 74 = 180$
    $2n + 202 = 180$
    $2n = -22$
    $n = -11$
    $m\angle X = 4(-11) + 61$ $m\angle Y = 67 - 3(-11)$
    $= 17$ $= 100$
    $m\angle Z = (-11) + 74$
    $= 63$
    The side opposite $\angle Y$, $\overline{XZ}$, is longest.

44. $NQ = \sqrt{(2 + 4)^2 + (-1 + 1)^2}$
    $= 6$
    $QD = \sqrt{(-4 + 1)^2 + (-1 - 3)^2}$
    $= 5$
    $DN = \sqrt{(-1 - 2)^2 + (3 + 1)^2}$
    $= 5$

45. $m = \dfrac{y_2 - y_1}{x_2 - x_1}$
    $= \dfrac{-11 - 9}{6 - 4}$
    $= \dfrac{-20}{2}$
    $= -10$

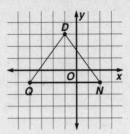

Acute, isosceles

46. Given: $\overline{PQ}$ bisects $\overline{AB}$ at M.
    Prove: $\overline{AM} \cong \overline{MB}$

STATEMENTS	REASONS
a. $\overline{PQ}$ bisects $\overline{AB}$.	a. Given
b. M is the midpoint of $\overline{AB}$.	b. Definition of bisect
c. $AM = MB$	c. Definition of midpoint
d. $\overline{AM} \cong \overline{MB}$	d. Definition of $\cong$ segments

47. x = angle; $90 - x$ = complement
    $x = 4(90 - x + 5$
    $5x = 365$
    $x = 73$
    $90 - x = 17$

48. See students' work.

Technology:
The Triangle Inequality

PAGE 251 EXERCISES
1. No   2. Yes   3. No   4. No
5. Checks to see if the sum of the two lesser measures is greater than the greatest measure.
6. If the sum of the two lesser measures is more than the greatest measure, then the other two inequalities will also be true.

5-7 Inequalities Involving Two Triangles

PAGES 254-255   CHECKING FOR UNDERSTANDING
1. a. See students' work.
   b. The triangle with a 100° vertex angle
   c. SAS Inequality

2. Answers will vary. A sample answer is given. As the angle between the edges of a hinge gets larger, the distance between ends of the sides gets longer.

3. Answers will vary. A sample answer is a pair of scissors.

4. $m\angle ALK < m\angle ALN$ 5. $m\angle ALK < m\angle NLO$

6. $m\angle OLK > m\angle NLO$ 7. $m\angle KLO = m\angle ALN$

8. AC
$$(5x + 20) + (8x - 100) = 180$$
$$x = 20$$
$$m\angle 1 = 5x + 20 = 120$$
$$m\angle 2 = 8x - 100 = 60$$

9. $m\angle B$; $AC > BC$

10. $m\angle 1$; $m\angle 1 = 120$, $m\angle 2 = 60$

11. Given: $\overline{PQ} \cong \overline{SQ}$
    Prove: $PR > SR$

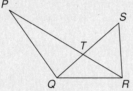

STATEMENTS	REASONS
a. $\overline{PQ} \cong \overline{SQ}$	a. Given
b. $\overline{QR} \cong \overline{QR}$	b. Congruence of segments is reflexive.
c. $m\angle PQR = m\angle PQS + m\angle SQR$	c. $\angle$ addition postulate
d. $m\angle PQR > m\angle SQR$	d. Definition of inequality
e. $PR > SR$	e. SAS inequality

PAGES 255-257   EXERCISES

12. $m\angle ADC < m\angle ADB$ 13. $AB > AC$

14. $PT < RS$ 15. $m\angle 1 < m\angle 2$

16. $ZR < XR$ 17. $m\angle DFE > m\angle DFG$

18. $0 < 5x - 14 < 46$ 19. $3x - 2 > 10$; $x > 4$
    $14 < 5x < 60$
    $2.8 < x < 12$
    $2.8 < x$ and $x < 12$

20. $x + 2 + 2x - 8 > x + 2$ and $2x - 8 < x + 2$
    $3x - 6 > x + 2$ $x < 10$
    $2x > 8$
    $x > 4$

21. Given: $\overline{PQ} \cong \overline{RS}$
    $QR < PS$
    Prove: $m\angle 3 < m\angle 1$

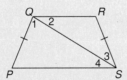

STATEMENTS	REASONS
a. $\overline{PQ} \cong \overline{RS}$	a. Given
b. $\overline{QS} \cong \overline{QS}$	b. Congruence of segments is reflexive.

c. $QR < PS$ c. Given

d. $m\angle 3 < m\angle 1$ d. SSS inequality

22. Given: $\overline{PR} \cong \overline{PQ}$
    $SQ > SR$
    Prove: $m\angle 1 < m\angle 2$

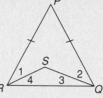

STATEMENTS	REASONS
a. $\overline{PR} \cong \overline{PQ}$	a. Given
b. $\angle PRQ \cong \angle PQR$	b. If 2 sides of a Δ are $\cong$, then the $\angle$s opposite the sides are $\cong$.
c. $m\angle PRQ = m\angle 1 + m\angle 4$ $m\angle PQR = m\angle 2 + m\angle 3$	c. $\angle$ addition postulate
d. $m\angle PRQ = m\angle PQR$	d. Definition of $\cong$ $\angle$s
e. $m\angle 1 + m\angle 4 = m\angle 2 + m\angle 3$	e. Substitution prop. of equality
f. $SQ > SR$	f. Given
g. $m\angle 4 > m\angle 3$	g. If one side of a Δ is longer than another side, then the $\angle$ opposite the longer side is greater than the $\angle$ opposite the shorter side.
h. $m\angle 4 = m\angle 3 + x$	h. Definition of inequality
i. $m\angle 1 + m\angle 4 - m\angle 4 = m\angle 2 + m\angle 3 - (m\angle 3 + x)$	i. Subtraction prop. of equality
j. $m\angle 1 = m\angle 2 - x$	j. Substitution prop. of equality
k. $m\angle 1 + x = m\angle 2$	k. Addition prop. of equality
l. $m\angle 1 < m\angle 2$	l. Definition of inequality

23. Given: ΔTER
    $\overline{TR} \cong \overline{EU}$
    Prove: $TE > RU$

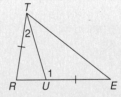

STATEMENTS	REASONS
a. $\overline{TR} \cong \overline{EU}$	a. Given
b. $\overline{TU} \cong \overline{TU}$	b. Congruence of segments is reflexive.
c. $m\angle 1 > m\angle 2$	c. If an $\angle$ is an ext. $\angle$ of a Δ, then its measure is greater than the measure of either of its corr. remote int. $\angle$s.
d. $TE > RU$	d. SAS Inequality

24. Given: $\overline{TU} \cong \overline{US}$

  $\overline{US} \cong \overline{SV}$

  $m\angle SVU > \angle USV$

Prove: $ST > UV$

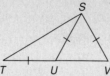

STATEMENTS	REASONS
a. $\overline{TU} \cong \overline{US}$, $\overline{US} \cong \overline{SV}$	a. Given
$m\angle SVU > m\angle USV$	
b. $m\angle SUT > m\angle SVU$	b. If an $\angle$ is an ext. $\angle$ of a $\triangle$, then its measure is greater than the measure of its corr. remote int. $\angle$s.
c. $\angle SUV \cong \angle SVU$	c. If 2 sides of a $\triangle$ are $\cong$, the $\angle$s opposite the sides are $\cong$.
d. $m\angle SUV = m\angle SVU$	d. Definition of $\cong$ $\angle$s
e. $m\angle SUT > m\angle USV$	e. Transitive prop. of inequality
f. $ST > UV$	f. SAS Inequality

25. Given: $\overline{ED} \cong \overline{DF}$

  $m\angle 1 > m\angle 2$

  D is the midpoint of $\overline{CB}$.

  $\overline{AE} \cong \overline{AF}$

Prove: $AC > AB$

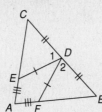

STATEMENTS	REASONS
a. $\overline{ED} \cong \overline{DF}$	a. Given
D is the midpoint of $\overline{CB}$.	
b. $CD = BD$	b. Definition of midpoint
c. $\overline{CD} \cong \overline{BD}$	c. Definition of $\cong$ segments
d. $m\angle 1 > m\angle 2$	d. Given
e. $EC > FB$	e. SAS inequality
f. $\overline{AE} \cong \overline{AF}$	f. Given
g. $AE = AF$	g. Definition of $\cong$ segments.
h. $AE + EC > AE + FB$	h. Addition prop. of inequality
i. $AE + EC > AF + FB$	i. Substitution prop. of equality
j. $AE + EC = AC$	j. Segment addition postulate
$AF + FB = AB$	
k. $AC > AB$	k. Substitution prop. of equality

26. Given: $m\angle DBC = m\angle DCB$

  $m\angle ADB < m\angle ADC$

Prove: $m\angle ACB < m\angle ABC$

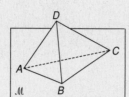

STATEMENTS	REASONS
a. $m\angle DBC = m\angle DCB$	a. Given
b. $\angle DBC \cong \angle DCB$	b. Definition of $\cong$ $\angle$s
c. $\overline{DB} \cong \overline{DC}$	c. If 2 $\angle$s are $\cong$, the sides opposite these $\angle$s are also $\cong$.
d. $\overline{DA} \cong \overline{DA}$	d. Congruence of segments is reflexive.
e. $m\angle ADB < m\angle ADC$	e. Given
f. $AB < AC$	f. SAS inequality
g. $m\angle ACB < m\angle ABC$	g. If one side of a $\triangle$ is longer than another side, the $\angle$ opposite the longer side is greater than the $\angle$ opposite the shorter side.

27. Given: $\overline{AC} \cong \overline{DF}$

  $\overline{BC} \cong \overline{EF}$

  $m\angle F > m\angle C$

Prove: $DE > AB$

We are given that $\overline{AC} \cong \overline{DF}$ and $\overline{BC} \cong \overline{EF}$. We also know that $m\angle F > m\angle C$. Now draw auxiliary ray $\overline{FZ}$ such that $m\angle DFZ = m\angle C$ and that $\overline{ZF} \cong \overline{BC}$. This leads to two cases.

Case I: If Z lies on $\overline{DE}$, then $\triangle FZD \cong \triangle CBA$ by SAS. Hence $ZD = BA$ by CPCTC and the definition of congruent segments. By the Segment Addition Postulate, $DE = EZ + ZD$ and hence $DE > ZD$ by the definition of inequality, then $DE > AB$ by substitution property of equality.

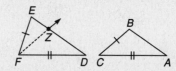

Case II: If Z does not lie on $\overline{DE}$, then let the intersection of $\overline{FZ}$ and $\overline{ED}$ be point T.

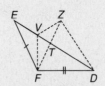

Now draw another auxiliary segment $\overline{FV}$ such that V is on $\overline{DE}$ and $\angle EFV \cong \angle VFZ$. Since $\overline{FZ} \cong \overline{BC}$ and $\overline{BC} \cong \overline{EF}$, we have $\overline{FZ} \cong \overline{EF}$ by the transitive theorem. Also $\overline{VF}$ is congruent to itself by the reflexive theorem. Hence, $\triangle EFV \cong \triangle ZFV$ by SAS. Then by CPCTC, $\overline{EV} \cong \overline{ZV}$. In $\triangle VZD$ the Triangle Inequality Theorem gives $VD + VZ > ZD$ and so by substitution $VD + EV > ZD$. By the Segment Addition Postulate $ED > ZD$. We also have $\triangle FZD \cong \triangle CBA$ by SAS which gives $\overline{ZD} \cong \overline{AB}$ by CPCTC. Making the substitution, we get $ED > BA$ or $DE > AB$.

86

28. $\overline{XZ}$ is not perpendicular to plane $\mathcal{P}$.

29. $\triangle ABC$ is equilateral, so $\overline{AB} \cong \overline{BC}$. Since $\overline{DB} \cong \overline{DB}$ and $\triangle ABD$ and $\triangle BCD$ are right triangles, $\triangle ABD \cong \triangle BCD$ by LL, and $\overline{AD} \cong \overline{CD}$ by CPCTC. Therefore, $\triangle CDA$ is isosceles and $\angle DCA \cong \angle DAC$.

30. a. 2.78 m/s; 3.08 m/s
    b.

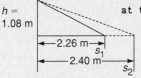

As the length of the stride increases, the angle formed at the hip increases.

$h = 1.08$ m
2.26 m s_1
2.40 m s_2

31. $AB = \sqrt{(1-7)^2 + (-1-7)^2} = 10$

    $BC = \sqrt{(7-2)^2 + (7-5)^2} = 13$

    $AC = \sqrt{(1-2)^2 + (-1-5)^2} = \sqrt{17} \approx 4.1$

    Yes; the measures satisfy the triangle inequality.

32. Given: $\overline{AC} \cong \overline{BD}$
    $\overline{AD} \cong \overline{BC}$
    Prove: $\triangle AXC \cong \triangle BXD$

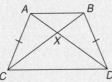

STATEMENTS	REASONS
a. $\overline{AC} \cong \overline{BD}$, $\overline{AD} \cong \overline{BC}$	a. Given
b. $\overline{AB} \cong \overline{AB}$	b. Congruence of segments is reflexive.
c. $\triangle ABC \cong \triangle BAD$	c. SSS
d. $\angle BCA \cong \angle ADB$	d. CPCTC
e. $\angle AXC \cong \angle BXD$	e. Vertical $\angle$s are $\cong$.
f. $\triangle AXC \cong \triangle BXD$	f. AAS

33. $(3n + 32) + (14n - 5) = 180$

    $17n = 153$

    $n = 9$

34. $(6x + 6) + (11x - 1) = 90$

    $17x = 85$

    $x = 5$

    $m\angle A = 36$; $m\angle B = 54$

35. See students' work.

Chapter 5 Summary and Review

PAGES 258-260   SKILLS AND CONCEPTS

1. $m\angle DBC = 2m\angle DBG = 2 \cdot 33 = 66$

   $m\angle BDC = m\angle BCD = 57$

2. $(3x + 11) + (7x + 9) = 90$

   $x = 7$

   $m\angle 2 = 58$

3. $3x - 14 = 2x - 1$

   $x = 13$

   $m\angle AED = 7 \cdot 13 + 1 = 92$

   No; $m\angle AED \neq 90$

4. $3x + 1 = 40$

   $x = 13$

   $3y - 1 = 50$

   $y = 17$

5. $4x + 3 = 47$

   $x = 11$

   $2y - 9 = 43$

   $y = 26$

6. $7x - 3 = 53$

   $x = 8$

   $5y - 2 = 2y + 7$

   $3y = 9$

   $y = 3$

7. $4x - 3 = x + 3$

   $3x = 6$

   $x = 2$

   $12y + 1 = 10y + 3$

   $2y = 2$

   $y = 1$

8. Given: $\overline{QP} \cong \overline{QR}$
   $\overline{QX}$ does not bisect $\angle PQR$,
   Prove: $\overline{QX}$ is not a median of $\triangle PQR$.

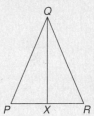

Proof: Assume $\overline{QX}$ is a median of $\triangle PQR$. By definition of median, X is the midpoint of $\overline{PR}$, and hence by the definition of midpoint, $\overline{PX} \cong \overline{XR}$. We are given that $\overline{QP} \cong \overline{QR}$ and we know $\overline{QX} \cong \overline{QX}$ since congruence of segments is reflexive. Therefore, $\triangle QXP \cong QXR$ by SSS and $\angle PQX \cong \angle RQX$ by CPCTC. By the definition of angle bisector $\overline{QX}$ bisects $\angle PQR$. But this contradicts our given statement. Therefore, the assumption must be false, and $\overline{QX}$ is not a median of $\triangle PQR$.

9. Given: $\triangle QXP \cong \triangle QXR$
   Prove: $\overline{QX}$ is an altitude of $\triangle PQR$.

Proof: Assume $\overline{QX}$ is not an altitude of $\triangle PQR$. This means that $\overline{QX}$ is not perpendicular to $\overline{PR}$ by the definition of altitude. By the definition of perpendicular, $\angle QXR$ is not a right angle. Therefore, $\angle QXR$ is either acute or obtuse. Since $\angle QXP$ and $\angle QXR$ form a linear pair, these two angles are supplementary. If $\angle QXP$ is acute, $\angle QXR$ is obtuse (or vice versa), by the definition of supplementary. In either case, $\angle QXP \ncong \angle QXR$. But we are given $\triangle QXP \cong \triangle QXR$ and by CPCTC, $\angle QXP \cong \angle QXR$. This is a contradiction, and hence our assumption must be false. Therefore, $\overline{QX}$ is an altitude of $\triangle PQR$.

10. $<$ 11. $>$ 12. $<$ 13. $<$ 14. $>$ 15. $\overline{SP}$

16. $\overline{AC}$, $\overline{AB}$, $\overline{CB}$ 17. $\angle D$, $\angle CBD$, $\angle BCD$

18. Given: $FG < FH$

Prove: $m\angle 1 > m\angle 2$

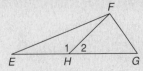

STATEMENTS	REASONS
a. $FG < FH$	a. Given
b. $m\angle FGH > m\angle 2$	b. If one side of a Δ is longer than another side, then the $\angle$ opp. the longer side is greater than the $\angle$ opp. the shorter side.
c. $m\angle 1 > m\angle FGH$	c. The measure of an ext. $\angle$ of a Δ is greater than the measure of either of its corr. remote int. $\angle$s.
d. $m\angle 1 > m\angle 2$	d. Transitive prop. of inequality

19. $11 - 5 = 6$; $11 + 5 = 16$
between 6 and 16

20. $24 - 7 = 17$; $24 + 7 = 31$
between 17 and 31

21. $AB = \sqrt{(-5 - 4)^2 + (12 + 3)^2} = \sqrt{306} \approx 17.5$
$BC = \sqrt{(4 - 0)^2 + (-3 - 0)^2} = 5$
$AC = \sqrt{(-5 - 0)^2 + (12 - 0)^2} = 13$
Yes

22. $DE = \sqrt{(-3 - 3)^2 + (4 + 5)^2} = \sqrt{117} \approx 10.8$
$EF = \sqrt{(3 + 1)^2 + (-5 - 1)^2} = \sqrt{52} \approx 7.2$
$DF = \sqrt{(-3 + 1)^2 + (4 - 1)^2} = \sqrt{13} \approx 3.6$
No, $\sqrt{52} + \sqrt{13} > \sqrt{117}$

23. 3 triangles: 2, 3, 4; 2, 4, 5; 3, 4, 5

24. $m\angle PNQ < m\angle QNR$ 25. $m\angle PNS < m\angle RNS$

26. $m\angle NPQ < m\angle NRS$

27. Given: $AD = BC$

Prove: $DB < AC$

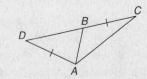

STATEMENTS	REASONS
a. $AD = BC$	a. Given
b. $\overline{AD} \cong \overline{BC}$	b. Definition of $\cong$ segments
c. $\overline{BA} \cong \overline{BA}$	c. Congruence of segments is reflexive.
d. $m\angle CBA > m\angle DAB$	d. If an $\angle$ is an ext. $\angle$ of a Δ then its measure is greater than the measure of either of its corr. remote int. $\angle$s.
e. $AC > DB$	e. SAS inequality

PAGE 260   APPLICATIONS AND CONNECTIONS

28. $\left(\frac{1}{2}\right)^8 \cdot x = \frac{5}{16}$
$x = 80$

29.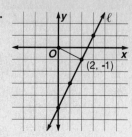

30. Since the cities are not in a straight line, three of them will form a triangle. Use the triangle inequality.

Blockburg–Pine City–Susanton
$9 - 6 < x < 9 + 6$
$3 < x < 15$

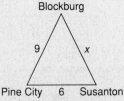

Susanton–Pine City–Leshville
$13 - 6 < y < 13 + 6$
$7 < y < 19$

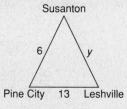

Leshville–Pine City–Blockburg
$13 - 9 < z < 13 + 9$
$4 < z < 22$

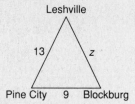

Bonnie's path $= x + y + z$ miles.
$3 + 7 + 4 < x + y + z < 15 + 19 + 22$
$14 < x + y + z < 56$
Bonnie will travel between 14 and 56 miles.

Chapter 5 Test

PAGE 261

1. $m\angle AQH = 90$ 2. $m\angle AHQ = 26$

3. $m\angle APW = 98$ 4. $m\angle HXW = 108$

5. $7y - 5 = 3y + 11$
$4y = 16$
$y = 4$
$(7y - 5) + (3y + 11)$
$10y + 6$; $y = 4$
46

6. >   7. <   8. >   9. <   10. >

11. $SR > SQ$ 12. $m\angle SPR < m\angle SPQ$

13. PS 14. $31 - 13 < PQ < 31 + 13$

  18 and 44

15. $(5x + 31) + (74 - 3x) + (4x + 9) = 180$

  $6x + 114 = 180$

  $x = 11$

$m\angle A = 86$, $m\angle B = 41$, $m\angle C = 53$

$\overline{BC}$ is longest segment in $\triangle ABC$.

16. $(3x + 8) + (5x + 2) > 8x - 10$

  x = all positive real numbers

  $(5x + 2) + (8x - 10) > 3x + 8$

  $x > \dfrac{8}{5}$

  $(8x - 10) + (3x + 8) > 5x + 2$

  $x > 0$

  Intersection of x = all positive numbers, $x > \dfrac{8}{5}$

  and $x > 0$ is $x > \dfrac{8}{5}$.

17. $13x - 5 > 7x + 25$

  $6x > 30$

  $x > 5$

18. Given: $\overline{FM}$ is a median
  of $\triangle DEF$.
  $m\angle 1 > m\angle 2$
  Prove: $DF \neq EF$

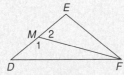

  Proof: Assume $DF = EF$. M is the midpoint of DE
  and $\overline{DM} \cong \overline{EM}$, since it is given that $\overline{FM}$ is
  a median of $\triangle DEF$. $\overline{FM} \cong \overline{FM}$ by the
  reflexive property of equality and
  $m\angle 1 > m\angle 2$ is given, so $DF > EF$ by SAS
  Inequality. But $DF = EF$ by assumption.
  This contradicts the comparison property.
  Therefore the assumption is false, and
  $DF \neq EF$.

19. Given: $NO = QP$
  $PN > OQ$
  Prove: $MP > MO$

STATEMENTS	REASONS
a. $NO = QP$	a. Given
b. $\overline{NO} \cong \overline{QP}$	b. Definition of congruence
c. $\overline{OP} \cong \overline{OP}$	c. Congruence of segments is reflexive.
d. $PN > OQ$	d. Given
e. $m\angle MOP > m\angle MPO$	e. SSS inequality
f. $MP > MO$	f. If one ∠ of a Δ is greater than another, the side opposite the greater ∠ is longer than the side opposite the lesser ∠.

20. Given: $\overline{AD} \perp \overline{DC}$
  $\overline{AB} \perp \overline{BC}$
  $AB = DC$
  Prove: $\overline{DC} \perp \overline{BC}$

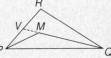

STATEMENTS	REASONS
a. $AD \perp DC$ $AB \perp BC$, $AB = DC$	a. Given
b. $\overline{AB} \cong \overline{DC}$	b. Definition of congruence
c. $\overline{AC} \cong \overline{AC}$	c. Congruence of segments is reflexive.
d. $\angle D$ and $\angle B$ are right angles.	d. ⊥ lines form 4 rt. ∠s.
e. $\triangle ADC$ and $\triangle CBA$ are right triangles.	e. Definition of rt Δ
f. $\triangle ADC \cong \triangle CBA$	f. HL
g. $\angle ACD \cong \angle CAB$	g. CPCTC
h. $AB \parallel CD$	h. If alt. int. ∠s are ≅, lines are ‖.
i. $DC \perp BC$	i. In a plane, if a line is ⊥ to one of 2 ‖ lines, then it is ⊥ to the other.

BONUS:

Given: $\triangle PQR$ with M in interior.

Prove: $PR + QR > PM + QM$

STATEMENTS	REASONS
1. Extend $\overline{QM}$ to intersect $\overline{PR}$ at V.	1. Through any 2 pts. there is 1 line.
2. $VR + QR > VQ$ $VP + VM > PM$	2. Δ inequality theorem
3. $VQ = VM + QM$	3. Segment Addition Postulate
4. $VR + QR > VM + QM$	4. Substitution prop. of equality
5. $VP + VM + VR + QR >$ $PM + VM + QM$	5. Addition prop. of inequality
6. $VP + VR + QR >$ $PM + QM$	6. Subtraction prop. of inequality
7. $VP + VP = PR$	7. Segment Addition Postulate
8. $PR + QR > PM + QM$	8. Substitution prop. of equality

Algebra Review

PAGES 262-263

1. $5a - 5 = 7a - 19$

  $14 = 2a$

  $7 = a$

2. $\dfrac{2}{3}x + 5 = \dfrac{1}{2}x + 4$

  $\dfrac{1}{6}x = -1$

  $x = -6$

89

3. $5(4 - n) = 2n - 1$

$\quad 20 - 5n = 2n - 1$

$\quad\quad 21 = 7n$

$\quad\quad 3 = n$

4. $2(2y - 3) = -9(y - 6) + y$

$\quad 4y - 6 = -9y + 54 + y$

$\quad\quad 12y = 60$

$\quad\quad y = 5$

5. $\dfrac{r}{100} = \dfrac{5}{20}$

$\quad r = \dfrac{5}{20}(100) = 25$

25% increase

6. $\dfrac{105}{100} = \dfrac{3.15}{x}$

$\quad 105x = 315$

$\quad\quad x = \$3.00$

7. $\dfrac{75}{100} = \dfrac{\$36}{x}$

$\quad 75x = 3,600$

$\quad\quad x = \$48$

8. $\dfrac{5}{7} = \dfrac{15}{y}$

$\quad 5y = 105$

$\quad\quad y = 21$

9. $\dfrac{175}{75} = \dfrac{35}{y}$

$\quad 175y = 2625$

$\quad\quad y = 15$

10. $\dfrac{21}{x} = \dfrac{1.2}{21}$

$\quad 1.2x = 441$

$\quad\quad x = 367.5$

11. $6x \le -24$

$\quad x \le -4$

12. $-7y \ge -91$

$\quad y \le 13$

13. $-0.8t < -0.96$

$\quad t > 1.2$

14. $\dfrac{4}{3}a < 16$

$\quad a < 12$

15. $\dfrac{2}{3}k \ge \dfrac{2}{15}$

$\quad k \ge \dfrac{1}{5}$

16. $\dfrac{4}{7}z > -\dfrac{2}{5}$

$\quad z > -\dfrac{7}{10}$

17. $(4a^2b)^3 = 4^3(a^2)^3(b)^3$

$\quad\quad = 64a^6b^3$

18. $(-3xy)^2(4x)^3 = (-3)^2x^2y^2 \cdot (4)^3x^3$

$\quad\quad\quad = 9x^2y^2 \cdot 64x^3$

$\quad\quad\quad = 576x^5y^2$

19. $(-2c^{-2}d)^4(-3cd^2)^3 = (-2)^4(c^{-2})^4d^4 \cdot (-3)^3c^3(d^2)^3$

$\quad\quad\quad = 16c^{-8}d^4 \cdot (-27)c^3d^6$

$\quad\quad\quad = \dfrac{-432d^{10}}{c^5}$

20. $\dfrac{(3a^3b^{-1}c^2)^2}{18a^2b^3c^4} = \dfrac{(3)^2(a^3)^2(b^{-1})^2(c^2)^2}{18a^2b^3c^4}$

$\quad\quad = \dfrac{9a^6b^{-2}c^4}{18a^2b^3c^4} = \dfrac{a^4}{2b^5}$

21. 2.4×10^5

22. 4.88×10^9

23. 3.14×10^{-5}

24. 1.87×10^{-6}

25. $(2x^2 - 5x + 7) - (3x^3 + x^2 + 2)$

$\quad = 2x^2 - 5x + 7 - 3x^3 - x^2 - 2$

$\quad = -3x^3 + x^2 - 5x + 5$

26. $(x^2 - 6xy + 7y^2) + (3x^2 + xy - y^2)$

$\quad = x^2 - 6xy + 7y^2 + 3x^2 + xy - y^2$

$\quad = 4x^2 - 5xy + 6y^2$

27. $11m^2n^2 + 4mn - 6) + 5m^2n^2 - 6mn + 17)$

$\quad = 11m^2n^2 + 4mn - 6 + 5m^2n^2 - 6mn + 17$

$\quad = 16m^2n^2 - 2mn + 11$

28. $(7a^2 + 4) - (3a^2 + 2a - 6)$

$\quad = 7a^2 + 4 - 3a^2 - 2a + 6$

$\quad = 4a^2 - 2a + 10$

29. $y^2 + 7y + 12 = (y + 4)(y + 3)$

30. $b^2 + 5b - 6 = (b + 6)(b - 1)$

31. $a^2 - 10ab + 9b^2 = a^2 + (-1 + (-9))ab + 9b^2$

$\quad\quad = (a^2 - ab) + (-9ab + 9b^2)$

$\quad\quad = a(a - b) + -9b(a - b)$

$\quad\quad = (a - b)(a - 9b)$

32. $2r^2 - 3r - 20 = 2r^2 + (-5 + 8)r - 20$

$\quad\quad = (2r^2 - 5r) + (8r - 20)$

$\quad\quad = r(2r - 5) + 4(2r - 5)$

$\quad\quad = (2r - 5)(r + 4)$

33. $6x^2 - 5x - 6 = 6x^2 + (4 + (-9))x - 6$

$\quad\quad = (6x^2 + 4x) + (-9x - 6)$

$\quad\quad = 2x(3x + 2) + -3(3x + 2)$

$\quad\quad = (3x + 2)(2x - 3)$

34. $56m^2 - 93mn + 27n^2$

$\quad = 56m^2 + (-72 - 21)mn + 27n^2$

$\quad = (56m^2 - 72mn) + (-21mn + 27n^2)$

$\quad = 8m(7m - 9n) + (-3n)(7m - 9n)$

$\quad = (7m - 9n)(8m - 3n)$

35. $\dfrac{2 \text{ cm}}{5 \text{ km}} = \dfrac{x}{16 \text{ km}}$

$\quad 5x = 32$

$\quad\quad x = 6.4 \text{ cm}$

36. $0 < 3.6d < 90$

$\quad 0 < d < 25$

37. $x + y = 16$

$\quad 2.79x + 2.99y = 46.04$

$\quad$ If $x + y = 16$, then $y = 16 - x$

$\quad 2.79x + 2.99(16 - x) = 46.04$

$\quad 2.79x + 47.84 - 2.99x = 46.04$

$\quad\quad -0.2x = -1.8$

$\quad\quad x = 9 \text{ at } \$2.79$

$\quad\quad y = 16 - 9 = 7 \text{ at } \$2.99$

38. x = number of minutes it takes to drive to work.

$\quad 40(x + 1) = 45(x - 1)$

$\quad 40x + 40 = 45x - 45$

$\quad\quad -5x = -85$

$\quad\quad x = 17, \ x + 1 = 18 \text{ min}$

$\quad d = rt = 40 \text{ mph} \cdot \dfrac{18}{60} \text{ hr} = 12 \text{ miles}$

Chapter 6   Quadrilaterals

PAGES 268-269   CHECKING FOR UNDERSTANDING

6-1   Parallelograms

1. A quadrilateral is a four-sided closed figure in one plane.

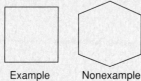

Example   Nonexample

2. Answers may vary. See students' work.
3. both pairs of opposite sides parallel
4. $\overline{FR} \cong \overline{CA}$, $\overline{FC} \cong \overline{RA}$, $\angle F \cong \angle A$, $\angle R \cong \angle C$
5. $\overline{DC}$; definition of parallelogram
6. $\overline{CB}$; Th. 6-1 (Opp. sides of a ▱ are ≅.)
7. $\triangle CBA$; SAS or SSS
8. $\angle ABC$; Th. 6-2 (Opp. ∠s of a ▱ are ≅.)
9. $\overline{EB}$; Th. 6-4 (Diagonals of a ▱ bisect each other.)
10. $\angle ACD$; alt. int. ∠s theorem
11. slope of $\overline{AB} = \dfrac{1 - 6}{1 - 3} = \dfrac{5}{2}$

    slope of $\overline{BC} = \dfrac{6 - 8}{3 - 8} = \dfrac{2}{5}$

    slope of $\overline{CD} = \dfrac{8 - 3}{8 - 6} = \dfrac{5}{2}$

    slope of $\overline{DA} = \dfrac{3 - 1}{6 - 1} = \dfrac{2}{5}$

    Since the opposite sides have the same slope, they are parallel and $ABCD$ is a parallelogram.
12. $m\angle L = 88$, $m\angle A = 92$, $m\angle M = 88$
13. Given: parallelogram $MNOP$
    Prove: $\triangle MNO \cong \triangle OPM$

STATEMENTS	REASONS
1. $MNOP$ is a parallelogram.	1. Given
2. $\overline{MN} \cong \overline{OP}$ $\overline{NO} \cong \overline{PM}$	2. Opp. sides of a ▱ are ≅.
3. $\angle MNO \cong \angle OPM$	3. Opp. ∠s of a ▱ are ≅.
4. $\triangle MNO \cong \triangle OPM$	4. SAS

14. $AB = CD = 31$ $AD = BC = 35$
    $2x + 5 = y + 1$ $3x - 4 = y + 5$
                            $3x - 9 = y$
    $2x + 5 = (3x - 9) + 1$ $y = 3(13) - 9$
         $x = 13$ $y = 30$
    $AB = 2x + 5 = 31$
    $CD = y + 1 = 31$
    $AD = y + 5 = 35$
    $BC = 3x - 4 = 35$

15. definition of parallelogram
16. Th. 6-4 (Diagonals of a ▱ bisect each other.)
17. Th. 6-2 (Opp. ∠s of a ▱ are ≅.)
18. Th. 6-3 (Consecutive ∠s in a ▱ are supp.)
19. $P = DU + UN + KN + KD$

    $3x + 6 = 8x - 4$ $8y - 4 = 2y + 14$
    $-5x = -10$ $6y = 18$
    $x = 2$ $y = 3$
    $DU = 3x + 6 = 12$ $UN = 8y - 4 = 20$
    $KN = 8x - 4 = 12$ $KD = 2y + 14 = 20$
    $P = 12 + 20 + 12 + 20 = 64$

PAGES 269-271   EXERCISES

20. true; definition of parallelogram
21. true; Th. 6-4 (Diagonals of a ▱ bisect each other.), vertical ∠s ≅, and SAS
22. true; Th. 6-2 (Opp. ∠s of a ▱ are ≅.)
23. false
24. false
25. true; Th. 6-4 (Diagonals of a ▱ bisect each other.)
26. $x = 80$; $y = 80$; $z = 100$
27. $x = 30$; $y = 45$; $z = 75$
28. $x = 25$; $y = 35$; $z = 120$
29. $y + (4y + 20) = 180$
    $5y = 160$
    $y = 32$
    $4y + 20 = 148$
    $m\angle R = 32$
    $m\angle S = 148$
30. $m\angle D + m\angle C = 180$
    $(3x - 199) + (x + 75) = 180$
    $4x = 304$
    $x = 76$
    $3x - 199 = 29$
    $x + 75 = 151$
    $m\angle A = 151$
    $m\angle B = 29$
    $m\angle C = 151$
    $m\angle D = 29$

31. (9,4)

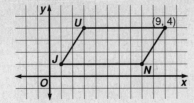

(5,-2)

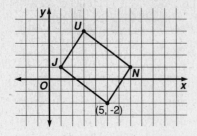

(-3,4)

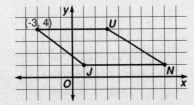

32. Given: Parallelogram $MATH$
    $\overline{MP} \cong \overline{TQ}$
    Prove: $\overline{PH} \parallel \overline{AQ}$

STATEMENTS	REASONS
1. $MATH$ is a ▱. $\overline{MP} \cong \overline{TQ}$	1. Given
2. $\overline{MH} \cong \overline{TA}$	2. Definition of parallelogram
3. $\angle HMP \cong \angle ATQ$	3. If 2 ∥ lines are cut by a transversal, alt. int. ∠s are ≅.
4. $\triangle HMP \cong \triangle ATQ$	4. SAS
5. $\angle MPH \cong \angle TQA$	5. CPCTC
6. $\overline{PH} \parallel \overline{AQ}$	6. If 2 lines are cut by a transversal and alt. ext. ∠s are ≅, then the lines are ∥.

33. Yes; $\overline{JU} \parallel \overline{YL}$ and $\overline{JY} \parallel \overline{UL}$ since if two lines are cut by a transversal so that corresponding angles are congruent, then the lines are parallel. Thus $JULY$ is a parallelogram by definition.

34. No; if $\overline{JU}$ and $\overline{EN}$ were parallel, then $\angle U$ and $\angle N$ would be supplementary. But $m\angle U + m\angle M \neq 180$. So $\overline{JU} \not\parallel \overline{EN}$, and $JUNE$ is not a parallelogram.

35. The opposite angles should be congruent.

36. The opposite sides should be congruent.

37. The opposite sides should be parallel, and if they were parallel, then $\angle ADC$ would be congruent to $\angle BCE$.

38. $(6x + 15y) + 9x = 180$

$15x + 15y = 180$

$x + y = 12$

$x = 12 - y$

$6x + 15y = 12x + 10y + 5$

$6x - 12x = -15y + 10y + 5$

$-6x = -5y + 5$

$x = \dfrac{-5y + 5}{-6}$

$12 - y = \dfrac{-5y + 5}{6}$

$-6(12 - y) = -5y + 5$

$-72 + 6y = -5y + 5$

$11y = 77$

$y = 7$

$x = 12 - y = 5$

$m\angle M = 9x = 45$

39. $2(4a + 20) = 13a \qquad a + b = 2b - 2$

$8a + 40 = 13a \qquad 8 + b = 2b - 2$

$40 = 5a \qquad 10 = b$

$8 = a$

$CM = (a + b) + (2b - 2)$

$= (8 + 10) + (2(10) - 2)$

$= 18 + 18$

$= 36$

40. $m\angle RSX = 55$ and $m\angle XRS = 70$ since opp. ∠s of a ▱ are ≅.

$m\angle SXR = 180 - (m\angle RSX + m\angle XRS)$

$= 180 - (55 + 70)$

$= 55$

41. Given: $ABCD$ is a parallelogram.
    Prove: $\angle BAD \cong \angle DCB$
    $\angle ABC \cong \angle CDA$

STATEMENTS	REASONS
1. $ABCD$ is a ▱.	1. Given
2. $\overline{AD} \cong \overline{BC}$ $\overline{AB} \cong \overline{CD}$	2. Opposite sides of a ▱ are ≅.
3. $\overline{BD} \cong \overline{BD}$ $\overline{AC} \cong \overline{AC}$	3. Congruence of segments is reflexive.
4. $\triangle BAD \cong \triangle DCB$ $\triangle ABC \cong \triangle CDA$	4. SSS
5. $\angle BAD \cong \angle DCB$ $\angle ABC \cong \angle CDA$	5. CPCTC

42. Given: $WXYS$ is a ▱.
    Prove: $\angle W$ and $\angle Z$,
    $\angle X$ and $\angle Y$,
    $\angle W$ and $\angle X$, and
    $\angle Z$ and $\angle Y$ are
    supplementary.

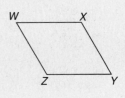

92

Proof: $\overline{WX}$ is parallel to $\overline{ZY}$ and $\overline{WZ}$ is parallel to $\overline{XY}$ by the definition of parallelogram. $\angle W$ and $\angle Z$, $\angle X$ and $\angle Y$, $\angle W$ and $\angle X$, and $\angle Z$ and $\angle Y$ are supplementary, since if two parallel lines are cut by a transversal, consecutive interior angles are supplementary.

43. Given: 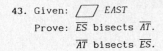 $EAST$
    Prove: $\overline{ES}$ bisects $\overline{AT}$.
    $\overline{AT}$ bisects $\overline{ES}$.

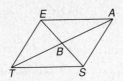

STATEMENTS	REASONS
1. $EAST$ is a ▱.	1. Given
2. $\overline{EA} \cong \overline{ST}$	2. Opp. sides of a ▱ are ≅.
3. $\overline{EA} \parallel \overline{ST}$	3. Definition of a ▱
4. $\angle AEB \cong \angle TSB$ $\angle EAB \cong \angle STB$	4. Alternate interior angle theorem
5. $\Delta EBA \cong \Delta SBT$	5. ASA
6. $\overline{EB} \cong \overline{SB}$ $\overline{AB} \cong \overline{TB}$	6. CPCTC
7. $\overline{ES}$ bisects $\overline{AT}$. $\overline{AT}$ bisects $\overline{ES}$.	7. Definition of bisector

44. Given: $PQST$ is a parallelogram.
    $\overline{RP}$ bisects $\angle QPT$.
    $\overline{VS}$ bisects $\angle QST$.
    Prove: $\overline{RP} \parallel \overline{VS}$

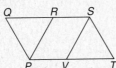

STATEMENTS	REASONS
1. $PQST$ is a ▱. $\overline{RP}$ bisects $\angle QPT$. $\overline{VS}$ bisects $\angle QST$.	1. Given
2. $\angle Q \cong \angle T$ $\angle QST \cong \angle QPT$	2. Opp. ∠s of a ▱ are ≅.
3. $m\angle QST = m\angle QPT$	3. Definition of congruent ∠s
4. $m\angle QST = m\angle QSV + m\angle VST$; $m\angle QPT = m\angle QPR + m\angle RPT$	4. Angle addition postulate
5. $m\angle QSV = m\angle VST$ $m\angle QPR = m\angle RPT$	5. Definition of angle bisector
6. $m\angle QST = 2m\angle VST$ $m\angle QPT = 2m\angle QPR$	6. Substitution
7. $2m\angle VST = 2m\angle QPR$	7. Substitution
8. $m\angle VST = m\angle QPR$	8. Division property of equality
9. $\angle VST \cong \angle QPR$	9. Definition of congruent ∠s
10. $\overline{QP} \cong \overline{ST}$	10. Opp. sides of a ▱ are ≅.
11. $\Delta QRP \cong \Delta TSV$	11. ASA
12. $\angle QRP \cong \angle SVT$	12. CPCTC

13. $\overline{QS} \parallel \overline{PT}$	13. Definition of parallelogram
14. $\angle QRP \cong \angle RPT$	14. If 2 ∥ lines are but by a transversal alt. int. ∠s are ≅.
15. $\angle SVT \cong \angle RPT$	15. Congruence of ∠s is transitive.
16. $\overline{RP} \parallel \overline{VS}$	16. If 2 lines are cut by a transversal and corr. ∠s are ≅, then the lines are ∥.

45. Given: $PQST$ is a parallelogram.
    $\overline{RP}$ bisects $\angle QPT$.
    $\overline{VS}$ bisects $\angle QST$.
    Prove: $\overline{RP} \cong \overline{VS}$

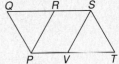

STATEMENTS	REASONS
1. $PQST$ is a ▱. $\overline{RP}$ bisects $\angle QPT$. $\overline{VS}$ bisects $\angle QST$.	1. Given
2. $\angle Q \cong \angle T$ $\angle QST \cong \angle QPT$	2. Opp. ∠s of a ▱ are ≅.
3. $m\angle QST = m\angle QPT$	3. Definition of congruent ∠s
4. $m\angle QST = m\angle QSV + m\angle VST$; $m\angle QPT = m\angle QPR + m\angle RPT$	4. Angle addition postulate
5. $m\angle QSV = m\angle VST$ $m\angle QPR = m\angle RPT$	5. Definition of angle bisector
6. $m\angle QST = 2m\angle VST$ $m\angle QPT = 2m\angle QPR$	6. Substitution
7. $2m\angle VST = 2m\angle QPR$	7. Substitution
8. $m\angle VST = m\angle QPR$	8. Division property of equality
9. $\angle VST \cong \angle QPR$	9. Definition of congruent ∠s
10. $\overline{QP} \cong \overline{ST}$	10. Opp. sides of a ▱ are ≅.
11. $\Delta QRP \cong \Delta TSV$	11. ASA
12. $\overline{RP} \cong \overline{VS}$	12. CPCTC

46.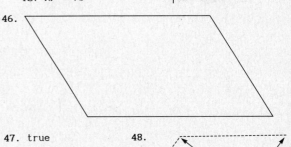

47. true

48.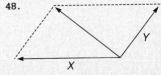

49. =; >

93

50. HA, LL, LA, and HL; see students' explanations.

51. $\overline{TA}$ 52. right; yes; no   53. $\dfrac{0-8}{3-(-4)} = -\dfrac{8}{7}$

54. parallel

55. If a quadrilateral has opposite sides parallel, then it is a parallelogram.

56. See students' work.

6-2 Problem-Solving Strategy: Look for a Pattern

PAGE 273   CHECKING FOR UNDERSTANDING

1. If you continue the pattern found in the example, the number of angles is 66.

2. Since 250 ÷ 4 gives a remainder of 2; the remainder of $3^{250} \div 5$ is 4.

3. yes; 3, 9, 7, 1, 3, 9, 7, 1, ...

4. The sequence is the powers of 2. The next one is 64.

5. The sequence adds the next whole number to the previous term. The next term is 29.

6. The pattern is 6, 2, 4, repeated. The next term is 2.

PAGES 273-274   EXERCISES

7. 7 tables: there are 7 other couples plus Shina and Jeff which makes 16 people. Two people are seated at each table except the end tables which each seat 3 people.

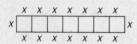

8. The pasture is $\frac{1}{4}$ the area of the cornfield, or 160 acres.

$\frac{1}{4} \times 640 = 160$

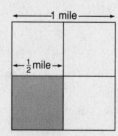

9. 56 pairs: 8 rays form 28 angles, so 8 distinct lines passing through a point will create twice as many pairs of vertical angles. 28 × 2 = 56

10. 1, 2, 3, 5, 7, 9, 11, 15   11. 47

12. Nathan. He caught Tim after he ran 100 yards and there were 5 yard left to the finish line. Since Nathan runs faster, he won.

13. $11^2 = 121$

    $111^2 = 12,321$

   $1111^2 = 1,234,321$

   continuing the pattern, $11,111^2 = 123,454,321$

Cooperative Learning Project

PAGE 274

Let h = hundreds digit;

   t = tens digit; and

   u = units digit.

The value of the number is

$100h + 10t + u$ and $h > u$.

$$
\begin{array}{r}
100h + 10t + u \\
- \quad 100u + 10t + h \\
\hline
100(h - u) + 0t + (u - h)
\end{array}
$$

Since $h > u$, $(u - h)$ will be negative. A ten must be regrouped to find the difference. The digit in the tens place is zero, so a hundred must be regrouped also.

The difference will be

$100(h - u - 1) + 10(9) + (10 + u - h)$.

Reverse the digits and find the sum.

$$
\begin{array}{l}
\quad 100(h - u - 1) + 10(9) + (10 + u - h) \\
+ \ 100(10 + u - h) + 10(9) + (h - u - 1) \\
\hline
\quad 100(10 - 1) \quad + 10(18) + 9 \quad = 900 + 180 + 9 \\
\hphantom{\quad 100(10 - 1) \quad + 10(18) + 9 \quad} = 1089
\end{array}
$$

The sum will be 1089 for any number chosen as long as $h > u$.

Suppose $h = u$. The difference is

$$
\begin{array}{r}
100h + 10t + u \\
- \quad 100u + 10t + h \\
\hline
100(h - u) + 0t + (u - h)
\end{array}
$$

then $(h - u) = 0$. So the result is 0.

6-3 Tests for Parallelograms

PAGES 277-278   CHECKING FOR UNDERSTANDING

1. Answers may vary. See students' work.

2. true

3. false; a sample answer:

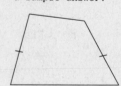

4. false; a sample answer:
ΔWXY ≅ ΔWZY

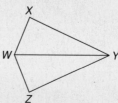

5. false; a sample answer:

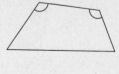

6. Yes; the diagonals bisect each other.

7. No; the top and bottom segments are parallel, but the other pair may not be.

8. No; the congruent sides may not be parallel.

9. Yes; both pairs of opposite angles are congruent.

10. $6y = 30$ $(5x + 10) + 6y = 180$

     $y = 5$ $5x + 10 + 6(5) = 180$

                             $5x = 140$

                              $x = 28$

11. $y^2 = 25$ $x^2 - 2x = 4x + 16$

     $y = \pm 5$ $x^2 - 6x - 16 = 0$

              $(x - 8)(x + 2) = 0$

              $x - 8 = 0$ $x + 2 = 0$

                 $x = 8$ or $x = -2$

12. Find the slopes of the opposite sides.

slope of $\overline{JK} = \dfrac{-2 - (-2)}{3 - 8} = 0$

slope of $\overline{KL} = \dfrac{-2 - (-4)}{8 - 7} = \dfrac{2}{1} = 2$

slope of $\overline{LM} = \dfrac{-4 - (-6)}{7 - 3} = \dfrac{2}{4} = \dfrac{1}{2}$

slope of $\overline{MJ} = \dfrac{6 - (-2)}{3 - 3}$ undefined

Since the slopes of the opposite sides are not the same, the sides are not parallel and $JKLM$ is not a parallelogram.

13. midpoint A of $\overline{JK} = \left(\dfrac{3 + 8}{2}, \dfrac{-2 + (-2)}{2}\right) = \left(\dfrac{11}{2}, -2\right)$

midpoint B of $\overline{KL} = \left(\dfrac{8 + 7}{2}, \dfrac{-2 + (-4)}{2}\right) = \left(\dfrac{15}{2}, -3\right)$

midpoint C of $\overline{LM} = \left(\dfrac{7 + 3}{2}, \dfrac{-4 + (-6)}{2}\right) = (5, -5)$

midpoint D of $\overline{MJ} = \left(\dfrac{3 + 3}{2}, \dfrac{-6 + (-2)}{2}\right) = (3, -4)$

slope of $\overline{AB} = \dfrac{-2 - (-3)}{\frac{11}{2} - \frac{15}{2}} = -\dfrac{1}{2}$

slope of $\overline{BC} = \dfrac{-3 - (-5)}{\frac{15}{2} - \frac{10}{2}} = \dfrac{2}{\frac{5}{2}} = \dfrac{4}{5}$

slope of $\overline{CD} = \dfrac{-5 - (-4)}{5 - 3} = -\dfrac{1}{2}$

slope of $\overline{DA} = \dfrac{-4 - (-2)}{3 - \frac{11}{2}} = \dfrac{-2}{\frac{-5}{2}} = \dfrac{4}{5}$

Since the opposite sides are parallel, $ABCD$ is a parallelogram.

14. Given: $\triangle AEU \cong \triangle OUE$

    Prove: $AEOU$ is a parallelogram.

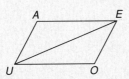

STATEMENTS	REASON
1. $\triangle AUE \cong \triangle OUE$	1. Given
2. $\overline{AE} \cong \overline{OU}$ $\overline{UA} \cong \overline{EO}$	2. CPCTC

3. $AEOU$ is a 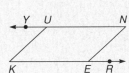.

3. If opposite sides of a quad. are $\cong$, it is a ▱.

15. Given: ▱ $PQRS$
         $\overline{XS} \cong \overline{QY}$

    Prove: $PYRX$ is a parallelogram.

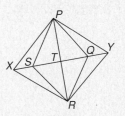

STATEMENTS	REASONS
1. $PQRS$ is a ▱. $\overline{XS} \cong \overline{QY}$	1. Given
2. $\overline{PT} \cong \overline{TR}$ $\overline{ST} \cong \overline{TQ}$	2. The diagonals of a ▱ bisect each other.
3. $ST = TQ$ $XS = QY$	3. Def. of $\cong$ segments
4. $XS + ST = TQ + QY$	4. Addition property of equality
5. $XT = XS + ST$ $TY = TQ + QY$	5. Segment addition postulate
6. $XT = TY$	6. Substitution prop. of equality
7. $PYRX$ is a ▱.	7. If the diagonals of a quad. bisect, it is a ▱.

16. Given: $\overline{UN} \parallel \overline{KE}$
          $\angle YUK \cong \angle REN$

    Prove: $UNEK$ is a parallelogram.

STATEMENTS	REASONS
1. $\overline{UN} \parallel \overline{KE}$ $\angle YUK \cong \angle REN$	1. Given
2. $\angle YUK$ and $\angle NUK$ are a linear pair. $\angle REN$ and $\angle NEK$ are a linear pair.	2. Definition of linear pair
3. $\angle YUK$ and $\angle NUK$ are supplementary. $\angle REN$ and $\angle NEK$ are supplementary.	3. If 2 $\angle$s form a linear pair, they are supp.
4. $\angle NUK \cong \angle NEK$	4. If 2 $\angle$s are supp. to $\cong$ $\angle$s then they are $\cong$.
5. $\angle NUK$ and $\angle UKE$ supp.	5. If 2 $\parallel$ lines are cut by a transversal, consec. int. $\angle$s are supp.
6. $\angle UKE \cong \angle UNE$	6. If 2 $\angle$s are supp. to $\cong$ $\angle$s then they are $\cong$.
7. $UNEK$ is a ▱.	7. If both pairs of opp. $\angle$s of a quad. are $\cong$, it is a ▱.

17. Given: $\overline{SR} \cong \overline{TA}$

$\overline{SR} \parallel \overline{TA}$

Prove: $STAR$ is a $\diagup\!\!\!\!\diagup$.

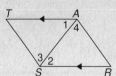

STATEMENTS	REASONS
1. $\overline{SR} \cong \overline{TA}$ $\overline{SR} \parallel \overline{TA}$	1. Given
2. $\angle 1 \cong \angle 2$	2. If 2 $\parallel$ lines are cut by a transversal, alt. int. $\angle$s are $\cong$.
3. $\overline{SA} \cong \overline{AS}$	3. Congruence of segments is reflexive.
4. $\triangle RSA \cong \triangle TAS$	4. SAS
5. $\angle 3 \cong \angle 4$	5. CPCTC
6. $\overline{ST} \parallel \overline{RA}$	6. If 2 lines are cut by a transversal and alt. int. $\angle$s are $\cong$, then the lines are $\parallel$.
7. $STAR$ is a $\diagup\!\!\!\!\diagup$.	7. Definition of $\diagup\!\!\!\!\diagup$

PAGES 278-280   EXERCISES

18. Yes; Theorem 6-5 (Both pairs of opposite sides are $\cong$.)

19. Yes; Theorem 6-8 (Both pairs of opp. $\angle$s are $\cong$.)

20. Yes; opposite sides are parallel.   21. No

22. $m\angle DAB = 180 - 137 = 43$

23. $AC = 2AT$

$5x - 12 = 2(14)$

$5x = 40$

$x = 8$

24. $CD = AB$

$CD = 6$

25. $4x + 7 = 8x - 5$ 26. $BD = 2BT$

$12 = 4x$ $4x + 8 = 2(3x + 1)$

$3 = x$ $4x + 8 = 6x + 2$

$6 = 2x$

$3 = x$

27. $m\angle BCD + m\angle ADC = 180$

$(3x + 14) + (x + 10) = 180$

$4x = 156$

$x = 39$

$m\angle ADC = x + 10 = 49$

28. $5x + y = 7$ $3x - 4y = 18$

$y = 7 - 5x$ $3x - 4(7 - 5x) = 18$

$3x - 28 + 20x = 18$

$23x = 46$

$x = 2$

$y = 7 - 5x$

$= 7 - 10$

$y = -3$

29. $x + y = 5$ $2x + 3y = 14$

$x = 5 - y$ $2(5 - y) + 3y = 14$

$10 - 2y + 3y = 14$

$y = 4$

$x = 5 - y$

$x = 5 - 4$

$x = 1$

30. false; sample answer: 31. false; sample answer:

     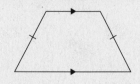

32. Yes; a pair of opp. sides are $\cong$ and $\parallel$. (Th. 6-6)

slope of $\overline{AB} = \dfrac{10 - 17}{8 - 16} = \dfrac{7}{8}$

slope of $\overline{CD} = \dfrac{11 - 4}{16 - 8} = \dfrac{7}{8}$

$AB = \sqrt{(8 - 16)^2 + (10 - 17)^2} = \sqrt{113}$

$CD = \sqrt{(16 - 8)^2 + (11 - 4)^2} = \sqrt{113}$

33. No

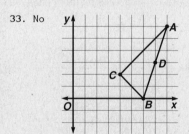

34. No; $AB \parallel CD$ but not $\cong$.

slope of $\overline{AB} = \dfrac{0 - 0}{-4 - 6} = 0$

slope of $\overline{BC} = \dfrac{0 - 4}{6 - 5} = -4$

slope of $\overline{CD} = \dfrac{4 - 4}{5 - 0} = 0$

slope of $\overline{DA} = \dfrac{4 - 0}{0 - (-4)} = 1$

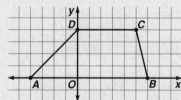

35. No; opp. sides $\not\parallel$

slope of $\overline{AB} = \dfrac{6 - 8}{-2 - 2}$

$= \dfrac{1}{2}$

slope of $\overline{BC} = \dfrac{8 - 8}{2 - 3}$

$= 0$

slope of $\overline{CD} = \dfrac{8 - 3}{3 - (-1)}$

$= \dfrac{5}{4}$

slope of $\overline{DA} = \dfrac{3 - 6}{-1 - (-2)}$

$= -3$

36. Sample answer:

37. Sample answer:

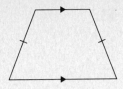

38. Given: $\square NCTM$
$\overline{NA} \cong \overline{ST}$

Prove: $ACSM$ is a parallelogram.

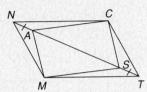

STATEMENTS	REASONS
1. $NCTM$ is a $\square$. $\overline{NA} \cong \overline{ST}$	1. Given
2. $\overline{NC} \cong \overline{TM}$ $\overline{CT} \cong \overline{MN}$	2. Opp. sides of a $\square$ are $\cong$.
3. $\overline{NC} \parallel \overline{TM}$ $\overline{CT} \parallel \overline{MN}$	3. Definition of $\square$
4. $\angle CNT \cong \angle NTM$ $\angle TNM \cong \angle NTC$	4. If 2 $\parallel$ lines are cut by a transversal, alt. int. $\angle$s are $\cong$.
5. $\triangle ANM \cong \triangle STC$ $\triangle ANC \cong \triangle STM$	5. SAS
6. $\overline{AM} \cong \overline{SC}$ $\overline{AC} \cong SM$	6. CPCTC
7. $ASCM$ is a $\square$.	7. If opp. sides of a quad. are $\cong$, it is a $\square$.

39. Given: $\triangle TWA$ is equilateral.
$TBWA$ is a parallelogram.
$TWAI$ is a parallelogram.

Prove: $\triangle IBM$ is equilateral.

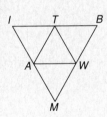

STATEMENTS	REASONS
1. $\triangle TWA$ is equilateral. $TBWA$ is a $\square$. $TWAI$ is a $\square$.	1. Given
2. $m\angle ATW = m\angle TWA =$ $m\angle WAT = 60$	2. Each $\angle$ of an equilateral $\triangle$ measures $60°$.
3. $\angle TAW \cong \angle IBW$ $\angle TWA \cong \angle BIA$	3. Opp. $\angle$s of a $\square$ are $\cong$.
4. $m\angle TAW = m\angle IBW$ $m\angle TWA = m\angle BIA$	4. Def. of $\cong \angle$s
5. $m\angle IBW = 60$ $m\angle BIA = 60$	5. Substitution prop. of equality
6. $m\angle IBW + m\angle BIA +$ $m\angle IMB = 180$	6. The sum of the $\angle$s in a $\triangle$ is 180.
7. $60 + 60 + m\angle IMB$ $= 180$	7. Substitution prop. of equality
8. $m\angle IMB = 60$	8. Subtraction prop. of equality
9. $\triangle IBM$ is equiangular.	9. Def. of equiangular
10. $\triangle IBM$ is equilateral.	10. An equiangular $\triangle$ is equilateral.

40. Given: $\triangle PQR \cong \triangle STV$
$\overline{PR} \parallel \overline{VS}$

Prove: $PRSV$ is a parallelogram.

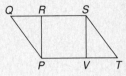

STATEMENTS	REASONS
1. $\triangle PQR \cong \triangle STV$ $\overline{PR} \parallel \overline{VS}$	1. Given
2. $\overline{PR} \cong \overline{VS}$	2. CPCTC
3. $PRSV$ is a $\square$.	3. If one pair of opp. sides of a quad. are $\cong$ and $\parallel$, it is a $\square$.

41. Given: $\overline{BD}$ bisects $\overline{AC}$.
$\overline{AC}$ bisects $\overline{BD}$.

Prove: $ABCD$ is a $\square$.

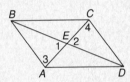

Proof: By the definition of segment bisector, $\overline{AE} \cong \overline{CE}$ and $\overline{BE} \cong \overline{DE}$. $\angle 1 \cong \angle 2$ because they are vertical angles. $\triangle BEA \cong \triangle DEC$ by SAS. Because corresponding parts in $\cong \triangle$s are $\cong$, $\angle 3 \cong \angle 4$ and $\overline{AB} \cong \overline{CD}$. Since $\angle 3$ and $\angle 4$ are are $\cong$ alt. int. $\angle$s, $\overline{AB} \parallel \overline{CD}$. Since a pair of opp. sides are $\cong$ and $\parallel$, $ABCD$ is a $\square$.

42. The opposite sides of the quadrilateral are always congruent, so it is always a parallelogram. The opposite sides of a parallelogram are parallel, so as long as the top bar is parallel to the ground, the glider will be, too.

43. The legs are made so that they bisect each other, so the quadrilateral formed by the ends of the legs is a parallelogram. Thus, the table top is parallel to the floor.

44. Yes; the opposite sides of the quadrilaterals are congruent, so they are parallelograms and opposite sides are parallel.

45. The pattern is to add next odd number, so the next term is 37.

46. $9x + 12 = 15x$ $15x = 30$
     $12 = 6x$ $9x + 12 = 30$
     $2 = x$
Both angles are $30°$.

47. no; triangle inequality; $30 + 35 \not> 66$

48. obtuse; one obtuse angle

$(7x - 8) + (3x + 3) + (18x - 11) = 180$

$28x = 196$

$x = 7$

$7x - 8 = 41$

$3x + 3 = 24$

$18x - 11 = 115$

49. $0 < y < 5$ 50. See students' work.

Technology: Parallelograms

1. yes   2. no

3. change lines 110-170 to use the distance formula to find the length of segments *AB* and *CD*.

6-4 Rectangles

1. Answers may vary. See students' work, A sample answer could be round or triangular books or beds.

2. They bisect each other and are congruent.

3. No; a rectangle is a parallelogram.

4. diagonals congruent, all right angles

5. $2(LP) = MK$ 6. $LJ = KM$

   $2(3x + 7) = 26$ $4x - 12 = 7x - 36$

    $6x + 14 = 26$ $-3x = -24$

        $x = 2$ $x = 8$

7.

           $KP = PJ$

           $x^2 = 7x - 10$

     $x^2 - 7x + 10 = 0$

   $(x - 5)(x - 2) = 0$

        $x = 5$ or $x = 2$

8.

9. No; sample answer:

10. Find the slope of each segment.

slope of $\overline{WX} = \dfrac{1 - 5}{1 - 5} = 1$

slope of $\overline{XY} = \dfrac{5 - 2}{5 - 8} = -1$

slope of $\overline{YZ} = \dfrac{2 - (-2)}{8 - 4} = 1$

slope of $\overline{ZW} = \dfrac{-2 - 1}{4 - 1} = -1$

Since the opposite segments are parallel, *WXYZ* is a parallelogram. The adjacent sides are perpendicular, so *WXYZ* is a rectangle.

11. Given: ▱ *WXYZ*

       ∠1 and ∠2 are complementary.

   Prove: *WXYZ* is a rectangle.

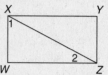

STATEMENTS	REASONS
1. ▱ *WXYZ* ∠1 and ∠2 are complementary.	1. Given
2. $m\angle 1 + m\angle 2 = 90$	2. Definition of complementary
3. $m\angle 1 + m\angle 2 + m\angle W = 180$	3. The sum of the ∠s in a Δ is 180.
4. $90 + m\angle W = 180$	4. Substitution prop. of equality
5. $m\angle W = 90$	5. Subtraction prop. of equality
6. $\angle W \cong \angle Y$	6. Opp. ∠s of a ▱ are ≅.
7. $m\angle W = m\angle Y$	7. Definition of congruent angles
8. $m\angle Y = 90$	8. Substitution prop. of equality
9. ∠W and ∠WXY are supplementary. ∠W and ∠YZW are supplementary.	9. Consec. int. ∠s in a ▱ are supp.
10. $m\angle W + m\angle WXY = 180$ $m\angle W + m\angle YZW = 180$	10. Definition of supplementary
11. $90 + m\angle WXY = 180$ $90 + m\angle YZW = 180$	11. Substitution prop. of equality
12. $m\angle WXY = 90$ $m\angle YZW = 90$	12. Subtraction prop. of equality
13. ∠W, ∠Y, ∠WXY, and ∠YZW are right angles.	13. Definition of right angle
14. *WXYZ* is a rectangle.	14. Definition of rectangle

12. $\angle CNR \cong \angle MNS \cong \angle CTQ \cong \angle MTP$ and $\angle NCR \cong \angle NMS \cong \angle TCQ \cong \angle TMP$. Since $\triangle NCR$, $\triangle NMS$, $\triangle TCQ$, and $\triangle TMP$ all have two angles congruent, the third angles are congruent by the third angle theorem. So, $\angle QRS \cong \angle NSM \cong \angle TQC \cong \angle SPQ$. Since they are vertical angles, $\angle NSM \cong \angle PSR$ and $\angle TQC \cong \angle PQR$.

Therefore, $\angle QRS \cong \angle PSR \cong \angle PQR \cong \angle SPQ$. $PQRS$ is a parallelogram since if both pairs of opposite angles of a quadrilateral are congruent, the quadrilateral is a parallelogram. Since all of the angles are congruent, and the consecutive angles are supplementary, the angles are all right. So $PQRS$ is a rectangle.

PAGES 285-287   EXERCISES

13. $HA = MT$
    $MT = 2(MP)$
    $HA = 2(MP)$
    $\quad = 2(6)$
    $\quad = 12$

14. $AT = MH$
    $\quad = 8$

15. $HP = PT$
    $3x = 18$
    $x = 6$

16. $m\angle 2 = \dfrac{180 - m\angle 1}{2} = \dfrac{18 - 55}{2} = 62.5$

17. $m\angle 4 = 180 - m\angle 3 = 180 - 110 = 70$

18.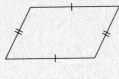

19.

20.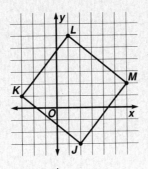

21. a. Use slopes to see if opposite sides are parallel and adjacent sides are perpendicular; use slopes to see if opposite sides are parallel and the distance formula to see if diagonals are congruent.

   b. midpoint of $\overline{JL} = \left(\dfrac{2 + 1}{2}, \dfrac{-3 + 6}{2}\right) = \left(\dfrac{3}{2}, \dfrac{3}{2}\right)$

   midpoint of $\overline{KM} = \left(\dfrac{-3 + 6}{2}, \dfrac{1 + 2}{2}\right) = \left(\dfrac{3}{2}, \dfrac{3}{2}\right)$

   $JKLM$ is a parallelogram because the diagonals bisect.

   $JL = \sqrt{(2 - 1)^2 + (-3 - 6)^2} = \sqrt{82}$

   $KM = \sqrt{(-3 - 6)^2 + (1 - 2)^2} = \sqrt{82}$

   Since the diagonals are congruent, $JKLM$ is a rectangle.

22. $PT = ST = TQ$
    $x + y = 5$ 　　　　 $3x - y = 5$
    $\quad x = 5 - y$ 　 $3(5 - y) - y = 5$
    　　　　　　　　 $15 - 3y - y = 5$
    　　　　　　　　　　 $-4y = -10$
    　　　　　　　　　　　 $y = 2\tfrac{1}{2}$
    　　　　　 $x = 5 - y = 2\tfrac{1}{2}$

23. $PS = QR$ 　　　　 $PQ = SR$
    $y = x + 7$ 　　 $y - 2x = x + 1$
    　　　　 $(x + 7) - 2x = x + 1$
    　　　　　　　 $-2x = -6$
    　　　　　　　　 $x = 3$
    　　　　 $y = x + 7 = 10$

24. $x + y = 2y - 7$ 　 $(x + y) + (2y - 7) = -3x$
    $\quad x = y - 7$ 　　　 $x + 3y - 7 = -3x$
    　　　　　　　　　　 $4x + 3y = 7$
    　　　　　　　 $4(y - 7) + 3y = 7$
    　　　　　　　 $4y - 28 + 3y = 7$
    　　　　　　　　　　　 $7y = 35$
    　　　　　　　　　　　 $y = 5$
    　　　　　　 $x = y - 7 = -2$

25. Since the diagonals of a rectangle are congruent and bisect each other, $\overline{TS} \cong \overline{TR}$ and $\overline{TR} \cong \overline{TN}$. Therefore, since if two sides of a triangle are congruent, the angles opposite them are congruent, $\angle 1 \cong \angle 2$ and $\angle 3 \cong \angle 4$.
    So $m\angle 2 = m\angle 1$
    　　　 $= 32$.
    $\angle 2$ and $\angle 3$ are complementary, so
    $m\angle 2 + m\angle 3 = 90$
    $\quad 32 + m\angle 3 = 90$
    　　　 $m\angle 3 = 58$
    　　　 $m\angle 4 = m\angle 3$
    　　　　　　 $= 58$

26. $MR = 2(ST)$
    $\quad = 2(14.25)$
    $\quad = 28.5$

27. 　　　　　　 $m\angle 1 = m\angle 2$
    　　　　　 $m\angle STR = m\angle MTN$
    $m\angle 1 + m\angle 2 + m\angle STR = 180$
    　　 $2m\angle 1 + m\angle MTN = 180$
    　　 $2m\angle 1 + 116 = 180$
    　　　　　　 $m\angle 1 = 32$
    　 $m\angle MTN + m\angle NTR = 180$
    　　 $116 + m\angle NTR = 180$
    　　　　 $m\angle NTR = 64$
    $m\angle 3 + m\angle 4 + m\angle NTR = 180$
    　　 $2m\angle 4 + 64 = 180$
    　　　　　 $m\angle 4 = 58$

28. slope of $\overline{AB} = \dfrac{2 - 8}{12 - 12}$ = undefined

slope of $\overline{BC} = \dfrac{8 - 8}{12 - (-3)}$ = 0

slope of $\overline{CD} = \dfrac{8 - 2}{-3 - (-3)}$ = undefined

slope of $\overline{DA} = \dfrac{2 - 2}{12 - (-3)}$ = 0

yes; opposite sides parallel, adjacent sides perpendicular, and all right angles

29. slope of $\overline{AB} = \dfrac{-3 - 8}{0 - 4} = \dfrac{11}{4}$

slope of $\overline{BC} = \dfrac{8 - (-4)}{4 - 7} = -4$

slope of $\overline{CD} = \dfrac{-4 - 7}{7 - 11} = \dfrac{11}{4}$

slope of $\overline{DA} = \dfrac{7 - (-3)}{11 - 0} = \dfrac{10}{11}$

no; only one pair of parallel sides and no right angles

30. slope of $\overline{AB} = \dfrac{0 - (-3)}{4 - 6} = -\dfrac{3}{2}$

slope of $\overline{BC} = \dfrac{-3 - 4}{6 - 8} = \dfrac{7}{2}$

slope of $\overline{CD} = \dfrac{4 - 1}{8 - 10} = -\dfrac{3}{2}$

slope of $\overline{DA} = \dfrac{1 - 0}{10 - 4} = \dfrac{1}{6}$

no; only one pair of parallel sides and no right angles

31. slope of $\overline{AB} = \dfrac{8 - 9}{-5 - 6} = \dfrac{1}{11}$

slope of $\overline{BC} = \dfrac{9 - (-2)}{6 - 7} = -\dfrac{11}{1}$

slope of $\overline{CD} = \dfrac{-2 - (-3)}{7 - (-4)} = \dfrac{1}{11}$

slope of $\overline{DA} = \dfrac{-3 - 8}{-4 - (-5)} = -\dfrac{11}{1}$

yes; opposite sides parallel and all right angles

32. yes   33. yes   34. yes   35. no   36. no

37. yes

38. Given: *READ* is a 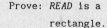.
    ∠R is a right angle.
Prove: *READ* is a rectangle.

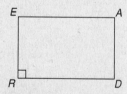

STATEMENTS	REASONS
1. *READ* is a ▱. ∠R is a right angle.	1. Given
2. m∠R = 90	2. Definition of right angle
3. ∠A ≅ ∠R	3. Opposite ∠s of a ▱ are ≅.
4. m∠A = m∠R	4. Definition of congruent ∠s

5. m∠A = 90	5. Substitution of property of equality
6. ∠R and ∠E are supplementary. ∠R and ∠D are supplementary.	6. Consec. ∠s in a ▱ are supp.
7. m∠R + m∠E = 180 m∠R + m∠D = 180	7. Definition of supp.
8. 90 + m∠E = 180 90 + m∠D = 180	8. Substitution prop. of equality
9. m∠E = 90 m∠D = 90	9. Subtraction prop. of equality
10. ∠A, ∠E, and ∠D are right ∠s.	10. Def. of right ∠
11. *READ* is a rectangle.	11. Definition of rectangle

39. a. (22, -2)

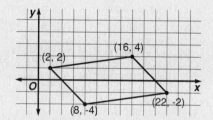

(10, 10)

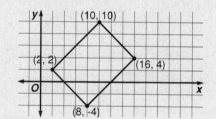

(-6, -6)

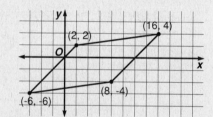

39. b. (10, 10) appears to complete a rectangle. Test this point to see if the quadrilateral has congruent diagonals.

distance from (10, 10) to (8, -4)

$= \sqrt{(10 - 8)^2 + (10 - (-4))^2}$

$= \sqrt{2^2 + 14^2}$

$= \sqrt{200}$

distance from (2, 2) to (16, 4)

$= \sqrt{(2 - 16)^2 + (2 - 4)^2}$

$= \sqrt{(-14)^2 + (-2)^2}$

$= \sqrt{200}$

The diagonals are congruent, so the point (10, 10) completes a rectangle.

40. Left; when stakes F and G are moved Left, $\overline{MK}$ will be extended and the midpoint of $\overline{MK}$ and $\overline{JL}$ will move downward making $\overline{JL}$ shorter.

41. Sample answer: Since all of the angles and the opposite sides are congruent, the bricks are interchangeable and can be installed in rows easily.

42. a. rectangular; 20 by 40 feet (20 feet high)
    b. circular
    c. rectangular; 300 by 200 yards
    d. rectangular; 29.5 by 59 feet
    e. rectangular; 36 by 78 feet
    f. rectangular; 62 feet $10\frac{3}{16}$ inches by 41 inches
    g. rectangular; 100 to 130 by 50 to 100 yards
    h. square infield; 90 by 90 feet
    i. rectangular; 176 by 55 feet (40 feet high)

43. slope of $\overline{AB} = \dfrac{4 - (-2)}{9 - 0} = \dfrac{2}{3}$

    slope of $\overline{BC} = \dfrac{-2 - 6}{0 - (-4)} = -2$

    slope of $\overline{CD} = \dfrac{6 - 6}{-4 - 5} = 0$

    slope of $\overline{DA} = \dfrac{6 - 4}{5 - 9} = -\dfrac{2}{7}$

    no; opposite sides not parallel

44. $P = WE + ES + ST + TW$
    $= 16 + 13 + 16 + 13$
    $= 58$

    $WE = ST$ $ES = TW$
    $3x + 7 = 6x - 2$ $7y - 1 = 2y + 9$
    $-3x = -9$ $5y = 10$
    $x = 3$ $y = 2$
    $WE = 3x + 7 = 16$ $ES = 7y - 1 = 13$
    $ST = 6x - 2 = 16$ $TW = 2y + 9 = 13$

45. $\dfrac{3 - (-4)}{9 - 8} = 7$

46. If a quadrilateral is a rectangle, then it is a parallelogram.

47. 16; possible pizzas: plain cheese; pepperoni; green peppers; mushrooms; onions; pepperoni & green peppers; pepperoni & mushrooms; pepperoni & onions; green peppers & mushrooms; green peppers & onions; mushrooms & onions; pepperoni, green peppers, & mushrooms; pepperoni, green peppers, & onions; pepperoni, mushrooms, & onions; green peppers, mushrooms, & onions; pepperoni, green peppers, mushrooms, & onions

48. See students' work.

Mid-Chapter Review

PAGE 287

1. $\overline{FE}$; definition of parallelogram
2. $\angle GFE$; Theorem 6-2 (Opp. $\angle$s of a $\square$ are $\cong$.)
3. $\overline{HD}$; Theorem 6-4 (The diagonals of a $\square$ bisect each other.)
4. $\triangle HDG$; Th. 6-4 and SAS
5. $\overline{FG}$; Theorem 6-1 (Opp. sides of a $\square$ are $\cong$.)
6. $\overline{HE}$; definition of parallelogram
7. 21 (pattern: add next consecutive whole number)
8. 125 (pattern: consecutive integers^3)
9. 32 (pattern: multiply by -2)
10. $\dfrac{-3}{2}$ $\left(\text{pattern: subtract } + \dfrac{3}{2}\right)$
11. Definition of parallelogram
12. Theorem 6-6 (One pair of opposite sides are both $\parallel$ and $\cong$.)
13. Theorem 6-8 (Both pairs of opp. $\angle$s are $\cong$.)
14. Theorem 6-7 (If the diagonals of a quad. bisect, it is a $\square$.)

15. Given: rectangle $JKLM$
    $\overline{KF} \cong \overline{MH}$
    $\overline{JE} \cong \overline{LG}$
    Prove: $EFGH$ is a parallelogram.

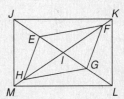

STATEMENTS	REASONS
1. $JKLM$ is a rectangle. $\overline{KF} \cong \overline{MH}$ $\overline{JE} \cong \overline{LG}$	1. Given
2. $\overline{KI} \cong \overline{MI}$ $\overline{JI} \cong \overline{LI}$	2. Diagonals of a $\square$ bisect each other.
3. $KI = MI$ $JI = LI$ $KF = MH$ $JE = LG$	3. Def. of $\cong$ segments
4. $KI = KF + FI$ $MI = MH + HI$ $JI = JE + EI$ $LI = LG + GI$	4. Segment addition postulate
5. $KF + FI = MH + HI$ $JE + EI = LG + GI$	5. Substitution prop. of equality
6. $FI = HI$ $EI = GI$	6. Subtraction prop. of equality
7. $\overline{FI} \cong \overline{HI}$ $\overline{EI} \cong \overline{GI}$	7. Def. of $\cong$ segments
8. $EFGH$ is a $\square$.	8. If the diagonals of a quad. bisect, it is a $\square$.

101

PAGE 290   CHECKING FOR UNDERSTANDING

1. A quadrilateral with four congruent sides has the opposite sides congruent. Since the opposite sides are congruent, it is a parallelogram.

2. Sample answer: Similarities: Both have opposite sides parallel and both have diagonals that bisect each other. Differences: A rhombus has diagonals that are perpendicular, all four sides are congruent, and the diagonals bisect the pairs of opposite angles.

3. A square is a rhombus that is also a rectangle. A rhombus is not always a square, but a square is always a rhombus.

4. square, rectangle, rhombus, parallelogram

5. parallelogram   6. rectangle, parallelogram

7. parallelogram   8. rhombus, parallelogram

9.

	Property	Parallelogram	Rectangle	Rhombus	Square
a.	The diagonals bisect each other.	yes	yes	yes	yes
b.	The diagonals are congruent.	no	yes	no	yes
c.	Each diagonal bisects a pair of opposite angles.	no	no	yes	yes
d.	The diagonals are ⊥.	no	no	yes	yes

10. 66.3

11. 51.8

12. $2x + 10 = 5x - 20$
$-3x = -30$
$x = 10$

13.
$x^2 = 2x + 24$
$x^2 - 2x - 24 = 0$
$(x - 6)(x + 4) = 0$
$x = 6$ or $x = -4$

PAGES 291-293   EXERCISES

14. rectangle, square

15. parallelogram, rectangle, rhombus, square

16. rhombus, square

17. parallelogram, rectangle, rhombus, square

18. square

19. False; the diagonals of a rhombus are not congruent unless it is also a square.

20. True; the diagonals of a parallelogram bisect each other.

21. True; the diagonals of a rhombus are perpendicular.

22. True; since the diagonals of a parallelogram bisect each other and all four sides of a rhombus are congruent, the triangles are congruent by SSS.

23. False; the consecutive angles of a rhombus are not congruent unless it is also a square.

24. **True; the consecutive angles in a parallelogram are supplementary.**

25. $EF = \sqrt{(0 - 2)^2 + (1 - 0)^2}$
$= \sqrt{(-2)^2 + 1^2}$
$= \sqrt{5}$
$= FG = \sqrt{(2 - 4)^2 + (0 - 4)^2}$
$= \sqrt{(-2)^2 + (-4)^2}$
$= \sqrt{20}$

$GH = \sqrt{(4 - 2)^2 + (4 - 5)^2}$
$= \sqrt{2^2 + (-1)^2}$
$= \sqrt{5}$

$EH = \sqrt{(0 - 2)^2 + (1 - 5)^2}$
$= \sqrt{(-2)^2 + (-4)^2}$
$= \sqrt{20}$

The opposite sides are congruent, so $EFGH$ is a parallelogram. However, all sides are not congruent, so it is not a square or a rhombus. We can test for a rectangle by finding the lengths of the diagonals.

$EG = \sqrt{(0 - 4)^2 + (1 - 4)^2}$
$= \sqrt{(-4)^2 + (-3)^2}$
$= \sqrt{25}$
$= 5$

$FH = \sqrt{(2 - 2)^2 + (0 - 5)^2}$
$= \sqrt{0^2 + (-5)^2}$
$= \sqrt{25}$
$= 5$

$EFGH$ is a parallelogram and a rectangle.

26. $EF = \sqrt{(0 - 4)^2 + (0 - (-3))^2}$
$= \sqrt{(-4)^2 + 3^2}$
$= \sqrt{25}$
$= 5$

$GH = \sqrt{(8 - 4)^2 + (0 - 3)^2}$
$= \sqrt{(-4)^2 + (-3)^2}$
$= \sqrt{25}$
$= 5$

$FG = \sqrt{(4-8)^2 + (-3-0)^2}$

$\quad = \sqrt{(-4)^2 + (-3)^2}$

$\quad = \sqrt{25}$

$\quad = 5$

$EH = \sqrt{(0-4)^2 + (0-3)^2}$

$\quad = \sqrt{(-4)^2 + (-3)^2}$

$\quad = \sqrt{25}$

$\quad = 5$

Since all four sides are congruent, *EFGH* is a rhombus and a parallelogram.

$EG = \sqrt{(0-8)^2 + (0-0)^2}$

$\quad = \sqrt{(-8)^2 + 0^2}$

$\quad = \sqrt{64}$

$\quad = 8$

$FH = \sqrt{(4-4)^2 + (-3-3)^2}$

$\quad = \sqrt{0^2 + (-6)^2}$

$\quad = \sqrt{36}$

$\quad = 6$

The diagonals are not congruent, so *EFGH* is not a rectangle or a square.

27. $EF = \sqrt{(2-(-3))^2 + (-3-1)^2}$

$\quad = \sqrt{5^2 + (-4)^2}$

$\quad = \sqrt{41}$

$GH = \sqrt{(1-6)^2 + (6-2)^2}$

$\quad = \sqrt{(-5)^2 + 4^2}$

$\quad = \sqrt{41}$

$FG = \sqrt{(-3-1)^2 + (1-6)^2}$

$\quad = \sqrt{(-4)^2 + (-5)^2}$

$\quad = \sqrt{41}$

$EH = \sqrt{(2-6)^2 + (-3-2)^2}$

$\quad = \sqrt{(-4)^2 + (-5)^2}$

$\quad = \sqrt{41}$

All sides are congruent, so *EFGH* is a rhombus and a parallelogram.

$EG = \sqrt{(2-1)^2 + (-3-6)^2}$

$\quad = \sqrt{1^2 + (-9)^2}$

$\quad = \sqrt{82}$

$FH = \sqrt{(-3-6)^2 + (1-2)^2}$

$\quad = \sqrt{(-9)^2 + (-1)^2}$

$\quad = \sqrt{82}$

The diagonals are congruent. Therefore, *EFGH* is a parallelogram, rhombus, rectangle, and a square.

28. $EF = \sqrt{(0-(-4))^2 + (-4-0)^2}$

$\quad = \sqrt{4^2 + (-4)^2}$

$\quad = \sqrt{32}$

$GH = \sqrt{(0-4)^2 + (4-0)^2}$

$\quad = \sqrt{(-4)^2 + 4^2}$

$\quad = \sqrt{32}$

$FG = \sqrt{(-4-0)^2 + (0-4)^2}$

$\quad = \sqrt{(-4)^2 + (-4)^2}$

$\quad = \sqrt{32}$

$EH = \sqrt{(0-4)^2 + (-4-0)^2}$

$\quad = \sqrt{(-4)^2 + (-4)^2}$

$\quad = \sqrt{32}$

All sides are congruent, so *EFGH* is a rhombus and a parallelogram.

$EG = \sqrt{(0-0)^2 + (-4-4)^2}$

$\quad = \sqrt{0^2 + (-8)^2}$

$\quad = \sqrt{64}$

$\quad = 8$

$FH = \sqrt{(-4-4)^2 + (0-0)^2}$

$\quad = \sqrt{(-8)^2 + 0^2}$

$\quad = \sqrt{64}$

$\quad = 8$

The diagonals are congruent, so *EFGH* is a parallelogram, rhombus, rectangle, and a square.

29. $\overline{IK} \perp \overline{LJ}$, so $m\angle 6 = 90$

$\quad m\angle 1 + m\angle 3 + 90 = 180$

$\qquad m\angle 1 + 62 = 90$

$\qquad\qquad m\angle 1 = 28$

$\qquad\qquad m\angle 4 = m\angle 3$

30. $\quad m\angle 3 = m\angle 4$

$\quad 2x + 30 = 3x - 1$

$\qquad 31 = x$

31. $4(x + 1) + 2(x + 1) = 90$

$\quad 4x + 4 + 2x + 2 = 90$

$\qquad\qquad 6x = 84$

$\qquad\qquad x = 14$

32. Since the diagonals of a square bisect opposite angles,

$m\angle ZXY = \frac{1}{2}(90)$ or 45.

33. $7x - 10 = 5x + 6$

$\quad 2x = 16$

$\quad x = 8$

34. $\quad x^2 = 5x + 24$

$\quad x^2 - 5x - 24 = 0$

$\quad (x - 8)(x + 3) = 0$

$\quad x = 8$ or $x = -3$

35. The diagonals are perpendicular.

Given: KITE is a quadrilateral.

$\overline{KI} \cong \overline{KE}$

$\overline{IT} \cong \overline{ET}$

Prove: $\overline{KT} \perp \overline{IE}$

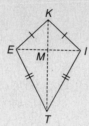

STATEMENTS	REASONS
1. $\overline{KI} \cong \overline{KE}$ $\overline{IT} \cong \overline{ET}$	1. Given
2. $\overline{KT} \cong \overline{KT}$	2. Congruence of segments is reflexive.
3. $\triangle KIT \cong \triangle KET$	3. SSS
4. $\angle IKM \cong \angle EKM$	4. CPCTC
5. $\overline{KM} \cong \overline{KM}$	5. Congruence of segments is reflexive.
6. $\triangle IKM \cong \triangle EKM$	6. SAS
7. $\angle IMK \cong \angle EMK$	7. CPCTC
8. $\angle IMK$ and $\angle EMK$ form a linear pair.	8. Def. of linear pair
9. $\angle IMK$ and $\angle EMK$ are supplementary.	9. If 2 ∠s form a linear pair, they are supp.
10. $m\angle IMK + m\angle EMK = 180$	10. Def. of supp.
11. $m\angle IMK = m\angle EMK$	11. Def. ≅ ∠s
12. $2m\angle IMK = 180$	12. Substitution prop. of equality
13. $m\angle IMK = 90$	13. Division prop. of equality
14. $\angle IMK$ is a right ∠.	14. Def. of right ∠
15. $\overline{KT} \perp \overline{IE}$	15. Def. of ⊥

36. Given: ABCD is a rhombus.

Prove: $\overline{AC} \perp \overline{BD}$

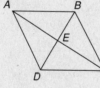

STATEMENTS	REASONS
1. ABCD is a rhombus.	1. Given
2. $\overline{AB} \cong \overline{BC}$	2. Def. of rhombus
3. $\overline{BD}$ bisects $\overline{AC}$ at E.	3. Diagonals of a ▱ bisect each other.
4. $\overline{AE} \cong \overline{CE}$	4. Def. of bisector
5. $\overline{BE} \cong \overline{BE}$	5. Congruence of segments is reflexive.
6. $\triangle ABE \cong \triangle CBE$	6. SSS
7. $\angle BEA \cong \angle BEC$	7. CPCTC
8. $\angle BEA$ and $\angle BEC$ form a linear pair.	8. Def. linear pair
9. $\angle BEA$ and $\angle BEC$ are supplementary.	9. If 2 ∠s form a linear pair, they are supp.
10. $m\angle BEA + m\angle BEC = 180$	10. Def. of supp.
11. $m\angle BEA = m\angle BEC$	11. Def. of ≅ ∠s
12. $2m\angle BEA = 180$	12. Substitution prop. of equality
13. $m\angle BEA = 90$	13. Division prop. of equality
14. $\angle BEA$ is a right ∠.	14. Def. of right ∠
15. $\overline{AC} \perp \overline{BD}$	15. Def. of ⊥

37. Given: ABCD is a rhombus.

$\overline{AF} \cong \overline{BF}$

$\overline{BG} \cong \overline{CH}$

$\overline{CH} \cong \overline{DE}$

$\overline{DE} \cong \overline{AF}$

Prove: EFGH is a parallelogram.

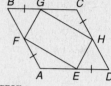

STATEMENTS	REASONS
1. ABCD is a rhombus. $\overline{AF} \cong \overline{BG}$, $\overline{BG} \cong \overline{CH}$, $\overline{CH} \cong \overline{DE}$, $\overline{DE} \cong \overline{AF}$	1. Given
2. $\overline{AB} \cong \overline{BC}$, $\overline{BC} \cong \overline{CD}$, $\overline{CD} \cong \overline{AD}$, $\overline{AD} \cong AB$	2. Definition of rhombus
3. $AF = BG$, $BG = CH$, $CH = DE$, $DE = AF$, $AB = BC$, $BC = CD$, $CD = AD$, $AD = AB$	3. Def. of ≅ segments
4. $AB = AF + FB$ $BC = BG + GC$ $CD = CH + HD$ $AD = DE + EA$	4. Segment addition postulate
5. $AF + FB = BG + GC$ $BG + GC = CH + HD$ $CH + HD = DE + EA$ $DE + EA = AF + FB$	5. Substitution property of equality
6. $FB = GC$, $GC = HD$, $HD = EA$, $EA = FB$	6. Subtraction prop. of equality
7. $\overline{FB} \cong \overline{GC}$, $\overline{GC} \cong \overline{HD}$, $\overline{HD} \cong \overline{EA}$, $\overline{EA} \cong \overline{FB}$	7. Def. of ≅ segments
8. $\angle A \cong \angle C$, $\angle B \cong \angle D$	8. Opp. ∠s of a ▱ are ≅.
9. $\overline{FB} \cong \overline{HD}$, $\overline{BG} \cong \overline{ED}$, $\overline{GC} \cong \overline{AE}$, $\overline{CH} \cong \overline{FA}$	9. Transitive prop. of equality
10. $\triangle FBG \cong \triangle HDE$ $\triangle GCH \cong \triangle EAF$	10. SAS
11. $\overline{FB} \cong \overline{HE}$, $\overline{FE} \cong \overline{GH}$	11. CPCTC
12. Quad. EFGH is a ▱.	12. If opp. sides of a quad. are ≅, it is a ▱.

104

38. two - the diagonals

39. a. $\overline{AC}$ becomes shorter and $\overline{BD}$ becomes longer.

   b. The base of the jack and the plate that supports the car are parallel to the rod between points A and C and perpendicular to the diagonal $\overline{BD}$. The diagonals of a rhombus are perpendicular. Changing the lengths of the diagonals doesn't affect the level of the car.

   c. no; See reason for 39 b. Since the diagonals of other parallelograms are not perpendicular, the car would remain parallel, but the load would shift as the jack was raised.

40.
$$m\angle 1 = m\angle 2 \qquad m\angle 2 + m\angle 3 = 90 \qquad m\angle 4 = m\angle 3$$
$$32 = m\angle 2 \qquad 32 + m\angle 3 = 90 \qquad = 5B$$
$$m\angle 3 = 58$$

41.
$$AC = BC$$
$$y + 5 = 3x - 4$$
$$y = 3x - 9$$

$$CD = AB \qquad\qquad AD = y + 5$$
$$y + 1 = 2x + 5 \qquad\qquad = 35$$
$$(3x - 9) + 1 = 2x + 5 \qquad BC = 3x - 4$$
$$x = 13 \qquad\qquad = 35$$
$$y = 3x - 9 \qquad CD = y + 1 = 31$$
$$= 30 \qquad AB = 2x + 5 = 31$$

42. no solution **43.** yes; LA or AAS

44. Transitive property of equality **45.** plane

46.

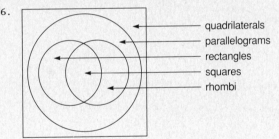

quadrilaterals
parallelograms
rectangles
squares
rhombi

6-6 Trapezoids

PAGES 296-297   CHECKING FOR UNDERSTANDING

1. a.

   b.

   c.

2.

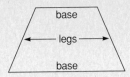

3. Any two positive numbers whose sum is 30. The sum of the measures of the bases is twice the measure of the median. **4.** 9 **5.** 21

6.
$$AC = BD$$
$$4y - 5 = 2y + 3$$
$$2y = 8$$
$$y = 4$$
$$AC = 4y - 5 = 11$$
$$BD = 2y + 3 = 11$$

7.
$$m\angle BAD + m\angle CBA = 180$$
$$123 + m\angle CBA = 180$$
$$m\angle CBA = 57$$

8. 105

9. Graph to find the bases.

endpoints of median $\left(\dfrac{1 + 3}{2}, \dfrac{0 + (-1)}{2}\right) = \left(2, -\dfrac{1}{2}\right)$

$\left(\dfrac{7 + 6}{2}, \dfrac{6 + 2}{2}\right) = \left(\dfrac{13}{2}, 4\right)$

median length $= \sqrt{\left(2 - \dfrac{13}{2}\right)^2 + \left(-\dfrac{1}{2} - 4\right)^2}$

$= \sqrt{\left(\dfrac{-9}{2}\right)^2 + \left(\dfrac{-9}{2}\right)^2} = \sqrt{\dfrac{81}{4} + \dfrac{81}{4}}$

$= \sqrt{\dfrac{162}{4}} = \dfrac{9\sqrt{2}}{2} = 6.364$

10. $x = \dfrac{14 + 27}{2}$

    $= 20.5$

11. $55 = \dfrac{(3x + 5) + (7x - 10)}{2}$

    $110 = 3x + 5 + 7x - 10$

    $115 = 10x$

    $11.5 = x$

12.
$$x^2 = \dfrac{48 + 10x}{2}$$
$$2x^2 = 48 + 10x$$
$$2x^2 - 10x - 48 = 0$$
$$x^2 - 5x - 24 = 0$$
$$(x - 8)(x + 3) = 0$$
$$x = 8 \text{ or } x = -3$$
$x \neq -3$ because $10x = -30$ and a length cannot be negative. Therefore, $x = 8$.

13.
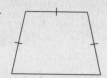

14. Cannot be drawn since the bases are parallel. If they were congruent, the quadrilateral would be a parallelogram.

15.

16. Cannot be drawn: if the diagonals bisected, it would be a parallelogram.

17.
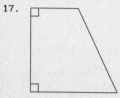

18. Cannot be drawn: no quadrilateral has four acute angles.

19. Cannot be drawn: it would be a parallelogram.

20. $TV = \dfrac{PS + QR}{2} = \dfrac{20 + 14}{2} = 17$

21. $TV = \dfrac{PS + QR}{2}$

23. $2 = \dfrac{PS + 14.3}{2}$

$46.4 = PS + 14.3$

$32.1 = PS$

22. $TV = \dfrac{PS + QR}{2}$

$x + 7 = \dfrac{5x + 2}{2}$

$2x + 14 = 5x + 2$

$12 = 3x$

$4 = x$

23. 57   24. 180 − a   25. 1, 8; 2, 7; 3, 6; 4, 5

26. T coordinates: $\dfrac{x + 0}{2} = 1$, $\dfrac{y + 0}{2} = 3$

$x = 2$, $y = 6$

(2, 6)

S coordinates: $\dfrac{x + 8}{2} = 8$, $\dfrac{y + 0}{2} = 3$

$x = 8$, $y = 6$

(8, 6)

27. Isosceles trapezoid; Justifications may vary.

28. Given: ABCD is an isosceles trapezoid.

Prove: $\overline{AC} \cong \overline{BD}$

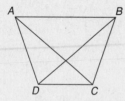

Proof: Since ABCD is an isosceles trapezoid, $\overline{AD} \cong \overline{BC}$. ∠ADC ≅ ∠BCD because the base angles of an isosceles trapezoid are congruent. $\overline{DC} \cong \overline{DC}$ because the congruence of segments is reflexive. So, ΔADC ≅ ΔBCD by SAS. Therefore, $\overline{AC} \cong \overline{BD}$ by CPCTC.

29. Given: Trapezoid RSPT is isosceles.

Prove: ΔRSQ is isosceles.

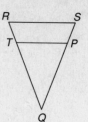

STATEMENTS	REASONS
1. Trapezoid RSPT is is isosceles.	1. Given
2. ∠R ≅ ∠S	2. Base ∠s of an isosceles trapezoid are ≅.
3. $\overline{RQ} \cong \overline{SQ}$	3. If two ∠s of a Δ are ≅, the sides opposite the ∠s are ≅.
4. ΔRSQ is isosceles.	4. Def. of isosceles Δ

30. Given: ΔSQR is isosceles. ΔPQT is isosceles. $\overline{TP} \parallel \overline{RS}$

Prove: RSPT is an isosceles trapezoid.

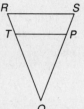

STATEMENTS	REASONS
1. ΔSQR is isosceles. ΔPQT is isosceles. $\overline{TP} \parallel \overline{RS}$	1. Given
2. RSPT is a trapezoid.	2. Definition of a trapezoid
3. $\overline{QP} \cong \overline{QT}$ $\overline{QS} \cong \overline{QR}$	3. Definition of isosceles Δ
4. QP = QT QS = QR	4. Def. of congruent segments
5. QR = QT + TR QS = QP + PS	5. Segment addition postulate
6. QT + TR = QP + PS	6. Substitution
7. TR = PS	7. Subtraction prop. of equality
8. $\overline{TR} \cong \overline{PS}$	8. Definition of congruent segments
9. RSPT is an isosceles trapezoid	9. Def. of isosceles trapezoid

31. a. 3; JKZX, IJXY, IKZY

b. Yes; the bases and legs mus be congruent if they are isosceles.

c. Answers may vary.

32. 100: since m∠SRQ = 120 and m∠RQS = 20, m∠RSQ = 40. Therefore m∠SQP = 40 and m∠QPS = 40, so m∠PSQ = 100.

33. a.

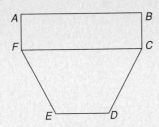 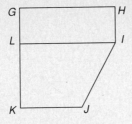

   b. Yes: *IJKL* from the end view is congruent to the trapezoid on the other end of the box.

34. $a = 162$; $b = 81$; $d = \dfrac{100 + 152}{2} = 125$;

   $e = \dfrac{150 + 125}{2} = 137.5$

35. a. 6.18   b. 4.74

36. false; any rhombus that is not a square

37. $(2x - 10) + (6x - 50) = 180$

   $8x = 240$

   $x = 30$

38. yes; detachment

39. $m\angle B = m\angle L$

   $7x + 29 = 9x - 1$

   $15 = x$

   $m\angle B = 7x + 29 = 134$; obtuse

40. See students' work.

Chapter 6 Summary and Review

PAGES 300-302   SKILLS AND CONCEPTS

1. $\overline{ED}$; Th. 6-4   2. $\overline{DC}$; Th. 6-1   3. $\angle ABC$; Th. 6-2

4. $\overline{AD}$; definition of parallelogram

5. $\triangle DAB$; SAS or SSS   6. $\angle 2$; Th. 3-1

7. $\overline{EA}$; Th. 6-4   8. $\angle DCB$ or $\angle DAB$; Th. 6-3

9. Given $\square$ PRSV

   $\triangle PQR \cong \triangle STV$

   Prove: Quadrilateral

   PQST is a

   parallelogram.

 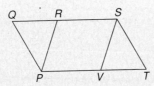

STATEMENTS	REASONS
1. $\square$PRSV $\triangle PQR \cong \triangle STV$	1. Given
2. $\overline{RS} \cong \overline{PV}$	2. Opp. sides of a $\square$ are $\cong$.
3. $\overleftrightarrow{QS} \parallel \overleftrightarrow{PT}$	3. Definition of parallelogram
4. $\overline{QR} \cong \overline{VT}$	4. CPCTC
5. $QR + RS = QS$ $PV + VT = PT$	5. Segment addition postulate
6. $QR + RS = PV + VT$	6. Addition property of equality

7. $QS = PT$	7. Substitution prop. of equality
8. $\overline{QS} \cong \overline{PT}$	8. Def. of $\cong$ segments
9. Quad. *PQST* is a $\square$.	9. If a pair of opp. sides of a quad. are $\cong$ and $\parallel$, it is a $\square$.

10. Given: $\square$PQST

   $\overline{QR} \cong \overline{TV}$

   Prove: Quadrilateral

   PRSV is a

   parallelogram.

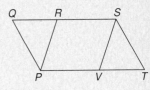

STATEMENTS	REASONS
1. PQST is a $\square$. $\overline{QR} \cong \overline{TV}$	1. Given
2. $\overline{QP} \cong \overline{ST}$	2. Opp. sides of a $\square$ are $\cong$.
3. $\angle Q \cong \angle T$	3. Opp. $\angle$s of a $\square$ are $\cong$.
4. $\triangle QPR \cong \triangle TSV$	4. SAS
5. $\overline{PR} \cong \overline{VS}$ $\angle QRP \cong \angle TVS$	5. CPCTC
6. $\overline{QS} \parallel \overline{PT}$	6. Def of $\square$.
7. $\angle TVS \cong \angle RSV$	7. If 2 $\parallel$ lines are cut by a transversal, alt. int. $\angle$s are $\cong$.
8. $\angle QRP \cong \angle RSV$	8. Congruence of $\angle$s is transitive.
9. $\overline{PR} \parallel \overline{VS}$	9. If 2 lines are cut by a trans. and corr. $\angle$s are $\cong$, the lines are $\parallel$.
10. Quad. *PRSV* is a $\square$.	10. If a pair of opp. sides of a quad. are $\cong$ and $\parallel$, it is a $\square$.

11. $DB = AC$

   $5x - 4 = 6x - 10$

   $6 = x$

12. $m\angle DAC + m\angle CAB = 90$

   $(12x + 1) + (6x - 1) = 90$

   $18x = 90$

   $x = 5$

13. $AB = 2EB$

   $24x - 8 = 2(8x + 4)$

   $24x - 8 = 16x + 8$

   $8x = 16$

   $x = 2$

107

14.
$$AB = DC$$
$$x^2 = 3x - 2$$
$$x^2 - 3x + 2 = 0$$
$$(x - 1)(x - 2) = 0$$
$$x = 1 \text{ or } x = 2$$

15.
$$m\angle BCD = m\angle CDA$$
$$10x^2 = 9x^2 + 9$$
$$x^2 - 9 = 0$$
$$(x + 3)(x - 3) = 0$$
$$x = -3 \text{ or } x = 3$$

16. $FH = 2FJ$
$$= 2(6)$$
$$= 12$$

17. $m\angle FGH = 2m\angle FGJ$
$$= 2(23)$$
$$= 46$$

18. The diagonals of a rhombus are perpendicular, so $m\angle IJF = 90$.

19. $HG = FG$
$$4x - 1 = 20 + x$$
$$3x = 21$$
$$x = 7$$

20. parallelogram **21.** rectangle, parallelogram

22. square, rhombus, rectangle, parallelogram

23. $m\angle SRX = m\angle RTW$
$$35 = m\angle RTW$$

24. $m\angle RSW = m\angle TWS$
$$45 = m\angle TWS$$

25. $m\angle RTW = m\angle SRT$
$$47 = m\angle SRT$$

26. measure of median $= \dfrac{RS + TW}{2}$
$$= \dfrac{23 + 19}{2}$$
$$= 21$$

27. $m\angle XWT + m\angle XTW + m\angle TXW = 180$
$$m\angle XWT + 23 + 127 = 180$$
$$m\angle XWT = 30$$

PAGE 302   APPLICATIONS AND CONNECTIONS

28. 55: (10 cans tall + 9 + 8 + ... + 1)

29. Yes; The corners will each have a 90° angle.

30. 50

Chapter 6 Chapter Test

PAGE 303

1. $\overline{EG}$; Th. 6-4   **2.** $\angle FGH$; Th. 6-2

3. $\overline{GH}$; def. of ▱   **4.** $\triangle HGD$; SAS

5. $\overline{FH}$; Th. 6-10   **6.** $\angle FDH$ and $\angle FGH$; Th. 6-11

7. 13, 21, 34, 55 (Pattern: add two previous numbers.)

8. slope of $\overline{AB} = \dfrac{6 - 11}{-2 - 2} = \dfrac{5}{4}$

slope of $\overline{BC} = \dfrac{11 - 8}{2 - 3} = -3$

slope of $\overline{CD} = \dfrac{8 - 3}{3 - (-1)} = \dfrac{5}{4}$

slope of $\overline{DA} = \dfrac{3 - 6}{-1 - (-2)} = -3$

$ABCD$ is a parallelogram because the slopes of the opposite sides are equal.

9. slope of $\overline{AB} = \dfrac{7 - 2}{-3 - 3} = -\dfrac{5}{6}$

slope of $\overline{BC} = \dfrac{2 - (-1)}{3 - 0} = 1$

slope of $\overline{CD} = \dfrac{-1 - 3}{0 - (-6)} = -\dfrac{2}{3}$

slope of $\overline{DA} = \dfrac{3 - 7}{-6 - (-3)} = \dfrac{4}{3}$

$ABCD$ is not a parallelogram because the slopes of the opposite sides are not equal.

10. slope of $\overline{AB} = \dfrac{-3 - (-2)}{7 - 4} = -\dfrac{1}{3}$

slope of $\overline{BC} = \dfrac{-2 - 4}{4 - 6} = 3$

slope of $\overline{CD} = \dfrac{4 - 2}{6 - 12} = -\dfrac{1}{3}$

slope of $\overline{DA} = \dfrac{2 - (-3)}{12 - 7} = 1$

$ABCD$ is not a parallelogram because the slopes of both pairs of opposite sides are not equal.

11. slope of $\overline{AB} = \dfrac{3 - 2}{11 - 4} = \dfrac{1}{7}$

slope of $\overline{BC} = \dfrac{2 - (-2)}{4 - 1} = \dfrac{4}{3}$

slope of $\overline{CD} = \dfrac{-2 - (-1)}{1 - 8} = \dfrac{1}{7}$

slope of $\overline{DA} = \dfrac{-1 - 3}{8 - 11} = \dfrac{4}{3}$

$ABCD$ is a parallelogram because the slopes of the opposite sides are equal.

12. true

13. false; sample answer:

14. false; sample answer:

15. true

16. $\dfrac{QR + PS}{2} = TV$

$\dfrac{QR + 32}{2} = TV$

$QR + 32 = 52$

$QR = 20$

17. $VR = PT$
$$= 18$$

18. The base angles of an isosceles trapezoid are congruent, so $m\angle QTV = m\angle RVT$. Since they are a linear pair, $\angle RVT$ and $\angle TVS$ are supplementary.

$m\angle RVT + m\angle TVS = 180$

$m\angle QTV + m\angle TVS = 180$

$79 + m\angle TVS = 180$

$m\angle TVS = 101$

19. $TV = \dfrac{QR + PS}{2}$

$= \dfrac{9x + 13x}{2}$

$= 11x$

20. $TV = \dfrac{PS + QR}{2}$

$3x - 10 = \dfrac{(2x + 4) + (x - 3)}{2}$

$6x - 20 = 2x + 4 + x - 3$

$3x = 21$

$x = 7$

$QR = x - 3 = 4$

$PS = 2x + 4 = 18$

$TV = 3x - 10 = 11$

BONUS

Given: $LMNP$

$\overline{MP} \perp \overline{LN}$

Prove: $LMNP$ is a rhombus.

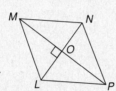

STATEMENTS	REASONS
1. $LMNP$ is a ▱. $\overline{MP} \perp \overline{LN}$	1. Given
2. $\angle MON$, $\angle MOL$ are right $\angle$s.	2. ⊥ lines form 4 right $\angle$s.
3. $\angle MON \cong \angle MOL$	3. All right $\angle$s are $\cong$.
4. $\overline{MO} \cong \overline{MO}$	4. Congruence of seg. is reflexive.
5. $\overline{LO} \cong \overline{NO}$	5. Diagonals of a ▱ bisect each other.
6. $\triangle LOM \cong \triangle NOM$	6. SAS
7. $\overline{LM} \cong \overline{MN}$	7. CPCTC
8. $\overline{LM} \cong \overline{NP}$ $\overline{MN} \cong \overline{LP}$	8. Opp. sides of a ▱ are $\cong$.
9. $\overline{LM} \cong \overline{MN} \cong \overline{NP} \cong \overline{LP}$	9. Trans. Prop. of $\cong$
10. ▱$LMNP$ is a rhombus.	10. Def. of rhombus

College Entrance Exam Preview

1. B; $\angle 1$ is an exterior angle of the triangle, so by the Exterior Angle Inequality Theorem, $m\angle 1 > m\angle 2$

2. A; $2x \boxtimes x^2$

$2 \boxtimes x$ Divide each side by x.

Since $0 < x < 1$, $2 > x$.

3. C; The average of three integers is the sum of the integers divided by 3. So the quanties are equal.

4. A; Simplify: $\dfrac{y^2 - 3y}{\frac{1}{2}(y - 3)} = \dfrac{y(y - 3)}{\frac{1}{2}(y - 3)}$

$= \dfrac{y}{\frac{1}{2}}$

$= 2y$

$2y + 1 > 2y$, so $2y + 1 > \dfrac{y^2 - 3y}{\frac{1}{2}(y - 3)}$.

5. D;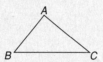

Since $m\angle A > m\angle B$ and $m\angle A > m\angle C$, $BC > AC$ and $BC > AB$. However, we cannot tell the relationship of AC and AB.

6. C; $\ell \parallel m$, $m\angle 1 = m\angle 3$ since they are corresponding angles.

$m\angle 2 + m\angle 3 - m\angle 1 = m\angle 2 + m\angle 3 - m\angle 3$

$= m\angle 2$

7. C; $S = 1 + 2 + 3 + \ldots + 19 + 20$

$= (1 + 20) + (2 + 19) + (3 + 18) + \ldots(10 + 11)$

$= 21 + 21 + \ldots + 21 + 21$

$= 10(21)$

$= 210$

8. B; $40 + 80 + m\angle 2 = 180$

$m\angle 2 = 60$

If the parallel lines are cut by a transversal, the alternate interior angles are congruent, so $m\angle 1 = 40$

Therefore, $m\angle 2 > m\angle 1$.

9. D; If $0 < a < 1$, $\frac{1}{a} > 1$. If $a > 1$, $\frac{1}{a} < 1$. So we cannot determine if $\frac{1}{a} > a$ or $\frac{1}{a} < a$.

10. D; Suppose $x = 1$ and $y = -2$. Then $x > y$, and $|x| = |1| = 1$, $|y| = |-2| = 2$. So $|x| < |y|$. If $x = 2$ and $y = 1$ then $|x| = |2| = 2$ and $|y| = |1| = 1$. So $|x| > |y|$. Therefore, we cannot determine if $|x| > |y|$ or $|x| < |y|$.

11. A; $m\angle 1 + 35 = 180$ $m\angle 2 = 35 + 90$ Exterior

$m\angle 1 = 155$ $m\angle 2 = 125$ Angle Thereom

So $m\angle 1 > m\angle 2$

12. B; $r + s \; \square \; r - s$

         $s \; \square \; -s$ Subtract r from each side.

Since $s < 0$, and the opposite of a negative number is positive, $s < 0$ and $-s > 0$. Therefore, $r + s < r - s$.

13. A; $a* = a^3 - 1$

     $5* = (5)^3 - 1$ $(-5)* = (-5)^3 - 1$

        $= 125 - 1$ $= -125 - 1$

        $= 124$ $= -126$

     So $5* > (-5)*$

14. B; $10^{11} - 10^{10} = 10(10^{10}) - 10^{10}$

                      $= 10^{10}(10 - 1)$

                      $= 10^{10}(9)$

        $10^{10}(9) > 10^{10}$

15. A; Prime factors of $858 = \{2, 3, 11, 13\}$

greatest prime factor = 13

Prime factors of $2310 = \{2, 3, 5, 7, 11\}$

greatest prime factor = 11

So the greatest prime factor of 858 is greater than the greatest prime factor of 2310.

16. C: $4x + 2y = 12$

       $2x + y = 6$

          $y = 6 - 2x$

      $3x - 4y = -2$

   $3x - 4(6 - 2x) = -2$

    $3x - 24 + 8x = -2$

           $11x = 22$

             $x = 2$

          $y = 6 - 2x = 2$

17. $625; \; 6.25 \times 10^2$ 18. $70°$

19. $x - 6y = -33$

     slope $= \dfrac{7 - 5}{9 - (-3)} = \dfrac{1}{6}$

     $y - 7 = \dfrac{1}{6}(x - 9)$

     $y - 7 = \dfrac{1}{6}x = \dfrac{9}{6}$

    $6y - 42 = x - 9$

     $6y - x = 33$

     $x - 6y = -33$

20. $h = 0.75(220 - a)$

21. $\sqrt{293} \approx 17.1$ units $d = \sqrt{(6 - (-11))^2 + (4 - 2)^2}$

                          $= \sqrt{289 + 4} = \sqrt{293}$

                          $= 17.1$ units

22. $S = \dfrac{d}{t}$ 2.5 min $= .041\overline{6}$ hr

    $= \dfrac{5}{.041\overline{6}}$

    $= 120$ mph

23. $\dfrac{x(x + 1)}{(x - 4)(x + 3)}$ is undefined when its denominator is zero.

    $(x - 4)(x + 3) = 0$

    $x - 4 = 0$ or $x + 3 = 0$

        $x = 4$ $x = -3$

Chapter 7   Similarity

7-1   Properties of Proportions

PAGES 310-311   CHECKING FOR UNDERSTANDING

1. $\frac{81}{72}$ and $\frac{1.125}{1}$

2. 72 and 1.125

3. 81 and 1

4. $72 \times 1.125 = 81$ and $81 \times 1 = 81$

5. There are 1.125 boys for every girl.

6. $\frac{78}{77} \approx 1.013$

7. $\frac{84}{84 + 71} = \frac{84}{155} \approx 0.542$

8. $\frac{92}{63} \approx 1.460$

9. $\frac{80}{82} \approx 0.976$

10. $\frac{b}{a} \stackrel{?}{=} \frac{d}{c}$
$\frac{2}{3} = \frac{4}{6}$ yes

11. $\frac{a}{c} \stackrel{?}{=} \frac{b}{d}$
$\frac{3}{6} = \frac{2}{4}$ yes

12. $\frac{c}{b} \stackrel{?}{=} \frac{d}{a}$
$\frac{6}{2} \stackrel{?}{=} \frac{4}{3}$
$3 \neq \frac{4}{3}$ no

13. $\frac{(a + b)}{b} \stackrel{?}{=} \frac{(c + d)}{d}$
$\frac{(3 + 2)}{2} \stackrel{?}{=} \frac{(6 + 4)}{4}$
$\frac{5}{2} = \frac{10}{4}$ yes

14. $\frac{d}{b} \stackrel{?}{=} \frac{c}{a}$
$\frac{4}{2} = \frac{6}{3}$ yes

15. $\frac{x}{3} = \frac{15}{10}$
$10x = 45$
$x = 4.5$

16. $\frac{5}{17} = \frac{2x}{51}$
$255 = 34x$
$7.5 = x$

17. $\frac{x + 1}{x} = \frac{7}{2}$
$2(x + 1) = 7x$
$2x + 2 = 7x$
$2 = 5x$
$0.4 = x$

18. $\frac{AB}{AC} = \frac{FT}{FE}$
$\frac{8}{8 + 6} = \frac{2}{FE}$
$8FE = 28$
$FE = 3.5$

PAGES 311-313   EXERCISES

19. $\frac{12}{24} = 0.50$

20. $\frac{15}{55} \approx 0.27$

21. $\frac{13}{52} = 0.25$

22. $\frac{20}{30} \approx 0.67$

23. $\frac{11}{24} = \frac{x}{24}$
$x = 11$

24. $\frac{5}{8} = \frac{20}{x}$
$5x = 160$
$x = 32$

25. $\frac{b}{3.24} = \frac{1}{8}$
$8b = 3.24$
$b = 0.405$

26. $\frac{4}{n} = \frac{7}{8}$
$7n = 32$
$n = \frac{32}{7}$

27. $\frac{m + 3}{12} = \frac{5}{4}$
$4(m + 3) = 60$
$m + 3 = 15$
$m = 12$

28. $\frac{1}{3} = \frac{t}{8 - t}$
$8 - t = 3t$
$8 = 4t$
$2 = t$

29. $BD = DC$, so $\frac{BD}{DC} = \frac{1}{1}$

30. $BC = 2DC$ so $\frac{DC}{BC} = \frac{1}{2}$.

31. $\triangle ABC$ is equilateral, So $m\angle ABD = 60$. In an equilateral triangle, a median is an altitude, so $m\angle ADC = 90$. So $\frac{m\angle ABD}{m\angle ADC} = \frac{60}{90} = \frac{2}{3}$.

32. a. $RP = RS + SP$
$= 2 + 3$
$= 5$
$\frac{RS}{SP} = \frac{RT}{TQ}$
$\frac{2}{3} = \frac{4}{TQ}$
$2TQ = 12$
$TQ = 6$
$RQ = RT + TQ$
$= 4 + 6$
$= 10$

b. $\frac{RS}{SP} = \frac{RT}{TQ}$
$\frac{RS}{45} = \frac{32}{40}$
$1440 = 40RS$
$36 = RS$
$RP = RS + SP$
$= 36 + 45$
$= 81$

c. $RQ - RT = TQ$
$24 - 16 = TQ$
$8 = TQ$
$\frac{RS}{SP} = \frac{RT}{TQ}$
$\frac{RS}{3 \cdot RS} = \frac{16}{8}$
$8RS = 48 - 16RS$
$24RS = 48$
$RS = 2$
$SP = RP - RS$
$= 3 - 2$
$= 1$

d. $\frac{RS}{SP} = \frac{RT}{TQ}$
$\frac{RS}{36 - RS} = \frac{36}{48}$
$48RS = 1296 - 36RS$
$84RS = 1296$
$RS = 15\frac{3}{7}$
$SP = RP - RS$
$= 36 - 15\frac{3}{7}$
$= 20\frac{4}{7}$
$RQ = RT + TQ$
$= 36 + 48$
$= 84$

33. $\frac{3}{8} = \frac{x}{100}$
$8x = 300$
$x = 37.5$
37.5%

34. $\frac{5}{12} = \frac{x}{100}$
$12x = 500$
$x \approx 41.7$
41.7%

35. $\frac{13}{4} = \frac{x}{100}$
$4x = 1300$
$x = 325$
325%

36. $\frac{a}{b} = \frac{c}{d}$
$ad = bc$
$\frac{a + b}{b} = \frac{c + d}{d}$
$(a + b)d = (c + d)b$
$ad + bd = bc + bd$
$ad + bd - bd = bc + bd - bd$
$ad = bc$

111

37.
$$\frac{a}{b} = \frac{c}{d}$$
$$ad = bc$$

$$\frac{a - b}{b} = \frac{c - d}{d}$$
$$(a - b)d = (c - d)b$$
$$ad - bd = bc - bd$$
$$ad - bd + bd = bc - bd + bd$$
$$ad = bc$$

38.
$$\frac{a}{b} = \frac{c}{d}$$
$$ad = bc$$

$$\frac{a}{b} = \frac{a + c}{b + d}$$
$$(b + d)a = (a + c)b$$
$$ab + ad = ab + bc$$
$$ab + ad - ab = ab + bc - ab$$
$$ad = bc$$

$$\frac{c}{d} = \frac{a + c}{b + d}$$
$$(b + d)c = (a + c)d$$
$$bc + cd = ad + cd$$
$$bc + cd - cd = ad + cd - cd$$
$$bc = ad$$
$$ad = bc$$

39.
$$8 = \frac{10}{x}$$
$$8x = 10$$
$$x = 1.25$$

$$\frac{10}{x} = \frac{y}{5}$$
$$\frac{10}{1.25} = \frac{y}{5}$$
$$1.25y = 50$$
$$y = 40$$

40.
$$\frac{x - 1}{x} = \frac{3}{4}$$
$$3x = 4x - 4$$
$$-x = -4$$
$$x = 4$$

$$\frac{3}{4} = \frac{y}{y + 1}$$
$$4y = 3y + 3$$
$$y = 3$$

41. Answers may vary. A sample answer is $\frac{x}{2} = \frac{11}{y}$.

42. The measures of the angles could be x, x, and $2x$ or x, $2x$, $2x$.

$$x + x + 2x = 180$$
$$4x = 180$$
$$x = 45$$
45, 45, 90

$$x + 2x + 2x = 180$$
$$5x = 180$$
$$x = 36$$
36, 72, 72

43. a. yes

    b. not necessarily; only if they are congruent

44. $\frac{3.5}{10.5}$ or $\frac{1}{3}$

45. $\frac{1}{5.9680} = \frac{500}{x}$

        $x = 2984$

$500 in U.S. dollars = 2984 Swedish kronas

46. $\frac{2.3}{52.6} = \frac{x}{1}$

    $52.6x = 2.3$

       $x \approx 0.044$

Since $0.044 > 0.04$, this is a strong bank.

47. $\frac{24}{54} = \frac{x}{3}$

    $54x = 72$

      $x \approx 1.3$

48. yes; if it is a square

49. No; it fails the triangle inequality since $19 + 31 \not> 55$.

50.

51. If a quadrilateral is a trapezoid, then it has exactly two opposite sides parallel.

52. ·——•————•————•——·
      S Q R

53. See student's work.

7-2   Applications of Proportions

PAGES 316–317   CHECKING FOR UNDERSTANDING

1. Sample answer: Measure the length and the width. Then divide the length by the width. If the quotient is about 1.618, it is a golden rectangle.

2. a. About 8.9 people in 1000 were married in 1895.

    b. 0.3 more people per 1000 were married in 1993 than in 1895.

    c. 92

3. The ratios of real distance to distance on the map should equal each other.

$$\frac{15 \text{ km}}{1 \text{ cm}} = \frac{x \text{ km}}{7.9 \text{ cm}}$$

4. c **5.** a

6.
$$\frac{AB}{AD} = \frac{PQ}{PS}$$
$$\frac{2}{5} = \frac{3}{PS}$$
$$2PS = 15$$
$$PS = 7.5$$

7.
$$\frac{RS}{CD} = \frac{QR}{BC}$$
$$\frac{4.5}{6.23} = \frac{QR}{7.0}$$
$$6.23QR = 31.5$$
$$QR \approx 5.06$$

8.
$$\frac{CD}{DA} = \frac{SR}{SP}$$
$$\frac{21.7}{SP + 4} = \frac{14.0}{SP}$$
$$21.7SP = 14SP + 56$$
$$7.7SP = 56$$
$$SP = \approx 7.27$$

9.
$$\frac{\text{sides of a rectangle}}{\text{diagonals}} \overset{?}{=} \frac{\text{sides of a pentagon}}{\text{diagonals}}$$
$$\frac{4}{2} \neq \frac{5}{3} \quad \text{no}$$

10.
$$\frac{\text{sides of a triangle}}{\text{exterior angles}} \overset{?}{=} \frac{\text{sides of a hexagon}}{\text{exterior angles}}$$
$$\frac{3}{6} = \frac{6}{12} \quad \text{yes}$$

11.
$$\frac{4 \text{ drinks}}{3 \text{ days}} = \frac{x \text{ drinks}}{365 \text{ days}}$$
$$3x = 1460$$
$$x \approx 487$$
about 487 drinks

12.
$$\frac{8 \text{ hits}}{9 \text{ games}} = \frac{x \text{ hits}}{108 \text{ games}}$$
$$9x = 864$$
$$x = 96$$
96 hits

13. $\dfrac{CD}{CT} \stackrel{?}{=} \dfrac{AC}{AT}$

$\dfrac{4}{8} = \dfrac{8}{16}$ yes

14. $\dfrac{BD}{BT} \stackrel{?}{=} \dfrac{AD}{AT}$

$\dfrac{8}{12} \neq \dfrac{12}{16}$ no

15. $\dfrac{AB}{AT} \stackrel{?}{=} \dfrac{BC}{BT}$

$\dfrac{4}{16} \neq \dfrac{4}{12}$ no

16. $\dfrac{AB}{AD} = \dfrac{PQ}{PS}$

$\dfrac{4}{8} = \dfrac{6}{PS}$

$4PS = 48$

$PS = 12$

17. $\dfrac{RS}{CD} = \dfrac{QR}{BC}$

$\dfrac{4.5}{6.3} = \dfrac{QR}{7}$

$6.3QR = 31.5$

$QR = 5$

18. $\dfrac{CD}{SR} = \dfrac{DA}{SP}$

$\dfrac{21.8}{33} = \dfrac{43.6}{SP}$

$21.8SP = 1438.8$

$SP = 66$

19. a. $\dfrac{15.8}{100,000} = \dfrac{x}{3,600,000}$

$100,000x = 56,880,000$

$x = 568.8$

about 569 people

b. $\dfrac{15.8}{100,000} = \dfrac{x}{255,000,000}$

$100,000x = 4,029,000,000$

$x = 40,290$

about 40,290 people

20. a. Tokyo: $\dfrac{26,952}{1089} \approx 24.7$

Sao Paulo: $\dfrac{18,052}{451} \approx 40.0$

New York: $\dfrac{14,622}{1274} \approx 11.5$

Mexico City: $\dfrac{20,207}{522} \approx 38.7$

Seoul: $\dfrac{16,268}{342} \approx 47.6$

b. Seoul; Sample answer: On the average, there are more people living in each square mile in Seoul than in other cities.

21. $\dfrac{QR}{PQ} = \dfrac{BC}{AB}$

$\dfrac{x+3}{4} = \dfrac{x+5}{5}$

$5x + 15 = 4x + 20$

$x = 5$

$BC = x + 5$
$= 5 + 5$
$= 10$

$QR = x + 3$
$= 5 + 3$
$= 8$

22. $\dfrac{DA}{AB} = \dfrac{PS}{PQ}$

$\dfrac{x+2}{x-3} = \dfrac{5}{3}$

$3x + 6 = 5x - 15$

$21 = 2x$

$10.5 = x$

$DA = x + 2$
$= 10.5 + 2$
$= 12.5$

$AB = x - 3$
$= 10.5 - 3$
$= 7.5$

23. $\dfrac{6}{3.25} = \dfrac{x}{10}$

$3.25x = 60$

$x \approx 18.5$

24. a. $\dfrac{20}{14} = \dfrac{x}{10}$

$14x = 200$

$x \approx 14.3$

about 14.3 inches

b. $\dfrac{\text{original} - \text{new width}}{\text{original width}} = \dfrac{x}{100}$

$\dfrac{14 - 10}{14} = \dfrac{x}{100}$

$\dfrac{4}{14} = \dfrac{x}{100}$

$14x = 400$

$x \approx 28.6$

about 28.6%

25. $PS = \sqrt{(2-2)^2 + (1-5)^2}$
$= \sqrt{0^2 + (-4)^2}$
$= \sqrt{16}$
$= 4$

$PD = \sqrt{(2-4)^2 + (1-1)^2}$
$= \sqrt{(-2)^2 + 0^2}$
$= \sqrt{4}$
$= 2$

$RS = \sqrt{(4-2)^2 + (5-5)^2}$
$= \sqrt{2^2 + 0^2}$
$= \sqrt{4}$
$= 2$

$BL = \sqrt{(-2-(-2))^2 + (-1-5)^2}$
$= \sqrt{0^2 + (-6)^2}$
$= \sqrt{36}$
$= 6$

$DR = \sqrt{(4-4)^2 + (1-5)^2}$
$= \sqrt{0^2 + (-4)^2}$
$= \sqrt{16}$
$= 4$

$\dfrac{PS}{BL} = \dfrac{PD}{BA}$

$\dfrac{4}{6} = \dfrac{2}{BA}$

$4BA = 12$

$BA = 3$

$\dfrac{PS}{BL} = \dfrac{DR}{AT}$

$\dfrac{4}{6} = \dfrac{4}{AT}$

$4AT = 24$

$AT = 6$

$\dfrac{PS}{BL} = \dfrac{RS}{TL}$

$\dfrac{4}{6} = \dfrac{2}{TL}$

$4TL = 12$

$TL = 3$

The two possible sets of points are $A(1, 1)$ and $T(1, 5)$ or $A(-5, -1)$ and $T(-5, 5)$.

26. Answers for measures may vary. The ratio closest to the golden ratio is $\dfrac{AC}{AB}$.

27. $\dfrac{76 + x}{90 + x} = \dfrac{90}{100}$

$7600 + 100x = 8100 + 90x$

$10x = 500$

$x = 50$

50 points

28. $3x + 4x + 5x = 72$

$12x = 72$

$x = 6$

The sides are 3(6), 4(6), and 5(6) or 18, 24, and 30 inches long.

29. Sample answer: The newspaper used the following method. If you find the percentage of the population involved in crime in 1991 (5.898%) and the percentage involved in 1992 (5.6%), there are 0.238% fewer people involved in crime. To find the decrease, you divide 0.238 (the change) by 5.898 (the original percentage). The percentage of decrease is about 0.4%. However, most often percentages of change are found by finding the amount of change, in this case 14,438,200 - 14,872,900 or -434,700 and dividing by the original amount, in this case 14,872,900. This method yields a change of $\dfrac{-434,700}{14,872,900}$ or about -0.03%.

30. $\dfrac{2}{1} = \dfrac{x}{82.5}$

$x = 165$

165 Hertz

31. $x + 3x + 2x = 1000$

$6x = 1000$

$x \approx 166.67$

CD component: $166.67, receiver: $500, speakers: $333.33

32. a. $\dfrac{2 \text{ cm}}{8000 \text{ mi}} = \dfrac{x \text{ cm}}{240,000 \text{ mi}}$

$8000x = 480,000$

$x = 60 \text{ cm}$

b. $\dfrac{2 \text{ cm}}{8000 \text{ mi}} = \dfrac{x \text{ cm}}{2200 \text{ mi}}$

$8000x = 4400$

$x = 0.55 \text{ cm}$

c. $\dfrac{2 \text{ cm}}{8000 \text{ mi}} = \dfrac{x}{93,000,000 \text{ mi}}$

$8000x = 186,000,000$

$x = 23,250 \text{ cm}$

d. $\dfrac{2 \text{ cm}}{8000 \text{ mi}} = \dfrac{x \text{ cm}}{864,000 \text{ mi}}$

$8000x = 1,728,000$

$x = 216 \text{ cm}$

33. $\dfrac{25}{36} = \dfrac{x}{30}$

$36x = 750$

$x \approx 20.8$

about 20.8 in.

34. $\dfrac{2 \text{ squares}}{\frac{3}{4} \text{ c. flour}} = \dfrac{6\frac{1}{2} \text{ squares}}{x \text{ c. flour}}$

$2x = \left(\dfrac{3}{4}\right)\left(6\dfrac{1}{2}\right)$

$2x = 4\dfrac{7}{8}$

$x = 2\dfrac{7}{16}$

$2\dfrac{7}{16}$ cups

35. $\dfrac{2000}{8000} = \dfrac{x}{100}$

$8000x = 200,000$

$x = 25$

25%

36. $\dfrac{1 \text{ cm}}{57 \text{ km}} = \dfrac{4.7 \text{ cm}}{x \text{ km}}$

$x = 267.9$

267.9 km

37. a. 1, 1, 2, 3, 5, 8, 13, 21, 34, 55, 89, 144, 233, 377, 610, 987, 1597, 2584, 4181, 6765

b. A term is the sum of the two previous terms.

c. 1, 2, 1.5, 1.666, 1.6, 1.625, 1.61538, 1.619047, 1.617647, 1.6181818, 1.6179775, 1.618055556, 1.6180258, 1.618037135, 1.618032787, 1.618034448, 1.618033813, 1.618032056, 1.618033963; They are closer and closer approximations of the golden ratio.

38. $\dfrac{t}{18} = \dfrac{5}{6}$

$6t = 90$

$t = 15$

39. $x + x + 104 = 180$

$2x = 76$

$x = 38$

$38°, 38°$

40. Answers may vary. A sample answer:

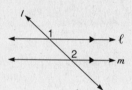

41.

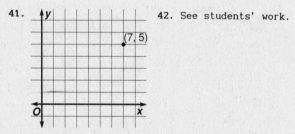

(7, 5)

42. See students' work.

7-3 **Similar Polygons**

PAGE 323   CHECKING FOR UNDERSTANDING

1. Sample answer: Congruence means that two figures are exactly alike. Similarity means that two figures have the same shape, but they may be different in size.

2. Yes; all the angles are congruent and the sides are in the ratio 1:1.

3. No; their sides may not be congruent.

4. No; they may not have the same number of sides.

5. $\angle A \cong \angle D$, $\angle B \cong \angle E$, $\angle C \cong \angle F$, $\frac{AB}{DE} = \frac{BC}{EF} = \frac{AC}{DF}$

6. $\angle R \cong \angle L$, $\angle S \cong \angle M$, $\angle T \cong \angle N$, $\angle V \cong \angle O$, $\angle W \cong \angle P$,

   $\angle X \cong \angle Q$, $\frac{RS}{LM} = \frac{ST}{MN} = \frac{TV}{NO} = \frac{VW}{OP} = \frac{WX}{PQ} = \frac{RX}{LQ}$

7. Yes; corresponding angles are congruent and

   $\frac{2.0}{3.0} = \frac{1.6}{2.4} = \frac{1.8}{2.7}$.

8. No; corresponding angles are not congruent.

9. No; their two pairs of acute angles may not be congruent.

10. **Yes; their corresponding angles are congruent and their corresponding sides are in the ratio 1:1.**

11. **No; they may not have sides with proportional measures.**

12. No; their angles may not be congruent.

13. scale factor: $\frac{LT}{CK} = \frac{8}{12} = \frac{2}{3}$

14. $\frac{LT}{CK} = \frac{TF}{KR}$ 15. $\frac{LT}{CK} = \frac{FE}{RO}$

    $\frac{8}{12} = \frac{10}{KR}$ $\frac{8}{12} = \frac{10}{RO}$

    $8KR = 120$ $8RO = 120$

    $KR = 15$ $RO = 15$

16. $\frac{LT}{CK} = \frac{LE}{CO}$

    $\frac{8}{12} = \frac{15}{CO}$

    $8CO = 180$

    $CO = 22.5$

17. a. perimeter of $LEFT = LE + EF + FT + LT$

       $= 15 + 10 + 10 + 8$

       $= 43$

    b. perimeter of $CORK = CO + OR + RK + CK$

       $= 22.5 + 15 + 15 + 12$

       $= 64.5$

    c. $\frac{\text{perimeter of } LEFT}{\text{perimeter of } CORK} = \frac{43}{64.5} = \frac{2}{3}$

PAGES 324-326   EXERCISES

18. $\frac{3}{1} = \frac{5}{x}$ $\frac{3}{1} = \frac{4}{y}$

    $3x = 5$ $3y = 4$

    $x = 1\frac{2}{3}$ $y = 1\frac{1}{3}$

19. $\frac{5}{7.5} = \frac{8}{x}$

    $5x = 60$

    $x = 12$

    Opposite angles are congruent, so the figures are parallelograms. The opposite sides of parallelograms are congruent, so $y = x$ or $y = 12$.

20.   21.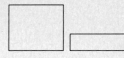

22. impossible   23.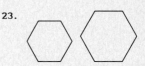

24.    25.

26. $\frac{6}{7} = \frac{17.6}{x}$ 27. $\frac{6.2}{7} = \frac{31}{88}$ or about 0.35

    $6.2x = 123.2$

    $x \approx 19.9$

    about 19.9 inches

28. a. Since the triangles are similar, $m\angle 1 = m\angle A$.

       $m\angle 1 = 25$

    b. $m\angle 1 + m\angle DCE + m\angle 2 = 180$

       $25 + 80 + m\angle 2 = 180$

       $m\angle 2 = 75$

    c. $m\angle 3 = m\angle DCE$

       $= 80$

    d. $\frac{DE}{AD} = \frac{DC}{DB}$

       $\frac{10 - 6}{10} = \frac{5}{DB}$

       $4DB = 50$

       $DB = 12.5$

    e. $\frac{EC}{AB} = \frac{2}{5}$ and $\overline{EC} \parallel \overline{AB}$

29. I.   II.

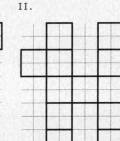

    III.   IV.

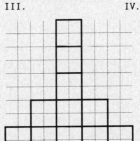   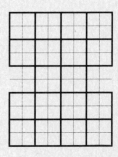

30. a.

	I	II	III	IV
Perimeter of Original	16	28	20	22
Perimeter of Enlargement	32	56	40	44

b.

	I	II	III	IV
Area of Original	10	13	11	18
Area of Enlargement	40	52	44	72

c. The perimeter of the englargement is twice the perimeter of the original.

d. The area of the enlargement is four times the area of the original.

e. The perimeters of the enlargements would be triple the perimeters of the originals.

f. The areas of the enlargements would be nine times the areas of the originals.

g. yes

31. 6 times

32. M is (6, 9) and N is (-6, 9)

or M is (6, -9) and N is (-6, -9)

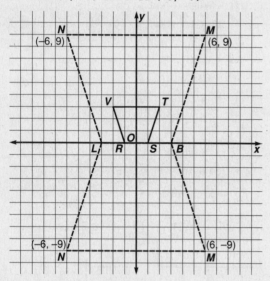

33. M is (0, -4) and N is (3, -2)

or M is (0, 4) and N is (3, 2)

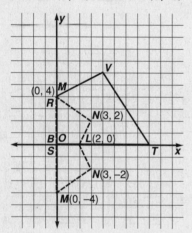

34. The student should draw a rectangle 91 mm by 46 mm.

35. The student should draw a rectangle $5\frac{1}{4}$ in. by $3\frac{1}{8}$ in.

36. The student should draw a rectangle $3\frac{3}{4}$ in. by 6 in.

37. The student should draw a rectangle $4\frac{1}{2}$ in. by $9\frac{3}{4}$ in.

38. a. Yes; the sides are 3:1.

b. No; the areas are in the ratio 9:1.

c. No; the volumes are in the ratio 27:1.

39. $\frac{20}{2} = \frac{x}{9}$

$2x = 180$

$x = 90$

90 cm

40. 8 feet = 96 inches

5 feet 2 inches = 62 inches

2 feet = 24 inches

$\frac{96}{62} = \frac{x}{24}$

$62x = 2304$

$x \approx 37$

about 37 inches

41. $\frac{4}{5} = \frac{3}{x}$

$4x = 15$

$x = 3.75$

3.75 inches

42. $\frac{8\frac{1}{2}}{x} = \frac{1}{8}$

$x = 68$

$\frac{11}{y} = \frac{1}{8}$

$y = 88$

68 by 88 inches

43. $\frac{2}{3} = \frac{x}{21}$

$3x = 42$

$x = 14$

14 seniors

44. trapezoid

45. It is less than 13 and greater than 3.

46. intersecting, parallel, skew

47. If it is cool, then I will wear a sweater.

48. the angle itself, the interior, the exterior

49. Two polygons are similar if their corresponding angles are congruent, and their corresponding sides are proportional.

Technology: Similarity

PAGE 327   EXERCISES

1-3. Answers will vary. See students' work.

4. Yes; the angles are congruent and the sides are proportional.

5. A line parallel to a side of a triangle forms a triangle similar to the original triangle.

7-4　Similar Triangles

1. Two triangles are similar if
   a. Two angles of one triangle are congruent to two corresponding angles of another triangle;
   b. corresponding sides of two triangles are proportional; or
   c. the measures of two sides of a triangle are proportional to measures of two corresponding sides of another triangle and the included angles are congruent.

2. SSS, SAS, ASA, AAS, HL, HA, LL, LA
   Sample answer: Two triangles are congruent and similar by SSS and SAS. To be congruent the parts must be congruent; to be similar the sides must be proportional and the angles be congruent. Two triangles can be also shown to be congruent by ASA and AAS. Two triangles can be shown to be similar by AA.

3. Sample answer: Because the triangles are similar, the sides are proportional. Therefore, $\frac{a}{d} = \frac{c}{f}$. By properties of proportions $\frac{a}{c} = \frac{d}{f}$.

4. $\angle MLP$, $\angle LPT$; $\angle LMT$, $\angle MTP$; $\angle LKM$, $\angle TKP$; $\angle LKT$, $\angle MKP$

5. $\overline{RA}$, $\overline{OF}$; $\overline{AT}$, $\overline{FT}$; $\overline{RT}$, $\overline{OT}$

6. yes; AA Similarity　　　7. no

8. yes; SSS Similarity　　　9. no

10. yes; SAS Similarity　　11. yes; AA Similarity

12. yes; SAS Similarity; $\frac{2}{4} = \frac{x}{9}$
$$4x = 18$$
$$x = 4.5$$

13. yes; AA Similarity;
$$\frac{2}{2 + 4} = \frac{x}{10} \qquad \frac{2}{2 + 4} = \frac{1.5}{1.5 + y}$$
$$6x = 20 \qquad 3 + 2y = 9$$
$$x = 3\frac{1}{3} \qquad 2y = 6$$
$$y = 3$$

14. yes; AA Similarity

15. yes; AA Similarity　　16. no

17. yes; SSS Similarity　　18. no

19. $\frac{QR}{RS} = \frac{QP}{TS}$ 　　　20. $\frac{TS}{QP} = \frac{RS}{QR}$

$\frac{x + 4}{2x + 3} = \frac{3}{5}$ 　　　$\frac{6}{4} = \frac{x + 1}{3x - 4}$

$5x + 20 = 6x + 9$ 　　$18x - 24 = 4x + 4$

$11 = x$ 　　　　　$14x = 28$

$x = 2$

21. $\triangle ABC \sim \triangle ADB$(AA Similarity); $\triangle ABC \sim \triangle BDC$ (AA Similarity); $\triangle ABD \sim \triangle BDC$(Th. 7-3)

22. $\triangle CHB \sim \triangle DHE$(AA Similarity); $\triangle ACE \sim \triangle ADB$ (AA Similarity); $\triangle EAC \sim \triangle BHC$(AA Similarity); $\triangle BAD \sim \triangle BHC$(Th. 7-3); $\triangle EHD \sim \triangle EAC$(Th. 7-3); $\triangle BAD \sim \triangle EHD$(Th. 7-3)

23. $\triangle AEB \sim \triangle ADC$; AA Similarity: 12, 22.5, 7.5

24. $\triangle BVR \sim \triangle BCS \sim \triangle VCT$; AAA Similarity; 9, 4, 3

25. Given: $\angle D$ is a right angle.
$\overline{BE} \perp \overline{AC}$
Prove: $\triangle ADC \sim \triangle ABE$

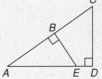

STATEMENTS	REASONS
1. $\angle D$ is a right angle. $\overline{BE} \perp \overline{AC}$	1. Given
2. $\angle EBA$ is a right angle.	2. Definition of perpendicular
3. $\angle A \cong \angle A$	3. Congruence of angles is reflexive.
4. $\triangle ADC \sim \triangle ABE$	4. AA Similarity

26. Given: $\overline{QS} \parallel \overline{PT}$
Prove: $\triangle QRS \sim \triangle TRP$

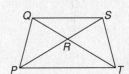

STATEMENTS	REASONS
1. $\overline{QS} \parallel \overline{PT}$	1. Given
2. $\angle SQR \cong \angle PTR$ $\angle QSR \cong \angle TPR$	2. If 2 $\parallel$ lines are cut by a transversal, alt. int. $\angle$s are $\cong$.
3. $\triangle QRS \sim \triangle TRP$	3. AA Similarity

27. Given: $\angle B \cong \angle E$; $\frac{AB}{DE} = \frac{BC}{EF}$
Prove: $\triangle ABC \sim \triangle DEF$

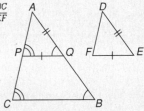

STATEMENTS	REASONS
1. Draw $\overline{QP} \parallel \overline{BC}$ so $\overline{QP} \cong \overline{EF}$.	1. Parallel Postulate
2. $\angle APQ \cong \angle C$; $\angle AQP \cong \angle B$	2. If 2 $\parallel$ lines are cut by a transversal, corr. $\angle$s are $\cong$.
3. $\angle B \cong \angle E$	3. Given
4. $\angle AQP \cong \angle E$	4. Congruence of angles is transitive.
5. $\triangle ABC \sim \triangle AQP$	5. AA Similarity
6. $\frac{AB}{AQ} = \frac{BC}{QP}$	6. Definition of similar
7. $\frac{AB}{DE} = \frac{BC}{EF}$	7. Given
8. $AB \cdot QP = AQ \cdot BC$; $AB \cdot EF = DE \cdot BC$	8. Equality of cross products

9. $QP = EF$ — 9. Definition of congruent segments

10. $AB \cdot EF = AQ \cdot BC$ — 10. Substitution

11. $AQ \cdot BC = DE \cdot BC$ — 11. Substitution

12. $AQ = DE$ — 12. Division property of equality

13. $\overline{AQ} \cong \overline{DE}$ — 13. Definition of congruent segments

14. $\triangle AQP \cong \triangle DEF$ — 14. SAS

15. $\angle APQ \cong \angle F$ — 15. CPCTC

16. $\angle C \cong \angle F$ — 16. Congruence of angles is transitive.

17. $\triangle ABC \sim \triangle DEF$ — 17. AA Similarity

28. Given: $\triangle BAC$ and $\triangle EDF$ are right triangles.

$\dfrac{AB}{DE} = \dfrac{AC}{DF}$

Prove: $\triangle ABC \sim \triangle DEF$

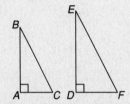

STATEMENTS	REASONS
1. $\triangle BAC$ and $\triangle EDF$ are right triangles.	1. Given
2. $\angle BAC$ and $\angle EDF$ are right angles.	2. Definition of right triangle
3. $\angle BAC \cong \angle EDF$	3. All right $\angle$s are $\cong$.
4. $\dfrac{AB}{DE} = \dfrac{AC}{DF}$	4. Given
5. $\triangle ABC \sim \triangle DEF$	5. SAS Similarity

29. Reflexive property

Given: $\triangle ABC$

Prove: $\triangle ABC \sim \triangle ABC$

STATEMENTS	REASONS
1. $\triangle ABC$	1. Given
2. $\angle A \cong \angle A$ $\angle B \cong \angle B$	2. Congruence of angles is reflexive.
3. $\triangle ABC \sim \triangle ABC$	3. AA Similarity

Symmetric property

Given: $\triangle ABC \sim \triangle DEF$

Prove: $\triangle DEF \sim \triangle ABC$

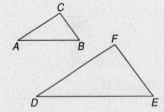

STATEMENTS	REASONS
1. $\triangle ABC \sim \triangle DEF$	1. Given
2. $\angle A \cong \angle D$ $\angle B \cong \angle E$	2. Definition of similar polygons
3. $\angle D \cong \angle A$ $\angle E \cong \angle B$	2. Congruence of angles is symmetric.
4. $\triangle DEF \sim \triangle ABC$	4. AA Similarity

Transitive property

Given: $\triangle ABC \sim \triangle DEF$

$\triangle DEF \sim \triangle GHI$

Prove: $\triangle ABC \sim \triangle GHI$

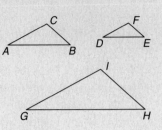

STATEMENTS	REASONS
1. $\triangle ABC \sim \triangle DEF$ $\triangle DEF \sim \triangle GHI$	1. Given
2. $\angle A \cong \angle D$ $\angle B \cong \angle E$ $\angle D \cong \angle G$ $\angle E \cong \angle H$	2. Definition of similar polygons
3. $\angle A \cong \angle G$ $\angle B \cong \angle H$	3. Congruence of angles is transitive.
4. $\triangle ABC \sim \triangle GHI$	4. AA Similarity

30. a. $AB = |7 - (-8)| = 15$

$BC = \sqrt{6^2 + 12^2} = \sqrt{36 + 144} = \sqrt{180} = 6\sqrt{5}$

$CA = \sqrt{6^2 + 3^2} = \sqrt{36 + 9} = \sqrt{45} = 3\sqrt{5}$

$TR = |6 - (-4)| = 10$

$RC = \sqrt{8^2 + 4^2} = \sqrt{64 + 16} = \sqrt{80} = 4\sqrt{5}$

$CT = \sqrt{2^2 + 4^2} = \sqrt{4 + 16} = \sqrt{20} = 2\sqrt{5}$

$\dfrac{AB}{TR} = \dfrac{15}{10} = \dfrac{3}{2}$

$\dfrac{BC}{RC} = \dfrac{6\sqrt{5}}{4\sqrt{5}} = \dfrac{3}{2}$

$\dfrac{CA}{CT} = \dfrac{3\sqrt{5}}{2\sqrt{5}} = \dfrac{3}{2}$

$\dfrac{AB}{TR} = \dfrac{BC}{RC} = \dfrac{CA}{CT}$; $\triangle ABC \sim \triangle TRC$ by SSS Similarity

b. $\dfrac{\text{perimeter of } \triangle ABC}{\text{perimeter of } \triangle TRC} = \dfrac{15 + 6\sqrt{5} + 3\sqrt{5}}{10 + 4\sqrt{5} + 2\sqrt{5}} = \dfrac{15 + 9\sqrt{5}}{10 + 6\sqrt{5}}$

$= \dfrac{3}{2}$

31. One angle must be congruent to its corresponding angle and its adjacent sides must be proportional to their corresponding sides.

32. $\dfrac{QA}{BA} = \dfrac{BA}{AP}$

$\dfrac{2}{6} = \dfrac{6}{AP}$

$2AP = 36$

$AP = 18$

18 ft

33. $\dfrac{1.8}{x} = \dfrac{0.9}{6.0}$

$0.9x = 10.8$

$x = 12$

12 m

34. a. $AB = CD = 8$ $BC = AD = 18$

Since $DCBA$ is a parallelogram, $\angle PAB \cong \angle TCB$.

Therefore, by SAS similarity, $\triangle PAB \sim \triangle TCB$.

b. $\dfrac{PB}{BT} = \dfrac{PA}{TC}$

$= \dfrac{4}{9}$ or $4:9$

35. false   36. true   37. true

38. true   39. false   40. true

41. See students' work.

Mid-Chapter Review

PAGE 335

1. $\frac{12}{16}$ or $\frac{3}{4}$

2. $\frac{1350 \text{ lira}}{1 \text{ dollar}} = \frac{3000 \text{ lira}}{x \text{ dollars}}$

   $1350x = 3000$

   $x \approx 2.22$

   about \$2.22

3. $\frac{29 \text{ miles}}{1 \text{ gallon}} = \frac{2700 \text{ miles}}{x \text{ gallons}}$

   $29x = 2700$

   $x \approx 93.1$

   about 93.1 gallons

4. $\frac{x}{5} = \frac{x - 1}{2}$

   $5x - 5 = 3x$

   $2x = 5$

   $x = 2.5$

5. Two polygons are similar if their corresponding angles are congruent and the measures of their corresponding sides are proportional.

6. yes; AA Similarity

7. David; the right angles are congruent, but the other two pairs of angles may not be.

16. $\frac{x}{16} = \frac{x + 4}{x + 4 + 12}$

   $16x + 64 = x^2 + 16x$

   $64 = x^2$

   $\pm 8 = x$

   -8 is not possible, so $x = 8$.

17.

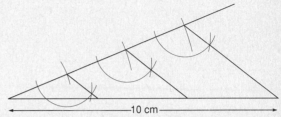

—10 cm—

PAGES 340-341 EXERCISES

18. ER
19. AR
20. AR
21. AE
22. AR
23. DE
24. 24, 30
25. 2, 12
26. 15, 7

27. $\frac{EQ}{QF} = \frac{PE}{DP}$

   $\frac{3}{8} = \frac{x + 2}{12}$

   $8x + 16 = 36$

   $8x = 20$

   $x = 2.5$

28. $\frac{PE}{DP} = \frac{EQ}{QF}$

   $\frac{7}{12 - 7} = \frac{x + 3}{x - 3}$

   $\frac{7}{5} = \frac{x + 3}{x - 3}$

   $7x - 21 = 5x + 15$

   $2x = 36$

   $x = 18$

29. $\frac{AB}{BC} = \frac{DE}{DC}$

   $\frac{6}{x} = \frac{8}{4}$

   $8x = 24$

   $x = 3$

30. $\frac{DC}{DE} = \frac{FA}{FE}$

   $\frac{7}{5} = \frac{8}{x}$

   $7x = 40$

   $x = \frac{40}{7}$

31. $BDAF$ is a parallelogram. So $BD = AF$ and $BA = DF$. $BDEF$ is also a parallelogram, so $BF = DE$. Since B, D, and F are midpoints, $AF = FE$, $ED = DC$, and $CB = BA$. Therefore, $AF = 7$, $FE = 7$, $ED = 12$, $DC = 12$, $CB = 16$ and $BA = 16$. The perimeter of $\triangle AEC = 7 + 7 + 12 + 12 + 16 + 16 = 70$. The perimeter of $\triangle BDF = 7 + 16 + 12 = 35$. perimeter of $\triangle BDF$: perimeter of $\triangle AEC = 35:70 = 1:2$

32. $BDAF$ and $CDFB$ are parallelograms, so $DF = BA$ and $DF = CB$. B is the midpoint of $\overline{CA}$, so $BA = CB = \frac{1}{2}(10)$ or 5. Hence, $DF = 5$. $BDAF$ and $BDEF$ are parallelograms so $AF = BD$ and $FE = BD$. So $AF = FE = 8$. $AE = AF + FE$ by the segment addition postulate, so $AE = 8 + 8$ or 16. $BDEF$ is a parallelogram, so $BF = DE$, so $BF = 4$.

7-5 Proportional Parts

PAGE 339 CHECKING FOR UNDERSTANDING

1. Sample answer: Segments AB and CD are separated proportionally if $\frac{AE}{EB} = \frac{CF}{FD}$.

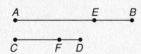

2. Sample answers: $\frac{a}{b} = \frac{c}{d}$, $\frac{a}{c} = \frac{b}{d}$

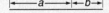 

3. If a line intersects two sides of a triangle and separates the sides into segments of

4. if it is parallel to the third side and intersects the other two sides in two different points.

5. if the endpoints of the segment are the midpoints of the other 2 sides

6. false; proportion does not use corresponding parts

7. true   8. true   9. true   10. yes

11. no   12. yes   13. yes

14. $\frac{10}{7 + 10} = \frac{12}{12 + x}$

   $120 + 10x = 204$

   $10x = 84$

   $x = 8.4$

15. $\frac{2x}{4x} = \frac{8x}{32}$

   $64x = 32x^2$

   $x = 2$

33.

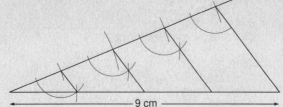

<------------------- 9 cm ------------------->

34. Given: $\frac{DB}{AD} = \frac{EC}{AE}$
Prove: $\overline{DE} \parallel \overline{BC}$

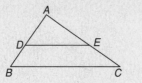

STATEMENTS	REASONS
1. $\frac{DB}{AD} = \frac{EC}{AE}$	1. Given
2. $\frac{AD + DB}{AD} = \frac{AE + EC}{AE}$	2. Addition property of equality
3. $AB = AD + DB$ $AC = AE + EC$	3. Segment addition postulate
4. $\frac{AB}{AD} = \frac{AC}{AE}$	4. Substitution property of equality
5. $\angle A \cong \angle A$	5. Congruence of angles is reflexive.
6. $\triangle ADE \cong \triangle ABC$	6. SAS similarity
7. $\angle ADE \cong \angle ABC$	7. Definition of similar polygons
8. $\overline{DE} \parallel \overline{BC}$	8. If 2 lines are cut by a transversal and corr. $\angle$s are $\cong$, then the lines are $\parallel$.

35. Given: D is the midpoint of $\overline{AB}$.
E is the midpoint of $\overline{AC}$.
Prove: $\overline{DE} \parallel \overline{BC}$
$DE = \frac{1}{2}BC$

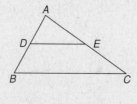

STATEMENTS	REASONS
1. D is the midpoint of $\overline{AB}$. E is the midpoint of $\overline{AC}$.	1. Given
2. $\overline{AD} \cong \overline{DB}$ $\overline{AE} \cong \overline{EC}$	2. Definition of midpoint
3. $AD = DB$ $AE = EC$	3. Definition of congruent segments
4. $AB = AD + DB$ $AC = AE + EC$	4. Segment addition postulate
5. $AB = AD + AD$ $AC = AE + AE$	5. Substitution property of equality
6. $AB = 2AD$ $AC = 2AE$	6. Substitution property of equality

STATEMENTS	REASONS
7. $\frac{AB}{AD} = 2$ $\frac{AC}{AE} = 2$	7. Division property of equality
8. $\frac{AB}{AD} = \frac{AC}{AE}$	8. Transitive property of equality
9. $\angle A \cong \angle A$	9. Congruence of angles is reflexive.
10. $\triangle ADE \sim \triangle ABC$	10. SAS Similarity
11. $\angle ADE \cong \angle ABC$	11. Definition of similar polygons
12. $\overline{DE} \parallel \overline{BC}$	12. If 2 lines are cut by a transversal so that corr. $\angle$s are $\cong$, the lines are $\parallel$.
13. $\frac{BC}{DE} = \frac{AB}{AD}$	13. Definition of similar polygons
14. $\frac{BC}{DE} = 2$	14. Substitution property of equality
15. $2DE = BC$	15. Multiplication property of equality
16. $DE = \frac{1}{2}BC$	16. Division property of equality

36.

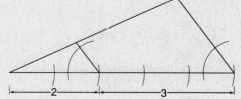

|<----- 2 ----->|<------- 3 ------->|

37.

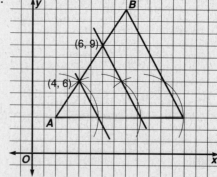

$P(4, 6)$ or $P(6, 9)$

38. $\overline{MN}$ must be parallel to to $\overline{BC}$.

$AM = \sqrt{(3 - 0)^2 + (7 - 10)^2}$
$\quad = \sqrt{3^2 + (-3)^2}$
$\quad = \sqrt{18}$

$\frac{AM}{MC} = \frac{3}{1}$

$\frac{\sqrt{18}}{MC} = \frac{3}{1}$

$3MC = \sqrt{18}$

$MC = \sqrt{2}$

120

slope of $\overleftrightarrow{AM} = \dfrac{7 - 10}{3 - 0}$

$= \dfrac{-3}{3}$

$= -1$

C is on $\overleftrightarrow{AM}$ so $\overleftrightarrow{AC}$ will be the same line. So, the slope of $\overleftrightarrow{AC} = -1$.

slope of $\overleftrightarrow{AC} = \dfrac{7 - y}{3 - x}$

$-1 = \dfrac{7 - y}{3 - x}$

$x - 3 = 7 - y$

$x = 10 - y$

$MC = \sqrt{(0 - x)^2 + (10 - y)^2}$

$\sqrt{2} = \sqrt{(0 - (10 - y))^2 + (10 - y)^2}$

$2 = (y - 10)^2 + (10 - y)^2$

$2 = y^2 - 20y + 100 + y^2 - 20y + 100$

$0 = 2y^2 - 40y + 198$

$y = 11$ or 9

If $y = 9$, $x = 1$, but $(1, 9)$ is between A and M, so $(1, 9)$ is not C. If $y = 11$, $x = -1$. $C = (-1, 11)$.

slope of $\overleftrightarrow{AN} = \dfrac{7 - 22}{3 - 8}$

$= \dfrac{-15}{-5}$

$= 3$

B is on $\overleftrightarrow{AN}$ so $\overleftrightarrow{AB}$ will be the same line. So the slope of $\overleftrightarrow{AB} = 3$.

slope of $\overleftrightarrow{AB} = \dfrac{7 - y}{3 - x}$

$3 = \dfrac{7 - y}{3 - x}$

$9 - 3x = 7 - y$

$y = 3x - 2$

$\overline{AC}$ and $\overline{AB}$ are divided proportionally,

so $\dfrac{AM}{MC} = \dfrac{AN}{NB} = \dfrac{3}{1}$.

$AN = \sqrt{(3 - 8)^2 + (7 - 22)^2}$

$= \sqrt{(-5)^2 + (-15)^2}$

$= \sqrt{250}$

$\dfrac{AN}{NB} = \dfrac{3}{1}$

$\dfrac{\sqrt{250}}{NB} = \dfrac{3}{1}$

$3NB = \sqrt{250}$

$NB = \dfrac{\sqrt{250}}{3}$

$NB = \sqrt{(8 - x)^2 + (22 - y)^2}$

$\dfrac{\sqrt{250}}{3} = \sqrt{(8 - x)^2 + (22 - (3x - 2))^2}$

$\dfrac{250}{9} = (8 - x)^2 + (24 - 3x)^2$

$\dfrac{250}{9} = 64 - 16x + x^2 + 576 - 144x + 9x^2$

$\dfrac{250}{9} = 10x^2 - 160x + 640$

$0 = 10x^2 - 160x + 612\tfrac{2}{9}$

$y = 9\tfrac{2}{3}$ or $6\tfrac{1}{3}$

If $y = 6\tfrac{1}{3}$, $x = 17$. But $\left(17, 6\tfrac{1}{3}\right)$ is between A and N. If $y = 9\tfrac{2}{3}$, $x = 27$. $B = \left(9\tfrac{2}{3}, 27\right)$.

39. parallelogram; Draw diagonal $\overline{SV}$. $\overline{AD}$ and $\overline{BC}$ are parallel to $\overline{SV}$ since they divide the sides of $\triangle RSV$ and $\triangle TSV$ proportionally and are therefore parallel to each other. $\overline{AD}$ and $\overline{BC}$ are equal to $\tfrac{1}{2}SV$ and therefore $\overline{AD} \cong \overline{BC}$. Since $\overline{AD} \parallel \overline{BC}$ and $\overline{AD} \cong \overline{BC}$, $ABCD$ is a parallelogram.

40. a.

b. the west side, there are fewer steps to get to the same height

c. $\dfrac{33}{44} = \dfrac{x}{52}$

$44x = 1715$

$x = 39$

39 steps

41. $\dfrac{60}{350} = \dfrac{w}{432}$ $\dfrac{70}{350} = \dfrac{y}{432}$

$350w = 25,920$ $350y = 30,240$

$w = 74.1$ ft $y = 86.4$ ft

$\dfrac{65}{350} = \dfrac{x}{432}$ $\dfrac{75}{350} = \dfrac{z}{432}$

$350x = 28,080$ $350z = 32,400$

$x = 80.2$ $z = 92.6$ ft

$v = 432 - 74.1 - 80.2 - 86.4 - 92.6 = 98.7$ ft

42. Draw a line 10 units long. Place 100-marks at the endpoints. Draw a line between the 35-marks. The length of the new line will be 35% of the length of the original line.

43. $\dfrac{3}{5} = \dfrac{15}{x}$ 44. $\angle R, \angle Q, \angle P$

$3x = 75$

$x = 25$

25 cm

121

45. $(7x - 1) + (18x + 2) + (5x + 10) = 180$

$$30x + 11 = 180$$
$$30x = 169$$
$$x = 5\frac{19}{30}$$
$$18x + 2 = 18\left(5\frac{19}{30}\right) + 2$$
$$= 103\frac{2}{5}$$

The triangle is obtuse.

46. slope $= \dfrac{14 - (-21)}{-22 - 8}$

$$= \frac{35}{-30}$$
$$= -\frac{7}{6}$$

47. Addition property of equality

48. See students' work.

7-6 Parts of Similar Triangles

PAGES 345-346   CHECKING FOR UNDERSTANDING

1.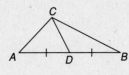

The ratio of medians is the same as the ratio of corresponding sides: $\dfrac{CD}{GH} = \dfrac{AB}{EF} = \dfrac{BC}{FG} = \dfrac{AC}{EG}$.

2.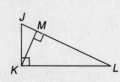

The ratio of the altitudes is the same as the ratio of corresponding sides: $\dfrac{KM}{OQ} = \dfrac{JK}{NO} = \dfrac{KL}{OP} = \dfrac{LJ}{PN}$.

3. only if $\triangle ABC$ is equiangular

4. true   5. false   6. true   7. true

8. $\dfrac{5}{8} = \dfrac{9}{x}$

$$5x = 72$$
$$x = 14.4$$

9. $\dfrac{x}{9} = \dfrac{8}{2x}$

$$2x^2 = 72$$
$$x^2 = 36$$
$$x = \pm 6$$

Since x is a measure it cannot be negative, so $x = 6$.

10. $\dfrac{PR}{AC} = \dfrac{\text{perimeter of } \triangle PQR}{\text{perimeter of } \triangle ABC}$

$$\frac{1.8}{1.2} = \frac{x}{3.4}$$
$$1.2x = 6.12$$
$$x = 5.1$$

perimeter of $\triangle PQR = 5.1$

PAGES 346-348   EXERCISES

11. true   12. false   13. false
14. true   15. true   16. true

17. $\dfrac{AC}{DF} = \dfrac{BR}{ES}$

$$\frac{20}{12} = \frac{x}{5}$$
$$12x = 100$$
$$x = 8\frac{1}{3}$$

18. $\dfrac{BC}{BR} = \dfrac{EF}{ES}$

$$\frac{x + 2}{x - 5} = \frac{16}{6}$$
$$16x - 80 = 6x + 12$$
$$10x = 92$$
$$x = 9.2$$

19. $\dfrac{18}{24} = \dfrac{x}{9}$

$$24x = 162$$
$$x = 6.75$$

20. $\dfrac{10}{12} = \dfrac{x}{18 - x}$

$$12x = 180 - 10x$$
$$22x = 180$$
$$x = 8\frac{2}{11}$$

21. $\dfrac{x}{4} = \dfrac{x + 3}{6}$

$$6x = 4x + 12$$
$$2x = 12$$
$$x = 6$$

22. $\dfrac{XZ}{WZ} = \dfrac{KM}{JM}$

$$\frac{4}{3} = \frac{2x - 5}{\frac{1}{2}(x + 2)}$$
$$2x + 4 = 6x - 15$$
$$19 = 4x$$
$$4.75 = x$$
$$JM = \frac{1}{2}(x + 2)$$
$$= \frac{1}{2}(4.75 + 2)$$
$$= 3.375$$

23. $\dfrac{AX}{AB} = \dfrac{DY}{DE}$

$$\frac{6}{8} = \frac{x + 1}{x^2}$$
$$6x^2 = 8x + 8$$
$$0 = 3x^2 - 4x - 4$$
$$x = 2 \text{ or } -\frac{2}{3}$$

If $x = 2$, $DY = 2 + 1$ or 3.

If $x = -\frac{2}{3}$, $DY = -\frac{2}{3} + 1$ or $\frac{1}{3}$.

24. $\dfrac{SU}{WY} = \dfrac{\text{perimeter of } \triangle STU}{\text{perimeter of } \triangle WZY}$

$$\frac{8}{12} = \frac{30}{12 + 2x + 1 + 4x - 4}$$
$$\frac{8}{12} = \frac{30}{6x + 9}$$
$$48x + 72 = 360$$
$$48x = 288$$
$$x = 6$$

122

25. In $\triangle UVT$,

$\dfrac{UV}{US} = \dfrac{VT}{TS}$

$\dfrac{10}{5} = \dfrac{VT}{12 - VT}$

$5VT = 120 - 10VT$

$15VT = 120$

$VT = 8$

$\triangle UVT \sim \triangle UWR$

$\dfrac{UW}{UV} = \dfrac{WR}{VT}$

$\dfrac{UW}{10} = \dfrac{15}{8}$

$8UW = 150$

$UW = 18.75$

26. perimeter of $\triangle LMN = LM + LN + MN$

$7.6 = 3.0 + LN + 2.8$

$1.8 = LN$

$\dfrac{LM}{XY} = \dfrac{LN}{XZ}$

$\dfrac{3.0}{2.7} = \dfrac{1.8}{XZ}$

$3.0XZ = 4.86$

$XZ = 1.62$

27. $\angle BAD \cong \angle CAD$

$\overline{BD} \cong \overline{DC}$

$\dfrac{BD}{DC} = \dfrac{BA}{AC}$

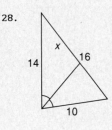

Since $BD = DC$, $\dfrac{BD}{DC} = 1$.

$1 = \dfrac{BA}{AC}$, so $BA = AC$ and

$\dfrac{BA}{AC} = \dfrac{1}{1}$.

28.

$\dfrac{14}{10} = \dfrac{x}{16 - x}$

$10x = 224 - 14x$

$24x = 224$

$x = 9\dfrac{1}{3}$

$16 - x = 16 - 9\dfrac{1}{3}$

$= 6\dfrac{2}{3}$

29. Given: $\triangle ABC \sim \triangle RST$

$\overline{AD}$ is a median
of $\triangle ABC$.

$\overline{RU}$ is a median
of $\triangle RST$.

Prove: $\dfrac{AD}{RU} = \dfrac{AB}{RS}$

Proof: We are given that $\triangle ABC \sim \triangle RST$, $\overline{AD}$ is a
median of $\triangle ABC$, and $\overline{RU}$ is a median of
$\triangle RST$. So, by the definition of median,
$CD = DB$ and $TU = US$. According to the
definition of similar polygons, $\dfrac{AB}{RS} = \dfrac{CB}{TS}$.
$CB = CD + DB$ and $TS = TU + US$ by the
segment addition postulate.

Substituting: $\dfrac{AB}{RS} = \dfrac{CD + DB}{TU + US}$

$\dfrac{AB}{RS} = \dfrac{DB + DB}{US + US}$

$\dfrac{AB}{RS} = \dfrac{2DB}{2US}$

$\dfrac{AB}{RS} = \dfrac{DB}{US}$

$\angle B \cong \angle S$ by the definition of similar
polygons, and $\triangle ABD \sim \triangle RSU$ using SAS
Similarity. Therefore, $\dfrac{AD}{RU} = \dfrac{AB}{RS}$ by the
definition of similar polygons.

30. Given: $\triangle ABC$

$\overline{DC}$ bisects $\angle ACB$.

Prove: $\dfrac{AD}{DB} = \dfrac{AC}{BC}$

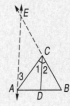

Proof: Construct a line through point A parallel
to $\overline{DC}$ meeting $\overleftrightarrow{BC}$ at E. Since $\overline{DC} \parallel \overline{AE}$,
$\dfrac{AD}{DB} = \dfrac{EC}{BC}$. We are given that $\overline{DC}$ bisects
$\angle ACB$. So by the definition of bisector,
$\angle 1 \cong \angle 2$. $\angle 1 \cong \angle 3$ because they are
alternate interior angles and $\angle 2 \cong \angle E$
because they are corresonding angles.
Therefore, since congruence of angles is
transitive, $\angle 3 \cong \angle E$. $\overline{EC} \cong \overline{AC}$ since if two
angles of a triangle are congruent, the
sides opposite the angles are congruent.
Therefore $EC = AC$ and $\dfrac{AD}{DB} = \dfrac{AC}{BC}$ by
substitution.

31. It is a trapezoid.

Given: $\overline{SV}$ bisects $\angle RST$.

$\overline{RA} \cong \overline{RV}$

$\overline{BT} \cong \overline{VT}$

Prove: $ABTR$ is a trapezoid.

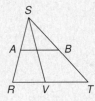

STATEMENTS	REASONS
1. $\overline{SV}$ bisects $\angle RST$. $\overline{RA} \cong \overline{RV}$ $\overline{BT} \cong \overline{VT}$	1. Given
2. $\dfrac{RV}{VT} = \dfrac{SR}{ST}$	2. An $\angle$ bisector in a $\triangle$ separates the opposite side into segments that have the same ratio as the other sides.
3. $\dfrac{ST}{VT} = \dfrac{SR}{RV}$	3. Property of proportions
4. $ST = SB + BT$ $SR = SA + AR$	4. Segment addition postulate
5. $\dfrac{SB + BT}{VT} = \dfrac{SA + AR}{RV}$	5. Substitution property of equality
6. $RA = RV$ $BT = VT$	6. Definition of congruent segments
7. $\dfrac{SB + BT}{BT} = \dfrac{SA + AR}{AR}$	7. Substitution property of equality

123

8. $\dfrac{SB}{BT} = \dfrac{SA}{AR}$ 8. Property of proportions

9. $\overline{AB} \parallel \overline{RT}$ 9. If a line intersects 2 sides of a $\triangle$ into corresponding segments of proportional lengths then the line is $\parallel$ to the third side.

10. $ABTR$ is a trapezoid.   10. Definition of trapezoid

32. Conjecture: $\dfrac{x}{z} = \dfrac{z}{y}$

Proof: Since $\overline{CD}$ is an altitude, $\angle CDA$ and $\angle CDB$ are right $\angle$s; $\triangle ABC$ is a right $\triangle$, so $\angle ACB$ is also right. Thus, $\angle CDA \cong \angle ACB$, and $\angle ACB \cong \angle CDB$. $\angle A \cong \angle A$, so $\triangle ACB \sim \triangle ADC$; $\angle B \cong \angle B$, so $\triangle ACB \sim \triangle CDB$ by AA Similarity. By the transitive property, $\triangle ADC \sim \triangle CDB$. By definition of similar $\triangle$s, corresponding parts are proportional, so $\dfrac{x}{z} = \dfrac{z}{y}$.

33. $\dfrac{1.3}{300} = \dfrac{x}{180}$

$300x = 234$

$x = 0.78$

0.78 cm

34. $\dfrac{1.3}{x} = \dfrac{4.5}{180}$

$4.5x = 234$

$x = 52$

52 cm

35. $\dfrac{2}{12} = \dfrac{1}{x}$

$2x = 12$

$x = 6$

Steve is 6 feet tall.

36. $\dfrac{AD}{DB} = \dfrac{AF}{FC}$

$\dfrac{3}{6} = \dfrac{4}{FC}$

$3FC = 24$

$FC = 8$

37. $\dfrac{AD}{AB} = \dfrac{DF}{BC}$

$\dfrac{3}{3+6} = \dfrac{DF}{15}$

$9DF = 45$

$DF = 5$

38. $\angle 2 \cong \angle 1$, $\angle 2 \cong \angle N$, $\overline{PQ} \parallel \overline{LN}$, $\angle 1 \cong \angle L$, $\angle 3 \cong \angle 4$, $\angle L \cong \angle N$, $\angle 2 \cong \angle 1$, $\triangle MPQ \sim \triangle MLN$, $\dfrac{MP}{ML} = \dfrac{PQ}{LN} = \dfrac{QM}{NM}$, $\triangle MPQ$ and $\triangle MLN$ are isosceles

39. $\overline{PQ} \perp \overline{QS}$, $\triangle RPQ$ and $\triangle RSQ$ are isosceles, $\overline{RP} \cong \overline{QP}$, $\overline{RS} \cong \overline{QS}$

40. $\triangle AEF$ and $\triangle DBC$ are right triangles, $\overline{CD} \perp \overline{AD}$, $\overline{AF} \perp \overline{AD}$, $\overline{CD} \parallel \overline{AF}$

41. $\overline{AB} \parallel \overline{DC}$, $\angle 1 \cong \angle 3$, $\triangle ADC \cong \triangle CBA$, $\angle 1$ and $\angle 2$ are complementary, $\angle 3$ and $\angle 4$ are complementary

42. See students' work.

7-7   Problem-Solving Strategy: Solve a Simpler Problem

PAGE 350   CHECKING FOR UNDERSTANDING

1. See students' work.

2. with a complicated or unfamilar problem

3. $1 + 2 + 3 + \ldots + 198 + 199 + 200$

$= (1 + 200) + (2 + 199) + (3 + 198) + \ldots + (100 + 101)$

$= 201 + 201 + 201 + \ldots + 201$

$= 100(201)$

$= 20{,}100$

4.
points	segments
1	0
2	1
3	3
4	6
5	10
n	$\dfrac{n(n-1)}{2}$

For 75 points, you would need $\dfrac{75(75-1)}{2}$ = 75(37) or 2775 segments.

5. You could choose a different color sock for eight choices. But on the 9th choice you must repeat colors. So you must pull 9 socks to ensure a pair that matches.

PAGES 350-351   **EXERCISES**

6. There are seven possible combinations: 1 half-dollar, 1 quarter, 1 nickel and 20 pennies; 1 half-dollar, 7 nickels, and 15 pennies; 2 quarters, 1 dime, 5 nickels, and 15 pennies; 1 quarter, 5 dimes, 2 nickels, and 15 pennies; 1 quarter, 1 dime, 11 nickels, and 10 pennies; 5 dimes, 8 nickels, and 10 pennies; or 1 dime, 17 nickels, and 5 pennies

7. The thousands digit must be 1, since the United States was founded in 1776. The hundreds digit is even, and must be greater than 7, so it is 8. The ones digit is 1 greater than the hundreds digit, so it is 8 + 1 or 9. If t is the tens digit, $1 + 8 + t + 9 = 24$, so $t = 6$. The year was 1869.

8. For a number to have 5 divisors, it must be the square of a composite number. The smallest whole composite number is 4, so its square, 16, is the smallest number with exactly 5 divisors. Its divisors are 1, 2, 4, 8, and 16.

9. If there are x people at the table, there are $\frac{x}{2}$ bowls of rice, $\frac{x}{3}$ bowls of vegetables, and $\frac{x}{4}$ bowls of entree.

$$\frac{x}{2} + \frac{x}{3} + \frac{x}{4} = 26$$

$$12\left(\frac{x}{2} + \frac{x}{3} + \frac{x}{4}\right) = 12(26)$$

$$6x + 4x + 3x = 312$$

$$13x = 312$$

$$x = 24$$

There are 24 people at the table.

10. Suppose there are 9 ladles full of soup in each pot. After the ladle of chili is added to the vegetable soup pot, there are 9 ladles of vegetable soup and 1 ladle of chili in the vegetable soup pot and 8 ladles of chili in the chili pot.

Wendy mixed the 10 ladles of soup in the vegetable soup pot. The pot was $\frac{9}{10}$ vegetable soup, so the ladle she pulled up was also. This left 9 ladles of soup in the pot, with $\frac{9}{10}$ of a ladle of chili.

When the ladle of chil & vegetable soup was added to the chili, it had 9 ladles of soup with $\frac{9}{10}$ of a ladle being vegetable soup.

So, the pots have the same amount of the other type of soup.

11. The series of fractions simplifies to $\frac{1}{2} + 1 + \frac{3}{2} + 2 + \ldots + \frac{99}{2}$. So, find the half of the sum of the series $1 + 2 + 3 + \ldots + 99$. $1 + 2 + 3 + \ldots + 99 = 49(100) + 50$ or 4950, since there are 49 pairs of addends with a sum of 100, 50 has no match. The sum of the series of fractions is $\frac{4950}{2}$ or 2475.

12. Work backward.

Let x = price before tennis privileges.

$$x + 0.05x = 463.05$$

$$1.05x = 463.05$$

$$x = 441$$

Let y = price before 10% corporate discount.

$$y - 0.10y = 441$$

$$0.9y = 441$$

$$y = 490$$

Let z = price before $75 sale.

$$z - 75 = 490$$

$$z = 565$$

The regular price is $565.

Cooperative Learning Project

PAGE 351

She could pull three of each color first, then the next sock pulled would make 4 of the same color, That is, $3(3) + 1$ or 10 socks.

If there were n sisters, she would need $2n$ socks of the same color. She could pull $(2n - 1)$ socks of each color, then the next sock makes $2n$ of the same color. That is $3(2n - 1) + 1$ socks Michelle needs to pull.

Chapter 7 Summary and Review

PAGES 352-354   SKILLS AND CONCEPTS

1. $\frac{5}{x} = \frac{2}{3}$

$$2x = 15$$
$$x = 7.5$$

2. $\frac{x}{9} = \frac{7}{15}$

$$15x = 63$$
$$x = 4.2$$

3. $\frac{1}{x} = \frac{5}{x + 5}$

$$5x = x + 5$$
$$4x = 5$$
$$x = 1.25$$

4. $\frac{n + 4}{3} = \frac{5n - 3}{8}$

$$15n - 9 = 8n + 32$$
$$7n = 41$$
$$n = \frac{41}{7}$$

5. $\frac{a}{b} = \frac{c}{d}$

$$ad = bc$$
$$\frac{a}{b} \overset{?}{=} \frac{d}{c}$$
$$ac \neq bd$$

false

6. $\frac{a + b}{b} \overset{?}{=} \frac{c + d}{d}$

$$\frac{a}{b} + \frac{b}{b} \overset{?}{=} \frac{c}{d} + \frac{d}{d}$$
$$\frac{a}{b} + 1 \overset{?}{=} \frac{c}{d} + 1$$
$$\frac{a}{b} = \frac{c}{d} \quad \text{true}$$

7. $\frac{AB}{XY} = \frac{AC}{XZ}$

$$\frac{7}{XY} = \frac{6}{8}$$
$$6XY = 56$$
$$XY = 9\frac{1}{3}$$

8. $\frac{AC}{BC} = \frac{XZ}{YZ}$

$$\frac{6}{7} = \frac{14}{YZ}$$
$$6YZ = 98$$
$$YZ = 16\frac{1}{3}$$

9. true

10. false

11. $\frac{AB}{GF} = \frac{CB}{EF}$

$$\frac{12}{6} = \frac{16}{x}$$
$$12x = 96$$
$$x = 8$$

12. $\frac{AB}{GF} = \frac{CA}{EG}$

$$\frac{12}{6} = \frac{20}{y}$$
$$12y = 120$$
$$y = 10$$

13. Given: $\dfrac{RP}{QS} = \dfrac{RS}{QP}$

$\overline{QR} \parallel \overline{PS}$

isosceles

trapezoid $PQRS$

Prove: $\triangle PQR \sim \triangle SRQ$

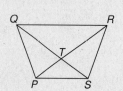

STATEMENTS	REASONS
1. isosceles trapezoid $PQRS$ $\overline{QR} \parallel \overline{PS}$	1. Given
2. $\overline{QP} \cong \overline{RS}$	2. Definition of isosceles trapezoid
3. $\overline{RQ} \cong \overline{RQ}$	3. Congruence of segments is reflexive.
4. $QP = RS$ $RQ = RQ$	4. Definition of congruent segments
5. $\dfrac{RQ}{RQ} = 1$, $\dfrac{QP}{RS} = 1$	5. Division property of equality
6. $\dfrac{RQ}{RQ} = \dfrac{QP}{RS}$	6. Substitution property of equality
7. $\dfrac{RP}{QS} = \dfrac{RS}{QP}$	7. Given
8. $\angle PQR \cong \angle SRQ$	8. Base $\angle$s of an iso. trap. are $\cong$.
9. $\triangle PQR \sim \triangle SRQ$	9. SAS Similarity

14. Given: $\overline{QR} \parallel \overline{PS}$

Prove: $\dfrac{QT}{TS} = \dfrac{TR}{PT}$

STATEMENTS	REASONS
1. $\overline{QR} \parallel \overline{PS}$	1. Given
2. $\angle QRT \cong \angle TPS$	2. If two $\parallel$ lines are cut by a trans., alt. int. $\angle$s are $\cong$.
3. $\angle QTR \cong \angle STP$	3. Vertical $\angle$s are $\cong$.
4. $\triangle QTR \sim \triangle STP$	4. AA Similarity
5. $\dfrac{QT}{TS} = \dfrac{TR}{PT}$	5. Definition of similar $\triangle$s

15. $\dfrac{TS}{SR} = \dfrac{TV}{VP}$

$\dfrac{5 + x}{3} = \dfrac{8 + x}{4}$

$24 + 3x = 20 + 4x$

$4 = x$

16. $\dfrac{PV}{TV} = \dfrac{PQ}{QR}$

$\dfrac{x}{7.29} = \dfrac{9}{27}$

$27x = 65.61$

$x = 2.43$

17. $\dfrac{BM}{BC} = \dfrac{YN}{YZ}$

$\dfrac{7}{9} = \dfrac{YN}{12}$

$9YN = 84$

$YN = 9\dfrac{1}{3}$

18. $\dfrac{ST}{PQ} = \dfrac{SV}{PM}$

$\dfrac{4}{10} = \dfrac{6x + 1}{2x + 9}$

$60x + 10 = 8x + 36$

$52x = 26$

$x = \dfrac{1}{2}$

perimeter of $\triangle STV = ST + SV + TV$

$= 4 + 6\left(\dfrac{1}{2}\right) + 1 + 3$

$= 11$

$\dfrac{ST}{PQ} = \dfrac{\text{perimeter of } \triangle STV}{\text{perimeter of } \triangle PQM}$

$\dfrac{4}{10} = \dfrac{11}{x}$

$4x = 110$

$x = 27.5$

PAGE 354   APPLICATIONS AND CONNECTIONS

19. $\dfrac{1}{6}(174)$ or 29 times

20. $\dfrac{1 \text{ cm}}{15 \text{ km}} = \dfrac{7.9 \text{ cm}}{x \text{ km}}$

$x = 118.5$

118.5 kilometers

21. $\triangle TAC \sim \triangle TBD$ by SAS Similarity. For $\dfrac{DB}{AC} = \dfrac{7}{4}$, you must set the divider so that $AT = TC = 4$ and $DT = TB = 7$.

22. $\dfrac{\text{wingspan}}{\text{length}} = \dfrac{\text{model wingspan}}{\text{model length}}$

$\dfrac{90}{78} = \dfrac{36}{x}$

$90x = 2808$

$x = 31.2$

31.2 cm

23.

n	2^n	units digit of 2^n
1	2	2
2	4	4
3	8	8
4	16	6
5	32	2
6	64	4
⋮		

The units digits repeat in a pattern of 4. Since $125 \div 4$ has a remainder of 1, the units digit of 2^{125} will be 2.

126

Chapter 7 Test

1. b

2. $\dfrac{x}{28} = \dfrac{60}{16}$

$16x = 1680$

$x = 105$

3. $\dfrac{21}{1-x} = \dfrac{7}{x}$

$21x = 7 - 7x$

$28x = 7$

$x = 0.25$

4. $\dfrac{14}{21} = \dfrac{18}{x}$

$14x = 378$

$x = 27$

5. $\dfrac{1 \text{ soda}}{4 \text{ alum}} = \dfrac{x \text{ soda}}{150 \text{ alum}}$

$4x = 150$

$x = 37.5$

37.5 grams

6. true **7.** true **8.** false **9.** false

10. $\dfrac{8}{12} = \dfrac{10}{15} = \dfrac{12}{18}$, so yes by SSS Similarity

11. $\dfrac{1.6}{2.4} = \dfrac{1.8}{2.7}$ and $\angle ABC \cong \angle PKM$, so yes by SAS Similarity

12. $\dfrac{PW}{QW} = \dfrac{ST}{SU}$

$\dfrac{x}{1} = \dfrac{x+5}{5}$

$5x = x + 5$

$4x = 5$

$x = 1\frac{1}{4}$

13. $\dfrac{SW}{SV} = \dfrac{RS}{SU}$

$\dfrac{3}{2} = \dfrac{1\frac{1}{3}}{x + \frac{2}{3}}$

$\dfrac{8}{3} = 3x + 2$

$\dfrac{2}{3} = 3x$

$\dfrac{2}{9} = x$

14. Given: $\triangle ABC \sim \triangle RSP$

D is the midpoint of $\overline{AC}$.

Q is the midpoint of $\overline{PR}$.

Prove: $\triangle SPQ \sim \triangle BCD$

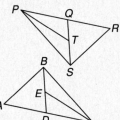

STATEMENTS	REASONS
1. $\triangle ABC \sim \triangle RSP$ D is the midpoint of $\overline{AC}$. Q is the midpoint of $\overline{PR}$.	1. Given
2. $\angle RSP \cong \angle ACB$	2. Definition of similar polygons
3. $\overline{BD}$ is a median of $\triangle ABC$. $\overline{QS}$ is a median of $\triangle RSP$.	3. Definition of median
4. $\dfrac{SQ}{BD} = \dfrac{SP}{BC} = \dfrac{PR}{AC}$	4. If two $\triangle$s are similar, then the measures of corresponding medians are proportional to the measures of corresponding sides.
5. $PQ = QR$ $DC = DA$	5. Definition of midpoint
6. $AD + DC = AC$ $PQ + QR = PR$	6. Segment addition postulate
7. $2(DC) = AC$ $2(PQ) = PR$	7. Substitution property of equality
8. $\dfrac{2(PQ)}{2(DC)} = \dfrac{SQ}{BD}$	8. Substitution property of equality
9. $\dfrac{PQ}{DC} = \dfrac{SQ}{BD}$	9. Substitution property of equality
10. $\triangle SPQ \sim \triangle BCD$	10. SSS Similarity

15. $\dfrac{DE}{AB} = \dfrac{DC}{AC}$

$\dfrac{0.3}{AB} = \dfrac{0.4}{48}$

$0.4AB = 14.4$

$AB = 36$

36 miles

BONUS

The ratio of the sides is 5:15 or 1:3. Since the ratio of the sides is in linear measure and the area is square units, the ratio will be $1^2 : 3^2$ or 1:9.

Algebra Review

1. $7xy(x^2 + 4xy - 8y^2) = 7x^3y + 28x^2y^2 - 56xy^3$

2. $x(3x - 5) + 7(x^2 - 2x + 9)$

$= 3x^2 - 5x + 7x^2 - 14x + 63$

$= 10x^2 - 19x + 63$

3. $4x^2(x + 8) - 3x(2x^2 - 8x + 3)$

$= 4x^3 + 32x^2 - 6x^3 + 24x^2 - 9x$

$= -2x^3 + 56x^2 - 9x$

4. $(r - 3)(r + 7) = r^2 + 7r - 3r - 21$

$= r^2 + 4r - 21$

5. $(x + 5)(3x - 2) = 3x^2 - 2x + 15x - 10$
$$= 3x^2 + 13x - 10$$

6. $(4n + 3)(3n - 4) = 12n^2 - 16n + 9n - 12$
$$= 12n^2 - 7n - 12$$

7. $(2x + 9y)(3x - y) = 6x^2 - 2xy + 27xy - 9y^2$
$$= 6x^2 + 25xy - 9y^2$$

8. $(a - 4)(a^2 + 5a - 7)$
$$= a^3 + 5a^2 - 7a - 4a^2 - 20a + 28$$
$$= a^3 + a^2 - 27a + 28$$

9. $x^2 + 18x + 81 = x^2 + 9x + 9x + 81$
$$= (x + 9)(x + 9)$$
$$= (x + 9)^2$$

10. $32n^2 - 80n + 50 = 2(16n^2 - 40n + 25)$
$$= 2(4n - 5)(4n - 5)$$
$$= 2(4n - 5)^2$$

11. $\frac{n^2}{4} - \frac{9}{16} = \frac{1}{4}\left(n^2 - \frac{9}{4}\right) = \frac{1}{4}\left(n - \frac{3}{2}\right)\left(n + \frac{3}{2}\right)$

12. $3x^3 - 192x = 3x(x^2 - 64) = 3x(x - 8)(x + 8)$

13. $16p^2 - 81r^4 = (4p - 9r^2)(4p + 9r^2)$

14. $54b^3 - 72b^2g + 24bg^2 = 6b(9b^2 - 12bg + 4g^2)$
$$= 6b(3b - 2g)^2$$

15. $\frac{3x^2y}{12xy^3z} = \frac{3xy \cdot x}{3xy \cdot 4y^3z} = \frac{x}{4y^3z}$; $12xy^3z \neq 0$, so
excluded values are $x = 0$, $y = 0$, $z = 0$

16. $\frac{z^2 - 3z}{z - 3} = \frac{z(z - 3)}{z - 3} = z$; $z - 3 \neq 0$, so excluded

value is $z = 3$

17. $\frac{a^2 - 25}{a^2 + 3a - 10} = \frac{(a - 5)(a + 5)}{(a + 5)(a - 2)} = \frac{a - 5}{a - 2}$;

$a^2 + 3a - 10 \neq 0$, so excluded values are $a = -5$
or $a = 2$

18. $\frac{x^2 + 10xy + 21y^2}{x^3 + x^2y - 42xy^2} = \frac{(x + 3y)(x + 7y)}{x(x + 7y)(x - 6y)}$

$$= \frac{x + 3y}{x(x - 6y)}$$

excluded values when denominator = 0:
$x^3 + x^2y - 42xy^2 = 0$
$x(x + 7y)(x - 6y) = 0$
$x = 0 \qquad x + 7y = 0 \quad$ or $\quad x - 6y = 0$
$\qquad\qquad x = -7y \qquad\qquad x = 6y$
So, excluded values are $x = 0$, $x = -7y$ and
$x = 6y$.

19. Domain: $\{-2, -1, 0\}$
Range: $\{-1, 0, 2\}$
Inverse: $\{(-1, -2), (0, -1), (2, 0)\}$

20. Domain: $\{-3, 4\}$
Range: $\{5, 6\}$
Inverse: $\{(5, -3), (6, -3) (5, 4), (6, 4)\}$

21. Domain: $\{4\}$
Range: $\{-2, -1, 1, 7\}$
Inverse: $\{(1, 4), (-2, 4), (7, 4), (-1, 4)\}$

22. $7x - 12 < 30$
$7x < 42$
$x < 6$
$\{x | x < 6\}$

23. $4y - 11 \geq 8y + 7$
$-18 \geq 4y$
$-\frac{9}{2} \geq y$
$\left\{y | y \leq -\frac{9}{2}\right\}$

24. $4(n - 1) < 7n + 8$
$4n - 4 < 7n + 8$
$-12 < 3n$
$-4 < n$
$\{n | n > -4\}$

25. $\frac{3}{10}(4 - d) \leq -\frac{4}{5}\left(\frac{1d}{5} + 2\right)$
$3(4 - d \leq -8\left(\frac{d}{5} + 2\right)$
$12 - 3d \leq -\frac{8d}{5} - 16$
$28 \leq \frac{7}{5}d$
$20 \leq d$
$\{d | d \geq 20\}$

26. $28 \cdot 42 = y \cdot 56$
$1176 = 56y$
$21 = y$

27. $y \cdot 35 = 35 \cdot 175$
$35y = 6125$
$y = \frac{245}{3}$ or $81.\overline{6}$

28. $x \cdot 3.6 = 2.7 \cdot 8.1$
$3.6x = 21.87$
$x = 6.075$

29. $\frac{x + y}{c} = d$
$x + y = cd$
$x = cd - y$

30. $5(2a + x) = 3b$
$10a + 5x = 3b$
$5x = 3b - 10a$
$x = \frac{3b - 10a}{5}$

31. $\frac{ax - 3}{2} = 7b - 6$
$ax - 3 = 14b - 12$
$ax = 14b - 9$
$x = \frac{14b - 9}{a}$

32. $\frac{2x - a}{3} = \frac{a + 3b}{4}$
$4(2x - a) = 3(a + 3b)$
$8x - 4a = 3a + 9b$
$8x = 7a + 9b$
$x = \frac{7a + 9b}{8}$

33. $\dfrac{26}{5} = \dfrac{x}{12}$

$5x = 312$

$x = 62.4$

$62.40

34. area $= \ell \cdot w$

perimeter $= 2\ell + 2w$

area $= 25x^2 - 9$

$= (5x - 3)(5x + 3)$

perimeter $= 2(5x - 3) + 2(5x + 3)$

$= 10x - 6 + 10x + 6$

$= 20x$

35. Let w = width of result

$w + 3$ = length of result

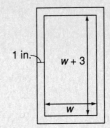

1 in.

$w + 3$

w

trimmed area $= 2w + 2(w + 3) + 4$

$46 = 2w + 2w + 6 + 4$

$36 = 4w$

$9 = w$

So, width of original $= 9 + 2$ or 11

length of original $= (9 + 3) + 2 = 14.$

The dimensions of the original were 14 in. by 11 in.

36. $3 < 1.75 + 0.08x < 4$

$1.25 < 0.08x < 2.25$

$15.625 < x < 28.125$

Sara must write an integral number of checks. So she can write between 16 and 28 checks and stay within her budget.

Chapter 8   Right Triangles and Trigonometry

1. If x is the geometric mean, $\dfrac{6}{x} = \dfrac{x}{10}$.

2. x and y

3. v

4. $\dfrac{4}{x} = \dfrac{x}{25}$

$x^2 = 100$

$x = 10$

5. $\dfrac{15}{x} = \dfrac{x}{3}$

$x^2 = 45$

$x = \sqrt{45} \approx 6.7$

6. $\dfrac{2}{x} = \dfrac{x}{10}$

$x^2 = 20$

$x = \sqrt{20} \approx 4.5$

7. $\dfrac{7}{x} = \dfrac{x}{22}$

$x^2 = 154$

$x = \sqrt{154} \approx 12.4$

8. $\dfrac{\frac{1}{2}}{x} = \dfrac{x}{\frac{2}{3}}$

$x^2 = \dfrac{1}{3}$

$x = \dfrac{1}{\sqrt{3}} \approx 0.6$

9. $\dfrac{8}{x} = \dfrac{x}{5}$

$x^2 = 40$

$x = \sqrt{40} \approx 6.3$

10. $\triangle XYZ \sim \triangle XWY$

$\triangle XYZ \sim \triangle YWZ$

$\triangle XWY \sim \triangle YWZ$

11. $\dfrac{4}{x} = \dfrac{x}{11}$

$x^2 = 44$

$x = \sqrt{44} \approx 6.6$

$\dfrac{4}{y} = \dfrac{y}{7}$

$y^2 = 28$

$y = \sqrt{28} \approx 5.3$

12. $\dfrac{6}{8} = \dfrac{8}{x - 6}$

$6(x - 6) = 64$

$6x - 36 = 64$

$6x = 100$

$x = 16\dfrac{2}{3}$

$\dfrac{6}{y} = \dfrac{y}{16\frac{2}{3}}$

$y^2 = 100$

$y = 10$

13. $\dfrac{3}{x} = \dfrac{x}{5}$

$x^2 = 15$

$x = \sqrt{15} \approx 3.9$

14. $\dfrac{4}{x} = \dfrac{x}{6}$

$x^2 = 24$

$x = \sqrt{24} \approx 4.9$

15. $\dfrac{\frac{1}{4}}{x} = \dfrac{x}{9}$

$x^2 = 2.25$

$x = 1.5$

16. $\dfrac{4}{x} = \dfrac{x}{\frac{1}{9}}$

$x^2 = \dfrac{4}{9}$

$x = \dfrac{2}{3}$

17. $\dfrac{\frac{3}{8}}{x} = \dfrac{x}{\frac{8}{3}}$

$x^2 = 1$

$x = 1$

18. $\dfrac{\frac{2}{3}}{x} = \dfrac{x}{\frac{1}{3}}$

$x^2 = \dfrac{2}{9}$

$x = \dfrac{\sqrt{2}}{3} \approx 0.5$

19. $\dfrac{5}{x} = \dfrac{x}{9}$

$x^2 = 45$

$x = \sqrt{45} \approx 6.7$

20. $\dfrac{3}{x} = \dfrac{x}{12}$

$x^2 = 36$

$x = 6$

21. $\dfrac{3}{x} = \dfrac{x}{10}$

$x^2 = 30$

$x = \sqrt{30} \approx 5.5$

22. $\dfrac{3}{x} = \dfrac{x}{8}$

$x^2 = 24$

$x = \sqrt{24} \approx 4.9$

23. $\dfrac{4}{x} = \dfrac{x}{8}$

$x^2 = 32$

$x = \sqrt{32} \approx 5.7$

24. $\dfrac{4}{x} = \dfrac{x}{7}$

$x^2 = 28$

$x = \sqrt{28} \approx 5.3$

25. $\dfrac{x}{6} = \dfrac{6}{9}$

$9x = 36$

$x = 4$

$y = 9 - 4 = 5$

26. $\dfrac{10}{x} = \dfrac{x + 21}{10}$

$x(x + 21) = 10 \cdot 10$

$x^2 + 21x - 100 = 0$

$(x - 4)(x + 25) = 0$

$x = 4$ or $x = -25$

$x = -25$ is not a reasonable answer, so $x = 4$.

$y = 21 + 4 = 25$

27. $\dfrac{16}{x} = \dfrac{4x}{16}$

$4x^2 = 256$

$x^2 = 64$

$x = 8$

$\dfrac{4x}{y} = \dfrac{y}{5x}$, $x = 8$

$\dfrac{32}{y} = \dfrac{y}{40}$

$y^2 = 1280$

$y = \sqrt{1280} \approx 35.8$

28. $\dfrac{x}{5} = \dfrac{25}{x}$

$x^2 = 125$

$x = \sqrt{125} \approx 11.2$

$\dfrac{20}{y} = \dfrac{y}{25}$

$y^2 = 500$

$y = \sqrt{500} \approx 22.4$

29. $\dfrac{x - 1}{x + 1} = \dfrac{x + 1}{x + 4}$

$(x - 1)(x + 4) = (x + 1)^2$

$x^2 + 3x - 4 = x^2 + 2x + 1$

$x = 5$

$$y^2 + (x - 1)^2 = (x + 1)^2, \quad x = 5$$
$$y^2 + 4^2 = 6^2$$
$$y^2 + 16 = 36$$
$$y^2 = 20$$
$$y = \sqrt{20} \approx 4.5$$

30.
$$\frac{6}{x - 9} = \frac{x}{6}$$
$$x(x - 9) = 36$$
$$x^2 - 9x - 36 = 0$$
$$(x - 12)(x + 3) = 0$$
$$x = 12 \quad \text{or} \quad x = -3$$
$x = -3$ is not a reasonable answer, so $x = 12$.
$$\frac{3}{y} = \frac{y}{9}$$
$$y^2 = 27$$
$$y = \sqrt{27} \approx 5.2$$

31.
$$\frac{6}{4} = \frac{PQ}{6}$$
$$4(PQ) = 36$$
$$PQ = 9$$
$$PR = PQ + QR$$
$$= 9 + 4$$
$$= 13$$
$$\frac{4}{VR} = \frac{VR}{13}$$
$$(VR)^2 = 52$$
$$VR = \sqrt{52} = 2\sqrt{13} \approx 7.2$$
$$\frac{9}{PV} = \frac{PV}{13}$$
$$(PV)^2 = 117$$
$$PV = \sqrt{117} = 3\sqrt{13} \approx 10.8$$

32.
$$\frac{AG}{AD} = \frac{AD}{AF} \qquad\qquad GF = AF - AG$$
$$\frac{AG}{12} = \frac{12}{15} \qquad\qquad\qquad = 15 - 9.6$$
$$15(AG) = 144 \qquad\qquad\qquad = 5.4$$
$$AG = 9.6$$
$$\frac{AG}{DG} = \frac{DG}{EF} \qquad\qquad \frac{EF}{GF} = \frac{GF}{DF}$$
$$\frac{9.6}{DG} = \frac{DG}{5.4} \qquad\qquad \frac{EF}{5.4} = \frac{5.4}{9}$$
$$(DG)^2 = 51.84 \qquad\qquad 9(EF) = 29.16$$
$$DG = 7.2 \qquad\qquad\qquad EF = 3.24$$
$$CD = GE \qquad\qquad\qquad CG = DE$$
$$\frac{3.24}{GE} = \frac{GE}{5.76} \qquad\qquad DE = 9 - 3.24$$
$$\qquad\qquad\qquad\qquad\quad CG = 5.76$$
$$(GE)^2 = 18.66$$
$$GE = 4.32$$
$$CD = 4.32$$

$$\frac{HG}{5.76} = \frac{5.76}{9.6} \qquad\qquad \frac{3.456}{CH} = \frac{CH}{AH}$$
$$9.6(HG) = 33.178 \qquad\qquad (CH)^2 = (3.456)(6.144)$$
$$HG = 3.456 \qquad\qquad\qquad CH = \sqrt{21.234}$$
$$\qquad\qquad\qquad\qquad\qquad\quad CH = 4.608$$
$$\frac{BC}{4.608} = \frac{4.608}{AC}$$
$$7.68(BC) = 21.234$$
$$BC = 2.7648$$

33. Given: $\triangle ADC$

$\angle ADC$ is a right angle.

$\overline{DB}$ is an altitude of $\triangle ADC$.

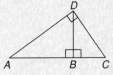

Prove: $\dfrac{AB}{DB} = \dfrac{DB}{CB}$

Proof: Given that $\triangle ADC$ is a right triangle and $\overline{DB}$ is an altitude of $\triangle ADC$. $\triangle ADC$ is a right triangle by the definition of a right triangle. Therefore, $\triangle ADB \sim \triangle DCB$, because if the altitude is drawn from the vertex of the right angle to the hypotenuse of a right triangle, then the two triangles formed are similar to the given triangle and to each other. So $\dfrac{AB}{DB} = \dfrac{DB}{CB}$ by definition of similar polygons.

34. Given: $\triangle ADC$

$\angle ADC$ is a right angle.

$\overline{DB}$ is an altitude of $\triangle ADC$.

Prove: $\dfrac{AB}{AD} = \dfrac{AD}{AC}$

$\dfrac{BC}{DC} = \dfrac{DC}{AC}$

STATEMENTS	REASONS
a. $\triangle ADC$ $\angle ADC$ is a right angle. $\overline{DB}$ is an altitude of $\triangle ADC$.	a. Given
b. $\triangle ADC$ is a right triangle.	b. Definition of right triangle
c. $\triangle ABD \sim \triangle ADC$ $\triangle DBC \sim \triangle ADC$	c. If the altitude is drawn from the vertex of the rt. $\angle$ to the hypotenuse of a rt. $\triangle$, then the 2 $\triangle$s formed are similar to the given $\triangle$ and to each other.
d. $\dfrac{AB}{AD} = \dfrac{AD}{AC}$ $\dfrac{BC}{DC} = \dfrac{DC}{AC}$	d. Definition of similar polygons

131

35.
$$\frac{a + b}{2} > \sqrt{ab}$$
$$a + b > 2\sqrt{ab}$$
$$a^2 + 2ab + b^2 > 4ab$$
$$a^2 - 2ab + b^2 > 0$$
$$(a - b)^2 > 0$$

The square of any real number except 0 is greater than 0. So, reverse the steps.

$$(a - b)^2 > 0$$
$$a^2 - 2ab + b^2 > 0$$
$$a^2 + 2ab + b^2 > 4ab$$
$$a + b > 2\sqrt{ab}$$
$$\frac{a + b}{2} > \sqrt{ab}$$

Therefore, if $a \neq b$, the arithmetic mean of a and b will always be greater than their geometric mean.

36. $\triangle FGH$ is a right triangle. $\overline{OG}$ is the altitude from the vertex of the right angle to the hypotenuse of that triangle. So, by Theorem 8-2, OG is the geometric mean between OF and OH.

37. $197 - 71 + 1 = 127$

38. $4:8:12 = 1:2:3$
$1 + 2 + 3 = 6$
$\frac{1}{6} = \frac{x}{180}$; $x = 30$
$\frac{2}{6} = \frac{x}{180}$; $x = 60$
$\frac{3}{6} = \frac{x}{180}$; $x = 90$

39. Distributive property

40. No; complementary angles have measures with a sum of 90 and the measure of an obtuse angle is greater than 90.

41. $AB + BC = AC$

42. See students' work.

8-2 The Pythagorean Theorem

1. Answers may vary. Sample answer: If c is the measure of the hypotenuse of a right triangle and a and b are the measures of the legs, then $a^2 + b^2 = c^2$.

2. See students' work.

3. $c^2 = 9^2 + 22^2$
$c^2 = 81 + 484 = 565$
$c = \sqrt{565} \approx 23.8$

4. $5^2 + 10^2 \overset{?}{=} 12^2$
$25 + 100 \overset{?}{=} 144$
$125 \neq 144$; No

5. $0.27^2 + 0.36^2 \overset{?}{=} 0.45^2$
$0.0729 + 0.1296 \overset{?}{=} -0.2025$
$0.2025 = 0.2025$; Yes

6. $1^2 + 2^2 \overset{?}{=} 3^2$
$1 + 4 \overset{?}{=} 9$
$5 \neq 9$; No

7. $9^2 + 40^2 \overset{?}{=} 41^2$
$81 + 1600 \overset{?}{=} 1681$
$1681 = 1681$; Yes

8. $10^2 + 13^2 \overset{?}{=} 17^2$
$100 + 169 \overset{?}{=} 289$
$269 \neq 289$; No

9. $25^2 + 60^2 \overset{?}{=} 65^2$
$625 + 3600 \overset{?}{=} 4225$
$4225 = 4225$; Yes

10. $y^2 + 12^2 = 13^2$
$y^2 + 144 = 169$
$y^2 = 25$
$y = 5$

11. $x^2 + 3^2 = 6^2$
$x^2 + 9 = 36$
$x^2 = 27$
$x = \sqrt{27} \approx 5.2$

12. $10^2 + 24^2 = x^2$
$100 + 576 = x^2$
$676 = x^2$
$26 = x$

13. $(x + 9)^2 + (x + 2)^2 = (x + 10)^2$
$x^2 + 18x + 81 + x^2 + 4x + 4 = x^2 + 20x + 100$
$2x^2 + 22x + 85 = x^2 + 20x + 100$
$x^2 + 2x - 15 = 0$
$(x - 3)(x + 5) = 0$
$x = 3$ or -5
Since $x = -5$ is impossible, $x = 3$.

14. $c^2 = 42^2 + 54^2$
$c^2 = 1764 + 2916 = 4680$
$c = \sqrt{4680} \approx 68$ in.

132

15.

$c^2 = 4^2 + 2^2$

$c^2 = 16 + 4 = 20$

$c = \sqrt{20} \approx 4.5$ miles

16. $12^2 + 16^2 \overset{?}{=} 20^2$

$144 + 256 \overset{?}{=} 400$

$400 = 400$; Yes

17. $1.6^2 + 3.0^2 \overset{?}{=} 3.4^2$

$2.56 + 9.00 \overset{?}{=} 11.56$

$11.56 = 11.56$; Yes

18. $3.87^2 + 4.47^2 \overset{?}{=} 5.91^2$

$14.9769 + 19.9809 \overset{?}{=} 34.9281$

$34.9578 \neq 34.9281$; No

19. $6^2 + 8^2 \overset{?}{=} 10^2$

$36 + 64 \overset{?}{=} 100$

$100 = 100$; Yes

20. $25^2 \overset{?}{=} 20^2 + 15^2$

$625 \overset{?}{=} 400 + 225$

$625 = 625$; Yes

21. $18^2 + 34^2 \overset{?}{=} 39^2$

$324 + 1156 \overset{?}{=} 1521$

$1480 \neq 1521$; No

22. $x^2 + 6^2 = 10^2$

$x^2 + 36 = 100$

$x^2 = 64$

$x = 8$

23. $x^2 + (\sqrt{12})^2 = (\sqrt{13})^2$

$x^2 + 12 = 13$

$x^2 = 1$

$x = 1$

24. $x^2 + (8.0)^2 = (9.4)^2$

$x^2 + 64.00 = 88.36$

$x^2 = 24.36$

$x = \sqrt{24.36} \approx 4.9$ cm

25. Let $y = \frac{1}{2}x$.

$y^2 + 11.3^2 = 13.2^2$

$y^2 + 127.69 = 174.24$

$y^2 = 46.55$

$y = \sqrt{46.55} \approx 6.8$ mm

$x = 2y$

$x \approx 2(6.8)$

$x \approx 13.6$

26. $x^2 = 12^2 + 5^2$

$x^2 = 144 + 25$

$x^2 = 169$

$x = 13$

27. $(6.7)^2 + (7.1)^2 = x^2$

$44.89 + 50.41 = x^2$

$95.3 = x^2$

$x = \sqrt{95.3} \approx 9.8$ m

28. $(x + 10)^2 = (x + 7)^2 + 8^2$

$x^2 + 20x + 100 = x^2 + 14x + 49 + 64$

$x^2 + 20x + 100 = x^2 + 14x + 113$

$6x = 13$

$x = \frac{13}{6}$

29. $c^2 = 15^2 + 8^2$

$c^2 = 225 + 64$

$c = \sqrt{289} = 17$ cm

$P = 4 \cdot 17 = 68$ cm

30. $\frac{a}{15} = \frac{15}{a + 16}$

$a^2 + 16a = 225$

$a^2 + 16a - 225 = 0$

$(a + 25)(a - 9) = 0$

$a = -25$ or $a = 9$

Since $a = -25$ is impossible, $a = 9$.

$9^2 + b^2 = 15^2$

$81 + b^2 = 225$

$b^2 = 144$

$b = 12$

$c^2 = 12^2 + 16^2$

$c^2 = 144 + 256 = 400$

$c = 20$

$a + b + c = 9 + 12 + 20 = 41$

31. $AB = 8$, $AC = 34$, $EF = 30$, $AD = BC$

Draw auxilliary lines $AR \perp DC$ and $BS \perp DC$.

In $\triangle ACR$,

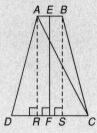

$30^2 + (RC)^2 = 34^2$

$900 + (RC)^2 = 1156$

$(RC)^2 = 256$

$RC = 16$

$RC = RS + SC$

$16 = 8 + SC$

$8 = SC$

In $\triangle BSC$, $30^2 + 8^2 = (BC)^2$

$900 + 64 = (BC)^2$

$964 = (BC)^2$

$2\sqrt{241} = BC$

In $\triangle ARD$, $30^2 + (RD)^2 = (2\sqrt{241})^2$

$900 + (RD)^2 = 964$

$(RD)^2 = 64$

$RD = 8$

$CD = RC + RD$

$= 16 + 8$

$= 24$

Perimeter $= AB + BC + CD + DA$

$= 8 + 2\sqrt{241} + 24 + 2\sqrt{241}$

$= 32 + 4\sqrt{241}$ units or

≈ 94.1 units

32. $24^2 + x^2 = 26^2$

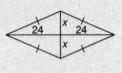

$576 + x^2 = 676$

$x^2 = 100$

$x = 10$

length of diagonal $= 2x = 2(10) = 20$

33. $(AC)^2 = 32^2 + 24^2$

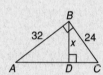

$(AC)^2 = 1024 + 576$

$(AC)^2 = 1600$

$AC = 40$

Since $\triangle ADB \sim \triangle ABC$,

$\dfrac{AB}{AC} = \dfrac{BD}{CB}$

$\dfrac{32}{40} = \dfrac{BD}{24}$

$40(BD) = 768$

$BD = 19.2$

The rise of the roof is 19.2 ft.

34. $\overline{AC}$ is on the y-axis, $\overline{CB}$ is on the x-axis, and C is at the origin. Since the axes are perpendicular,

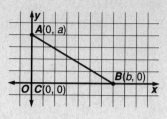

$\angle ACB$ is a right angle, making $\triangle ACB$ a right triangle. By the Pythagorean Theorem,

$(AC)^2 + (BC)^2 = (AB)^2$

$(0 - a)^2 + (b - 0)^2 = (AB)^2$

$\sqrt{(0 - a)^2 + (b - 0)^2} = AB$

Therefore, the distance from A to B is

$\sqrt{(0 - a)^2 + (b - 0)^2}$ or $\sqrt{a^2 + b^2}$.

35. Let x = length of diagonal of bottom face of container.

Let y = length of the longest rod.

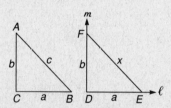

$x^2 = 4^2 + 12^2$

$x^2 = 16 + 144$

$x^2 = 160$

$y^2 = 3^2 + x^2$

$y^2 = 9 + 160$

$y^2 = 169$

$y = 13$

13 feet

36. The sum of the areas of the two smaller squares $(a^2 + b^2)$, is equal to the area of the larger square (c^2).

37. The proof requires an auxiliary figure.

Given: $\triangle ABC$ with sides of measure a, b, and c, where $a^2 + b^2 = c^2$

Prove: $\triangle ABC$ is a right triangle.

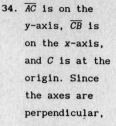

Proof: Draw $\overline{DE}$ on line ℓ with measure equal to a. At D, draw line $m \perp \overline{DE}$. Locate point F on m so that $DF = b$. Draw $\overline{FE}$ and call its measure x. Because $\triangle FED$ is a right triangle, $a^2 + b^2 = x^2$. But $a^2 + b^2 = c^2$, so $x^2 = c^2$ or $x = c$. Thus, $\triangle ABC \cong \triangle FED$ by SSS. This means $\angle C \cong \angle D$. Therefore, $\angle C$ must be a right angle, making $\triangle ABC$ a right triangle.

38. a. See students' work.

  b. For acute triangles, $a^2 + b^2 > c^2$.

   For obtuse triangles, $a^2 + b^2 < c^2$.

39. $c^2 = 12^2 + 5^2$

  $c^2 = 144 + 25 = 169$

  $c = \sqrt{169} = 13$ ft

40. $c^2 = 8^2 + 15^2$

  $c^2 = 64 + 225 = 289$

  $c = 17$ ft

41. The area of a trapezoid

42. (3,4,5), (6,8,10), (12,16,20), (24,32,40), (27,36,45)

43. a. Yes

  b. Yes

  c. Answers will vary. Conjecture is true.

  d. No: 1, 2, and 30 have a product of 60, but

   $1^2 + 2^2 \neq 30^2$

44. $\dfrac{9}{x} = \dfrac{x}{15}$

  $x^2 = 135$

  $x = \sqrt{135}$

   $= 3\sqrt{15} \approx 11.6$

45. $m = \dfrac{b_1 + b_2}{2}$

  $m = \dfrac{8 + 22}{2}$

   $= 15$ meters

46. $\overleftrightarrow{XT} \parallel \overleftrightarrow{WY}$ since $\angle 2 \cong \angle 4$ and these are alternate interior angles.

  $\overleftrightarrow{TZ} \parallel \overleftrightarrow{SY}$ since $\angle 3 \cong \angle 5$ and these are alternate exterior angles.

47. $8x - 9 = 6x - 1$

   $2x = 8$

   $x = 4$

48. A duck-billed platypus is a mammal that lays eggs; syllogism.

49. See students' work.

8-3 Special Right Triangles

1. $l \cdot \sqrt{2}$

2. $s \cdot \sqrt{3}$; $2s$

3. $s = \dfrac{14}{\sqrt{3}} \approx 8.08$; $h = 2\left(\dfrac{14}{\sqrt{3}}\right) \approx 16.17$

4. $x = \dfrac{1}{2} \cdot 10 = 5$

  $y = 5\sqrt{3}$

5. $x = 2 \cdot 18 = 16$

  $y = 8\sqrt{3}$

---

6. $c = (1)\sqrt{2}$

  $c = \sqrt{2}$

  $c \approx 1.4$ ft

7. $c = 31.2\sqrt{2}$

  $c \approx 44.1$ m

8. $c = \left(\dfrac{14}{3}\right)\sqrt{2}$

  $c = \dfrac{14\sqrt{2}}{3}$

  $c \approx 6.6$ yd

9. hypotenuse = 4 ft   short leg = $\dfrac{1}{2}(4) = 2$ ft

  long leg = $2\sqrt{3} \approx 3.5$ ft

10. hypotenuse = 27.4 m

  short leg = $\dfrac{1}{2}(27.4) = 13.7$ m

  long leg = $13.7\sqrt{3} \approx 23.7$ m

11. hypotenuse = $\dfrac{2}{3}$ yd   short leg = $\dfrac{1}{2}\left(\dfrac{2}{3}\right) = \dfrac{1}{3}$ yd

  long leg = $\dfrac{1}{3} \cdot \sqrt{3} = \dfrac{\sqrt{3}}{3} \approx 0.6$ yd

12. One side of equilateral triangle is 24 ÷ 3 or 8 units. The altitude divides the triangle into two 30°-60°-90° triangles.

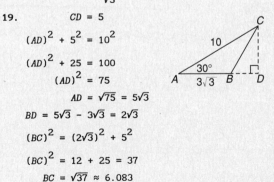

  hypotenuse = 8 units, short legs = 4 units, long leg = $4\sqrt{3} \approx 6.9$ units

13. short leg = 3 ft, hypotenuse = 2(3) = 6 ft,

  long leg = $3\sqrt{3} \approx 5.2$ ft

14. leg = 5.0 cm   hypotenuse = $5.0\sqrt{2} \approx 7.1$ cm

15. hypotenuse = 7.0 m, leg = $\dfrac{7.0}{\sqrt{2}} = \dfrac{7.0\sqrt{2}}{2} \approx 4.9$ m

16. hypotenuse = 6.0 in., leg = $\dfrac{6.0}{\sqrt{2}} = \dfrac{6.0\sqrt{2}}{2}$

   $= 3\sqrt{2} \approx 4.2$ in.

17. hypotenuse = 15.0 in., short leg = $\dfrac{1}{2}(15.0)$

   $= 7.5$ in.

  long leg = $7.5\sqrt{3} \approx 13.0$ in.

18. long leg = 31.2 cm

  short leg = $\dfrac{31.2}{\sqrt{3}} = \dfrac{31.2\sqrt{3}}{3} = 10.4\sqrt{3} \approx 18.0$ cm

19. $CD = 5$

  $(AD)^2 + 5^2 = 10^2$

  $(AD)^2 + 25 = 100$

   $(AD)^2 = 75$

   $AD = \sqrt{75} = 5\sqrt{3}$

  $BD = 5\sqrt{3} - 3\sqrt{3} = 2\sqrt{3}$

  $(BC)^2 = (2\sqrt{3})^2 + 5^2$

  $(BC)^2 = 12 + 25 = 37$

   $BC = \sqrt{37} \approx 6.083$

20. $SQ = \dfrac{8\sqrt{3}}{\sqrt{3}} = 8$, $PQ = 2 \cdot 8 = 16$

$RP = 2 \cdot (8\sqrt{3}) = 16\sqrt{3}$

$RS = 8\sqrt{3}(\sqrt{3}) = 24$

$RP + PQ + QS + SR = 16\sqrt{3} + 16 + 8 + 24$
$$= 48 + 16\sqrt{3} \approx 75.713 \text{ units}$$

21. $2x^2 + 2y^2 = 1458$

$x^2 + y^2 = 729$

diagonal $= \sqrt{729} = 27$ units

22. $DC = \dfrac{5.2}{\sqrt{3}} = \dfrac{5.2\sqrt{3}}{3}$

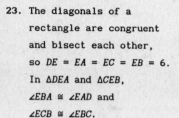

$BC = 2\left(\dfrac{5.2\sqrt{3}}{3}\right) \approx 6.0$

Perimeter $\approx 3(6.0) \approx 18.0$ m

23. The diagonals of a rectangle are congruent and bisect each other, so $DE = EA = EC = EB = 6$.

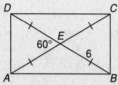

In $\triangle DEA$ and $\triangle CEB$,

$\angle EBA \cong \angle EAD$ and

$\angle ECB \cong \angle EBC$.

Since $m\angle DEA = 60$ and $m\angle CEB = 60$, $m\angle EDA = m\angle EAD = 60$ and $m\angle ECB = m\angle EBC = 60$. Therefore, $DA = DE = EA = 6$ and $CB = EC = EB = 6$. $\triangle CDA$ and $\triangle ABC$ are $30°-60°-90°$ triangles, so $DC = AD\sqrt{3} = 6\sqrt{3}$ and $AB = CB\sqrt{3} = 6\sqrt{3}$.

perimeter of rectangle $= AB + BC + CD + DA$
$$= 6\sqrt{3} + 6 + 6\sqrt{3} + 6$$
$$= 12 + 12\sqrt{3} \text{ or about}$$
$$32.8 \text{ units}$$

24. $RS = 2(10\sqrt{3}) = 20\sqrt{3} \approx 34.641$ units

$TS = 10\sqrt{3}(\sqrt{3}) = 30$

$TV = \dfrac{10\sqrt{3}}{\sqrt{3}} = 10$

$VS = TS - TV$

$VS = 30 - 10 = 20$ units

25. Side of equilateral triangle is 14 cm.

$DC = \dfrac{1}{2}(14) = 7$

$BD = 7\sqrt{3} \approx 12.1$ cm

26. $u^2 = 1^2 + 1^2$

$u^2 = 2$

$u = \sqrt{2}$

27. $v^2 = 1^2 + (\sqrt{2})^2$

$v^2 = 1 + 2 = 3$

$v = \sqrt{3}$

28. $w^2 = 1^2 + (\sqrt{3})^2$

$w^2 = 1 + 3 = 4$

$w = 2$

29. $x^2 = 1^2 + 2^2$

$x^2 = 1 + 4 = 5$

$x = \sqrt{5}$

30. $y^2 = 1^2 + (\sqrt{5})^2$

$y^2 = 1 + 5 = 6$

$y = \sqrt{6}$

31. $z^2 = 1^2 + (\sqrt{6})^2$

$z^2 = 1 + 6 = 7$

$z = \sqrt{7}$

32. $(AE)^2 = (AD)^2 + (DE)^2$

$(AE)^2 = s^2 + s^2 = 2s^2$

$AE = s\sqrt{2}$

$(AF)^2 = (AE)^2 + (EF)^2$

$(AF)^2 = (s\sqrt{2})^2 + s^2$

$(AF)^2 = 2s^2 + s^2 = 3s^2$

$AF = s\sqrt{3}$

33. $\overline{BF}$, $\overline{DF}$ and $\overline{BD}$, the three sides that make the triangle which contains $\angle BFD$, all have length $s\sqrt{2}$. Therefore, $\triangle BFD$ is equilateral and $m\angle BFD = 60$.

34. Given: $\triangle ABC$ is a $45°-45°-90°$ triangle.

Prove: Measure of the hypotenuse is $\sqrt{2}$ times the length of a leg.

Let ℓ = the length of a leg.

Let h = the length of the hypotenuse.

Since the angles opposite them are congruent, the legs are congruent. Using the Pythagorean Theorem:

$\ell^2 + \ell^2 = h^2$

$2\ell^2 = h^2$

$\ell\sqrt{2} = h$

Therefore, the length of the hypotenuse is $\sqrt{2}$ times the length of a leg.

35. $1 + 2\left(\dfrac{\sqrt{2}}{2}\right) = 1 + \sqrt{2}$
$$\approx 2.4 \text{ ft}$$

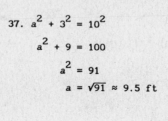

36. $3\sqrt{3} + 3\sqrt{3} =$
$$6\sqrt{3} \approx 10.4 \text{ mm}$$

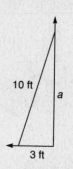

37. $a^2 + 3^2 = 10^2$

$a^2 + 9 = 100$

$a^2 = 91$

$a = \sqrt{91} \approx 9.5$ ft

38. $\angle QPR \cong \angle APB$

$$\frac{3+5}{5} \overset{?}{=} \frac{12}{12-4.5}$$

$$\frac{8}{5} = \frac{12}{7.5}$$

$$60 = 60$$

Therefore $\angle BPA \sim \angle RPQ$ by SAS Similarity.

39. $10y = 3y + 21$

$7y = 21$

$y = 3$

$10y = 3y + 21 = 30$

Perimeter $= 30 + 30 + 18 = 78$ in.

40. Given: $m\angle BAC = 90$

$m\angle ABC = 30$

$m\angle EDC = 60$

Prove: ℓ is parallel

to m.

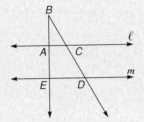

Proof: Since $m\angle BAC = 90$, $\triangle BAC$ is a right triangle. Thus, $m\angle BAC + m\angle ABC + m\angle ACB = 180$, and since $m\angle ABC = 30$, it follows that $90 + 30 + m\angle ACB = 180$. By subtraction, $m\angle ACB = 60$. Since $\angle ACB$ and $\angle EDC$ are congruent corresponding angles, ℓ is parallel to m.

41. See students' work.

8-4 Trigonometry

1. Triangle measurement

2. $\overline{BC}$; $\overline{AC}$

3. $\sin A = \cos B$

4. They are reciprocals.

5. $\sin A = \frac{15}{17} \approx 0.882$

6. $\cos A = \frac{8}{17} \approx 0.471$

7. $\tan A = \frac{15}{8} = 1.875$

8. $\sin B = \frac{8}{17} \approx 0.471$

9. $\cos B = \frac{15}{17} \approx 0.882$

10. $\tan B = \frac{8}{15} \approx 0.533$

11. $\tan Q$

12. $\cos Q$

13. $\sin P$

14. $\tan P$

15. 0.174

16. 0.809

17. 0.781

18. $m\angle A = 6$

19. $m\angle S = 35$

20. $m\angle C = 26$

---

21. $\tan 19 = \frac{28,000}{x}$

$$x = \frac{28,000}{\tan 19}$$

$$x \approx 81,317.9 \text{ ft} \approx \frac{81317.9}{5280} \text{ or } 15.4 \text{ miles}$$

22. $\sin A = \frac{21}{29} \approx 0.724$

23. $\sin B = \frac{20}{29} \approx 0.690$

24. $\tan A = \frac{21}{20} = 1.050$

25. $\cos B = \frac{21}{29} \approx 0.724$

26. $\cos E = \frac{24}{40} = 0.600$

27. $\tan F = \frac{24}{32} = 0.750$

28. $\tan C$

29. $\cos T$

30. $\sin T$

31. $\tan T$

32. $\sin 60° = \frac{\sqrt{3}}{2}$

33. $\cos 60° = \frac{1}{2}$

34. $\tan 60° = \dfrac{\frac{\sqrt{3}}{2}}{\frac{1}{2}} = \frac{\sqrt{3}}{2} \cdot \frac{2}{1} = \sqrt{3}$

35. $\sin 30° = \frac{1}{2}$

36. $\cos 30° = \frac{\sqrt{3}}{2}$

37. $\tan 30° = \dfrac{\frac{1}{2}}{\frac{\sqrt{3}}{2}} = \frac{1}{2} \cdot \frac{2}{\sqrt{3}} = \frac{1}{\sqrt{3}} \cdot \frac{\sqrt{3}}{\sqrt{3}} = \frac{\sqrt{3}}{3}$

38. $\sin x° = \frac{7}{13}$; $x \approx 33°$

39. $\cos 17° = \frac{x}{9.7}$

$$x = 9.7(\cos 17°)$$

$$x \approx 9.3$$

40. $\tan x = \frac{16}{10}$

$$x \approx 58°$$

41. $\sin x = \frac{12}{18}$

$$x \approx 42°$$

$$12^2 + \left(\frac{1}{2}y\right)^2 = 18^2$$

$$144 + \frac{1}{4}y^2 = 324$$

$$\frac{1}{4}y^2 = 180$$

$$y^2 = 720$$

$$y = \frac{720}{\sqrt{720}} \approx 26.8$$

42. $\sin 63° = \frac{y}{50}$

$$y = 50(\sin 63°)$$

$$y \approx 44.6$$

$$\cos 63° = \frac{x}{50}$$

$$x = 50(\cos 63°)$$

$$x \approx 22.7$$

43. $\sin x = \frac{2}{4}$

$$x \approx 30°$$

$$\cos 40° = \frac{y}{4}$$

$$y = 4(\cos 40°)$$

$$y \approx 3.1$$

44. $\sin x = \frac{18}{27}$

$\quad\quad x \approx 42°$

$\quad a^2 + 18^2 = 27^2$

$\quad a^2 + 324 = 729$

$\quad\quad a^2 = 405$

$\quad\quad\quad a \approx 20.1$

$\quad \frac{1}{2}a \approx 10.0$ (side opp. $y°$ angle)

$\quad \tan y = \frac{10}{18}$

$\quad\quad y \approx 29°$

45. $\tan 55° = \frac{x}{9}$

$\quad\quad x = 9(\tan 55°)$

$\quad\quad x \approx 12.9$

$\quad \sin 47° = \frac{12.9}{y}$

$\quad\quad y = \frac{12.9}{\sin 47°}$

$\quad\quad y \approx 17.6$

46. $\tan 32° = \frac{24}{x}$

$\quad\quad x = \frac{24}{\tan 32°}$

$\quad\quad x \approx 38.4$

$\quad \cos 32° = \frac{y}{38.4}$

$\quad\quad y = 38.4(\cos 32°)$

$\quad\quad y \approx 32.6$

47. $\sin 55° = \frac{100}{x}$

$\quad\quad x = \frac{100}{\sin 55°}$

$\quad\quad x \approx 122$ ft

48. $\sin 25° = \frac{x}{30}$

$\quad\quad x = 30(\sin 25°)$

$\quad\quad x \approx 12.7$ units

$\quad \overline{BD} = 2(12.7)$

$\quad\quad = 25.4$ units

$\quad \cos 25° = \frac{y}{30}$

$\quad\quad y = 30(\cos 25°)$

$\quad\quad y \approx 27.2$

$\quad \overline{AC} \approx 2(27.2) \approx 54.4$ units

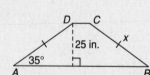

49. $\sin 35° = \frac{25}{x}$

$\quad\quad x = \frac{25}{\sin 35°}$

$\quad\quad x \approx 43.6$ inches

50. $3^2 + y^2 = 4^2$

$\quad 9 + y^2 = 16$

$\quad\quad y^2 = 7$

$\quad\quad y = \sqrt{7}$

$\quad \tan Y = \frac{\sqrt{7}}{3} \approx 0.88$

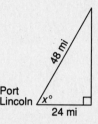

51. a. $m\angle A < 45$

b. $m\angle A = 45$

c. $\tan A > 1$

d. $0 \le \sin A \le 1;\ 0 \le \cos A \le 1$

52. $\cos x = \frac{24}{48}$

$\quad\quad x \approx 60°$

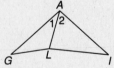

53.

$\quad \sin 15° = \frac{x}{2}$

$\quad\quad x = 2(\sin 15°)$

$\quad\quad x \approx 0.5176$ miles

$\quad 0.5176(5280) \approx 2733$ ft

54. $P = IV \cos θ$

$\quad P = 2(120) \cos 67°$

$\quad P \approx 93.775$ watts

55. hypotenuse $= 2(8) - 16$ units

$\quad$ longer leg $= \sqrt{3}(8) \approx 13.9$ units

56. $\frac{8}{x} = \frac{x}{13}$

$\quad x^2 = 104$

$\quad x = \sqrt{104} \approx 10.2$

$\quad \frac{5}{y} = \frac{y}{13}$

$\quad y^2 = 65$

$\quad y = \sqrt{65} \approx 8.1$

57. No, $\frac{AB}{AC} \ne \frac{AE}{AD}$

$\quad \frac{9.6}{15} \stackrel{?}{=} \frac{6.8}{10}$

$\quad\quad 96 \ne 102$

58. $\frac{10 + 22}{2} = 16$ inches

59. False; the diagonals of a rhombus bisect opposite angles.

60. Given: $\overline{GA} \cong \overline{AI}$

$\quad\quad GL < IL$

$\quad$ Prove: $m\angle 1 < m\angle 2$

$\quad$ Proof: $\triangle GAL$ and $\triangle IAL$ satisfy the SSS Inequality. That is, $\overline{GA} \cong \overline{AI}$, $\overline{AL} \cong \overline{AL}$, and $GL < IL$. It follows that $m\angle 1 < m\angle 2$.

61. $2x - 75 = x + 25$

$\quad\quad\quad x = 100$

62. $7x + 12 = 4x + 42$

$\quad\quad\quad 3x = 30$

$\quad\quad\quad\quad x = 10$

63. $\sin Y = \dfrac{XZ}{YZ}$

$\cos Y = \dfrac{XY}{YZ}$

$\tan Y = \dfrac{XZ}{XY}$

Mid-Chapter Review

PAGE 382

1. $\dfrac{8}{HK} = \dfrac{HK}{14}$

   $(HK)^2 = 112$

   $HK = \sqrt{112} \approx 10.6$

2. $\dfrac{9}{GH} = \dfrac{GH}{15}$

   $(GH)^2 = 135$

   $GH = \sqrt{135} \approx 11.6$

3. $\dfrac{7}{HJ} = \dfrac{HJ}{11}$

   $(HJ)^2 = 77$

   $HJ = \sqrt{77} \approx 8.8$

4. $\dfrac{8}{HG} = \dfrac{HG}{16}$

   $(HG)^2 = 128$

   $HG = \sqrt{128} \approx 11.3$

5. $12^2 + 16^2 \overset{?}{=} 20^2$

   $144 + 256 \overset{?}{=} 400$

   $400 = 400$

   Yes

6. $(2.2)^2 + (2.4)^2 \overset{?}{=} (3.3)^2$

   $4.84 + 5.76 \overset{?}{=} 10.89$

   $10.6 \neq 10.89$

   No

7. $1^2 + (\sqrt{2})^2 \overset{?}{=} (\sqrt{3})^2$

   $1 + 2 \overset{?}{=} 3$

   $3 = 3$

   Yes

8. $(\sqrt{3})^2 + (\sqrt{4})^2 \overset{?}{=} (\sqrt{5})^2$

   $3 + 4 \overset{?}{=} 5$

   $7 \neq 5$

   No

9. $(1.6)^2 + (3.0)^2 \overset{?}{=} (3.4)^2$

   $2.56 + 9 \overset{?}{=} 11.56$

   $11.56 = 11.56$

   Yes

10. $15^2 + 20^2 \overset{?}{=} 25^2$

    $225 + 400 \overset{?}{=} 625$

    $625 = 625$

    Yes

11. Work with the right triangle formed by one side and an altitude.

    short leg $= \dfrac{12\sqrt{3}}{\sqrt{3}} = 12$

    hypotenuse $= 2(12) = 24$

    perimeter of equilateral triangle

    $= 3(24)$

    $= 72$ units

12. $8\sqrt{2} \approx 11.3$ cm

13. 12 ft 6 in. $= 12.5$ ft

    $\sin x = \dfrac{12.5}{16}$

    $x \approx 51°$

    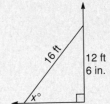

    16 ft

    12 ft 6 in.

    $x°$

Technology: Tangent Ratio

PAGE 383   EXERCISES

1. 8, 83°

2. $\dfrac{2}{3}$, 34°

3. $\dfrac{2}{5}$, 22°

8-5 Application: Using Trigonometry

PAGE 386   CHECKING FOR UNDERSTANDING

1. See students' work.

2. See students' work.

3. It depends on what information is given.
   If you were given: opposite and hypotenuse, use sine;
   opposite and adjacent, use tangent;
   adjacent and hypotenuse, use cosine.

4. Elevation, $\angle GEF$; depression, $\angle HFE$

5. Elevation $\angle ZXY$; depression, $\angle WYX$

6. Elevation $\angle RUS$; depression $\angle TSU$

7. Elevation $\angle KHJ$; depression $\angle IJH$

8. $\sin 15° = \dfrac{QR}{37}$

   $QR = 37(\sin 15°)$

   $QR \approx 9.6$

9. $\sin 47° = \frac{10}{PQ}$

$PQ = \frac{10}{\sin 47°}$

$PQ \approx 13.7$

10. $\cos 16° = \frac{13.4}{PQ}$

$PQ = \frac{13.4}{\cos 16°}$

$PQ \approx 13.9$

11. $\tan 72° = \frac{13}{QR}$

$QR = \frac{13}{\tan 72°}$

$QR \approx 4.2$

12. $\tan 74° = \frac{PR}{33.6}$

$PR = 33.6(\tan 74°)$

$PR \approx 117.2$

13. $\cos 24° = \frac{43.7}{PQ}$

$PQ = \frac{43.7}{\cos 24°}$

$PQ \approx 47.8$

14. $\tan 35° = \frac{BC}{100}$

$BC = 100(\tan 35°)$

$BC \approx 70.02$ m

$CD \approx 70.02 + 1.45$

≈ 71.47 m

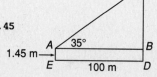

15. $\cos 65° = \frac{8}{AC}$

$AC = \frac{8}{\cos 65°}$

$AC \approx 19$ feet

PAGES 387–388   EXERCISES

16. $\tan Y = \frac{54}{28}$

$Y \approx 63°$

17. $\tan X = \frac{28}{54}$

$X \approx 27°$

18. $90°$

19. $XZ^2 + YZ^2 = XY^2$

$54^2 + 28^2 = XY^2$

$2916 + 784 = XY^2$

$3700 = XY^2$

$\sqrt{3700} = XY$

$61 \approx XY$

20. $90°$

21. $\tan 71° = \frac{6.3}{UV}$

$UV = \frac{6.3}{\tan 71°}$

$UV \approx 2$

22. $\sin 71° = \frac{6.3}{WV}$

$WV = \frac{6.3}{\sin 71°}$

$WV \approx 7$

23. $m\angle W + m\angle V = 90$

$m\angle W + 71 = 90$

$m\angle W = 19$

24. $\tan 23° = \frac{x}{100}$

$x = 100(\tan 23°)$

$x \approx 42.45$ m

height of building $\approx 42.4 + 1.55 \approx 44.00$ m

25. $\tan 15° = \frac{d}{495}$

$d = 495(\tan 15°)$

$d \approx 132.63$ meters

26. $\sin 50° = \frac{x}{50}$

$x = 50(\sin 50°)$

$x \approx 38.30$ meters

27. $\sin x = \frac{10}{75}$

$x \approx 8°$

28.

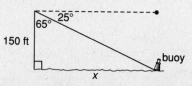

$\tan 65° = \frac{x}{150}$

$x = 150(\tan 65°)$

$x \approx 321.68$ feet

29. $\tan 44° = \frac{30}{x}$

$x = \frac{30}{\tan 44°}$

$x \approx 31.07$ meters

30. $\tan x = \frac{40}{630}$

$x \approx 4°$

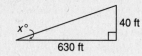

31. $\tan 29° = \frac{1353}{x}$

$x = \frac{1353}{\tan 29°}$

$x \approx 2440.88$ feet

$\tan 42° = \frac{1353}{x}$

$x = \frac{1353}{\tan 42°}$

$x \approx 1502.66$ feet

Distance between boats is

$2440.88 - 1502.66 \approx 938.22$ feet

32.

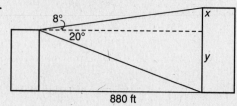

$\tan 8° = \frac{x}{880}$

$x = 880(\tan 8°)$

$x \approx 124$ feet

$$\tan 20° = \frac{y}{880}$$

$$y = 880(\tan 20°)$$

$$y \approx 320 \text{ ft}$$

$$x + y \approx 124 + 320 \approx 444 \text{ feet}$$

33. a.

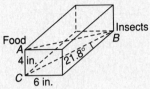

$$\sin 21.8° = \frac{6}{BC}$$

$$BC = \frac{6}{\sin 21.8°}$$

$$BC \approx 16.16 \text{ inches}$$

$$(AB)^2 = 4^2 + (16.16)^2$$

$$(AB)^2 = 277.15$$

$$AB = \sqrt{277.15} \approx 16.6 \text{ inches}$$

b. Find the side of the box, y.

$$\tan 21.8° = \frac{6}{y}$$

$$y = \frac{6}{\tan 21.8°}$$

$$y \approx 15$$

Open up the box to see how the ant could crawl. He could take one of the two paths. Look at the right triangles formed.

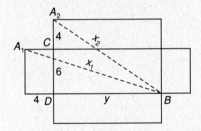

If he took the path of length x_1, then

$$(y + 4)^2 + 6^2 = (x_1)^2$$

$$(15 + 4)^2 + 6^2 = (x_1)^2$$

$$(19)^2 + 6^2 = (x_1)^2$$

$$361 + 36 = (x_1)^2$$

$$397 = (x_1)^2$$

$$\sqrt{397} = x_1$$

$$19.9 \approx x_1$$

If he took the path of length x_2, then

$$(4 + 6)^2 + y^2 = (x_2)^2$$

$$10^2 + 15^2 = (x_2)^2$$

$$325 = (x_2)^2$$

$$18.03 \approx x_2$$

x_2 is shorter so ant would crawl about 18.03 inches.

34. $d^2 = 160^2 + 40^2$
$d^2 = 27,200$
$d = 164.92 \text{ km}$

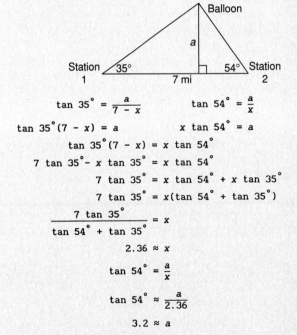

35. $\cos 40° = \dfrac{x}{50}$

$$x = 50(\cos 40°)$$

$$x \approx 38.3$$

$$50 - x \approx 50 - 38.3 \approx 11.7$$

The tip of the pendulum rose about 11.7 cm.

36. Let x = distance from station 2 to point directly below balloon.

$$\tan 35° = \frac{a}{7 - x} \qquad \tan 54° = \frac{a}{x}$$

$$\tan 35°(7 - x) = a \qquad x\tan 54° = a$$

$$\tan 35°(7 - x) = x\tan 54°$$

$$7\tan 35° - x\tan 35° = x\tan 54°$$

$$7\tan 35° = x\tan 54° + x\tan 35°$$

$$7\tan 35° = x(\tan 54° + \tan 35°)$$

$$\frac{7\tan 35°}{\tan 54° + \tan 35°} = x$$

$$2.36 \approx x$$

$$\tan 54° = \frac{a}{x}$$

$$\tan 54° \approx \frac{a}{2.36}$$

$$3.2 \approx a$$

The altitude of the balloon is about 3.2 miles.

37. $\cos A = \frac{2}{6} = \frac{1}{3} \approx 0.333$

$$a^2 + 2^2 = 6^2$$
$$a^2 + 4 = 36$$
$$a^2 = 32$$
$$a = \sqrt{32} = 4\sqrt{2}$$

$\sin A = \frac{4\sqrt{2}}{6} = \frac{2\sqrt{2}}{3} \approx 0.943$

$\tan A = \frac{4\sqrt{2}}{2} = 2\sqrt{2} \approx 2.828$

38. $\frac{1}{20} = \frac{12.7}{x}$

$x = 254$ miles

39. $RT = 2(7.6) = 15.2$ units

40. Given: $\overline{CI} \cong \overline{MI}$

$\overline{IT}$ is a median
of $\triangle CIM$.

Prove: $\angle CIT \cong \angle MIT$

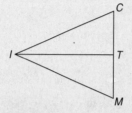

STATEMENTS	REASONS
a. $\overline{CI} \cong \overline{MI}$ $\overline{IT}$ is a median of $\triangle CIM$.	a. Given
b. $\overline{IT} \cong \overline{IT}$	b. Congruence of segments is reflexive.
c. $\overline{TC} \cong \overline{TM}$	c. Definition of median
d. $\triangle CTI \cong \triangle MTI$	d. SSS
e. $\angle CIT \cong \angle MIT$	e. CPCTC

41. See students' work.

8-6 Law of Sines

PAGES 391-392 CHECKING FOR UNDERSTANDING

1. $\frac{\sin M}{m} = \frac{\sin L}{l} = \frac{\sin K}{k}$

2. The law of sines can be used on any triangle, but it is usually used on non-right triangles.

3. Case 1: You know the measure of two angles and any side of a triangle.

Case 2: You know the measure of two sides and an angle opposite one of the known sides of the triangle.

4. $\frac{\sin 22^\circ}{a} = \frac{\sin 49^\circ}{4.7}$

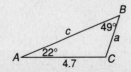

5. $\frac{\sin 50^\circ}{14} = \frac{\sin B}{10}$

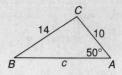

6. $\frac{\sin 40^\circ}{20} = \frac{\sin 60^\circ}{b}$

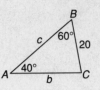

7. $\frac{\sin 42^\circ}{16} = \frac{\sin C}{12}$

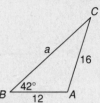

8. $m\angle A = 52$

$$\frac{\sin 52^\circ}{84} = \frac{\sin 70^\circ}{b}$$
$$b(\sin 52^\circ) = 84(\sin 70^\circ)$$
$$b = \frac{84(\sin 70^\circ)}{\sin 52^\circ}$$
$$b \approx 100.2$$
$$\frac{\sin 52^\circ}{84} = \frac{\sin 58^\circ}{c}$$
$$c(\sin 52^\circ) = 84(\sin 58^\circ)$$
$$c = \frac{84(\sin 58^\circ)}{\sin 52^\circ}$$
$$c \approx 90.4$$

9. $\frac{\sin 106}{17} = \frac{\sin B}{10}$

$$17(\sin B) = 10(\sin 106)$$
$$\sin B = \frac{10(\sin 106)}{17}$$
$$B \approx 34^\circ$$
$$m\angle C \approx 180 - (106 + 34) \approx 40$$
$$\frac{\sin 106^\circ}{17} = \frac{\sin 40^\circ}{c}$$
$$c = \frac{17(\sin 40^\circ)}{\sin 106^\circ}$$
$$c \approx 11.4$$

10. $m\angle C = 74$

$$\frac{\sin 49^\circ}{8} = \frac{\sin 57^\circ}{b}$$
$$b(\sin 49^\circ) = 8(\sin 57^\circ)$$
$$b = \frac{8(\sin 57^\circ)}{\sin 49^\circ}$$
$$b \approx 8.9$$

$$\frac{\sin 49°}{8} = \frac{\sin 74°}{c}$$

$$c(\sin 49°) = 8(\sin 74°)$$

$$c = \frac{8(\sin 74°)}{\sin 49°}$$

$$c \approx 10.2$$

11. $m\angle C = 80$

$$\frac{\sin 80°}{20} = \frac{\sin 40°}{a}$$

$$a(\sin 80°) = 20(\sin 40°)$$

$$a = \frac{20(\sin 40°)}{\sin 80°}$$

$$a \approx 13.1$$

$$\frac{\sin 80°}{20} = \frac{\sin 60°}{b}$$

$$b(\sin 80°) = 20(\sin 60°)$$

$$b = \frac{20(\sin 60°)}{\sin 80°}$$

$$b \approx 17.6$$

12. $m\angle A = m\angle C = 72$

$$\frac{\sin 36°}{22} = \frac{\sin 72°}{a}$$

$$a(\sin 36°) = 22(\sin 72°)$$

$$a = \frac{22(\sin 72°)}{\sin 36°}$$

$$a \approx 35.6 \text{ cm}$$

Perimeter $\approx 2(35.6) + 22 \approx 93.2$ cm

PAGES 392-393   EXERCISES

13. $\dfrac{\sin 53°}{a} = \dfrac{\sin 61°}{2.8}$

$$a(\sin 61°) = 2.8(\sin 53°)$$

$$a = \frac{2.8(\sin 53°)}{\sin 61°}$$

$$a \approx 2.6$$

14. $\dfrac{\sin 98°}{36} = \dfrac{\sin C}{12}$

$$36(\sin C) = 12(\sin 98°)$$

$$\sin C = \frac{12(\sin 98°)}{36}$$

$$C \approx 19°$$

15. $m\angle C = 87$

$$\frac{\sin 87°}{2.2} = \frac{\sin 70°}{a}$$

$$a(\sin 87°) = 2.2(\sin 70°)$$

$$a = \frac{2.2(\sin 70°)}{\sin 87°}$$

$$a \approx 2.1$$

16. $\dfrac{\sin 55°}{11} = \dfrac{\sin A}{9}$

$$11(\sin A) = 9(\sin 55°)$$

$$\sin A = \frac{9(\sin 55°)}{11}$$

$$A \approx 42°$$

17. $m\angle B = 80$

$$\frac{\sin 70°}{8} = \frac{\sin 30°}{a}$$

$$a(\sin 70°) = 8(\sin 30°)$$

$$a = \frac{8(\sin 30°)}{\sin 70°}$$

$$a \approx 4.3$$

$$\frac{\sin 70°}{8} = \frac{\sin 80°}{b}$$

$$b(\sin 70°) = 8(\sin 80°)$$

$$b = \frac{8(\sin 80°)}{\sin 70°}$$

$$b \approx 8.4$$

18. $\dfrac{\sin 124°}{25} = \dfrac{\sin A}{10}$

$$25(\sin A) = 10(\sin 124°)$$

$$\sin A = \frac{10(\sin 124°)}{25}$$

$$A \approx 19°$$

$$m\angle B \approx 37$$

$$\frac{\sin 124°}{25} = \frac{\sin 37°}{b}$$

$$b(\sin 124°) = 25(\sin 37°)$$

$$b = \frac{25(\sin 37°)}{\sin 124°}$$

$$b \approx 18.1$$

19. $m\angle C = 89$

$$\frac{\sin 29°}{a} = \frac{\sin 89°}{11.5}$$

$$a(\sin 89°) = 11.5(\sin 29°)$$

$$a = \frac{11.5(\sin 29°)}{\sin 89°}$$

$$a \approx 5.6$$

$$\frac{\sin 89°}{11.5} = \frac{\sin 62°}{b}$$

$$b(\sin 89°) = 11.5(\sin 62°)$$

$$b = \frac{11.5(\sin 62°)}{\sin 89°}$$

$$b \approx 10.2$$

20. $\dfrac{\sin 35°}{24} = \dfrac{\sin A}{7.5}$

$24(\sin A) = 7.5(\sin 35°)$

$\sin A = \dfrac{7.5(\sin 35°)}{24}$

$A \approx 10°$

$m\angle B \approx 135$

$\dfrac{\sin 35°}{24} = \dfrac{\sin 135°}{b}$

$b(\sin 35°) = 24(\sin 135°)$

$b = \dfrac{24(\sin 135°)}{\sin 35°}$

$b \approx 29.6$

21. $m\angle A = 25°$

$\dfrac{\sin 36°}{8} = \dfrac{\sin 25°}{a}$

$a(\sin 36°) = 8(\sin 25°)$

$a = \dfrac{8(\sin 25°)}{\sin 36°}$

$a \approx 5.8$

$\dfrac{\sin 36°}{8} = \dfrac{\sin 119°}{c}$

$c(\sin 36°) = 8(\sin 119°)$

$c = \dfrac{8(\sin 119°)}{\sin 36°}$

$c \approx 11.9$

22. $m\angle A = 60$

$\dfrac{\sin 60°}{0.9} = \dfrac{\sin 47°}{b}$

$b(\sin 60°) = 0.9(\sin 47°)$

$b = \dfrac{0.9(\sin 47°)}{\sin 60°}$

$b \approx 0.8$

$\dfrac{\sin 60°}{0.9} = \dfrac{\sin 73°}{c}$

$c(\sin 60°) = 0.9(\sin 73°)$

$c = \dfrac{0.9(\sin 73°)}{\sin 60°}$

$c \approx 1.0$

23. $\dfrac{\sin 103°}{20} = \dfrac{\sin C}{9.2}$

$20(\sin C) = 9.2(\sin 103°)$

$\sin C = \dfrac{9.2(\sin 103°)}{20}$

$C \approx 27°$

$m\angle A \approx 50$

$\dfrac{\sin 103°}{20} = \dfrac{\sin 50°}{a}$

$a = (\sin 103°) = 20(\sin 50°)$

$a = \dfrac{20(\sin 50°)}{\sin 103°}$

$a \approx 15.7$

24. $\dfrac{\sin 95°}{14} = \dfrac{\sin A}{12}$

$14(\sin A) = 12(\sin 95°)$

$\sin A = \dfrac{12(\sin 95°)}{14}$

$A \approx 59°$

$m\angle C \approx 26$

$\dfrac{\sin 95°}{14} = \dfrac{\sin 26°}{c}$

$c(\sin 95°) = 14(\sin 26°)$

$c = \dfrac{14(\sin 26°)}{\sin 95°}$

$c \approx 6.2$

25. $m\angle A = m\angle C = 47.5$

$\dfrac{\sin 47.5°}{160} = \dfrac{\sin 85°}{b}$

$b(\sin 47.5°) = 160(\sin 85°)$

$b = \dfrac{160(\sin 85°)}{\sin 47.5°}$

$b \approx 216 \text{ ft}$

Perimeter $\approx 2(160) + 216 \approx 536$

26. $\dfrac{\sin 75°}{34} = \dfrac{\sin 40°}{a}$

$a(\sin 75°) = 34(\sin 40°)$

$a = \dfrac{34(\sin 40°)}{\sin 75°}$

$a \approx 22.6 \text{ ft}$

$\dfrac{\sin 75°}{34} = \dfrac{\sin 65°}{b}$

$b(\sin 75°) = 34(\sin 65°)$

$b = \dfrac{34(\sin 65°)}{\sin 75°}$

$b \approx 31.9 \text{ ft}$

27. $\dfrac{\sin 100.4°}{30} = \dfrac{\sin 45.6°}{x}$

$x(\sin 100.4°) = 30(\sin 45.6°)$

$x = \dfrac{30(\sin 45.6°)}{\sin 100.4°}$

$x \approx 21.8 \text{ miles}$

28. $m\angle BDC = 90 - m\angle DBC$
$= 90 - 6.7$
$= 83.3$
$m\angle ADB = 180 - m\angle BDC$
$= 180 - 83.3$
$= 96.7$

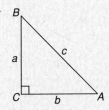

$m\angle ABD + m\angle ADB + m\angle BAD = 180$
$(37.2 - 6.7) + 96.7 + m\angle BAD = 180$
$m\angle BAD = 52.8$

Use the law of sines.
$$\frac{\sin m\angle BAD}{x} = \frac{\sin m\angle ABD}{AD}$$
$$\frac{\sin 52.8}{x} = \frac{\sin 30.5}{35}$$
$$x = \frac{35 \sin 52.8}{\sin 30.5}$$
$$x \approx 54.9$$
The shadow is about 54.9 feet long.

29. Yes. By definition, $\sin A = \frac{a}{c}$
and $\sin B = \frac{b}{c}$. According to the

law of sines
$$\frac{\sin A}{a} = \frac{\sin B}{b}$$
$$\frac{\frac{a}{c}}{a} \; ? \; \frac{\frac{b}{c}}{b}$$
$$c = c$$

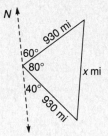

So the law of sines holds true for the acute angles of a right triangle.

30. a.

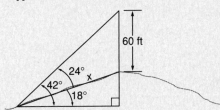

b. $$\frac{\sin 50°}{930} = \frac{\sin 80°}{x}$$
$$x(\sin 50°) = 930(\sin 80°)$$
$$x = \frac{930(\sin 80°)}{\sin 50°}$$
$$x \approx 1196 \text{ miles}$$

31. Let x = distance surveyor is from base of support.

$$\frac{\sin 24°}{60} = \frac{\sin 48°}{x}$$
$$x(\sin 24°) = 60(\sin 48°)$$
$$x = \frac{60(\sin 48°)}{\sin 24°}$$
$$x \approx 109.6 \text{ feet}$$

32. $$\frac{\sin 64°}{100} = \frac{\sin 26°}{x}$$
$$x(\sin 64°) = 100(\sin 26°)$$
$$x = \frac{100(\sin 26°)}{\sin 64°}$$
$$x \approx 48.77 \text{ meters}$$
height of dam $\approx 48.77 + 1.73 \approx 50.50$ meters

33. $$\frac{34}{14} = \frac{YZ}{4}$$
$$14(YZ) = 136$$
$$YZ \approx 9.7 \text{ inches}$$

34. See students' work.

35. Given: $\overline{AB} \perp \overline{BD}$
$\overline{DE} \perp \overline{DB}$
$\overline{DB}$ bisects $\overline{AE}$.
Prove: $\angle A \cong \angle E$

STATEMENTS	REASONS
1. $\overline{AB} \perp \overline{BD}$ $\overline{DE} \perp \overline{DB}$	1. Given
2. $\angle B$ is a right angle. $\angle D$ is a right angle.	2. $\perp$ lines form four rt. $\angle$s.
3. $\angle B \cong \angle D$	3. All rt. $\angle$s are $\cong$.
4. $\angle 1 \cong \angle 2$	4. Vertical $\angle$s are $\cong$.
5. $\overline{DB}$ bisects $\overline{AE}$.	5. Given
6. $\overline{AC} \cong \overline{EC}$	6. Definition of bisector
7. $\triangle ABC \cong \triangle EDC$	7. AAS
8. $\angle A \cong \angle E$	8. CPCTC

36. See students' work.

8-7 Law of Cosines

PAGES 396-397   CHECKING FOR UNDERSTANDING

1. The law of cosines can be used to solve a triangle in the following cases.
   1. To find the length of the third side of any triangle if the lengths of the two sides and the included angle are given.
   2. To find an angle of a triangle if the lengths of the three sides are given.

2. See students' work.

3. The law of sines and law of cosines are most appropriate for non-right triangles. The trigonometric ratios are only appropriate for right triangles.

Use	Given
law of sines	the measures of two angles and any side; or two sides and an angle opposite one of the known sides
law of cosines	the measures of two sides and the included angle; or the lengths of all three sides

4. Law of sines

$$\frac{\sin 40^\circ}{10} = \frac{\sin C}{8}$$

$$10(\sin C) = 8(\sin 40^\circ)$$

$$\sin C = \frac{8(\sin 40^\circ)}{10}$$

$$C \approx 31^\circ$$

$$m\angle B \approx 109$$

$$\frac{\sin 40^\circ}{10} = \frac{\sin 109^\circ}{b}$$

$$b(\sin 40^\circ) = 10(\sin 109^\circ)$$

$$b = \frac{10(\sin 109^\circ)}{\sin 40^\circ}$$

$$b \approx 14.7$$

5. Law of cosines

$$a^2 = 6^2 + 7^2 - 2(6)(7)\cos 55^\circ$$

$$a^2 \approx 36.8$$

$$a \approx 6.1$$

$$\frac{\sin 55^\circ}{6.1} = \frac{\sin B}{6}$$

$$\sin B = \frac{6 \sin 55^\circ}{6.1}$$

$$\sin B \approx 0.8057$$

$$B \approx 54^\circ$$

$$m\angle A + m\angle B + m\angle C = 180$$

$$55 + 54 + m\angle C = 180$$

$$m\angle C \approx 71$$

6. Law of cosines

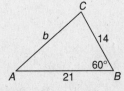

$$b^2 = (14)^2 + (21)^2 - 2(14)(21)\cos 60^\circ$$

$$b^2 = 343$$

$$b \approx 18.5$$

$$14^2 = (18.5)^2 + (21)^2 - 2(18.5)(21)\cos A$$

$$196 = 784 - 777\cos A$$

$$-588 = -777\cos A$$

$$41^\circ \approx A$$

$$m\angle C \approx 79$$

7. Law of cosines

$$c^2 = a^2 + b^2 - 2ab \cos C$$

$$16^2 = 14^2 + 15^2 - 2(14)(15)\cos C$$

$$256 = 196 + 225 - 420\cos C$$

$$-165 = -420\cos C$$

$$0.3929 \approx \cos C$$

$$67^\circ \approx C$$

$$\frac{\sin C}{c} = \frac{\sin A}{a}$$

$$\frac{\sin 67^\circ}{16} = \frac{\sin A}{14}$$

$$\sin A = \frac{14\sin 67^\circ}{16}$$

$$\sin A \approx 0.8054$$

$$A \approx 54^\circ$$

$$m\angle A + m\angle B + m\angle C = 180$$

$$54 + m\angle B + 67 = 180$$

$$m\angle B \approx 59$$

8. Law of sines

$$\frac{\sin 51^\circ}{40} = \frac{\sin C}{35}$$

$$40(\sin C) = 35(\sin 51^\circ)$$

$$\sin C = \frac{35(\sin 51^\circ)}{40}$$

$$C \approx 43^\circ$$

$$m\angle B \approx 86$$

$$\frac{\sin 51^\circ}{40} = \frac{\sin 86^\circ}{b}$$

$$b(\sin 51^\circ) = 40(\sin 86^\circ)$$

$$b = \frac{40(\sin 86^\circ)}{\sin 51^\circ}$$

$$b \approx 51.3$$

9. Law of cosines

$$5^2 = 6^2 + 7^2 - 2(6)(7)\cos A$$

$$25 = 85 - 84 \cos A$$

$$-60 = -84 \cos A$$

$$44^\circ \approx A$$

$$\frac{\sin 44^\circ}{5} = \frac{\sin B}{6}$$

$$\sin B = \frac{65\sin 44^\circ}{5}$$

$$\sin B \approx 0.8336$$

$$B \approx 56^\circ$$

$$m\angle A + m\angle B + m\angle C = 180$$

$$44 + 56 + m\angle C = 180$$

$$m\angle C = 80$$

10. Law of sines

$$\frac{\sin 66°}{185} = \frac{\sin A}{140}$$

$$185(\sin A) = 140(\sin 66°)$$

$$\sin A = \frac{140(\sin 66°)}{185}$$

$$A \approx 44°$$

$m\angle C \approx 70$

$$\frac{\sin 66°}{185} = \frac{\sin 70°}{c}$$

$$c(\sin 66°) = 185(\sin 70°)$$

$$c = \frac{185(\sin 70°)}{\sin 66°}$$

$$c \approx 190.3$$

11. Law of cosines

$$c^2 = (21.5)^2 + (13)^2 - 2(21.5)(13)\cos 78°$$

$$c^2 \approx 515.03$$

$$c \approx 22.7$$

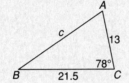

$$(21.5)^2 = (13)^2 + (22.7)^2 - 2(13)(22.7)\cos A$$

$$462.25 = 684.29 - 590.2 \cos A$$

$$-222.04 = -590.2 \cos A$$

$$68° \approx A$$

$$m\angle B \approx 34$$

PAGES 397-398   EXERCISES

12. Law of sines

$$m\angle B = 70$$

$$\frac{\sin 70°}{4} = \frac{\sin 40°}{a}$$

$$a(\sin 70°) = 4(\sin 40°)$$

$$a = \frac{4(\sin 40°)}{\sin 70°}$$

$$a \approx 2.7$$

$$\frac{\sin 70°}{4} = \frac{\sin 70°}{b}$$

$$b \approx 4.0$$

13. Law of cosines

$$c^2 = 11^2 + (10.5)^2 - 2(11)(10.5)\cos 35°$$

$$c^2 \approx 42.03$$

$$c \approx 6.5$$

$$\frac{\sin 35°}{6.5} = \frac{\sin A}{11}$$

$$\sin A = \frac{11\sin 35°}{6.5}$$

$$\sin A \approx 0.9707$$

$$A \approx 76°$$

$$m\angle A + m\angle B + m\angle C = 180$$

$$76 + m\angle B + 35 = 180$$

$$m\angle B = 69$$

14. Law of sines

$$\frac{\sin 42°}{17} = \frac{\sin A}{11}$$

$$17(\sin A) = 11(\sin 42°)$$

$$\sin A = \frac{11(\sin 42°)}{17}$$

$$A \approx 26°$$

$m\angle C \approx 112$

$$\frac{\sin 42°}{17} = \frac{\sin 112°}{c}$$

$$c(\sin 42°) = 17(\sin 112°)$$

$$c = \frac{17(\sin 112°)}{\sin 42°}$$

$$c \approx 23.6$$

15. Law of sines

$$m\angle B = 98$$

$$\frac{\sin 26°}{12.2} = \frac{\sin 56°}{a}$$

$$a(\sin 26°) = 12.2(\sin 56°)$$

$$a = \frac{12.2(\sin 56°)}{\sin 26°}$$

$$a \approx 23.1$$

$$\frac{\sin 26°}{12.2} = \frac{\sin 98°}{b}$$

$$b(\sin 26°) = 12.2(\sin 98°)$$

$$b = \frac{12.2(\sin 98°)}{\sin 26°}$$

$$b \approx 27.6$$

16. $$\frac{\sin 19°}{61} = \frac{\sin A}{51}$$

$$61(\sin A) = 51(\sin 19°)$$

$$\sin A = \frac{51(\sin 19°)}{61}$$

$$A \approx 16°$$

$m\angle C \approx 145$

$$\frac{\sin 19°}{61} = \frac{\sin 145°}{c}$$

$$c(\sin 19°) = 61(\sin 145°)$$

$$c = \frac{61(\sin 145°)}{\sin 19°}$$

$$c \approx 107.5$$

147

17. $5^2 = 12^2 + 13^2 - 2(12)(13)\cos A$

$25 = 313 - 312\cos A$

$-288 = -312\cos A$

$23° \approx A$

$12^2 = 5^2 + 13^2 - 2(5)(13)\cos B$

$144 = 194 - 130\cos B$

$-50 = -130\cos B$

$67° \approx B$

$m\angle C = 90$

18. $b^2 = 20^2 + 24^2 - 2(20)(24)\cos 47°$

$b^2 \approx 321.28$

$b \approx 17.9$

$20^2 = (17.9)^2 + (24)^2 - 2(17.9)(24)\cos A$

$400 = 896.41 - 859.2\cos A$

$-496.41 = -859.2\cos A$

$55° \approx A$

$m\angle C \approx 78$

19. $m\angle C = 180 - 40 - 59 = 81$

$\dfrac{\sin 81°}{14} = \dfrac{\sin 40°}{a}$

$a(\sin 81°) = 14(\sin 40°)$

$a = \dfrac{14(\sin 40°)}{\sin 81°}$

$a \approx 9.1$

$\dfrac{\sin 81°}{14} = \dfrac{\sin 59°}{b}$

$b(\sin 81°) = 14(\sin 59°)$

$b = \dfrac{14(\sin 59°)}{\sin 81°}$

$b \approx 12.1$

20. $(345)^2 = (648)^2 + (442)^2 - 2(648)(442)\cos A$

$119,025 = 615,268 - 572,832\cos A$

$-496,243 = -572,832\cos A$

$30 \approx m\angle A$

$(648)^2 = (345)^2 + (442)^2 - 2(345)(442)\cos B$

$419,904 = 314,389 - 304,980\cos B$

$105,515 = -304,980\cos B$

$110 \approx m\angle A$

$(442)^2 = (345)^2 + (648)^2 - 2(345)(648)\cos C$

$195,364 = 538,929 - 447,120\cos C$

$-343,565 = -447,120\cos C$

$40 \approx m\angle C$

21. $a^2 = 5^2 + (4.9)^2 - 2(5)(4.9)\cos 29°$

$a^2 \approx 6.15$

$a \approx 2.5$

$\dfrac{\sin 29°}{2.5} = \dfrac{\sin B}{5}$

$\sin B = \dfrac{5\sin 29°}{2.5}$

$\sin B \approx 0.9696$

$B \approx 76°$

$m\angle A + m\angle B + m\angle C = 180$

$29 + 76 + m\angle C \approx 180$

$m\angle C \approx 75$

22. $m\angle C = 180 - 17 - 71 = 92$

$\dfrac{\sin 17°}{8} = \dfrac{\sin 71°}{b}$

$b(\sin 17°) = 8(\sin 71°)$

$b = \dfrac{8(\sin 71°)}{\sin 17°}$

$b \approx 25.9$

$\dfrac{\sin 17°}{8} = \dfrac{\sin 92°}{c}$

$c(\sin 17°) = 8(\sin 92°)$

$c = \dfrac{8(\sin 92°)}{\sin 17°}$

$c \approx 27.3$

23. $(12.50)^2 = (16.71)^2 + (10.30)^2$
$\qquad - 2(16.71)(10.30)\cos A$

$462.25 = 385.3141 - 344.266\cos A$

$76.9359 = -344.266\cos A$

$103 \approx m\angle A$

$(16.71)^2 = (21.50)^2 + (10.30)^2$
$\qquad - 2(21.50)(10.30)\cos B$

$279.2241 = 568.34 - 442.9\cos B$

$-289.1159 = -442.9\cos B$

$49 \approx m\angle B$

$m\angle C = 180 - 103 - 49 = 28$

24. $a^2 = 7^2 + (14.1)^2 - 2(7)(14.1)\cos B$

$a^2 \approx 75.16$

$a \approx 8.7$

$7^2 = (8.7)^2 + (14.1)^2 - 2(8.7)(14.1)\cos B$

$49 = 274.5 - 245.34\cos B$

$-225.5 = -245.34\cos B$

$23 \approx m\angle B$

$m\angle C = 180 - 23 - 29 = 128$

25. $8^2 = 24^2 + 18^2 - 2(24)(18)\cos A$

$64 = 900 - 864\cos A$

$-836 = -864\cos A$

$15 \approx m\angle A$

$24^2 = 8^2 + 18^2 - 2(8)(18)\cos B$

$576 = 388 - 288\cos B$

$188 = -288\cos B$

$131 \approx m\angle B$

$m\angle C = 180 - 131 - 15 = 34$

26. $x^2 = (400)^2 + (600)^2 - 2(400)(600)\cos 46.3°$

$x^2 \approx 188,376.44$

$x \approx 434$

Perimeter $\approx 434 + 600 + 400 \approx 1434$ feet

27. $(4.9)^2 = (6.8)^2 + (8.4)^2 - 2(6.8)(8.4)\cos A$

$24.01 = 116.8 - 114.24\cos A$

$-92.79 = -114.24\cos A$

$36 \approx m\angle A$

28. $a^2 = 71^2 + 55^2 - 2(71)(55)\cos 106°$

$a^2 \approx 10,218.72$

$a \approx 101.1$ cm

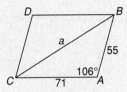

$c^2 = 55^2 + 71^2 - 2(55)(71)\cos 74°$

$c^2 \approx 5913.27$

$c \approx 76.9$ cm

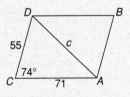

29. $(AB)^2 = 15^2 + 15^2 - 2(15)(15)\cos 123°$

$(AB)^2 \approx 695.09$

$AB \approx 26$ cm

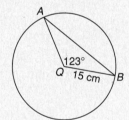

30. $85^2 = 50^2 + 70^2 - 2(50)(70)\cos A$

$7225 = 7400 - 7000\cos A$

$-175 = -7000\cos A$

$89 \approx m\angle A$

31. Let x = distance from point on ground to top of building.

$\dfrac{\sin 34°}{x} = \dfrac{\sin 14°}{40}$

$x(\sin 14°) = 40(\sin 34°)$

$x = \dfrac{40(\sin 34°)}{\sin 14°}$

$x \approx 92.5$ ft

$\sin 42° = \dfrac{h}{92.5}$

$h \approx 61.9$ feet

32. $d^2 = 70^2 + 130^2 - 2(70)(130)\cos 130°$

$d^2 = 33,498.7345$

$d \approx 183$ miles

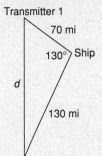

33. It is not possible because there are many triangles that have angles with these measures.

34. $a^2 = (b - x)^2 + h^2$ Use the Pythagorean Theorem for ΔBDC.

$= b^2 - 2bx + x^2 + h^2$ Expand $(b - x)^2$.

$= b^2 - 2bx + c^2$ In ΔADB,

$c^2 = x^2 + h^2$.

$= b^2 - 2b(c\cos A) + c^2$ $\cos A = \dfrac{x}{c}$,

so $x = c\cos A$

$= b^2 + c^2 - 2bc\cos A$

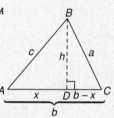

35. $a^2 = 36^2 + 48^2 - 2(36)(48)\cos 105°$

$a^2 = 4494.47862$

$a \approx 67$ nautical miles

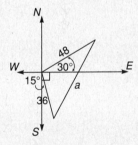

36. $a^2 = (900)^2 + (1150)^2 - 2(900)(1150)\cos 165°$

$a^2 = 4,131,966.46$

$a \approx 2032.7$ km

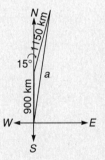

37. $t^2 = 180^2 + 240^2 - 2(180)(240)\cos 12°$

$t^2 = 5488.047297$

$t \approx 74$ yards

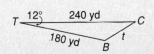

38.
$$\frac{\sin 84°}{38} = \frac{\sin 40°}{x}$$

$$x(\sin 84°) = 38(\sin 40°)$$

$$x = \frac{38(\sin 40°)}{\sin 84°}$$

$$x \approx 24.56 \text{ cm}$$

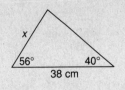

39. $\frac{8}{x} = \frac{x}{18}$

$x^2 = 144$

$x = 12$

40. $3x - 2 = 2x + 3$

$x = 5$

$LN = 3(5) - 2 = 13$

41. $KL = \sqrt{(5 - 0)^2 + (8 + 4)^2}$

$KL = \sqrt{169} = 13$

$LM = \sqrt{(0 + 1)^2 + (-4 - 1)^2}$

$LM = \sqrt{26} \approx 5.1$

$MK = \sqrt{(-1 - 5)^2 + (1 - 8)^2}$

$MK = \sqrt{85} \approx 9.2$

$5.1 + 9.2 \overset{?}{>} 13$

$14.3 > 13$

Yes, the lengths of the segments satisfy the triangle inequality.

42. Given: $\overline{AB} \cong \overline{BC}$

Prove: $\angle 3 \cong \angle 4$

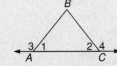

Proof: We are given that $\overline{AB} \cong \overline{BC}$. So $\angle 1 \cong \angle 2$ since if two sides of a triangle are congruent, then the angles opposite those sides are congruent. $\angle 1$ and $\angle 3$ and $\angle 2$ and $\angle 4$ form a linear pair. The angles in a linear pair are supplementary, so $\angle 1$ and $\angle 3$ are supplementary and $\angle 2$ and $\angle 4$ are supplementary. If two angles are supplementary to the same or congruent angles, then they are congruent. So $\angle 3 \cong \angle 4$.

43. See students' work.

8-8 Problem-Solving Strategy: Decision-Making

PAGE 400   CHECKING FOR UNDERSTANDING

1. No; but there is usually one way that is more efficient than the others.

2. Use experience with other problems and the way they were solved and look at the wording of the problem.

3. Look for a pattern, act it out, make a chart; 220 cans.

4. Act it out, draw a diagram; twice.

5. 2730; multiply the previous term by 4 and add 2.

6. 9; 1 half-dollar, 1 quarter, 2 dimes, 1 nickel, 4 pennies

7. Start the 7-minute and 3-minute timer together. At the end of 3 minutes, start the spaghetti. The time remaining on the 7-minute timer is 4 minutes. At the end of 4 minutes, turn the timer over and boil the spaghetti another 7 minutes, for a total of 11 minutes.

8. 38; $n^2 + 2$

9. Let x = Mrs. Sterling's estate.

$\frac{3}{4}x$ was left to the son, \$24,000 was left to niece.

$x - \left(\frac{3}{4}x + 24,000\right) = \frac{1}{4}x - 24,000$ = remainder

$\frac{1}{2}\left(\frac{1}{4}x - 24,000\right) = \frac{1}{8}x - 12,000$ left to her church

$\left(\frac{1}{4}x - 24,000\right) - \left(\frac{1}{8}x - 12,000\right)$

$\quad = \frac{1}{8}x - 12,000$ = remainder

$\frac{1}{3}\left(\frac{1}{8}x - 12,000\right) = \frac{1}{24}x - 4000$ left to alma mater

$\left(\frac{1}{8}x - 12,000\right) - \left(\frac{1}{24}x - 4000\right) = 4000$

$\frac{1}{12}x - 8000 = 4000$

$\frac{1}{12}x = 12,400$

$x = \$144,000$

10. Solutions will vary. A sample solution is
$297 \times 18 = 5346$

11. $xy = 95$, $xz = 140$, $yz = 532$

$x = \frac{95}{y}$ $x = \frac{140}{z}$ $z = \frac{532}{y}$

$\frac{95}{y} = \frac{140}{z}$

$95z = 140y$

$95\left(\frac{532}{y}\right) = 140y$

$\frac{50540}{y} = 140y$

$50540 = 140y^2$

$361 = y^2$

$19 = y$

Since $y = 19$, $xy = 95$ becomes $19x = 95$ and $x = 5$. $yz = 532$ becomes $19z = 532$ and $z = 28$.

Volume = $5(19)(28) = 2,660 \text{ cm}^3$

150

12. Rectangle has length of x and width of y. Square has one side $x - 0.2x = 0.8x$ and other side $y + 0.2y = 1.2y$. Area of rectangle is xy; area of square is $0.8x(1.2y) = 0.96xy$.

$$\frac{0.96xy}{xy} = 0.96 = 96\%$$

The area of the square is 96% the area of the rectangle.

13. 70; It is the only number divisible by both

$$5 \left(20\% = \frac{1}{5} \text{ are shoe stores}\right) \text{ and}$$

$$7 \left(\frac{1}{7} \text{ are toy stores}\right) \text{ that is between 50 and 100.}$$

14. Let v = number of varsity players.
Let j = number of junior varsity players.
total team = $v + j$

We are looking for $\frac{v}{j + v}$. Convert to inches, and write an equation. The sum of the heights of each group is the average for the group multiplied by the number of members.

$$72j + 80v = 75(j + v)$$
$$72j + 80v = 75j + 75v$$
$$5v = 3j$$
$$\frac{5v}{3} = j$$

So $\dfrac{v}{j + v} = \dfrac{v}{\dfrac{5v}{3} + v}$

$$= \frac{v}{\dfrac{8v}{3}}$$

$$= \frac{3}{8}$$

Therefore $\frac{3}{8}$ of the players are varsity players.

Cooperative Learning Project

PAGE 401

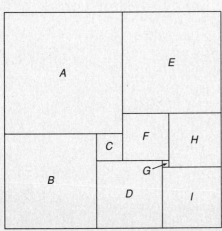

A side of square H is $\sqrt{64}$ or 8 units long and a side of square F is $\sqrt{49}$ or 7 units long.

A side of square G is the difference between the sides of F and H, so it equals $8 - 7$ or 1. The area of square $G = 1^2$ or 1.

A side of square I is the sum of the sides of G and H. $8 + 1 = 9$. The area of square I is 9^2 or 81.

A side of square D is the sum of the sides of squares G and I. $1 + 9 = 10$. The area of square D is 10^2 or 100.

A side of square C is the sum of the sides of squares G and D minus the side of square F. $(1 + 10) - 7 = 4$. The area of square C is 4^2 or 16.

A side of square B is the sum of the sides of squares C and D. $4 + 10 = 14$. The area of square B is 14^2 or 196.

A side of square E is the sum of the sides of squares F and G. $7 + 8 = 15$. The area of square E is 15^2 or 225.

A side of square A is the sum of the sides of squares B and C. $14 + 4 = 18$. The area of square A is 18^2 or 324.

Chapter 8 Summary and Review

PAGES 402–404   SKILLS AND CONCEPTS

1. $\dfrac{12}{x} = \dfrac{x}{27}$

    $x^2 = 324$
    $x = 18$

2. $\dfrac{9}{x} = \dfrac{x}{27}$

    $x^2 = 243$
    $x = \sqrt{243} \approx 15.6$

3. $\dfrac{60}{x} = \dfrac{x}{52}$

    $x^2 = 3120$
    $x = \sqrt{3120} \approx 55.9$

4. $\dfrac{20}{x} = \dfrac{x}{75}$

    $x^2 = 1500$
    $x = \sqrt{1500} \approx 38.7$

5. $\dfrac{1}{x} = \dfrac{x}{4}$

    $x^2 = 4$
    $x = 2$

6. $\dfrac{13}{x} = \dfrac{x}{39}$

    $x^2 = 507$
    $x = \sqrt{507} \approx 22.5$

7. $\dfrac{99}{x} = \dfrac{x}{121}$

    $x^2 = 11,979$
    $x = \sqrt{11,979}$
    ≈ 109.4

8. $\dfrac{8}{x} = \dfrac{x}{6}$

    $x^2 = 48$
    $x = \sqrt{48} \approx 6.9$

9. $\dfrac{m}{x} = \dfrac{x}{n}$

$x^2 = mn$

$x = \sqrt{mn}$

10. $\dfrac{4p}{x} = \dfrac{x}{16p}$

$x^2 = 64p^2$

$x = 8p$

11. $\dfrac{4}{LN} = \dfrac{LN}{6}$

$(LN)^2 = 24$

$LN = \sqrt{24} \approx 4.9$

12. $\dfrac{4}{KL} = \dfrac{KL}{18}$

$(KL)^2 = 72$

$KL = \sqrt{72} \approx 8.5$

13. $\dfrac{3}{LM} = \dfrac{LM}{10}$

$(LM)^2 = 30$

$LM = \sqrt{30} \approx 5.5$

14. $\dfrac{\frac{1}{3}}{x} = \dfrac{x}{\frac{7}{12}}$

$x^2 = \dfrac{7}{36}$

$x = \dfrac{\sqrt{7}}{6} \approx 0.4$

15. $\dfrac{19}{14} = \dfrac{KM}{19}$

$14(KM) = 361$

$KM \approx 25.8$

16. $\dfrac{0.6}{KN} = \dfrac{1.5}{0.6}$

$1.5(KN) = 0.36$

$KN = 0.24$

17. $c^2 = (7.1)^2 + (6.7)^2$

$c^2 = 95.3$

$c \approx 9.8$

18. $c^2 = (9.4)^2 + (8.0)^2$

$c^2 = 152.36$

$c \approx 12.3$

19. $c^2 = (8.0)^2 + (15.0)^2$

$c^2 = 289.00$

$c = 17.0$

20. $c^2 = (94)^2 + (88)^2$

$c^2 = 16,580$

$c \approx 128.8$

21. $9^2 + 21^2 \overset{?}{=} 23^2$

$81 + 441 \overset{?}{=} 529$

$522 \neq 529$

No

22. $4^2 + (7.5)^2 \overset{?}{=} (8.5)^2$

$16 + 56.25 \overset{?}{=} 72.25$

$72.25 = 72.25$

Yes

23. $17^2 + 144^2 \overset{?}{=} 145^2$

$289 + 20,736 \overset{?}{=} 21,025$

$21,025 = 21,025$

Yes

24. $19^2 + 14^2 \overset{?}{=} 30^2$

$361 + 196 \overset{?}{=} 900$

$557 \neq 900$

No

25. shorter leg $= \dfrac{1}{2} \cdot 3.1 = 1.55$

$x = 1.55\sqrt{3} \approx 2.7$ cm

26. $x = 3.0\sqrt{2} \approx 4.2$

27. $x = \dfrac{14.2}{\sqrt{2}} = 7.1\sqrt{2} \approx 10.0$ m

28. $x = \dfrac{1}{2} \cdot 42 = 21$ inches

29. $\sin Q = \dfrac{15.0}{17.0} \approx 0.882$

30. $\tan Q = \dfrac{15.0}{8.0} = 1.875$

31. $\cos R = \dfrac{15.0}{17.0} \approx 0.882$

32. $\tan R = \dfrac{8.0}{15.0} \approx 0.533$

33. $\dfrac{\sin 46°}{65} = \dfrac{\sin 83°}{c}$

$c(\sin 46°) = 65(\sin 83°)$

$c = \dfrac{65(\sin 83°)}{\sin 46°}$

$c \approx 89.7$

$m\angle A = 180 - 46 - 83 = 51$

$\dfrac{\sin 46°}{65} = \dfrac{\sin 51°}{a}$

$a(\sin 46°) = 65(\sin 51°)$

$a = \dfrac{65(\sin 51°)}{\sin 46°}$

$a \approx 70.2$

34. $\dfrac{\sin 65°}{80} = \dfrac{\sin B}{10}$

$80(\sin B) = 10(\sin 65°)$

$\sin B = \dfrac{10(\sin 65°)}{80}$

$m\angle B \approx 7$

$m\angle C = 180 - 65 - 7 = 108$

$\dfrac{\sin 65°}{80} = \dfrac{\sin 108°}{c}$

$c(\sin 65°) = 80(\sin 108°)$

$c = \dfrac{80(\sin 108°)}{\sin 65°}$

$c \approx 83.9$

35. $\dfrac{\sin 22°}{6.8} = \dfrac{\sin A}{4.2}$

$6.8(\sin A) = 4.2(\sin 22°)$

$\sin A = \dfrac{4.2(\sin 22°)}{6.8}$

$m\angle A \approx 13$

$m\angle C = 180 - 22 - 13 = 145$

$\dfrac{\sin 22°}{6.8} = \dfrac{\sin 145°}{c}$

$c(\sin 22°) = 6.8(\sin 145°)$

$c = \dfrac{6.8(\sin 145°)}{\sin 22°}$

$c \approx 10.4$

36.
$$c^2 = 8^2 + 12^2 - 2(8)(12)\cos 55°$$
$$c^2 \approx 97.87$$
$$c \approx 9.9$$
$$8^2 = 12^2 + (9.9)^2 - 2(12)(9.9)\cos A$$
$$64 = 242.01 - 237.6\cos A$$
$$-178.01 = -237.6\cos A$$
$$41 \approx m\angle A$$
$$m\angle B = 180 - 55 - 41 = 84$$

37.
$$b^2 = 44^2 + 32^2 - 2(44)(32)\cos 44°$$
$$b^2 \approx 934.34$$
$$b \approx 30.6$$
$$44^2 = (30.6)^2 + 32^2 - 2(30.6)(32)\cos A$$
$$1936 = 1960.36 - 1958.4\cos A$$
$$-24.36 = -1958.4\cos A$$
$$89 \approx m\angle A$$
$$m\angle C \approx 180 - 44 - 89 = 47$$

38.
$$c^2 = (4.5)^2 + (4.9)^2 - 2(4.5)(4.9)\cos 78°$$
$$c^2 = 35.09$$
$$c \approx 5.9$$
$$(4.5)^2 = (4.9)^2 + (5.9)^2 - 2(4.9)(5.9)\cos A$$
$$20.25 = 58.82 - 57.82\cos A$$
$$-38.57 = -57.82\cos A$$
$$48 \approx m\angle A$$
$$m\angle B = 180 - 78 - 48 = 54$$

39.
$$6^2 = 9^2 + 8^2 - 2(9)(8)\cos A$$
$$36 = 145 - 144\cos A$$
$$-109 = -144\cos A$$
$$41 \approx m\angle A$$
$$9^2 = 6^2 + 8^2 - 2(6)(8)\cos B$$
$$81 = 100 - 96\cos B$$
$$-19 = -96\cos B$$
$$79 \approx m\angle B$$
$$m\angle C = 180 - 41 - 79 = 60$$

PAGE 404   APPLICATIONS AND CONNECTIONS

40.
$$\sin 70° = \frac{h}{65}$$
$$h = 65(\sin 70°)$$
$$h \approx 61 \text{ meters}$$

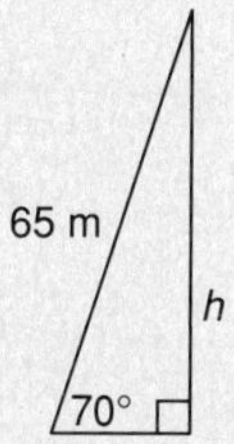

41.
$$\sin x = \frac{30}{400}$$
$$x \approx 4°$$

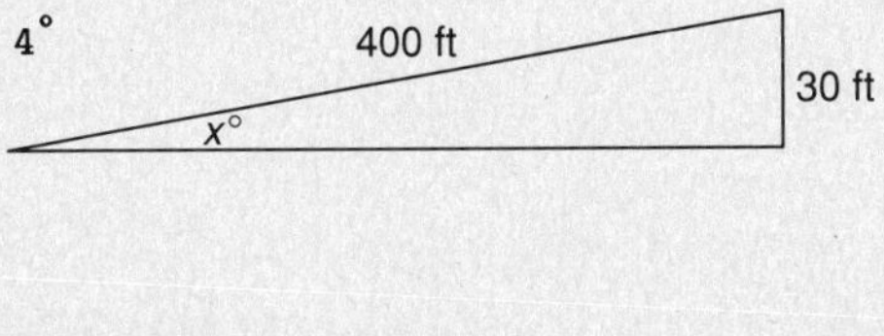

42.
$$\tan 67° = \frac{x}{120}$$
$$x = 120(\tan 67°)$$
$$x \approx 283 \text{ meters}$$

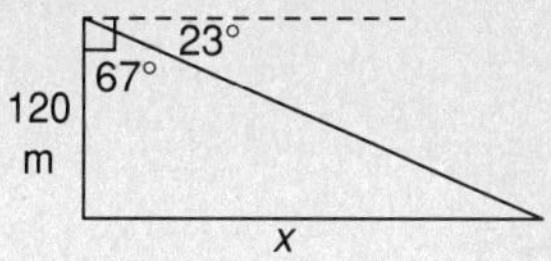

43.
$$x^2 = 700^2 + 1000^2 - 2(700)(1000)\cos 160°$$
$$x \approx 1,675 \text{ km}$$

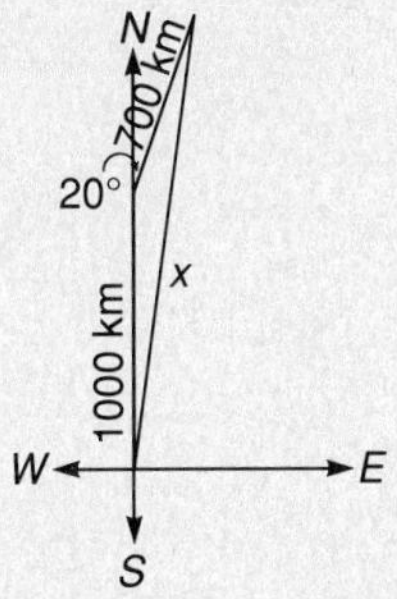

44. Answers will vary. Sample answer is look for a pattern;

n	5^n	Remainder of $5^n + 7$
1	5	5
2	25	4
3	125	6
4	625	2
5	3125	3
6	15,625	1
7	78,125	5
8	390,625	4

The remainders repeat in a pattern of 6. Since $100 + 6$ has a remainder of 4, the remainder of $5^{100} + 7$ has a remainder of 2.

Chapter 8 Test

PAGE 405

1.
$$\frac{3}{x} = \frac{x}{12}$$
$$x^2 = 36$$
$$x = 6$$

2.
$$\frac{5}{x} = \frac{x}{4}$$
$$x^2 = 20$$
$$x = \sqrt{20} \approx 4.5$$

3.
$$\frac{28}{x} = \frac{x}{56}$$
$$x^2 = 1568$$
$$x = \sqrt{1568} = 28\sqrt{2} \approx 39.6$$

4.
$$\frac{5}{QS} = \frac{QS}{8}$$
$$(QS)^2 = 40$$
$$QS = \sqrt{40} \approx 6.3$$

5.
$$\frac{9.5}{QP} = \frac{QP}{12.5}$$
$$(QP)^2 = 118.75$$
$$QP = \sqrt{118.75} \approx 10.9$$

153

6. $c^2 = 39^2 + 80^2$
   $c^2 = 7921$
   $c = 89$

7. $c^2 = (1.5)^2 + (11.2)^2$
   $c^2 = 127.69$
   $c = 11.3$

8. $c^2 = (6.9)^2 + (7.2)^2$
   $c^2 = 99.45$
   $c \approx 10.0$

9. $c^2 = (14.7)^2 + (18.1)^2$
   $c^2 = 543.7$
   $c \approx 23.3$

10. shorter leg $= \frac{1}{2}(6.8) = 3.4$ ft
    $x = 3.4\sqrt{3} \approx 5.9$

11. $x^2 = (4.2)^2 + (5.1)^2$
    $x^2 = 43.65$
    $x = \sqrt{43.65} \approx 6.6$

12. $x = \frac{7.3}{\sqrt{2}} = \frac{7.3\sqrt{2}}{2} = 3.65\sqrt{2} \approx 5.2$

13. $\sin A = \frac{60}{61} \approx 0.984$

14. $\tan B = \frac{11}{60} \approx 0.183$

15. $\cos A = \frac{11}{61} \approx 0.180$

16. $\tan A = \frac{60}{11} \approx 5.455$

17. $\sin x = \frac{28}{36}$
    $x \approx 51°$

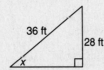

18. angle $= 180 - 45 - 79 = 56°$
    $\frac{\sin 79°}{30} = \frac{\sin 45°}{x}$
    $x = \frac{30(\sin 45°)}{\sin 79°}$
    $x \approx 21.6$ cm
    $\frac{\sin 79°}{30} = \frac{\sin 56°}{y}$
    $y = \frac{30(\sin 56°)}{\sin 79°}$
    $y \approx 25.3$ cm

19. $28^2 = 22^2 + 22^2 - 2(22)(22)\cos x$
    $784 = 968 - 968\cos x$
    $-184 = -968\cos x$
    $79° \approx x$

20. Answers will vary. A sample answer is make a
    list; $\frac{5}{50}$ or $\frac{1}{10}$.

BONUS:

$\sin A = \frac{x\sqrt{3}}{2x} = \frac{\sqrt{3}}{2} \approx 0.866$

$\cos A = \frac{x}{2x} = \frac{1}{2} = 0.500$

$\tan A = \frac{x\sqrt{3}}{x} = \sqrt{3} \approx 1.732$

College Entrance Exam Preview

PAGES 406-407

1. D; $8 + 12 = 20$; Sum of the measures two sides of
   a triangle must be greater than the measure of
   the third side.

2. B; $\frac{1}{x} - \frac{2}{y} = \frac{y}{xy} - \frac{2x}{xy} = \frac{y - 2x}{xy}$

3. C; $\frac{BC}{DC} = \frac{AC}{EC}$

   $\frac{x}{x + 6} = \frac{10 + x}{(x + 3) + (x + 6)}$

   $\frac{x}{x + 6} = \frac{10 + x}{2x + 9}$ $(x + 6)(x + 10)$

   $x^2 + 16x + 60$

   $2x^2 + 9x = x^2 + 16x + 60$

   $x^2 - 7x - 60 = 0$

   $(x + 5)(x - 12) = 0$

   $x = -5$ or $x = 12$

4. A; $2x - y - 8 = 0$
   $2x = y + 8$
   $x = \frac{1}{2}y + 4$
   $y = 0, x = 4$

5. C; $x - \frac{2}{x - 3} = \frac{x - 1}{3 - x}$

   $x - \frac{2}{x - 3} = \frac{x - 1}{-(x - 3)}$; Multiply each term
   by $x - 3$.

   $x(x - 3) - 2 = -(x - 1)$

   $x^2 - 2x - 3 = 0$

   $(x - 3)(x + 1) = 0$

   $x = 3$ or $x = -1$

   Since division by 0 is undefined, the only
   solution is $x = -1$.

6. $|-a| = 7$
   $-a = 7$ or $-a = -7$
   $a = -7$ or $a = 7$

7. D;

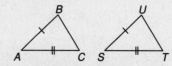

8. A; $x^2 = 4^2 + 8^2$

$x^2 = 80$

$x = \sqrt{80}$

$8 < x < 9$

9. C; $12^2 + 15^2 \overset{?}{=} 18^2$

$144 + 225 \overset{?}{=} 324$

$369 \neq 324$

10. D; 5, 6, 8, 11, 15, 20, 26, 33
   +1 +2 +3 +4 +5 +6 +7 +8

$33 + 8 = 41$

11. B; $8^2 + 8(2) = 80$

12. A; $\frac{1}{3}$ to $\frac{5}{12}$, multiply both fractins by 12;

4 to 5

13. $\dfrac{82 + 81 + 79 + 87 + x}{5} = 85$

$\dfrac{329 + x}{5} = 85$

$329 + x = 425$

$x = 96$

14. $(DE)^2 + 4^2 = 5^2$

$(DE)^2 = 9$

$DE = 3$

$DC = 3 + 16 + 3 = 22$

$A = \frac{1}{2}(16 + 22)4 = 76$ units^2

15. $\dfrac{9}{21} = \dfrac{24}{x}$

$9x = 504$

$x = 56$ units

16. $\dfrac{x}{30} + \dfrac{x}{20} = 1$

$2x + 3x = 60$

$5x = 60$

$x = 12$ minutes

17. $(5^2 + 5 \cdot 5) - [(-1)^2 + 5(-1)]$

$50 - (-4) = 54$

18. Let 1 represent the amount of water in the fish bowl.

$1 - \dfrac{1}{10} = \dfrac{9}{10}$ remains after first day

$\dfrac{1}{12} \cdot \dfrac{9}{10} = \dfrac{3}{40}$ evaporates

$\dfrac{9}{10} - \dfrac{3}{40}$ or $\dfrac{33}{40}$ remains after the second day

19. Area of rectangle – Area of triangle
   = remaining area

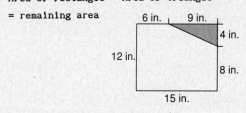

$12(15) - \left(\dfrac{1}{2} \cdot 9 \cdot 4\right) = 162$ in^2

20. $62(2.5) - 55(2.5) = 17.5$ miles

Chapter 9   Circles

Parts of Circles

PAGE 413   CHECKING FOR UNDERSTANDING

1. No; A is the center of the circle but it is not on the circle.

2. The point stays in one place and is the center of the circle. The tip of the pencil moves around the point, always at the same distance from the point.

3. Both tangents and secants are lines that intersect a circle. A tangent intersects a circle in one point, and a secant intersects a circle in two points.

4. a. The radius is $\sqrt{6}$ because the general equation for a circle is $(x - h)^2 + (y - k)^2 = r^2$.

   b. $K(-5, 0)$

5. P 6. $\overline{PD}$, $\overline{PB}$, $\overline{PC}$

7. $\overline{DB}$ 8. $\overline{EA}$ or $\overline{DB}$

9. $\overleftrightarrow{HB}$ 10. $\overleftrightarrow{EA}$ or $\overleftrightarrow{BD}$

11. G, P 12. F, H

13. A, B, C, D, E 14. $DB = 2(PC)$
                                          $= 12$

15. $(x + 2)^2 + (y + 7)^2 = 81$

    $(x - (-2))^2 + (y - (-7))^2 = 9^2$

                          $r = 9$

    Center is $(-2, -7)$.

16. $(x + 5)^2 + (y - 7)^2 = 100$

    $(x - (-5))^2 + (y - 7)^2 = 10^2$

                          $r = 10$

    Center is $(-5, 7)$.

PAGES 414-415   EXERCISES

17. true   18. false   19. false

20. false   21. false   22. false

23. $d = 2r$ 24. $d = 2r$ 25. $d = 2r$
    $d = 7.6$ $1.75 = r$ $= x$

26. $(x - 0)^2 + (y - 0)^2 = 5^2$
                   $x^2 + y^2 = 25$

27. $(x - 0)^2 + (y - 0)^2 = 7^2$
                   $x^2 + y^2 = 49$

28. $(x - 3)^2 + (y - 4)^2 = 6^2$
    $(x - 3)^2 + (y - 4)^2 = 36$

29. $(x - 0)^2 + (y - 0)^2 = (\sqrt{14})^2$
                   $x^2 + y^2 = 14$

30.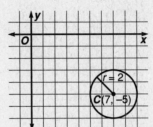

31.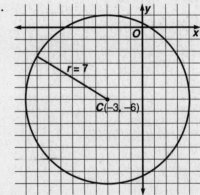

32. 2   33. 15 units $(7 + 5 + 3)$

34. diameter   35. QB

36. 8.5 $(5 + 5 - 1.5)$ 37. 15 $(10 + 6 - 1)$

38. $<$ 39. $>$ 40. $>$

41. exterior   42. exterior   43. on the circle

44. interior

45. 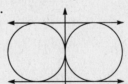   46.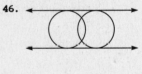

47.

48. $(x - (-4))^2 + (y - (-7))^2 = \left(\frac{12}{2}\right)^2$
         $(x + 4)^2 + (y + 7)^2 = 36$

156

49. center $= \left(\dfrac{-6 + 2}{2}, \dfrac{15 + 7}{2}\right)$

$= (-2, 11)$

$d = \sqrt{(-6 - 2)^2 + (15 - 7)^2}$

$= \sqrt{64 + 64}$

$d = \sqrt{128}$

$r = \dfrac{\sqrt{128}}{2}$

$r^2 = \dfrac{128}{4} = 32$

$(x + 2)^2 + (y - 11)^2 = 32$

50. Look for a pattern.

n	1	2	3	4	...	n
regions	4	7	10	13	...	$3n + 1$

For any n, there are $3n + 1$ regions.

51. $5\frac{1}{4}$ in.   **52.** 113.75 mm; 7.5 in.

53. 16; since the square of an odd number is odd, the number of odd perfect squares between 0 and 1000 will be the number of odd integers between $\sqrt{0}$ and $\sqrt{1000}$. There are 16 odd integers between 0 and $\sqrt{1000}$.

54. true   **55.** false   **56.** true

57. false   **58.** false   **59.** false

60. See students' work.

9-2   Angles and Arcs

PAGES 418-419   CHECKING FOR UNDERSTANDING

1. $\overset{\frown}{TC}$ or $\overset{\frown}{JT}$ **2.** $\overset{\frown}{JTC}$; $\overline{JC}$ is a diameter

3. $\angle CRT$ or $\angle TRJ$

4. Subtract 123 from 360; 237.

5. Less than 180; the minor arc contains all the points of a circle that are in the interior of an angle.

6. minor; $m\overset{\frown}{AB} = m\overset{\frown}{AC} - m\overset{\frown}{BC}$

$= 180 - m\angle BMC$ $m\angle BMC = m\overset{\frown}{BC}$

$= 180 - 40$

$= 140$

7. major; $m\overset{\frown}{ECA} = 360 - m\overset{\frown}{EA}$

$= 360 - m\overset{\frown}{BC}$

$= 360 - 40$

$= 320$

8. semicircle; 180   **9.** semicircle; 180

10. major; $m\overset{\frown}{DCE} = 360 - m\overset{\frown}{DE}$

$= 360 - (m\overset{\frown}{DA} - m\overset{\frown}{EA})$

$= 360 - (90 - m\overset{\frown}{BC})$

$= 360 - (90 - 40)$

$= 310$

11. major; $m\overset{\frown}{CBD} = 360 - m\overset{\frown}{DC}$

$= 360 - 90$

$= 270$

12. major; $m\overset{\frown}{DAB} = 360 - m\overset{\frown}{DB}$

$= 360 - (m\overset{\frown}{DC} + m\overset{\frown}{CB})$

$= 360 - (90 + m\angle BMC)$

$= 360 - (90 + 40)$

$= 360 - 130$

$= 230$

13. minor; $m\overset{\frown}{AE} = m\angle AME$

$= m\angle BMC$

$= 40$

14. minor; $m\overset{\frown}{BC} = m\angle BMC$

$= 40$

15. minor; $m\overset{\frown}{BD} = m\overset{\frown}{DC} + m\overset{\frown}{BC}$

$= m\angle DMC + 40$

$= 90 + 40$

$= 130$

16. major; $m\overset{\frown}{BDC} = 360 - m\overset{\frown}{BC}$

$= 360 - 40$

$= 320$

17. minor; $m\overset{\frown}{AD} = m\angle AMC$

$= 90$

PAGES 419-421   EXERCISES

18. $m\overset{\frown}{YZ} = m\angle YPZ$
$= 38$

19. $m\overset{\frown}{WX} = m\angle WPX$
$= 28$

20. $m\angle VPZ = m\angle WPX$
$= 28$

21. $m\overset{\frown}{XWY} = m\overset{\frown}{WZ} + m\overset{\frown}{WX} + m\overset{\frown}{YZ}$
$= 180 + 28 + 38$
$= 246$

22. $m\overset{\frown}{VZ} = m\overset{\frown}{WX}$
$= 28$

23. $m\overset{\frown}{VWX} = 180$

24. $m\overset{\frown}{ZVW} = 180$

25. $m\overset{\frown}{VPW} = m\overset{\frown}{ZW} - m\overset{\frown}{ZV}$
$= 180 - 28$
$= 152$

26. $m\overset{\frown}{WYZ} = 180$ **27.** $m\overset{\frown}{ZXW} = 180$

28. $m\angle XPY = m\overset{\frown}{WYZ} - m\overset{\frown}{WX} - m\overset{\frown}{YZ}$
$= 180 - 28 - 38$
$= 114$

29. $m\overset{\frown}{XY} = m\angle XPY$
$= 114$

30. $2x + (4x + 15) + (2x + 5) = 180$
$8x = 160$
$x = 20$

31. $m\overset{\frown}{BY} = m\angle BCY$
$= 2x$
$= 40$

32. $m\overset{\frown}{BQ} = m\angle BCQ$
$= 4x + 15$
$= 95$

33. $\overset{\frown}{mQA} = m\angle QCX + m\angle XCA$
    $= m\angle QCX + m\angle BCY$
    $= (2x + 5) + 40$
    $= 85$

34. $\overset{\frown}{mQX} = m\angle QCX$
    $= 2x + 5$
    $= 45$

35. $\overset{\frown}{mYQ} = \overset{\frown}{mYX} - \overset{\frown}{mQX}$
    $= 180 - 45$
    $= 135$

36. $m\angle YCQ = \overset{\frown}{mYQ}$
    $= 135$

37. $m\angle QCA = \overset{\frown}{mQX} + \overset{\frown}{mXA}$
    $= 45 + \overset{\frown}{mBY}$
    $= 45 + 40$
    $= 85$

38. $\overset{\frown}{mBX} = \overset{\frown}{mYX} - \overset{\frown}{mBY}$
    $= 180 - 40$
    $= 140$

39. $m\angle BCX = \overset{\frown}{mBX}$
    $= 140$

40. $\overset{\frown}{mXA} = \overset{\frown}{mBY}$
    $= 40$

41. $\overset{\frown}{mXYA} = 360 - \overset{\frown}{mXA}$
    $= 360 - 40$
    $= 320$

42. false   43. false   44. true   45. true

46. false   47. false   48. false   49. true

50. $\overset{\frown}{mSR} = m\angle SAR$
    $= 32$

51. $\overset{\frown}{mTX} = m\angle XAQ + m\angle QAT$
    $= m\angle WAR + m\angle SAR$
    $= 112 + 32$
    $= 144$

52. $\overset{\frown}{mSW} = m\angle SAR + m\angle RAW$
    $= 32 + 112$
    $= 144$

53. $\overset{\frown}{mTQ} = m\angle TAQ$
    $= m\angle SAR$
    $= 32$

54. $\overset{\frown}{mXQ} = m\angle XAQ$
    $= m\angle WAR$
    $= 112$

55. $\overset{\frown}{mWR} = m\angle WAR$
    $= 112$

56. $\overset{\frown}{mTYX} = 360 - \overset{\frown}{mTX}$
    $= 360 - 144$
    $= 216$

57. $\overset{\frown}{mSZW} = 360 - \overset{\frown}{mSW}$
    $= 360 - 144$
    $= 216$

58. Yes; if they are in circles with radii of different lengths.

59. $OP = OQ$, so $m\angle Q = m\angle P$
  $m\angle Q + m\angle P + m\angle POQ = 180$
    $m\angle Q + m\angle Q + \overset{\frown}{mPQ} = 180$
       $2m\angle Q + 120 = 180$
           $m\angle Q = 30$

60. Let x = length of each side.
  since $a^2 + b^2 = c^2$
     $x^2 + x^2 = 1$
        $2x^2 = 1$
         $x^2 = \frac{1}{2}$
          $x = \sqrt{\frac{1}{2}} = \frac{\sqrt{2}}{2} \approx 0.71$

61. $\triangle BXY$ is a right triangle.
  $\frac{XA}{BA} = \frac{BA}{AY}$
              $(AB)^2 + (AY)^2 = (BY)^2$
                $5^2 + 12^2 = (BY)^2$
              $25 + 144 = (BY)^2$
                   $13 = BY$

  $\frac{2\frac{1}{12}}{BA} = \frac{BA}{12}$
  $(BA)^2 = \frac{25}{12} \cdot \frac{12}{1} = 25$
    $BA = 5$

62. given $m\angle B = 65$, so $m\angle A = 65$
  given $m\angle D = 50$, so $m\angle E = 50$
  $m\angle BCA = 180 - 65 - 65 = 50$
  $m\angle ECD = 180 - 50 - 50 = 80$
  $m\angle ECB + m\angle ACD = 360 - m\angle BCA - m\angle ECD$
                    $= 360 - 50 - 80$
                    $= 230$

63. $\frac{360}{6} = 60$

64. Spokes 1-14 contain 13 angles.
  $13\left(\frac{360}{30}\right) = 13(12)$
             $= 156$

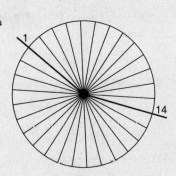

65. $2(35 - 12) = 46$

66. bean soup-$28.8°$
  chicken soup-$115.2°$
  tomato soup-$36°$
  vegetable soup-$180°$

Favorite Soup

Chicken

Tomato   32%

10%   8% Bean

Vegetable
50%

67. $(x - 1)^2 + (y - 2)^2 = 9$

68. $\frac{3}{4} = \frac{x}{6}$
  $4x = 18$
  $x = 4.5$

69. -3, subtract 2 from the previous term

70. $2x - 1 = x + 7$
     $x = 8$

71. Obtuse triangles have one obtuse angle, and all the angles in an acute triangle are acute.

72. If circles are concentric, then they have the same center.

73. $d = \sqrt{(-11 - (-3))^2 + (6 - 7)^2}$
   $= \sqrt{64 + 1}$
   $= \sqrt{65} \approx 8.1$

74. See students' work.

PAGE 425   CHECKING FOR UNDERSTANDING

1. $\overline{PA}$ and $\overline{PB}$ are congruent because they are both radii of $\odot P$. Therefore, $\triangle PAB$ is isosceles.

2. The arc of a chord is the arc that has the same endpoints as a chord. $\overset{\frown}{AB}$ is the arc of chord $\overline{AB}$; $\overset{\frown}{CD}$ is the arc of chord $\overline{CD}$.

3. $\overset{\frown}{AM} \cong \overset{\frown}{MB}$; $\overset{\frown}{AR} \cong \overset{\frown}{RB}$; $\triangle APM \cong \triangle BPM$; $\angle APR \cong \angle BPR$

4. $\overset{\frown}{AB} \cong \overset{\frown}{CD}$; $\overline{AB}$ and $\overline{CD}$ are equidistant from point P.

5. Theorem 9-2   6. Theorem 9-2

7. Theorem 9-3   8. Theorem 9-1

9. Theorem 9-1   10. Theorem 9-3

11. Theorem 9-1   12. $AC = 2(7)$
$$= 14$$

13. 75   14. $6^2 + 8^2 = (ON)^2$
$$36 + 64 = (ON)^2$$
$$10 = ON$$

PAGES 425-427   EXERCISES

15. $\overline{QV}$ 16. 5   17. V 18. $\overset{\frown}{QS}$

19. $\overset{\frown}{YT}$ 20. $\overline{YS}$ 21. $\overline{WA}$ 22. $\overline{QT}$

23. no   24. $\dfrac{360 - 100}{4} = 65$ 25. 16

26. $JL = 2(KL)$
$$= 2\left(\sqrt{5^2 - 3^2}\right)$$
$$= 2\sqrt{16} = 2 \cdot 4$$
$$= 8$$

27. Yes; in a circle, 2 minor arcs are congruent if their corresponding chords are congruent.

28. No; because circle O may not be congruent to circle Q.

29. $r^2 = 5^2 + 12^2$ 30. $9^2 + 12^2 = r^2$
$= 25 + 144$ $81 + 144 = r^2$
$r = \sqrt{169} = 13$ $\sqrt{225} = r$
$15 = r$

31. $d^2 + 8^2 = 10^2$
$$d^2 = 10^2 - 8^2$$
$$d^2 = 100 - 64 = 36$$
$$d = \sqrt{36} = 6$$

32. $d^2 + 3^2 = 5^2$
$$d^2 = 5^2 - 3^2$$
$$d^2 = 25 - 9 = 16$$
$$d = \sqrt{16} = 4$$

33. longer chord

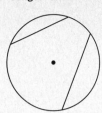

34.

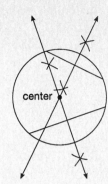

center

35. $\overline{MN} = \overline{PQ}$
$7x + 13 = 10x - 8$
$21 = 3x$
$7 = x$
$PS = \dfrac{PQ}{2} = \dfrac{10x - 8}{2} = 31$

36. Given: $\odot O$
$\overline{AB} \cong \overline{CD}$

Prove: $\overset{\frown}{AB} \cong \overset{\frown}{CD}$

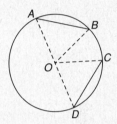

Proof: Draw radii $\overline{OA}$, $\overline{OB}$, $\overline{OC}$ and $\overline{OD}$. Since all radii are congruent, $\overline{OA} \cong \overline{OC}$ and $\overline{OB} \cong \overline{OD}$. $\overline{AB} \cong \overline{CD}$ and $\triangle ABO \cong \triangle CDO$ by SSS. $\angle AOB \cong \angle COD$ because they are corresponding angles in congruent triangles. Therefore, $\overset{\frown}{AB} \cong \overset{\frown}{CD}$.

37. Given: $\odot O$
$\overline{OS} \perp \overline{RT}$
$\overline{OV} \perp \overline{UW}$
$\overline{OS} \cong \overline{OV}$

Prove: $\overline{RT} \cong \overline{UW}$

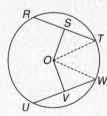

Proof: Draw radii $\overline{OT}$ and $\overline{OW}$. Since $\overline{OT} \cong \overline{OW}$ and $\overline{OS} \cong \overline{OV}$, $\triangle STO \cong \triangle VWO$ by HL. Then $\overline{ST} \cong \overline{VW}$ and $ST = VW$. Since a diameter perpendicular to a chord bisects the chord, $\overline{OS}$ bisects $\overline{RT}$ and $\overline{OV}$ bisects $\overline{UW}$. So, $RT = 2(ST)$ and $UW = 2(VW)$. Therefore, $RT = UW$ and $\overline{RT} \cong \overline{UW}$.

38. Given: ⊙O

    $\overline{MN} \cong \overline{PQ}$

   Prove: $\overline{MN}$ and $\overline{PQ}$ are
       equidistant
       from O.

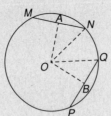

Proof: Draw radii $\overline{ON}$ and $\overline{OQ}$, $\overline{OA} \perp \overline{MN}$, and $\overline{OB} \perp \overline{PQ}$. Then $\overline{OA}$ bisects $\overline{MN}$ and $\overline{OB}$ bisects $\overline{PQ}$ because $\overline{OA}$ and $\overline{OB}$ can be extended to form radii, and a radius perpendicular to a chord bisects the chord. $AN = \frac{1}{2}MN$ and $BQ = \frac{1}{2}PQ$. Since $\overline{MN} \cong \overline{PQ}$, $MN = PQ$, and $AN = BQ$. Since $\overline{AN} \cong \overline{BQ}$ and $\overline{ON} \cong \overline{OQ}$, $\triangle AON \cong \triangle BOQ$ by HL. Therefore, $\overline{OA} \cong \overline{OB}$ and $\overline{MN}$ and $\overline{PB}$ are equidistant from O.

39.

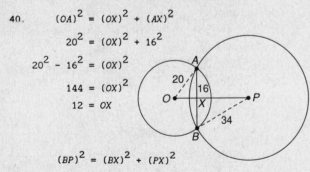

$$(OP)^2 + (HP)^2 = (OH)^2$$
$$10^2 + (HP)^2 = 20^2$$
$$(HP)^2 = 20^2 - 10^2$$
$$(HP)^2 = 400 - 100 = 300$$
$$HP = \sqrt{300} = 10\sqrt{3} \approx 17.3$$
$$HC = 2HP = 20\sqrt{3} \approx 34.6 \text{ units}$$

40. $(OA)^2 = (OX)^2 + (AX)^2$
$$20^2 = (OX)^2 + 16^2$$
$$20^2 - 16^2 = (OX)^2$$
$$144 = (OX)^2$$
$$12 = OX$$

$$(BP)^2 = (BX)^2 + (PX)^2$$
$$34^2 = 16^2 + (PX)^2$$
$$34^2 - 16^2 = (PX)^2$$
$$900 = (PX)^2$$
$$30 = PX$$
$$OP = OX + PX$$
$$= 12 + 30$$
$$= 42$$

41. 3 chords: Draw a chord between the two points where the circles intersect and draw one more chord for each circle. Construct the perpendicular bisectors of these chords. The two points where these bisectors intersect are the centers of the circles.

42.

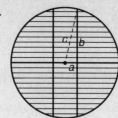

Locate the center of the grill which is also halfway between the support wires. Construct a rt. △ by drawing a radius to connect the center of the grill and one of the support wires. The hypotenuse of the triangle is the radius, one leg is half the length of one support wire, and the other leg is half the distance between the support wires.

$$c^2 = a^2 + b^2$$
$$27^2 = 6^2 + b^2$$
$$27^2 - 6^2 = b^2$$
$$729 - 36 = b^2$$
$$26.325 = b$$

length of support wire $= 2b = 52.65$ cm

43.   Let $x = \perp$ distance from the center of picture to center of chord;

    $x + 4 = $ final height of picture.
$$4^2 = (2.5)^2 + x^2$$
$$16 - 6.25 = x^2$$
$$9.75 = x^2$$
$$3.1 \approx x$$
$$7.1 \approx x + 4$$

44. Draw two nonparallel chords and then draw the perpendicular bisector of each chord. The point of intersection is the center of the circle.

45. $m\overset{\frown}{MN} = m\angle MQN$
$$= 90 - m\angle CQM - m\angle BQN$$
$$= 90 - 15 - 18$$
$$= 57$$

46. $\frac{9}{x} = \frac{x}{21}$
$$x^2 = 189$$
$$x = \sqrt{189} \approx 13.7$$

47.

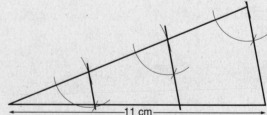

48. Division or multiplication property of equality

49. $CA = BA - BC = 17 - 12 = 5$

50. See students' work.

1. $m\angle 1 = \frac{1}{2}m\overset{\frown}{BC}$

    $= \frac{1}{2}(42)$

    $= 21$

2. They are inscribed angles that intercept the same arc.

3. Right triangle; because $\angle DBC$ is inscribed in a semicircle it is a right angle.

4. $\angle DFE$ is neither a central angle nor an inscribed angle.

5. No; vertex is not on circle.

6. Yes; vertex is on circle and sides are chords.

7. No; one side is not a chord.

8. $m\overset{\frown}{KS} = 2m\angle KUT$

    $= 2(60)$

    $= 120$

9. $m\angle KTS = \frac{1}{2}m\overset{\frown}{KS}$

    $= \frac{1}{2}(120)$

    $= 60$

10. $m\overset{\frown}{UK} = 2(m\angle UTK)$

    $= 2(30)$

    $= 60$

11. $m\angle USK = \frac{1}{2}m\overset{\frown}{UK}$

    $= \frac{1}{2}(60)$

    $= 30$

12. $m\angle TSK = \frac{1}{2}m\overset{\frown}{TK}$

    $= \frac{1}{2}(140)$

    $= 70$

13. $m\angle TSU = \frac{1}{2}m\overset{\frown}{TU}$

    $= \frac{1}{2}(80)$

    $= 40$

14. $m\overset{\frown}{UT} = 2m\angle UKT$

    $= 2(40)$

    $= 80$

15. $m\overset{\frown}{TS} = 2m\angle TUS$

    $= 2(50)$

    $= 100$

16. $m\angle TKS = \frac{1}{2}m\overset{\frown}{TS}$

    $= \frac{1}{2}(100)$

    $= 50$

17. See students' work.

18. $m\overset{\frown}{AB} = m\angle AXB$

    $= 104$

19. $m\angle BAC = \frac{1}{2}m\overset{\frown}{BC}$

    $= \frac{1}{2}(94)$

    $= 47$

20. $m\angle BDC = \frac{1}{2}m\overset{\frown}{BC}$

    $= \frac{1}{2}(94)$

    $= 47$

21. $m\angle BCA = \frac{1}{2}m\overset{\frown}{AB}$

    $= \frac{1}{2}(104)$

    $= 52$

22. $m\angle ADB = \frac{1}{2}m\overset{\frown}{AB}$

    $= \frac{1}{2}(104)$

    $= 52$

23. $m\angle ADC = \frac{1}{2}m\overset{\frown}{ABC}$

    $= \frac{1}{2}(198)$

    $= 99$

24. $m\angle XAB = \dfrac{180 - m\angle AXB}{2}$

    $= \dfrac{180 - 104}{2}$

    $= 38$

25. $m\angle ABX = \dfrac{180 - m\angle AXB}{2}$

    $= \dfrac{180 - 104}{2}$

    $= 38$

26. $m\angle ACD = m\angle CAB$

    $= 47$

27. $m\angle BCD = m\angle BCA + m\angle ACD$

    $= 52 + 47$

    $= 99$

28. $m\angle DEC = 180 - m\angle CDE - m\angle ECD$

    $= 180 - 47 - 47$

    $= 86$

29. $m\angle AED = 180 - m\angle EDA - m\angle DAE$

    $= 180 - 52 - 34$

    $= 94$

30. $m\angle EAD = 180 - m\angle ADC - m\angle DCE$

    $= 180 - 99 - 47$

    $= 34$

31. $m\overset{\frown}{DC} = 360 - m\overset{\frown}{BC} - m\overset{\frown}{AB} - m\overset{\frown}{AD}$

    $= 360 - 94 - 104 - 94$

    $= 68$

32. $m\angle BAD = \frac{1}{2}m\overset{\frown}{BCD}$

    $= \frac{1}{2}(162)$

    $= 81$

33. $m\angle DBC = \frac{1}{2}m\overset{\frown}{DC}$

    $= \frac{1}{2}(68)$

    $= 34$

34. $m\overset{\frown}{AD} = 2m\angle DCA$

    $= 2(47)$

    $= 94$

35. $m\angle ABD = \frac{1}{2}m\overset{\frown}{AD}$

    $= \frac{1}{2}(94)$

    $= 47$

36. $m\angle GHI + m\angle IJG = 180$

    $2x + (2x + 10) = 180$

    $4x = 170$

    $x = 42.5$

    $m\angle GHI = 2x = 85$

37. $m\angle IJG = 2x + 10$

    $= 2(42.5) + 10$

    $= 95$

38. $m\angle HGJ = 2x - 10$

    $= 2(42.5) - 10$

    $= 75$

39. $m\angle JIH = 360 - m\angle IJG - m\angle JGH - m\angle GHI$

    $= 360 - 95 - 75 - 85$

    $= 105$

40. $m\overset{\frown}{JGH} = 2m\angle JIH$

    $= 2(105)$

    $= 210$

41. $m\overset{\frown}{GHI} = 2m\angle GJI$

    $= 2(95)$

    $= 190$

42. $m\overset{\frown}{GJI} = 2m\angle GHI$

    $= 2(85)$

    $= 170$

43. $m\overset{\frown}{JIH} = 2m\angle HGJ$

    $= 2(75)$

    $= 150$

44. See students' work.

45. Yes; yes; the perpendicular bisectors of the sides of the triangle intersect inside the triangle. The center of the circle is the point where the bisectors intersect.

46. 90, 90, 90, 90; opposite angles of a quadrilateral inscribed in a circle are supplementary and the consecutive angles of a parallelogram are supplementary. So, each angle must have a measure of 90.

47. Given: $\overline{MH} \parallel \overline{AT}$
Prove: $\widehat{AM} \cong \widehat{HT}$

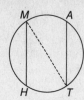

Proof: Draw $\overline{MT}$. Since $\overline{MH} \parallel \overline{AT}$, $\angle HMT \cong \angle MTA$ and $m\angle HMT = m\angle MTA$. But $m\angle HMT = \frac{1}{2}m\widehat{HT}$ and $m\angle MTA = \frac{1}{2}m\widehat{AM}$. Therefore, $\frac{1}{2}m\widehat{HT} = \frac{1}{2}m\widehat{AM}$ and $m\widehat{HT} = m\widehat{AM}$. The arcs are in the same circle, so $\widehat{AM} \cong \widehat{HT}$.

48. Given: inscribed $\angle XAZ$
$\overline{AY}$ bisects $\angle XAZ$.
Prove: Y bisects $\widehat{XZ}$.

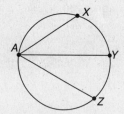

Proof: Since $\overline{AY}$ bisects $\angle XAZ$, $m\angle XAY = m\angle YAZ$. $m\angle XAY = \frac{1}{2}m\widehat{XY}$ and $m\angle YAZ = \frac{1}{2}m\widehat{YZ}$. Therefore, $\frac{1}{2}m\widehat{XY} = \frac{1}{2}m\widehat{YZ}$ and $m\widehat{XY} = m\widehat{YZ}$. Therefore Y bisects $\widehat{XZ}$.

49. $m\angle PRQ = m\angle PRK + m\angle KRQ$

$= \frac{1}{2}(m\widehat{PK}) + \frac{1}{2}(m\widehat{KQ})$

$= \frac{1}{2}(m\widehat{PK} + m\widehat{KQ})$

$= \frac{1}{2}m\widehat{PQ}$

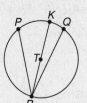

50. $m\angle PRQ = m\angle QRK - m\angle PRK$

$= \frac{1}{2}(m\widehat{QK}) - \frac{1}{2}(m\widehat{PK})$

$= \frac{1}{2}(m\widehat{QK} - m\widehat{PK})$

$= \frac{1}{2}m\widehat{PQ}$

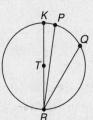

51. Given: inscribed $\angle MLN$
inscribed $\angle CED$
$\widehat{CD} \cong \widehat{MN}$
Prove: $\angle MLN \cong \angle CED$

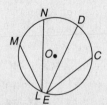

STATEMENTS	REASONS
1. $\angle MLN$ and $\angle CED$ are inscribed $\angle$s. $\widehat{CD} \cong \widehat{MN}$	1. Given

2. $m\angle MLN = \frac{1}{2}m\widehat{MN}$

$m\angle CED = \frac{1}{2}m\widehat{CD}$

2. If an $\angle$ is inscribed in a $\odot$, the measure of the $\angle = \frac{1}{2}$ the measure of the intercepted arc.

3. $m\angle MLN = \frac{1}{2}m\widehat{CD}$ | 3. Substitution

4. $m\angle MLN = m\angle CED$ | 4. Transitive property of equality

5. $\angle MLN \cong \angle CED$ | 5. Definition of congruence

52. Given: $\widehat{PQR}$ is a semicircle of $\odot C$.
Prove: $\angle PQR$ is a right $\angle$.

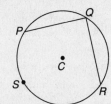

Proof: Since $\widehat{PQR}$ is a semicircle, $\widehat{PSR}$ is also a semicircle and has a degree measure of 180. From the diagram, $\angle PQR$ is an inscribed angle, and $m\angle PQR = \frac{1}{2}(m\widehat{PSR})$ or 90. As a result, $\angle PQR$ is a right angle.

53. Given: Quadrilateral $ABCD$ inscribed in $\odot O$.
Prove: $\angle A$ and $\angle C$ are supplementary.
$\angle B$ and $\angle D$ are supplementary.

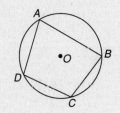

Proof: In $\odot O$, $m\widehat{DCB} + m\widehat{DAB} = 360$. Since $m\angle C = \frac{1}{2}m\widehat{DAB}$ and $m\angle A = \frac{1}{2}m\widehat{DCB}$, $m\angle C + m\angle A = \frac{1}{2}m\widehat{DAB} + \frac{1}{2}m\widehat{DCB}$ or $m\angle C + m\angle A = \frac{1}{2}(m\widehat{DAB} + m\widehat{DCB}) = \frac{1}{2}(360)$ or 180. Since $m\angle C + m\angle A = 180$, the angles are supplementary. A similar proof holds for angles B and D.

54. It is a rectangle. $m\widehat{YZ} = 120$, $m\widehat{ZB} = 60$, $m\widehat{BX} = 60$, $m\widehat{XA} = 60$, and $m\widehat{AY} = 60$.

$m\angle AYZ = \frac{1}{2}m\widehat{ABZ}$

$= \frac{1}{2}(60 + 60 + 60) = \frac{1}{2}(180) = 90$

$m\angle YZB = \frac{1}{2}m\widehat{YAB}$

$= \frac{1}{2}(60 + 60 + 60) = \frac{1}{2}(180) = 90$

$m\angle ZBA = \frac{1}{2}m\widehat{AYZ}$

$= \frac{1}{2}(60 + 120) = \frac{1}{2}(180) = 90$

$m\angle YAB = \frac{1}{2}m\widehat{YZB}$

$= \frac{1}{2}(120 + 60) = \frac{1}{2}(180) = 90$

55. a. $\overset{\frown}{mEMY} = m\angle ELY$ b. $\overset{\frown}{mENY} = 2(m\angle ELY)$
             $= 60$ $= 2(60)$
                                       $= 120$

56. $r^2 = 60^2 + 25^2$ 57. No; $6^2 + 9^2 \neq 11^2$
      $= 3600 + 625$
      $= 4225$
    $r = \sqrt{4225}$
      $= 65$ cm

58. Yes; all angles are congruent since they each measure 90°, and corresponding sides will always have the same ratio since all four sides of a square are congruent.

59. median $= \dfrac{\text{base} + \text{base}}{2}$

     $18 = \dfrac{29 + b}{2}$

   $29 + b = 36$
        $b = 7$ inches

60. hypothesis: an angle is inscribed in a semicircle
     conclusion: the angle is a right angle

61. $AB = \sqrt{(7 - (-3))^2 + (4 - 1)^2}$
       $= \sqrt{10^2 + 3^2}$
       $= \sqrt{109}$
   $AB \approx 10.4$

62. A central angle has its vertex at the center of the circle and an inscribed angle has its vertex on the circle. If an inscribed angle and a central angle intercept the same arc, the measure of the central angle will be twice the measure of the inscribed angle.

Mid-Chapter Review

PAGE 433

1.

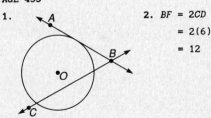

2. $BF = 2CD$
       $= 2(6)$
       $= 12$

3. $\overset{\frown}{mAFE} = 180$

4. $\overset{\frown}{mAD} = m\angle 2 + m\angle 3$
        $= m\angle 2 + m\angle 1$
        $= 32 + 32$
        $= 64$

5. $\overset{\frown}{mAF} = 180 - m\angle 1$
       $= 180 - 32$
       $= 148$

6. $\overset{\frown}{mDE} = 180 - m\angle 1 - m\angle 2$
       $= 180 - 32 - 32$
       $= 116$

7. $m\angle 4 = 180 - m\angle 2 - m\angle 1$
        $= 180 - 32 - 32$
        $= 116$

8. $4^2 + d^2 = 5^2$
         $d^2 = 5^2 - 4^2$
         $d^2 = 25 - 16 = 9$
          $d = \sqrt{9} = 3$ cm

9. Draw $\overline{AQ}$ which bisects $\angle A$ and draw a perpendicular from Q to X, the midpoint of $\overline{AC}$. $\triangle AQX$ is a 30°-60°-90° right $\triangle$.
   $AQ = $ radius $= 12$
   $QX = \dfrac{12}{2} = 6$
   $AX = 6\sqrt{3}$
   Therefore side $AC = 2AX = 12\sqrt{3} \approx 20.8$ units

10. QB, QA and QC are radii, so the distance $= 12$ units.

11. $\overset{\frown}{mAB} = 2(m\angle ACB)$
        $= 2(60)$
        $= 120$

PAGES 436-437   CHECKING FOR UNDERSTANDING

1. 2; A tangent can be drawn to each "side" of the circle from the point outside of the circle.

2. 0; A tangent cannot pass through a point inside the circle.

3. 1; Only one line can be drawn perpendicular to the endpoint of a radius.

4. inscribed   5. neither   6. circumscribed

7. Two tangent segments from the same exterior point to a circle are congruent, so $x = 12$.

8. $x^2 = 12^2 + 7^2$
     $= 144 + 49 = 193$
   $x = \sqrt{193} \approx 13.9$

9. The sides of a square are all congruent, so $x = 14$.

10. $x = 2(6)$
     $= 12$

11. $(x + 12)^2 = 12^2 + 16^2$
   $x^2 + 24x + 144 = 144 + 256$
   $x^2 + 24x - 256 = 0$
   $(x + 32)(x - 8) = 0$
     $x = -32$ or $x = 8$
           $x = 8$

12. $x^2 + 12^2 = (8 + 12)^2$

$x^2 = 20^2 - 12^2$

$x^2 = 400 - 144 = 256$

$x = \sqrt{256} = 16$

PAGES 437-439   EXERCISES

13. $m\overset{\frown}{CE} = m\angle CPE$
    $= 45$

14. $mPCG = 90$

15. $m\angle CGP = 180 - m\angle PCG - m\angle CPE$
    $= 180 - 90 - 45$
    $= 45$

16. $CG = PC$
    $= 8$

17. $m\angle QDC = 90$

18. $m\angle FGD = m\angle CGP$
    $= 45$

19. $m\angle FQD = 180 - m\angle QDC - m\angle FGD$
    $= 180 - 90 - 45$
    $= 45$

20. $m\overset{\frown}{DF} = m\angle FDQ$
    $= 45$

21. $DQ = BQ$
    $= 5$

22. $DG = DQ$
    $= 5$

23. $DC = DG + GC$
    $= 5 + 8$
    $= 13$

24. $8^2 + 8^2 = (PG)^2$
    $64 + 64 = (PG)^2$
    $128 = (PG)^2$
    $8\sqrt{2} = PG \approx 11.3$

25. $5^2 + 5^2 = (GQ)^2$
    $25 + 25 = (GQ)^2$
    $\sqrt{50} = GQ = 5\sqrt{2}$
    ≈ 7.1

26. $\overline{PQ} = PG + GQ$
    $= 8\sqrt{2} + 5\sqrt{2}$
    $= 13\sqrt{2} \approx 18.4$

27. Quadrilateral $ABQP$ is a trapezoid.
    $3^2 + x^2 = (13\sqrt{2})^2$
    $9 + x^2 = 338$
    $x^2 = 329$
    $x = \sqrt{329} \approx 18.1$
    $AB = \sqrt{329} \approx 18.1$

28. $\overline{OK} \parallel \overline{CL}$: Two lines perpendicular to a given line are parallel.

29. $\triangle OKM \sim \triangle CLM$: A line parallel to a side of a triangle forms a triangle similar to the original triangle by AA Similarity.

30. $\overline{BX} \cong \overline{BZ}$ so $BZ = 6$, $\overline{CX} \cong \overline{CY}$ so $CY = 7$, $\overline{AZ} \cong \overline{AY}$ so $AZ = AY$. Let $x = AZ$ and AY.
    $AB = BZ + AZ$ $AC = CY + AY$
    $= 6 + x$ $= 7 + x$

$AB + AC + BC = 42$

$(6 + x) + (7 + x) + 13 = 42$

$2x = 16$

$x = 8$

$AB = 6 + x = 14$

$AC = 7 + x = 15$

31. $AB + BC + CA = 50$
    $(10 + x) + (12 + x) + 22 = 50$
    $2x = 6$
    $x = 3$
    $BC = 12 + x = 15$

32. $AB + BC + CA = 48$
    $(6 + x) + (9.5 + x) + 15.5 = 48$
    $2x = 17$
    $x = 8.5$
    $BZ = 8.5$

33. $TB = TS$ and $TA = TR$ (If two segments from the same exterior point are tangent to a circle, then they are congruent.) $TA - TB = TR - TS$ (Substitution property of equality). Therefore, $AB = RS$.

34. $AT = RT$ and $TB = TS$ (If two segments from the same exterior point are tangent to a circle, then they are congruent.) $AT + TB = RT + TS$ (Addition property of equality). Therefore, $AB = RS$.

35.

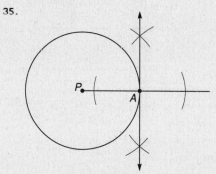

36.

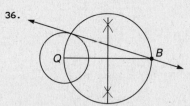

37. Given: $\overleftrightarrow{CA}$ is tangent to the circle at A.
    Prove: $\overline{XA} \perp \overleftrightarrow{CA}$

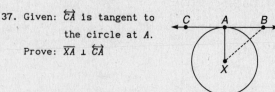

Proof: Pick any point on $\overleftrightarrow{CA}$ other than A and call it B. Draw $\overline{XB}$. From the definition of tangent, we know that $\overleftrightarrow{CA}$ intersects $\odot X$ at exactly one point, A, and B lies in the exterior of $\odot O$. Therefore, $XA < XB$. Thus, since $\overline{XA}$ is the shortest segment from X to $\overline{CA}$, it follows that $\overline{XA} \perp \overleftrightarrow{CA}$.

164

38. Given: $\overline{AB}$ and $\overline{AC}$ are
tangent to $\odot X$
at B and C.
Prove: $\overline{AB} \cong \overline{AC}$

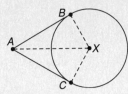

Proof: Draw $\overline{BX}$, $\overline{CX}$, and $\overline{AX}$. $\angle ABX$ and $\angle ACX$ are
right $\angle$s. Since $\overline{BX}$ and $\overline{CX}$ are radii, $BX \cong$
CX. $\overline{AX} \cong \overline{AX}$ and right Δs AXB and AXC are
congruent by HL. Finally, $\overline{AB} \cong \overline{AC}$ by
CPCTC.

39. Given: $\ell \perp \overline{AB}$
$\overline{AB}$ is a radius of $\odot A$.
Prove: ℓ is tangent to $\odot A$.

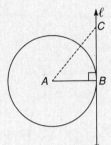

Proof: Assume that ℓ is not tangent to $\odot A$. Since
ℓ touches $\odot A$ at B, it must touch the
circle in another place. Call this point
C. Then $AB = AC$. But if AB is
perpendicular to ℓ, AB must be the
shortest distance between A and ℓ. There
is a contradiction. Therefore, ℓ is
tangent to $\odot A$.

40. a. $(x - 11)^2 + (y + 8)^2 = 49$

b.

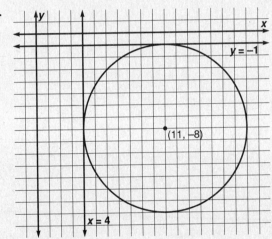

41.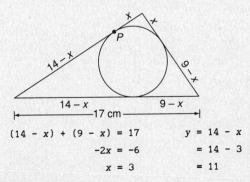

$(14 - x) + (9 - x) = 17$ $y = 14 - x$
$\qquad\qquad -2x = -6$ $= 14 - 3$
$\qquad\qquad\quad x = 3$ $= 11$

$x:y = 3:11$

42.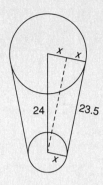

$x^2 + (23.5)^2 = 24^2$
$\qquad x^2 = 576 - 552.25$
$\qquad x^2 = 23.75$
$\qquad\quad x \approx 4.9$ cm smaller radius
$\qquad 2x \approx 9.7$ cm larger radius

43. Sample answer: Everyone is his or her own
person, an individual and alone. However, each
person touches the lives of others, just as a
tangent touches a circle in one place. Each
person is changed by his or her relationships
with others but is still alone.

44. The measure of an inscribed angle is half the
measure of its intercepted arc.

So $m\angle ABC = \frac{1}{2}m\widehat{AC}$

$\qquad\quad 84 = m\widehat{AC}$

45. $15^2 + 8^2 = s^2$ 46. Yes; AA Similarity
$\quad 225 + 64 = s^2$
$\qquad\quad 17 = s$
perimeter $= 4s = 68$ in.

47. Yes; isosceles   48. $\frac{-9 - 3}{2 - 0} = -6$

49. See students' work.

9-6   More Angle Measures

1. in the circle:

$m\angle IHJ = \frac{1}{2}(m\widehat{JI} + m\widehat{GF})$

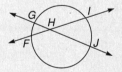

on the circle:

$m\angle LNM = \frac{1}{2}m\widehat{LM}$

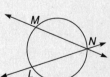

outside the circle:

$m\angle ACE = \frac{1}{2}(m\widehat{AE} - m\widehat{DB})$

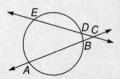

2. Sample answer: The measures of both angles equal half the intercepted arc. The sides of inscribed angles are both secants, unlike angles formed by a secant and a tangent.

3. Sample answer: Subtract the arc with the smaller measure from the arc with the larger measure.

4. $m\angle 1 = \frac{1}{2}(126) = 63$

5. $360 - 117 - 125 = 118$

$m\angle 2 = \frac{1}{2}(118) = 59$

6. $360 - 100 - 120 - 90 = 50$

$m\angle 3 = \frac{1}{2}(120 - 50) = 35$

7. $360 - 150 = 210$

$m\angle 4 = \frac{1}{2}(210) = 105$

8. $360 - 175 - 110 = 75$

$m\angle 5 = \frac{1}{2}(110 - 75) = 17.5$

9. $360 - 220 = 140$

$m\angle 6 = \frac{1}{2}(220 - 140) = 40$

10. $80 = \frac{1}{2}(110 + x)$

$160 = 110 + x$

$50 = x$

11. $35 = \frac{1}{2}[(360 - x) - x]$

$70 = 360 - x - x$

$-290 = -2x$

$145 = x$

12. $15 = \frac{1}{2}(55 - x)$

$30 = 55 - x$

$25 = x$

PAGES 443-446   EXERCISES

13. $m\overset{\frown}{BF} = 360 - (84 + 38 + 64 + 60)$

$= 360 - 246$

$= 114$

14. $m\overset{\frown}{BDF} = 360 - m\overset{\frown}{BF}$

$= 360 - 114$

$= 246$

15. $m\angle 1 = \frac{1}{2}(m\overset{\frown}{BDF} - m\overset{\frown}{BF})$

$= \frac{1}{2}(246 - 114)$

$= \frac{1}{2}(132)$

$= 66$

16. $m\overset{\frown}{BFC} = 360 = m\overset{\frown}{BC}$

$= 360 - 84$

$= 276$

17. $m\angle 2 = \frac{1}{2}(m\overset{\frown}{BFC})$

$= \frac{1}{2}(276)$

$= 138$

18. $m\angle GBC = \frac{1}{2}(m\overset{\frown}{BC})$

$= \frac{1}{2}(84)$

$= 42$

19. $m\overset{\frown}{BFE} = m\overset{\frown}{BF} + m\overset{\frown}{FE}$

$= 114 + 60$

$= 174$

20. $m\angle 3 = \frac{1}{2}(m\overset{\frown}{BFE})$

$= \frac{1}{2}(174)$

$= 87$

21. $m\angle 4 = \frac{1}{2}(m\overset{\frown}{CD} + m\overset{\frown}{EF})$

$= \frac{1}{2}(38 + 60)$

$= 49$

22. $m\angle 5 = \frac{1}{2}(m\overset{\frown}{DE} + m\angle CBF)$

$= \frac{1}{2}(64 + 198)$

$= 131$

23. $m\overset{\frown}{FBC} = m\overset{\frown}{BC} + m\overset{\frown}{BF}$

$= 84 + 114$

$= 198$

24. $m\angle 6 = \frac{1}{2}(m\overset{\frown}{CBF} - m\overset{\frown}{EF})$

$= \frac{1}{2}(198 - 60)$

$= \frac{1}{2}(138)$

$= 69$

25. $m\overset{\frown}{FBD} = m\overset{\frown}{FB} + m\overset{\frown}{BC} + m\overset{\frown}{CD}$

$= 114 + 84 + 38$

$= 236$

26. $m\angle 7 = \frac{1}{2}(m\overset{\frown}{FBD})$

$= \frac{1}{2}(236)$

$= 118$

27. $m\angle 8 = \frac{1}{2}(m\overset{\frown}{BF} - m\overset{\frown}{CD})$

$= \frac{1}{2}(114 - 38)$

$= \frac{1}{2}(76)$

$= 38$

28. $m\angle RST = \frac{1}{2}(m\overset{\frown}{RWT} - m\overset{\frown}{RT})$

$m\angle 1 + m\angle 2 = \frac{1}{2}[360 - (4x + 4) - (4x + 4)]$

$2x + 2x = \frac{1}{2}[360 - 4x - 4 - 4x - 4]$

$4x + 4x = 360 - 4x - 4 - 4x - 4$

$8x = 352 - 8x$

$16x = 352$

$x = 22$

29. $m\angle 1 = 2x = 2(22) = 44$

30. $m\overset{\frown}{RV} = 360 - [m\overset{\frown}{RYT} + m\overset{\frown}{TWV}]$

$= 360 - [(4x + 4) + 2(3x + 14)]$

$= 360 - 4x - 4 - 6x - 28$

$= 328 - 10x$

$= 328 - 10(22)$

$= 328 - 220$

$= 108$

31. $m\angle 2 = 2x = 2(22) = 44$

32. $m\overset{\frown}{RYT} = 4x + 4$

$= 4(22) + 4$

$= 92$

33. $m\overset{\frown}{TRV} = 360 - m\overset{\frown}{TWV}$

$= 360 - 2(m\angle 4)$

$= 360 - 2(3x + 14)$

$= 360 - (6x + 28)$

$= 360 - [6(22) + 28]$

$= 360 - (132 + 28)$

$= 200$

34. $m\overset{\frown}{YT} = 3x - 20$

$= 3(22) - 20$

$= 46$

35. $m\overset{\frown}{YR} = m\overset{\frown}{RYT} - m\overset{\frown}{YT}$

$= 92 - 46$

$= 46$

36. $m\angle 1 = \frac{1}{2}(m\overset{\frown}{RW} - m\overset{\frown}{YR})$

$44 = \frac{1}{2}(m\overset{\frown}{RW} - 46)$

$88 = m\overset{\frown}{RW} - 46$

$134 = m\overset{\frown}{RW}$

$m\angle 5 = \frac{1}{2}(m\overset{\frown}{VW} + m\overset{\frown}{YT})$

$= \frac{1}{2}[m\overset{\frown}{RW} - m\overset{\frown}{RV}) + 46]$

$= \frac{1}{2}[(134 - 108) + 46]$

$= \frac{1}{2}(72)$

$= 36$

37. $m\angle 2 = \frac{1}{2}(m\overset{\frown}{TW} - m\overset{\frown}{YT})$ 38. $m\angle 1 = \frac{1}{2}(m\overset{\frown}{RW} - m\overset{\frown}{RY})$

$44 = \frac{1}{2}(m\overset{\frown}{TW} - 46)$ $44 = \frac{1}{2}(m\overset{\frown}{RW} - 46)$

$88 = m\overset{\frown}{TW} - 46$ $88 = m\overset{\frown}{RW} - 46$

$134 = m\overset{\frown}{TW}$ $134 = m\overset{\frown}{RW}$

39. $m\angle 5 + m\angle 6 = 180$ 40. $m\angle 4 = 3x + 14$

$36 + m\angle 6 = 180$ $= 3(22) + 14$

$m\angle 6 = 144$ $= 80$

41. $m\angle 4 = \frac{1}{2}(m\overset{\frown}{TWV})$ 42. $m\overset{\frown}{YV} = m\overset{\frown}{YR} + m\overset{\frown}{RV}$

$80 = \frac{1}{2}(m\overset{\frown}{TWV})$ $= 46 + 108$

$= 154$

$160 = m\overset{\frown}{TWV}$

43. $m\overset{\frown}{VW} + m\overset{\frown}{TW} = m\overset{\frown}{TWV}$ 44. $m\angle 3 + m\angle 4 = 180$

$m\overset{\frown}{VW} + 134 = 160$ $m\angle 3 + 80 = 180$

$m\overset{\frown}{VW} = 26$ $m\angle 3 = 100$

45. $m\angle 7 = m\angle 6 = 144$

46. $x + (275 - 3x) + 2x + (110 - 2x) = 360$

$-2x = -25$

$x = 12.5$

$m\angle CED = \frac{1}{2}(m\overset{\frown}{CD} + m\overset{\frown}{AB})$

$= \frac{1}{2}(x + 2x)$

$= \frac{1}{2}(3x)$

$= \frac{1}{2}[3(12.5)]$

$= 18.75$

47. Let $x = m\overset{\frown}{RS}$

Let $2x = m\overset{\frown}{AB}$

$2x + 120 + x = 180$

$3x = 60$

$x = 20 = m\overset{\frown}{RS}$

$2x = 40 = m\overset{\frown}{AB}$

$m\angle RTS = \frac{1}{2}(m\overset{\frown}{AB} - m\overset{\frown}{RS})$ $m\angle UTV = \frac{1}{2}(m\overset{\frown}{CD} - m\overset{\frown}{UV})$

$= \frac{1}{2}(40 - 20) = 10$ $10 = \frac{1}{2}(35 - m\overset{\frown}{UV})$

$m\angle RTS = m\angle UTV$ $20 = 35 - m\overset{\frown}{UV}$

$15 = m\overset{\frown}{UV}$

48. $m\overset{\frown}{AC} = 2m\angle R$ $m\angle B = \frac{1}{2}(m\overset{\frown}{CRA} - m\overset{\frown}{CA})$

$= 2(40)$ $x = \frac{1}{2}(132 + 148 - 80)$

$= 80$ $x = 100$

$m\overset{\frown}{RC} = 360 - 132 - 80$ $m\angle RCB = \frac{1}{2}m\overset{\frown}{RAC}$

$= 148$ $z = \frac{1}{2}(132 + 80)$

$z = 106$

$m\angle RAB = \frac{1}{2}m\overset{\frown}{RCA}$

$y = \frac{1}{2}(148 + 80)$

$y = 114$

49. $m\angle SAE = \frac{1}{2}(m\overset{\frown}{SE} - m\overset{\frown}{ST})$

$12 = \frac{1}{2}(70 - x)$

$24 = 70 - x$

$46 = x$

$m\overset{\frown}{CT} = 360 - (162 + 70 + 46) = 82$

$m\angle ACS = \frac{1}{2}(m\overset{\frown}{CS})$ $m\angle CAE = \frac{1}{2}(m\overset{\frown}{CE} - m\overset{\frown}{CT})$

$y = \frac{1}{2}(46 + 82)$ $z = \frac{1}{2}(162 - 82)$

$y = 64$ $z = 40$

50. $m\angle APB = 180 - m\angle CPB$

$= 180 - 115$

$= 65$

$m\angle APB = \frac{1}{2}(m\overset{\frown}{AB} + m\overset{\frown}{CD})$

$= \frac{1}{2}[(6x + 16) + (3x - 12)]$

$65 = \frac{1}{2}(9x + 4)$

$130 = 9x + 4$

$126 = 9x$

$14 = x$

$m\overset{\frown}{AB} = 6x + 16$ $m\overset{\frown}{CD} = 3x - 12$

$= 6(14) + 16$ $= 3(14) - 12$

$= 100$ $= 30$

51. Given: Secants $\overleftrightarrow{AC}$ and $\overleftrightarrow{BD}$ intersect at X inside $\odot P$.

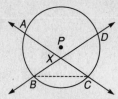

Prove: $m\angle AXB = \frac{1}{2}(m\widehat{AB} + m\widehat{CD})$

Proof: We are given that secants $\overleftrightarrow{AC}$ and $\overleftrightarrow{BD}$ intersect at X inside $\odot P$. Draw $\overline{BC}$. Because an angle inscribed has the measure of $\frac{1}{2}$ the measure of its intercepted arc, $m\angle XBC = \frac{1}{2}m\widehat{CD}$ and $m\angle XCB = \frac{1}{2}m\widehat{AB}$. By the Exterior Angle Theorem, $m\angle AXB = m\angle XCB + m\angle XBC$. By substitution, $m\angle AXB = \frac{1}{2}m\widehat{AB} + \frac{1}{2}m\widehat{CD}$. Then by use of the distribute property, $m\angle AXB = \frac{1}{2}(m\widehat{AB} + m\widehat{CD})$.

52. Given: $\overleftrightarrow{AC}$ and $\overleftrightarrow{AT}$ are secants to the circle.

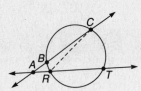

Prove: $m\angle CAT = \frac{1}{2}(m\widehat{CT} - m\widehat{BR})$

Proof: We are given that $\overleftrightarrow{AC}$ and $\overleftrightarrow{AT}$ are secants to a circle. Draw $\overline{CR}$. $m\angle CRT = \frac{1}{2}m\widehat{CT}$ and $m\angle ACR = \frac{1}{2}m\widehat{BR}$ because the measure of an inscribed angle equals $\frac{1}{2}$ the measure of the intercepted arc. By the Exterior Angle Theorem, $m\angle CRT = m\angle ACR + m\angle CAT$. Then by substitution, $\frac{1}{2}m\widehat{CT} = \frac{1}{2}m\widehat{BR} + m\angle CAT$, and by the subtraction property of equality, $\frac{1}{2}m\widehat{CT} - \frac{1}{2}m\widehat{BR} = m\angle CAT$. Finally, by the distributive property of equality, $\frac{1}{2}(m\widehat{CT} - m\widehat{BR}) = m\angle CAT$.

53. Given: $\overleftrightarrow{DG}$ is a tangent to the circle. $\overrightarrow{DF}$ is a secant to the circle.

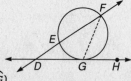

Prove: $m\angle FDG = \frac{1}{2}m\widehat{FG} - m\widehat{EG})$

Proof: We are given that $\overleftrightarrow{DG}$ is a tangent to a circle, and $\overrightarrow{DF}$ is a secant to that circle. Draw $\overline{FG}$. $m\angle DFG = \frac{1}{2}m\widehat{GE}$ and $m\angle FGH = \frac{1}{2}m\widehat{FG}$ because the measure of an inscribed angle equals $\frac{1}{2}$ the measure of the intercepted arc. By the Exterior

Angle Theorem, $m\angle FGH = m\angle DFG + m\angle FDG$. Then by substitution $\frac{1}{2}m\widehat{FG} = \frac{1}{2}m\widehat{GE} + m\angle FDG$, and by the subtraction property of equality $\frac{1}{2}m\widehat{FG} - \frac{1}{2}m\widehat{GE} = m\angle FDG$. Finally, by the distributive property of equality, $\frac{1}{2}(m\widehat{FG} - m\widehat{GE}) = m\angle FDG$.

54. Given: $\overleftrightarrow{HI}$ and $\overleftrightarrow{HJ}$ are tangents to the circle.

Prove: $m\angle IHJ = \frac{1}{2}(m\widehat{IXJ} - m\widehat{IJ})$

Proof: We are given that $\overleftrightarrow{HI}$ and $\overleftrightarrow{HJ}$ are tangents to a circle. Draw $\overline{IJ}$. $m\angle IJK = \frac{1}{2}m\widehat{IXJ}$ and $m\angle HIJ = \frac{1}{2}m\widehat{IJ}$ because the measure of an inscribed angle equals $\frac{1}{2}$ the measure of the intercepted arc. By the Exterior Angle Theorem, $m\angle IJK = m\angle HIJ + m\angle IHJ$. Then by substitution, $\frac{1}{2}m\widehat{IXJ} = \frac{1}{2}m\widehat{IJ} + m\angle IHJ$ and by the subtraction property of equality, $\frac{1}{2}m\widehat{IXJ} - \frac{1}{2}m\widehat{IJ} = m\angle IHJ$. Finally, by the distributive property of equality, $\frac{1}{2}(m\widehat{IXJ} - m\widehat{IJ}) = m\angle IHJ$.

55. Theorem 9-11. Case 1
Given: $\overleftrightarrow{AB}$ is a tangent of $\odot O$. $\overline{AC}$ is a secant of $\odot O$. $\angle CAB$ is acute.

Prove: $m\angle CAB = \frac{1}{2}m\widehat{CA}$

Proof: Construct diameter $\overline{AD}$. $\angle DAB$ is a right $\angle$ with measure 90, and $\widehat{DCA}$ is a semicircle with measure 180, since if a line is tangent to a $\odot$, it is $\perp$ to the radius at the point of tangency. Since $\angle CAB$ is acute, C is in the interior of $\angle DAB$, so by the angle and arc addition postulates, $m\angle DAB = m\angle DAC + m\angle CAB$ and $m\widehat{DCA} = m\widehat{DC} + m\widehat{CA}$. By substitution, $90 = m\angle DAC + m\angle CAB$ and $180 = m\widehat{DC} + m\widehat{CA}$. Thus, $90 = \frac{1}{2}m\widehat{DC} + \frac{1}{2}m\widehat{CA}$ by division, so $m\angle DAC + m\angle CAB = \frac{1}{2}m\widehat{DC} + \frac{1}{2}m\widehat{CA}$ by substitution. $m\angle DAC = \frac{1}{2}\widehat{DC}$ since $\angle DAC$ is inscribed, so substitution yields $\frac{1}{2}m\widehat{DC} + m\angle CAB = \frac{1}{2}m\widehat{DC} + \frac{1}{2}m\widehat{CA}$. By subtraction, $m\angle CAB = \frac{1}{2}m\widehat{CA}$.

Case 2

Given: $\overleftrightarrow{AB}$ is a tangent of ⊙O.

$\overline{AC}$ is a secant of ⊙O.

∠CAB is a right angle.

Prove: $m\angle CAB = \frac{1}{2}m\overarc{CA}$

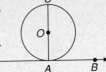

Proof: ∠CAB is a right angle, so $\overline{CA} \perp \overline{AB}$ and $m\angle CAB = 90$. If a line is tangent to a ⊙, then it is ⊥ to the radius drawn to the point of tangency, so $\overline{AC}$ must be a diameter. Thus, $m\overarc{CA} = 180$, so $\frac{1}{2}m\overarc{CA} = 90$. By substitution, $m\angle CAB = \frac{1}{2}m\overarc{CA}$.

Case 3

Given: $\overleftrightarrow{AB}$ is a tangent of ⊙O.

$\overline{AC}$ is a secant of ⊙O.

∠CAB is obtuse.

Prove: $m\angle CAB = \frac{1}{2}m\overarc{CDA}$

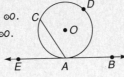

Proof: ∠CAB and ∠CAE form a linear pair, so $m\angle CAB + m\angle CAE = 180$. Since ∠CAB is obtuse, ∠CAE is acute and Case 1 applies, so $m\angle CAE = \frac{1}{2}m\overarc{CA}$. $m\overarc{CA} + m\overarc{CDA} = 360$, so $\frac{1}{2}m\overarc{CA} + \frac{1}{2}m\overarc{CDA} = 180$ by division, and $m\angle CAE + \frac{1}{2}m\overarc{CDA} = 180$ by substitution. By the transitive property, $m\angle CAB + m\angle CAE = m\angle CAE + \frac{1}{2}m\overarc{CDA}$, so by subtraction $m\angle CAB = \frac{1}{2}m\overarc{CDA}$.

56.

$m\angle ADB = \frac{1}{2}(m\overarc{ACB} - m\overarc{AB})$	Theorem 9-13
$x = \frac{1}{2}[(360 - y) - y]$	Substitution
$x = \frac{1}{2}(360 - 2y)$	Substitution
$2x = 360 - 2y$	Multiplication prop.
$2x + 2y = 360$	Addition prop.
$x + y = 180$	Division prop.

57. a. Yes; the ship is safe. If the measure of the angle formed by the lighthouses and ship is smaller than the published measure, then the ship must be outside the danger circle. (An angle outside the circle is smaller than an inscribed angle.)

b. No; the ship is not safe. The only way this angle can be greater than the published measure is for the ship to be within the danger circle. (An angle inside the circle is larger than an inscribed angle.)

58. It is tangent to the circle.

59. $2x = 35$

$x = 17.5$

60. Yes; the sum of any two sides is greater than the third side.

61. the vertex angle, $m\angle V = 116$, since:

$7x - 3 = 4x + 12$ $32 + 32 + m\angle V = 180$

$3x = 15$ $m\angle V = 116$

$x = 5$

$7x - 3 = 32$

$4x + 12 = 32$

62. $180 - 115 = 65$

Since the Δ is isosceles (from diagram):

$65 + 65 + x = 180$

$x = 50$

63. Congruence of angles is reflexive.

64.

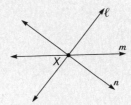

65. $m\angle XYZ = \frac{1}{2}(m\overarc{XWZ} - m\overarc{XZ})$ $m\angle AOB = m\overarc{AB}$

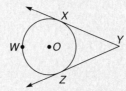

$m\angle RTV = \frac{1}{2}(m\overarc{RV} - m\overarc{SU})$ $m\angle CDE = \frac{1}{2}m\overarc{CE}$

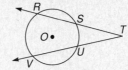

$m\angle KLM = \frac{1}{2}m\overarc{KL}$ $m\angle FGJ = \frac{1}{2}(m\overarc{FJ} + m\overarc{HI})$

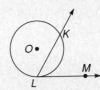

66. $x^2 - 7x - 8 = 0$

$x = \dfrac{-(-7) \pm \sqrt{(-7)^2 - 4(1)(-8)}}{2(1)}$

$= \dfrac{7 \pm \sqrt{49 + 32}}{2}$

$= \dfrac{7 \pm \sqrt{81}}{2}$

$= \dfrac{7 \pm 9}{2}$

$= \dfrac{7 + 9}{2}$ or $\dfrac{7 - 9}{2}$

$x = 8$ or $x = -1$

The solution set is {8, -1}.

169

67. $3x^2 + 14x - 5 = 0$

$$x = \frac{-14 \pm \sqrt{14^2 - 4(3)(-5)}}{2(3)}$$

$$= \frac{-14 \pm \sqrt{196 + 60}}{6}$$

$$= \frac{-14 \pm \sqrt{256}}{6}$$

$$= \frac{-14 \pm 16}{6}$$

$$= \frac{-14 + 16}{6} \text{ or } \frac{-14 - 16}{6}$$

$$x = \frac{1}{3} \text{ or } x = -5$$

The solution set is $\left\{\frac{1}{3}, -5\right\}$.

68. $n^2 - 13n - 32 = 0$

$$n = \frac{-(-13) \pm \sqrt{(-13)^2 - 4(1)(-32)}}{2(1)}$$

$$= \frac{13 \pm \sqrt{169 + 128}}{2}$$

$$= \frac{13 \pm \sqrt{297}}{2}$$

$$= \frac{13 \pm 3\sqrt{33}}{2}$$

$$n = \frac{13 + 3\sqrt{33}}{2} \text{ or } n = \frac{13 - 3\sqrt{33}}{2}$$

The solution set is $\left\{\frac{13 + 3\sqrt{33}}{2}, \frac{13 - 3\sqrt{33}}{2}\right\}$.

69. $-4y^2 + 16y + 13 = 0$

$$y = \frac{-16 \pm \sqrt{16^2 - 4(-4)(13)}}{2(-4)}$$

$$= \frac{-16 \pm \sqrt{256 + 208}}{-8}$$

$$= \frac{-16 \pm \sqrt{464}}{-8}$$

$$= \frac{-16 \pm 4\sqrt{29}}{-8}$$

$$y = \frac{-16 + 4\sqrt{29}}{-8} \text{ or } y = \frac{-16 - 4\sqrt{29}}{-8}$$

$$= \frac{4 - \sqrt{29}}{2} \qquad\qquad = \frac{4 + \sqrt{29}}{2}$$

The solution set is $\left\{\frac{4 - \sqrt{29}}{2}, \frac{4 + \sqrt{29}}{2}\right\}$.

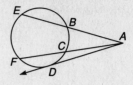

9-7 | Special Segments in a Circle

PAGE 450   CHECKING FOR UNDERSTANDING

1. A secant segment is a segment from an exterior point to the farthest point of intersection with the circle. An exterior secant segment is just the part of the secant segment outside of the

circle. Examples of secant segments are $\overline{AE}$ and $\overline{AF}$. Examples of exterior secant segments are $\overline{AB}$ and $\overline{AC}$.

2. $AB \cdot AE = AC \cdot AF$

3. A tangent segment is a segment from an exterior point to the point of tangency. $\overline{AD}$ is an example of a tangent segment.

4. The measure of the secant segment times the measure of the exterior secant segment equals the square of the measure of the tangent segment.

5. Sample answer:
   $RV \cdot VT = SV \cdot VU$

6. $3x = 4 \cdot 9$
   $x = 12$

7. $3x = 7 \cdot 2$
   $x = 4\frac{2}{3}$

8. $5(x + 5) = 4(8 + 4)$
   $5x + 25 = 48$
   $5x = 23$
   $x = 4.6$

9. $4(x + 4) = 3(5 + 3)$
   $4x + 16 = 24$
   $4x = 8$
   $x = 2$

10. $10(x + 10) = 20^2$
    $10x + 100 = 400$
    $10x = 300$
    $x = 30$

11. $3x = 7 \cdot 3$
    $x = 7$

12. $x(5 + x) = 3(9 + 3)$
    $5x + x^2 = 36$
    $x^2 + 5x - 36 = 0$
    $(x + 9)(x - 4) = 0$
    $x = 4$

13. $x^2 = 8(8 + 8)$
    $x^2 = 128$
    $x = 8\sqrt{2} \approx 11.31$

14. $x(12 + x) = 8^2$
    $12x + x^2 = 64$
    $x^2 + 12x - 64 = 0$
    $(x + 16)(x - 4) = 0$
    $x = 4$

PAGES 451-453   EXERCISES

15. $8(8 + x) = 9^2$
    $64 + 8x = 81$
    $8x = 17$
    $x = \frac{17}{8}$

16. $5(3x + 5) = 10^2$
    $15x + 25 = 100$
    $15x = 75$
    $x = 5$

17. $0.5(x + 0.5) = 0.4(0.8 + 0.4)$

$0.5x + 0.25 = 0.32 + 0.16$

$0.5x = 0.23$

$x = 0.46$

18. $2x \cdot 2x = 20 \cdot 5$

$4x^2 = 100$

$x^2 = 25$

$x = 5$

19. $x^2 = 0.8(0.8 + 1.0)$

$x^2 = 1.44$

$x = 1.2$

20. $x(5 + x) = 5(x + 5)$

$5x + x^2 = 5x + 25$

$x^2 = 25$

$x = 5$

21. $x(5 + x) = 2(4 + 2)$

$5x + x^2 = 12$

$x^2 + 5x - 12 = 0$

$x = \dfrac{-5 \pm \sqrt{5^2 - 4(1)(-12)}}{2(1)}$

$= \dfrac{-5 \pm \sqrt{73}}{2}$

$= \dfrac{-5 + \sqrt{73}}{2} \approx 1.77$

22. $1.2^2 = 0.4x(0.5x + 0.4x)$

$1.44 = 0.2x^2 + 0.16x^2$

$1.44 = 0.36x^2$

$4 = x^2$

$2 = x$

23. $x(3x + x) = 0.5(2 + 0.5)$

$3x^2 + x^2 = 1.25$

$4x^2 = 1.25$

$x^2 = \dfrac{5}{16}$

$x = \dfrac{\sqrt{5}}{4} \approx 0.56$

24. $FH \cdot HD = CH \cdot HE$

$6 \cdot 2 = CH \cdot 3$

$12 = 3CH$

$4 = CH$

25. $AD \cdot AF = AC \cdot AG$

$16 \cdot 8 = AC \cdot 6$

$128 = 6AC$

$21.3 \approx AC$

$AG + GC = AC$

$GC \approx 21.3 - 6$

$GC \approx 15.3$

26. $AD \cdot AF = AC \cdot AG$

$(8 + 8)8 = 21 \cdot AG$

$128 = 21AG$

$6.1 \approx AG$

27. $EH \cdot HC = DH \cdot FH$

$10.5(20) = 8 \cdot FH$

$210 = 8FH$

$26.3 \approx FH$

28. $(BA)^2 = AD \cdot AF$

$(BA)^2 = (16 + 6 + 2)(16)$

$(BA)^2 = 384$

$BA = \sqrt{384} \approx 19.6$

29. $(ST)^2 + (TU)^2 = (SU)^2$

$4^2 + (TU)^2 = 9^2$

$(TU)^2 = 65$

$(TU)^2 = RT \cdot ST$

$65 = (4 + x)4$

$65 = 16 + 4x$

$49 = 4x$

$12.25 = x$

30. $(AB)^2 = AF \cdot AE$

$x^2 = (6 + 2)6$

$x^2 = 48$

$x = \sqrt{48} \approx 6.9$

$AD \cdot AC = AF \cdot AE$

$(y + 4)4 = (6 + 2)6$

$4y + 16 = 48$

$4y = 32$

$y = 8$

31. If $\overline{LO}$ were extended to a point P on the circle,

$LP \cdot LO = MO \cdot ON$

$LP \cdot 5 = 4 \cdot 10$

$LP = 8$

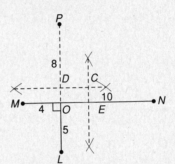

Draw the perpendicular bisectors of $\overline{LP}$ and $\overline{MN}$. Call the midpoints of $\overline{LP}$ and $\overline{MN}$ D and E respectively. The point of intersection is the center, C. $\overline{CM}$ is a radius. In $\triangle CME$,

$CM^2 = CE^2 + EM^2$

$CM^2 = (PO - PD)^2 + \left(\dfrac{1}{2}MN\right)^2$

$CM^2 = \left(8 - \dfrac{1}{2}PL\right)^2 + \left(\dfrac{1}{2}(14)\right)^2$

$CM^2 = \left(8 - \dfrac{1}{2}(13)\right)^2 + 7^2$

$CM^2 = (1.5)^2 + 49$

$CM^2 = 2.25 + 49$

$CM = \sqrt{51.25} \approx 7.16$

32. $x^2 + (12 - 5)^2 = 12^2$

$x^2 + 7^2 = 12^2$

$x^2 = 144 - 49$

$x^2 = 95$

$x = \sqrt{95} \approx 9.7$ units

33. Given: $\overline{RP}$ and $\overline{RT}$ are
secant segments.

Prove: $RQ \cdot RP = RS \cdot RT$

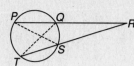

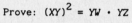

STATEMENTS	REASONS
1. Draw $\overline{PS}$ and $\overline{TQ}$.	1. Through any 2 pts. there is 1 line.
2. $\angle SRP \cong \angle QRT$	2. Congruence of $\angle$s is reflexive.
3. $\angle RPS \cong \angle RTQ$	3. If 2 inscribed $\angle$s of a $\odot$ or $\cong$ $\odot$s intercept $\cong$ arcs or the same arc, then the $\angle$s are $\cong$.
4. $\triangle PSR \sim \triangle TQR$	4. AA Similarity
5. $\dfrac{RQ}{RS} = \dfrac{RT}{RP}$	5. Def. similar polygons
6. $RQ \cdot RP = RS \cdot RT$	6. Cross products

34. Given: $\overline{XY}$ is a tangent.

$\overline{YW}$ is a secant.

Prove: $(XY)^2 = YW \cdot YZ$

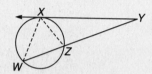

Proof: Draw $\overline{XZ}$ and $\overline{XW}$: $m\angle YXZ = \frac{1}{2}m\overparen{XZ}$ and $m\angle XWZ$

$= \frac{1}{2}m\overparen{XZ}$ since they are inscribed angles.

By substitution, $m\angle YXZ = m\angle XWZ$, and $\angle YXZ \cong \angle XWZ$ by the definition of congruent angles. $\angle Y \cong \angle Y$, since congruence of angles is reflexive. Therefore, $\triangle YXZ \sim \triangle YWZ$ by AA Similarity. $\frac{XY}{YW} = \frac{YZ}{XY}$ by definition of similar polygons. Cross products give us

$(XY)^2 = YW \cdot YZ.$

35. $3y = 4x$

$y = \dfrac{4}{3}x$

$(6 + x)(4 + 6) = (3 + 5)(5 + y)$

$(6 + x)10 = 8(5 + y)$

$60 + 10x = 40 + 8y$

$60 + 10x = 40 + 8\left(\dfrac{4}{3}x\right)$

$60 + 10x = 40 + \dfrac{32}{3}x$

$180 + 30x = 120 + 32x$

$60 = 2x$

$30 = x$

$y = \dfrac{4}{3}x$

$= \dfrac{4}{3}(30)$

$y = 40$

36. $50 \cdot x = 90 \cdot 90$

$50x = 8100$

$x = 162$

radius $= \dfrac{1}{2}(50 + 162)$

$= 106$ cm

37. $x^2 = 150(8000 + 150)$

$x^2 = 150(8150)$

$= 1,222,500$

$x = \sqrt{1,222,500}$

≈ 1106 mi

38. $20 \cdot x = (25)(25)$

$20x = 625$

$x = 31.25$

diameter $= x + 20$

$= 31.25 + 20$

$= 51.25$

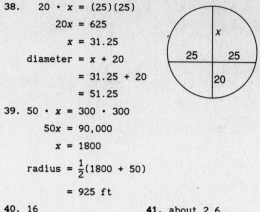

39. $50 \cdot x = 300 \cdot 300$

$50x = 90,000$

$x = 1800$

radius $= \dfrac{1}{2}(1800 + 50)$

$= 925$ ft

40. 16

41. about 2.6

42. about 16.7

43. about 1

44. Change line 10 to ask for AB, AC, and AD. Change ED in 40 to AE.

45. $m\angle ABC = \dfrac{1}{2}(m\overparen{AC} - m\overparen{DE})$

$= \dfrac{1}{2}[100 - (360 - 120 - 100 - 90)]$

$= \dfrac{1}{2}(50)$

$= 25$

46. $m\angle ECD = \dfrac{1}{2}(m\overparen{DE})$

$= \dfrac{1}{2}[360 - (120 + 100 + 90)]$

$= \dfrac{1}{2}(360 - 310)$

$= \dfrac{1}{2}(50)$

$= 25$

47. $\sin 62° = \dfrac{x}{15}$

$0.8829 = \dfrac{x}{15}$

$x = 13.24$

$\sin 70° = \dfrac{y}{15}$

$0.9397 = \dfrac{y}{15}$

$y = 14.09$

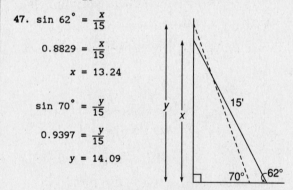

$y - x = 14.09 - 13.24 = 0.85$ ft or 10.2 in.

48.

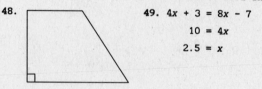

49. $4x + 3 = 8x - 7$

$10 = 4x$

$2.5 = x$

50. The friend is wrong. The measure of the exterior secant segment times the measure of the secant segment equals the measure of the other exterior secant segment times the measure of the other secant segment.

Technology: Circles

1.-3. Answers will vary. See students' work.

4. yes   5. no

9-8   Problem-Solving Strategy: Using Graphs

1. Rugged; less

2. Fashionable; they sell the least.

3. Sample answers: yes, because Prestige Jeans are already high in sales; no, because Best Jeans do not have good sales.

4. Sample answer: The circle graph helps you to visualize the situation.

5. Sample answers: bar graphs, line graphs, pictographs

6. a. Glamorous Fashions

   b. Funky Records

   c. up

   d. down

   e. Sample answer: Sell the Glamorous Fashions stock, since it is going down.

7.

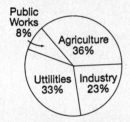

Water Use in the U.S.

8. 1,000,000,000 seconds $\times \dfrac{1 \text{ minute}}{60 \text{ seconds}} \times \dfrac{1 \text{ hour}}{60 \text{ minutes}}$

$\times \dfrac{1 \text{ day}}{24 \text{ hours}} \times \dfrac{1 \text{ year}}{365 \text{ days}} \approx 31.7$

You would be about 32 years old.

9. a.

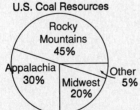

U.S. Coal Resources

   b. Sample answers: quality and price of the coal, accessibility and cost of transporting the coal, types of coal in different parts of the country, and ease in mining

10. typed 10^2 as 102: $101 - 10^2 = 1$; or omitted negative sign: $101 - 102 = -1$

11. 40; dividing by 2, 3, 4, 5, ...

12. $\dfrac{\$502,191}{\$4,000,000} \approx 12.6\%$ 13. $\dfrac{\$134,751}{\$748,817} \approx 18.0\%$

14. $\dfrac{\$111,343}{\$12,000} \approx 9.3$ times more

Cooperative Learning Project

a. The line graph indicates that sales are rapidly increasing. However, only January, February, and March are included. Perhaps sales decrease after March. Also, there is no zero on the scale, and no break to show discontinuity.

b. The circle graph is not drawn to scale. Example: Techtonics' percentage (Market Share) is only slightly greater than that of Worldwide's, but the graph shows Techtonics' share as much greater. Someone might want to use this graph to make Techtonics look like it has a larger lead in market share over their competition.

c. The graph is meant to show that the purchasing power of a U.S. dollar has changed drastically from 1950 to 1990. The area of the 1950 dollar should be 5.42 times greater than the area of the 1990 dollar. However, the area of the 1950 dollar is only about 3.3 times the area of the 1990 dollar. The graph makes the change in the purchasing power look smaller than it is. Someone might draw the graph this way to make the economy look better than it is.

Chapter 9 Summary and Review

1. no   2. yes   3.

4. $3x + (3x - 3) + (2x + 15) = 180$

                        $8x = 168$

                        $x = 21$

5. $m\widehat{YAX}$ = semicircle = 180

6. $m\angle BPY = m\overarc{BY}$
$\quad = 3x = 3(21)$
$\quad = 63$

7. $m\overarc{BX} = m\angle YPC + m\angle CPA$
$\quad = (3x - 3) + (2x + 15)$
$\quad = 3(21) - 3 + 2(21) + 15$
$\quad = 117$

8. $m\angle CPA = 2x + 15$
$\quad = 2(21) + 15$
$\quad = 57$

9. $m\overarc{BC} = m\overarc{BY} + m\overarc{YC}$
$\quad = m\angle BPY + m\angle YPC$
$\quad = 3x + 3x - 3$
$\quad = 3(21) + 3(21) - 3$
$\quad = 123$

10. $13^2 = 5^2 + x^2$
$\quad 169 = 25 + x^2$
$\quad 144 = x^2$
$\quad 12 = x$
$\quad chord = 2x = 24$

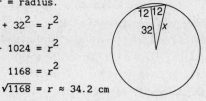

11. Let r = radius.
$\quad 12^2 + 32^2 = r^2$
$\quad 144 + 1024 = r^2$
$\quad 1168 = r^2$
$\quad \sqrt{1168} = r \approx 34.2$ cm

12. $m\angle DAB = \frac{1}{2}(m\overarc{BD})$
$\quad = \frac{1}{2}(72)$
$\quad = 36$

13. $m\overarc{CD} = m\angle CPD$
$\quad = 144$

14. $m\overarc{CA} = m\overarc{BD}$
$\quad = 72$

15. $m\angle CDA = \frac{1}{2}(m\overarc{CA})$
$\quad = \frac{1}{2}(72)$
$\quad = 36$

16. $m\overarc{AB} = 360 - (m\overarc{BD} + m\overarc{DC} + m\overarc{CA})$
$\quad = 360 - (72 + 144 + 72)$
$\quad = 360 - 288$
$\quad = 72$

17. $x^2 + 9^2 = (6 + 9)^2$
$\quad x^2 + 81 = 225$
$\quad x^2 = 144$
$\quad x = 12$

18. $2 + x = 8$
$\quad x = 6$

19. $m\angle DEC = m\angle AEB$
$\quad = 42$

20. $m\angle DEC = \frac{1}{2}(m\overarc{CD} + m\overarc{AB})$
$\quad 42 = \frac{1}{2}(m\overarc{CD} + 29)$
$\quad 84 = m\overarc{CD} + 29$
$\quad 55 = m\overarc{CD}$

21. $m\angle GFD = \frac{1}{2}(m\overarc{CD} - m\overarc{BG})$
$\quad = \frac{1}{2}(55 - 18)$
$\quad = \frac{1}{2}(37)$
$\quad = 18.5$

22. $m\overarc{AD} = m\overarc{AC} - m\overarc{CD}$
$\quad = 180 - 55$
$\quad = 125$

23.
$\quad m\angle AED = 360 - (m\angle AEB + m\angle BEC + m\angle CED)$
$\quad m\angle AED = 360 - (42 + m\angle AED + 42)$
$\quad m\angle AED = 360 - 42 - m\angle AED - 42$
$\quad m\angle AED + m\angle AED = 360 - 84$
$\quad 2m\angle AED = 276$
$\quad m\angle AED = 138$

24. $m\overarc{GC} = 360 - (m\overarc{BG} + m\overarc{AB} + m\overarc{AD} + m\overarc{DC})$
$\quad = 360 - (18 + 29 + 125 + 55)$
$\quad = 360 - 227$
$\quad = 133$

25. $4x = 3 \cdot 8$
$\quad x = 6$

26. $x^2 = 0.5(0.8 + 0.5)$
$\quad x^2 = 0.65$
$\quad x \approx 0.81$

27. $3(x + 3) = 5(5 + 6)$
$\quad 3x + 9 = 25 + 30$
$\quad 3x = 46$
$\quad x = 15\frac{1}{3}$

28. $5(x + 5) = 7^2$
$\quad 5x + 25 = 49$
$\quad 5x = 24$
$\quad x = 4.8$

PAGE 460   APPLICATIONS AND CONNECTIONS

29. $\frac{360}{10} = 36$

30. $x^2 + 3^2 = 4^2$
$\quad x^2 = 16 - 9$
$\quad x^2 = 7$
$\quad x = \sqrt{7} \approx 2.6$
$\quad height = 4 + x \approx 4 + 2.6$
$\quad \approx 6.6$ cm

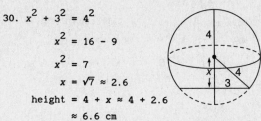

31. $5(2x + 5) = 14^2$
$\quad 10x + 25 = 196$
$\quad 10x = 171$
$\quad x = 17.1$
$\quad radius = x + 5 = 17.1 + 5$
$\quad = 22.1$ m

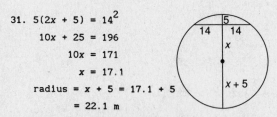

32.

Portion of Sales per Recording Type

Cassettes 49%

12-inch singles 2%

LPs 4%

45s 6%

Compact disks 39%

PAGE 461

1. Sample answer: A segment is the radius of the circle if its endpoints are the center of the circle and a point on the circle.

2.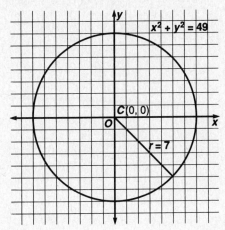

3. $x + 10$

4. $x(x + 6 + 6) = 8^2$
$x^2 + 6x + 6x = 64$
$x^2 + 12x - 64 = 0$
$(x - 4)(x + 16) = 0$
$x = 4$

5. $x = 15$

6. $5x = 6 \cdot 8$
$5x = 48$
$x = 9.6$

7. $x(x + 5) = 6^2$
$x^2 + 5x - 36 = 0$
$(x - 4)(x + 9) = 0$
$x = 4$

8. $5(x + 5) = 4(4 + 3)$
$5x + 25 = 28$
$5x = 3$
$x = \frac{3}{5} = 0.6$

9. $m\angle BPD = m\overset{\frown}{BD}$
$= 42$

10. $m\overset{\frown}{AC} = m\overset{\frown}{BD}$
$= 42$

11. $m\angle APC = m\overset{\frown}{AC}$
$= 42$

12. $m\overset{\frown}{CD} = m\overset{\frown}{AB} - (m\overset{\frown}{AC} + m\overset{\frown}{BD})$
$= 180 - (42 + 42)$
$= 96$

13. $m\angle BPF = m\angle APC$
$= 42$

14. $m\overset{\frown}{FB} = m\angle FPB$
$= 42$

15. $m\overset{\frown}{AF} = m\overset{\frown}{AFB} - (m\overset{\frown}{BE} + m\overset{\frown}{EF})$
$= 180 - (12 + 30)$
$= 138$

16. $m\overset{\frown}{FE} = m\overset{\frown}{BEF} - m\overset{\frown}{BE}$
$= 42 - 12$
$= 30$

17. $m\angle FCD = \frac{1}{2}(m\overset{\frown}{DB} + m\overset{\frown}{BEF})$
$= \frac{1}{2}(42 + 42)$
$= 42$

18. $m\angle EDC = \frac{1}{2}(m\overset{\frown}{EF} + m\overset{\frown}{FAC})$
$= \frac{1}{2}(30 + 180)$
$= 105$

19. $(5 + x)(5 - x) = 3 \cdot 3$
$25 - x^2 = 9$
$-x^2 = -16$
$x = 4$ inches

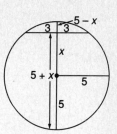

20. chords

BONUS

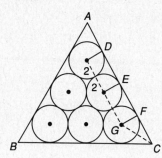

$AD = FC = 2\sqrt{3}$. Therefore,

Since $\overline{AC}$ is tangent to the circles, the radii of the circles form rectangles on side $\overline{AC}$. $DE = 4$; $EF = 4$

ΔFCG is a $30°$-$60°$-$90°$ Δ, so if $FG = 2$, $FC = 2\sqrt{3}$.

$AC = AD + DE + EF + FC$
$= 2\sqrt{3} + 4 + 4 + 2\sqrt{3}$
$= 8 + 4\sqrt{3} \approx 14.9$

Algebra Review

PAGES 462-463

1.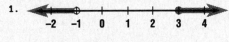

2.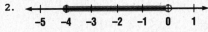

3. (number line from 6 to 12)

4. (number line from -3 to 3)

5. $a^2 + 17a = 0$ $0^2 + 17(0) = 0$
$a(a + 17) = 0$ $0 + 0 = 0$
$a = 0$ or $a + 17 = 0$ $0 = 0$
$a = -17$

$-17 + 17 = 0$
$0 = 0$

$\{0, -17\}$

6. $(y + 5)(y + 8) = 0$ $(-5)^2 + 13(-5) + 40 = 0$
$y = -5$ or $y = -8$ $0 = 0$

$-8^2 + 13(-8) + 40 = 0$
$0 = 0$

$\{-5, -8\}$

7.
$$2x^2 + 13x - 24 = 0 \qquad 2\left(\tfrac{3}{2}\right)^2 + 13\left(\tfrac{3}{2}\right) - 24 = 0$$
$$(2x - 3)(x + 8) = 0 \qquad \tfrac{9}{2} + \tfrac{39}{2} - 24 = 0$$
$$2x - 3 = 0 \text{ or } x + 8 = 0 \qquad 24 - 24 = 0$$
$$2x = 3 \qquad x = -8$$
$$x = \tfrac{3}{2}$$

$$2(-8)^2 + 13(-8) - 24 = 0$$
$$128 - 104 - 24 = 0$$
$$0 = 0$$

$$\left\{\tfrac{3}{2}, \ -8\right\}$$

8.
$$x^2 + 5x - 6 = 78 \qquad (-12)^2 + 5(-12) - 6 = 78$$
$$x^2 + 5x - 84 = 0 \qquad 144 - 60 - 6 = 78$$
$$(x + 12)(x - 7) = 0 \qquad 78 = 78$$
$$x + 12 = 0 \text{ or } x - 7 = 0$$
$$x = -12 \qquad x = 7$$

$$7^2 + 5(7) - 6 = 78$$
$$49 + 35 - 6 = 78$$
$$78 = 78$$

$$\{-12, \ 7\}$$

9. $r(25r^2 + 20r + 4) = 0$
$$r(5r + 2)(5r + 2) = 0$$
$$r = 0 \text{ or } 5r + 2 = 0$$
$$5r = -2$$
$$r = -\tfrac{2}{5}$$

$$25(0)^3 + 20(0) + 4(0) = 0$$
$$0 = 0$$

$$25\left(-\tfrac{2}{5}\right)^3 + 20\left(-\tfrac{2}{5}\right)^2 + 4\left(-\tfrac{2}{5}\right) = 0$$
$$25\left(-\tfrac{8}{125}\right) + 20\left(\tfrac{4}{25}\right) - \tfrac{8}{5} = 0$$
$$-\tfrac{200}{125} + \tfrac{80}{25} - \tfrac{8}{5} = 0$$
$$-\tfrac{8}{5} + \tfrac{16}{5} - \tfrac{8}{5} = 0$$
$$-\tfrac{16}{5} + \tfrac{16}{5} = 0$$
$$0 = 0$$

$$\left\{-\tfrac{2}{5}, \ 0\right\}$$

10.
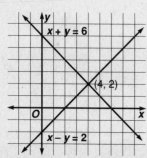

11.
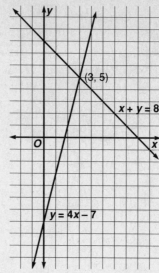

12.
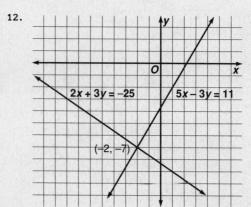

13. $\sqrt{108} = \sqrt{4 \cdot 9 \cdot 3}$
$$= \sqrt{2^2} \cdot \sqrt{3^2} \cdot \sqrt{3}$$
$$= 2 \cdot 3\sqrt{3}$$
$$= 6\sqrt{3}$$

14. $\sqrt{720} = \sqrt{9 \cdot 16 \cdot 5}$
$$= \sqrt{3^2} \cdot \sqrt{4^2} \cdot \sqrt{5}$$
$$= 3 \cdot 4 \cdot \sqrt{5}$$
$$= 12\sqrt{5}$$

15. $\dfrac{\sqrt{5}}{\sqrt{55}} = \dfrac{\sqrt{5}}{\sqrt{55}} \cdot \dfrac{\sqrt{55}}{\sqrt{55}}$
$$= \dfrac{\sqrt{5 \cdot 5 \cdot 11}}{\sqrt{55 \cdot 55}}$$
$$= \dfrac{\sqrt{5^2 \cdot 11}}{\sqrt{55^2}}$$
$$= \dfrac{5\sqrt{11}}{55}$$
$$= \dfrac{\sqrt{11}}{11}$$

16. $\sqrt{\dfrac{20}{7}} = \dfrac{\sqrt{20}}{\sqrt{7}}$
$$= \dfrac{\sqrt{20}}{\sqrt{7}} \cdot \dfrac{\sqrt{7}}{\sqrt{7}}$$
$$= \dfrac{\sqrt{2^2 \cdot 5 \cdot 7}}{\sqrt{7^2}}$$
$$= \dfrac{2\sqrt{35}}{7}$$

17. $\sqrt{96x^4} = \sqrt{4^2 \cdot 6 \cdot x^2 \cdot x^2}$
$$= 4x^2\sqrt{6}$$

18. $\sqrt{\dfrac{60}{y^2}} = \dfrac{\sqrt{2^2 \cdot 3 \cdot 5}}{\sqrt{y \cdot y}}$
$$= \dfrac{2\sqrt{15}}{|y|}$$

19. $\dfrac{5x^2y}{8ab} \cdot \dfrac{12a^2b}{25x} = \dfrac{3axy}{10}$

176

20. $\dfrac{r^2 + 3r - 18}{r + 2} \cdot \dfrac{r + 5}{r^2 - r - 6}$

$= \dfrac{(r + 6)\cancel{(r - 3)}}{r + 2} \cdot \dfrac{r + 6}{\cancel{(r - 3)}(r + 2)}$

$= \dfrac{(r + 6)^2}{(r + 2)^2}$

21. $\dfrac{b^2 + 19b + 84}{b - 3} \cdot \dfrac{b^2 - 9}{b^2 + 15b + 36}$

$= \dfrac{(b + 7)\cancel{(b + 12)}}{\cancel{b - 3}} \cdot \dfrac{\cancel{(b + 3)}\cancel{(b - 3)}}{\cancel{(b + 12)}\cancel{(b + 3)}}$

$= b + 7$

22. $\dfrac{p^3 r}{2q} \div \dfrac{-(p^2)}{4q}$

$= \dfrac{p^{\cancel{3}\,-p}r}{\cancel{2q}} \cdot \dfrac{\cancel{4q}^{\,2}}{-(\cancel{p^2})}$

$= -2pr$

23. $\dfrac{7a^2 b}{x^2 + x - 30} \div \dfrac{3a}{x^2 + 15x + 54}$

$= \dfrac{7a^2 b}{x^2 + x - 30} \cdot \dfrac{x^2 + 15x + 54}{3a}$

$= \dfrac{7\cancel{a^2}^{\,a} b}{\cancel{(x + 6)}(x - 5)} \cdot \dfrac{(x + 9)\cancel{(x + 6)}}{3\cancel{a}}$

$= \dfrac{7ab(x + 9)}{3(x - 5)}$

24. $\dfrac{n^2 + 4n - 21}{n^2 + 8n + 15} \div \dfrac{n^2 - 9}{n^2 + 12n + 35}$

$= \dfrac{n^2 + 4n - 21}{n^2 + 8n + 15} \cdot \dfrac{n^2 + 12n + 35}{n^2 - 9}$

$= \dfrac{(n + 7)\cancel{(n - 3)}}{\cancel{(n + 5)}(n + 3)} \cdot \dfrac{(n + 7)\cancel{(n + 5)}}{(n + 3)\cancel{(n - 3)}}$

$= \dfrac{(n + 7)^2}{(n + 3)^2}$

25. $f(2) = 2^2 - 2 + 1$
   $= 4 - 2 + 1$
   $= 3$

26. $f(-1) = (-1)^2 - (-1) + 1$
   $= 1 + 1 + 1$
   $= 3$

27. $f\left(\dfrac{1}{2}\right) = \left(\dfrac{1}{2}\right)^2 - \dfrac{1}{2} + 1$

$= \dfrac{1}{4} - \dfrac{1}{2} + 1$

$= \dfrac{3}{4}$

28. $f(a + 2) = (a + 2)^2 - (a + 2) + 1$
   $= a^2 + 4a + 4 - a - 2 + 1$
   $= a^2 + 3a + 3$

29. Let x = ounces of solution.
   $0.06x + (0.10)(12) = 0.07(x + 12)$
   $0.06x + 1.2 = 0.07x + 0.84$
   $-0.01x = -0.36$
   $x = 36$ ounces

30. $4m^2 - 3mp + 3p - 4m$
   $= 4m^2 - 3pm - 4m + 3p$
   $= (4m - 3p)(m - 1)$
   $4m - 3p$ units by $m - 1$ units

31. Let x = price of shirts.
   Let y = price of ties.

   $8x + 3y = 155 \qquad\qquad 8(16) + 3y = 155$
   $5x + 3y = 107 \qquad\qquad\qquad\quad 3y = 27$
   $3x = 48 \qquad\qquad\qquad\quad\ y = 9$
   $x = 16$

   Shirts cost \$16; ties cost \$9.

32. Let x = width of sidewalk.

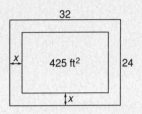

$(32 - 2x)(24 - 2x) = 425$

$768 - 48x - 64x + 4x^2 = 425$

$4x^2 - 112x + 343 = 0$

$x = \dfrac{-(-112) \pm \sqrt{(-112)^2 - 4(4)(343)}}{2(4)}$

$= \dfrac{112 \pm \sqrt{12{,}544 = 5488}}{8}$

$= \dfrac{112 - 84}{8}$

$= \dfrac{28}{8}$

$= 3.5$ ft

33.

t	h
0	0
1	67.1
2	124.4
3	171.9
4	209.6
5	237.5
6	255.6
7	263.9
8	262.4
9	251.1
10	230
11	199.1
12	158.4
13	107.4
14	47.6
15	-22.5

Since the height changes from positive to negative between 14 and 15 seconds after throwing the ball, the height must be zero for some time between 14 and 15 seconds. Since the absolute value of the height is closer to zero for 15 seconds, the time at which the height is zero rounded to the nearest second is 15.

Chapter 10   Polygons and Area

10-1   Polygons and Polyhedra

PAGES 469-470   CHECKING FOR UNDERSTANDING

1. a. yes

   b. No; sides must be line segments.

   c. No; sides must meet at only one point.

   d. yes

2. The polygon in a. is convex because none of the lines containing the sides pass through the interior.

3. Decagon *ABCDEFGHIJ*; yes; yes; it is convex and all sides and angles appear congruent.

4. no

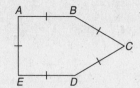

5. They are all congruent and are shaped like regular polygons.

6. convex polygon   7. not a polygon

8. convex polygon   9. concave polygon

10. not a polygon   11. concave polygon

12. convex polygon   13. not a polygon

14. faces: $\triangle ABD$, $\triangle ADC$, $\triangle DBC$, and $\triangle ABC$

    edges: $\overline{DB}$, $\overline{DA}$, $\overline{DC}$, $\overline{BA}$, $\overline{BC}$, and $\overline{AC}$

    vertices: A, B, C, and D

15. faces: quadrilaterals *ABFE*, *FBCG*, *HGCD*, *EHDA*, *ABCD*, and *EFGH*;

    edges; $\overline{AE}$, $\overline{EF}$, $\overline{FB}$, $\overline{AB}$, $\overline{FG}$, $\overline{GC}$, $\overline{CB}$, $\overline{HG}$, $\overline{CD}$, $\overline{DH}$, $\overline{EH}$, and $\overline{AD}$;

    vertices: A, B, C, D, E, F, G, and H

16. faces: $\triangle DEF$, $\triangle DAF$, $\triangle DBE$, $\triangle DBA$, $\triangle BAC$, $\triangle EBC$, $\triangle FEC$ and $\triangle CAF$

    edges: $\overline{EC}$, $\overline{CA}$, $\overline{CB}$, $\overline{CF}$, $\overline{AB}$, $\overline{BE}$, $\overline{FA}$, $\overline{EF}$, $\overline{DA}$, $\overline{DF}$, $\overline{DE}$, and $\overline{DB}$

    vertices: A, B, C, D, E, and F

PAGES 470-472   EXERCISES

17. triangle   18. decagon   19. 20-gon

20. octagon   21. hexagon   22. *x*-gon

23. not a polygon   24. concave heptagon

25. convex pentagon   26. concave quadrilateral

27. not a polygon   28. convex hexagon

29. *M*, *N*, *O*, *P*, *Q*   30. $\angle M$, $\angle N$, $\angle O$, $\angle P$, $\angle Q$

31. $\overline{MN}$, $\overline{NO}$, $\overline{OP}$, $\overline{PQ}$, $\overline{QM}$ 32. convex

33. pentagon

34. No; its sides are not all congruent.

35. It is not regular; not all of the sides are congruent.

36. It is regular; it is convex, all the sides are congruent, and all the angles are congruent.

37. It is regular; it is convex, all the sides are congruent, and all the angles are congruent.

38. It is not regular; the polygon is not convex.

39. a square   40. a rhombus

          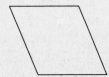

41. not possible   42.

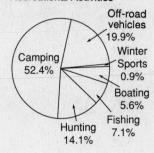

43. a. triangles; b. squares; c. triangles;
    d. pentagons; e. triangles

44. a. 3; b. 3; c. 4; d. 3; e. 5

45. a. 4, 4, 6   b. 6, 8, 12   c. 8, 6, 12
    d. 12, 20, 30   e. 20, 12, 30

46. yes;

    a. 4 + 4 = 6 + 2   b. 6 + 8 = 12 + 2

    c. 8 + 6 = 12 + 2   d. 12 + 20 = 30 + 2

    e. 20 + 12 = 30 + 2

47. Answers may vary. A sample answer is a rectangle that is not a square.

48. a. 6; rectangles; opposite faces congruent

    b. 18; rectangles and triangles; all rectangles congruent; all triangles congruent

    c. 12; triangles; all faces congruent

49. National Parks Recreational Activities

Off-road vehicles 19.9%
Winter Sports 0.9%
Camping 52.4%
Boating 5.6%
Fishing 7.1%
Hunting 14.1%

50. $c^2 = a^2 + b^2$

$c^2 = (4.0)^2 + (5.6)^2$

$c^2 = 16 + 31.36$

$c^2 = 47.36$

$c \approx 6.9$

51. Not enough information is given.

52. $m = \dfrac{0 - (-2)}{5 - 5} = \dfrac{2}{0}$; undefined

53. If a polygon is regular, then it is convex and has all sides congruent.

54. Answers may vary. A sample answer:

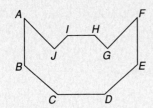

10-2   Angles of Polygons

1. No; the sum of the measures of the exterior angles of any convex polygon is 360.

2. 2070 is not divisible by 180, and a polygon must have an integral number of sides.

3. Let s represent the number of sides.

$180(s - 2) = 24{,}840$

$180s - 360 = 24{,}840$

$s = 140$

4. $180(5 - 2) = 180(3)$
$= 540$

5. $180(6 - 2) = 180(4)$
$= 720$

6. $180(12 - 2) = 180(10)$
$= 1800$

7. $180(25 - 2) = 180(23)$
$= 4140$

8. $180(36 - 2) = 180(34)$
$= 6120$

9. $180(x - 2)$

10. $\dfrac{180(5 - 2)}{5} = \dfrac{180(3)}{5}$
$= 108$

11. $\dfrac{180(7 - 2)}{7} = \dfrac{180(5)}{7}$
$= 128\frac{4}{7}$

12. $\dfrac{180(15 - 2)}{15} = \dfrac{180(13)}{15}$
$= 156$

13. $\dfrac{180(x - 2)}{x} = \dfrac{180x - 360}{x}$

14. $\dfrac{360}{45} = 8$

15. $\dfrac{360}{72} = 5$

16. $\dfrac{360}{60} = 6$

17. $\dfrac{360}{n}$

18. $720 = 180(x - 2)$
$720 = 180x - 360$
$1080 = 180x$
$6 = x$

19. $1440 = 180(x - 2)$
$1440 = 180x - 360$
$1800 = 180x$
$10 = x$

20. $2880 = 180(x - 2)$
$2880 = 180x - 360$
$3240 = 180x$
$18 = x$

21. $3240 = 180(x - 2)$
$3240 = 180x - 360$
$3600 = 180x$
$20 = x$

22. $180(17 - 2) = 180(15)$
$= 2700$

23. $180(20 - 2) = 180(18)$
$= 3240$

24. $180(13 - 2) = 180(11)$
$= 1980$

25. $180(15 - 2) = 180(13)$
$= 2340$

26. $180(59 - 2) = 180(57)$
$= 10{,}260$

27. $180(2t - 2) = 360t - 360$

28. $\dfrac{360}{180 - 160} = \dfrac{360}{20}$
$= 18$

29. $\dfrac{360}{180 - 120} = \dfrac{360}{60}$
$= 6$

30. $\dfrac{360}{180 - 156} = \dfrac{360}{24}$
$= 15$

31. $\dfrac{360}{180 - 165} = \dfrac{360}{15}$
$= 24$

32. $\dfrac{360}{180 - 144} = \dfrac{360}{36}$
$= 10$

33. $\dfrac{360}{180 - 179} = \dfrac{360}{1}$
$= 360$

34. $\dfrac{180(4 - 2)}{4} = \dfrac{180(2)}{4}$
$= 90;$
$180 - 90 = 90$

35. $\dfrac{180(8 - 2)}{8} = \dfrac{180(6)}{8}$
$= 135;$
$180 - 135 = 45$

36. $\dfrac{180(10 - 2)}{10} = \dfrac{180(8)}{10}$
$= 144;$
$180 - 144 = 36$

37. $\dfrac{180(20 - 2)}{20} = \dfrac{180(18)}{20}$
$= 162;$
$180 - 162 = 18$

38. $\dfrac{180(18 - 2)}{18} = \dfrac{180(16)}{18}$
$= 160;$
$180 - 160 = 20$

39. $\dfrac{180(x - 2)}{x}; \dfrac{360}{x}$

40. $180(9 - 2) = 1190 + x$
$1260 = 1190 + x$
$70 = x$

41. $360 = 339 + x$
$21 = x$

42. $360 = x + 2x + 3x + 4x$
$360 = 10x$
$36 = x$
angles: 36; 2(36) or 72; 3(36) or 108; 4(36) or 144

43. $10(x + 10) = 360$
$10x + 100 = 360$
$10x = 260$
$x = 26$ $x + 10 = 26 + 10$ or 36

179

44. $4x + 2x = 180$

$6x = 180$

$x = 30$

$\dfrac{360}{2(30)} = \dfrac{360}{60} = 6$ The polygon has 6 sides.

45. $\dfrac{180(5 - 2)}{5} = z$

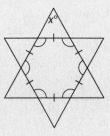

$\dfrac{180(3)}{5} = z$

$108 = z$

$y + z = 180$

$y + 108 = 180$

$y = 72$

$x + 2y = 180$

$x + 2(72) = 180$

$x = 36$

46. All of the sides and angles of the hexagon are congruent. Since the base angles of the triangles form linear pairs with the angles of the hexagon they are all congruent.

Therefore, the triangles are all congruent by ASA and the angles of the points of the star are congruent by CPCTC.

exterior angle of hexagon $= \dfrac{360}{6} = 60$

$x + 2(60) = 180$

$x = 60$

47. a. $7300 < 180(x - 2) < 7500$

$7300 < 180x - 360 < 7500$

$7660 < 180x < 7860$

$42\dfrac{5}{9} < x < 43\dfrac{2}{3}$

Since x must be an integer, $x = 43$.

b. $180(43 - 2) = 180(41)$

$= 7380$

48. $890 + x + (90 - x) + (180 - x) = 180(8 - 2)$

$890 + x + 90 - x + 180 - x = 180(6)$

$1160 - x = 1080$

$-x = -80$

$x = 80$

angles: 80; (90 - 80) or 10; (180 - 80) or 100

49. a. 1010

b. $11 \times 10 = 110$

c. They don't always work; no.

50. a. increases   **b.** less   **c.** stays 360

51. a.

Regular Polygon	triangle	square	pentagon	hexagon	heptagon	octagon
Does it tessellate the plane?	yes	yes	no	yes	no	no
Measure, m, of one interior angle	60	90	108	120	$128\dfrac{4}{7}$	135
Is m a factor of 360?	yes	yes	no	yes	no	no

b. If the measure of an interior angle of a regular polygon is a factor of 360, the polygon will tessellate the plane.

52. concave polygon; heptagon

53. $\left(\dfrac{10}{2}\right)^2 + 12^2 = r^2$

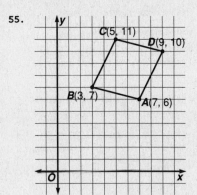

$5^2 + 12^2 = r^2$

$25 + 144 = r^2$

$169 = r^2$

$13 = r$

radius = 13 in.

54. $\dfrac{x}{75} = \dfrac{6}{10}$

$10x = 450$

$x = 45$ The tree is 45 feet tall.

55.

slope of $\overline{AB} = \dfrac{7 - 6}{3 - 7} = -\dfrac{1}{4}$

slope of $\overline{CD} = \dfrac{11 - 10}{5 - 9} = -\dfrac{1}{4}$

$AB = \sqrt{(3 - 7)^2 + (7 - 6)^2}$

$= \sqrt{(-4)^2 + 1^2}$

$= \sqrt{16 + 1}$

$= \sqrt{17}$

$CD = \sqrt{(5 - 9)^2 + (11 - 10)^2}$

$= \sqrt{(-4)^2 + 1^2}$

$= \sqrt{16 + 1}$

$= \sqrt{17}$

A pair of opposite sides are parallel and congruent, so $ABCD$ is a parallelogram.

56. $x + x + 88 = 180$
$$2x = 92$$
$$x = 46$$

57. $180 - x = x + 58$
$$122 = 2x$$
$$61 = x$$

58. sample drawing:

The sum of the measures is 360. This agrees with the exterior angle sum theorem.

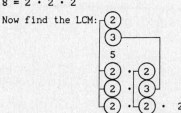

10-3	**Problem-Solving Strategy: Guess and Check**

PAGES 481-482   CHECKING FOR UNDERSTANDING

1. Answers may vary. A sample answer is when another, more direct method is not obvious.

2. Look at the results and see how close you are. Adjust guesses accordingly.

3. The first three prime numbers are 2, 3, and 5. The first three composite numbers are 4, 6, and 8. Find the LCM of these numbers. First write each composite as a product of its prime factors.

$4 = 2 \cdot 2$

$6 = 2 \cdot 3$

$8 = 2 \cdot 2 \cdot 2$

Now find the LCM:

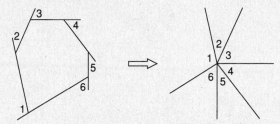

LCM = $2 \cdot 2 \cdot 2 \cdot 3 \cdot 5$ or 120

4. One answer is $35 - 64 + 752 + 6 - 17 = 712$.

5. Answers may vary. A sample answer is shown.

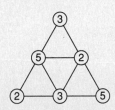

---

6. $(x + 1)^2 - x^2 = 75$
$$x^2 + 2x + 1 - x^2 = 75$$
$$2x + 1 = 75$$
$$2x = 74$$
$$x = 37$$

The numbers are 37 and 38.

7. 35; 25, 30, 20, 35, 15, 40, 10
$+ 5$ $- 10$ $+ 15$ $- 20$ $+ 25$ $- 30$

8. If the number for the day is less than 12, it would be a confusing date. So there are 12×12 dates that have a day number less than 12. But a date where the month and the day have the same number would be the same day in either country. There are 12 of these. So there are $144 - 12$ or 132 confusing dates.

9. 0, 1; 4, 5; 12, 13; 24, 25; 40, 41

10. Sample answers are $9802 + 9802 = 19604$ or $9703 + 9703 = 19406$.

Cooperative Learning Project

PAGE 482

A possible strategy: Make a list of the numbers on the dominos and cross off each one as it is located. When no more dominos can be deduced, guess at the numbers on one and see if this leads you to a contradiction.

1	0	2	0	0	5	4	1
1	1	5	3	6	2	4	2
3	3	1	0	3	5	3	4
0	6	6	4	6	5	1	1
0	4	0	2	5	4	2	6
1	2	3	2	6	4	5	2
3	5	5	0	3	4	6	6

10-4	**Area of Parallelograms**

PAGE 486   CHECKING FOR UNDERSTANDING

1. A square is a special rectangle.

2. $(a + b)$ square units

3. No; 6 is not the measure of the altitude.

4. $(5 \text{ m})^2 = 25 \text{ m}^2$

5. $(5 \text{ in.})(11.2 \text{ in.}) = 56 \text{ in}^2$

6. $(16 \text{ yd})(9 \text{ yd}) = 144 \text{ yd}^2$

7. (15 mm)(6 mm) + (3 mm)(3 mm) + (1 mm)(1 mm)

= 100 mm^2

8. (8 m)^2 − (3 m)(5 m) = 64 m^2 − 15 m^2 = 49 m^2

9. (6 ft)(12 ft) − 2(4 ft)(2 ft) = 72 ft^2 − 16 ft^2

= 56 ft^2

PAGES 486-488   EXERCISES

10. (6 ft)(2 ft) = 12 ft^2

11. 36 m^2 = (9 m)(x m)   **12.** 20 yd^2 = (4 yd)(x yd)

4 m = x 5 yd = x

13. 3810 mm^2 = (120 mm)(x mm)

31.75 mm = x

14. a parallelogram;

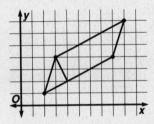

length of base = $\sqrt{(8 - 2)^2 + (4 - 1)^2}$

= $\sqrt{(6)^2 + (3)^2}$

= $\sqrt{45}$

height = $\sqrt{(4 - 3)^2 + (2 - 4)^2}$

= $\sqrt{1 + 4}$

= $\sqrt{5}$

A = $\sqrt{45} \cdot \sqrt{5}$

= $\sqrt{225}$

= 15 units^2

15. a square;

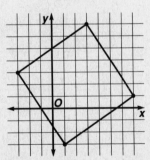

length of one side

= $\sqrt{[(-3) - 3]^2 + [1 - (-3)]^2}$

= $\sqrt{(-6)^2 + (4)^2}$

= $\sqrt{36 + 16}$

= $\sqrt{52}$

A = $(\sqrt{52})^2$

= 52 units^2

16. a parallelogram;

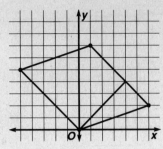

length of base = $\sqrt{(6 - 1)^2 + (2 - 7)^2}$

= $\sqrt{25 + 25}$ or $\sqrt{50}$

height = $\sqrt{(4 - 0)^2 + (4 - 0)^2}$

= $\sqrt{16 + 16}$ or $\sqrt{32}$

A = $\sqrt{50} \cdot \sqrt{32}$ or 40 units^2

17. a rectangle;

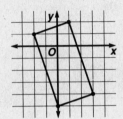

length = $\sqrt{(0 - (-2))^2 + (-5 - 1)^2}$

= $\sqrt{(2)^2 + (-6)^2}$

= $\sqrt{40}$

width = $\sqrt{(0 - 3)^2 + (-5 - (-4))^2}$

= $\sqrt{(3)^2 + (-1)^2}$

= $\sqrt{10}$

A = $(\sqrt{40})(\sqrt{10})$

= $\sqrt{400}$ or 20 units^2

18. (8 m)(6 m) = (12 m)(x m)

48 m^2 = 12x m^2

4 m = x

19. 2x^2 + 9x + 9 cm^2 = (2x + 1 cm)(a cm)

x + 4 cm = a

20. Let w = width.

$w(w + 4)$ = 117

$w^2 + 4w$ = 117

$w^2 + 4w - 117$ = 0

$(w - 9)(w + 13)$ = 0

w = 9 or w = −13

Since w = −13 is not reasonable, w = 9.

width = 9 cm   length = 9 + 4 or 13 cm

21. $(2x)^2 - x^2$ = 363

$4x^2 - x^2$ = 363

$3x^2$ = 363

x^2 = 121

x = 11

The side of the original square was 11 in. long.

22.

$$(x + 5)^2 = 2.25x^2$$
$$x^2 + 10x + 25 = 2.25x^2$$
$$-1.25x^2 + 10x + 25 = 0$$
$$x^2 - 8x - 20 = 0$$
$$(x - 10)(x + 2) = 0$$
$$x = 10 \text{ or } x = -2$$

Since $x = -2$ is not reasonable, $x = 10$. A side of the original square was 10 inches, so its area was $(10)^2$ or 100 square inches.

23. The triangles can be assembled to form a square that is congruent to *MNOP*. So the area of the new square equals the area of *MNOP*. Since the area of *ABCD* is the sum of these two areas, it is twice the area of *MNOP*.

24. The area of each square is $\frac{486}{6}$ or 81 square centimeters. If s is the length of a side of a square, $s^2 = 81$ and $s = 9$. The perimeter of the figure contains 14 sides of the squares, so the perimeter of the figure is 14(9) or 126 cm.

25. $A = s^2$

$= (1.5)^2$

$= 2.25 \text{ in}^2$

$S = \frac{F}{A}$

$= \frac{3550 \text{ pounds}}{2.25 \text{ in}^2}$

≈ 1577.8 pounds per square inch

26. a. (20 ft)(14 ft) + (14 ft)(12 ft)

$= 280 \text{ ft}^2 + 168 \text{ ft}^2$

$= 448 \text{ ft}^2$

b. They need 448 square feet of carpet. That is $\frac{448}{9}$ or about 49.8 square yards. Adding 4 yards for waste is 53.8 square yards. Since they cannot buy a fraction of a yard, they will buy 54 square yards of carpet.

c. 54(16.99) = $917.46

27. $4 \cdot (5 - 2) + 7 = 19$

28. An exterior angle measures 180 - 160 or 20. There are $\frac{360}{20}$ or 18 sides.

29. Given: trapezoid *ABCD*

$\overline{AB} \parallel \overline{CD}$

Prove: ∠*A* and ∠*D* are supplementary.

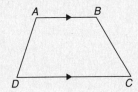

STATEMENTS	REASONS
1. trapezoid *ABCD* $\overline{AB} \parallel \overline{DC}$	1. Given
2. ∠*A* and ∠*D* are supp.	2. When 2 ∥ lines are cut by a transversal, consecutive interior interior ∠s are supp.

30. See students' work.

Mid-Chapter Review

PAGE 488

1. concave; pentagon

2. not a polygon

3. convex; quadrilateral

4. not a polygon

5. $\frac{180(6 - 2)}{6} = \frac{180(4)}{6} = 120$; 180 - 120 = 60

6. $\frac{180(16 - 2)}{16} = \frac{180(14)}{16} = 157.5$;

180 - 157.5 = 22.5

7. $\frac{180(30 - 2)}{30} = \frac{180(28)}{30} = 168$; 180 - 168 = 12

8. 727

9. area of lawn = area of property - area of house

$= [18(5 + 20 + 8)$

$+ 12(5 + 20 + 8 - 15)]$

$- 20(18 - 5 - 5)$

$= 18(33) + 12(18) - 20(8)$

$= 594 + 216 - 160$

$= 650$ square yards

Mr. Jackson will need more than one bag, since the area of the lawn is 650 square yards.

10-5 ## Area of Triangles, Rhombi, and Trapezoids

PAGE 492 CHECKING FOR UNDERSTANDING

1. 76 sq. units; Postulate 10-2 says that congruent figures have equal areas.

2. Yes; the length of a median is $\frac{1}{2}(b_1 + b_2)$ units.

3. She could use the same formula, but the value of h would be different.

4. $\frac{1}{2}(8)(13) = 4(13) = 52 \text{ cm}^2$

5. $\frac{1}{2}(5)(7 + 14) = \frac{1}{2}(5)(21) = 52.5 \text{ ft}^2$

6. $\frac{1}{2}(4 + 4)(7 + 7) = \frac{1}{2}(8)(14) = (4)(14) = 56 \text{ in}^2$

7.

$3^2 + x^2 = 5^2$

$x^2 = 16$

$x = 4$

$A = \frac{1}{2}(6)(4 + 4)$

$= 3(8)$

$= 24 \text{ ft}^2$

8. $(10)(14) = 140 \text{ m}^2$

9.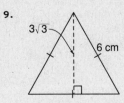

$\frac{1}{2}(6)(3\sqrt{3}) = 3(3\sqrt{3})$

$= 9\sqrt{3}$

$\approx 15.6 \text{ m}^2$

10. The diagonals form 30°-60°-90° triangles with the long legs 5 inches long. The short legs are $\frac{5}{\sqrt{3}}$ inches long.

$A = \frac{1}{2}(10)\left(2\left(\frac{5}{\sqrt{3}}\right)\right)$

$= 10\left(\frac{5}{\sqrt{3}}\right)$

$\approx 28.9 \text{ in}^2$

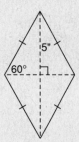

11.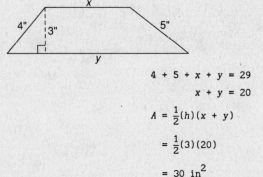

$4 + 5 + x + y = 29$

$x + y = 20$

$A = \frac{1}{2}(h)(x + y)$

$= \frac{1}{2}(3)(20)$

$= 30 \text{ in}^2$

PAGES 493-494   EXERCISES

12. $A = \frac{1}{2}bh$

$88 = \frac{1}{2}b(16)$

$11 = b$

13. $A = \frac{1}{2}(19)(12)$

$= 114 \text{ cm}^2$

14. $A = \frac{1}{2}h(b_1 + b_2)$

$96 = \frac{1}{2}(6)(b_1 + b_2)$

$16 = \frac{1}{2}(b_1 + b_2)$

The median is $\frac{1}{2}(b_1 + b_2)$ units long, so the median is 16 units.

15. $A = \frac{1}{2}(11)(16 + 11)$

$= 148.5 \text{ m}^2$

16. $997.5 = \frac{1}{2}(21)(40 + b_1)$

$997.5 = 10.5(40 + b_1)$

$95.0 = 40 + b_1$

$55.0 \text{ cm} = b_1$

17.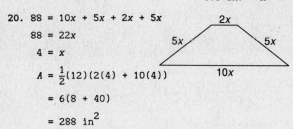

$P = 4s$

$52 = 4s$

$13 = s$

$x^2 + 12^2 = 13^2$

$x^2 + 144 = 169$

$x^2 = 25$

$x = 5$

$A = \frac{1}{2}(10)(24)$

$= 120 \text{ square units}$

18. $850 = \frac{1}{2}b(30 + 20)$

$1700 = b(50)$

$34 \text{ mi} = b$

19. $A = \frac{1}{2}(7)(4)$

$= 14$

$14 = \frac{1}{2}(8)(h)$

$14 = 4h$

$3.5 \text{ in.} = h$

20. $88 = 10x + 5x + 2x + 5x$

$88 = 22x$

$4 = x$

$A = \frac{1}{2}(12)(2(4) + 10(4))$

$= 6(8 + 40)$

$= 288 \text{ in}^2$

21. $P = 2(5) + b_1 + b_2$

$28 = 10 + b_1 + b_2$

$18 = b_1 + b_2$

$A = \frac{1}{2}h(b_1 + b_2)$

$36 = \frac{1}{2}h(18)$

$36 = 9h$

$4 \text{ cm} = h$

22. It shows how the area of a triangle is related to the area of a rectangle.

23. Let b_1 = base of parallelogram,

b_2 = base of triangle,

and n = height of parallelogram and triangle.

area of parallelogram = $b_1 h$

area of triangle = $\frac{1}{2}b_2 h$

$b_1 h = \frac{1}{2}b_2 h$

$b_1 = \frac{1}{2}b_2$

The base of the triangle is twice as long as the base of the parallelogram.

24. Let $RA = b_1$ and $TP = b_2$. Let h represent the height of $TRAP$.

area of $TRAP$ = area of $\triangle TRP$ + area of $\triangle RAP$

area of $TRAP$ = $\frac{1}{2}(b_1)h + \frac{1}{2}(b_2)h$

area of $TRAP$ = $\frac{1}{2}h(b_1 + b_2)$

25. $ABCD$ is a rhombus. The diagonals of a rhombus are perpendicular, so $\overline{AE} \perp \overline{BD}$ and $\overline{CE} \perp \overline{DB}$. Therefore, $\overline{AE}$ is an altitude of $\triangle ABD$ and $\overline{CE}$ is an altitude of $\triangle BCD$. Since the diagonals of a rhombus bisect each other,

$\overline{AE} \cong \overline{EC}$. So $AE = \frac{1}{2}AC$

and $EC = \frac{1}{2}AC$.

area of $ABCD$ = area of $\triangle ABD$ + area of $\triangle BCD$

$= \frac{1}{2}(BD)(AE) + \frac{1}{2}(BD)(EC)$

$= \frac{1}{2}(BD)\left(\frac{1}{2}AC\right) + \frac{1}{2}(BD)\left(\frac{1}{2}AC\right)$

$= \frac{1}{4}(BD)(AC) + \frac{1}{4}(BD)(AC)$

$= \frac{1}{2}(BD)(AC)$

The area is one-half the product of the diagonals.

26. no; area $MQRP = \frac{1}{2}\left(\frac{1}{2}h\right)(MP + QR)$

area $QNOR = \frac{1}{2}\left(\frac{1}{2}h\right)(QR + NO)$

Since $MP \neq NO$, the areas are not equal.

27. works for a rectangle; $a = \ell$, $b = w$, $c = \ell$, and $d = w$, so

$\frac{(a + c)(b + d)}{4} = \frac{(\ell + \ell)(w + w)}{4}$

$= \frac{(2\ell)(2w)}{4} = \frac{4\ell w}{4} = \ell w$

Area is equal to the product of the length and the width.

doesn't work for a rhombus; all sides are congruent, so $a = b = c = d$.

$\frac{(a + c)(b + d)}{4} = \frac{(s + s)(s + s)}{4}$

$= \frac{(2s)(2s)}{4} = \frac{4s^2}{4} = s^2$

Area is not equal to the length of a side squared, unless the rhombus is a square.

28. area of lawn = area of property - area of house - area of drive

$= \frac{1}{2}(65)(55 + 60) - (20)(40)$

$- (20)(25)$

$= (32.5)(115) - 800 - 500$

$= 3737.5 - 800 - 500$

$= 2437.5$ square feet

Hector should mix $\frac{2437.5}{50}$ or 48.75 gallons of fertilizer.

29. a. 35 sq. units   b. 27.125 sq. units

30. The triangle formed is a 45°-45°-90° triangle, so the altitude is $\frac{18}{\sqrt{2}}$ or $9\sqrt{2}$ units.

$A = (32)(9\sqrt{2})$

$= 288\sqrt{2}$

≈ 407.3 in^2

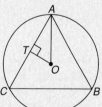

31. $\frac{7}{x} = \frac{x}{14}$

$x^2 = 98$

$x = \sqrt{98} \approx 9.9$

32. Divide a term by -3 to get the next term.

$\left(-\frac{2}{9}\right) \div -3 = \frac{2}{27}$

33. No; $4 + 9 < 21$; it fails the triangle inequality.

34. See students' work.

10-6   Area of Regular Polygons

PAGE 498   CHECKING FOR UNDERSTANDING

1. A radius is a segment between the center and a vertex and an apothem is a segment from the center perpendicular to a side.

2. 36; 15; $\frac{360}{n}$

3. The formula for the area of a polygon is based on the sum of the areas of several triangles in a polygon.

4. Let $x = \frac{180}{\text{number of sides}}$, then $a = r \cos x°$.

5. $p = 35 = 3(10)$ or 30 cm

6.

7. 30°-60°-90°; central angle COA would measure 120°; $\overline{OT}$ bisects $\angle COA$, so $m\angle TOA = 60$.

8. 5 feet; it is half the length of $\overline{AC}$

9. OT, $\frac{5}{\sqrt{3}}$ or about 2.89 cm;

OA, $\frac{10}{\sqrt{3}}$ or about 5.77 cm

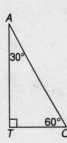

10. $A = \frac{1}{2}Pa$

$= \frac{1}{2}(30)\left(\frac{5}{\sqrt{3}}\right)$

$= \frac{75}{\sqrt{3}}$

≈ 43.3 cm^2

11. $P = 35$ central angle $= \frac{360}{3}$

$= 3(6)$ $= 120°$

$= 18$ cm

The triangle formed is a 30°-60°-90°

triangle, so the apothem is $\frac{3}{\sqrt{3}}$ or $\sqrt{3}$ centimeters

long.

$A = \frac{1}{2}Pa$

$= \frac{1}{2}(18)(\sqrt{3})$

$= 9\sqrt{3}$

≈ 15.6 cm^2

12. $P = 4s$ central angle $= \frac{360}{4}$

$= 4(9)$ $= 90°$

$= 36$ in.

The triangle formed is a 45°-45°-90° triangle,

so the apothem is 4.5 in.

$A = \frac{1}{2}Pa$

$= \frac{1}{2}(36)(4.5)$

$= 81$ in^2

13. $P = 5s$ central angle $= \frac{360}{5}$

$= 5(2)$ $= 72°$

$= 10$ m

Use the small triangle
to find the apothem.

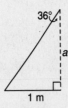

$\tan 36° = \frac{1}{a}$ $A = \frac{1}{2}Pa$

$a = \frac{1}{\tan 36°}$ $= \frac{1}{2}(10)(1.4)$

$a \approx 1.4$ m $= 7$ m^2

14. $A = \frac{1}{2}(3 \cdot 20)(5.8)$

$= 174$ cm^2

15. $A = s^2$

$= 16^2$

$= 256$ in^2

16. $A = \frac{1}{2}(6 \cdot 19.1)(16.5)$

≈ 945.5 mm^2

17. $A = \frac{1}{2}(5 \cdot 13)(8.9)$

≈ 289.3 mi^2

18. $A = \frac{1}{2}(6 \cdot 10)(8.7)$

$= 261$ m^2

19. $A = \frac{1}{2}(8 \cdot 6.2)(7.5)$

$= 186$ ft^2

20. The apothem, a radius,
and $\frac{1}{2}$ of a side of a
hexagon form a
30°-60°-90° triangle.
So the apothem of the
large hexagon is $4\sqrt{3}$
units and the apothem
of the small hexagon is $3\sqrt{3}$ units.

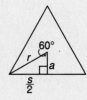

area of shaded region = area of large hexagon
                       - area of small hexagon

$= \frac{1}{2}(8 \cdot 6)(4\sqrt{3}) - \frac{1}{2}(6 \cdot 6)(3\sqrt{3})$

$= 96\sqrt{3} - 54\sqrt{3}$

$= 42\sqrt{3}$

≈ 72.7 units^2

21. area of shaded region = area of pentagon
                       - area of triangle

$= \frac{1}{2}(8.0 \cdot 5)(5.5) - \frac{1}{2}(8.0)(5.5)$

$= 110 - 22$

$= 88$ units^2

22. A radius, the apothem,
and $\frac{1}{2}$ of a side form a
30°-60°-90° triangle,
so the apothem of the
large triangle is $\frac{1.3}{\sqrt{3}}$
units and the apothem of
the small triangle is $\frac{0.6}{\sqrt{3}}$ units.

area of shaded region = area of large triangle
                       - area of small triangle

$= \frac{1}{2}(3 \cdot 2.6)\left(\frac{1.3}{\sqrt{3}}\right) - \frac{1}{2}(3 \cdot 1.2)\left(\frac{0.6}{\sqrt{3}}\right)$

$= 1.69\sqrt{3} - 0.36\sqrt{3}$

$= 1.33\sqrt{3}$

≈ 2.3 units^2

23. The apothem of the triangle is $\frac{2}{\sqrt{3}}$ units long.

area of shaded region = area of large square
    + area of triangle
    - area of small square

$= (4)^2 + \frac{1}{2}(4 \cdot 3)\left(\frac{2}{\sqrt{3}}\right) - (2)^2$

$= 16 + 4\sqrt{3} - 4$

$= 12 + 4\sqrt{3}$

$\approx 18.9 \text{ units}^2$

24. An apothem of the octagon forms a $22.5°$ angle with a radius.

$\tan 22.5° = \frac{6}{a}$

$a = \frac{6}{\tan 22.5°}$

$a \approx 14.485$

area of shaded region = area of octagon -
        area of square

$= \frac{1}{2}(12 \cdot 8)(14.485) - (12)^2$

$= 695.28 - 144$

$\approx 551.3 \text{ units}^2$

25. The apothem, radius, and $\frac{1}{2}$ of a side of the hexagon form a $30°$-$60°$-$90°$ triangle. So the apothem of the hexagon is $6\sqrt{3}$ units long, and the radius is 12 units.

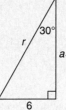

The apothem, radius, and $\frac{1}{2}$ of a side of the triangle form a $30°$-$60°$-$90°$ triangle also. The radius is 12, so the apothem is 6 units and $\frac{1}{2}$ a side is $6\sqrt{3}$ units.

area of shaded region = area of hexagon -
        area of triangle

$= \frac{1}{2}(12 \cdot 6)(6\sqrt{3}) - \frac{1}{2}(3 \cdot (2 \cdot 6\sqrt{3}))(6)$

$= 216\sqrt{3} - 108\sqrt{3}$

$= 108\sqrt{3}$

$\approx 187.1 \text{ units}^2$

26. $a = \frac{10}{2}$

$= 5 \text{ cm}$

$\frac{s}{2} = a\sqrt{3}$

$\frac{s}{2} = 5\sqrt{3}$

$s = 10\sqrt{3} \text{ cm}$

$P = 3s$

$= 3(10\sqrt{3})$

$= 30\sqrt{3} \text{ cm}$

$A = \frac{1}{2}(30\sqrt{3})(5)$

$= 75\sqrt{3} \text{ cm}^2$

27. $\frac{s}{2} = \frac{10}{2}$

$s = 10 \text{ cm}$

$P = 6s$

$= 6(10)$

$= 60 \text{ cm}$

$a = \frac{s}{2}(\sqrt{3})$

$= \frac{10}{2}\sqrt{3}$

$= 5\sqrt{3} \text{ cm}$

$A = \frac{1}{2}(60)(5\sqrt{3})$

$= 150\sqrt{3} \text{ cm}^2$

28. $\sin 22.5° = \frac{2}{10}$

$10 \sin 22.5° = \frac{s}{2}$

$7.65 \text{ cm} \approx 5$

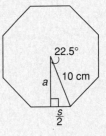

$P = 8s$

$= 8(7.65)$

$\approx 61.2 \text{ cm}$

$\cos 22.5° = \frac{a}{10}$

$10 \cos 22.5° = a$

$9.2 \text{ cm} \approx a$

$A \approx \frac{1}{2}(61.2)(9.24)$

$\approx 281.5 \text{ cm}^2$

29. apothem = 6 in.

$\frac{s}{2} = \frac{6}{\sqrt{3}}$

$\frac{s}{2} = 2\sqrt{3}$

$s = 4\sqrt{3} \text{ in.}$

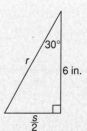

30. area of $ABCD = x^2$

$\triangle EBC$ is a $45°$-$45°$-$90°$ triangle, so

$EB = EC = \frac{x}{12}$.

area of $BFEC = \left(\frac{x}{\sqrt{2}}\right)^2 = \frac{x^2}{2}$

area of $ABCD$: area of $BFEC = x^2 : \frac{x^2}{2}$ or $2:1$.

187

31. $\sin 18° = \dfrac{\frac{s}{2}}{4}$

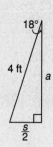

$4 \sin 18° = \dfrac{s}{2}$

$8 \sin 18° = s$

$2.472 \approx s$

$P = 10s$
$\approx 10(2.472)$
≈ 24.72 ft

$\cos 18° = \dfrac{a}{4}$
$4 \cos 18° = a$
$3.804 \approx a$

$A = \dfrac{1}{2}(24.72)(3.804)$

≈ 47.02 ft^2

32. Looking at the 30°-60°-90° triangle formed by the apothem, a radius, and $\frac{1}{2}$ a side of the large hexagon, the apothem is a radius of the circle. So if s_1 = a side of the hexagon,

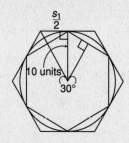

$\dfrac{s_1}{2} = \dfrac{10}{\sqrt{3}}$

$s_1 = \dfrac{20}{\sqrt{3}}$

$P = 6\left(\dfrac{20}{\sqrt{3}}\right)$

$= 40\sqrt{3}$ units

$A = \dfrac{1}{2}(40\sqrt{3})(10)$

$= 200\sqrt{3}$ units^2

Looking at the 30°-60°-90° triangle formed by the apothem, a radius, and $\frac{1}{2}$ a side of the smaller hexagon, the radius is a radius of the circle. So if s_2 = a side of the hexagon,

$\dfrac{s_2}{2} = \dfrac{10}{2}$

$s_2 = 10$

$P = 6(10)$
$= 60$ units

If a = the apothem, $a = \dfrac{s}{2}\sqrt{3}$

$= 5\sqrt{3}$ units

$A = \dfrac{1}{2}(60)(5\sqrt{3})$

$= 150\sqrt{3}$ units^2

area of smaller hexagon:area of larger hexagon
= $150\sqrt{3}:200\sqrt{3}$ or 3:4.

33. a. square

   b. Use the triangle to find the length of the apothem, a, of the octagon.

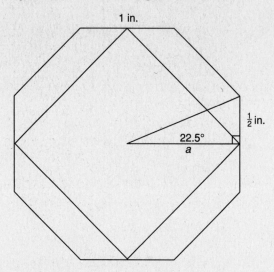

$\tan 22.5° = \dfrac{\frac{1}{2}}{a}$

$a = \dfrac{\frac{1}{2}}{\tan 22.5°}$

$a \approx 1.207$ in.

a is half the diagonal of the square. So, the side of the square is $a\sqrt{2}$ or about 1.707 in. The area of the square is $(1.707)^2 \approx 2.914$ or about 2.91 in^2

   c. area of octagon not in square
   = area of octagon - area of square
   $= \dfrac{1}{2}(8 \cdot 1)(1.207) - 2.914$
   ≈ 1.91 in^2

34. $a = \dfrac{s}{2\sqrt{3}}$

$P = 3s$

The triangle is a 30°-60°-90° triangle, so $a = \dfrac{\sqrt{3}}{6}s$.

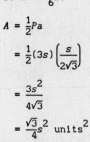

$A = \dfrac{1}{2}Pa$

$= \dfrac{1}{2}(3s)\left(\dfrac{s}{2\sqrt{3}}\right)$

$= \dfrac{3s^2}{4\sqrt{3}}$

$= \dfrac{\sqrt{3}}{4}s^2$ units^2

35. a. $P = 3s$
   $= 3(18)$
   $= 54$ feet

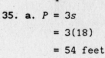

b. $A = \frac{1}{2}Pa$

$\quad = \frac{1}{2}(54)(3\sqrt{3})$

$\quad = 81\sqrt{3}$

$\quad \approx 140.3 \text{ ft}^2$

$a = \dfrac{9}{\sqrt{3}}$

$\quad = 3\sqrt{3} \text{ feet}$

36.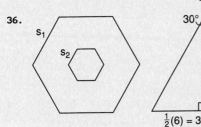

Let s_1 be the length of a side of the large hexagon; s_2 be the length of a side of the small hexagon; a_1 be the apothem of the large hexagon; and a_2 be the apothem of the small hexagon.

$36 = 6s_1 \qquad 12 = 6s_2 \qquad a_1 = 3\sqrt{3} \qquad a_2 = \sqrt{3}$

$6 = s_1 \qquad\quad 2 = s_2$

area of bench = area of large hexagon −
$\qquad\qquad\qquad$ area of small hexagon

$\quad = \frac{1}{2}(36)(3\sqrt{3}) - \frac{1}{2}(12)(\sqrt{3})$

$\quad = 54\sqrt{3} - 6\sqrt{3}$

$\quad = 48\sqrt{3}$

$\quad \approx 83.14$

Total area of benches = 14(83.14)

$\qquad\qquad\qquad\qquad\quad \approx 1163.96$

Ms. Nystrom will need $\dfrac{1163.96}{175}$ or about 6.65 cans. Since she cannot order a fraction of a can, she should order 7 cans of stain for the seats.

37. $A = \frac{1}{2}(17)(24)$

$\quad = 204 \text{ ft}^2$

38. No; $18 + 32 \le 67$, so these lengths fail the triangle inequality.

39. If two figures are congruent, then they have equal areas. Two figures are congruent. They have equal areas.

40. center, apothem, radius, central angle; apothem

Technology: Area

PAGE 501

1. 0.5 * C3 * D3
2. The polygon is regular, so to find the perimeter, multiply the number of sides by the length of a side.
3. See students' work.

| 10-7 | Area and Circumference of a Circle |

PAGE 504 CHECKING FOR UNDERSTANDING

1. Answers may vary; A sample answer is that the circumference is the measure around the outside of a circle.
2. The measure of the diameter is twice the measure of the radius.
3. The circumference is 24π feet, but the area is 144π square feet.
4. $d = 24$ cm; $C = 24\pi$ cm; $A = 144\pi$ cm^2
5. $r = 2.4$ km; $C = 4.8\pi$ km; $A = 5.76$ km^2
6. $r = 10$ in.; $d = 20$ in.; $A = 100\pi$ in^2
7. $r = 9$ ft; $d = 18$ ft; $C = 18\pi$ ft
8. $\quad A = \pi r^2 \qquad\qquad$ fence $= 2\pi(r + 5)$

$\quad 7850 = \pi r^2 \qquad\qquad\qquad = 2\pi(50.0 + 5)$

$\quad 50.0 \approx r \qquad\qquad\qquad\quad \approx 346$ feet

PAGE 504 EXERCISES

9. $C = 2\pi r$

$\quad = 2\pi(10)$

$\quad \approx 62.8$ m

10. $C = 2\pi r$

$\quad = 2\pi(4)$

$\quad \approx 25.1$ in.

11. $C = 2\pi r$

$\quad = 2\pi(7)$

$\quad \approx 44.0$ yd

12. $C = 2\pi r$

$\quad = 2\pi(3.6)$

$\quad \approx 22.6$ km

13. $C = 2\pi r$

$\quad = 2\pi(1.1)$

$\quad \approx 6.9$ mm

14. $C = 2\pi r$

$\quad = 2\pi\left(\frac{1}{4}\right)$

$\quad \approx 1.6$ mi

15. $A = \pi r^2$

$\quad = \pi(18)^2$

$\quad \approx 1017.9$ in^2

16. $A = \pi r^2$

$\quad = \pi(5.8)^2$

$\quad \approx 105.7$ m^2

17. $A = \pi r^2$

$\quad = \pi(9.7)^2$

$\quad \approx 295.6$ km^2

18. $A = \pi r^2$

$\quad = \pi(0.4)^2$

$\quad \approx 0.5$ in^2

19. $A = \pi r^2$

$\quad = \pi\left(3\frac{1}{3}\right)^2$

$\quad \approx 34.9$ yd^2

20. $A = \pi r^2$

$\quad = \pi(4\sqrt{5})^2$

$\quad \approx 251.3$ cm^2

21. 11; $A = \pi(11)^2 = 121\pi$

22. 7; $A = \pi(7)^2 = 49\pi$

23. $\sqrt{11}$; $A = \pi(\sqrt{11})^2 = 11\pi$

24. $\sqrt{15}$; $A = \pi(\sqrt{15})^2 = 15\pi$

25. 25; $A = \pi(25)^2 = 625\pi$

26. $\sqrt{68}$; $A = \pi(\sqrt{68})^2 = 68\pi$

27. $2r = 6$ m

   $r = 3$ m

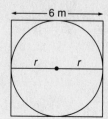

   $C = 2\pi r \qquad A = \pi r^2$

   $\quad = 2\pi(3) \qquad = \pi(3)^2$

   $\quad = 6\pi$ m $\qquad = 9\pi$ m^2

28. $r\sqrt{2} = 4$

   $r = \dfrac{4}{\sqrt{2}}$

   $\quad = 2\sqrt{2}$ feet

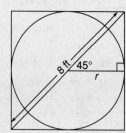

   $C = 2\pi r \qquad A = \pi r^2$

   $\quad = 2\pi(2\sqrt{2}) \qquad = \pi(2\sqrt{2})^2$

   $\quad = 4\sqrt{2}\pi$ ft $\qquad = 8\pi$ ft^2

29. area of shaded region = area of circle −

   area of square

   $= \pi(3\sqrt{2})^2 - 6^2$

   $= 18\pi - 36$ units^2

   ≈ 20.55 units^2

30. Let a = apothem of hexagon.

   $a = \left(\dfrac{1}{2}\right)(12)(\sqrt{3})$

   $\quad = 6\sqrt{3}$

   $s = 2(6) = 12$

   $P = 6(12) = 72$

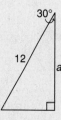

   area of shaded region = area of circle −

   area of hexagon

   $= \pi(12)^2 - \dfrac{1}{2}(72)(6\sqrt{3})$

   $= 144\pi - 216\sqrt{3}$ units^2

   ≈ 78.27 units^2

31. radius of circle = $\dfrac{1}{2}$ side of square

   $= \dfrac{1}{2}(7)$

   $= 3.5$

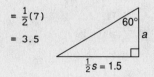

apothem of triangle = a

   $a = \dfrac{\frac{1}{2}s}{\sqrt{3}}$

   $\quad = \dfrac{1.5}{\sqrt{3}}$

   $\quad = \dfrac{\sqrt{3}}{2}$

area of shaded region = area of circle −

   area of triangle

   $= \pi(3.5)^2 - \dfrac{1}{2}(3 \cdot 3)\left(\dfrac{\sqrt{3}}{2}\right)$

   $= 12.25\pi - 2.25\sqrt{3}$ units^2

   ≈ 34.59 units^2

32. side of square = 2(radius)

   $= 2(7)$

   $= 14$

area of shaded region = area of square −

   area of circle

   $= (14)^2 - \pi(7)^2$

   $= 196 - 49\pi$ units^2

   ≈ 42.06 units^2

33. radius of large circle = $\dfrac{1}{2}(20)$

   $= 10$ units

radius of small circles = $\dfrac{1}{4}(20)$

   $= 5$ units

area of shaded region = area of large circle −

   area of small circles

   $= \pi(10)^2 = 2[\pi(5)^2]$

   $= 100\pi - 50\pi$

   $= 50\pi$ units^2

   ≈ 157.08 units^2

34. radius of circles = $\dfrac{1}{4}(6)$

   $= 1.5$ units

area of shaded region = area of square −

   area of circles

   $= (6)^2 - 4[\pi(1.5)^2]$

   $= 36 - 9\pi$ units^2

   ≈ 7.73 units^2

35. This figure can be drawn like the one at the right. The radius of the unshaded circle is $\dfrac{1}{2}(20)$ or 10 and the radius of the small shaded circle is $\dfrac{1}{2}(10)$ or 5.

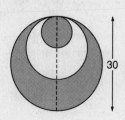

area of shaded region = area of large circle
$\qquad$ - area of medium circle
$\qquad$ + area of small circle

$$= \pi(15)^2 - \pi(10)^2 + \pi(5)^2$$

$$= 225\pi - 100\pi + 25\pi$$

$$= 150\pi \text{ units}^2$$

$$\approx 471.24 \text{ units}^2$$

36. radius of each small semicircle $= \frac{1}{2}\left(\frac{15}{3}\right)$
$\qquad\qquad\qquad\qquad\qquad = 2.5$ units

area of shaded region
= area of large semicircle -
$\quad$ area of small semicircles

$$= \frac{1}{2}\pi\left(\frac{15}{2}\right)^2 - 3\left[\frac{1}{2}\pi(2.5)^2\right]$$

$$= 28.125\pi - 9.375\pi$$

$$= 18.75\pi \text{ units}^2$$

$$\approx 58.90 \text{ units}^2$$

37. A diagonal of the square is a diameter of the circle. Let d = the length of the diameter.

$$9^2 + 12^2 = d^2$$

$$225 = d^2$$

$$15 = d$$

area of shaded region = area of circle -
$\qquad\qquad\qquad\qquad$ area of rectangle

$$= \pi\left(\frac{15}{2}\right)^2 - (9)(12)$$

$$= 56.25\pi - 108 \text{ units}^2$$

$$\approx 68.71 \text{ units}^2$$

38. a. Let s = a side of the rhombus

$$\left(\frac{32}{2}\right)^2 + \left(\frac{24}{2}\right)^2 = s^2$$

$$400 = s^2$$

$$20 = s$$

The side of the rhombus will be tangent to the circle. The radius drawn to the point of tangency will be perpendicular to the side of the rhombus. Looking at the triangle formed by one side of the rhombus and half of each diagonal, the length of the radius, r, can be found using the following proportion.

$$\frac{r}{\left(\frac{32}{2}\right)} = \frac{\left(\frac{24}{2}\right)}{20}$$

$$20r = \left(\frac{32}{2}\right)\left(\frac{24}{2}\right)$$

$$20r = \frac{768}{4}$$

$$20r = 192$$

$$r = 9.6 \text{ feet}$$

area of circle $= \pi(9.6)^2$
$\qquad\qquad\qquad = 92.16\pi \text{ ft}^2$

b. area inside rhombus but outside circle
$\quad$ = area of rhombus - area of circle

$$= \frac{1}{2}(32)(24) - 92.16\pi$$

$$= 384 - 92.16\pi \text{ ft}^2$$

39. radius of small circles $= \frac{1}{2}r$

area of shaded region = area of large circle -
$\qquad\qquad\qquad\qquad\qquad$ area of small circles

$$= \pi r^2 - 2\left[\pi\left(\frac{1}{2}r\right)^2\right]$$

$$= \pi r^2 - 2\left(\frac{1}{4}\pi r^2\right)$$

$$= \pi r^2 - \frac{1}{2}\pi r^2$$

$$= \frac{1}{2}\pi r^2$$

r	Area of shaded region	Area of circle
2	4π	2π
3	9π	$\frac{9}{2}\pi$
4	16π	8π
5	25π	$\frac{25}{2}\pi$
6	36π	18π
8	64π	32π

$$\frac{\text{area of shaded region}}{\text{area of large circle}} = \frac{\frac{1}{2}\pi r^2}{\pi r^2}$$

$$= \frac{1}{2}$$

The area of the shaded region is one-half the area of the large circle.

40. No; let $3x$ represent the circumference of one circle and $5x$ represent the circumference of the other.

Smaller circle $\qquad\qquad$ Larger circle

$C = 3x$ $\qquad\qquad\qquad\qquad$ $C = 5x$

$2\pi r = 3x$ $\qquad\qquad\qquad\quad$ $2\pi r = 5x$

$r = \frac{3x}{2\pi}$ $\qquad\qquad\qquad\quad$ $r = \frac{5x}{2\pi}$

$A = \pi r^2$ $\qquad\qquad\qquad\quad$ $A = \pi r^2$

$A = \pi\left(\frac{3x}{2\pi}\right)^2$ $\qquad\qquad\quad$ $A = \pi\left(\frac{5x}{2\pi}\right)^2$

$A = \pi\frac{9x^2}{4\pi}$ $\qquad\qquad\qquad$ $A = \pi\frac{25x^2}{4\pi}$

ratio of the areas $= \dfrac{\frac{9x^2}{4\pi}}{\frac{25x^2}{4\pi}}$ or $\dfrac{9}{25}$

41. $A = \pi r^2$

$\quad = \pi(1.5)^2$

$\quad \approx 7.06$

The area that will benefit is about 7 square miles.

42. The area is a 80 by 110 yard rectangle and a circle with a diameter of 80 yards.

area of field = area of rectangle
$\qquad\qquad\qquad$ + area of circle

$\qquad\qquad = 80(110) + \pi(40)^2$

$\qquad\qquad = 8800 + 1600\pi$

$\qquad\qquad \approx 13,827$ square yards

43. area of 14-inch pizza $= \pi(7)^2$

$\qquad\qquad\qquad\qquad = 49\pi$

area of 10-inch pizza $= \pi(5)^2$

$\qquad\qquad\qquad\qquad = 25\pi$

Set up a proportion.

$\dfrac{15 \text{ ounces}}{49\pi} = \dfrac{x \text{ ounces}}{25\pi}$

$\qquad 49x\pi = 375\pi$

$\qquad\quad x = \dfrac{375\pi}{49\pi}$

$\qquad\quad x \approx 7.7$ ounces

44. The diameter of the tablecloth must be 28 + 48 + 28 or 104 inches, since it must cover the table and go to the floor on each side. Find the circumference to find the amount of lace.

$C = 2\pi\left(\dfrac{104}{2}\right)$

$\quad = 104\pi$

$\quad \approx 326.7$ inches or 9.1 yards

45. The apothem of a hexagon with sides 10 inches long is $\left(\dfrac{10}{2}\right)\sqrt{3}$ or $5\sqrt{3}$ inches long.

$A = \dfrac{1}{2}Pa$

$\quad = \dfrac{1}{2}(6 \cdot 10)(5\sqrt{3})$

$\quad = 150\sqrt{3}$

$\quad \approx 259.81 \text{ in}^2$

46. $6^2 + \left(\dfrac{16}{2}\right)2 = r^2$

$\qquad 36 + 64 = r^2$

$\qquad\quad 100 = r^2$

$\qquad\quad 10 = r$

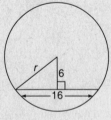

The radius is 10 centimeters.

47. $m\angle A = 103$, $a = 14$, $b = 7.5$

$\dfrac{\sin A}{a} = \dfrac{\sin B}{b}$

$\dfrac{\sin 103°}{14} = \dfrac{\sin B}{7.5}$

$\sin B = \dfrac{7.5 \sin 103°}{14}$

$\sin B \approx 0.5220$

$m\angle B \approx 31$

$m\angle A + m\angle B + m\angle C = 180$

$103 + 31 + m\angle C = 180$

$m\angle C = 46$

$\dfrac{\sin 103°}{14} = \dfrac{\sin 46°}{C}$

$C = \dfrac{14 \sin 46°}{\sin 103}$

$C \approx 10.3$

The remaining side and angles are 10.3 feet and 31° and 46°.

48. $(x + 16) + (8x + 7) + (11x - 3) = 180$

$\qquad\qquad\qquad\qquad 20x + 20 = 180$

$\qquad\qquad\qquad\qquad\quad 20x = 160$

$\qquad\qquad\qquad\qquad\qquad x = 8$

$x + 16 = 8 + 16$ or 24

$8x + 7 = 8(8) + 7$ or 71

$11x - 3 = 11(8) - 3$ or 85

Since all the angles are acute, the triangle is acute.

49. $(6y + 14) + (22y - 2) = 180$

$\qquad\qquad\quad 28y + 12 = 180$

$\qquad\qquad\qquad\quad 28y = 168$

$\qquad\qquad\qquad\qquad y = 6$

50. See students' work.

10-8   Geometric Probability

PAGES 509-510   CHECKING FOR UNDERSTANDING

1. probability $= \dfrac{\text{area of region } Y}{\text{area of region } X}$

2. Red area: probability $= \dfrac{\text{area of red circle}}{\text{area of target}}$

$\qquad\qquad\qquad = \dfrac{\pi(14)^2}{\pi(32)^2}$

$\qquad\qquad\qquad = \dfrac{196\pi}{1024\pi}$

$\qquad\qquad\qquad = \dfrac{49}{256}$ or about 0.19

192

Blue area: probability $= \dfrac{\text{area of blue ring}}{\text{area of target}}$

$$= \frac{\pi(24)^2 - \pi(14)^2}{\pi(32)^2}$$

$$= \frac{576\pi - 196\pi}{1024\pi}$$

$$= \frac{380\pi}{1024\pi}$$

$$= \frac{95}{256} \text{ or about } 0.37$$

Green area: probability $= \dfrac{\text{area of blue ring}}{\text{area of target}}$

$$= \frac{\pi(32)^2 - \pi(24)^2}{\pi(32)^2}$$

$$= \frac{1024\pi - 576\pi}{1024\pi}$$

$$= \frac{448\pi}{1024\pi}$$

$$= \frac{7}{16} \text{ or about } 0.44$$

The probability of winning a jumbo squirtgun is about 0.19; the probability of winning a yo-yo is about 0.37; and the probability of winning a candy bar is about 0.44.

3. Answers may vary. A sample answer is carnival games.

4. $\dfrac{\text{length of } \overline{AC}}{\text{length of } \overline{AG}} = \dfrac{3}{10}$

5. $\dfrac{\text{length of } \overline{AE}}{\text{length of } \overline{AG}} = \dfrac{8}{10}$ or $\dfrac{4}{5}$

6. $\dfrac{\text{length of } \overline{CF}}{\text{length of } \overline{AG}} = \dfrac{6}{10}$ or $\dfrac{3}{5}$

7. $\dfrac{\text{length of } \overline{DE}}{\text{length of } \overline{AG}} = \dfrac{2}{10}$ or $\dfrac{1}{5}$

8. $\dfrac{\text{length of } \overline{AG}}{\text{length of } \overline{AG}} = \dfrac{10}{10}$ or 1

9. $\dfrac{\text{length of } \overline{GC}}{\text{length of } \overline{AG}} = \dfrac{7}{10}$

10. Suppose a side of the square is 2 units long. One of the four shaded triangles would have an area of $\frac{1}{2}(1)(1) = \frac{1}{2}$. The total area of the shaded triangles would be $4\left(\frac{1}{2}\right)$ or 2 units^2.

probability of shaded region

$= \dfrac{\text{area of shaded region}}{\text{total area}}$

$= \dfrac{2}{2^2}$

$= \dfrac{2}{4}$ or 0.50

11. First find the area of the two semicircles as shown. This is the area of a circle of radius 2. $A = \pi(2)^2$ or 4π units^2. The area of the unshaded region is $(4)^2 - 4\pi$ or $16 - 4\pi$ units^2. If we subtract this area from the area of the two semicircles, this is the area of the shaded portion of the original figure.

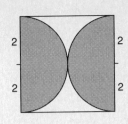

probability $= \dfrac{\text{area of shaded region}}{\text{total area}}$

$$= \frac{4\pi - (16 - 4\pi)}{16}$$

$$= \frac{4\pi - 16 + 4\pi}{16}$$

$$= \frac{8\pi - 16}{16}$$

$$\approx 0.57$$

12. probability $= \dfrac{\text{area of sector}}{\text{area of circle}}$

$$= \frac{\frac{70}{360}\pi r^2}{\pi r^2}$$

$$= \frac{70}{360}$$

$$\approx 0.19$$

PAGE 510   EXERCISES

13. If $XY - 10$, $XZ = 5$, $XW = WZ = 2.5$, $WY = 7.5$, and $WV = 3.75$

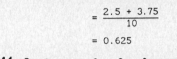

probability $= \dfrac{\text{length of } \overline{XV}}{\text{length of } \overline{XY}}$

$$= \frac{2.5 + 3.75}{10}$$

$$= 0.625$$

14. a.

C   A   D   E   B

b. $CD = DB$, so $\dfrac{CD}{CB} = \dfrac{1}{2}$.

c. Since $CA = AE = EB$, $\dfrac{AB}{CB} = \dfrac{2}{3}$.

15. a. See students' work.

b. probability $= \dfrac{\text{total area of cards}}{\text{area of board}}$

$$= \frac{25(2.5)(3.5)}{(6 \cdot 12)(3 \cdot 12)}$$

$$= \frac{218.75}{2592} \approx 0.08$$

c. No; as long as the dart is randomly thrown and the cards do not overlap, the area of the board and the cards is always the same.

193

16. a. $\frac{90}{360} = 0.25$ b. $\frac{65}{360} \approx 0.18$

c. $\frac{65}{360} \approx 0.18$ d. $\frac{10}{360} \approx 0.03$

17.

A		C		D	B
12:00	12:10		12:20	12:30	

If you arrive before 12:15 or after 12:25 you will miss your friend.

probability = $\frac{15 + 5}{30}$

= $\frac{20}{30}$ or $\frac{2}{3}$

18. a. $\frac{25}{252}(2,962,000) = 293,849$ sq. mi

b. $\frac{13}{252}(2,962,000) = 152,802$ sq. mi

c. Yes; more trials make the approximation more accurate.

19. probability of hitting bull's eye in one throw

$= \frac{\text{probability of hitting bull's eye}}{\text{probability of hitting dart board}}$

$= \frac{\frac{1}{16}}{\frac{2}{3}}$

$= \frac{3}{32}$

20. $A = \frac{N}{360}\pi r^2$

$= \frac{150}{360}\pi (5)^2$

$\approx 32.7 \text{ m}^2$

21. The center of the quarter must land more than 12 mm from the edge of the square. That is the shaded area. It is a square with sides 32 − 12 − 12 or 8 mm long.

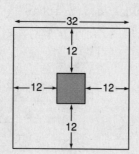

probability = $\frac{\text{shaded area}}{\text{area of square}}$

$= \frac{8^2}{32^2}$

$= \frac{1}{16}$ or 0.0625

22. $C = \pi d$ $A = \pi r^2$

$= \pi(1.6)$ $= \pi(0.8)^2$

≈ 5.0 in. $\approx 2.0 \text{ in}^2$

23. $\frac{26}{x} = \frac{x}{44}$

$x^2 = 1144$

$x = \sqrt{1144}$

$x \approx 33.8$

24. See students' work.

PAGES 514-515   CHECKING FOR UNDERSTANDING

1. See students' work.

2. All of the nodes have even degrees or exactly two nodes in the network have odd degrees.

3. No; nodes L and O are not connected by an edge.

4. July; node L has odd degree and M has even degree.

5. $A − 1$, $M − 1$, $C − 0$

6. $N − 3$, $C − 2$, $O − 4$, $M − 2$, $T − 1$

7. $A − 1$, $B − 2$, $C − 2$, $D − 2$, $E − 2$, $F − 1$

8. Yes; the degrees of all the nodes are even.

9. No; the degrees of all the nodes are odd.

10. Yes; exactly two nodes have even degrees.

11. Not complete; add edges between C and M and I and T.

12. Not complete; add edges between C and I, C and N, and U and N.

13. complete

PAGES 515-517   EXERCISES

14. $A − 3$, $B − 4$, $C − 2$, $D − 4$, $E − 3$, $F − 4$

15. $A − 3$, $B − 2$, $C − 3$, $D − 2$, $E − 5$, $F − 2$, $G − 3$

16. $A − 3$, $B − 6$, $C − 3$

17. edges between: P and E, E and N, and P and N

18. edges between: Y and Z, Y and V, Y and X, Z and V, Z and W, and X and W

19. edges between: R and U, R and N, R and K, E and U, E and N, and K and U

20. a. 3 and 3; 4 and 6; 5 and 10; 6 and 15

b. add 3, add 4, add 5, ...

c. 45

21. yes

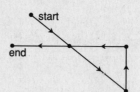

22. yes

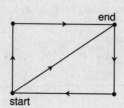

23. yes

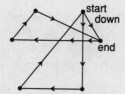

24. Yes. This network is traceable because exactly two nodes, E and W, have odd degrees.

25. Answers will vary. Network must have all nodes with even degrees or exactly two with odd degrees. A sample answer is given:

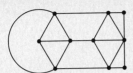

26. Answers will vary.
A sample answer
is given:

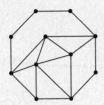

27. a. yes;

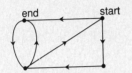

b. no
c. No; if a network has an Euler circuit, each node has an even degree, so any path will return to its starting node.

28.

Node	Degree
A	2
B	3
C	3
D	2
E	3
F	3
Total	16

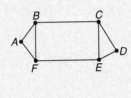

There are 8 edges.
So, the sum of the degrees of the nodes is twice the number of edges.

29. a.

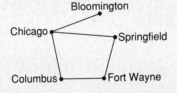

b. yes – through Fort Wayne or Chicago
30. No; it is not traceable since 6 nodes have odd degrees.
31. a. complete
b. 21

32. The area of the two unshaded semicircles is the area of a circle of diameter 10.

$A = \pi(5)^2$ or 25π cm^2

probability $= \dfrac{\text{area of red region}}{\text{area of square}}$

$= \dfrac{10^2 - 25\pi}{10^2}$

$= \dfrac{100 - 25\pi}{100}$

≈ 0.21

33. Given: Lines ℓ and m intersect at P.
Prove: Plane $\mathcal{R}$ contains both ℓ and m.

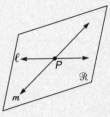

Assume there is no plane containing both ℓ and m.
34. reflexive property of equality
35.

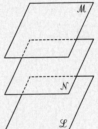

36. See students' work.

Chapter 10 Summary and Review

PAGES 518-520   SKILLS AND CONCEPTS
1. L, M, N, O, P; $\overline{LM}$, $\overline{LP}$, $\overline{LN}$, $\overline{LO}$, $\overline{OP}$, $\overline{PM}$, $\overline{MN}$, and $\overline{NO}$
2. $\triangle LMP$, $\triangle LNM$, $\triangle LNO$, $\triangle LOP$, and quadrilateral $MNOP$
3. No; all of the faces are not congruent.
4. $\dfrac{180(10-2)}{10} = \dfrac{180(8)}{10} = 144$
5. $180(n-2) = 1980$
$180n - 360 = 1980$
$180n = 2340$
$n = 13$
6. $\dfrac{180(20-2)}{20} = \dfrac{180(18)}{20} = 162$; $180 - 162 = 18$
7. $(7)(2.9) = 20.3$ ft^2
8. $18.9(h) = 134.19$
$n = 7.1$ in.

195

9. $(3x)^2 = x^2 + 648$

$9x^2 = x^2 + 648$

$8x^2 = 648$

$x^2 = 81$

$x = 9$ m

10. $A = \frac{1}{2}bh$

$48 = \frac{1}{2}b(6)$

$48 = 3b$

16 mm $= b$

11. $A = \frac{1}{2}d_1 \cdot d_2$

$= \frac{1}{2}(8.6)(6.3)$

$= 27.09$ cm^2

12. $6.8 = 1.9 + 1.9 + b_1 + b_2$

$3 = b_1 + b_2$

$A = \frac{1}{2}h(b_1 + b_2)$

$7.2 = \frac{1}{2}h(3)$

$7.2 = 1.5h$

4.8 ft $= h$

13. $A = \frac{1}{2}Pa$

$= \frac{1}{2}(6 \cdot 8.9\sqrt{3})(8.9)$

≈ 411.6 in^2

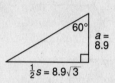

$\frac{1}{2}s = 8.9\sqrt{3}$, $60°$, $a = 8.9$

14. $\tan 36° = \dfrac{\frac{1}{2}s}{0.4}$

$0.8 \tan 36° = s$

$0.58 \approx s$

$A = \frac{1}{2}Pa$

$= \frac{1}{2}(5 \cdot 0.58)(0.4)$

≈ 0.6 ft^2

$36°$, $a = 0.4$, $\frac{1}{2}s$

15. $A = \frac{1}{2}Pa$

$= \frac{1}{2}(6 \cdot 64)(32\sqrt{3})$

$\approx 10{,}641.7$ mm^2

$30°$, $a = 32\sqrt{3}$, $\frac{1}{2}s = 32$

16. $A = s^2$

$= (2n)^2$

$= 4n^2$ cm^2

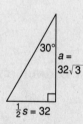

$2n$ cm, n cm

17. $C = 2\pi r$

$= 2\pi(7)$

≈ 44.0 mm

$A = \pi r^2$

$= \pi(7)^2$

≈ 153.9 mm^2

18. $C = 2\pi r$

$= 2\pi(19)$

≈ 119.4 in.

$A = \pi r^2$

$= \pi(19)^2$

≈ 1134.1 in^2

19. $C = 2\pi r$

$= 2\pi(0.9)$

≈ 5.7 ft

$A = \pi r^2$

$= \pi(0.9)^2$

≈ 2.5 ft^2

20. A C ———————————— B
1 2 3 4 5 6 7

probability $= \dfrac{\text{length of } \overline{AB}}{\text{length of } \overline{AC}} = \dfrac{\frac{1}{2}}{7} = \dfrac{1}{14}$

21. A, B, C, D, E and $\overline{AB}$, $\overline{BC}$, $\overline{BD}$, $\overline{BE}$, $\overline{CD}$

22. yes

23. No; add edges between A and C, A and D, A and E, C and E, and D and E.

PAGE 520   **APPLICATIONS AND CONNECTIONS**

24. 631 and 542

25. Area $= 3(8 \cdot 8) + (10 \cdot 8)$

$= 192 + 80$

$= 272$ ft^2

Yes, one gallon will cover all of the walls.

26. Total area $=$ area of square base $+$
areas of trapezoid sides

$= 8^2 + 4\left[\frac{1}{2}(12)(8 + 10)\right]$

$= 64 + 4(108)$

$= 496$ in^2

Chapter 10 Test

PAGE 521

1. Q, R, S, T, U

2. $\overline{QR}$, $\overline{RS}$, $\overline{ST}$, $\overline{TU}$, $\overline{UQ}$

3. pentagon

4. convex

5. regular; all sides and angles congruent and convex

6. $180(5 - 2) = 180(3)$
$= 540$

7. $\dfrac{360}{5} = 72$

8. 727

9. $A = bh$
$= (4.95)(0.51)$
$= 2.5245$ ft^2

10. $P = 4s$
$258 = 4s$
64.5 in. $= s$

$A = s^2$
$= (64.5)^2$
$= 4160.25$ in^2

11. $A = \frac{1}{2}bh$

$= \frac{1}{2}(16)(30.6)$

$= 244.8$ ft^2

12. $A = \frac{1}{2}bh$

$3x^2 + 6x = \frac{1}{2}b(3x + 6)$

$6x^2 + 12x = b(3x + 6)$

$2x = b$

13. $A = (10)(13.5)$

$= 135 \text{ ft}^2$

14. $A = \frac{1}{2}Pa$

$= \frac{1}{2}(6 \cdot 10)(5\sqrt{3})$

$\approx 259.8 \text{ cm}^2$

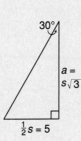

30°

$a = s\sqrt{3}$

$\frac{1}{2}s = 5$

15. $A = \pi r^2$

$= \pi(2)^2$

$\approx 12.6 \text{ in}^2$

16. $C = 2\pi r$

$= 2\pi(2)$

$\approx 12.6 \text{ in.}$

17. $A = \frac{N}{360}\pi r^2$

$= \frac{30}{360}\pi(2)^2$

$\approx 1.0 \text{ in}^2$

18. probability $= \dfrac{\text{area of bull's eye}}{\text{area of target}}$

$= \dfrac{\pi(1.5)^2}{\pi(9)^2}$

$= \dfrac{2.25}{81}$ or about 0.028

19. probability $= \dfrac{\text{area of blue ring}}{\text{area of target}}$

$= \dfrac{\pi(5.5)^2 - \pi(1.5)^2}{\pi(9)^2}$

$= \dfrac{28}{81}$ or about 0.346

20. Sample answer:

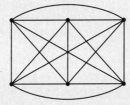

15 edges

BONUS

Assume a side of the large square is 1 unit long.
Then the radius of the large circle is $\frac{1}{2}$ unit and
half of the diagonal of the blue square is $\frac{1}{2}$ unit.

Two sides of the green
square and a diagonal
form a 45°-45°-90°
triangle. So a side of
the square is $\frac{1}{\sqrt{2}}$ units
long. The radius of the

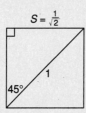

$S = \frac{1}{\sqrt{2}}$

1

45°

small circle is $\frac{1}{2}\left(\frac{1}{\sqrt{2}}\right)$ or $\frac{\sqrt{2}}{4}$ units long.

---

probability

$= \dfrac{\text{area of green region}}{\text{area of target}}$

$= \dfrac{\text{area of small square} - \text{area of small circle}}{\text{area of target}}$

$= \dfrac{\left(\frac{1}{\sqrt{2}}\right) - \pi\left(\frac{\sqrt{2}}{4}\right)^2}{(1)^2}$

$= \dfrac{\frac{1}{2} - \frac{1}{8}\pi}{1}$

$= \frac{1}{2} - \frac{1}{8}\pi \approx 0.107$

Out of 92 balls, about 92(0.107) or about 10 balls
will fall in the green region.

College Entrance Exam Preview

PAGES 522-523

1. C $\quad x^2 + 3 = (4)^2 + 3 \qquad 5x - 1 = 5(4) - 1$

$= 19 \qquad\qquad\qquad = 19$

2. D $\quad$ Suppose $x = 1$, $y = \frac{1}{2}$; then $x > y$,

and $x^2 > y^2$.

Suppose $x = 1$, $y = -1$; then $x > y$,

and $x^2 = y^2$.

Suppose $x = -1$, $y = -2$; then $x > y$,

and $x^2 < y^2$.

3. B $\quad \left(\frac{3}{4}\right)\#6 = 5\left(\frac{3}{4}\right) - 2(6)$

$= -8\frac{1}{4}$

$5\#\left(\frac{3}{4}\right) = 5(5) - 2\left(\frac{3}{4}\right) = 23\frac{1}{2}$

4. D $\quad$ A chord could be shorter than a radius,
the same length as a radius, or longer
than a radius.

5. A $\quad$ area of shaded region

$= $ area of square $-$ area of triangle

$= (4)^2 - \frac{1}{2}(4 \cdot 3)\left(\frac{2}{\sqrt{3}}\right)$

$= 16 - 4\sqrt{3}$

$\approx 9.07 \text{ cm}^2$

area of unshaded region $= \frac{1}{2}(4 \cdot 3)\left(\frac{2}{\sqrt{3}}\right)$

$= 4\sqrt{3}$

$\approx 6.93 \text{ cm}^2$

6. D   Suppose $a = 2$. Then $|-a| = |-2| = 2$.
Then $|-a| = a$.
Suppose $a = -2$. Then $|-a| = |-(-2)| = 2$.
Then $|-a| > a$.

7. C   Since $XY = XZ$, $m\angle XYZ = m\angle XZY$. $m\angle XYZ + m\angle 1$
$= 180$ and $m\angle XZY + m\angle 2 = 180$. Since these
angles are linear pairs, $m\angle 1 = m\angle 2$ because
they are supplementary to congruent
angles.

8. C $C = 2\pi r$ $P = 4s$
    $= 2\pi(2x)$ $= 4(\pi x)$
    $= 4\pi x$ $= 4\pi x$

9. B   The product of a positive and a negative
number is negative, so $st < 0$.
The quotient of a positive and a negative
number is negative, so since $-\dfrac{s}{t}$ is the
opposite of a negative, it is positive.

10. A $x + 30 + 80 = 180$
          $x = 70$
$m\angle A < m\angle C < m\angle B$ so $BC < AB < AC$.

11. A   The area of the triangle
is less than the
area of the circle.

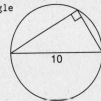

12. A   The first number is zero, so no matter
what the twentieth number is, their
product is 0.
If n is even, then the nth term is
negative. So the fourth term is negative.
If n is odd, then the nth term is
positive. So the nineteenth term is
positive. The product of a negative and a
positive is negative, so the product of
the fourth and nineteenth terms is
negative.

13. B
$\underbrace{0 + (-1)}_{-1} + \underbrace{2 + (-3)}_{(-1)} + \underbrace{4 + (-5)}_{(-1)} + \ldots + \underbrace{18 + (-19)}_{(-1)}$
$= 10(-1)$
$= -10$
$-10 < 0$

14. D   Since $\overline{DE}$ and $\overline{AB}$ are not corresponding
sides, their relationship cannot be
determined.

15. A $x - y \overset{?}{=} y - x$
       $x - y + y \overset{?}{=} y - x + y$
           $x \overset{?}{=} 2y - x$
       $x + x \overset{?}{=} 2y - x + x$
         $2x \overset{?}{=} 2y$
           $x > y$

16. Area of figure
$= $ area of semicircle + area of rectangle
$= \dfrac{1}{2}\left[\pi\left(\dfrac{3x}{2}\right)^2\right] + x(3x)$
$= \dfrac{1}{2}\left(\dfrac{9\pi x^2}{4}\right) + 3x^2$
$= \dfrac{9\pi x^2}{8} + 3x^2$

17. $\dfrac{1716 \text{ feet}}{3 \text{ seconds}} \times \dfrac{60 \text{ seconds}}{1 \text{ minute}} \times \dfrac{60 \text{ minutes}}{1 \text{ hour}} \times \dfrac{1 \text{ mile}}{5280 \text{ feet}}$
$= 390 \dfrac{\text{miles}}{\text{hour}}$

18. $C = 2\pi r$
   $= 2\pi(8)$
   $= 16\pi$
area length $= \dfrac{80}{360}(16\pi)$
            $= \dfrac{32}{9}\pi$ or about 11.2 units

19. $\dfrac{7}{x - 3} - \dfrac{1}{2} > \dfrac{3}{x - 4}$
If $x - 3 > 0$ and $x - 4 > 0$ or $x - 3 < 0$ and
$x - 4 < 0$ then
$2(7)(x - 4) - (x - 3)(x - 4) > 3(2)(x - 3)$
   $14x - 56 - x^2 + 7x - 12 > 6x - 18$
                 $0 > x^2 - 15x - 50$
                 $0 > (x - 5)(x - 10)$
  $x - 5 > 0$ and $x - 10 < 0$
      $x > 5$ and $x < 10$
or $x - 5 < 0$ and $x - 10 > 0$
      $x < 5$ and $x > 10$
$\{x | 5 < x < 10\}$ is a solution set.
If $x - 3 < 0$ and $x - 4 > 0$ then
$2(7)(x - 4) - (x - 3)(x - 4) < 3(2)(x - 3)$
   $14x - 56 - x^2 + 7x - 12 < 6x - 18$
                 $0 < (x - 5)(x - 10)$
  $x - 5 > 0$ and $x - 10 > 0$
      $x > 5$ and $x > 10$
                 $x > 10$
or $x - 5 < 0$ and $x - 10 < 0$
      $x < 5$ and $x < 10$
      $x < 5$
We are given that $x - 3 < 0$ and $x - 4 < 0$ so
$3 < x < 4$. So $x < 5$ will always be true so
$\{x | 3 < x < 4$ or $5 < x < 10\}$ is the solution set.

20. registered voters
$= 0.65(\text{women surveyed}) + 0.55(\text{men surveyed})$
$= 0.65(100 - 40)$ $+ 0.55(40)$
$= 39 + 22$
$= 61$ people registered
not registered $= 100 -$ registered
              $= 100 - 61$
              $= 39$ people

Chapter 11   Surface Area and Volume

11-1   Problem Solving Strategy: Make a Model

PAGE 527   CHECKING FOR UNDERSTANDING

1. Sample answer: No; because the area seems to get bigger as the figure becomes "closer" to a square.

2. Sample answer: Use 16 small squares made out of paper or other material. Move these squares around until you find one with a perimeter of 22 units.

3. a. Sample answer: Moving paper is easier than moving furniture. If you find out that something is too big or too little for the space, you will know not to buy it.

   b. Sample answer: It is hard to visualize three-dimensional objects on a two-dimensional drawing. Colors and designs are not shown on the drawing so it is hard to tell how everything will look.

4. $r = 4.5 + 3 + 2 = 9.5$ feet

   $A = \pi(9.5)^2$

   $A = 90.25\pi \approx 283.5$ ft^2

5. All of the teams except the champion lose one game, so there are $32 - 1$ or 31 games.

6.

```
 |___1 mile___|___1 mile___|
   length of      length of
     train          tunnel
```

   distance = length of train + length of tunnel

   $d = 2$ miles, $r = 60$ mph

   $d = rt$

   $2 = 60(t)$

   $\dfrac{2}{60} = t$

   $\dfrac{1}{30}$ hr or 2 min $= t$

PAGE 527   EXERCISES

7. $12 - 34 + 56 - 7 + 89 = 116$

8. $x =$ steps per second

   $10(x + 1) = 6(x + 3)$

   $10x + 10 = 6x + 18$

   $4x = 8$

   $x = 2$

   Number of steps $= 10(2 + 1) = 30$ steps

9. $1600 \div 2 = 800$
   $800 \div 2 = 400$ $\Big\}$ Day 1
   $400 \div 2 = 200$

   $200 \div 2 = 100$
   $100 \div 2 = 50$ $\Big\}$ Day 2
   $50 \div 2 = 25$

   Lisa had 25 bacteria at the beginning of the first day.

10. Pattern: An odd number squared equals an odd number.

    An even number squared equals an even number.

    From 1^2 to 70^2, half the numbers are even and half are odd, so 50% of the perfect squares between 0 and 5000 are odd.

11. 15 moves:

	1	2	3	4	5	6	7
start	○	○	○		●	●	●
move 1	○	○		○	●	●	●
2	○	○	●	○		●	●
3	○	○	●	○	●		●
4	○	○	●		●	○	●
5	○		●	○	●	○	●
6		○	●	○	●	○	●
7	●	○		○	●	○	●
8	●	○	●	○		○	●
9	●	○	●	○	●	○	
10	●	○	●	○	●		○
11	●	○	●		●	○	○
12	●		●	○	●	○	○
13	●	●		○	●	○	○
14	●	●	●	○		○	○
15	●	●	●		○	○	○

12. 24 moves:

	1	2	3	4	5	6	7	8	9
start	○	○	○	○		●	●	●	●
move 1	○	○	○		○	●	●	●	●
2	○	○	○	●	○		●	●	●
3	○	○	○	●	○	●		●	●
4	○	○	○	●		●	○	●	●
5	○	○		●	○	●	○	●	●
6	○		○	●	○	●	○	●	●
7	○	●	○		○	●	○	●	●
8	○	●	○	●	○		○	●	●
9	○	●	○	●	○	●	○		●
10	○	●	○	●	○	●	○	●	
11	○	●	○	●	○	●		●	○
12	○	●	○	●		●	○	●	○
13	○	●		●	○	●	○	●	○
14		●	○	●	○	●	○	●	○
15	●		○	●	○	●	○	●	○
16	●	●	○		○	●	○	●	○
17	●	●	○	●	○		○	●	○
18	●	●	○	●	○	●	○		○
19	●	●	○	●	○	●		○	○
20	●	●	○	●		●	○	○	○
21	●	●		●	○	●	○	○	○
22	●	●	●		○	●	○	○	○
23	●	●	●	●	○		○	○	○
24	●	●	●	●		○	○	○	○

13.

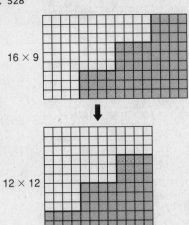

14. John, Sally, Andy, Lisa

15. P = 1 cent, N = 5 cents, D = 10 cents

PPN = 7 cents	PNQ = 31 cents
PPD = 12 cents	PDQ = 36 cents
PPQ = 27 cents	NDQ = 40 cents
PND = 16 cents	

Cooperative Learning Project

PAGE 528

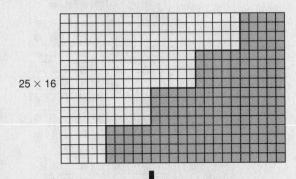

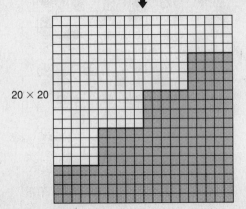

11-2	**Exploring Surface Area**

PAGES 531-532   CHECKING FOR UNDERSTANDING

1. On isometric dot paper, the dots are arranged in triangles, which aid in drawing three-dimensional objects. On rectangular dot paper, the dots are arranged in squares, which aid in drawing two-dimensional objects such as nets.

2. A net is the unfolded two-dimensional pattern of a three-dimensional object. The sum of the areas of the polygonal shapes in the net is the surface area of the polyhedron.

3. Wing-loading is the total weight of the aircraft on take-off divided by the total surface of its wings.

4. The net won't fold into a cube because two of the squares will overlap instead of folding to become the top and bottom.

5. 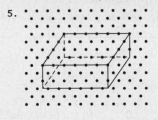   6.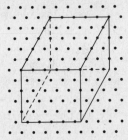

7.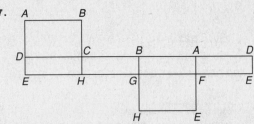

8.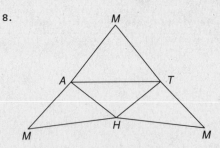

9. 2 pentagons, 5 rectangles
10. 2 triangles, 3 rectangles
11. c
12. c
13.

200

14.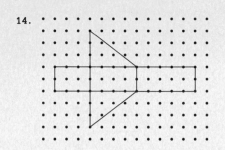

PAGES 532-534   EXERCISES

15. yes   **16.** no   **17.** no   **18.** no

19. no   **20.** yes   **21.** b   **22.** c

23. 2 pentagons, 5 rectangles

24. 2 triangles, 3 rectangles

25. 2 hexagons, 6 rectangles

26. 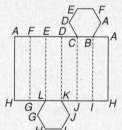   **27.**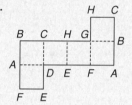

28.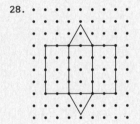

29.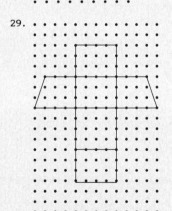

30.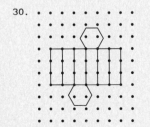

31. yes

32. No; 4 and 2 would be opposite and their sum is not 7.

33. Yes

34. No; 3 and 5 would be opposite and their sum is not 7.

35. Yes

36. No; 4 and 2 would be opposite and their sum is not 7.

37. Answers will vary. Sample answers given.

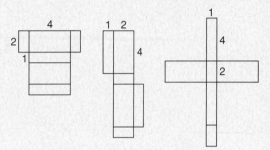

On our 18 × 30 grid we arranged 15 nets.

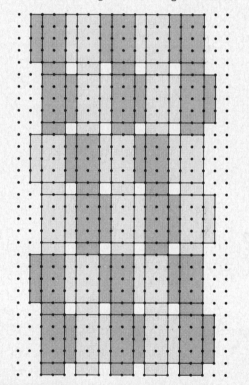

38. Sample answer:

In the net, every polygon is an entire face in the solid. In the cardboard box cutout, some of the polygons are part of a face and parts of faces are covered twice. This gives the cardboard box more stability when it is folded.

39. Wright brothers' plane = $\frac{750}{532} \approx 1.41$

Four-passenger plane = $\frac{1150}{117} \approx 9.83$

Supersonic transport = $\frac{750,000}{7700} \approx 97.40$

40. $46(36) = 1656$ in^2

41. $C = \pi \cdot 12 = 12\pi \approx 37.7$ inches

42. $A = \frac{1}{2}(7)(2) = 7$ ft^2

43. a. <   **b.** >

44. The total surface area of a geometric solid is the sum of the areas of the shapes that make up its faces. A net gives a two-dimensional view of these faces, which allows us to use area formulas to compute total surface area. Although there are several ways to arrange the polygons that will fold up into the geometric solid, all of these nets have the same surface area.

Technology: Drawing Three-Dimensional Figures

PAGE 535   EXERCISES

1.–3. See students' work.

11-3 **Surface Area of Prisms and Cylinders**

PAGE 539   CHECKING FOR UNDERSTANDING

1. a. 2 rhombi and 4 parallelograms

b. two faces are rhombi

c.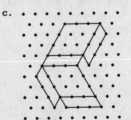

2. Sample answer: Lateral area is the area of all the lateral faces. Surface area is the area of the entire surface including the bases (the lateral area plus the area of the bases).

3. Sample answer: To make the label, the printer needs to know the circumference of the circular base and the height of the cylinder. The area of the label is closely associated with the lateral area of the cylinder.

4. Sample answer: In a right prism, the lateral edges of the prism are also altitudes of the prism. If this is not the case, then the prism is an oblique prism.

5. Sample answer: The endpoints of the axis are the center of the circular bases of the cylinder.

6. $P = 2(20 + 5)$ $L = 50(3)$
$P = 50$ $L = 150$
$B = 20(5)$ $T = 150 + 2(100)$
$B = 100$
$T = 350$ cm^2

7. $P = 2(7.5 + 14.5)$ $L = 44(8)$
$P = 44$ $L = 352$
$B = 7.5(14.5)$ $T = 352 + 2(108.75)$
$B = 108.75$
$T = 569.5$ cm^2

8. $P = 3(5)$
$P = 15$
$B = \frac{1}{2}(5)(2.5\sqrt{3})$
$B \approx 10.83$
$L = 15(12)$
$L = 180$
$T \approx 180 + 2(10.83)$
$T \approx 201.7$ cm^2

9. $P = 3(6.2)$
$P = 18.6$
$B = \frac{1}{2}(6.2)(3.1\sqrt{3})$
$B \approx 16.65$
$L = (18.6)(20.4)$
$L = 379.4$
$T \approx 379.4 + 2(16.65)$
$T \approx 412.7$ cm^2

10. $T = 2\pi rh + 2\pi r^2$
$T = 2\pi \cdot 4 \cdot 8 + 2\pi \cdot 4^2$
$T \approx 301.6$ cm^2

11. $T = 2\pi rh + 2\pi r^2$
$T = 2\pi \cdot (6.8) \cdot 17 + 2\pi \cdot (6.8)^2$
$T \approx 1016.9$ cm^2

12. $A = 2\pi rh$
$630 = 2\pi \cdot r \cdot 35$
$r = \frac{630}{2\pi \cdot 35}$
$r \approx 2.86$ inches

202

13. right prism

14. heptagons, rectangles

15. $7(6) = 42$ units

16. $56(7) = 392$ units^2

17. $2\pi \cdot 3 = 6\pi$ cm

18. $2\pi \cdot 3 \cdot 8 = 48\pi$ cm^2

19. $3^2 \cdot \pi = 9\pi$ cm^2

20. $48\pi + 2 \cdot 9\pi = 66\pi$ cm^2

21. $L = 36(12)$

$\quad = 432$ in^2

$B = \frac{1}{2} \cdot 36 \cdot 3\sqrt{3}$

$\quad = 54\sqrt{3}$

$T = 43 + 2(54\sqrt{3})$

$\quad = 432 + 108\sqrt{3}$

$\quad \approx 619.1$ in^2

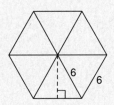

$30°$-$60°$-$90°$ triangle

hypotenuse $= 6$

shorter leg $= 3$

longer leg $= 3\sqrt{3}$

22. $L = 12(21)$

$\quad = 252$ m^2

$B = \frac{1}{2}(4)(3)$

$\quad = 6$

$T = 252 + 2(6)$

$\quad = 264$ m^2

23. $L = (30 + 10\sqrt{3})(5)$

$\quad = 150 + 50\sqrt{3}$

$\quad \approx 236.6$ ft^2

$B = \frac{1}{2} \cdot 10 \cdot 10\sqrt{3}$

$\quad = 50\sqrt{3}$

$T = (150 + 50\sqrt{3}) + 2(50\sqrt{3})$

$\quad = 150 + 150\sqrt{3}$

$\quad \approx 409.8$ ft^2

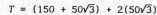

24. $L = 8(16) + 16(8) + 24(8) + 8(6) + 8(8) + 8(10)$

$\quad = 640$ yd^2

$B = 6(24) + 10(16)$

$\quad = 304$ yd^2

$T = 640 + 2(304)$

$\quad = 1248$ yd^2

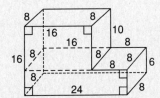

25. $L = 32(8)$

$\quad = 256$

$B = 8^2$

$\quad = 64$

$T = 256 + 2(64)$

$\quad = 384$ units^2

26. $8x(2x) = 144$

$\quad 16x^2 = 144$

$\quad x^2 = 9$

$\quad x = 3$

$3x = 9,\ 2x = 6$

$B = 9(3)$

$\quad = 27$

$T = 144 + 2(27)$

$\quad = 198$ cm^2

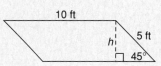

27. $T = 2\pi rh + 2\pi r^2$

$T = 2\pi \cdot 4 \cdot 8 + 2\pi \cdot 16$

$T = 96\pi$

$\quad \approx 301.6$ m^2

28. $h = \dfrac{5}{\sqrt{2}}$

$\quad = \dfrac{5\sqrt{2}}{2}$

$T = $ (area of front lateral face)2 +

(area of side lateral face)2 +

(area of base)2

$T = \left(10 \cdot \dfrac{5\sqrt{2}}{2}\right)2 + (5 \cdot 5)2 + (10 \cdot 5)2$

$\quad = 50\sqrt{2} + 50 + 100$

$\quad \approx 220.7$ units^2

29. $h = 6\sqrt{3}$

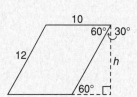

$T = (10 \cdot 6\sqrt{3}) \cdot 2 + (12 \cdot 8) \cdot 2 + (10 \cdot 8) \cdot 2$

$\quad = 120\sqrt{3} + 192 + 160$

$\quad \approx 559.8$ units^2

30. $L = 44(6) = 264$

$B = 14(8) = 112$

$T = 264 + 2(112)$

$\quad = 488$

$488 - 2$(area of circles) + lateral area of cylinder

$488 - 2\pi \cdot 2^2 + 2\pi \cdot 2 \cdot 14 \approx 638.8$ units^2

31. The base is circular. Sample answer: Compare the area of bases that are square, regular hexagonal, regular 12-gon, and circular.

32. $(9 \cdot 13) + 2(2 \cdot 13) + 2(2 \cdot 9) = 205$ in^2

33. $L = 2\pi \cdot 8 \cdot 40$

$\quad \approx 2010.6$ ft^2

34. a. $L = 188(2) = 376$

$B = 20(74) = 1480$

$T = 376 + 2(1480)$

$= 3336$ mm^2

b. $6.5 + 74 + 6.5 = 87$

$2 + 20 + 2 + 20 + 2 = 46$

dimensions: 87 mm × 46 mm

Area $= 87(46) = 4002$ mm^2

35. Sample answer:

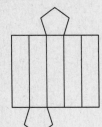

36. $\dfrac{8}{6} = \dfrac{10}{(ED) + 6}$

$8(ED) + 48 = 60$

$8(ED) = 12$

$ED = 1.5$

$EC = 1.5 + 6 = 7.5$

37. $(BC)^2 = 8^2 + 6^2$

$(BC)^2 = 100$

$BC = 10$

38. $\dfrac{7.5}{(AB) + 10} = \dfrac{6}{10}$

$6(AB) + 60 = 75$

$6(AB) = 15$

$AB = 2.5$

39. area $ABDE$ = area $\triangle AEC$ − area $\triangle BDC$

$= \dfrac{1}{2}(7.5)(10) - \dfrac{1}{2}(6)(8)$

$= 13.5$

40. See students' work.

11-4 | Surface Area of Pyramids and Cones

PAGE 545   CHECKING FOR UNDERSTANDING

1. The lateral edge of a pyramid is the side of a triangle where one endpoint is on the base, while the other is the vertex. The lateral edge of a prism is the side of a parallelogram, and its endpoints are both on bases.

2. As the number of sides increases, the base resembles a circle. As this takes place, the lateral faces become narrower so the lateral surface looks rounder.

3. lateral edges

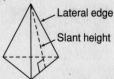

Lateral edge

Slant height

4. if the cone were oblique and not a right cone

5. pyramid   **6.** both   **7.** prism   **8.** neither

9. $L = \dfrac{1}{2} \cdot 9 \cdot 6$

$= 27$ cm^2

10. $L = \pi \cdot 6 \cdot 10$

$= 60\pi \approx 188.5$ cm^2

11. $L = \dfrac{1}{2} \cdot 35 \cdot 8.2$

$= 143.5$ cm^2

12. $\ell^2 = 15^2 + 8^2$

$\ell^2 = 289$

$\ell = 17$ inches

$T = \pi \cdot 8 \cdot 17 + \pi \cdot 64$

$= 200\pi \approx 628.3$ in^2

13. $\ell^2 = 17^2 - 8^2$

$\ell^2 = 225$

$\ell = 15$

$L = \dfrac{1}{2} \cdot 64 \cdot 15$

$= 480$

$T = 480 + 16^2$

$= 736$ cm^2

14. $\ell^2 = 5^2 + 3^2$

$\ell^2 = 34$

$\ell = \sqrt{34}$

$T = \pi r \ell + 2\pi rh + \pi r^2$

$= \pi \cdot 3 \cdot \sqrt{34} + 2\pi \cdot 3 \cdot 10 \cdot \pi \cdot 9$

$= (3\sqrt{34} + 69)\pi$

≈ 271.7 in^2

PAGES 545-547   EXERCISES

15. Prism   **16.** Pyramid   **17.** Neither   **18.** Pyramid

19. Pyramid

20. $\ell^2 = 17^2 - 12^2$

$\ell^2 = 145$

$\ell = \sqrt{145} \approx 12.0$ units

21. $A = \dfrac{1}{2} \cdot 24 \cdot \sqrt{145}$

$A \approx 144.5$ units^2

22. $L = \dfrac{1}{2}(4 \cdot 24)\sqrt{145}$

$L \approx 578.0$ units^2

23. $578 + 24^2 \approx 1154$ units^2

24. $L = \dfrac{1}{2} \cdot 21 \cdot 5\dfrac{3}{8}$

$= 56\dfrac{7}{16}$ in^2

≈ 56.4 in^2

25. $\ell^2 = 10^2 - 8^2$

$\ell^2 = 36$

$\ell = 6$

$L = \dfrac{1}{2} \cdot 48 \cdot 6$

$= 144$ cm^2

26. $\ell^2 = 12^2 + 5^2$

$\ell^2 = 169$

$\ell = 13$

$L = \pi \cdot 5 \cdot 13$

$= 65\pi \approx 204.2$ ft^2

27. $r^2 = 13^2 - 12^2$

$r^2 = 25$

$r = 5$

$T = \pi \cdot 5 \cdot 13 + \pi \cdot 25$

$= 90\pi \approx 282.7$ cm^2

28. $\ell^2 = 8^2 + 2^2$

$\ell^2 = 68$

$\ell = \sqrt{68} = 2\sqrt{17}$

$T = \pi r^2 + 2\pi rh + \pi r\ell$

$\quad = \pi \cdot 4 + 2\pi \cdot 2 \cdot 8 + \pi \cdot 2 \cdot 2\sqrt{17}$

$\quad = (36 + 4\sqrt{17})\pi \approx 164.9$ ft^2

29. $s^2 = 100$

$s = 10$

$T = \frac{1}{2} \cdot 40 \cdot 16 + 100$

$\quad = 420$ ft^2

30. $(TP)^2 = 16^2 + 16^2$

$(TP)^2 = 512$

$TP = 16\sqrt{2}$

$\ell^2 = 16^2 - (8\sqrt{2})^2$

$\ell^2 = 128$

$\ell = 8\sqrt{2}$

$L = \frac{1}{2} \cdot 48\sqrt{2} \cdot 8\sqrt{2}$

$L = 384$ units^2

$T = 384 + \frac{1}{2} \cdot 16\sqrt{2} \cdot 8\sqrt{6}$

$T = 384 + 128\sqrt{3}$

$T = 605.7$ units^2

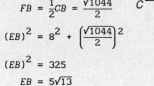

31. $(CB)^2 = 30^2 + 12^2$

$(CB)^2 = 1044$

$CB = \sqrt{1044}$

$FB = \frac{1}{2}CB = \frac{\sqrt{1044}}{2}$

$(EB)^2 = 8^2 + \left(\frac{\sqrt{1044}}{2}\right)^2$

$(EB)^2 = 325$

$EB = 5\sqrt{13}$

$(\ell_1)^2 = (5\sqrt{13})^2 - 6^2$

$(\ell_1)^2 = 325 - 36 = 289$

$\ell_1 = 17$

$(\ell_2)^2 = (5\sqrt{13})^2 - 15^2$

$(\ell_2)^2 = 325 - 225 = 100$

$\ell_2 = 10$

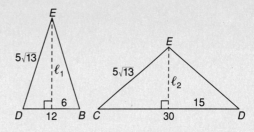

area of $\Delta EDB = \frac{1}{2} \cdot 12 \cdot 17$

$\quad = 102$

area of ΔEDB + area of $\Delta ECA = 2(102)$

$\quad\quad\quad = 204$

area of $\Delta ECD = \frac{1}{2} \cdot 30 \cdot 10$

$\quad = 150$

area of ΔECD + area of $\Delta EAB = 2(150)$

$\quad\quad\quad = 300$

Area of rectangular base = 30(12) = 360

$T = 204 + 300 + 360$

$\quad = 864$ in^2

32. area of trapezoid $= \frac{1}{2}(2 + 4) \cdot 8$

$\quad\quad = 24$

area of 5 trapezoids = 5(24) = 120 yd^2

33. $\frac{x}{x + 13} = \frac{7}{12}$

$12x = 7(x + 13)$

$5x = 91$

$x = 18.2$ m

T(frustrum) $= L$(entire cone) $- L$(small cone) $+$

$\quad\quad A$(large circle) $+ A$(small circle)

$\quad = \pi(12)(31.2) - \pi(7)(18.2) +$

$\quad\quad \pi(12^2) + \pi(7^2)$

$\quad = 374.4\pi - 127.4\pi + 144\pi + 49\pi$

$\quad = 440\pi$

$\quad \approx 1382.3$ m^2

34. The lateral area approaches the area of the base. This can be seen by showing a series of cones cut on their slant heights and folded out into sectors. As the altitude approaches zero, the slant height approaches the radius of the base, and the sector narrows, approaching a complete circle.

35.

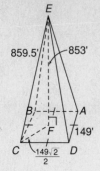 

$(AC)^2 = (AB)^2 + (BC)^2$

$(AC)^2 = 149^2 + 149^2$

$AC = 149\sqrt{2}$

$FC = \frac{1}{2}AC = \frac{149\sqrt{2}}{2}$

$(EC)^2 = (EF)^2 + (FC)^2$

$(EC)^2 = 853^2 + \left(\frac{149\sqrt{2}}{2}\right)2$

$EC \approx 859.48$

$859.48^2 = \ell^2 + (74.5)^2$

$\ell \approx 856.247$

$L = \frac{1}{2}P\ell$

$= \frac{1}{2}(596)(856.247)$

$\approx 255,161.7 \text{ ft}^2$

36. $\ell^2 = 250^2 + 210^2$

$\ell^2 = 106,600$

$\ell \approx 326.5$

$L = \pi r\ell$

$= \pi(210)(326.5)$

$\approx 215,401 \text{ ft}^2$

37. $r^2 = 56^2 - 32^2$

$r^2 = 2112$

$r \approx 46 \text{ ft}$

$\ell = 56'$ $h = 32'$ r

38. False

39. $A = \pi \cdot 2^2$

$= 4\pi$

$\approx 12.6 \text{ yd}^2$

40. The measure of the inscribed angle is half the measure of the central angle.

41. They are perpendicular.

42. See students' work.

Mid-Chapter Review

PAGE 547

1. T 2. $\overline{TO}$ 3. 6

4.

5. $T = 2\pi rh + 2\pi r^2$

$= 2\pi \cdot 6 \cdot 3 + 2\pi \cdot 36$

$= 108\pi \text{ in}^2$

6. $T = \pi r\ell + \pi r^2$

$= \pi \cdot 8 \cdot 14 + \pi \cdot 8^2$

$= 176\pi \text{ cm}^2$

7. $L = \frac{1}{2}P\ell$

$= \frac{1}{2} \cdot 96 \cdot 15$

$= 720 \text{ units}^2$

11-5   Volume of Prisms and Cylinders

PAGE 550   CHECKING FOR UNDERSTANDING

1. Sample answers: Topsoil, sand, and gravel are sold in cubic yards. Crude oil is sold in barrels. Grain and apples are sold in bushels and pecks. Milk is sold in pints, quarts, and gallons. Gasoline is sold in gallons.

2. 27 ft^3

3. Sample answer: A deck of playing cards might be used to develop the volume formula for a prism.

4. The volumes of two congruent geometric solids are equal.

5. $V = Bh$

$= 4^2 \cdot 3$

$= 48 \text{ m}^3$

6. $a^2 + 12^2 = 15^2$ $V = Bh$

$a^2 = 81$ $V = \frac{1}{2}(9 \cdot 12) \cdot 10$

$a = 9$

$= 540 \text{ cm}^3$

7. $V = Bh$ 8. $V = Bh$

$= \pi\left(3\frac{1}{2}\right)^2 \cdot 2$ $= 12(3.5)$

$\approx 77.0 \text{ in}^3$ $= 42 \text{ m}^3$

9. $V = Bh$

$\quad = \pi \cdot 2^2 \cdot 8$

$\quad = 32\pi \approx 100.5 \text{ m}^3$

10. $a^2 = 8^2 - 4^2$

$\quad a^2 = 48$

$\quad a = 4\sqrt{3}$

$\quad V = Bh$

$\quad V = \frac{1}{2} \cdot 48 \cdot 4\sqrt{3} \cdot 20$

$\quad \approx 3326 \text{ cm}^3$

11. $V = \frac{3}{4}(\pi r^2 h)$

$\quad = \frac{3}{4}(\pi \cdot 6^2 \cdot 23)$

$\quad \approx 1950.9 \text{ ft}^3$

12. $V = Bh$

$\quad = (5 \cdot 4) \cdot 2$

$\quad = 40 \text{ m}^3$

PAGES 551–553   EXERCISES

13. $V = Bh$

$\quad = 68(4)$

$\quad = 272 \text{ cm}^3$

14. $V = Bh$

$\quad = (9 \cdot 9) \cdot 9$

$\quad = 729 \text{ in}^3$

15. $\quad V = Bh$

$\quad 962 = 52 \cdot h$

$\quad 18.5 \text{ cm} = h$

16. $V = Bh$

$\quad = 17.5(14)$

$\quad = 245 \text{ cm}^3$

17. $V = 16(4.2)$

$\quad = 67.2 \text{ ft}^3$

18. $V = Bh$

$\quad = \pi(3.2)^2 \cdot 10.5$

$\quad = 107.52\pi \approx 337.8 \text{ cm}^3$

19. $V = Bh$

$\quad = \pi \cdot (1.5)^2 \cdot 4$

$\quad = 9\pi \approx 28.3 \text{ ft}^3$

20. $h^2 = 36^2 - 20^2$

$\quad h^2 = 896$

$\quad h = 8\sqrt{14}$

$\quad V = Bh$

$\quad = \left(\frac{1}{2} \cdot 40 \cdot 8\sqrt{14}\right) \cdot 25$

$\quad \approx 14{,}966.6 \text{ ft}^3$

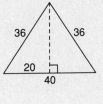

21. $h^2 = 17^2 - 8^2$

$\quad h^2 = 225$

$\quad h = 15$

$\quad V = \pi r^2 h$

$\quad V = \pi \cdot 4^2 \cdot 15$

$\quad = 240\pi \approx 754.0 \text{ cm}^3$

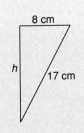

22. $V = Bh$

$\quad = \left(\frac{1}{2} \cdot 10 \cdot 10\sqrt{3}\right) \cdot 5$

$\quad \approx 433.0 \text{ in}^3$

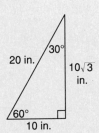

23. $V = (15 \cdot 10 \cdot 3) + (5 \cdot 10 \cdot 3)$

$\quad = 450 + 150$

$\quad = 600 \text{ m}^3$

24. $V = (16 \cdot 16 \cdot 8) + (8 \cdot 8 \cdot 6)$

$\quad = 2048 + 384$

$\quad = 2432 \text{ in}^3$

25. $V = Bh$

$\quad = \left(\frac{1}{2} \cdot 30 \cdot 2.5\sqrt{3}\right)40$

$\quad \approx 2598.1 \text{ in}^3$

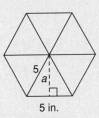

5 in.

$a = 2.5\sqrt{3}$

26. $V = Bh$

$\quad = \left[\frac{1}{2}(9 + 5) \cdot 3\right]20$

$\quad = 420 \text{ cm}^3$

27. a. $V = V(\text{block}) - V(\text{hole})$

$\quad = (10 \cdot 8 \cdot 15) - (\pi \cdot 2^2 \cdot 15)$

$\quad = 1200 - 188.5$

$\quad \approx 1011.5 \text{ mm}^3$

b. $1011.5 \text{ mm}^3 = 1.0115 \text{ cm}^3$

$\quad 1.0115(8.9) \approx 9.0 \text{ grams}$

28. $x^2 + x^2 = 12^2$

$\quad 2x^2 = 144$

$\quad x^2 = 72$

$\quad x = 6\sqrt{2}$

$\quad V = (6\sqrt{2})^3$

$\quad \approx 610.9 \text{ cm}^3$

29. $V = Bh$

$\quad = (12)(10)(3)$

$\quad = 360 \text{ cm}^3$

30. $V = \pi r^2 h$

$\quad = \pi \cdot (1.3)^2 \cdot 4.2$

$\quad = 7.098\pi$

$\quad \approx 22.3 \text{ in}^2$

31. $V(\text{pitcher}) = \pi \cdot 3^2 \cdot 14$

$\quad = 126\pi \approx 395.8 \text{ in}^3$

$V(\text{pan}) = 9 \cdot 12 \cdot 2$

$\quad = 216 \text{ in}^3$

No, the cake pan will not hold all the water.

32. $T = 6s^2$

$\quad 54 = 6s^2$

$\quad 9 = s^2$

$\quad 3 = s$

$\quad V = 3^3$

$\quad = 27 \text{ in}^3$

33. $s^3 = 6s^2$

$\quad s^3 - 6s^2 = 0$

$\quad s^2(s - 6) = 0$

$\quad s^2 = 0 \text{ or } s - 6 = 0$

$\quad s = 0 \qquad s = 6$

The edge of the cube is 6 units.

34. If one dimension is doubled, the volume would double. If two dimensions are doubled, the volume would quadruple.

35. Sample answer: Slice the oblique prism or cylinder parallel to its base to form a large number of pieces. Slide the pieces so that they stack as a right prism or cylinder. This sliding has not changed the volume or the height, and the volume of a right prism or cylinder is the area of the base times the height.

36. $V = \pi r^2 h$

$\quad = \pi \cdot 10^2 \cdot 6$

$\quad = 600\pi$

$V(\text{wedge}) = \dfrac{50}{360} \cdot \dfrac{600\pi}{1}$

$\qquad\qquad = \dfrac{250\pi}{3}$

$\qquad\qquad \approx 261.8 \text{ in}^3$

37. $V = \pi r^2 h$

$\quad = \pi \cdot 2^2 \cdot 30$

$\quad \approx 377 \text{ ft}^3$

1 cord $= 4 \times 4 \times 8 = 128 \text{ ft}^3$

$377 \div 128 \approx 2.9$ cords of wood

almost 3 cords

38. $V = 8 \cdot 12 \cdot 4$

$\quad - 384 \text{ ft}^3$

In one hour tank loses $3600(0.1) = 360 \text{ ft}^3$ of water.

$384 - 360 = 24 \text{ ft}^3$ of water left in tank

$\dfrac{24}{384} = 6.25\%$

39. a. $c^2 = 12^2 + 5^2$

$\quad c^2 = 169$

$\quad\ \ c = 13$

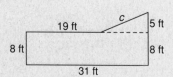

Perimeter $= 31 + 8 + 19 + 13 + 5 + 8$

$\qquad\qquad\ = 84$ feet

b. $V(\text{cement}) = V(\text{rectangle}) + V(\text{triangle})$

$\qquad = 8 \cdot 31 \cdot \dfrac{1}{2} + \dfrac{1}{2} \cdot 5 \cdot 12 \cdot \dfrac{1}{2}$

$\qquad = 139 \text{ ft}^3$ or about 5.15 yd^3

c. $\$2.65 \cdot 139 = \$368.35$

40. $L = \pi r \ell$

$\quad = \pi \cdot 3.2 \cdot 5.2$

$\quad = 16.64\pi$

$\quad \approx 52.3 \text{ mm}^2$

41. $x^2 = 5^2 - 4^2$

$\quad x^2 = 9$

$\quad\ \ x = 3$ cm

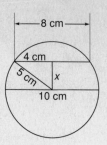

42. $\dfrac{6}{x} = \dfrac{10}{15}$ 43. $x^2 = 13^2 - 5^2$ 44. 42

$\quad 10x = 90$ $\qquad x^2 = 144$

$\quad\ \ x = 9$ $\qquad\ \ x = 12$

45. Area is a two-dimensional measurement, while volume is a three-dimensional measurement.

Prisms: $L = Ph$; $T = Ph + 2B$; $V = Bh$;

Cylinders: $L = 2\pi rh$; $T = 2\pi rh + 2\pi r^2$; $V = \pi r^2 h$

11-6 Volume of Pyramids and Cones

PAGES 556-557   CHECKING FOR UNDERSTANDING

1. Sample answer: Measure the radius and the height and use the formula for the volume of a cone.

2. The volume of a cone is one-third the volume of a cylinder with the same altitude and congruent bases.

3. Sample answer: Use an open pyramid and an open prism with the same base and the same height. Fill the pyramid with sand and pour the sand into the prism. Repeat this procedure until the prism is filled. The pyramid will have to be filled three times in order to fill the prism.

4. $V = \dfrac{1}{3}Bh$

$\quad = \dfrac{1}{3}(12 \cdot 10) \cdot 8$

$\quad = 320 \text{ in}^3$

5. $h^2 + r^2 = \ell^2$

$\quad h^2 + 5^2 = 13^2$

$\qquad\quad h^2 = 144$

$\qquad\qquad h = 12$

$\qquad V = \dfrac{1}{3}Bh$

$\qquad\quad = \dfrac{1}{3}(\pi \cdot 5^2) \cdot 12$

$\qquad\quad = 100\pi$

$\qquad\quad \approx 314.2 \text{ in}^3$

6. $A = \dfrac{1}{3}Bh$

$\quad = \dfrac{1}{3}\left(\dfrac{1}{2} \cdot 4\sqrt{3} \cdot 48\right)11$

$\quad \approx 609.7 \text{ cm}^3$

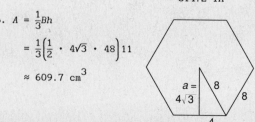

7. $V = V(\text{larger cone}) - V(\text{smaller cone})$

$\quad = \frac{1}{3}\pi \cdot 8^2 \cdot 11 - \frac{1}{3}\pi \cdot 8^2 \cdot 3$

$\quad = \frac{704\pi}{3} - \frac{192\pi}{3}$

$\quad = \frac{512\pi}{3}$

$\quad \approx 536.2 \text{ in}^3$

8. $V = \frac{1}{3}Bh$

$\quad = \frac{1}{3}\left(\frac{1}{2} \cdot 8 \cdot 4\sqrt{3}\right) \cdot 30$

$\quad \approx 277.1 \text{ m}^3$

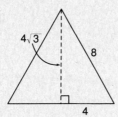

9. $V = \frac{1}{3}Bh$

$\quad = \frac{1}{3} \cdot \pi \cdot 9^2 \cdot 9\sqrt{3}$

$\quad \approx 1322.3 \text{ units}^3$

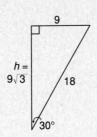

PAGES 557-559   EXERCISES

10. $V = \frac{1}{3}Bh$

$\quad = \frac{1}{3} \cdot 27.9 \cdot 18.5$

$\quad \approx 172.1 \text{ mm}^3$

11. $V = \frac{1}{3} \cdot 15 \cdot 7$

$\quad = 35 \text{ ft}^3$

12. $V = \frac{1}{3}B \cdot h$

$\quad = \frac{1}{3} \cdot \pi \cdot 5^2 \cdot 16$

$\quad \approx 418.9 \text{ ft}^3$

13. $V = \frac{1}{3} \cdot \pi \cdot (4.2)^2 \cdot 10.3$

$\quad \approx 190.3 \text{ m}^3$

14. $\qquad V = \frac{1}{3}Bh$

$\qquad 729 = \frac{1}{3} \cdot 243 \cdot h$

$\qquad \frac{729}{81} = h$

$\quad 9 \text{ units} = h$

15. $V = \frac{1}{3}Bh$

$\quad = \frac{1}{3} \cdot \pi \cdot 8^2 \cdot 21$

$\quad \approx 1407.4 \text{ units}^3$

16. $V = \frac{1}{3}Bh$

$\quad = \frac{1}{3} \cdot 30 \cdot 12 \cdot 8$

$\quad \approx 960 \text{ units}^3$

17. $V = V(\text{cylinder}) + V(\text{cone})$

$\quad = \pi \cdot 2^2 \cdot 8 + \frac{1}{3}\pi \cdot 2^2 \cdot 8$

$\quad \approx 134.0 \text{ cm}^3$

18. $r^2 = \ell^2 - h^2 \qquad\qquad V = \frac{1}{3}Bh$

$\quad r^2 = 13^2 - 12^2 \qquad\quad = \frac{1}{3} \cdot \pi \cdot 5^2 \cdot 12$

$\quad r^2 = 25 \qquad\qquad\qquad \approx 314.2 \text{ in}^3$

$\quad r = 5$

19. diagonal of base of pyramid:

$\quad d^2 = 16^2 + 16^2$

$\quad d^2 = 512$

$\quad d = \sqrt{512}$

$\quad \frac{1}{2}d = \frac{\sqrt{512}}{2}$

height of pyramid:

$\quad h^2 = 17^2 - \left(\frac{\sqrt{512}}{2}\right)^2 \qquad V = \frac{1}{3}Bh + s^3$

$\quad h^2 = 161 \qquad\qquad\qquad\quad = \frac{1}{3} \cdot 16^2 \cdot \sqrt{161} + 16^3$

$\quad h = \sqrt{161} \qquad\qquad\qquad\quad \approx 5178.8 \text{ m}^3$

20. $a^2 = 17^2 - 15^2$

$\quad a^2 = 64$

$\quad a = 8$

$\quad b = 16$

$\quad h^2 = 15^2 - 8^2 \qquad\qquad V = \frac{1}{3}Bh$

$\quad h^2 = 161 \qquad\qquad\qquad = \frac{1}{3} \cdot 16^2\sqrt{161}$

$\quad h = \sqrt{161} \qquad\qquad\qquad \approx 1082.8 \text{ m}^3$

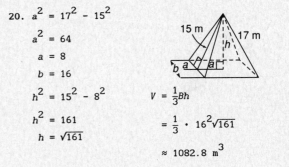

21. $d^2 = 24^2 + 24^2$

$\quad d^2 = 1152$

$\quad d = \sqrt{1152}$

$\quad \frac{1}{2}d = \frac{\sqrt{1152}}{2}$

$\quad h^2 = 17^2 - \left(\frac{\sqrt{1152}}{2}\right)^2$

$\quad h^2 = 1$

$\quad h = 1$

$\quad V = \frac{1}{3}Bh$

$\quad = \frac{1}{3} \cdot 24^2 \cdot 1$

$\quad = 192 \text{ units}^3$

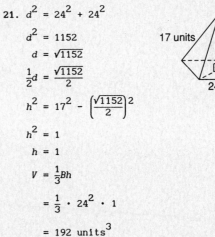

209

22. Divide the regular octahedron into 2 congruent pyramids. Base of the pyramids is a square whose side is 12 cm.

diagonal of base of pyramid:

$d^2 = 12^2 + 12^2$

$d^2 = 288$

$d = 12\sqrt{2}$

$\frac{1}{2}d = 6\sqrt{2}$ (base of triangle formed to find height of pyramid)

$h^2 = 12^2 - (6\sqrt{2})^2$

$h^2 = 72$

$h = 6\sqrt{2}$

volume of $\frac{1}{2}$ regular octahedron:

$V = \frac{1}{3}Bh$

$= \frac{1}{3} \cdot 12^2 \cdot 6\sqrt{2}$

$\approx 407.3 \text{ cm}^3$

$V(\text{octahedron}) \approx 2 \cdot 407.3$

$\approx 814.6 \text{ cm}^3$

23. **a.** $B(\text{shaded pyramid}) = \frac{1}{2} \cdot 6 \cdot 9$

$= 27$

$V = \frac{1}{3} \cdot 27 \cdot 12$

$= 108 \text{ units}^3$

b. 108 : 648

1 : 6

24. $V = \frac{1}{3}Bh$

$80 = \frac{1}{3}B \cdot 5$

$48 = B$

$48 = 1 \cdot 48$

$= 2 \cdot 24$

$= 3 \cdot 16$

$= 4 \cdot 12$

$= 6 \cdot 8$

5 possibilities

25. $V = V(\text{larger cone}) - V(\text{smaller cone})$

$V = \frac{1}{3}\pi \cdot \left(\frac{9}{2}\right)^2 \cdot 5 - \frac{1}{3}\pi \cdot 3^2 \cdot 5$

$= 33.75\pi - 15\pi$

$= 18.75\pi$

$\approx 58.9 \text{ in}^3$

26. $\sin 40° = \frac{h}{12}$

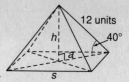

$h = 12 \sin 40°$

$h \approx 7.71$

$\cos 40° = \frac{a}{12}$

$a = 12 \cos 40°$

$a \approx 9.2$

diagonal of square base:

$2 \times 9.2 = 18.4$

Use Pythagorean Theorem to find s.

$s^2 + s^2 = (18.4)^2$

$2s^2 \approx 338$

$s^2 \approx 169$

$s \approx 13$

$V = \frac{1}{3}Bh$

$= \frac{1}{3} \cdot 13^2(12 \sin 40°)$

$\approx 435 \text{ units}^3$

27. $h^2 = 13^2 - 12^2$

$h^2 = 25$

$h = 5$

altitude of base = a

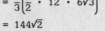

$a^2 = 12^2 - 2.5^2$

$a^2 = 137.75$

$a \approx 11.74$

area of base = B

$B \approx \frac{1}{2}(11.7)(5)$

≈ 29.35

$V = \frac{1}{3}Bh$

$= \frac{1}{3}(29.35)(5)$

$\approx 48.9 \text{ units}^3$

28. $h^2 = (6\sqrt{3})^2 - (2\sqrt{3})^2$

$h^2 = 96$

$h = \sqrt{96}$

$V = \frac{1}{3}Bh$

$= \frac{1}{3}\left(\frac{1}{2} \cdot 12 \cdot 6\sqrt{3}\right) \cdot \sqrt{96}$

$= 144\sqrt{2}$

$\approx 203.6 \text{ units}^3$

29. $h_1^{\,2} = 10^2 - 6^2$

$h_1^{\,2} = 64$

$h_1 = 8$

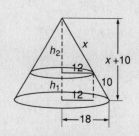

210

$$\frac{x}{x + 10} = \frac{12}{18}$$

$$18x = 12(x + 10)$$

$$6x = 120$$

$$x = 20$$

$$h_2{}^2 = 20^2 - 12^2$$

$$h_2{}^2 = 256$$

$$h_2 = 16$$

$V(\text{frustrum}) = V(\text{large cone}) - V(\text{small cone})$

$V(\text{frustrum}) = \frac{1}{3}\pi(18^2)(24) - \frac{1}{3}\pi(12^2)(16)$

$$= 2592\pi - 768\pi$$

$$= 1824\pi$$

$$\approx 5730.3 \text{ units}^3$$

30. Pyramid has 1 inch decrease in width for a 3 inch increase in height. There is a 6 inch decrease from base to top. So,

$$\frac{1}{3} = \frac{6}{x}$$

$x = 18$ inches
Pyramid is 18 inches high.

$V(\text{frustrum}) = V(\text{large pyramid})$
$\qquad\qquad\qquad - V(\text{small pyramid})$

$$= \frac{1}{3}(36)(18) - \frac{1}{3}(25)(15)$$

$$= 91 \text{ in}^3$$

31. $\ell = d$

$AB = CB$

If D is the center of the sphere,

$AD = CD = DB = 8$

By $30°$-$60°$-$90°$ Δ's

$$DE = \frac{1}{2}DB$$

$$= 4$$

$$EB = DB\sqrt{3}$$

$$= 4\sqrt{3}$$

$AE = AD + DE$

$AE = 8 + 4$

$AE = 12$

radius $= EB = 4\sqrt{3}$

$\qquad h = AE = 12$ in.

$B = \pi r^2 \qquad\qquad V = \frac{1}{3}Bh$

$\quad = \pi(4\sqrt{3})^2 \qquad\quad = \frac{1}{3}(48\pi)(12)$

$\quad = 48\pi \text{ in}^2 \qquad\qquad = 192\pi$

$\qquad\qquad\qquad\qquad\qquad \approx 603.2 \text{ in}^3$

32. a. $V = \frac{1}{3}(\pi r^2)h$

$\quad = \frac{1}{3}\pi \cdot 210^2 \cdot 250$

$\quad \approx 11{,}545{,}353 \text{ ft}^3$

b. $\dfrac{11{,}545{,}353 \text{ ft}^3}{\dfrac{10 \text{ ft}^3}{T}} \approx 1{,}154{,}535.3$ Tons

$\quad 1{,}154{,}535.3(0.115) \approx 132{,}771.6$ oz

c. $132{,}771.6(\$350) \approx \$46{,}470{,}060$

33. $V = \frac{1}{3}Bh$

$\quad = \frac{1}{3} \cdot 750^2 \cdot 481$

$\quad = 90{,}187{,}500 \text{ ft}^3$

34. Since the pile is 12 feet across at the building, the diameter of the semicircle is 12 feet. The pile is half of a cone.

$V = \frac{1}{2}\left(\frac{1}{3}\pi \cdot r^2 \cdot h\right)$

$\quad = \frac{1}{2}\left(\frac{1}{3}\pi(6^2)5\right)$

$\quad = 30\pi$

$\quad \approx 94.2 \text{ ft}^3$

35. The formula for the volume of a cone rounded to the nearest unit

36. Change line 30 to V = INT(3.14159 * R ^ 2 * H + 0.5)

37. See students' work.

38. $V = \ell wh$

$\quad = 3 \cdot 5 \cdot 8$

$\quad = 120 \text{ ft}^3$

39. area of unshaded regions

$= 2(\text{area of sector} - \text{area of triangle})$

$= 2\left(\frac{90}{360}(\pi)(3\sqrt{2})^2 - \frac{1}{2}(6)(3)\right)$

$= 2(4.5\pi - 9)$

$= 9\pi - 18$

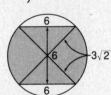

probability $= \dfrac{\text{area of shaded region}}{\text{area of circle}}$

$\qquad = \dfrac{\pi(3\sqrt{2})^2 - (9\pi - 18)}{\pi(3\sqrt{2})^2}$

$\qquad \approx 0.82$

40. They are complementary.

41. $AB = \sqrt{(0 - (-8))^2 + (4 - 1)^2}$

$\quad = \sqrt{8^2 + 3^2}$

$\quad = \sqrt{73}$

$\quad \approx 8.5$

42. If a cone and a cylinder have the same base and altitude, the volume of the cone is one-third the volume of the cylinder. If a pyramid and a prism have the same base and altitude, the volume of the pyramid is one-third the volume of the prism.

Surface Area and Volume of Spheres

PAGES 562-563   CHECKING FOR UNDERSTANDING

1. A transoceanic flight between two cities follows the great circle formed by a plane intersecting the sphere and passing through the two cities and the center of the sphere.

2. A plane and a sphere can intersect in a point (tangent) or a circle.

3. The intersection of a plane that contains the center of the sphere and the sphere is a great circle.

4. The volume of a sphere was generated by summing the volumes of an infinite number of small pyramids. Each pyramid has its base on the surface of the sphere and its height from the base to the center of the sphere.

5. True   6. False   7. True

8. $(RS)^2 = 25^2 - 7^2$ 9. $(PR)^2 = 13^2 - 12^2$

   $(RS)^2 = 576$ $(PR)^2 = 25$

     $RS = 24$ $PR = 5$

10. $T = 4\pi r^2$ $V = \frac{4}{3}\pi r^3$

     $= 4\pi \cdot 10^2$ $= \frac{4}{3}\pi \cdot 10^3$

     $\approx 1256.6 \text{ cm}^2$ $\approx 4188.8 \text{ cm}^3$

11. $A = \pi r^2$

      $50.24 = \pi \cdot r^2$

      $\frac{50.24}{\pi} = r^2$

      $\sqrt{\frac{50.24}{\pi}} = r$

        $T = 4\pi r^2$

         $= 4 \cdot \pi \cdot \left(\frac{50.24}{\pi}\right)$

         $\approx 200.96 \text{ cm}^2$

      $V = \frac{4}{3}\pi r^3$

         $= \frac{4}{3}\pi \cdot \left(\sqrt{\frac{50.24}{\pi}}\right)^3$

         $\approx 267.9 \text{ cm}^3$

12. $T = 4\pi r^2$ 13. $V = \frac{4}{3}\pi r^3$

   $256\pi = 4\pi r^2$ $= \frac{4}{3}\pi \cdot (4.75)^3$

     $64 = r^2$ $\approx 448.9 \text{ in}^3$

      $8 = r$

      $V = \frac{4}{3}\pi r^3$

        $= \frac{4}{3}\pi \cdot 8^3$

        $\approx 2144.7 \text{ cm}^3$

PAGES 563-565   EXERCISES

14. Sphere   15. Circle   16. Circle   17. Circle

18. Sphere   19. Circle   20. Sphere   21. Neither

22. Sphere   23. Neither   24. True   25. True

26. False   27. True   28. True   29. True

30. False   31. True   32. False

33. $(RS)^2 = 15^2 - 9^2$ 34. $(PR)^2 = 26^2 - 24^2$

    $(RS)^2 = 144$ $(PR)^2 = 100$

      $RS = 12$ $PR = 10$

35. $T = 4\pi r^2$ $V = \frac{4}{3}\pi r^3$

    $= 4\pi \cdot (2000)^2$ $= \frac{4}{3}\pi \cdot (2000)^3$

    $\approx 50,265,482 \text{ ft}^2$ $\approx 33,510,321,640 \text{ ft}^3$

36. $C = 2\pi r$

   $18.84 = 2\pi r$

    $\frac{9.42}{\pi} = r$

      $T = 4\pi r^2$

        $= 4\pi \cdot \left(\frac{9.42}{\pi}\right)^2$

        $\approx 113.0 \text{ m}^2$

      $V = \frac{4}{3}\pi r^3$

        $= \frac{4}{3}\pi \cdot \left(\frac{9.42}{\pi}\right)^3$

        $\approx 112.9 \text{ m}^3$

37. $V = \frac{4}{3}\pi r^3$

    $\frac{32}{3}\pi = \frac{4}{3}\pi r^3$

    $\frac{\frac{32}{3}\pi}{\frac{4}{3}\pi} = r^3$

       $8 = r^3$

    $2 \text{ in.} = r$

38. surface area of smaller sphere $= 4\pi r_1^2$

    surface area of larger sphere $= 4\pi r_2^2$

    $4(4\pi r_1^2) = 4\pi r_2^2$

     $16\pi r_1^2 = 4\pi r_2^2$

      $4r_1^2 = r_2^2$

      $2r_1 = r_2$

The ratio of the radii is 2:1.

39. $V(\text{hemisphere}) = \frac{1}{2} \cdot \frac{4}{3}\pi r^3 = \frac{2}{3}\pi r^3$

    $V(\text{cone}) = \frac{1}{3}\pi r^3$

     $\frac{2}{3}\pi r^3 : \frac{1}{3}\pi r^3$

       $\frac{2}{3} : \frac{1}{3}$

        $2 : 1$

40. $s^3 = 1728$

$s = 12$

diameter of sphere $= 12$

$r = 6$

$V = \frac{4}{3}\pi r^3$

$= \frac{4}{3}\pi \cdot 6^3$

$\approx 905 \text{ cm}^3$

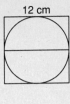

12 cm

41. d = diagonal of cube and diameter of sphere

c = diagonal of square

$c = 12\sqrt{2}$

$d^2 = 12^2 + (12\sqrt{2})^2$

$d^2 = 432$

$d = 12\sqrt{3}$

radius of sphere $= 6\sqrt{3}$

$V = \frac{4}{3}\pi r^3$

$= \frac{4}{3}\pi \cdot (6\sqrt{3})$

$\approx 4701 \text{ cm}^3$

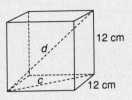

12 cm

12 cm

42. x = edge of cube, diameter and height of cylinder, and diameter of sphere

$T(\text{cube}) = 6x^2$

$T(\text{cylinder}) = 2\pi rh + 2\pi r^2$

$= 2\pi\left(\frac{x}{2}\right)x + 2\pi \cdot \left(\frac{x}{2}\right)^2$

$= \frac{3x^2}{2}\pi$

$T(\text{sphere}) = 4\pi r^2$

$= 4\pi\left(\frac{x}{2}\right)^2$

$= x^2\pi$

The sphere has the least surface area.

$V(\text{cube}) = x^3$

$V(\text{cylinder}) = \pi r^2 h$

$= \pi \cdot \left(\frac{x}{2}\right)^2 \cdot x$

$= \frac{\pi}{4}x^3$

$V(\text{sphere}) = \frac{4}{3}\pi r^3$

$= \frac{4}{3}\pi\left(\frac{x}{2}\right)^3$

$= \frac{\pi}{6}x^3$

The sphere has the least volume.

43. Answers will vary. Sample answers are given.

Labrador Sea; Glasgow, Scotland; Essen, Germany

44. $C = 2\pi r$

$27 = 2\pi r$

$\frac{27}{2\pi} = r$

$T = 4\pi r^2$

$= 4\pi\left(\frac{27}{2\pi}\right)^2$

$\approx 232.05 \text{ in}^2$

$V = \frac{4}{3}\pi r^3$

$= \frac{4}{3}\pi\left(\frac{27}{2\pi}\right)^3$

$\approx 332.38 \text{ in}^3$

45. $V(\text{hemisphere}) = \frac{1}{2} \cdot \frac{4}{3}\pi r^3$

$= \frac{2}{3}\pi\left(\frac{200}{3}\right)^3$

$\approx 620{,}561.5 \text{ yd}^3$

46. a. $V(\text{cone}) = \frac{1}{3}\pi r^2 h$

$= \frac{1}{3}\pi(2)^2 \cdot 10$

$\approx 41.89 \text{ cm}^3$

$V(\text{ice cream}) = \frac{4}{3}\pi r^3$

$= \frac{4}{3}\pi(2)^3$

$\approx 33.51 \text{ cm}^3$

No, the cone will not overflow.

b. $\frac{33.51}{41.89} \approx 80\%$

47. $T(\text{hemisphere}) = \frac{1}{2} \cdot 4\pi r^2$

$= 2\pi(40)^2$

$\approx 10{,}053.1 \text{ ft}^2$

48. a. $T = 4\pi r^2$

$= 4\pi(4000)^2$

$\approx 201{,}061{,}930 \text{ mi}^2$

b. $\frac{57{,}900{,}000}{201{,}061{,}930} \approx 28.8\%$

49. $V = \frac{1}{3}\pi r^2 h$

$= \frac{1}{3}\pi \cdot 5^2 \cdot 16$

$\approx 418.9 \text{ ft}^3$

50. median $= \frac{1}{2}(b_1 + b_2)$

$A = (\text{median})h$

$= 8.5(7.1)$

$= 60.35 \text{ ft}^2$

51. No, $(2.7)^2 + (3.0)^2 \overset{?}{=} (5.3)^2$

$16.29 \neq 28.09$

52. No; the bases may not be congruent.

53. $(11x - 45) + (8x + 35) = 180$

$19x - 10 = 180$

$19x = 190$

$x = 10$

54. The volume, since the radius is cubed. In the formula for surface area, the radius is only squared.

Chapter 11 Summary and Review

PAGES 566-568   SKILLS AND CONCEPTS

1. c   2. a   3. b

4. $L = Ph$ $T = Ph + 2B$

    $= 10(6)$ $= 60 + 2(3 \cdot 2)$

    $= 60 \text{ cm}^2$ $= 72 \text{ cm}^2$

5. $c^2 = 6^2 + 8^2$

    $c^2 = 100$

    $c = 10$

    $L = 24(11)$ $T = Ph + 2B$

      $= 264 \text{ in}^2$ $= 264 + 2\left(\frac{1}{2} \cdot 6 \cdot 8\right)$

                       $= 312 \text{ in}^2$

6. $L = 2\pi rh$ $T = 2\pi rh + 2\pi r^2$

    $= 2\pi \cdot 7 \cdot 10$

    $\approx 439.8 \text{ cm}^2$ $= 439.8 + 2\pi \cdot (7)^2$

                   $\approx 747.7 \text{ cm}^2$

7. $L = 2\pi rh$

    $= 2\pi \cdot (4.5)(7)$

    $\approx 197.9 \text{ ft}^2$

    $T = 2\pi rh + 2\pi r^2$

    $= 2\pi \cdot (4.5)(7) + 2\pi(4.5)^2$

    $\approx 325.2 \text{ ft}^2$

8. $L = \frac{1}{2}P\ell$ $T = L + B$

   $= \frac{1}{2} \cdot 12 \cdot 6$ $= 36 + 9$

                  $= 45 \text{ cm}^2$

    $= 36 \text{ cm}^2$

9. $\ell^2 = 5^2 - 3^2$ $T = L + B$

    $\ell^2 = 16$ $= 48 + 36$

    $\ell = 4$ $= 84 \text{ in}^2$

    $L = \frac{1}{2}P\ell$

     $= \frac{1}{2} \cdot 24 \cdot 4$

     $= 48 \text{ in}^2$

10. $L = \pi r\ell$ $T = \pi r\ell + \pi r^2$

    $= \pi \cdot 5 \cdot 13$

    $= 65\pi$ $= 65\pi + \pi \cdot 5^2$

    $\approx 204.2 \text{ ft}^2$ $\approx 282.7 \text{ ft}^2$

11. $L = \pi r\ell$ $T = \pi r\ell + \pi r^2$

    $= \pi \cdot 3.2 \cdot 5.2$

    $\approx 52.3 \text{ mm}^2$ $= 16.64\pi + \pi \cdot (3.2)^2$

                    $\approx 84.4 \text{ mm}^2$

12. $V = Bh$

    $= \frac{1}{2} \cdot 60 \cdot 5\sqrt{3} \cdot 20$

    $\approx 5196.2 \text{ cm}^3$

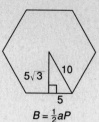

$B = \frac{1}{2}aP$

13. $V = \pi r^2 h$ 14. $V = \pi r^2 h$

    $= \pi \cdot 10^2 \cdot 20$ $= \pi \cdot 5^2 \cdot 13$

    $\approx 6283.2 \text{ cm}^3$ $\approx 1021.0 \text{ ft}^3$

15. $V = \frac{1}{3}Bh$

    $= \frac{1}{3} \cdot \frac{1}{2} \cdot 9 \cdot 4.5\sqrt{3} \cdot 15$

    $\approx 175.4 \text{ cm}^3$

16. $V = \frac{1}{3}Bh$

    $= \frac{1}{3} \cdot \pi \cdot 11^2 \cdot 22$

    $\approx 2787.6 \text{ cm}^3$

17. $C = 2\pi r$ $V = \frac{1}{3}Bh$

   $62.8 = 2\pi r$

   $\dfrac{62.8}{2\pi} = r$ $\approx \frac{1}{3}[\pi(10.0)^2] \cdot 15$

   $10.0 \approx r$ $\approx 1570.8 \text{ mm}^3$

18. Yes

19. $T = 4\pi r^2$ 20. $V = \frac{4}{3}\pi r^3$

    $= 4\pi \cdot 1080^2$ $= \frac{4}{3}\pi \cdot 20^3$

    $\approx 14,657,415 \text{ mi}^2$ $\approx 33,510.3 \text{ ft}^3$

PAGE 568   APPLICATIONS AND CONNECTIONS

21. 64 blocks, because $8^2 = 64$ and $4^3 = 64$

22. $T(\text{rectangular prism}) = Ph + 2B$

                      $= 10(2.5) + 2(2 \cdot 3)$

                      $= 37 \text{ units}^2$

  $T(\text{hexagonal prism}) = Ph + 2B$

                      $= 6(2.1)(2.3) + 2 \cdot \frac{1}{2} \cdot$

                      $1.05\sqrt{3} \cdot 12.6$

                      $\approx 51.9 \text{ units}^2$

Crystal with hexagonal base has the greater surface area.

23. $V = \ell wh$

    $= 6.5(5.5)(1)$

    $= 35.75 \text{ ft}^3$

Weight of waterbed $= 35.75(60)$

                      $= 2145 \text{ lb}$

24. volume of larger ball:

$$V = \frac{4}{3}\pi r^3$$

$$= \frac{4}{3}\pi \cdot (4.25)^3$$

$$\approx 321.6 \text{ cm}^3$$

volume of smaller ball:

$$V = \frac{4}{3}\pi r^3$$

$$= \frac{4}{3}\pi \cdot 4^3$$

$$\approx 268.1 \text{ cm}^3$$

volume of ball:

$$321.6 - 268.1 \approx 53.5 \text{ cm}^3$$

Chapter 11 Test

PAGE 569

1.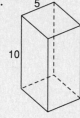

2.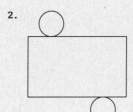

3. $T = Ph + 2B$

$$= 30 \cdot 10 + 2 \cdot \frac{1}{2} \cdot 2.5\sqrt{3} \cdot 30$$

$$\approx 429.9 \text{ ft}^2$$

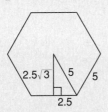

4. $T = 2\pi rh + 2\pi r^2$

$$= 2\pi \cdot 5 \cdot 10 + 2\pi \cdot 5^2$$

$$\approx 471.2 \text{ ft}^2$$

5. $T = \frac{1}{2}P\ell + B$

$$= \frac{1}{2} \cdot 69 \cdot 40 + \frac{1}{2} \cdot 23 \cdot 11.5\sqrt{3}$$

$$\approx 1609.1 \text{ cm}^2$$

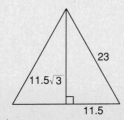

6. $\ell^2 = 30^2 + 27^2$

$$\ell^2 = 1629$$

$$\ell = \sqrt{1629}$$

$$T = \pi r\ell + \pi r^2$$

$$= \pi(27)\sqrt{1629} + \pi(27)^2$$

$$\approx 5713.8 \text{ mm}^2$$

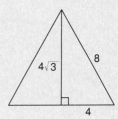

7. $T = 4\pi r^2$

$$= 4\pi(3)^2$$

$$\approx 113.1 \text{ in}^2$$

8. $V = Bh$

$$= \frac{1}{2} \cdot 8 \cdot 4\sqrt{3} \cdot 4$$

$$\approx 110.9 \text{ yd}^3$$

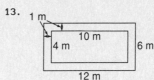

9. $V = \frac{1}{3}Bh$

$$= \frac{1}{3} \cdot 4^2 \cdot 6$$

$$= 32 \text{ in}^3$$

10. $V = \frac{1}{3}\pi r^2 h$

$$= \frac{1}{3}\pi(19.5)^2(50)$$

$$\approx 19,909.8 \text{ cm}^3$$

11. $V = \pi r^2 h$

$$= \pi(19.5)^2(50)$$

$$\approx 59,729.5 \text{ cm}^3$$

12. $V = \frac{4}{3}\pi r^3$

$$= \frac{4}{3}\pi(18)^3$$

$$\approx 24,429.0 \text{ mm}^3$$

13.

$V(\text{larger rectangle}) = \ell wh$

$$= 12(6)(0.1)$$

$$= 7.2 \text{ m}^3$$

$V(\text{smaller rectangle}) = \ell wh$

$$= 10(4)(0.1)$$

$$= 4 \text{ m}^3$$

$V(\text{concrete}) = 7.2 \text{ m}^3 - 4 \text{ m}^3$

$$= 3.2 \text{ m}^3$$

14. $c^2 = 8^2 + 6^2$

$$c^2 = 100$$

$$c = 10$$

$$L = Ph$$

$$= 24(16)$$

$$= 384 \text{ in}^2$$

15. $V(\text{cylinder}) = \pi r^2 h$

$\quad\quad = \pi \cdot 5^2 \cdot 15$

$\quad\quad \approx 1178.1 \text{ cm}^3$

$h^2 = 13^2 - 5^2$

$h^2 = 144$

$\quad h = 12$

$V(\text{cone}) = \frac{1}{3}\pi r^2 h$

$\quad\quad = \frac{1}{3}\pi \cdot 5^2 \cdot 12$

$\quad\quad \approx 314.2 \text{ cm}^3$

$V = V(\text{cylinder}) + V(\text{cone})$

$\quad = 1178.1 + 314.2$

$\quad = 1492.3 \text{ cm}^3$

BONUS

width $= x$

length $= 2x$

height $= 2(2x) = 4x$

$\quad V = Bh$

$216 = x(2x)(4x)$

$216 = 8x^3$

$\quad 27 = x^3$

$\quad\; 3 = x$

width $= 3$, length $= 6$, height $= 12$

$T = Ph + 2B$

$\quad = 18(12) + 2(18)$

$\quad = 252 \text{ ft}^2$

Algebra Review

PAGES 570-571

1. $|y - 1| \le 5$

$\quad y - 1 \le 5$ or $-(y - 1) \le 5$

$\quad\quad y \le 6 \quad\quad -y + 1 \le 5$

$\quad\quad\quad\quad\quad\quad\quad -y \le 4$

$\quad\quad\quad\quad\quad\quad\quad\quad y \ge -4$

$\{y | -4 \le y \le 6\}$

2. $|2 - n| = 5$

$\quad 2 - n = 5$ or $-(2 - n) = 5$

$\quad\quad -n = 3 \quad\quad -2 + n = 5$

$\quad\quad\; n = -3 \quad$ or $\quad n = 7$

$\{n | n = -3 \text{ or } n = 7\}$

3. $\left| 2p - \frac{1}{2} \right| > \frac{9}{2}$

$\quad 2p - \frac{1}{2} > \frac{9}{2}$ or $-\left(2p - \frac{1}{2}\right) > \frac{9}{2}$

$\quad\quad 2p > 5 \quad\quad -2p + \frac{1}{2} > \frac{9}{2}$

$\quad\quad p > \frac{5}{2} \quad\quad\quad -2p > 4$

$\quad\quad\quad\quad\quad\quad\quad p < -2$

$\left\{ p \middle| p < -2 \text{ or } p > \frac{5}{2} \right\}$

4. $|7a - 10| < 0$

$\quad 7a - 10 < 0$ or $-(7a - 10) < 0$

$\quad\quad 7a < 10 \quad\quad -7a + 10 < 0$

$\quad\quad a < \frac{10}{7} \quad\quad\quad -7a < -10$

$\quad\quad\quad\quad\quad\quad\quad a > \frac{10}{7}$

$\varnothing$

5. $\dfrac{x}{x^2 + 3x + 2} + \dfrac{1}{x^2 + 3x + 2}$

$\quad = \dfrac{x + 1}{x^2 + 3x + 2}$

$\quad = \dfrac{x + 1}{(x + 1)(x + 2)}$

$\quad = \dfrac{1}{x + 2}$

6. $\dfrac{2x}{4x^2 - 9} - \dfrac{3}{9 - 4x^2}$

$\quad = \dfrac{2x}{4x^2 - 9} + \dfrac{3}{4x^2 - 9}$

$\quad = \dfrac{2x + 3}{4x^2 - 9}$

$\quad = \dfrac{2x + 3}{(2x + 3)(2x - 3)}$

$\quad = \dfrac{1}{2x - 3}$

7. $\dfrac{x}{x + 3} - \dfrac{5}{x - 2}$

$\quad = \dfrac{x(x - 2) - 5(x + 3)}{(x + 3)(x - 2)}$

$\quad = \dfrac{x^2 - 2x - 5x - 15}{(x + 3)(x - 2)}$

$\quad = \dfrac{x^2 - 7x + 15}{x^2 + x - 6}$

8. $\dfrac{2x + 3}{x^2 - 4} + \dfrac{6}{x + 2}$

$\quad = \dfrac{2x + 3}{(x + 2)(x - 2)} + \dfrac{6}{x + 2}$

$\quad = \dfrac{2x + 3 + 6(x - 2)}{(x + 2)(x - 2)}$

$\quad = \dfrac{2x + 3 + 6x - 12}{(x + 2)(x - 2)}$

$\quad = \dfrac{8x - 9}{x^2 - 4}$

9. $x = 2y$

$x + y = 6$

$2y + y = 6$

$3y = 6$

$y = 2$

$x = 2y$

$x = 2 \cdot 2 = 4$

(4, 2)

10. $2m + n = 1$

$m - n = 8$

$m = 8 + n$

Substitute: $2m + n = 1$

$2(8 + n) + n = 1$

$16 + 2n + n = 1$

$3n = -15$

$n = -5$

$m = 8 + n$

$m = 8 + (-5) = 3$

(3, -5)

11. $3a - 2b = -4$

$3a + b = 2$

Solve $3a + b = 2$ for b:

$b = 2 - 3a$

Substitute in $3a - 2b = -4$

$3a - 2(2 - 3a) = -4$

$3a - 4 + 6a = -4$

$9a = 0$

$a = 0$

$b = 2 - 3a$

$b = 2 - 3(0) = 2$

(0, 2)

12. $3x - y = 1$

$2x + 4y = 3$

Solve $3x - y = 1$ for y.

$-y = -3x + 1$

$y = 3x - 1$

Substitute in $2x + 4y = 3$

$2x + 4(3x - 1) = 3$

$2x + 12x - 4 = 3$

$14x = 7$

$x = \frac{1}{2}$

$y = 3x - 1$

$y = 3\left(\frac{1}{2}\right) - 1$

$y = \frac{3}{2} - \frac{2}{2} = \frac{1}{2}$

$\left(\frac{1}{2}, \frac{1}{2}\right)$

13. $\frac{11}{20}$ or 0.55   14. $\frac{25}{100}$ or 0.25

15.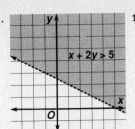

16.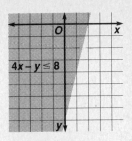

17.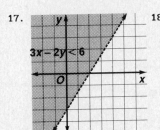

18.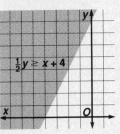

19. $2\sqrt{13} + 8\sqrt{15} - 3\sqrt{15} + 3\sqrt{13} = 5\sqrt{13} + 5\sqrt{15}$

20. $4\sqrt{27} + 6\sqrt{48}$

$= 4\sqrt{9} \cdot \sqrt{3} + 6\sqrt{16} \cdot \sqrt{3}$

$= 4 \cdot 3 \cdot \sqrt{3} + 6 \cdot 4 \cdot \sqrt{3}$

$= 12\sqrt{3} + 24\sqrt{3}$

$= 36\sqrt{3}$

21. $5\sqrt{18} - 3\sqrt{112} - 3\sqrt{98}$

$= 5 \cdot \sqrt{9} \cdot \sqrt{2} - 3 \cdot \sqrt{16} \cdot \sqrt{7} - 3\sqrt{49} \cdot \sqrt{2}$

$= 5 \cdot 3 \cdot \sqrt{2} - 3 \cdot 4 \cdot \sqrt{7} - 3 \cdot 7 \cdot \sqrt{2}$

$= 15\sqrt{2} - 12\sqrt{7} - 21\sqrt{2}$

$= -6\sqrt{2} - 12\sqrt{7}$

22. $\sqrt{8} + \sqrt{\dfrac{1}{8}}$

$= \sqrt{4} \cdot \sqrt{2} + \sqrt{\dfrac{1}{4}} \cdot \sqrt{\dfrac{1}{2}}$

$= 2\sqrt{2} + \dfrac{1}{2} \cdot \dfrac{\sqrt{1}}{\sqrt{2}}$

$= 2\sqrt{2} + \dfrac{1}{2\sqrt{2}}$

$= 2\sqrt{2} + \dfrac{1}{2\sqrt{2}} \cdot \dfrac{\sqrt{2}}{2}$

$= 2\sqrt{2} + \dfrac{\sqrt{2}}{4}$

$= \dfrac{8\sqrt{2}}{4} + \dfrac{\sqrt{2}}{4}$

$= \dfrac{9\sqrt{2}}{4}$

23. $x = \dfrac{-b \pm \sqrt{b^2 - 4ac}}{2a}$

$x^2 - 8x - 20 = 0$

$x = \dfrac{-(-8) \pm \sqrt{(-8)^2 - 4(1)(-20)}}{2(1)}$

$x = \dfrac{8 \pm \sqrt{144}}{2}$

$x = \dfrac{8 + 12}{2}$ or $x = \dfrac{8 - 12}{2}$

$x = 10$ or $x = -2$

24. $5b^2 + 9b + 3 = 0$

$b = \dfrac{-9 \pm \sqrt{9^2 - 4(5)(3)}}{2(5)}$

$b = \dfrac{-9 \pm \sqrt{21}}{10}$

$b = \dfrac{-9 \pm \sqrt{21}}{10}$ or $\dfrac{-9 - \sqrt{21}}{10}$

≈ -0.44 or -1.36

25. $9k^2 - 12k - 1 = 0$

$k = \dfrac{-(-12) \pm \sqrt{(-12)^2 - 4(9)(-1)}}{2(9)}$

$k = \dfrac{12 \pm \sqrt{180}}{18}$

$k = \dfrac{12 + 6\sqrt{5}}{18}$ or $\dfrac{12 - 6\sqrt{5}}{18}$

$k = \dfrac{2 + \sqrt{5}}{3}$ or $\dfrac{2 - \sqrt{5}}{3}$

≈ 1.41 or -0.08

26. $2m^2 - \dfrac{17m}{6} + 1 = 0$

$12m^2 - 17m + 6 = 0$

$m = \dfrac{-(-17) \pm \sqrt{(-17)^2 - 4(12)(6)}}{2(12)}$

$m = \dfrac{17 \pm \sqrt{1}}{24}$

$m = \dfrac{17 + 1}{24}$ or $\dfrac{17 - 1}{24}$

$m = \dfrac{3}{4}$ or $\dfrac{2}{3}$

27. x = part invested at 8%

$10,000 - x$ = part invested at 6%

$0.08x + 0.06(10,000 - x) = 760$

$0.08x + 600 - 0.06x = 760$

$0.02x = 160$

$x = 8000$

$10,000 - x = 2000$

$2000 at 6%, $8000 at 8%

28.
$$h = 1440t - 16t^2$$
$$25,000 = 1440t - 16t^2$$

$16t^2 - 1440t + 25,000 = 0$

$8(2t^2 - 180t + 3125) = 0$

$t = \dfrac{-(-180) \pm \sqrt{(-180)^2 - 4(2)(+3125)}}{2(2)}$

$t = \dfrac{180 \pm \sqrt{7400}}{4}$

$t \approx \dfrac{180 \pm 86.0}{4}$

$t \approx 66.5$ sec or 23.5 sec

$16t^2 - 1440t + 35,000 = 0$

$8(2t^2 - 180t + 4375) = 0$

$t = \dfrac{-(-180) \pm \sqrt{(-180)^2 - 4(2)(4375)}}{2(2)}$

$t = \dfrac{180 \pm \sqrt{-2600}}{4}$

This rocket will never reach a height of 35,000 ft.

29.

difference		3	2	5	
miles	2		5		10
cost	6.30		11.25		19.50
difference		4.95	3.3	8.25	

It cost $3.30 to travel 2 miles or $1.65 per mile.

Total cost - cost for 2 miles = base charge

$6.30 - 3.30 = $3 base charge

Let x = number of miles traveled and

y = total cost.

$y = 1.65x + 3$

It cost $4.65 for a one-mile trip.

30. area of entire region:

$A = 2x(x + 3)$

$= 2x^2 + 6x$

area of white region:

$A = x(x + 2)$

$= x^2 + 2x$

area of shaded region:

$A = (2x^2 + 6x) - (x^2 + 2x)$

$= x^2 + 4x$

Chapter 12   More Coordinate Geometry

PAGES 576-577   CHECKING FOR UNDERSTANDING

1. $x = 4$; A vertical line means x always equals one value, in this case 4, and y can equal anything.
2. False; horizontal lines are parallel to the x-axis.
3. They have the same value for m when expressed in slope-intercept form.
4. intercepts, slope-intercept; Answers may vary.
5. Sample answer: Move down 1 and to the left 2; move up 2 and to the right 4.
6. Yes; x and y are to the first power.
7. No; y is squared.
8. No; x is cubed.
9. Yes; x is to the first power.
10. No; x and y are both squared.
11. Yes; x and y are to the first power.

12.

x-intercept	y-intercept
$y = x$	$y = x$
$0 = x$	$y = 0$

13.

x-intercept	y-intercept
$4x - y = 4$	$4x - y = 4$
$4x - 0 = 4$	$4(0) - y = 4$
$4x = 4$	$-y = 4$
$x = 1$	$y = -4$

14.

x-intercept	y-intercept
$x + 2y = 6$	$x + 2y = 6$
$x + 2(0) = 6$	$0 + 2y = 6$
$x = 6$	$2y = 6$
	$y = 3$

15.

x-intercept	y-intercept
$x = 4$	none

16.

x-intercept	y-intercept
$y + 3 = x$	$y + 3 = x$
$0 + 3 = x$	$y + 3 = 0$
$3 = x$	$y = -3$

17.

x-intercept	y-intercept
$3x - 6y = 6$	$3x - 6y = 6$
$3x - 6(0) = 6$	$3(0) - 6y = 6$
$3x = 6$	$-6y = 6$
$x = 2$	$y = -1$

18. parallel; -3, -3

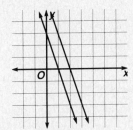

19. neither; 1, $\frac{1}{2}$

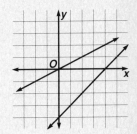

20. parallel; $\frac{1}{2}$, $\frac{1}{2}$

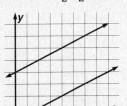

21. parallel; 0, 0

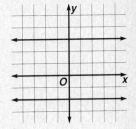

22. perpendicular; $\frac{3}{4}$, $-\frac{4}{3}$

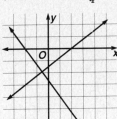

23. parallel; -1, -1

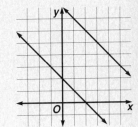

PAGES 577-579   EXERCISES

24.

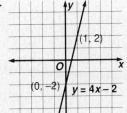

25.

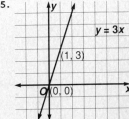

26.

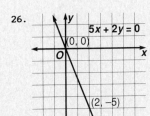

27.

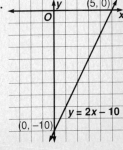

219

28.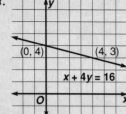

29.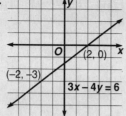

30. parallel; −1, −1

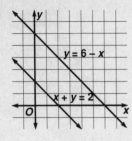

31. parallel; 5, 5

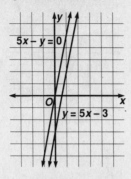

32. perpendicular; $-\frac{1}{2}$**, 2**

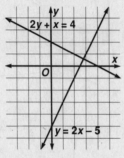

33. $y = x$
$m = 1; b = 0$

34. $3x + y = 5$
$\qquad y = -3x + 5$
$m = -3; b = 5$

35. $3x + 4y = 8$
$\qquad y = -\frac{3}{4}x + 2$
$m = -\frac{3}{4}; b = 2$

36. $y = 6$
$m = 0; b = 6$

37. $x = 9$
$m = $ undefined;
$b = $ none

38. $2x + y = 6$
$\qquad y = -2x + 6$
$m = -2; b = 6$

39.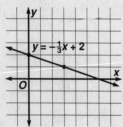

40.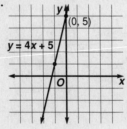

41.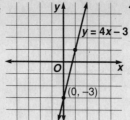

42.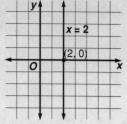

43.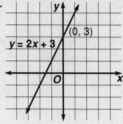

44.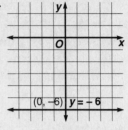

45.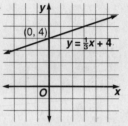

46.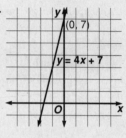

47.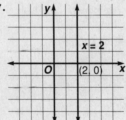

48. Student graphs will vary. All are of the form $y = 2x + b$, but all have a different value for b.

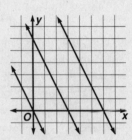

49. Student graphs will vary. All are of the form $y = mx + 3$, but all have a different value for m.

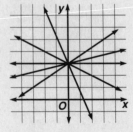

220

50. $x = a$

51. The line with equation $y = \frac{2}{3}x$ is perpendicular to both of the given lines. Find the points where this line intersects the given lines.

$$3x + 2y = 10 \qquad\qquad 3x + 2y = 4$$
$$3x + 2\left(\frac{2}{3}x\right) = 10 \qquad 3x + 2\left(\frac{2}{3}x\right) = 4$$
$$3x + \frac{4}{3}x = 10 \qquad\qquad 3x + \frac{4}{3}x = 4$$
$$\frac{13}{3}x = 10 \qquad\qquad\quad \frac{13}{3}x = 4$$
$$x = \frac{30}{13} \qquad\qquad\quad x = \frac{12}{13}$$
$$y = \frac{2}{3}x \qquad\qquad\qquad y = \frac{2}{3}x$$
$$= \frac{2}{3}\left(\frac{30}{13}\right) \qquad\qquad = \frac{2}{3}\left(\frac{12}{13}\right)$$
$$= \frac{20}{13} \qquad\qquad\qquad = \frac{8}{13}$$
$$\left(\frac{30}{13}, \frac{20}{13}\right) \qquad\qquad \left(\frac{12}{13}, \frac{8}{13}\right)$$

Find the midpoint of the segment with endpoints $\left(\frac{30}{13}, \frac{20}{13}\right)$ and $\left(\frac{12}{13}, \frac{8}{13}\right)$.

$$M = \left(\frac{\frac{30}{13} + \frac{12}{13}}{2}, \frac{\frac{20}{13} + \frac{8}{13}}{2}\right) = \left(\frac{\frac{42}{13}}{2}, \frac{\frac{28}{13}}{2}\right) =$$
$$\left(\frac{21}{13}, \frac{14}{13}\right)$$

The line with a slope of $-\frac{3}{2}$ passing through the point $\left(\frac{21}{13}, \frac{14}{13}\right)$ is parallel to the given lines and midway between them.

$$y = mx + b$$
$$\frac{14}{13} = \left(-\frac{3}{2}\right)\left(\frac{21}{13}\right) + b$$
$$\frac{14}{13} = -\frac{63}{26} + b$$
$$\frac{7}{2} = b$$
$$y = -\frac{3}{2}x + \frac{7}{2}$$
$$2y = -3x + 7$$
$$3x + 2y = 7$$

52. The road has an 8% grade, so the slope of the road is $\frac{8}{100}$ or $\frac{2}{25}$. So, if the horizontal change is represented by x, then the vertical change is $\frac{2}{25}x$.

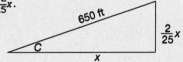

Use the tangent ratio to find the measure of angle C.

$$\tan C = \frac{\frac{2}{25}x}{x} \text{ or } \frac{2}{25}$$
$$C \approx 4.57$$

Use the sine ratio to find the rise of the road.

$$\sin 4.57° \approx \frac{\text{rise}}{650}$$
$$\text{rise} \approx 650 \sin 4.57°$$
$$\approx 51.8 \text{ feet}$$

53. a. 200
    b. 1400
    c.
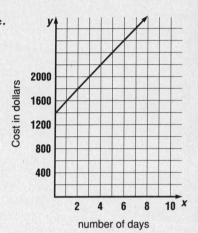

54. $V = \frac{4}{3}\pi r^3$
$$= \frac{4}{3}\pi(5)^3$$
$$= \frac{500}{3}\pi$$
$$\approx 523.6 \text{ in}^3$$

55. $T = 4\pi r^2$
$$= 4\pi(3)^2$$
$$= 36\pi$$
$$\approx 113.1 \text{ ft}^2$$

56. $m = \frac{0 - (-2)}{3 - 8}$
$$= \frac{2}{-5}$$
$$= -\frac{2}{5}$$

57.
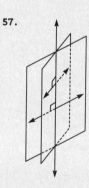

58. $\qquad m\angle 1 + m\angle 2 = 180$
$$2x + 15 + 8x - 5 = 180$$
$$10x + 10 = 180$$
$$10x = 170$$
$$x = 17$$
$$m\angle 1 = 2x + 15$$
$$= 2(17) + 15$$
$$= 49$$
$$m\angle 2 = 8x - 5$$
$$= 8(17) - 5$$
$$= 131$$

59. If it snows Saturday, then we will have to rent skis; law of syllogism.

60. See students' work.

221

Writing Equations of Lines

1. a. No; many lines pass through a point.

   b. No; many lines have the same slope.

   c. Yes; use the 2 points to determine the slope. Then substitute the slope and the coordinates of one point in $y = mx + b$ and solve for b.

   d. Yes; substitute the slope and coordinates of the point in $y = mx + b$ and solve for b.

2. a. $y = 1.2x + 5.3$ b. $y = 1.2x + 5.3$
   $$= 1.2(10) + 5.3$$
   $$= 17.3 \text{ million}$$

3. $m = \dfrac{8 - 4}{6 - 2}$
   $$= \dfrac{4}{4} \text{ or } 1$$

4. $m = \dfrac{-3 - (-2)}{6 - 3}$
   $$= \dfrac{-1}{3} \text{ or } -\dfrac{1}{3}$$
   $$b = -1$$
   $$y = -\dfrac{1}{3}x - 1$$

5. $y = mx + b$
   $$y = 4x + 2$$

6. $y = mx + b$
   $$y = -\dfrac{1}{2}x + 1$$

7. $y - y_1 = m(x - x_1)$
   $$y - 3 = 5(x - (-1))$$
   $$y - 3 = 5x + 5$$
   $$y = 5x + 8$$

8. $y - 0 = -3(x - 6)$
   $$y = -3x + 18$$

9. $m = \dfrac{4 - (-6)}{-7 - (-5)}$
   $$= \dfrac{10}{-2} \text{ or } -5$$
   $$y - 4 = -5(x - (-7))$$
   $$y - 4 = -5x - 35$$
   $$y = -5x - 31$$

10. $m = \dfrac{-1 - (-7)}{6 - (-3)}$
   $$= \dfrac{6}{9} \text{ or } \dfrac{2}{3}$$
   $$y - (-1) = \dfrac{2}{3}(x - 6)$$
   $$y + 1 = \dfrac{2}{3}x - 4$$
   $$y = \dfrac{2}{3}x - 5$$

11. $m = 3$
   $$y - 7 = 3(x - 3)$$
   $$y - 7 = 3x - 9$$
   $$y = 3x - 2$$

12. $m = 3$
   $$y - 2 = 3(x - 1)$$
   $$y - 2 = 3x - 3$$
   $$y = 3x - 1$$

13. $m = \dfrac{1 - 3}{2 - 3}$
   $$= \dfrac{-2}{-1} \text{ or } 2$$
   $$b = -3$$
   $$y = 2x - 3$$

14. $m = \dfrac{5 - 4}{4 - 0}$
   $$= \dfrac{1}{4}$$
   $$b = 4$$
   $$y = \dfrac{1}{4}x + 4$$

15. $m = \dfrac{0 - (-1)}{1 - 0}$
   $$= \dfrac{1}{1} \text{ or } 1$$
   $$b = -1$$
   $$y = x - 1$$

16. $y - y_1 = m(x - x_1)$
   $$y - (-4) = 3(x - 1)$$
   $$y + 4 = 3x - 3$$
   $$y = 3x - 7$$

17. $y - (-3) = \dfrac{1}{6}(x - 12)$
   $$y + 3 = \dfrac{1}{6}x - 2$$
   $$y = \dfrac{1}{6}x - 5$$

18. $y - 2 = -\dfrac{2}{3}(x - (-3))$
   $$y - 2 = -\dfrac{2}{3}x - 2$$
   $$y = -\dfrac{2}{3}x$$

19. $y - (-2) = -4(x - (-3))$
   $$y + 2 = -4x - 12$$
   $$y = -4x - 14$$

20. $y - 0 = -1(x - 5)$
   $$y = -x + 5$$

21. $y - 7 = 0(x - 7)$
   $$y - 7 = 0$$
   $$y = 7$$

22. $y = 0x + 7$
   $$y = 7$$

23. $y = -2x + 1$

24. $y = \dfrac{3}{4}x + 8$

25. $y - 3 = -\dfrac{1}{2}(x - 5)$
   $$y - 3 = -\dfrac{1}{2}x + \dfrac{5}{2}$$
   $$y = -\dfrac{1}{2}x + \dfrac{11}{2}$$

26. $y - 1 = 6(x - (-3))$
   $$y - 1 = 6x + 18$$
   $$y = 6x + 19$$

27. $m = -4$
   $$y - 1 = -4(x - (-3))$$
   $$y - 1 = -4x - 12$$
   $$y = -4x - 11$$

28. m is undefined
   $$x = 3$$

29. $m = 0$
   $$y = 2$$

30. $m = \dfrac{3 - (-3)}{0 - 4}$
   $$= \dfrac{6}{-4} \text{ or } -\dfrac{3}{2}$$
   $$y - 3 = -\dfrac{3}{2}(x - 0)$$
   $$y = -\dfrac{3}{2}x + 3$$

31. $m = \dfrac{-4 - 7}{9 - (-2)}$
   $$= \dfrac{-11}{11} \text{ or } -1$$
   $$y - (-4) = -1(x - 9)$$
   $$y + 4 = -x + 9$$
   $$y = -x + 5$$

32. slope of segment $= \dfrac{5 - (-1)}{2 - (-2)}$
   $$= \dfrac{6}{4} \text{ or } \dfrac{3}{2}$$

   slope of perpendicular $= -\dfrac{2}{3}$

   midpoint $= \left(\dfrac{2 + (-2)}{2}, \dfrac{5 + (-1)}{2}\right)$ or $(0, 2)$

   $$y - 2 = -\dfrac{2}{3}(x - 0)$$
   $$y = -\dfrac{2}{3}x + 2$$

33. midpoint $= \left(\dfrac{-4 + 5}{2},\ \dfrac{10 + (-7)}{2}\right)$ or $\left(\dfrac{1}{2},\ \dfrac{3}{2}\right)$

$y - \dfrac{3}{2} = -5\left(x - \dfrac{1}{2}\right)$

$y - \dfrac{3}{2} = -5x + \dfrac{5}{2}$

$y = -5x + 4$

34. slope of segment $= \dfrac{-7 - 1}{-3 - 5}$

$\qquad\qquad\qquad = \dfrac{-8}{-8}$ or 1

slope of perpendicular $= -1$

midpoint $= \left(\dfrac{-3 + 5}{2},\ \dfrac{-7 + 1}{2}\right)$ or $(1, -3)$

$y - (-3) = -1(x - 1)$

$\quad y + 3 = -x + 1$

$\qquad\quad y = -x - 2$

35. $m = \dfrac{3}{4}$

$y - 5 = \dfrac{3}{4}(x - (-4))$

$y - 5 = \dfrac{3}{4}x + 3$

$\quad\; y = \dfrac{3}{4}x + 8$

36. The center of the circle is $(0, 3)$. The segment from the center to a point on the circle is perpendicular to the line tangent to the circle at that point.

slope of segment from center to $(4, 0) = \dfrac{0 - 3}{4 - 0}$

or $-\dfrac{3}{4}$

The slope of the tangent is $\dfrac{4}{3}$.

$y - 0 = \dfrac{4}{3}(x - 4)$

$\quad\; y = \dfrac{4}{3}x - \dfrac{16}{3}$

37. The line passes through points $(s, 0)$ and $(0, t)$.

So the slope is $\dfrac{t - 0}{0 - s}$ or $-\dfrac{t}{s}$.

$y - 0 = -\dfrac{t}{s}(x - s)$

$\quad\; y = -\dfrac{tx}{s} + t$

38. a. $360x$ gallons   **b.** $y = 2880 - 360x$

c.

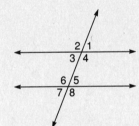

d. Without getting new stock, they would run out of paint in 8 weeks. So they should order paint in 5 weeks.

39. $y = 12x + 900$

40. See students' work.

41. $m = \dfrac{3}{2},\ b = -\dfrac{3}{4}$

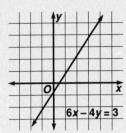

$6x - 4y = 3$

42.

$b^2 = a^2 + c^2 - 2ac \cos B$

$b^2 = 8^2 + 5^2 - 2(8)(5) \cos 116°$

$b^2 \approx 124.1$

$b = AC \approx 11.1$

$\dfrac{\sin A}{a} = \dfrac{\sin B}{b}$

$\dfrac{\sin A}{8} = \dfrac{\sin 116°}{11.1}$

$\sin A = \dfrac{8 \sin 116°}{11.1}$

$A \approx 40.4°$

$\dfrac{\sin C}{c} = \dfrac{\sin B}{b}$

$\dfrac{\sin C}{5} = \dfrac{\sin 116°}{11.1}$

$C \approx 23.9°$

43. Given: $\angle 4 \cong \angle 6$

Prove: $\angle 3 \cong \angle 5$

STATEMENTS	REASONS
1. $\angle 4 \cong \angle 6$	1. Given
2. $\angle 3$ and $\angle 4$ form a linear pair. $\angle 5$ and $\angle 6$ form a linear pair.	2. Definition of linear pair
3. $\angle 3$ and $\angle 4$ are supplementary. $\angle 5$ and $\angle 6$ are supplementary.	3. If 2 $\angle$s form a linear pair, they are supp.
4. $m\angle 3 + m\angle 4 = 180$ $m\angle 5 + m\angle 6 = 180$	4. Definition of supplementary
5. $m\angle 3 + m\angle 4 = m\angle 5 + m\angle 6$	5. Substitution property of equality
6. $m\angle 3 = m\angle 5$	6. Subtraction property of equality
7. $\angle 3 \cong \angle 5$	7. Definition of congruent angles

44. $AB = \sqrt{(5 - (-2))^2 + (-1 - (-6))^2}$

$= \sqrt{7^2 + 5^2}$

$= \sqrt{74}$

≈ 8.6

45. midpoint of $\overline{MN} = \left(\dfrac{2 + (-5)}{2}, \dfrac{3 + (-1)}{2} \right)$

$= \left(\dfrac{-3}{2}, \dfrac{2}{2} \right)$

$= (-1.5, 1)$

46. See students' work.

12-3   Connections to Algebra and Statistics

1. Sample answer:

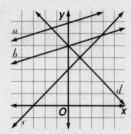

The slopes of the two parallel lines, a and b, are equal. The product of the slopes of the perpendicular lines, c and d, equals -1.

2. Sample answer: **a.** Make $x = 0$, and solve $5y = 10$, $y = 2$. **b.** Change this equation to the slope-intercept form and find the y-intercept.

3. scatter plots

4. midpoint of $\overline{ST} = \left(\dfrac{2 + (-4)}{2}, \dfrac{3 + 5}{2} \right)$ or $(-1, 4)$

midpoint of $\overline{RT} = \left(\dfrac{-4 + (-4)}{2}, \dfrac{-3 + 5}{2} \right)$ or $(-4, 1)$

midpoint of $\overline{RS} = \left(\dfrac{-4 + 2}{2}, \dfrac{-3 + 3}{2} \right)$ or $(-1, 0)$

equation of median through R:

slope $= \dfrac{4 - (-3)}{-1 - (-4)} = \dfrac{7}{3}$

$y - (-3) = \dfrac{7}{3}(x - (-4))$

$y + 3 = \dfrac{7}{3}x + \dfrac{28}{3}$

$y = \dfrac{7}{3}x + \dfrac{19}{3}$

equation of median through S:

slope $= \dfrac{3 - 1}{2 - (-4)} = \dfrac{2}{6}$ or $\dfrac{1}{3}$

$y - 3 = \dfrac{1}{3}(x - 2)$

$y - 3 = \dfrac{1}{3}x - \dfrac{2}{3}$

$y = \dfrac{1}{3}x + \dfrac{7}{3}$

equation of median through T:

slope $= \dfrac{5 - 0}{-4 - (-1)} = \dfrac{5}{-3}$ or $-\dfrac{5}{3}$

$y - 5 = -\dfrac{5}{3}(x - (-4))$

$y - 5 = -\dfrac{5}{3}x - \dfrac{20}{3}$

$y = -\dfrac{5}{3}x - \dfrac{5}{3}$

5. slope of $\overline{ST} = \dfrac{5 - 3}{-4 - 2} = \dfrac{2}{-6}$ or $-\dfrac{1}{3}$

Slope of perpendicular is 3.

slope of $\overline{RT} = \dfrac{5 - (-3)}{-4 - (-4)} =$ undefined

Slope of perpendicular is 0.

slope of $\overline{RS} = \dfrac{3 - (-3)}{2 - (-4)} = \dfrac{6}{6}$ or 1

Slope of perpendicular is -1.

From Exercise 4,

midpoint of $\overline{ST}$ is $(-1, 4)$, midpoint of $\overline{RT}$ is $(-4, 1)$, and midpoint of $\overline{RS}$ is $(-1, 0)$.

equation of perpendicular bisector of $\overline{ST}$:

$y - 4 = 3(x - (-1))$

$y - 4 = 3x + 3$

$y = 3x + 7$

equation of perpendicular bisector of $\overline{RT}$:

$y - 1 = 0(x - (-4))$

$y - 1 = 0$

$y = 1$

equation of perpendicular bisector of $\overline{RS}$:

$y - 0 = -1(x - (-1))$

$y = -x - 1$

6. a.

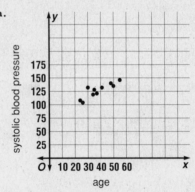

b. Sample answer: Choose points $(24, 108)$ and $(48, 140)$ to write the equation.

$m = \dfrac{140 - 108}{48 - 24}$

$= \dfrac{32}{24}$ or $\dfrac{4}{3}$

$y - 108 = \dfrac{4}{3}(x - 24)$

$y - 108 = \dfrac{4}{3}x - 32$

$y = \dfrac{4}{3}x + 76$

c. Use sample equation from **6b**.

$y = \frac{4}{3}x + 76$

$\quad = \frac{4}{3}(54) + 76$

$\quad = 148$

d. Sample answers: exercise, diet, heredity

PAGES 589-591   EXERCISES

7. slope of $\overleftrightarrow{AB} = \frac{2 - 0}{4 - 9} = \frac{2}{-5}$ or $-\frac{2}{5}$

slope of $\overleftrightarrow{BC} = \frac{2 - (-1)}{4 - 2} = \frac{3}{2}$

not collinear

8. slope of $\overleftrightarrow{XY} = \frac{9 - (-1)}{6 - 3} = \frac{10}{3}$

slope of $\overleftrightarrow{YZ} = \frac{0 - (-1)}{4 - 3} = \frac{1}{1}$ or 1

not collinear

9. slope of $\overleftrightarrow{LM} = \frac{4 - 3}{0 - 2} = \frac{1}{-2}$ or $-\frac{1}{2}$

slope of $\overleftrightarrow{MN} = \frac{6 - 3}{-4 - 2} = \frac{3}{-6}$ or $-\frac{1}{2}$

collinear

10. slope of $\overleftrightarrow{DE} = \frac{8 - (-3)}{4 - 9} = \frac{11}{-5}$ or $-\frac{11}{5}$

slope of $\overleftrightarrow{EF} = \frac{8 - 0}{4 - 0} = \frac{8}{4}$ or 2

not collinear

11. a.

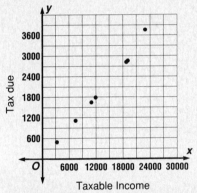

Taxable Income

b. Sample answer: Choose points (3268, 491) and (18753, 2816) to write the equation.

$m = \frac{2816 - 491}{18753 - 3268} = \frac{2325}{15485} \approx 0.15$

$y - 2816 = 0.15(x - 18753)$

$y - 2816 = 0.15x - 2812.95$

$\quad\quad y \approx 0.15x + 3$

c. Use sample answer from **11b**.

$y = 0.15x + 3$

$y = 0.15(12982) + 3$

$y \approx 1950$

12. slope of segment between (2, 5) and (-2, -1) =

$\frac{5 - (-1)}{2 - (-2)} = \frac{6}{4}$ or $\frac{3}{2}$

slope of perpendicular is $-\frac{2}{3}$.

midpoint of segment between (2, 5) and (-2, -1)

$= \left(\frac{2 + (-2)}{2}, \frac{5 + (-1)}{2} \right)$

$= \left(\frac{0}{2}, \frac{4}{2} \right)$ or (0, 2)

$y - 2 = -\frac{2}{3}(x - 0)$

$\quad y = -\frac{2}{3}x + 2$

13. vertex at (0, 6)

length of leg $= \sqrt{(0 - 4)^2 + (6 - (-2))^2}$

$\quad\quad\quad\quad\quad = \sqrt{4^2 + 8^2} = \sqrt{80}$

slope of line through (0, 6) and (4, -2)

$= \frac{6 - (-2)}{0 - 4} = \frac{8}{-4}$ or -2

equation of line through (0, 6) and (4, -2):

$y - 6 = -2(x - 0)$

$\quad y = -2x + 6$

There are an infinite number of possible third vertices. (-4, -2) is one possible vertex.

slope of line through (-4, -2) and (4, -2)

$= \frac{-2 - (-2)}{-4 - 4} = \frac{0}{-8}$ or 0

equation of line through (-4, -2) and (4, -2):

$y - (-2) = 0(x - (-4))$

$\quad y + 2 = 0$

$\quad\quad y = -2$

slope of line through (-4, -2) and (0, 6)

$= \frac{6 - (-2)}{0 - (-4)} = \frac{8}{4} = 2$

$y - 6 = 2(x - 0)$

$\quad y = 2x + 6$

14. slope of $\overline{BC} = \frac{-4 - 2}{2 - 6} = \frac{-6}{-4}$ or $\frac{3}{2}$

slope of altitude to $\overline{BC} = -\frac{2}{3}$

equation of line containing altitude to $\overline{BC}$:

$y - 14 = -\frac{2}{3}(x - 0)$

$y - 14 = -\frac{2}{3}x$

$\quad\quad y = -\frac{2}{3}x + 14$

225

15. slope of $\overline{AB} = \dfrac{14 - (-4)}{0 - 2} = \dfrac{18}{-2}$ or -9

slope of perpendicular to $\overline{AB} = \dfrac{1}{9}$

midpoint of $\overline{AB} = \left(\dfrac{0 + 2}{2}, \dfrac{14 + (-4)}{2}\right)$ or $(1, 5)$

equation of perpendicular bisector of $\overline{AB}$:

$y - 5 = \dfrac{1}{9}(x - 1)$

$y - 5 = \dfrac{1}{9}x - \dfrac{1}{9}$

$y = \dfrac{1}{9}x + \dfrac{44}{9}$

16. $E = \left(\dfrac{0 + 6}{2}, \dfrac{14 + 2}{2}\right) = \left(\dfrac{6}{2}, \dfrac{16}{2}\right) = (3, 8)$

slope of $\overleftrightarrow{BE} = \dfrac{8 - (-4)}{3 - 2} = \dfrac{12}{1}$ or 12

equation of $\overleftrightarrow{BE}$:

$y - 8 = 12(x - 3)$

$y - 8 = 12x - 36$

$y = 12x - 28$

17. slope of $\overleftrightarrow{RS} = \dfrac{-8 - 4}{-6 - 6} = \dfrac{-12}{-12}$ or 1

slope of $\overleftrightarrow{RT} = \dfrac{-8 - 10}{-6 - (-6)} = \dfrac{-18}{0}$ undefined

slope of $\overleftrightarrow{ST} = \dfrac{4 - 10}{6 - (-6)} = \dfrac{-6}{12}$ or $-\dfrac{1}{2}$

equation of $\overleftrightarrow{RS}$

$y - (-8) = 1(x - (-6))$

$y + 8 = x + 6$

$y = x - 2$

equation of $\overleftrightarrow{RT}$

$x = -6$

equation of $\overleftrightarrow{ST}$

$y - 4 = -\dfrac{1}{2}(x - 6)$

$y - 4 = -\dfrac{1}{2}x + 3$

$y = -\dfrac{1}{2}x + 7$

18. Let M be the midpoint of $\overline{RS}$, N be the midpoint of $\overline{RT}$, and O be the midpoint of $\overline{ST}$.

$M = \left(\dfrac{-6 + 6}{2}, \dfrac{-8 + 4}{2}\right) = \left(\dfrac{0}{2}, \dfrac{-4}{2}\right)$ or $(0, -2)$

$N = \left(\dfrac{-6 + (-6)}{2}, \dfrac{-8 + 10}{2}\right) = \left(\dfrac{-12}{2}, \dfrac{2}{2}\right)$ or $(-6, 1)$

$O = \left(\dfrac{6 + (-6)}{2}, \dfrac{4 + 10}{2}\right) = \left(\dfrac{0}{2}, \dfrac{14}{2}\right)$ or $(0, 7)$

slope of $\overleftrightarrow{TM} = \dfrac{10 - (-2)}{-6 - 0} = \dfrac{12}{-6}$ or -2

slope of $\overleftrightarrow{SN} = \dfrac{4 - 1}{6 - (-6)} = \dfrac{3}{12}$ or $\dfrac{1}{4}$

slope of $\overleftrightarrow{RO} = \dfrac{-8 - 7}{-6 - 0} = \dfrac{-15}{-6}$ or $\dfrac{5}{2}$

equation of $\overleftrightarrow{TM}$

$y - (-2) = -2(x - 0)$

$y + 2 = -2x$

$y = -2x - 2$

equation of $\overleftrightarrow{SN}$

$y - 1 = \dfrac{1}{4}(x - (-6))$

$y - 1 = \dfrac{1}{4}x + \dfrac{3}{2}$

$y = \dfrac{1}{4}x + \dfrac{5}{2}$

equation of $\overleftrightarrow{RO}$

$y - 7 = \dfrac{5}{2}(x - 0)$

$y - 7 = \dfrac{5}{2}x$

$y = \dfrac{5}{2}x + 7$

19. From Exercise 17, the slopes of $\overleftrightarrow{RS}$, $\overleftrightarrow{RT}$, and $\overleftrightarrow{ST}$, are 1, undefined, and $-\dfrac{1}{2}$ respectively. So the altitudes to the sides contained in these lines will have slopes of -1, 0, and 2 respectively.

equation of line containing altitude to T:

$y - 10 = -1(x - (-6))$

$y - 10 = -x - 6$

$y = -x + 4$

equation of line containing altitude to S:

$y - 4 = 0(x - 6)$

$y - 4 = 0$

$y = 4$

equation of line containing altitude to R:

$y - (-8) = 2(x - (-6))$

$y + 8 = 2x + 12$

$y = 2x + 4$

20. a.

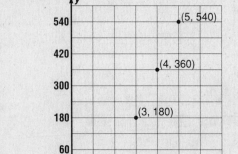

The slope of the line between $(3, 180)$ and $(4, 360)$ is 180. Therefore, $y = 180x + b$. Using $(3, 180)$, $180 = 180(3) + b$ and $b = -360$. The equation of the line is $y = 180x - 360$. Since $540 = 180(5) - 360$, the points are collinear.

b. $y = 180x - 360$

c. $y = 180x - 360$

$= 180(10) - 360$

$= 1800 - 360$

$= 1440$

21. $(x + 1)^2 + (y - 2)^2 = 25$

$((3) + 1)^2 + ((5) - 2)^2 \overset{?}{=} 25$

$4^2 + 3^2 \overset{?}{=} 25$

$16 + 9 \overset{?}{=} 25$

$25 = 25$

The point (3, 5) is on the circle since (3, 5) satisfies the equation.

22. The segment from the center of the circle, (−1, 2) to the point of tangency, (3, 5) is perpendicular to the tangent.

slope of line through (−1, 2) and (3, 5)

$= \dfrac{5 - 2}{3 - (-1)} = \dfrac{3}{4}$

slope of tangent $= -\dfrac{4}{3}$

equation of tangent:

$y - 5 = -\dfrac{4}{3}(x - 3)$

$y - 5 = -\dfrac{4}{3}x + 4$

$y = -\dfrac{4}{3}x + 9$

23. No; the distance between parallel lines is the length of a perpendicular line segment between the parallel lines.

24. a. Suppose Terry invests x dollars in the investment that pays 7% and y dollars in the investment that pays 10%. Then $0.07x + 0.10y = 210$.

b.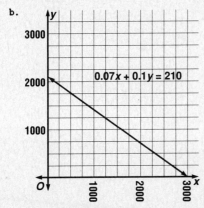

c. The intercepts are (0, 2100) and (3000, 0). They mean that Terry could invest $2100 in the 10% investment or $3000 in the 7% investment to earn $210 in interest.

d. The equation becomes the inequality $0.07x + 0.1y \geq 210$. The graph would be the line and all the points above it.

25. a.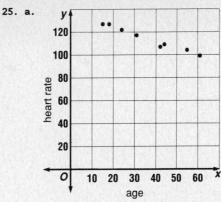

b. Sample answer: Choose points (42, 107) and (18, 127) to write the equation.

$m = \dfrac{127 - 107}{18 - 42} = \dfrac{20}{-24}$ or $-\dfrac{5}{6}$

$y - 107 = -\dfrac{5}{6}(x - 42)$

$y - 107 = -\dfrac{5}{6}x + 35$

$y = -\dfrac{5}{6}x + 142$

c. Use sample equation from 25b.

$y = -\dfrac{5}{6}x + 142$

$y = -\dfrac{5}{6}(19) + 142$

$y \approx -16 + 142$

$y \approx 126$

26. Let x = original price.

$274 = \dfrac{1}{2}x + 60$

$214 = \dfrac{1}{2}x$

$\$428 = x$

27. $T = 2(10)(6) + 2(10)(4) + 2(6)(4)$

$= 120 + 80 + 48$

$= 248 \text{ cm}^2$

28. $m\angle RTS = 180 - 75$ or 105

So, since $\overline{QT} \cong \overline{TS}$ and $\overline{RT} \cong \overline{RT}$, $RS > QR$ by SAS Inequality.

29. See students' work.

12-4 **Problem-Solving Strategy: Write an Equation**

PAGE 593   CHECKING FOR UNDERSTANDING

1. Sample answer: You need to know what the variable represents in order to write the equation.

2. First, the distributive property is used. Then $6x$ and $2x$ are added using the distributive property and 150 is added to each side of the equation. Finally, each side of the equation is divided by 8.

227

3. x = average; $\frac{1}{2}x - 7 = 53$

4. $835 + 30x = 1165$

   $30x = 330$

   $x = 11$

   The peas will be ready 11 days after June 1, or June 12.

5. $3(45) + 55x = 300$

   $135 + 55x = 300$

   $55x = 165$

   $x = 3$

   3 hours

6. Let w = width

   $2(2w - 40) + 2w = 220$

   $4w - 80 + 2w = 220$

   $6w = 350$

   $w = 50$

   $2w - 40 = 2(50) - 40$ or 60

   The dimensions are 60 m by 50 m.

7. Let x = number of adult tickets

   $3.5x + 2.5(x + 4) = 58$

   $3.5x + 2.5x + 10 = 58$

   $6x = 48$

   $x = 8$

   8 adult tickets and $8 + 4$ or 12 student tickets

PAGE 594   EXERCISES

8.

9. Let x represent the radius of Earth in feet. His feet would travel the circumference of Earth. His head would travel the circumference of a circle with a radius of $x + 5$.

   Units head travels   Units feet travel

   $C_1 = 2\pi r$ $C_2 = 2\pi r$

   $\quad = 2\pi(x + 5)$ $\quad = 2\pi x$

   $\quad = 2\pi x + 10\pi$

   Difference = $C_1 - C_2$

   $\quad = (2\pi x + 10\pi) - 2\pi x$

   $\quad = 10\pi$

   $\quad \approx 31.4$ feet

10. Sample answer:

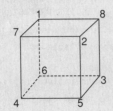

11. Let x be the speed of the passenger train in miles per hour.

    $2.5x + 2.5(x + 10) = 470$

    $2.5x + 2.5x + 25 = 470$

    $5x = 445$

    $x = 89$

    The trains are traveling at 89 mph and 99 mph.

12. There are 9 8-hour periods in 3 days, so the bacteria will double 9 times. There will be 2^9 or 512 times as many bacteria in the end as there were in the beginning.

    $512x = 12800$

    $x = 25$ There were 25 bacteria.

13. Let t represent the tens digit and u represent the units digit.

    $t + u = 10 \longrightarrow u = 10 - t$

    $3t = 2u$

    $3t = 2(10 - t)$

    $3t = 20 - 2t$

    $5t = 20$

    $t = 4$

    $u = 10 - t$

    $\quad = 10 - 4$

    $\quad = 6$ The number is 46.

14. 4 inches

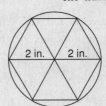

Cooperative Learning Project

PAGE 594

Volume of balloon with radius 5 cm

$$V = \frac{4}{3}\pi r^3$$

$$= \frac{4}{3}\pi(5)^3$$

$$= \frac{500}{3}\pi \text{ cm}^3$$

If the volume is $\frac{500}{3}\pi$ cm^3 after 3 seconds, $\frac{1}{3}\left(\frac{500}{3}\pi\right)$ or $\frac{500}{9}\pi$ cm^3 of helium enter the balloon each second.

Volume of balloon with radius 10 cm

$$V = \frac{4}{3}\pi r^3$$

$$= \frac{4}{3}\pi(10)^3$$

$$= \frac{4000}{3}\pi \text{ cm}^3$$

It will take $\dfrac{\frac{4000}{3}\pi}{\frac{500}{9}\pi}$ or 24 seconds to inflate the balloon to a radius of 10 cm.

1. Sample answer: because some of the coordinates will be 0 which will make the computations easier.

2. Sample answers:

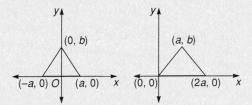

3. Sample answer: B is better because there are fewer variables.

4. $B(-a, 0)$

5. $E(d - f, r)$

6. a. right isosceles; the sides are congruent and lie on the perpendicular axes.

   b. (b, b)

   c. 1

   d. -1

   e. The median $\overline{TM}$ is perpendicular to the hypotenuse $\overline{LP}$.

7.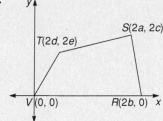

Midpoint A of $\overline{TS}$ is $\left(\dfrac{2d + 2a}{2}, \dfrac{2e + 2c}{2}\right)$ or $(d + a,$ etc.$)$.

Midpoint B of $\overline{SR}$ is $\left(\dfrac{2a + 2b}{2}, \dfrac{2c + 0}{2}\right)$ or $(a + b, c)$.

Midpoint C of $\overline{VR}$ is $\left(\dfrac{0 + 2b}{2}, \dfrac{0 + 0}{2}\right)$ or $(b, 0)$.

Midpoint D of $\overline{TV}$ is $\left(\dfrac{0 + 2d}{2}, \dfrac{0 + 2e}{2}\right)$ or (d, e).

Slope of $\overline{AB}$ is $\dfrac{e + c - c}{d + a - (a + b)}$ or $\dfrac{e}{d - b}$.

Slope of $\overline{DC}$ is $\dfrac{e - 0}{d - b}$ or $\dfrac{e}{d - b}$.

Slope of $\overline{DA}$ is $\dfrac{e + c - e}{d + a - d}$ or $\dfrac{c}{a}$.

Slope of $\overline{CB}$ is $\dfrac{c - 0}{a + b - b}$ or $\dfrac{c}{a}$.

Since opposite sides are parallel, $ABCD$ is a parallelogram.

8. Midpoint of $\overline{AC}$ is $\left(\dfrac{d + a + b}{2}, \dfrac{e + c + 0}{2}\right)$ or $\left(\dfrac{a + b + d}{2}, \dfrac{c + e}{2}\right)$

Midpoint of $\overline{DB}$ is $\left(\dfrac{d + a + b}{2}, \dfrac{e + c}{2}\right)$ or $\left(\dfrac{a + b + d}{2}, \dfrac{c + e}{2}\right)$

$\overline{AC}$ and $\overline{DB}$ bisect each other.

9.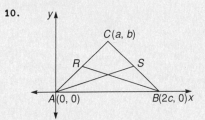

$DB = \sqrt{(a - b)^2 + (0 - c)^2} = \sqrt{(a - b)^2 + c^2}$

$AC = \sqrt{((a - b) - 0)^2 + (c - 0)^2}$

$\quad = \sqrt{(a - b)^2 + c^2}$

$DB = AC$ and $\overline{DB} \cong \overline{AC}$

10.

Midpoint R of $\overline{AC}$ is $\left(\dfrac{a + 0}{2}, \dfrac{b + 0}{2}\right)$ or $\left(\dfrac{a}{2}, \dfrac{b}{2}\right)$.

Midpoint S of $\overline{BC}$ is $\left(\dfrac{2a + a}{2}, \dfrac{0 + b}{2}\right)$ or $\left(\dfrac{3a}{2}, \dfrac{b}{2}\right)$.

$BR = \sqrt{\left(2a - \dfrac{a}{2}\right)^2 + \left(0 - \dfrac{b}{2}\right)^2} = \sqrt{\left(\dfrac{3a}{2}\right)^2 + \left(\dfrac{b}{2}\right)^2}$

$AS = \sqrt{\left(\dfrac{3a}{2} - 0\right)^2 + \left(\dfrac{b}{2} - 0\right)^2} = \sqrt{\left(\dfrac{3a}{2}\right)^2 + \left(\dfrac{b}{2}\right)^2}$

$BR = AS$ and $\overline{BR} \cong \overline{AS}$

11. $A(0, 0)$, $Y(b, 0)$ 12. $E(a, a)$, $S(0, a)$

13. $R(-b, 2b)$ 14. $D(a - b, c)$, $E(0, 0)$

15. $AB = \sqrt{(a - 0)^2 + (b - 0)^2} = \sqrt{a^2 + b^2}$

$BC = \sqrt{(2a - a)^2 + (0 - b)^2} = \sqrt{a^2 + b^2}$

$AB = BC$ and $\triangle ABC$ is isosceles.

16. Slope of $\overline{HK}$ is $\dfrac{0 - 0}{d - 0}$ or $\dfrac{0}{d}$ or 0.

Slope of $\overline{IJ}$ is $\dfrac{b - b}{a + d - a}$ or $\dfrac{0}{d}$ or 0.

Slope of $\overline{HI}$ is $\dfrac{b - 0}{a - 0}$ or $\dfrac{b}{a}$.

Slope of $\overline{KJ}$ is $\dfrac{b - 0}{a + d - d}$ or $\dfrac{b}{a}$.

$\overline{HK} \parallel \overline{IJ}$ and $\overline{HI} \parallel \overline{KJ}$

$HIJK$ is a parallelogram.

17. $DE = \sqrt{(a - 0)^2 + (a\sqrt{3} - 0)^2} = \sqrt{a^2 + 3a^2}$

$\qquad = \sqrt{4a^2} = 2a$

$\quad EF = \sqrt{(2a - a)^2 + (0 - a\sqrt{3})^2} = \sqrt{a^2 + 3a^2}$

$\qquad = \sqrt{4a^2} = 2a$

$\quad DF = \sqrt{(2a - 0)^2 + (0 - 0)^2} = \sqrt{4a^2} = 2a$

$\quad DE = EF = DF$ and $\overline{DE} \cong \overline{EF} \cong \overline{DF}$

$\quad \triangle DEF$ is equilateral.

18. Slope of $\overline{PQ}$ is $\dfrac{a - 0}{a - 0}$ or $\dfrac{a}{a}$ or 1.

Slope of $\overline{QR}$ is $\dfrac{0 - a}{2a - a}$ or $\dfrac{-a}{a}$ or -1.

$\overline{PQ}$ and $\overline{QR}$ are perpendicular and $\triangle PQR$ is a right triangle.

19.

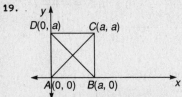

Slope of $\overline{AC}$ is $\dfrac{a - 0}{a - 0}$ or $\dfrac{a}{a}$ or 1.

Slope of $\overline{BD}$ is $\dfrac{a - 0}{0 - a}$ or $\dfrac{a}{-a}$ or -1.

$\overline{AC} \perp \overline{BD}$

20.

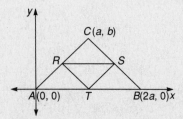

Midpoint R is $\left(\dfrac{a + 0}{2}, \dfrac{b + 0}{2}\right)$ or $\left(\dfrac{a}{2}, \dfrac{b}{2}\right)$.

Midpoint S is $\left(\dfrac{a + 2a}{2}, \dfrac{b + 0}{2}\right)$ or $\left(\dfrac{3a}{2}, \dfrac{b}{2}\right)$.

Midpoint T is $\left(\dfrac{2a + 0}{2}, \dfrac{0 + 0}{2}\right)$ or $(a, 0)$.

$RT = \sqrt{\left(\dfrac{a}{2} - a\right)^2 + \left(\dfrac{b}{2} - 0\right)^2} = \sqrt{\left(-\dfrac{a}{2}\right)^2 + \left(\dfrac{b}{2}\right)^2}$

$\qquad = \sqrt{\left(\dfrac{a}{2}\right)^2 + \left(\dfrac{b}{2}\right)^2}$

$ST = \sqrt{\left(\dfrac{3a}{2} - a\right)^2 + \left(\dfrac{b}{2} - 0\right)^2} = \sqrt{\left(\dfrac{a}{2}\right)^2 + \left(\dfrac{b}{2}\right)^2}$

$RT = ST$ and $\overline{RT} \cong \overline{ST}$

$\triangle RST$ is isosceles.

21.

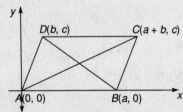

Midpoint of $\overline{AC}$ is $\left(\dfrac{(a + b) + 0}{2}, \dfrac{c + 0}{2}\right)$ or

$\left(\dfrac{a + b}{2}, \dfrac{c}{2}\right)$.

Midpoint of $\overline{DB}$ is $\left(\dfrac{a + b}{2}, \dfrac{0 + c}{2}\right)$ or $\left(\dfrac{a + b}{2}, \dfrac{c}{2}\right)$.

$\overline{AC}$ and $\overline{DB}$ bisect each other.

22.

Midpoint Q is $\left(\dfrac{b + 0}{2}, \dfrac{c + 0}{2}\right)$ or $\left(\dfrac{b}{2}, \dfrac{c}{2}\right)$.

Midpoint R is $\left(\dfrac{a - b + b}{2}, \dfrac{c + c}{2}\right)$ or $\left(\dfrac{a}{2}, c\right)$.

Midpoint S is $\left(\dfrac{a - b + a}{2}, \dfrac{c + 0}{2}\right)$ or $\left(\dfrac{2a - b}{2}, \dfrac{c}{2}\right)$.

Midpoint T is $\left(\dfrac{a + 0}{2}, \dfrac{0 + 0}{2}\right)$ or $\left(\dfrac{a}{2}, 0\right)$.

Slope of $\overline{QR}$ is $\dfrac{c - \frac{c}{2}}{\frac{a}{2} - \frac{b}{2}}$ or $\dfrac{\frac{c}{2}}{\frac{a - b}{2}}$ or $\dfrac{c}{a - b}$.

Slope of $\overline{TS}$ is $\dfrac{\frac{c}{2} - 0}{\frac{2a - b}{2} - \frac{a}{2}}$ or $\dfrac{\frac{c}{2}}{\frac{a - b}{2}}$ or $\dfrac{c}{a - b}$.

Slope of $\overline{QT}$ is $\dfrac{\frac{c}{2} - 0}{\frac{b}{2} - \frac{a}{2}}$ or $\dfrac{\frac{c}{2}}{\frac{b - a}{2}}$ or $\dfrac{c}{b - a}$.

Slope of $\overline{RS}$ is $\dfrac{c - \frac{c}{2}}{\frac{a}{2} - \frac{2a - b}{2}}$ or $\dfrac{\frac{c}{2}}{\frac{-a + b}{2}}$ or

$\dfrac{c}{b - a}$.

$\overline{QR} \parallel \overline{TS}$ and $\overline{QT} \parallel \overline{RS}$

$QRST$ is a parallelogram.

$QR = \sqrt{\left(\dfrac{a}{2} - \dfrac{b}{2}\right)^2 + \left(c - \dfrac{c}{2}\right)^2} = \sqrt{\left(\dfrac{a - b}{2}\right)^2 + \left(\dfrac{c}{2}\right)^2}$

$RS = \sqrt{\left(\dfrac{2a - b}{2} - \dfrac{a}{2}\right)^2 + \left(\dfrac{c}{2} - c\right)^2}$

$\qquad = \sqrt{\left(\dfrac{a - b}{2}\right)^2 + \left(-\dfrac{c}{2}\right)^2} = \sqrt{\left(\dfrac{a - b}{2}\right)^2 + \left(\dfrac{c}{2}\right)^2}$

$ST = \sqrt{\left(\dfrac{2a - b}{2} - \dfrac{a}{2}\right)^2 + \left(\dfrac{c}{2} - 0\right)^2}$

$\qquad = \sqrt{\left(\dfrac{a - b}{2}\right)^2 + \left(\dfrac{c}{2}\right)^2}$

$QT = \sqrt{\left(\dfrac{a}{2} - \dfrac{b}{2}\right)^2 + \left(0 - \dfrac{c}{2}\right)^2}$

$\qquad = \sqrt{\left(\dfrac{a - b}{2}\right)^2 + \left(-\dfrac{c}{2}\right)^2} = \sqrt{\left(\dfrac{a - b}{2}\right)^2 + \left(\dfrac{c}{2}\right)^2}$

$QR = RS = ST = QT$ and $\overline{QR} \cong \overline{RS} \cong \overline{ST} \cong \overline{QT}$

$QRST$ is a rhombus.

23.

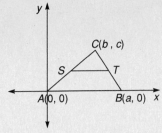

Midpoint S is $\left(\dfrac{b+0}{2}, \dfrac{c+0}{2}\right)$ or $\left(\dfrac{b}{2}, \dfrac{c}{2}\right)$.

Midpoint T is $\left(\dfrac{a+b}{2}, \dfrac{0+c}{2}\right)$ or $\left(\dfrac{a+b}{2}, \dfrac{c}{2}\right)$.

Slope of $\overline{ST}$ is $\dfrac{\frac{c}{2} - \frac{c}{2}}{\frac{a+b}{2} - \frac{b}{2}}$ or $\dfrac{0}{\frac{a}{2}}$ or 0.

Slope of $\overline{AB}$ is $\dfrac{0-0}{a-0}$ or $\dfrac{0}{a}$ or 0.

$\overline{ST} \parallel \overline{AB}$

24.

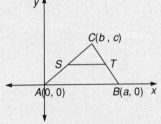

$ST = \sqrt{\left(\dfrac{a+b}{2} - \dfrac{b}{2}\right)^2 + \left(\dfrac{c}{2} - \dfrac{c}{2}\right)^2} = \sqrt{\left(\dfrac{a}{2}\right)^2 + 0^2}$

$\quad = \sqrt{\left(\dfrac{a}{2}\right)^2} = \dfrac{a}{2}$

$AB = \sqrt{(a-0)^2 + (0-0)^2} = \sqrt{a^2 + 0^2} = \sqrt{a^2}$

$\quad = a$

$ST = \dfrac{1}{2}AB$

25.

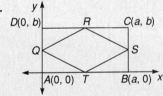

Midpoint Q is $\left(\dfrac{0+0}{2}, \dfrac{b+0}{2}\right)$ or $\left(0, \dfrac{b}{2}\right)$.

Midpoint R is $\left(\dfrac{a+0}{2}, \dfrac{b+b}{2}\right)$ or $\left(\dfrac{a}{2}, \dfrac{2b}{2}\right)$ or $\left(\dfrac{a}{2}, b\right)$.

Midpoint S is $\left(\dfrac{a+a}{2}, \dfrac{b+0}{2}\right)$ or $\left(\dfrac{2a}{2}, \dfrac{b}{2}\right)$ or $\left(a, \dfrac{b}{2}\right)$.

Midpoint T is $\left(\dfrac{a+0}{2}, \dfrac{0+0}{2}\right)$ or $\left(\dfrac{a}{2}, 0\right)$.

Slope of $\overline{QR}$ is $\dfrac{b - \frac{b}{2}}{\frac{a}{2} - 0}$ or $\dfrac{\frac{b}{2}}{\frac{a}{2}}$ or $\dfrac{b}{a}$.

Slope of $\overline{TS}$ is $\dfrac{\frac{b}{2} - 0}{a - \frac{a}{2}}$ or $\dfrac{\frac{b}{2}}{\frac{a}{2}}$ or $\dfrac{b}{a}$.

Slope of $\overline{RS}$ is $\dfrac{b - \frac{b}{2}}{\frac{a}{2} - a}$ or $\dfrac{\frac{b}{2}}{-\frac{a}{2}}$ or $-\dfrac{b}{a}$.

Slope of $\overline{QT}$ is $\dfrac{\frac{b}{2} - 0}{0 - \frac{a}{2}}$ or $\dfrac{\frac{b}{2}}{-\frac{a}{2}}$ or $-\dfrac{b}{a}$.

$\overline{QR} \parallel \overline{TS}$ and $\overline{RS} \parallel \overline{QT}$

$QRST$ is a parallelogram.

$QR = \sqrt{\left(\dfrac{a}{2} - 0\right)^2 + \left(b - \dfrac{b}{2}\right)^2} = \sqrt{\left(\dfrac{a}{2}\right)^2 + \left(\dfrac{b}{2}\right)^2}$

$RS = \sqrt{\left(a - \dfrac{a}{2}\right)^2 + \left(\dfrac{b}{2} - b\right)^2} = \sqrt{\left(\dfrac{a}{2}\right)^2 + \left(-\dfrac{b}{2}\right)^2}$

$\quad = \sqrt{\left(\dfrac{a}{2}\right)^2 + \left(\dfrac{b}{2}\right)^2}$

$ST = \sqrt{\left(a - \dfrac{a}{2}\right)^2 + \left(\dfrac{b}{2} - 0\right)^2} = \sqrt{\left(\dfrac{a}{2}\right)^2 + \left(\dfrac{b}{2}\right)^2}$

$QT = \sqrt{\left(\dfrac{a}{2} - 0\right)^2 + \left(0 - \dfrac{b}{2}\right)^2} = \sqrt{\left(\dfrac{a}{2}\right)^2 + \left(-\dfrac{b}{2}\right)^2}$

$\quad = \sqrt{\left(\dfrac{a}{2}\right)^2 + \left(\dfrac{b}{2}\right)^2}$

$QR = RS = ST = QT$ and $\overline{QR} \cong \overline{RS} \cong \overline{ST} \cong \overline{QT}$

$QRST$ is a rhombus.

26.

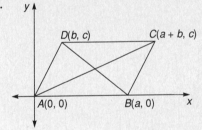

$AC = \sqrt{(a + b - 0)^2 + (c - 0)^2}$

$BD = \sqrt{(b - a)^2 + (c - 0)^2}$

But $AC = BD$ and

$\sqrt{(a + b - 0)^2 + (c - 0)^2}$

$\qquad\qquad\qquad = \sqrt{(b - 0)^2 + (c - 0)^2}$

$(a + b - 0)^2 + (c - 0)^2 = (b - a)^2 + (c - 0)^2$

$(a + b)^2 + (c)^2 = (b - a)^2 + (c)^2$

$a^2 + 2ab + b^2 + c^2 = b^2 - 2ab + a^2 + c^2$

$2ab = -2ab$

$4ab = 0$

$a = 0$ or $b = 0$

$a \neq 0$

$b = 0$

$\angle DAB$ is a right angle.

$ABCD$ is a rectangle.

27.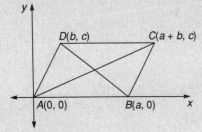

Slope of $\overline{BD}$ is $\dfrac{c - 0}{b - a}$ or $\dfrac{c}{b - a}$.

Slope of $\overline{AC}$ is $\dfrac{c - 0}{a + b - 0}$ or $\dfrac{c}{a + b}$.

But $\overline{BD} \perp \overline{AC}$ and

$\dfrac{c}{b - a} = -\dfrac{a + b}{c}$

$\dfrac{c}{b - a} = \dfrac{a + b}{-c}$

$-c^2 = b^2 - a^2$

$a^2 = b^2 + c^2$ and $\sqrt{a^2} = \sqrt{b^2 + c^2}$

$AD = \sqrt{(b - 0)^2 + (c - 0)^2} = \sqrt{b^2 + c^2}$

$DC = \sqrt{((a + b) - b)^2 + (c - c)^2} = \sqrt{a^2}$

$BC = \sqrt{((a + b) - a)^2 + (c - 0)^2} = \sqrt{b^2 + c^2}$

$AB = \sqrt{(a - 0)^2 + (0 - 0)^2} = \sqrt{a^2}$

$AD = DC = BC = AB$ and $\overline{AD} \cong \overline{DC} \cong \overline{BC} \cong \overline{AB}$

$ABCD$ is a rhombus.

28.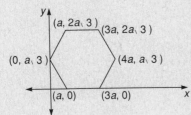

29. $x = 20$

30. $M(2, 4)$

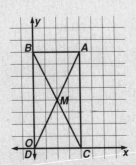

31. $d = \sqrt{(5 - (-2))^2 + (3 - 6)^2}$

$= \sqrt{7^2 + (-3)^2}$

$= \sqrt{58} \approx 7.6$ km

32. false   **33.** false   **34.** true   **35.** true

36. true   **37.** false   **38.** false   **39.** false

40. a. Sample answer:

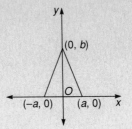

b. Sample answer:

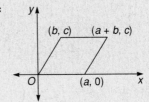

c. Sample answer:

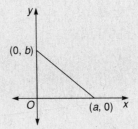

Mid-Chapter Review

PAGE 600

1. (3, 0), (0, -4)

2. no x-intercept; (0, 15)

3. $m = \dfrac{2 - 4}{2 - (-1)} = \dfrac{-2}{3}$ or $-\dfrac{2}{3}$

$y - 2 = -\dfrac{2}{3}(x - 2)$

$y - 2 = -\dfrac{2}{3}x + \dfrac{4}{3}$

$y = -\dfrac{2}{3}x + \dfrac{10}{3}$

4. $m = 3$

$y - 0 = 3(x - 0)$

$y = 3x$

5. $y - 0 = -\dfrac{1}{2}(x - 6)$

$y = -\dfrac{1}{2}x + 3$

6. slope of $\overleftrightarrow{AB} = \dfrac{0 - (-2)}{8 - 9} = \dfrac{2}{-1}$ or -2

slope of $\overleftrightarrow{BC} = \dfrac{16 - (-2)}{0 - 9} = \dfrac{18}{-9}$ or -2

collinear

7. slope of $\overleftrightarrow{XY} = \dfrac{2 - (-1)}{-2 - 8} = \dfrac{3}{-10}$ or $-\dfrac{3}{10}$

slope of $\overleftrightarrow{YZ} = \dfrac{3 - (-1)}{4 - 8} = \dfrac{4}{-4}$ or -1

not collinear

8. She drove 88 ÷ 40 or 2.2 hours. That is 2 hours and 12 minutes. She was 15 minutes early; so she left her office 2 hours and 27 minutes before 1:00 PM, that is 10:33 AM.

9. $A(-b, 0)$, $C(b, 2b)$, $D(-b, 2b)$

10. $E(0, 0)$, $G(a, b + c)$

11.

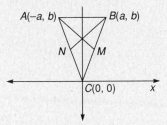

$N = \left(\dfrac{-a + 0}{2}, \dfrac{b + 0}{2}\right)$ or $\left(-\dfrac{a}{2}, \dfrac{b}{2}\right)$

$M = \left(\dfrac{a + 0}{2}, \dfrac{b + 0}{2}\right)$ or $\left(\dfrac{a}{2}, \dfrac{b}{2}\right)$

$BN = \sqrt{\left(-\dfrac{a}{2} - a\right)^2 + \left(\dfrac{b}{2} - b\right)^2}$

$= \sqrt{\left(\dfrac{-3a}{2}\right)^2 + \left(\dfrac{-b}{2}\right)^2}$

$= \sqrt{\dfrac{9a^2}{4} + \dfrac{b^2}{4}}$ or $\dfrac{\sqrt{9a^2 + b^2}}{2}$

$AM = \sqrt{\left(-a - \dfrac{a}{2}\right)^2 + \left(b - \dfrac{b}{2}\right)^2}$

$= \sqrt{\left(\dfrac{-3a}{2}\right)^2 + \left(\dfrac{b}{2}\right)^2}$

$= \sqrt{\dfrac{9a^2}{4} + \dfrac{b^2}{4}}$ or $\dfrac{\sqrt{9a^2 + b^2}}{2}$

Therefore, $\overline{BN} \cong \overline{AM}$.

12-6 Vectors

PAGE 604   CHECKING FOR UNDERSTANDING

1. A vector has direction and a line segment does not.

2. No, the 2 vectors are going in the opposite directions.

3. Parallel vectors have the same direction, but may or may not have the same magnitude. Equal vectors have both the same direction and the same magnitude.

4. Scalar multiplication changes the magnitude, but not the direction.

5. Sample answers:

$\vec{u} + \vec{v} = \vec{t}$ $\vec{u} + \vec{v} = \vec{t}$

6. Sample answer:

7. Sample answer:

8. $|\overrightarrow{SL}| = \sqrt{(5 - 0)^2 + (1 - 0)^2}$

$= \sqrt{5^2 + 1^2}$

$= \sqrt{26} \approx 5.1$

direction of $\overrightarrow{SL}$: $\tan x = \dfrac{1}{5}$

$x \approx 11°$

9. $|\overrightarrow{AB}| = \sqrt{(3 - 0)^2 + (8 - 0)^2}$

$= \sqrt{3^2 + 8^2}$

$= \sqrt{73} \approx 8.5$

direction of $\overrightarrow{AB}$: $\tan x = \dfrac{8}{3}$

$x \approx 69°$

10. $|\overrightarrow{RT}| = \sqrt{(-2 - 1)^2 + (-5 - 7)^2}$

$= \sqrt{(-3)^2 + (-12)^2}$

$= \sqrt{153} \approx 12.4$

direction of $\overrightarrow{RT}$: $\tan x = \dfrac{-5 - 7}{-2 - 1}$

$\tan x = \dfrac{-12}{-3}$ or 4

$x \approx 76°$

11.

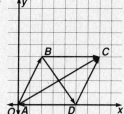

$|\overrightarrow{AB}| = \sqrt{(2 - 0)^2 + (4 - 0)^2}$

$= \sqrt{2^2 + 4^2}$

$= \sqrt{20} \approx 4.5$

direction of $\overrightarrow{AB}$: $\tan x = \dfrac{4 - 0}{2 - 0}$

$\tan x = \dfrac{4}{2}$

$x \approx 63°$

$|\overrightarrow{BC}| = \sqrt{(7 - 2)^2 + (4 - 4)^2}$

$= \sqrt{5^2 + 0^2}$

$= \sqrt{25} = 5$

direction of $\overrightarrow{BC}$: $\tan x = \dfrac{4 - 4}{7 - 2}$

$\tan x = \dfrac{0}{5}$

$x = 0$

$|\overrightarrow{DC}| = \sqrt{(7 - 5)^2 + (4 - 0)^2}$

$= \sqrt{2^2 + 4^2}$

$= \sqrt{20} \approx 4.5$

direction of $\overrightarrow{DC}$: $\tan x = \frac{4 - 0}{7 - 5}$

$\tan x = \frac{4}{2}$

$x \approx 63°$

$|\overrightarrow{DA}| = \sqrt{(5 - 0)^2 + (0 - 0)^2}$

$= \sqrt{5^2 + 0^2}$

$= \sqrt{25} = 5$

direction of $\overrightarrow{DA}$: $\tan x = \frac{0 - 0}{5 - 0}$

$\tan x = 0$

$x = 0$

$|\overrightarrow{AC}| = \sqrt{(7 - 0)^2 + (4 - 0)^2}$

$= \sqrt{7^2 + 4^2}$

$= \sqrt{65} \approx 8.1$

direction of $\overrightarrow{AC}$: $\tan x = \frac{4 - 0}{7 - 0}$

$\tan x = \frac{4}{7}$

$x \approx 30°$

$|\overrightarrow{BD}| = \sqrt{(2 - 5)^2 + (4 - 0)^2}$

$= \sqrt{(-3)^2 + 4^2}$

$= \sqrt{25} = 5$

direction of $\overrightarrow{BD}$: $\tan x = \frac{4 - 0}{2 - 5}$

$\tan x = \frac{4}{-3}$

$x \approx -53°$

Vectors $\overrightarrow{AB}$ and $\overrightarrow{DC}$ have the same direction, so they are parallel.

12. $\overrightarrow{AB}$ and $\overrightarrow{DC}$ have the same direction and magnitude, so they are equal.

13. Answers may vary. A sample answer is $\overrightarrow{AB}$ and $\overrightarrow{BC}$.

14. Answers may vary. A sample answer is $\overrightarrow{DA}$ and $\overrightarrow{BC}$. They both have a magnitude of 5, but they have opposite directions.

15.    16.

17.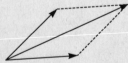

18. $\overrightarrow{W} + \overrightarrow{S} = (2, -4) + (2, 7)$

$= (2 + 2, -4 + 7)$

$= (4, 3)$

19. $2\overrightarrow{v} + \overrightarrow{t} = (2 \times 3, 2 \times 2) + (-5, 6)$

$= (6, 4) + (-5, 6)$

$= (6 + (-5), 4 + 6)$

$= (1, 10)$

20. $3\overrightarrow{v} + \overrightarrow{s} = (3 \times 3, 3 \times 2) + (2, 7)$

$= (9, 6) + (2, 7)$

$= (9 + 2, 6 + 7)$

$= (11, 13)$

21. $\overrightarrow{w} + \overrightarrow{s} + \overrightarrow{t} = (2, -4) + (2, 7) + (-5, 6)$

$= (2 + 2 + (-5), -4 + 7 + 6)$

$= (-1, 9)$

PAGES 605-606   EXERCISES

22. length = 6 + 6 or 12 units

23. Let $C = (0, 0)$, $A = (0, 6)$, $B = (-6, 6)$

$|\overrightarrow{CB}| = \sqrt{(-6 - 0)^2 + (6 - 0)^2}$

$= \sqrt{(-6)^2 + 6^2}$

$= \sqrt{72}$

$= 6\sqrt{2} \approx 8.5$ units

24. direction: $\tan x = \frac{6 - 0}{-6 - 0}$

$\tan x = \frac{6}{-6}$

$x = -45°$

The direction is 45° north of west.

25.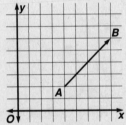

$|\overrightarrow{AB}| = \sqrt{(8 - 4)^2 + (6 - 2)^2}$

$= \sqrt{4^2 + 4^2}$

$= \sqrt{32}$

$= 4\sqrt{2} \approx 5.7$ units

direction of $\overrightarrow{AB}$: $\tan x = \frac{6 - 2}{8 - 4}$

$\tan x = \frac{4}{4}$

$x = 45°$

26.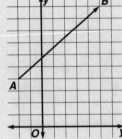

$|\overrightarrow{AB}| = \sqrt{(5 - (-2))^2 + (10 - 4)^2}$

$= \sqrt{7^2 + 6^2}$

$= \sqrt{85} \approx 9.2$ units

direction of $\overrightarrow{AB}$: $\tan x = \dfrac{10 - 4}{5 - (-2)}$

$\tan x = \dfrac{6}{7}$

$x \approx 41°$

27. $\overrightarrow{BC}$ and $\overrightarrow{AD}$ are parallel since they have the same direction.

28. $\overrightarrow{BC}$ and $\overrightarrow{AD}$ are equal since they have the same direction and magnitude.

29. $\overrightarrow{RT}$ 30. $\overrightarrow{TR}$ 31. $\overrightarrow{PR}$ 32. $\overrightarrow{RQ}$

33. $\vec{v} + \vec{u} = (2,\ 5) + (7,\ 1)$

$= (2 + 7,\ 5 + 1)$

$= (9,\ 6)$

34. $\vec{v} + 2\vec{u} = (2,\ 5) + (2 \times 7,\ 2 \times 1)$

$= (2,\ 5) + (14,\ 2)$

$= (2 + 14,\ 5 + 2)$

$= (16,\ 7)$

35. $2\vec{u} + 3\vec{v} = (2 \times 7,\ 2 \times 1) + (3 \times 2,\ 3 \times 5)$

$= (14,\ 2) + (6,\ 15)$

$= (14 + 6,\ 2 + 15)$

$= (20,\ 17)$

36. a. 1. Definition of vector addition
   2. Definition of vector addition
   3. Given
   4. Substitution prop. of equality
   5. Distributive prop.
   6. Substitution prop. of equality
   7. Multiplication prop. of equality

   b. If a segment has as its endpoints the midpoints of two sides of a triangle, its length is one-half the length of the third side.

37. direction of $\overrightarrow{CD}$: $\tan a = \dfrac{3 - 1}{4 - 6}$

$\tan a = \dfrac{2}{-2}$

$\tan a = -1$

direction of $\overrightarrow{AB}$: $\tan b = \dfrac{5 - (-4)}{2 - x}$

$\tan b = \dfrac{9}{2 - x}$

If $\overrightarrow{CD} \parallel \overrightarrow{AB}$, then the directions, a and b, of $\overrightarrow{CD}$ and $\overrightarrow{AB}$ are the same.

$a = b$

$\tan a = \tan b$

$-1 = \dfrac{9}{2 - x}$

$-2 + x = 9$

$x = 11$

38. The magnitudes are the same since the distance between the points is constant. But the directions are opposite.

39.

$\overrightarrow{AB}$ and $2\overrightarrow{AB}$ are parallel, and $\overrightarrow{AB} + \overrightarrow{BL}$ and $\overrightarrow{SR}$ are parallel since they have the same direction.

40. $\overrightarrow{AB} + \overrightarrow{BL}$ and $\overrightarrow{SR}$ are equal since they have the same magnitude and direction.

41. $\vec{v} \cdot \vec{w} = 7 \cdot 4 + (-2) \cdot 14$

$= 28 + (-28)$

$= 0$

$\vec{v} \perp \vec{w}$

$\vec{v} \cdot \vec{u} = 7 \cdot (-2) + (-2) \cdot 7$

$= -14 + (-14)$

$= -28$

$\vec{v} \not\perp \vec{u}$

$\vec{v} \cdot \vec{t} = 7 \cdot 2 + (-2) \cdot 7$

$= 14 + (-14)$

$= 0$

$\vec{v} \perp \vec{t}$

$\vec{w} \cdot \vec{u} = 4 \cdot (-2) + 14 \cdot 7$

$= -8 + 98$

$= 90$

$\vec{w} \not\perp \vec{u}$

$\vec{w} \cdot \vec{t} = 4 \cdot 2 + 14 \cdot 7$

$= 8 + 98$

$= 106$

$\vec{w} \not\perp \vec{t}$

$\vec{u} \cdot \vec{t} = -2 \cdot 2 + 7 \cdot 7$

$= -4 + 49$

$= 45$

$\vec{u} \not\perp \vec{t}$

42. Sample answer:

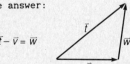

$\vec{t} - \vec{v} = \vec{w}$

If $\vec{t} = (x_1,\ y_1)$ and $\vec{v} = (x_2,\ y_2)$,

$\vec{t} - \vec{v} = (x_1 - x_2,\ y_1 - y_2)$

43.

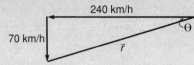

$\vec{r}$ is the path of the plane.

$|\vec{r}| = \sqrt{(240 - 0)^2 + (0 - (-70))^2}$

$= \sqrt{240^2 + 70^2}$

$= \sqrt{62500}$

$= 250$ km/h

direction: $\tan \theta = \dfrac{70}{240}$

$\theta \approx 16°$

The resulting speed is 250 km/h and the direction is 16° south of west.

44.

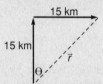

direction: $\tan \theta = \dfrac{15}{15}$

$\theta = 45°$

The direction is 45° east of north.

$|\vec{r}| = \sqrt{(15 - 0)^2 + (15 - 0)^2}$

$= \sqrt{15^2 + 15^2}$

$= 15\sqrt{2} \approx 21.2$ km

45.

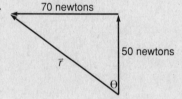

$|\vec{r}| = \sqrt{(0 - (-70))^2 + (0 - 50)^2}$

$= \sqrt{(-70)^2 + 50^2}$

$= \sqrt{7400}$

≈ 86 newtons

direction: $\tan \theta = \dfrac{70}{50}$

$\theta \approx 54°$

The direction is 54° west of north.

46.

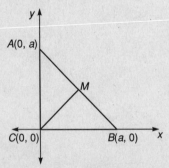

Midpoint M is $\left(\dfrac{0 + a}{2}, \dfrac{a + 0}{2}\right)$ or $\left(\dfrac{a}{2}, \dfrac{a}{2}\right)$.

Slope of $\overline{AB}$ is $\dfrac{0 - a}{a - 0}$ or $\dfrac{-a}{a}$ or -1.

Slope of $\overline{CM}$ is $\dfrac{\frac{a}{2} - 0}{\frac{a}{2} - 0}$ or $\dfrac{\frac{a}{2}}{\frac{a}{2}}$ or 1.

Since $-1 \cdot 1 = -1$, $\overline{CM}$ is perpendicular to $\overline{AB}$.

47. $V = \pi r^2 h$

$= \pi(5)^2(2)$

$= 50\pi$

≈ 157.1 m^2

48. $C = 2\pi r$

$= 2\pi(8)$

$= 16\pi$

≈ 50.3 in.

49. $\dfrac{6}{12} = \dfrac{9}{x}$

$6x = 108$

$x = 18$

$\dfrac{6}{12} = \dfrac{11}{y}$

$6y = 132$

$y = 22$

50. See students' work.

12-7 Coordinates in Space

PAGE 610   CHECKING FOR UNDERSTANDING

1. The 3 axes intersect at the same point and are perpendicular to each other.

2. The distance formula in a plane is the square root of the sum of the squares of the differences of the x and y values. The distance formula in space is the square root of the sum of the squares of the differences of the x, y, and z values.

3. The x value of the midpoint is the sum of the x values divided by 2. The y value of the midpoint is the sum of the y values divided by 2. The z value of the midpoint is the sum of the z values divided by 2.

4. A circle is 2-dimensional and a sphere is 3-dimensional. The equation of a sphere has a z term as well as x and y terms. The equation of a circle has just x and y terms.

5.

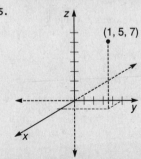

236

6.

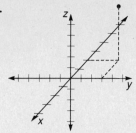

7. $AB = \sqrt{(0 - 0)^2 + (5 - 0)^2 + (0 - 0)^2}$

   $= \sqrt{5^2} = 5$

8. $PQ = \sqrt{(0 - 1)^2 + (2 - 0)^2 + (3 - (-3))^2}$

   $= \sqrt{(-1)^2 + 2^2 + 6^2}$

   $= \sqrt{41} \approx 6.4$

9. $M = \left(\dfrac{0 + 3}{2}, \dfrac{-4 + 0}{2}, \dfrac{2 + 2}{2}\right)$

   $= \left(\dfrac{3}{2}, -2, 2\right)$

10. $N = \left(\dfrac{-6 + 6}{2}, \dfrac{3 + 3}{2}, \dfrac{-1 + 1}{2}\right)$

   $= (0, 3, 0)$

11. $(0, 3, 4); 9$ 12. $(-2, -4, 4); 5$

13. $(x - 4)^2 + (y - 1)^2 + (z - (-2))^2 = 6^2$

   $(x - 4)^2 + (y - 1)^2 + (z + 2)^2 = 36$

14. $(x - 0)^2 + (y - 0)^2 + (z - 4)^2 = 16^2$

   $x^2 + y^2 + (z - 4)^2 = 256$

15. $PQ = \sqrt{(3 - 0)^2 + (4 - 0)^2 + (\sqrt{11} - 0)^2}$

   $= \sqrt{3^2 + 4^2 + (\sqrt{11})^2}$

   $= \sqrt{36}$

   $= 6$

   $PR = \sqrt{(0 - 0)^2 + (5 - 0)^2 + (0 - 0)^2}$

   $= \sqrt{0^2 + 5^2 + 0^2}$

   $= \sqrt{25}$

   $= 5$

   $QR = \sqrt{(3 - 0)^2 + (4 - 5)^2 + (\sqrt{11} - 0)^2}$

   $= \sqrt{3^2 + (-1)^2 + (\sqrt{11})^2}$

   $= \sqrt{21}$

   perimeter of $\triangle PQR = PQ + PR + QR$

   $= 6 + 5 + \sqrt{21}$

   $= 11 + \sqrt{21} \approx 15.6$ units

16. diameter $= \sqrt{(4 - 0)^2 + (7 - (-2))^2 + (-3 - 9)^2}$

   $= \sqrt{4^2 + 9^2 + (-12)^2}$

   $= \sqrt{241}$ units

   radius $= \dfrac{\sqrt{241}}{2} \approx 7.8$ units

17.

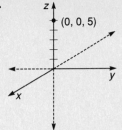

18.

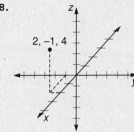

19.

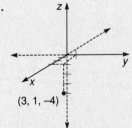

20. $AB = \sqrt{(2 - 2)^2 + (4 - 4)^2 + (7 - 5)^2}$

   $= \sqrt{0^2 + 0^2 + 2^2}$

   $= \sqrt{4}$

   $= 2$ units

21. $AB = \sqrt{(0 - (-3))^2 + (-2 - 4)^2 + (5 - (-2))^2}$

   $= \sqrt{3^2 + (-6)^2 + 7^2}$

   $= \sqrt{94} \approx 9.7$ units

22. $AB = \sqrt{(9 - 5)^2 + (1 - (-7))^2 + (0 - 4)^2}$

   $= \sqrt{4^2 + 8^2 + (-4)^2}$

   $= \sqrt{96} \approx 9.8$ units

23. $AB = \sqrt{(8 - 1)^2 + (10 - 12)^2 + (-3 - 6)^2}$

   $= \sqrt{7^2 + (-2)^2 + (-9)^2}$

   $= \sqrt{134} \approx 11.6$ units

24. $M = \left(\dfrac{1 + 7}{2}, \dfrac{3 + (-3)}{2}, \dfrac{-2 + 2}{2}\right)$

   $= (4, 0, 0)$

25. $M = \left(\dfrac{-5 + 5}{2}, \dfrac{4 + (-4)}{2}, \dfrac{-2 + 2}{2}\right)$

   $= (0, 0, 0)$

26. $M = \left(\dfrac{5 + 11}{2}, \dfrac{-6 + (-2)}{2}, \dfrac{3 + 7}{2}\right)$

   $= (8, -4, 5)$

27. $M = \left(\dfrac{22 + 0}{2}, \dfrac{5 + (-3)}{2}, \dfrac{-1 + 6}{2}\right)$

   $= (11, 1, 2.5)$

28. $(6, -5, 1)$; 9

29. $(-2, -3, 2)$; 10

30. $(0, 2, 4)$; 2

31. $(-8, 0, -4)$; $\sqrt{18} \approx 4.2$

32. $(x - (-1))^2 + (y - 2)^2 + (z - 4)^2 = 3^2$

$\quad (x + 1)^2 + (y - 2)^2 + (z - 4)^2 = 9$

33. $(x - 6)^2 + (y - (-1))^2 + (z - 3)^2 = 12^2$

$\quad (x - 6)^2 + (y + 1)^2 + (z - 3)^2 = 144$

34. $(x - 0)^2 + (y - 3)^2 + (z - (-2))^2 = 11^2$

$\quad\quad x^2 + (y - 3)^2 + (z + 2)^2 = 121$

35. $(x - (-2))^2 + (y - 4)^2 + (z - 1)^2 = (\sqrt{13})^2$

$\quad (x + 2)^2 + (y - 4)^2 + (z - 1)^2 = 13$

36. $AB = \sqrt{(6 - 4)^2 + (4 - 6)^2 + (1 - 0)^2}$

$\quad\quad = \sqrt{2^2 + (-2)^2 + 1^2}$

$\quad\quad = \sqrt{9}$

$\quad\quad = 3$

$\quad BC = \sqrt{(4 - 3)^2 + (6 - (-2))^2 + (0 - 3)^2}$

$\quad\quad = \sqrt{1^2 + 8^2 + (-3)^2}$

$\quad\quad = \sqrt{74}$

$\quad AC = \sqrt{(6 - 3)^2 + (4 - (-2))^2 + (1 - 3)^2}$

$\quad\quad = \sqrt{3^2 + 6^2 + (-2)^2}$

$\quad\quad = \sqrt{49}$

$\quad\quad = 7$

perimeter of $\triangle ABC = AB + BC + AC$

$\quad\quad\quad\quad = 3 + \sqrt{74} + 7$

$\quad\quad\quad\quad = 10 + \sqrt{74} \approx 18.6$ units

37. a. $C = \left(\dfrac{-3 + 5}{2}, \dfrac{5 + (-1)}{2}, \dfrac{7 + 5}{2}\right)$

$\quad\quad = (1, 2, 6)$

b. radius $= \sqrt{(1 - (-3))^2 + (2 - 5)^2 + (6 - 7)^2}$

$\quad\quad = \sqrt{4^2 + (-3)^2 + (-1)^2}$

$\quad\quad = \sqrt{26} \approx 5.1$ units

c. $(x - 1)^2 + (y - 2)^2 + (z - 6)^2 = (\sqrt{26})^2$

$\quad (x - 1)^2 + (y - 2)^2 + (z - 6)^2 = 26$

d.

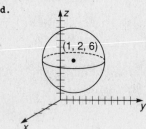

e. $T = 4\pi r^2$

$\quad = 4\pi(\sqrt{26})^2$

$\quad = 104\pi$

$\quad \approx 326.7$ units^2

f. $V = \dfrac{4}{3}\pi r^3$

$\quad = \dfrac{4}{3}\pi(\sqrt{26})^3$

$\quad \approx 555.3$ units^3

38. $T = 2(4)(4) + 2(4)(4) + 2(4)(4) \quad V = (4)(4)(4)$

$\quad = 96$ units^2 $\quad\quad\quad\quad\quad\quad\quad = 64$ units^3

39. $9 = \sqrt{(3t - 5)^2 + (5 - (-3))^2 + (-t - t)^2}$

$\quad 81 = (3t - 5)^2 + 8^2 + (-2t)^2$

$\quad 81 = 9t^2 - 30t + 25 + 64 + 4t^2$

$\quad 0 = 13t^2 - 30t + 8$

$\quad 0 = (13t - 4)(t - 2)$

$\quad t = \dfrac{4}{13}$ or 2

40. Midpoint M of $\overline{ST}$

$\quad = \left(\dfrac{-3 + 7}{2}, \dfrac{8 + 2}{2}, \dfrac{1 + (-3)}{2}\right) = (2, 5, -1)$

median from R to M

$\quad = \sqrt{(2 - 9)^2 + (5 - 4)^2 + (-1 - 11)^2}$

$\quad = \sqrt{(-7)^2 + 1^2 + (-12)^2}$

$\quad = \sqrt{194} \approx 13.9$ units

Midpoint N of $\overline{RS}$

$\quad = \left(\dfrac{9 + (-3)}{2}, \dfrac{4 + 8}{2}, \dfrac{11 + 1}{2}\right) = (3, 6, 6)$

median from T to N

$\quad = \sqrt{(3 - 7)^2 + (6 - 2)^2 + (6 - (-3))^2}$

$\quad = \sqrt{(-4)^2 + 4^2 + 9^2}$

$\quad = \sqrt{113} \approx 10.6$ units

Midpoint O of $\overline{RT}$

$\quad = \left(\dfrac{9 + 7}{2}, \dfrac{4 + 2}{2}, \dfrac{11 + (-3)}{2}\right) = (8, 3, 4)$

median from S to O

$\quad = \sqrt{(8 - (-3))^2 + (3 - 8)^2 + (4 - 1)^2}$

$\quad = \sqrt{11^2 + (-5)^2 + 3^2}$

$\quad = \sqrt{155} \approx 12.4$ units

41. $\dfrac{\sqrt{36}}{\sqrt{100}} = \dfrac{6}{10} = \dfrac{3}{5}$

42. $\dfrac{\pi(6)^2}{\pi(10)^2} = \dfrac{36\pi}{100\pi} = \dfrac{9}{25}$

43. $\dfrac{\frac{4}{3}\pi(6)^3}{\frac{4}{3}\pi(10)^3} = \dfrac{6^3}{10^3} = \dfrac{27}{125}$

44. The change in the x-, y-, and z-coordinates between $(4, -6, 10)$ and $(0, 1, -4)$ are -4, 7, and -14 respectively. So $(0 - 4, 1 + 7, -4 - 14)$ or $(-4, 8, -18)$ is collinear to these points.

radius $= \sqrt{(4 - 0)^2 + (-6 - 1)^2 + (10 - (-4))^2}$

$\quad = \sqrt{4^2 + (-7)^2 + 14^2}$

$\quad = \sqrt{261}$

equation of the circle

$\quad = (x - 0)^2 + (y - 1)^2 + (z - (-4))^2 = (\sqrt{261})^2$

$\quad\quad x^2 + (y - 1)^2 + (z + 4)^2 = 261$

Is (-4, 8, -18) on the circle?

$$(-4)^2 + ((8) - 1)^2 + ((-18) + 4)^2 \overset{?}{=} 261$$

$$(-4)^2 + 7^2 + (-14)^2 \overset{?}{=} 261$$

$$16 + 49 + 196 \overset{?}{=} 261$$

$$261 = 261$$

The other endpoint of the diameter is (-4, 8, -18).

45. planes' locations: (7, -9, 2) and (-4, -4, 1)

distance

$$= \sqrt{(7 - (-4))^2 + (-9 - (-4))^2 + (2 - 1)^2}$$

$$= \sqrt{11^2 + (-5)^2 + 1^2}$$

$$= \sqrt{147} \approx 12.1 \text{ miles}$$

46. (1, 2, 2) to block a row of Xs.

47. $2\vec{t} + \vec{u} = (2 \times 1, 2 \times (-5)) + (-4, 2)$

$$= (2, -10) + (-4, 2)$$

$$= (2 + (-4), -10 + 2)$$

$$= (-2, -8)$$

48. $A = \pi r^2$

$$= \pi(5)^2$$

$$= 25\pi$$

$$\approx 78.5 \text{ cm}^2$$

49. $\tan 36° = \dfrac{\frac{1}{2}}{5.5}$

$$s \approx 7.99 \text{ cm}$$

$$A = \frac{1}{2}Pa$$

$$\approx \frac{1}{2}(5 \cdot 7.99)(5.5)$$

$$\approx 109.9 \text{ cm}^2$$

50. $A = \frac{1}{2}bh$

$$= \frac{1}{2}(7)(3)$$

$$= 10.5 \text{ in}^2$$

51. Two lines intersect and more than one plane contains them.

52. $x + 25 = 2x - 75$

$$100 = x$$

53. See students' work.

Technology: Perspective Drawing

1. a. $A(-4, 1)$, $B(1, 1)$, $C(1, -4)$, $D(-4, -4)$, $E(0, 5)$, $F(5, 5)$, $G(5, 0)$, $H(0, 0)$

   b. See students' work.

2. a. $A(-7, -5)$, $B(1, -5)$, $C(8, -1)$, $D(0, 3)$

   b. See students' work.

Chapter 12 Summary and Review

1. 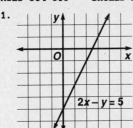   2.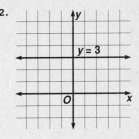

3. perpendicular; $2, -\frac{1}{2}$ 4. parallel; 5, 5

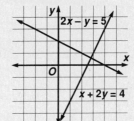   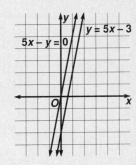

5. $m = 1$, $b = 8$ 6. $m = -\frac{1}{3}$

$y = x + 8$ $y - 0 = -\frac{1}{3}(x - 6)$

$y = -\frac{1}{3}x + 2$

7. $m = 0$ 8. $m = $ undefined

$y - 2 = 0(x - 5)$ $x = 5$

$y - 2 = 0$

$y = 2$

9. slope of $\overleftrightarrow{XY} = \dfrac{-1 - 1}{2 - 6} = \dfrac{-2}{-4} = \dfrac{1}{2}$

$y - (-1) = \frac{1}{2}(x - 2)$

$y + 1 = \frac{1}{2}x - 1$

$y = \frac{1}{2}x - 2$

slope of $\overleftrightarrow{YZ} = \dfrac{1 - (-3)}{6 - 0} = \dfrac{4}{6} = \dfrac{2}{3}$

$y - 1 = \frac{2}{3}(x - 6)$

$y - 1 = \frac{2}{3}x - 4$

$y = \frac{2}{3}x - 3$

slope of $\overleftrightarrow{XZ} = \dfrac{-1 - (-3)}{2 - 0} = \dfrac{2}{2} = 1$

$y - (-1) = 1(x - 2)$

$y + 1 = x - 2$

$y = x - 3$

10. midpoint of $\overleftrightarrow{XY} = \left(\dfrac{2 + 6}{2}, \dfrac{-1 + 1}{2}\right) = (4, 0)$

slope of median through $Z = \dfrac{0 - (-3)}{4 - 0} = \dfrac{3}{4}$

$y - 0 = \dfrac{3}{4}(x - 4)$

$y = \dfrac{3}{4}x - 3$

midpoint of $\overleftrightarrow{YZ} = \left(\dfrac{6 + 0}{2}, \dfrac{1 + (-3)}{2}\right) = (3, -1)$

slope of median through $X = \dfrac{-1 - (-1)}{3 - 2} = \dfrac{0}{1} = 0$

$y - (-1) = 0(x - 3)$

$y + 1 = 0$

$y = -1$

midpoint of $\overleftrightarrow{XZ} = \left(\dfrac{2 + 0}{2}, \dfrac{-1 + (-3)}{2}\right) = (1, -2)$

slope of median through $Y = \dfrac{-2 - 1}{1 - 6} = \dfrac{-3}{-5} = \dfrac{3}{5}$

$y - (-2) = \dfrac{3}{5}(x - 1)$

$y + 2 = \dfrac{3}{5}x - \dfrac{3}{5}$

$y = \dfrac{3}{5}x - \dfrac{13}{5}$

11. From Exercise 9, slope of $\overleftrightarrow{XY} = \dfrac{1}{2}$, slope of $\overleftrightarrow{YZ} = \dfrac{2}{3}$, and slope of $\overleftrightarrow{XZ} = 1$. So, the slopes of the altitudes to $\overleftrightarrow{XY}$, $\overleftrightarrow{YZ}$, and $\overleftrightarrow{XZ}$ are -2, $-\dfrac{3}{2}$, and -1 respectively.

altitude to $\overleftrightarrow{XY}$:   altitude to $\overleftrightarrow{YZ}$:

$y - (-3) = -2(x - 0)$ $y - (-1) = -\dfrac{3}{2}(x - 2)$

$y + 3 = -2x$

$y = -2x - 3$ $y + 1 = -\dfrac{3}{2}x + 3$

                          $y = -\dfrac{3}{2}x + 2$

altitude to $\overleftrightarrow{XZ}$:

$y - 1 = -1(x - 6)$

$y - 1 = -x + 6$

$y = -x + 7$

12. From Exercise 11, the slopes of the perpendiculars to $\overleftrightarrow{XY}$, $\overleftrightarrow{YZ}$, and $\overleftrightarrow{XZ}$ are -2, $-\dfrac{3}{2}$, and -1 respectively. And from Exercise 10, the midpoints are $(4, 0)$, $(3, -1)$ and $(1, -2)$ respectively.

perpendicular bisector of $\overleftrightarrow{XY}$

$y - 0 = -2(x - 4)$

$y = -2x + 8$

perpendicular bisector of $\overleftrightarrow{YZ}$

$y - (-1) = -\dfrac{3}{2}(x - 3)$

$y + 1 = -\dfrac{3}{2}x + \dfrac{9}{2}$

$y = -\dfrac{3}{2}x + \dfrac{7}{2}$

perpendicular bisector of $\overleftrightarrow{XZ}$

$y - (-2) = -1(x - 1)$

$y + 2 = -x + 1$

$y = -x - 1$

13.

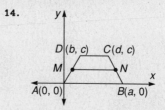

Midpoint M is $\left(\dfrac{b + 0}{2}, \dfrac{c + 0}{2}\right)$ or $\left(\dfrac{b}{2}, \dfrac{c}{2}\right)$.

Midpoint N is $\left(\dfrac{a + d}{2}, \dfrac{c + 0}{2}\right)$ or $\left(\dfrac{a + d}{2}, \dfrac{c}{2}\right)$.

Slope of $\overline{DC}$ is $\dfrac{c - c}{d - b}$ or $\dfrac{0}{d - b}$ or 0.

Slope of $\overline{MN}$ is $\dfrac{\frac{c}{2} - \frac{c}{2}}{\frac{a + d}{2} - \frac{b}{2}}$ or $\dfrac{0}{\frac{a + d - b}{2}}$ or 0.

Slope of $\overline{AB}$ is $\dfrac{0 - 0}{a - 0}$ or $\dfrac{0}{a}$ or 0.

$\overline{DC} \parallel \overline{MN} \parallel \overline{AB}$

14.

$DC = \sqrt{(d - b)^2 + (c - c)^2} = \sqrt{(b - d)^2 + 0}$

$= d - b$

$AB = \sqrt{(a - 0)^2 + (0 - 0)^2} = \sqrt{a^2 + 0^2} = a$

$MN = \sqrt{\left(\dfrac{a + d}{2} - \dfrac{b}{2}\right)^2 + \left(\dfrac{c}{2} - \dfrac{c}{2}\right)^2}$

$= \sqrt{\left(\dfrac{a + d - b}{2}\right)^2 + 0} = \dfrac{a + d - b}{2}$

$\dfrac{1}{2}(DC + AB) = \dfrac{1}{2}((d - b) + a) = \dfrac{d - b - a}{2}$ or

$\dfrac{a + d - b}{2} = MN$

15. $|\vec{v}| = \sqrt{(7 - 0)^2 + (1 - 0)^2}$

$= \sqrt{7^2 + 1^2}$

$\sqrt{50} \approx 7.1$ units

direction of $\vec{v}$: $\tan \theta = \dfrac{1}{7}$

$\theta \approx 8.1°$

16. $|\overrightarrow{AB}| = \sqrt{(7 - 1)^2 + (5 - 0)^2}$

$= \sqrt{6^2 + 5^2}$

$= \sqrt{61} \approx 7.8$ units

direction of $\overrightarrow{AB} = \tan \theta = \dfrac{5}{6}$

$\theta \approx 39.8°$

17. $\vec{a} + \vec{b} = (2, 4) + (5, -3)$

$= (2 + 5, 4 + (-3))$

$= (7, 1)$

18. $\vec{r} + \vec{s} = (0, 8) + (4, 0)$
$= (0 + 4, 8 + 0)$
$= (4, 8)$

19. $d = \sqrt{(3 - 7)^2 + (-3 - (-3))^2 + (1 - 5)^2}$
$= \sqrt{(-4)^2 + 0^2 + (-4)^2}$
$= \sqrt{32}$
$= 4\sqrt{2} \approx 5.7$ units
$M = \left(\dfrac{3 + 7}{2}, \dfrac{-3 + (-3)}{2}, \dfrac{1 + 5}{2}\right)$
$= (5, -3, 3)$

20. $d = \sqrt{(2 - 0)^2 + (4 - 2)^2 + (6 - 4)^2}$
$= \sqrt{2^2 + 2^2 + 2^2}$
$= \sqrt{12}$
$= 2\sqrt{3} \approx 3.5$ units
$M = \left(\dfrac{2 + 0}{2}, \dfrac{4 + 2}{2}, \dfrac{6 + 4}{2}\right)$
$= (1, 3, 5)$

21. $(x - 0)^2 + (y - 0)^2 + (z - 0)^2 = 5^2$
$x^2 + y^2 + z^2 = 25$

22. $(x - (-1))^2 + (y - 2)^2 + (z - (-3))^2 = 4^2$
$(x + 1)^2 + (y - 2)^2 + (z + 3)^2 = 16$

PAGE 616   APPLICATIONS AND CONNECTIONS

23.

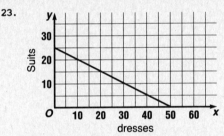

Sample answer: The x-intercept represents the situation that no suits were made that week. The y-intercept represents the situation that no dresses were made that week.

24. 6(0.21) or about 1.26 miles

25. (20, 20)

26. planes' positions: (-8, -10, 2) and (4, -8, 1)
distance
$= \sqrt{(-8 - 4)^2 + (-10 - (-8))^2 + (2 - 1)^2}$
$= \sqrt{(-12)^2 + (-2)^2 + 1^2}$
$= \sqrt{149} \approx 12.2$ miles

Chapter 12 Test

1. $-\dfrac{1}{2}$; 3   **2.** none; none

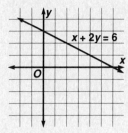 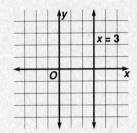

3. -3; 0

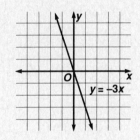

4. $y - (-2) = -4(x - 3)$
$y + 2 = -4x + 12$
$y = -4x + 10$

5. $m = \dfrac{11 - 3}{-4 - (-6)} = \dfrac{8}{2} = 4$
$y - 11 = 4(x - (-4))$
$y - 11 = 4x + 16$
$y = 4x + 27$

6. $m = 2$ **7.** $m = $ undefined
$y - (-4) = 2(x - (-1))$ $x = -4$
$y + 4 = 2x + 2$
$y = 2x - 2$

8.   **9.**

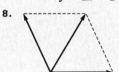

10. $\vec{a} + \vec{b} = (-3, 5) + (0, 7)$
$= (-3 + 0, 5 + 7)$
$= (-3, 12)$

11. (4, 5, -2); $\sqrt{81} = 9$

12. (0, 0, 0); $\sqrt{7} \approx 2.6$

13. $|\vec{v}| = \sqrt{(0 - (-5))^2 + (0 - (-3))^2}$
$= \sqrt{5^2 + 3^2}$
$= \sqrt{34} \approx 5.8$ units

14. $|\overrightarrow{AB}| = \sqrt{(3 - (-2))^2 + (7 - 5)^2}$
$= \sqrt{5^2 + 2^2}$
$= \sqrt{29} \approx 5.4$ units

15. $\sqrt{(2-2)^2 + (4-4)^2 + (5-7)^2}$

$= \sqrt{0^2 + 0^2 + (-2)^2}$

$= \sqrt{4}$

$= 2$ units

16. $M = \left(\dfrac{0+3}{2}, \dfrac{-4+0}{2}, \dfrac{2+2}{2}\right)$

$= \left(\dfrac{3}{2}, -2, 2\right)$

17. diameter $= \sqrt{(-3-5)^2 + (5-(-11))^2 + (7-5)^2}$

$= \sqrt{(-8)^2 + 6^2 + 2^2}$

$= \sqrt{104}$

radius $= \dfrac{\sqrt{104}}{2}$

$= \sqrt{26}$

center $= \left(\dfrac{-3+5}{2}, \dfrac{5+(-1)}{2}, \dfrac{7+5}{2}\right)$

$= (1, 2, 6)$

equation of sphere:

$(x-1)^2 + (y-2)^2 + (z-6)^2 = (\sqrt{26})^2$

$(x-1)^2 + (y-2)^2 + (z-6)^2 = 26$

18. Slope of segment between $(5, 2)$ and $(1, -4)$

$= \dfrac{-4-2}{1-5} = \dfrac{-6}{-4}$ or $\dfrac{3}{2}$

Slope of perpendicular $= -\dfrac{2}{3}$

midpoint of segments $= \left(\dfrac{5+1}{2}, \dfrac{2+(-4)}{2}\right)$

$= (3, -1)$

equation of perpendicular bisector:

$y - (-1) = -\dfrac{2}{3}(x-3)$

$y + 1 = -\dfrac{2}{3}x + 2$

$y = -\dfrac{2}{3}x + 1$

19. $(a + b, c)$

20.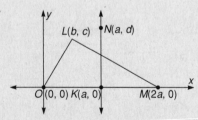

slope of $\overleftrightarrow{NK} = \dfrac{d-0}{a-a} = \dfrac{d}{0}$; undefined

slope of $\overline{OM} = \dfrac{0-0}{0-2a} = \dfrac{0}{-2a} = 0$

$\overleftrightarrow{NK} \perp \overline{OM}$ because vertical and horizontal lines are perpendicular.

$OK = \sqrt{(a-0)^2 + (0-0)^2} = a$

$KM = \sqrt{(2a-a)^2 + (0-0)^2} = a$

Since $OK = KM$ and $\overleftrightarrow{NK} \perp \overline{OM}$, $\overleftrightarrow{NK}$ is a perpendicular bisector of $\overline{OM}$.

BONUS

$NR = \sqrt{(7-3)^2 + (5-2)^2 + (-1-(-1))^2}$

$= \sqrt{4^2 + 3^2 + 0^2}$

$= \sqrt{25}$

$= 5$

$NM = \sqrt{(7-(-5))^2 + (5-(-4))^2 + (-1-(-1))^2}$

$= \sqrt{12^2 + 9^2 + 0^2}$

$= \sqrt{225}$

$= 15$

$(NT)^2 = NR \cdot NM$

$(NT)^2 = 5 \cdot 15$

$(NT)^2 = 75$

$NT = \sqrt{75}$

$NT \approx 8.7$ units

College Entrance Exam Preview

PAGES 618–619

1. D $T = 2(x^2) + 2(x)(h) + 2(x)(h)$

$= 2x^2 + 2xh + 2xh$

$= 2x^2 + 4xh$

2. C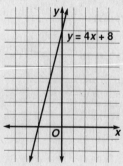

3. D   Let ℓ and w represent the length and width of the original rectangle. Then the dimensions of the new rectangle will be 3ℓ and $3w$.

area of original   area of new

$A = \ell w$ $A = (3\ell)(3w)$

$= 9\ell w$

242

4. A
$$\frac{s}{3s + 6} - \frac{s}{5s - 10} = \frac{2}{5}$$

$s(5)(5s - 10) - s(3s + 6)(5)$

   $= 2(3s + 6)(5s - 10)$

$25s^2 - 50s - 15s^2 + 30s$

   $= 30s^2 - 60s + 60s - 120$

$0 = 20s^2 + 20s - 120$

$0 = s^2 + s - 6$

$0 = (s + 3)(s - 2)$

$s = -3$ or 2

But if $s = 2$, then $\frac{s}{3s + 6}$ is undefined.

Therefore, $s = -3$.

5. C

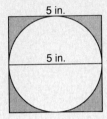

5 in.

5 in.

Area of square $= 5^2$

   $= 25$ in^2

Area of circle $= \pi r^2$

   $= \pi(2.5)^2$

   $= 6.25\pi$ in^2

Area of scrap $= 25 - 6.25\pi$

   ≈ 5.4 in^2

6. B
$$\frac{(8a + 7) + (2a + 4) + (a - 3) + 5a}{4}$$

$$= \frac{16a + 8}{4}$$

$= 4a + 2$

7. B   The slope of the segment between A and B is 0. So if the coordinates of B are x and y, $0 = \frac{y - 8}{x - 5}$ then $y = 8$. The line $x = -1$ is the perpendicular bisector, so the x-coordinate of the midpoint of $\overline{AB}$ is -1. Therefore, $x = -1 - (5 - (-1))$ or -7. B is $(-7, 8)$.

8. A $-3 - x < 2x < 3 + x$

$-3 - x < 2x$ and $2x < 3 + x$

   $-3 < 3x \qquad\quad x < 3$

   $-1 < x$

$\{x \mid -1 < x < 3\}$

9. D   The belt is traveling at a constant rate, so each pulley must cover the same distance in the same amount of time. Circumference of small pulley

$C = \pi d$

   $= \pi(4)$

   $= 4\pi$ in.

Circumference of large pulley

$C = \pi d$

   $= \pi(6)$

   $= 6\pi$ in.

In one minute, the small pulley travels $180(4\pi)$ or 720π inches. Suppose the large pulley makes x revolutions per minute.

$x(6\pi) = 720\pi$

   $x = 120$ rpm

10. A $x + 1$ increases as x increases.

x^2 increases as x increases if $x > 0$, so since $0 < x < 1$, $1 - x^2$ decreases as x increases.

$\frac{1}{x}$ decreases as x increases.

11. D
$$x^2 + kx - 51 = 0$$

$(-3)^2 + k(-3) - 51 = 0$

$9 - 3k - 51 = 0$

   $-3k = 42$

   $k = -14$

12. $68 + x + 3x = 180$

   $4x = 112$

   $x = 28$

The angles measure $28°$ and $3(28)$ or $84°$.

13. $\frac{\text{sum of six numbers}}{6} = 10$

sum of six numbers $= 60$

$\frac{\text{sum of ten numbers}}{10} = 6$

sum of ten numbers $= 60$

average of all sixteen $= \frac{\text{sum of six + sum of ten}}{16}$

   $= \frac{60 + 60}{16}$

   $= \frac{120}{16}$

   $= 7.5$

14. volume of space to be filled $= (80)(45)\left(\frac{3}{12}\right)$

   $= 900$ ft^2

$900(7.5)$ or 6750 gallons of water will be needed.

15. $75 + 9(x + 4) = 183$

   $75 + 9x - 36 = 183$

   $9x = 144$

   $x = 16$ ounces

16. $AM = 1$, $MB = 1$, $BN = 1$, and $CN = 1$.

area of $\triangle MND$ = area of square − area of $\triangle AMD$ − area of $\triangle MBN$ − area of $\triangle NCD$

$$= 2^2 - \frac{1}{2}(2)(1) - \frac{1}{2}(1)(1) - \frac{1}{2}(2)(1)$$

$$= 2^2 - 1 - \frac{1}{2} - 1$$

$$= 1.5$$

$$\frac{\text{area of } \triangle MND}{\text{area of square}} = \frac{1.5}{2^2}$$

$$= \frac{1.5}{4}$$

$$= \frac{3}{8}$$

17. $\dfrac{8x^5y^{-2}z}{16x^{-2}yz^2} = \dfrac{x^7}{2y^3z}$

18. $V = \pi r^2 h$

$$= \pi\left(\frac{12}{2}\right)^2(8)$$

$$= 288\pi$$

$$\approx 904.77 \text{ in}^3$$

The can holds about $\dfrac{904.77}{231}$ or 3.9 gallons.

19. $\dfrac{30}{50} + \dfrac{30}{x} = 1$

$$30x + 1500 = 50x$$

$$1500 = 20x$$

$$75 = x$$

75 minutes or 1 hour 15 minutes

20. Let x represent the number of hours it takes to travel to the first stop at 50 miles per hour. The distance to the stop is constant, so

$$45\left(x + \frac{2}{60}\right) = 50x$$

$$45x + \frac{3}{2} = 50x$$

$$\frac{3}{2} = 5x$$

$$0.3 = x$$

The first stop is 0.3(50) or 15 miles from the station.

244

Chapter 13 Loci and Transformations

13-1	Locus

1. A locus of points is the set of all points that satisfy given conditions.

2. A circle with radius of 3 in. and center at point C

3. The locus of points will be a sphere with radius of 3 in. instead of a circle with a radius of 3 in.

4. A cylindrical surface with $\overleftrightarrow{AB}$ as the axis and a radius of 5 cm

5. The locus of points will be two parallel lines, one on each side of $\overleftrightarrow{AB}$ and 5 cm from $\overleftrightarrow{AB}$, instead of a cylindrical surface.

6. 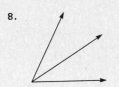 a line parallel to the given lines and halfway between the lines

7. 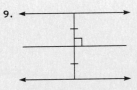 the perpendicular bisector of the line segment

8.  A ray that bisects the given angle

9.  Two parallel lines to the base, one on each side of the base and each at a distance equal to the altitude from the line that contains the base

10. A plane parallel to the given lines and halfway between the lines

11. A plane that is the perpendicular bisector of the given line segment

12. 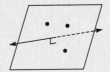 A line perpendicular to the plane determined by the three points that intersects the plane at a point equidistant from the points

13. 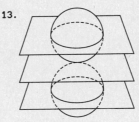 Two planes parallel to the given plane and each r units from the given plane

14. The portion of the plane, inside the classroom, that is parallel to the floor and the ceiling of the classroom and halfway between them.

15. A line segment perpendicular to the floor at the intersection of the diagonals of the floor of the classroom with endpoints on the floor and ceiling

16. Two parallel lines, one on each side of m and 4 meters from m

17. The 50-yard line of the football field

18. A sphere with a radius of one meter and a center at C

19. A cylindrical surface with line ℓ as the axis and a radius of 4 inches

20. The center line of the road

21. 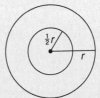 A circle concentric to the given circle with a radius that is half the radius of the given circle

22. 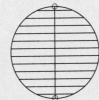 The perpendicular bisector of the chords; a diameter of the circle not including the endpoints that lie on the circle

245

23. 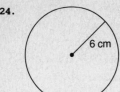 Two circles, one with a radius of three inches and the other with a radius of nine inches and concentric to the given circle

24. 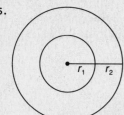 The interior of a circle with radius of 6 centimeters

25. 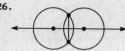 The circle with a radius equal to the sum of the radii of the 2 gears and center at the center of the large gear

26. 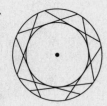 The line that is the perpendicular bisector of the chord with endpoints at the points of intersection; the line passing through the centers of the given circles

27. 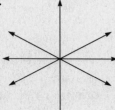 A circle concentric to the given circle and with a radius equal to the distance that the chords are from the center of the given circle

28. 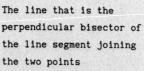 Two perpendicular lines which bisect the angles formed by the given intersecting lines

29. 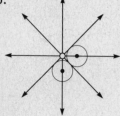 The line that is the perpendicular bisector of the line segment joining the two points

30. Two perpendicular lines which bisect the angles formed by the intersecting lines, not including the point of intersection of these lines

31. 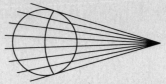 A curve which has endpoints on the circle at the points of tangency of the tangents to the circle from the given point and passing through the center of the circle; the endpoints are not part of the locus.

32. 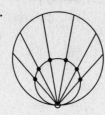 A circle whose diameter is half that of the given circle and is internally tangent to the given circle at the given point; the given point is not part of the locus

33. Two planes parallel to the given plane, one on each side of the given plane and the given distance from the plane

34. Two perpendicular planes that bisect the angles formed by the given intersecting planes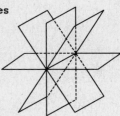

35. A line perpendicular to the plane at the point of tangency except the point itself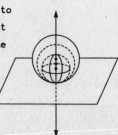

36. 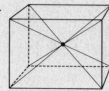 The point of intersection of the diagonals of the prism

246

37. 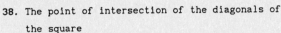 A line perpendicular to the plane of the circle at the center of the circle

38. The point of intersection of the diagonals of the square

39. A line perpendicular to $\mathcal{R}$ at the point of intersection of the diagonals of the square

40. Two perpendicular lines, one parallel to $\overline{AB}$ and $\overline{DC}$ and the other parallel to $\overline{AD}$ and $\overline{BC}$ and intersecting the center of the square

41. Two planes perpendicular to $\mathcal{R}$ and passing through the lines described in the answer for Exercise 40

42. A line parallel to $\overline{AB}$ and $\overline{DC}$ and halfway between them

43. All points on a circle with center at the vertex and radius half the length of the hypotenuse except the points on the given line and the points on the line perpendicular to the given line at the vertex

44. A part of a great circle

45. A curve that repeats itself every time the wheel makes one complete rotation

46. An arc of the circle with center at O and a radius of 100 cm followed by an arc of a circle with center B and a radius of 50 cm

47.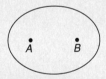

48. The interior of a rectangle that makes up the basketball court, minus a semicircle with center at the midpoint of the end with the basket and a radius of 19 ft 9 in.

49. A great circle crossing the great circle passing through Chicago and London such that their tangents at the point of intersection are perpendicular to each other

50. A circle and its interior with center at the broadcasting tower and a radius of 80 mi

51. The points on the perpendicular bisector of the line segment between the two students

52. slope

53. $T = 4\pi r^2$

$= 4(3.1416)(10)^2$

$\approx 1256.6 \text{ cm}^2$

54. 90

55. diameters

56. right triangle

57. skew

58. See students' work.

13-2 Locus and Systems of Equations

PAGE 631   CHECKING FOR UNDERSTANDING

1. If the lines are not parallel, the intersection will be one point. If both equations represent the same line, the locus will be the entire line. If the lines are parallel, there will be no points of intersection.

2. Replace x with -2 and y with 3 in both equations and check to see if the resulting equations are correct.

3. See students' work.

4.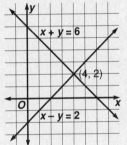

5.

6.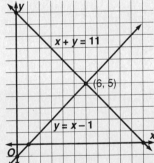

7.

$$y = 3x \qquad y = 3x$$
$$x + 2y = -21 \qquad y = 3(-3)$$
$$x + 2(3x) = -21 \qquad y = -9$$
$$x + 6x = -21$$
$$7x = -21$$
$$x = -3$$

$(-3, -9)$

8.

$$x - y = 5 \qquad x - y = 5$$
$$\underline{x + y = 25} \qquad 15 - y = 5$$
$$2x \quad\;\; = 30 \qquad -y = -10$$
$$x = 15 \qquad y = 10$$

$(15, 10)$

9.

$$4x - 10y = -40 \qquad 4x - 10y = -40$$
$$\underline{4x - 3y = -12} \qquad 4x - 10(4) = -40$$
$$-7y = -28 \qquad 4x = 0$$
$$y = 4 \qquad x = 0$$

$(0, 4)$

PAGES 631-633   EXERCISES

10. $(-2, -2)$ **11.** $(-2, 2)$ **12.** $(2, 0)$

13. $(6, 2)$ **14.** $(-2, 4)$ **15.** $(0, -1)$

16. $(-2, 0)$

17. a.
$$x + 3y = 6 \qquad \textbf{b.} \qquad x + 3y = 6$$
$$(0) + 3(2) \overset{?}{=} 6 \qquad (-1) + 3(4) \overset{?}{=} 6$$
$$6 = 6 \qquad -1 + 12 \overset{?}{=} 6$$
$$11 \neq 6$$

c.
$$x + 3y = 6 \qquad \textbf{d.} \qquad x + 3y = 6$$
$$(6) + 3(0) \overset{?}{=} 6 \qquad (-3) + 3(3) \overset{?}{=} 6$$
$$6 + 0 \overset{?}{=} 6 \qquad -3 + 9 \overset{?}{=} 6$$
$$6 = 6 \qquad 6 = 6$$

a, c, and d satisfy the equation.

18. a.
$$2x - 5y = -1 \qquad \textbf{b.} \qquad 2x - 5y = -1$$
$$2(0) - 5(5) \overset{?}{=} 1 \qquad 2(2) - 5(1) \overset{?}{=} -1$$
$$0 - 25 \overset{?}{=} 1 \qquad 4 - 5 \overset{?}{=} -1$$
$$-25 \neq 1 \qquad -1 = -1$$

c.
$$2x - 5y = -1 \qquad \textbf{d.} \qquad 2x - 5y = -1$$
$$2(0.5) - 5(0) \overset{?}{=} -1 \qquad 2(-2) - 5(-1) \overset{?}{=} -1$$
$$-1 - 0 \overset{?}{=} -1 \qquad -4 + 5 \overset{?}{=} -1$$
$$-1 = -1 \qquad 1 \neq -1$$

b and c satisfy the equation.

19. a.
$$3x = 15 \qquad \textbf{b.} \qquad 3x = 15$$
$$3(5) \overset{?}{=} 15 \qquad 3(5) \overset{?}{=} 15$$
$$15 = 15 \qquad 15 = 15$$

c.
$$3x = 15 \qquad \textbf{d.} \qquad 3x = 15$$
$$3(0) \overset{?}{=} 15 \qquad 3(5) \overset{?}{=} 15$$
$$0 \neq 15 \qquad 15 = 15$$

a, b, and d satisfy the equation.

20.

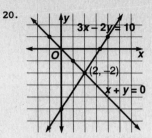

21.

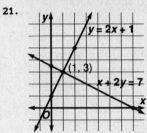

22.

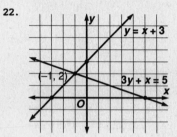

23.
$$x - y = 6 \qquad\qquad x + y = 5$$
$$\underline{x + y = 5} \qquad\qquad \frac{11}{2} + y = 5$$
$$2x \quad\;\; = 11 \qquad\qquad 11 + 2y = 10$$
$$x = \frac{11}{2} \qquad\qquad 2y = -1$$
$$y = -\frac{1}{2}$$

$\left(\dfrac{11}{2}, -\dfrac{1}{2}\right)$ or $\left(5\dfrac{1}{2}, -\dfrac{1}{2}\right)$

24.
$$x + 2y = 5$$
$$2x + y = 7$$
$$y = -2x + 7$$
$$x + 2(-2x + 7) = 5$$
$$x - 4x + 14 = 5$$
$$-3x = -9$$
$$x = 3$$
$$(3) + 2y = 5$$
$$2y = 2$$
$$y = 1$$

$(3, 1)$

25.
$$3x + 4y = -7$$
$$2x + y = -3$$
$$y = -2x - 3$$
$$3x + 4(-2x - 3) = -7$$
$$3x - 8x - 12 = -7$$
$$-5x = 5$$
$$x = -1$$
$$2(-1) + y = -3$$
$$y = -3 + 2 = -1$$

$(-1, -1)$

248

26.
$$y = x - 1$$
$$4x - y = 19$$
$$4x - (x - 1) = 19$$
$$4x - x + 1 = 19$$
$$3x = 18$$
$$x = 6$$
$$y = (6) - 1$$
$$y = 5$$
$$(6, 5)$$

27.
$$x = y + 10$$
$$2y = x - 6$$
$$2y = (y + 10) - 6$$
$$2y = y + 4$$
$$y = 4$$
$$x = (4) + 10$$
$$x = 14$$
$$(14, 4)$$

28.
$$9x + y = 20$$
$$3x + 3y = 12$$
$$y = -9x + 20$$
$$3x + 3(-9x + 20) = 12$$
$$3x - 27x + 60 = 12$$
$$-24x = -48$$
$$x = 2$$
$$9(2) + y = 20$$
$$18 + y = 20$$
$$y = 2$$
$$(2, 2)$$

29.
$$x - 2y = 5$$
$$3x - 5y = 8$$
$$x = 2y + 5$$
$$3(2y + 5) - 5y = 8$$
$$6y + 15 - 5y = 8$$
$$y = -7$$
$$x - 2(-7) = 5$$
$$x = -9$$
$$(-9, -7)$$

30.
$$3x + 7y = 16$$
$$x - 6y = 11$$
$$x = 6y + 11$$
$$3(6y + 11) + 7y = 16$$
$$18y + 33 + 7y = 16$$
$$25y = -17$$
$$y = -\frac{17}{25}$$
$$x - 6\left(-\frac{17}{25}\right) = 11$$
$$x + \frac{102}{25} = 11$$
$$25x + 102 = 275$$
$$25x = 173$$
$$x = \frac{173}{25}$$
$$\left(\frac{173}{25}, -\frac{17}{25}\right)$$

31.
$$6x + 5 = y$$
$$x - y = 0$$
$$x = y$$
$$6x + 5 = x$$
$$5x = -5$$
$$x = -1$$
$$6(-1) + 5 = y$$
$$-1 = y$$
$$(-1, -1)$$

32.
$$9x + 7y = 4 \longrightarrow 27x + 21y = 12$$
$$6x - 3y = 18 \longrightarrow \underline{42x - 21y = 126}$$
$$69x = 138$$
$$x = 2$$
$$27(2) + 21y = 12$$
$$21y = -42$$
$$y = -2$$
$$(2, -2)$$

33.
$$2x - 5y = -6 \longrightarrow -6x + 15y = 18$$
$$6x - 6y = 18 \longrightarrow \underline{6x - 6y = 18}$$
$$9y = 36$$
$$y = 4$$
$$2x - 5(4) = -6$$
$$2x = 14$$
$$x = 7$$
$$(7, 4)$$

34.
$$6x + 7y = -9 \longrightarrow -66x - 77y = 99$$
$$-9x + 11y = 78 \longrightarrow \underline{-63x + 77y = 546}$$
$$-129x = 645$$
$$x = -5$$
$$6(-5) + 7y = -9$$
$$7y = 21$$
$$y = 3$$
$$(-5, 3)$$

35.

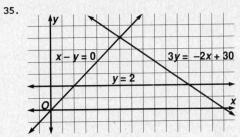

a. (2, 2), (12, 2), (6, 6)

$$y = 2 \qquad x - y = 0$$
$$x - y = 0 \qquad x = y$$
$$x - 2 = 0 \qquad 3y = -2x + 30$$
$$x = 2 \qquad 3y = -2(y) + 30$$
$$(2, 2) \qquad 5y = 30$$
$$y = 6$$
$$x = 6$$
$$(6, 6)$$

$$3y = -2x + 30$$
$$y = 2$$
$$3(2) = -2x + 30$$
$$6 - 30 = -2x$$
$$-24 = -2x$$
$$12 = x$$
$$3y = -2(12) + 30$$
$$3y = -24 + 30$$
$$3y = 6$$
$$y = 2$$
$$(12, 2)$$

b. $A = \frac{1}{2}bh$
$$= \frac{1}{2}(12 - 2)(4)$$
$$= \frac{1}{2}(10)(4)$$
$$= 20 \text{ units}^2$$

249

36.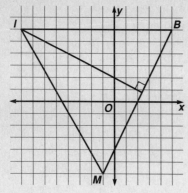

slope of $\overline{MB} = \dfrac{6-(-6)}{5-(-1)} = \dfrac{12}{6} = 2$

slope of $\perp$ to $\overline{MB} = -\dfrac{1}{2}$

equation of line $\perp$ to $\overline{MB} \longrightarrow \quad y = mx + b$

$$y = -\dfrac{1}{2}x + b$$

$$6 = -\dfrac{1}{2}(-8) + b$$

$$6 - 4 = b$$

$$2 = b$$

$$y = -\dfrac{1}{2}x + 2$$

equation of $\overleftrightarrow{MB} \longrightarrow \quad y = 2x + b$

$$-6 = 2(-1) + b$$

$$-4 = b$$

$$y = 2x - 4$$

using the two equations to find the intersection of $\overleftrightarrow{MB}$ and $\perp$ to $\overleftrightarrow{MB}$:

$$-\dfrac{1}{2}x + 2 = 2x - 4$$

$$6 = \dfrac{5}{2}x$$

$$12 = 5x$$

$$\dfrac{12}{5} = x$$

$$y = -\dfrac{1}{2}\left(\dfrac{12}{5}\right) + 2$$

$$y = -\dfrac{6}{5} + 2$$

$$y = \dfrac{4}{5}$$

Solution: $\left(\dfrac{12}{5}, \dfrac{4}{5}\right)$

37.
$$x - y = 0$$
$$x = y$$
$$(x + 1)^2 + (y - 4)^2 = 25$$
$$(x + 1)^2 + (x - 4)^2 = 25$$
$$x^2 + 2x + 1 + x^2 - 8x + 16 = 25$$
$$2x^2 - 6x - 8 = 0$$
$$x^2 - 3x - 4 = 0$$
$$(x - 4)(x + 1) = 0$$
$$x = 4 \text{ or } x = -1$$

$(4, 4)$ and $(-1, -1)$

38.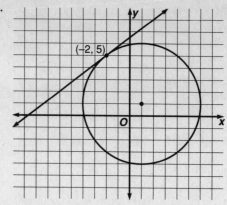

39. Find the endpoints of a line perpendicular to the parallel lines.

$y = 3x + 1$ so the perpendicular is $y = -\dfrac{1}{3}x + 1$.

$3x + 1 = -\dfrac{1}{3}x + 1 \qquad 3x - 8 = -\dfrac{1}{3}x + 1$

$\dfrac{10}{3}x = 0 \qquad\qquad 3x + \dfrac{1}{3}x = 8 + 1$

$x = 0 \qquad\qquad\qquad \dfrac{10}{3}x = 9$

$y = 1 \qquad\qquad\qquad 10x = 27$

$\qquad\qquad\qquad\qquad x = 2.7$

$\qquad\qquad y = -\dfrac{1}{3}(2.7) + 1 = 0.1$

Find the distance between $(0, 1)$ and $(2.7, 0.1)$

$$d = \sqrt{(0 - 2.7)^2 + (1 - 0.1)^2}$$

$$= \sqrt{7.29 + .81}$$

$$= \sqrt{8.1} \approx 2.8$$

40. Answers may vary. See students' work. Sample answers:

a. $y = -1$

b. any line parallel to $y = 2x - 3$

c. same line, $y = 2x - 3$

41. $y = mx + b$

$y = -22,300x + 4,050,000$

$y = 118,900x + 3,262,000$

$-22,300x + 4,050,000 = 118,900x + 3,262,000$

$\qquad\qquad -141,200x = -788,000$

$\qquad\qquad\qquad x = 5.58$ years

42. $y = 0.25x + 20$

$y = 0.20x + 25$

$0.20x + 25 < 0.25x + 20$

$\qquad -0.05x < -5$

$\qquad\quad x > 100$ miles

43.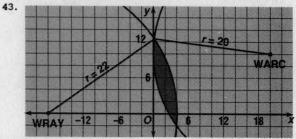

Yes; their areas of coverage overlap.

250

44. See students' work.

45. Two circles concentric to the given circle, one with a radius of 2 in. and the other with a radius of 8 in.

46.
$$\frac{4}{y} = \frac{y}{23} \qquad y^2 + z^2 = (4 + 19)^2$$
$$y^2 = 92 \qquad (\sqrt{92})^2 + z^2 = (23)^2$$
$$y = \sqrt{92} \approx 9.6 \qquad z^2 = -92 + 529$$
$$z = \sqrt{437} \approx 20.9$$

$$x^2 + (19)^2 = z^2$$
$$x^2 = (\sqrt{437})^2 - (19)^2$$
$$x^2 = 437 - 361 = 76$$
$$x = \sqrt{76} \approx 8.7$$

47.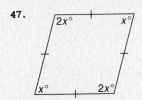

48. If three points lie in the same plane, then they are coplanar.

49. Let x = measure of angle
Let $4x$ = measure of supplement
$$x + 4x = 180$$
$$5x = 180$$
$$x = 36$$

50. Sample answer: To solve the system by graphing, graph each equation on the same coordinate plane and find the intersection of the two graphs. To solve the system by substitution, replace x with $y + 10$ in the second equation. Solve for y and then for x. To solve the system by elimination, change the equations so that the x and y values are on the right side of the equations and the constants are on the left. Add the two equations to eliminate the x values. Solve for y and then for x.

13-3 Intersection of Loci

PAGES 636-637   CHECKING FOR UNDERSTANDING

1. Sample answer: Draw the perpendicular bisector of the line segment between the two points. This represents all the points equidistant from the two points. Then draw a line parallel to the two given lines and halfway between them. The intersection of the lines drawn is the locus of points requested.

2. $(x - 4)^2 + (y - 1)^2 = 25$ is a circle with radius 5 and center $(4, 1)$; $(x - 4)^2 + (y - 1)^2 = 0$ is the point $(4, 1)$.

3. $(x - 4)^2 + (y - 1)^2 = 25$ is a circle with radius 5 and center $(4, 1)$; $(x - 4)^2 + (y - 1)^2 + (2 + 2)^2 = 25$ is a sphere with radius 5 and center $(4, 1, -2)$.

4. They may have no points of intersection; one or both lines may be tangents of the circle; one or both lines may be secants of the circle; number of possible intersections: 0, 1, 2, 3, or 4.

5. A sphere of radius 7 with center $(2, -6, 5)$

6. A plane perpendicular to the xy-plane intersecting the xy-plane at $x = 2$

7. A cylinder with radius 3 and an axis passing through points $(5, 7, z)$

8. A plane perpendicular to the xy-plane intersecting the xy-plane in the line $y + x = 0$

9. They may have no points of intersection; the plane may be tangent to the sphere or it may intersect the sphere in a circle; number of possible points of intersection: 0, 1, infinite

10. They may have no points of intersection; the circles may be tangent; the circles may intersect at 2 points; number of possible points of intersection: 0, 1, or 2

11. They may have no points of intersection; one or both lines may be tangent to the outer circle; one or both lines may be tangent to the inner circle and intersect the outer circle in 2 places; one or both lines may be secants of both circles; number of possible points of intersection: 0, 1, 2, 3, 4, 5, 6, 7, or 8

12.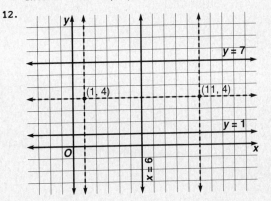

The locus is the set of points $(1, 4)$ and $(11, 4)$.

13.

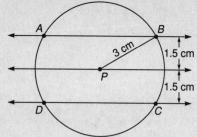

The locus is the set of 4 points that are on the circle of radius 3 cm which is centered at the given point on the given line and which lie on either of the two lines parallel to the given line and 1.5 cm from it.

14.

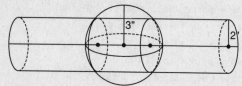

The locus meeting both conditions is the two circles formed by the intersection of the sphere with radius 3 inches centered at the given point and the cylinder with radius 2 inches centerd around the given line.

15.

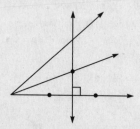

The locus is the point inside the angle where the ray that bisects the angle intersects the line that is the perpendicular bisector of the segment that has the given points as endpoints.

16.

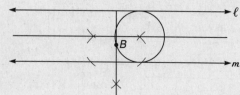

PAGES 637-639   EXERCISES

17. a cylinder with radius 6 and whose axis is perpendicular to the xy-plane through the point $(2, -4, 0)$

18. A plane perpendicular to the xy-plane whose intersection with the xy-plane is the line $y = 2x - 10$

19. A sphere with radius 4 and center $(3, 4, 5)$

20. A plane perpendicular to the xy-plane which intersects the y-axis at $y = 6$

21. $(x - (-1))^2 + (y - (-6))^2 = (4)^2$

$(x + 1)^2 + (y + 6)^2 = 16$

22. $(x - (-2))^2 + (y - 5)^2 + (z - 1)^2 = (6)^2$

$(x + 2)^2 + (y - 5)^2 + (z - 1)^2 = 36$

23. They may have no points of intersection; the line may be tangent to either circle; the line may be a secant to the outer circle; the line may be a secant of both circles; number of possible points of intersection: 0, 1, 2, 3, or 4

24. They may have no points of intersection; they may be tangent; they may intersect in a circle; number of possible points of intersection: 0 or 1

25. They may have no points of intersection; one or both lines may be tangent to the sphere; one or both lines may be secants of the sphere; number of possible points of intersection: 0, 1, 2, 3, or 4

26. They may have no points of intersection; the circle may be tangent to the sphere; the circle may lie on the sphere; the circle may intersect the sphere at 2 points; number of possible points of intersection: 0, 1, 2, or infinite

27. They may have no points of intersection; one or both planes may be tangent to the sphere; one or both planes may intersect the sphere in a circle; number of possible points of intersection: 0, 1, 2, or infinite

28. They may have no points of intersection; the plane may be tangent to the circle; the plane may intersect the circle at 2 points; the circle may lie in the plane; number of possible points of intersection: 0, 1, 2, or infinite

29. The locus is the 4 points at the intersection of a circle of radius 5 cm which has its center at the given point on the given line and 2 parallel lines which are 2 cm from the given line.

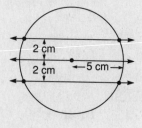

30.

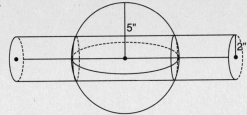

The locus is the two circles formed by the intersection of a sphere with a radius of 5 inches which is centered at the given point on the given line, and a cylinder with a radius of 2 inches.

31.

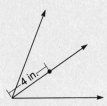

The locus is a single point 4 inches from the vertex and on the bisector of the angle.

32.

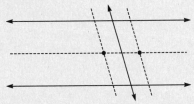

The locus is 2 points which lie on the line parallel to the given parallel lines and midway between them and also on the intersecting lines which are parallel to the given intersecting line.

33.

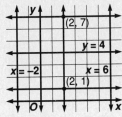

The locus of the points is (2, 1) and (2, 7).

34.

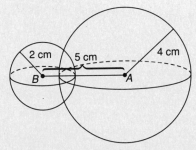

The locus is a circle with center on $\overline{AB}$ and perpendicular to $\overline{AB}$.

35. The locus is two circles on perpendicular planes. The radii of the circles are 3 units centered at the point of intersection.

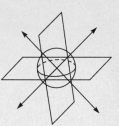

36.

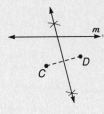

37.

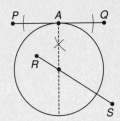

38.

39. $x + y = 4$
$$y = 4 - x$$

$$x^2 + (y + 1)^2 = 4$$
$$x^2 + (4 - x + 1)^2 = 4$$
$$x^2 + (5 - x)^2 = 4$$
$$x^2 + 25 - 10x - x^2 = 4$$
$$25 - 10x = 4$$
$$-10x = -21$$
$$x = 2.1$$

$$x^2 + (y + 1)^2 = 4$$
$$(2.1)^2 + (y + 1)^2 = 4$$
$$4.41 + (y + 1)^2 = 4$$
$$(y + 1)^2 = -0.41$$

There is no real number whose square is -0.41. Therefore, the solution set for this system is empty.

40.

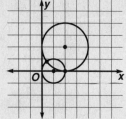

$(x - 1)^2 + y^2 = 1$

$$y^2 = 1 - (x - 1)^2$$

$$y = \sqrt{1 - (x - 1)^2}$$

$$(x - 2)^2 + (y - 2)^2 = 4$$

$$x^2 - 4x + 4 + y^2 - 4y + 4 = 4$$

$$x^2 - 4x + 4 + 1 - (x - 1)^2 - 4\sqrt{1 - (x - 1)^2} + 4 = 4$$

$$x^2 - 4x + 5 - x^2 + 2x - 1 - 4\sqrt{1 - (x - 1)^2} + 4 = 4$$

$$-2x + 8 - 4\sqrt{1 - (x - 1)^2} = 4$$

$$-4\sqrt{1 - (x - 1)^2} = 4 - 8 + 2x$$

$$-4\sqrt{1 - (x - 1)^2} = -4 + 2x$$

$$16[1 - (x - 1)^2] = (-4 + 2x)^2$$

$$16[1 - (x^2 - 2x + 1)] = 16 - 16x + 4x^2$$

$$16 - 16(x^2 - 2x + 1) = 16 - 16x + 4x^2$$

$$16 - 16x^2 + 32x - 16 = 16 - 16x + 4x^2$$

$$-20x^2 + 48x - 16 = 0$$

$$5x^2 - 12x + 4 = 0$$

$$(5x - 2)(x - 2) = 0$$

$$5x - 2 = 0 \text{ or } x - 2 = 0$$

$$5x = 2 \qquad\qquad x = 2$$

$$x = \frac{2}{5} = 0.4$$

$y = \sqrt{1 - (x - 1)^2}$

$= \sqrt{1 - (0.4 - 1)^2}$

$= \sqrt{1 - 0.36}$

$y = \sqrt{0.64} = 0.8$

$y = \sqrt{1 - (2 - 1)^2}$

$= \sqrt{1 - 1}$

$y = 0$

locus is (2, 0) and (0.4, 0.8)

41. 5 points

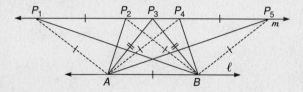

42.

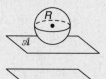
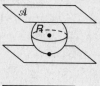

4 points

43. 0 points

44. no points   one point

a circle

45.   **46.**

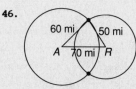

47.

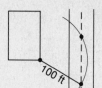

48. a circle and its interior

49. sometimes   **50.** never   **51.** always

52. never   **53.** always   **54.** sometimes

55. sometimes   **56.** always

57. Sample answer: Divide the problem into two
separate locus problems. Draw the locus of
points for the first problem. Then draw the
locus of points for the second problem. The
intersection of the two drawings is the answer
to the problem. To draw the locus of points
5 units from the line, first draw the 2
parallel lines 5 units from the given line. Then
draw the circle 5 units from the given point.
The 2 drawings intersect at 2 points.

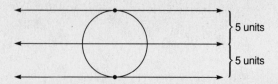

Mappings

1. Sample answer: A transformation maps each point of a plane to exactly one other point.

2. Sample answer: Each point of a preimage corresponds to one point of the image and each point of an image corresponds to one point of the preimage.

3. Sample answer: A figure can be

reflected

rotated

slid

enlarged or reduced

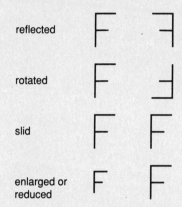

4. Sample answer: The image of an isometry is congruent to its preimage. The image of a similarity transformation is similar to its preimage.

5. $\overline{DC}$ 6. U 7. $\angle S$ 8. $\angle C$ 9. $\overline{RS}$
10. E 11. B 12. D 13. $\angle DEB$ 14. $\angle BDE$
15. $\overline{ED}$ 16. A 17. B 18. C 19. $\overline{BA}$
20. $\overline{CA}$ 21. $\angle CBA$

PAGES 642-643   EXERCISES

22. $\overline{RS}$ 23. $\angle T$ 24. $\overline{AE}$ 25. $\angle B$
26. $\overline{QR}$ 27. $\triangle RQS$ 28. $\triangle EFD$ 29. $\triangle NMW$
30. $\triangle YXZ$ 31. $\triangle XZY$ 32. $\triangle KLM$ 33. $CDAB$
34. $UTSR$ 35. $\overline{WY}$ 36. W and Y
37. $\triangle XYW \longrightarrow \triangle ZYW$
38. a. A gray; B gray   b. A gray; B gray
    c. A blue; B gray
39. yes
40. Angel A is reflected to form Angel B.
41. Angel D is rotated or reflected to form Angel C.
42. The print of the left foot is the reflection of the print of the right foot. As Sam walks down the beach, the prints of the feet slide in the direction he is going.
43. For each frame of the cartoon, slide the picture of the ball just slightly in one direction.
44. a circle

45. $A = \frac{1}{2}(18)(2 \cdot 17.5)$ 46. $4(x + 1) = 3 \cdot 8$
$\qquad = \frac{1}{2}(630)$ $\qquad 4x + 4 = 24$
$\qquad\qquad\qquad\qquad\quad 4x = 20$
$\qquad = 315 \text{ cm}^2$ $\qquad\qquad x = 5$

47. $\frac{18}{x} = \frac{x}{31}$
$x^2 = 558$
$x = \sqrt{558} \approx 23.6$

48. If a mapping is a transformation, then it is one-to-one.

49. See students' work.

Reflections

1. The line of reflection is the perpendicular bisector of the line segment joining the image point and its preimage point.

2. Sample answer: Point A has a reflection image with respect to point Q if Q is the midpoint of the line segment joining A and its image.

3. Sample answer: A reflection is an isometry, because a preimage and its reflection image are congruent.

4. Sample answers: isosceles triangles, butterflies, hearts

5. Sample answers: Squares, sunflowers, bicycle wheels

6. A 7. C 8. $\overline{AC}$

9.
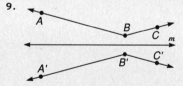

10.

11.   12.
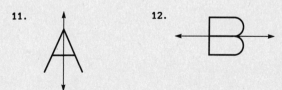

13.   14.
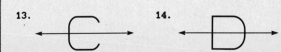

15.

16.

17.

PAGES 648-651   EXERCISES

18. *L*   **19.** *J*   **20.** $\overline{JL}$ **21.** ∠*IHG*

22. $\overline{HG}$ **23.** Δ*CXA*   **24.** *N*   **25.** $\overline{IH}$

26.-27. No; not all points are the same distance from *ℓ*.

28.-31. Yes; for any point *A* on each figure, it is possible to find another point *B* on the figure so that *ℓ* is the perpendicular bisector of $\overline{AB}$.

32. both   **33.** both   **34.** point

35.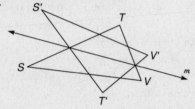

36.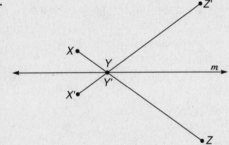

37.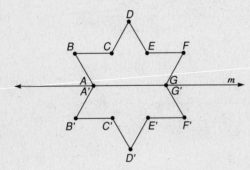

38.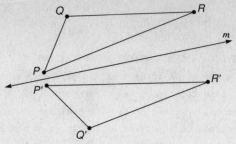

39.

40.
none

41.

42.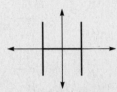

43.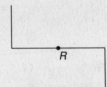

44.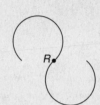

45.

46.

47.
none

48.

49.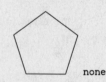
none

50.
none

51.
none

52.
none

53.

54.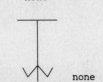
none

256

55.

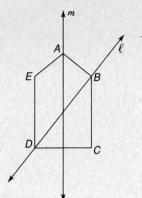

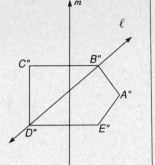

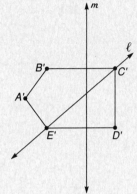

56. Sample answer: Find the reflection image of the 3 ball with respect to the line of one of the long sides of the pool table. Aim the cue ball for the reflection image of the 3 ball.

57. 168 cm   **58.** ∠S   **59.** $\overline{CD}$ **60.** HA   **61.** SSS

62. AAS   **63.** not enough information

64. HL   **65.** not enough information

66. See students' work.

Mid-Chapter Review

PAGE 651

1. a. Read the problem carefully.
   b. Draw the given figure.
   c. Locate the points that satisfy the given conditions.
   d. Draw a smooth curve or line.
   e. Describe the locus.

2. A line that is the perpendicular bisector of the segment joining the two given points

3. A plane that is the prependicular bisector of the segment joining the two given points

4.
$$y = x + 4 \qquad\qquad 13 - 4 = x$$
$$y - 4 = x \qquad\qquad 9 = x$$
$$y = 2(y - 4) - 5$$
$$y = 2y - 8 - 5$$
$$-y = -13$$
$$y = 13$$
$$(9, 13):a$$

5.
$$x = y - 6 \qquad\qquad 12 + 6 = y$$
$$x + 6 = y \qquad\qquad 18 = y$$
$$x = 30 - y$$
$$x = 30 - (x + 6)$$
$$x = 30 - x - 6$$
$$2x = 24$$
$$x = 12$$
$$(12, 18):b$$

6. A doughnut shape 6 cm wide

7. If the two points are more than 8 units apart, there are no points in the locus. If the two points are 8 units apart, the locus is one point at the point of tangency of the two spheres. If the two points are less than 8 units apart but more than 2 units apart, the locus is a circle formed by the intersection of the two spheres. If the two points are 2 units apart, the locus is one point of tangency of the two spheres. If the two points are less than 2 units apart, the locus has no points of tangency.

8.

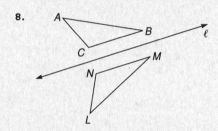

9. $\overline{BC}$ **10.** ∠B

Technology: Reflections

PAGE 652   EXERCISES

1.

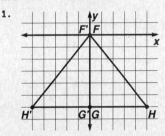

2.

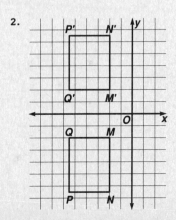

257

13-6 Translations

1. Sample answer: Yes, the designs on wallpaper keep repeating the same pictures. The pictures are usually translations of each other.

2. In the first reflection, the picture is flipped. In the second reflection, the picture is flipped again, putting the image in the same orientation as the original picture. The second image is a translation image of the original picture.

3. Collinearity, angle and distance measure, and betweeness of points

4. yes

5. No, the green image is incorrect.

6. $\overline{CD}$ 7. none   8. none   9. none

10.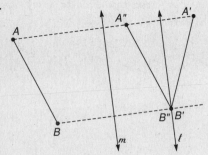

11.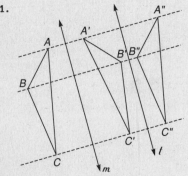

12. B   13. F   14. G   15. C   16. H   17. P

18. D   19. Q   20. R   21. C   22. Q   23. P

24. Yes; $\overline{XY}$ is a composite of two reflections of $\overline{TU}$.

25. Yes; $\triangle KJL$ is a composite of two reflections of $\triangle EDF$.

26. No; $\triangle PQR$ is not a reflection of $\triangle NMO$.

27. Yes; $IJKLM$ is a composite of two reflections of $ABCDE$.

28. $\overline{WV}$ 29. $\triangle HGI$

30. none   31. pentagon $AHGFE$

32. $\overline{XY}$ 33. $\triangle JKL$

34. $\triangle STU$ 35. pentagon $IJKLM$

36.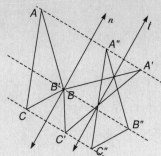

37.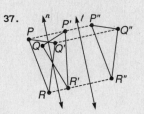

38.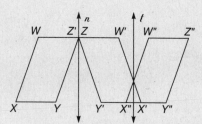

39.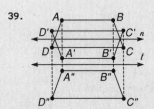

40. $\triangle PQR$ 41. $\triangle STU$ 42. $\triangle LMN$ 43. $\triangle LMN$ 44. $\triangle STU$

45. A translation is composed of two successive reflections over parallel lines. The first reflection with respect to line ℓ preserves collinearity. The second reflection with respect to line m preserves collinearity. Therefore, by transitivity, collinearity is preserved from preimage to image.

46. A translation is composed of two successive reflections over parallel lines. The first reflection with respect to line ℓ preserves betweeness of points. The second reflection with respect to line m preserves betweeness of points. Therefore, by transitivity, betweeness of points is preserved from preimage to image.

47. A translation is composed of two successive reflections over parallel lines. The first reflection with respect to line ℓ preserves angle and distance measure. The second reflection with respect to line m preserves angle and distance measure. Therefore, by transitivity, angle and distance measure is preserved from preimage to image.

48.

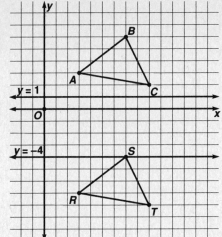

49.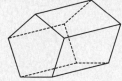

50.

51.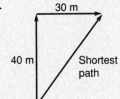

52.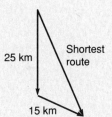

53.

54. $A = bh$

$\quad = (12)(6)$

$\quad = 72 \text{ ft}^2$

55. $A = \frac{1}{2}Pa$

$\quad = \frac{1}{2}(8 \cdot 6)(4\sqrt{3})$

$\quad \approx 166.3 \text{ cm}^2$

56. $A = \frac{1}{2}bh$

$\quad = \frac{1}{2}(4)(3)$

$\quad = 6 \text{ in}^2$

57. $\angle P$ since side QR is the longest side

58. $\frac{180 - 67}{2} = 56.5$

59. See students' work.

Developing Reasoning Skills: Möbius Strips

PAGE 658

When you cut down a pencil line through the center of a Möbius Strip, you get two intertwining strips, each with two surfaces.

13-7 ### Rotations

PAGES 661–662   CHECKING FOR UNDERSTANDING

1. When the lines are parallel

2. When the lines are intersecting

3. The measure of the angle of rotation is twice the measure of the angle between the intersecting lines.

4. You can find the reflection image with respect to the first line and then the reflection image of that image with respect to the second line. You could also draw angles of rotation to find the rotation image.

5. quadrilateral *EFCD*   6. quadrilateral *JKHG*

7. quadrilateral *HGJK*   8. quadrilateral *CDEF*

9. quadrilateral *CDAB*   10. 140

11. 140   12. 140   13. 140   14. *C*   15. $\overline{GK}$

16. 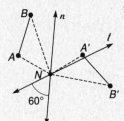   **17.**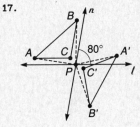

PAGES 662–664   EXERCISES

18.–19. In both cases, there are proper successive reflections with respect to two intersecting lines.

20. 60°   21. 90°   22. 120°   23. 74°

24. yes   25. yes   26. yes   27. yes

28. Sample answer: 29. Sample answer:

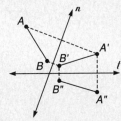   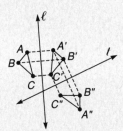

30. 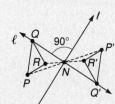   **31.**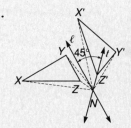

32. 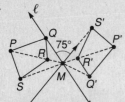 33.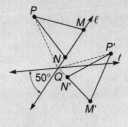

34. reflection   35. rotation   36. translation

37. It preserves orientation, because if vertices are in clockwise order, the vertices of the image will be in clockwise order.

38. $\overleftrightarrow{AD}$ and $\overleftrightarrow{BE}$; $\overleftrightarrow{BE}$ and $\overleftrightarrow{CF}$; $\overleftrightarrow{CF}$ and $\overleftrightarrow{AD}$.

39. $m\angle AOC$ is 120, so the measure of the angle of intersecting lines will be 60.

40. 9: Since $m\angle BAC = 40$ in $\triangle ABC$ and since $\triangle AB'C'$ is the rotation image of $\triangle ABC$, it would take $360 \div 40$ or 9 rotations to map $\triangle ABC$ onto itself.

41. a. right circular cone
    b. right cylinder with hollowed out right cone

42. $72°$: There are 10 seats on the Ferris Wheel and 10 angles formed by each two seats. The measure of the angle between each two seats is $36°$. There are two angles between seats 1 and 3. The measure of the angle of rotation from seat 1 to seat 3 is $72°$.

43. $108°$: The same reasoning holds as for Exercise 42 except that the angle of rotation from seat one to seat four is three times the measure of the angle formed. ($3 \times 36° = 108°$)

44. 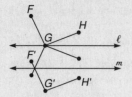   45. 75

46. $x = \frac{1}{2}(75) = 37.5$ 47. $x = \frac{1}{2}(50 + 80) = 65$

48. No; the sum of their measures would have to be both 90 and 180

49. Successive reflections with respect to two intersecting lines will produce a rotation. Successive reflections with respect to two parallel lines will produce a translation.

13-8   Dilations

PAGES 667-668   CHECKING FOR UNDERSTANDING

1. Sample answer: A dilation does not preserve distance measure, and the other transformations do.

2. If the absolute value of the scale factor is greater than 1, the dilation is an enlargement. If the absolute value of the scale factor is between 0 and 1, the dilation is a reduction.

3. Sample answer: No, all figures would have a single point, namely the center of the dilation, as dilation images.

4. $6 \times 8 = 48$ 5. similar   6. $BC < YZ$

7. $32 \div 8 = 4$ 8. 62   9. 2; enlargement

10. $\frac{3}{2}$; enlargement   11. $\frac{1}{4}$; reduction

12.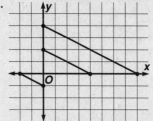

13. 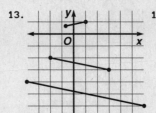   14.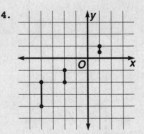

PAGES 668-670   EXERCISES

15. enlargement   16. reduction   17. reduction

18. enlargement   19. reduction   20. enlargement

21. congruence   22. enlargement   23. 30

24. $\frac{1}{3}$ 25. 24   26. 15.5   27. 3   28. 30   29. A

30. G 31. T 32. C 33. S 34. B 35. F 36. D

37. 2; enlargement   38. 5; enlargement

39. $\frac{1}{3}$; reduction   40. $\frac{4}{3}$; enlargement

41. $\frac{1}{4}$; reduction   42. 3; enlargement

43. $\frac{4}{3}$ 44. 2

45. 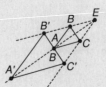   46.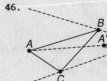

47. 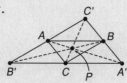   48.

260

49.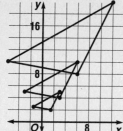

50.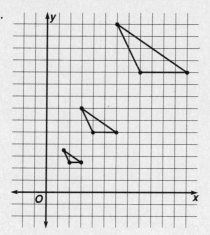

51.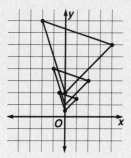

52.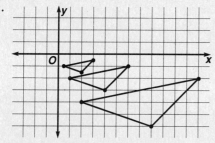

53.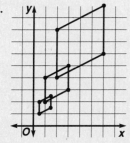

54.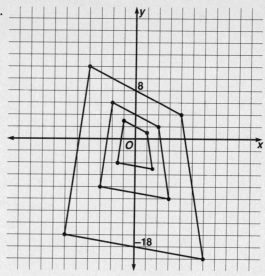

55. a. The perimeter of the image will be 4 times that of the preimage.

b. The area of the image will be 16 times that of the preimage.

56. a. The surface area of the image will be 16 times that of the preimage.

b. The volume of the image will be 64 times that of the preimage.

57. Given: Dilation with center C and scale factor k

Prove: $ED = k(AB)$

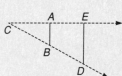

Proof: $CE = k(CA)$ and $CD = k(CB)$ by the definition of a dilation. $\frac{CE}{CA} = k$ and $\frac{CD}{CB} = k$. So, $\frac{CE}{CA} = \frac{CD}{CB}$ by substitution.

$\angle ACB \cong \angle ECD$, since congruence of angles is reflexive. Therefore, by SAS Similarity, $\triangle ACB \sim \triangle ECD$. The corresponding sides of similar triangles are proportional, so $\frac{ED}{AB} = \frac{CE}{CA}$. We know that $\frac{CE}{CA} = k$, so $\frac{ED}{AB} = k$ by substitution.

Therefore, $ED = k(AB)$ by the multiplication property of equality.

58.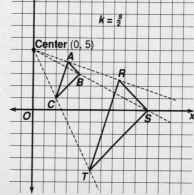

261

59. Sample answer: The fish are dilations of each other.

60. $\left(\frac{3}{4} \cdot 8\right)$ by $\left(\frac{3}{4} \cdot 10\right)$ = 6 in. by $7\frac{1}{2}$ in.

61. $\frac{3}{5}$

62.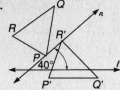

63. $\frac{4}{x} = \frac{x}{9}$

$x^2 = 36$

$x = 6$

64. $5^2 + 7^2 = x^2$

$25 + 49 = x^2$

$\sqrt{74} = x$

$8.6 \approx x$

65. $\cos 68° = \frac{8}{x}$

$0.3764 = \frac{8}{x}$

$0.3764x = 8$

$x = \frac{8}{.3764}$

$x = 21.4$

66. Drawn at $\frac{1}{2}$ scale

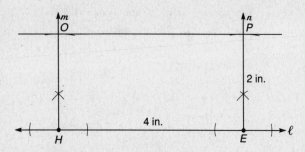

67. a triangle with one obtuse angle; no

68. $(20 + 5x) + (x + 10) = 180$

$6x + 30 = 180$

$6x = 150$

$x = 25$

69. A dilation with a scale factor with an absolute value greater than 1 will be an enlargement. In other words, the image will be larger than its preimage. A dilation with a scale factor with an absolute value between 0 and 1 will be a reduction. In other words, the image will be smaller than its preimage.

13-9 Problem-Solving Strategy: Make a Table

PAGE 672   CHECKING FOR UNDERSTANDING

1. Sample answer: Making a table is a good strategy, because it helps to organize the information so you can see if all the criteria are met.

2. Sample answer: In the first example, the information is put into a table to help solve the problem. In the second example, the information is organized in a table for others to gain information.

3.
Name	Sun.	Mon.	Tues.	Wed.	Thurs.	Fri.	Sat.
Rita		x	x	x	x	x	
Tony	x	x			x	x	x
Beth	x			x			x
Cam	x					x	x
Joshua	x		x				x

4.
	30°	45°	60°
Sine	$\frac{1}{2}$	$\frac{\sqrt{2}}{2}$	$\frac{\sqrt{3}}{2}$
Cosine	$\frac{\sqrt{3}}{2}$	$\frac{\sqrt{2}}{2}$	$\frac{1}{2}$
Tangent	$\frac{\sqrt{3}}{3}$	1	$\sqrt{3}$

5.
A	B	C	D	F
3	0	0	1	1
2	1	1	0	1
2	1	0	2	0
2	0	2	1	0
1	3	0	0	1
1	2	1	1	0
1	1	3	0	0
0	4	0	1	0
0	3	2	0	0

PAGES 672-673   EXERCISES

6. If the dots are labeled as shown, the following triangles are isosceles.

A• B• C•
D• E• F•
G• H• I•

$\triangle ABD$	$\triangle ABE$	$\triangle BCE$	$\triangle BCF$	$\triangle DEB$	$\triangle DEA$	$\triangle DEG$
$\triangle DEH$	$\triangle EFB$	$\triangle EFC$	$\triangle EFH$	$\triangle EFI$	$\triangle GHD$	$\triangle GHE$
$\triangle HIE$	$\triangle HIF$	$\triangle ACE$	$\triangle DBF$	$\triangle DHF$	$\triangle GEI$	$\triangle AGE$
$\triangle BHD$	$\triangle BHF$	$\triangle CIE$	$\triangle ACH$	$\triangle GBI$	$\triangle AFG$	$\triangle CDI$
$\triangle ACG$	$\triangle ICG$	$\triangle AGI$	$\triangle ACI$			

There are 32 isosceles triangles that could be drawn.

7. Sample answer: 2, 3, 6

8.
Homerun	Triple	Double	Single
2	0	1	5
1	2	0	5
1	1	2	4
1	0	4	3
0	3	1	4
0	2	3	3
0	1	5	2
0	0	7	1

9. If the eight points represent the student council members, there are $7 + 6 + 5 + 4 + 3 + 2 + 1$ or 28 handshakes.

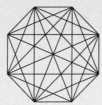

10.

	Bell	Thornton	Arnold	Terri
lead guitar player	X	X	X	✓
rhythm guitar player	X	X	✓	X
keyboard player	✓	X	X	X
drummer	X	✓	X	X

Bell, keyboard; Thornton, drummer; Arnold, rhythm guitar; Terri, lead guitar

11.

Name	number of sides	number of diagonals	interior ∡ measure	exterior ∡ measure
equilateral Δ	3	0	60	120
square	4	2	90	90
pentagon	5	5	108	72
hexagon	6	9	120	60
heptagon	7	14	$128\frac{4}{7}$	$51\frac{3}{7}$
octagon	8	20	135	45
nonagon	9	27	140	40
decagon	10	35	144	36

12. Let x = width
Let $x + 8$ = length
$$x(x + 8) = 2(x + 8)(x - 12)$$
$$x^2 + 8x = 2(x^2 - 4x - 96)$$
$$x^2 + 8x = 2x^2 - 8x - 192$$
$$-x^2 + 16x + 192 = 0$$
$$x^2 - 16x - 192 = 0$$
$$(x - 24)(x + 8) = 0$$
$$x = 24$$
$$x + 8 = 32 \qquad \text{32 ft by 24 ft}$$

13. A four-digit palindrome will take the form $xyyx$ with x and y as digits. x cannot be zero, or this would be a 3-digit, not a 4-digit, number. There are 9 possible values for x. y could be any digit, so it has 10 possible values. Therefore, there are $9 \cdot 10$ or 90 4-digit palindrones.

14. Make fewer cuts and look for a pattern.

number of cuts	0	1	2	3	4	5
maximum number of pieces	1	2	4	7	11	16

+1 +2 +3 +4 +5

15. $2 + 4 + 6 + \ldots + 96 + 98 + 100$
$= (2 + 100) + (4 + 98) + (6 + 96) + \ldots$
$\quad + (50 + 52)$
$= 102 + 102 + 102 + \ldots + 102$
$= 25(102)$
$= 2550$

16. Draw $\overline{AC}$ which bisects the 60° angle. Draw $\overline{BC}$ making a 30°-60°-90° right triangle. The short leg (the radius) is 5. The hypotenuse is 10. The distance between ℓ and m is $10 + 5$ or 15. Therefore, $x = 15 - 12$ or 3.

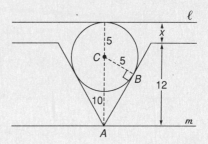

Cooperative Learning Project

PAGE 673

10; *RRCCCC, RCRCCC, RCCRCC, RCCCRC, CCCRRC, CCRCRC, CRCRCC, CRCCRC, CRRCCC, CCRRCC*

4 games – 1 way

1	2	3	4
C	C	C	C

5 games – 4 ways

1	2	3	4	5
R	C	C	C	C
C	R	C	C	C
C	C	R	C	C
C	C	C	R	C

6 games – 10 ways

1	2	3	4	5	6
R	R	C	C	C	C
C	R	R	C	C	C
C	C	R	R	C	C
C	C	C	R	R	C
R	C	R	C	C	C
R	C	C	R	C	C
R	C	C	C	R	C
C	R	C	R	C	C
C	R	C	C	R	C
C	C	R	C	R	C

7 games - 20 ways

1	2	3	4	5	6	7
R	R	R	C	C	C	C
C	R	R	R	C	C	C
C	C	R	R	R	C	C
C	C	C	R	R	R	C
R	C	R	C	R	C	C
C	R	C	R	C	R	C
C	C	R	C	R	R	C
R	C	R	C	C	R	C
R	C	C	R	C	R	C
R	C	C	R	R	C	C
C	R	C	R	R	C	C
R	C	C	C	R	R	C
C	R	C	C	R	R	C
R	C	R	R	C	C	C
R	R	C	C	R	C	C
R	R	C	R	C	C	C
R	R	C	C	C	R	C
C	R	R	C	R	C	C
C	R	R	C	C	R	C
C	C	R	R	C	R	C

There are 1 + 4 + 10 + 20 or 35 ways for the Cubs to win the series.

There are 35 ways for the Cubs to win and 35 ways for the Red Sox to win. So there are 70 ways for either team to win.

Chapter 13 Summary and Review

PAGES 674-676   SKILLS AND CONCEPTS

1. A plane that is the perpendicular bisector of the segment joining the two points

2. The interior of a circle with center at the given point and radius 6 cm

3.
$$y = x - 2$$
$$2x + y = 13$$
$$2x + (x - 2) = 13$$
$$3x = 15$$
$$x = 5$$
$$y = x - 2$$
$$ = 5 - 2$$
$$y = 3$$
(5, 3)

4.
$$y = 2x - 1$$
$$x + y = 7$$
$$x + (2x - 1) = 7$$
$$3x = 8$$
$$x = \frac{8}{3}$$
$$x + y = 7$$
$$\frac{8}{3} + y = 7$$
$$y = \frac{13}{3}$$
$$\left(\frac{8}{3}, \frac{13}{3}\right)$$

5.
$$-2x + y = -1$$
$$y = 2x - 1$$
$$3x - 4y = -1$$
$$3x - 4(2x - 1) = -1$$
$$3x - 8x + 4 = -1$$
$$-5x = -5$$
$$x = 1$$
$$y = 2x - 1$$
$$ = 2(1) - 1$$
$$y = 1$$
(1, 1)

6.
$$3x + y = 5$$
$$y = 5 - 3x$$
$$2x + 3y = 8$$
$$2x + 3(5 - 3x) = 8$$
$$2x + 15 - 9x = 8$$
$$-7x = -7$$
$$x = 1$$
$$y = 5 - 3x$$
$$y = 5 - (3)(1)$$
$$y = 2$$ (1, 2)

7. They may have no points of intersection; the line may be tangent to the circle, the line may intersect the circle in two points; number of possible points of intersection: 0, 1, or 2.

8. They may have no points of intersection, the line may be tangent to the sphere, the line may intersect the sphere at two points; number of possible points of intersection: 0, 1, or 2.

9. They may have no points of intersection, the plane may be tangent to the outside circle; the plane may intersect the outside circle at two points and not touch the inside circle; the plane may be tangent to the inside circle and intersect the outside circle at two points; the plane may intersect both cirles at two points; the circles may lie in the plane; number of possible intersections: 0, 1, 2, 3, 4, or infinite.

10. They may have no points of intersection, one plane may be tangent to the circle and the other plane may not touch the circle; both planes may be tangent to the circle; one plane may intersect the outside circle at two points and the other plane may not touch the circle; one plane may be tangent to the circle and the other plane may intersect the circle at two points; both planes may intersect the circle at two points; the circle may lie in one of the planes; number of possible intersections: 0, 1, 2, 3, 4, or infinite.

11. E 12. $\angle ABE$ 13. B 14. $\triangle ABE$

15.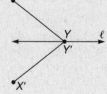

16.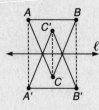

17.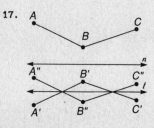

264

18.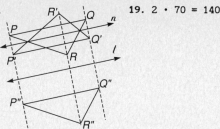

19. 2 · 70 = 140

20.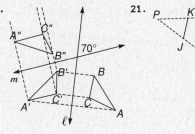

21.

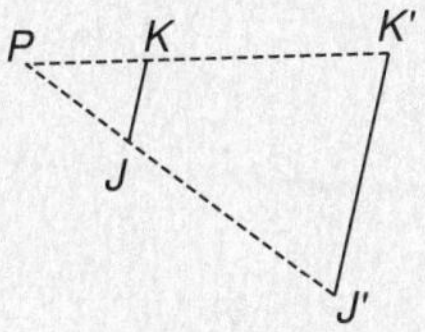

22. enlargement; |3| > 1

PAGE 676   APPLICATIONS AND CONNECTIONS

23. Imagine the reflection of the 5 ball with respect to the line formed by one side of the billiard table, and aim for the reflection.

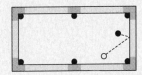

24. The stake should be placed at least 18 feet from the line on the ground that is directly beneath the horizontal pole.

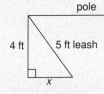

4 ft   5 ft leash $4^2 + x^2 = 5^2$
                       $x = 3$

Overhead view of Spot's range

Overhead view of Bruno's range

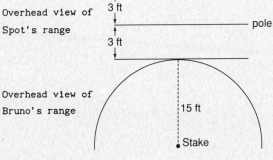

25.

25¢	10¢	5¢
2	0	1
1	3	0
1	2	2
1	1	4
1	0	6
0	5	1
0	4	3
0	3	5
0	2	7
0	1	9
0	0	11

Chapter 13 Test

PAGE 667

1. Two lines parallel to ℓ, each 5 inches from ℓ

2. A circle centered at A with a radius of 4 cm

3. A sphere centered at C with a radius of 3 meters

4. A cylinder whose axis is line n with a radius of 10 feet

5. Four points if the line crosses both spheres; three points if the line is tangent to the inner sphere, two points if the line intersects only the outer sphere; one point if the line is tangent to the outer sphere.

6. Two circles if both planes intersect the sphere; a circle and a point if one plane intersects the sphere and the other is tangent; a circle if only one plane intersects the sphere; two points if both planes are tangent; one point if one plane is tangent and the other plane does not intersect the sphere.

7.
$$y = 4x$$
$$x + y = 5$$
$$x + 4x = 5$$
$$5x = 5$$
$$x = 1$$
$$y = 4x$$
$$= 4(1)$$
$$y = 4$$
$$(1, 4)$$

8.
$$3x - 2y = 10$$
$$x + y = 0$$
$$x = -y$$
$$3(-y) - 2y = 0$$
$$-3y - 2y = 10$$
$$-5y = 10$$
$$y = -2$$
$$x + y = 0$$
$$x + (-2) = 0$$
$$x = 2$$
$$(2, -2)$$

9.
$$x - 4y = 7$$
$$x = 4y + 7$$
$$2x + y = -4$$
$$2(4y + 7) + y = -4$$
$$8y + 14 + y = -4$$
$$9y = -18$$
$$y = -2$$

$$x = 4(-2) + 7$$
$$x = -1$$

$$(-1, -2)$$

10. yes   11. yes   12. yes   13. no

14. translation   15. reflection

16. rotation   17.

18. enlargement

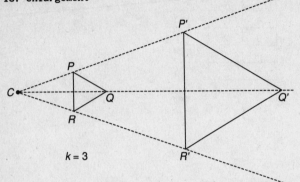

$k = 3$

19. reduction

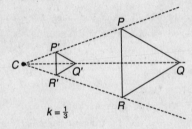

$k = \frac{1}{3}$

20. Congruence
    transformation

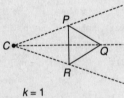

$k = 1$

BONUS
Reflected over x-axis

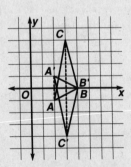

The coordinates of the reflection of $\triangle ABC$ over the
x-axis are $A'(2, 1), B'(4, 0)$, and $C'(3, -4)$.

Rotated 90° clockwise

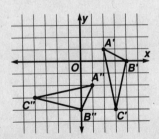

The coordinates of $\triangle A'B'C'$ rotated 90° clockwise
about the origin are $A''(1, -2), B''(0, -4)$, and
$C''(-4, -3)$.

Algebra Review

PAGES 678-679

1. $\frac{4x}{3} + \frac{7}{2} = \frac{7x}{12}$

$$12\left(\frac{4x}{3} + \frac{7}{2}\right) = 12\left(\frac{7x}{12}\right)$$

$$4(4x) + 6(7) = 7x$$

$$16x + 42 = 7x$$

$$9x = -42$$

$$x = -\frac{42}{9} = -\frac{14}{3}$$

check: $\frac{4}{3}\left(-\frac{14}{3}\right) + \frac{7}{2} = \dfrac{7\left(-\frac{14}{3}\right)}{12}$

$$-\frac{56}{9} + \frac{7}{2} = -\frac{98}{36}$$

$$-224 + 126 = -98$$

$$-98 = -98$$

2. $\frac{1}{h + 1} + \frac{2}{3} = \frac{2h + 5}{h - 1}$

$$3(h - 1)(h + 1)\left(\frac{1}{h + 1} + \frac{2}{3}\right)$$

$$= 3(h + 1)(h - 1)\left(\frac{2h + 5}{h - 1}\right)$$

$$3(h - 1) + 2(h - 1)(h + 1) = 3(h + 1)(2h + 5)$$

$$3h - 3 + 2(h^2 - 1) = 3(2h^2 + 7h + 5)$$

$$3h - 3 + 2h^2 - 2 = 6h^2 + 21h + 15$$

$$-4h^2 - 18h - 20 = 0$$

$$4h^2 + 18h + 20 = 0$$

$$2h^2 + 9h + 10 = 0$$

$$(2h + 5)(h + 2) = 0$$

$2h + 5 = 0 \qquad h + 2 = 0$

$2h = -5 \qquad\qquad h = -2$

$$h = -\frac{5}{2}$$

check: $\frac{1}{-2 + 1} + \frac{2}{3} = \frac{2(-2) + 5}{-2 - 1}$

$$-1 + \frac{2}{3} = -\frac{1}{3}$$

$$-\frac{1}{3} = -\frac{1}{3}$$

$$\frac{1}{-\frac{5}{2} + 1} + \frac{2}{3} = \frac{2\left(-\frac{5}{2}\right) + 5}{-\frac{5}{2} - 1}$$

$$\frac{1}{-\frac{3}{2}} + \frac{2}{3} = 0$$

$$-\frac{2}{3} + \frac{2}{3} = 0$$

$$0 = 0$$

3. $\dfrac{3a + 2}{a^2 + 7a + 6} = \dfrac{1}{a + 6} + \dfrac{4}{a + 1}$

$(a + 6)(a + 1)\dfrac{3a + 2}{(a + 6)(a + 1)}$

$\qquad = (a + 6)(a + 1)\left(\dfrac{1}{a + 6} + \dfrac{4}{a + 1}\right)$

$\qquad 3a + 2 = a + 1 + 4(a + 6)$

$\qquad 3a + 2 = a + 1 + 4a + 24$

$\qquad\qquad -2a = 23$

$\qquad\qquad\quad a = -\dfrac{23}{2}$

check: $\dfrac{3\left(-\frac{23}{2}\right) + 2}{\left(-\frac{23}{2}\right)^2 + 7\left(-\frac{23}{2}\right) + 6}$

$\qquad\qquad = \dfrac{1}{-\frac{23}{2} + 6} + \dfrac{4}{-\frac{23}{2} + 1}$

$\qquad \dfrac{-\frac{65}{2}}{\frac{231}{4}} = -\dfrac{2}{11} + -\dfrac{8}{21}$

$\qquad\quad -\dfrac{130}{231} = -\dfrac{130}{231}$

4. $\dfrac{3m - 2}{(2m + 1)(m - 3)} - \dfrac{2}{2m + 1} = \dfrac{4}{m - 3}$

$(2m + 1)(m - 3)\left(\dfrac{3m - 2}{(2m + 1)(m - 3)}\right)$

$- (2m + 1)(m - 3)\left(\dfrac{2}{2m + 1}\right) = \dfrac{4}{m - 3}(2m + 1)(m - 3)$

$3m - 2 - 2(m - 3) = 4(2m + 1)$

$3m - 2 - 2m + 6 = 8m + 4$

$\qquad\qquad -7m = 0$

$\qquad\qquad\quad m = 0$

check: $\dfrac{3(0) - 2}{2(0)^2 - 5(0) - 3} - \dfrac{2}{2(0) + 1} = \dfrac{4}{0 - 3}$

$\qquad\qquad\qquad \dfrac{-2}{-3} - 2 = -\dfrac{4}{3}$

$\qquad\qquad\qquad \dfrac{2}{3} - \dfrac{6}{3} = -\dfrac{4}{3}$

$\qquad\qquad\qquad\quad -\dfrac{4}{3} = -\dfrac{4}{3}$

5. $6x + 5y = 35 \qquad 6x + 5(1) = 35$

$\underline{-6x + 9y = -21} \qquad 6x = 30$

$\qquad\quad 14y = 14 \qquad\qquad x = 5$

$\qquad\qquad y = 1$

$(5, 1)$

6. $3x - 7y = -6 \qquad 3x - 7(3) = -6$

$\underline{-3x - 6y = -33} \qquad 3x = 15$

$\qquad\quad 13y = -39 \qquad\qquad x = 5$

$\qquad\qquad y = 3$

$(5, 3)$

7. $6a + 7b = 5 \qquad 6a + 7(-1) = 5$

$\underline{-6a + 9b = -21} \qquad 6a = 12$

$\qquad\quad 16b = -16 \qquad\qquad a = 2$

$\qquad\qquad b = -1$

$(2, -1)$

8. $15m + 6n = -24 \qquad\qquad -8(-4) - 6n = -4$

$\underline{-8m - 6n = -4} \qquad\qquad 32 - 6n = -4$

$\quad 7m \quad\; = -28 \qquad\qquad\qquad -6n = -36$

$\qquad\; m = -4 \qquad\qquad\qquad\qquad n = 6$

$(-4, 6)$

9. $\dfrac{-b}{a} = 1 - 8 = -7 \qquad \dfrac{c}{a} = -8$

try $a = 1$, $b = 7$, $c = -8$

$x^2 + 7x - 8 = 0$

check: $\quad 1^2 + 7(1) - 8 = 0$

$\qquad\qquad\qquad\qquad 0 = 0$

$\qquad (-8)^2 + 7(-8) - 8 = 0$

$\qquad\qquad\qquad\qquad 0 = 0$

10. $\dfrac{-b}{a} = \dfrac{3}{2} - \dfrac{8}{2} = \dfrac{-5}{2}$ \qquad check: $2\left(\dfrac{3}{2}\right)^2 + \dfrac{3}{2}(5) - 12 = 0$

$\dfrac{c}{a} = \dfrac{3}{2}\left(\dfrac{-4}{1}\right) = \dfrac{-12}{2}$ \qquad\qquad $\dfrac{18}{4} + \dfrac{30}{4} - 12 = 0$

try $a = 2$, $b = 5$, \qquad\qquad\qquad\qquad $0 = 0$

$\quad c = -12$ \qquad\qquad $2(-4)^2 + 5(-4) - 12 = 0$

$2x^2 + 5x - 12 = 0$ \qquad\qquad $32 - 20 - 12 = 0$

$\qquad\qquad\qquad\qquad\qquad\qquad 0 = 0$

11. $\dfrac{-b}{a} = \dfrac{-2}{3} - \dfrac{3}{2} = \dfrac{-4}{6} - \dfrac{9}{6} = \dfrac{-13}{6}$

$\dfrac{c}{a} = \left(-\dfrac{2}{3}\right)\left(-\dfrac{3}{2}\right) = \dfrac{6}{6}$

try $a = 6$, $b = 13$, $c = 6$

$6x^2 + 13x + 6 = 0$

check: $6\left(-\dfrac{2}{3}\right)^2 + 13\left(-\dfrac{2}{3}\right) + 6 = 0$

$\qquad\qquad \dfrac{24}{9} - \dfrac{26}{3} + 6 = 0$

$\qquad\qquad\qquad\qquad 0 = 0$

$\quad 6\left(-\dfrac{3}{2}\right)^2 + 13\left(-\dfrac{3}{2}\right) + 6 = 0$

$\qquad\qquad \dfrac{54}{4} - \dfrac{39}{3} + 6 = 0$

$\qquad\qquad\qquad\qquad 0 = 0$

12. $\dfrac{-b}{a} = (3 + \sqrt{5}) + (3 - \sqrt{5}) = \dfrac{6}{1}$

$\dfrac{c}{a} = (3 + \sqrt{5})(3 - \sqrt{5}) = 9 - 5 = \dfrac{4}{1}$

try $a = 1$, $b = -6$, $c = 4$

$x^2 - 6x + 4 = 0$

check: $(3 + \sqrt{5})^2 - 6(3 + \sqrt{5}) + 4 = 0$

$\qquad 9 + 6\sqrt{5} + 5 - 18 - 6\sqrt{5} + 4 = 0$

$\qquad\qquad\qquad 14 - 18 + 4 = 0$

$\qquad\qquad\qquad\qquad\quad 0 = 0$

$\quad (3 - \sqrt{5})^2 - 6(3 - \sqrt{5}) + 4 = 0$

$\quad 9 - 6\sqrt{5} + 5 - 18 + 6\sqrt{5} + 4 = 0$

$\qquad\qquad\quad 14 - 18 + 4 = 0$

$\qquad\qquad\qquad\qquad 0 = 0$

13. $\sqrt{3x} = 6$ check: $\sqrt{3(12)} = 6$

    $3x = 36$ $\sqrt{36} = 6$

    $x = 12$ $6 = 6$

14. $\sqrt{7x - 1} = 5$ check: $\sqrt{7\left(\dfrac{26}{7}\right) - 1} = 5$

    $7x - 1 = 25$ $\sqrt{26 - 1} = 5$

      $7x = 26$ $\sqrt{25} = 5$

       $x = \dfrac{26}{7}$ $5 = 5$

15. $\sqrt{\dfrac{4a}{3}} - 2 = 0$ check: $\sqrt{\dfrac{4(3)}{3}} - 2 = 0$

     $\sqrt{\dfrac{4a}{3}} = 2$ $\sqrt{4} - 2 = 0$

      $\dfrac{4a}{3} = 4$ $2 - 2 = 0$

       $4a = 12$ $0 = 0$

        $a = 3$

16. $\sqrt{x + 4} = x - 8$ check: $\sqrt{12 + 4} = 12 - 8$

    $x + 4 = x^2 - 16x + 64$ $\sqrt{16} = 4$

      $0 = x^2 - 17x + 60$ $4 = 4$

      $0 = (x - 12)(x - 5)$ $\sqrt{5 + 4} = 5 - 8$

   $x - 12 = 0$ $x - 5 = 0$ $\sqrt{9} = -3$

      $x = 12$ $x = 5$ $3 \neq -3$

Solution is $x = 12$.

17. 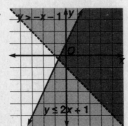 18.

19.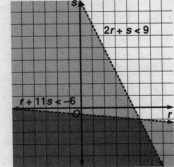

20.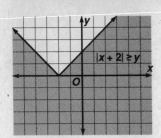

21. mean $= \dfrac{4 + 5 + 6 + 8 + 12}{5} = \dfrac{35}{5}$ or 7

    median = 6

    mode = no mode

22. mean $= \dfrac{9 + 9 + 9 + 9 + 8}{5} = \dfrac{44}{5}$ or 8.8

    median = 9

    mode = 9

23. mean $= \dfrac{0 + 2 + 2 + 2 + 3 + 3 + 4 + 5 + 7 + 8 + 8}{11}$

        $= \dfrac{44}{11}$ or 4

    median = 3

    mode = 2

24. mean $= \dfrac{9 + 2 + 17 + 1 + 9 + 5 + 12 + 17}{8}$

        $= \dfrac{72}{8}$ or 9

    median = 9

    mode = 9, 17

25. $(30 - 8):8 = 22:8$ or $11:4$

26.   Let x = hours to clean garage

      $\dfrac{x}{9}$ = Kiko's time

      $\dfrac{x}{6}$ = Marcus's time

     $\dfrac{x}{9} + \dfrac{x}{6} = 1$

     $6x + 9x = 54$

       $15x = 54$

        $x = 3.6$ hours

27. $55 \overset{?}{=} \sqrt{15(240)}$

    $55 \overset{?}{=} \sqrt{3600}$

    $55 \neq 60$

    No, it would skid 240 ft at 60 mph.

28. Let x = measure of side of square

         $2x^2 = (x + 3)(x + 2)$

         $2x^2 = x^2 + 5x + 6$

     $x^2 - 5x - 6 = 0$

    $(x - 6)(x + 1) = 0$

          $x = 6$

    6 cm by 6 cm

29. If the odds of winning are 1:5, then $\dfrac{1}{1 + 5}$ or $\dfrac{1}{6}$

    of the people will win. They will need $\dfrac{1}{6}(180)$ or

    30 prizes.